D0935071

FRAGMENTS OF ROMAN POETRY c.60 BC–AD 20

TO ROBIN NISBET

Fragments of Roman Poetry c.60 BC–AD 20

Edited with an Introduction, Translation, and Commentary
By ADRIAN S. HOLLIS

OXFORD
UNIVERSITY PRESS

OXFORD
UNIVERSITY PRESS

Great Clarendon Street, Oxford OX2 6DP

Oxford University Press is a department of the University of Oxford.
It furthers the University's objective of excellence in research, scholarship,
and education by publishing worldwide in

Oxford New York

Auckland Cape Town Dar es Salaam Hong Kong Karachi
Kuala Lumpur Madrid Melbourne Mexico City Nairobi
New Delhi Shanghai Taipei Toronto

With offices in

Argentina Austria Brazil Chile Czech Republic France Greece
Guatemala Hungary Italy Japan Poland Portugal Singapore
South Korea Switzerland Thailand Turkey Ukraine Vietnam

Oxford is a registered trade mark of Oxford University Press
in the UK and in certain other countries

Published in the United States
by Oxford University Press Inc., New York

British Library Cataloguing in Publication Data

Data available

Library of Congress Cataloging in Publication Data

Data available

Typeset by RefineCatch Limited, Bungay, Suffolk
Printed in Great Britain
on acid-free paper by
Biddles Ltd, King's Lynn

ISBN 978–0–19–814698–8

1 3 5 7 9 10 8 6 4 2

Preface

This work could be referred to as *FRP* (*Fragments of Roman Poetry*), to distinguish it from *FPR* (*Fragmenta Poetarum Romanorum*, ed. E. Baehrens, 1886), *FPL* (*Fragmenta Poetarum Latinorum*, ed. W. Morel, 1927, revised by K. Büchner, 1982, and J. Blänsdorf, 1995) and *FLP* (*The Fragmentary Latin Poets*, ed. E. Courtney, 1993).

I have set the time-limits *c.*60 BC to AD 20, the same duration (80 years) and approximately the same dates which Velleius Paterculus allowed for the great age of Latin poetry (1.17.2; cf. 2.36.2–3 where the earliest poets named are Varro Atacinus, Lucretius and Catullus, the latest Rabirius). One or two poets on the edge of the period have been excluded (M. Cicero, and with him the astronomical fragment of Q. Cicero (Courtney, pp. 178–81)). I have not included 'Versus Populares', e.g. the rude songs chanted by soldiers at their general's triumph, or the fragments of poets who have for the most part survived (e.g. Catullus, Tibullus, Ovid). On the other hand I have admitted the tragic remains of Varius Rufus and Gracchus. The likelihood that some of the items in this book are not 'fragments' but complete short poems (e.g. Calvus, **39**, Furius, **84**, **85**, Octavian, **161**, Marsus, **174**, **180**, Laurea, **194**) troubles me not at all.

The text is not divided between 'testimonia' and 'fragmenta', but simply has 'items' (like *Supplementum Hellenisticum*, ed. Lloyd-Jones and Parsons, 1983), whether or not they contain verbatim quotations. Consequently some of my 'items' do not have exact counterparts in the 'fragments' of Blänsdorf and Courtney (see my Comparative Table). I have, however, fixed the minimum subscription to the main section at one word of poetry, even though Q. Hortensius gains admission on the basis of **99**, whereas the much more significant Valerius Cato is relegated to the Appendix (p. 429). The first item under a poet's name often just establishes that he wrote poetry, his approximate dates, origins, and connections, the genres which he patronized and his overall poetic reputation. My citations from the quoting sources are sometimes longer than in other collections (including Courtney, despite ibid., p. viii) in order to make clear precisely why these words are quoted—even if the reason appears misguided or puerile.

In the Commentary (which is the heart of this book) I have suggested contexts, even for some quite small fragments, in a way which may seem rash, but is usually based upon a possible model or imitation in another poet. For example, to suggest that the single line of Cornelius Severus (**216**) 'pinea frondosi coma murmurat Appennini' comes from a simile, and illustrated a crowd reacting with disapproval to a speech, may seem a hit in the air, but gains plausibility from Ovid, *Met.* 15.603–4 (the Romans waxing indignant at the thought that they might again be ruled by a king) 'qualia succinctis, ubi trux insibilat Eurus, / murmura pinetis fiunt'. If such suggestions are proved wrong, that will be for the welcome reason that new evidence has emerged. Meanwhile it is worth remembering that a quotation, however small, was once part of a living poem, and not just an exhibit in a grammarian's dusty catalogue of unusual genders, declensions, conjugations or forms of the ablative.

Wherever possible I have tried to relate these fragmentary poets to a poet whose work has survived—e.g. to Catullus (Cinna, Calvus, Maecenas), Lucretius (Egnatius, Varius Rufus), Virgil (Varius Rufus, Cornelius Gallus), Ovid (Tullius Laurea, Cornelius Severus). The section containing Adespota Selecta follows the same chronological sequence as the main section, though of course in a much more tentative way (some of the items may be later than our period). I hope that the translation will be of use: often it is no more than provisional because it necessitates taking a view about the context, or the relationship between individual words, when other views are quite possible. Another new feature is the alphabetical Appendix of named poets from whom no verbatim quotation has survived. My purpose throughout this book has been to attempt some integration of the poetic scene in Rome during this period, so that we can gain some idea of what it might have looked like in e.g. 44 BC, 35 BC, or AD 8.

Work on this book started about 1989, before I discovered that Edward Courtney's project was much more advanced. We met, and agreed that our approaches were sufficiently different to leave room for two books. Thereafter I deliberately worked on other things, in order to allow a time-gap between Courtney's volume and mine. In the interval several other relevant and valuable books appeared: above all R. Kaster, *Suetonius, De Grammaticis et Rhetoribus* (Oxford, 1995) and Jane Lightfoot, *Parthenius of Nicaea* (Oxford, 1999); also J. Blänsdorf's third edition of Morel (1995, in some respects disappointing). From all of these I have profited.

I am most grateful to Mrs Rachel Chapman (Miss R. E. Woodrow) for typing the manuscript (as she did for my Callimachus, *Hecale*). Professor Harry Jocelyn, shortly before his death, gave me an offprint of his *Eikasmos* article on Calvus, **39**. My American former pupil, Mel Field, generously presented me with a copy of Morel at a time when it was out of print and virtually unobtainable—if he will get in touch, he certainly deserves a copy of this volume in return. Other debts are acknowledged in their place. More generally I have profited down the years from discussions with friends and colleagues—among them Peter Brown, Stephen Harrison, Stephen Heyworth, Gregory Hutchinson, and Oliver Lyne.

This book is dedicated to Professor Robin Nisbet, who read almost all of the first draft (mention of his name without source usually refers to his comments thereon). I discovered only at his retirement dinner that I had been his first graduate pupil; certainly he is the scholar to whom I owe most. Perhaps this is the place to add that he did *not* forge the Cornelius Gallus papyrus. How can I be so sure? Because in 1963 he told me that *his* papyrus of Cornelius Gallus would include the line 'sunt apud infernos tot carminis heroinae' (to provide a parallel for taking 'fabulae' as genitive in Horace, *Odes* 1.4.16).

A.S.H.
Keble College, Oxford
December 2005

Postscript: In September 2003 the Clarendon Press published a paperback version of Courtney's *Fragmentary Latin Poets*, with Addenda (pp. 499 ff.). A few misprints in the actual Latin text of the hardback remain uncorrected in the paperback. From the authors whom I include, in Tullius Laurea, fr. 1.5 Courtney (p. 182) 'arte' for the correct 'ante'; in Furius Bibaculus, fr. 11 C. (p. 196) 'hic' for 'hoc'; and in Aemilius Macer, fr. 8.1 C. (p. 296) 'fumantia' for the correct 'spumantia'. Note also that on p. 289 (Valgius Rufus), in the quotation of Propertius 1.9.16, 'gurgite' is a slip for 'flumine'.

Finally I would like to thank the staff of OUP, in particular Kathleen McLaughlin, Jane Robson and David Carles, who coped with a complicated typescript and an untechnological author. Miss Ruth Dry of Keble kindly typed the Index and did much photocopying.

Contents

List of Poets in Alphabetical Order (including names in the Appendix)

Numbering of Items: Comparative Table

Hollis	Blänsdorf	Courtney
Cinna, 1	–	–
2	Cinna 2	Cinna 2
3	3	3
4	5	4
5	5	4
6	1	1
7	–	–
8	8	8
9	7	7
10	6	6
11	9	9
12	10	10
13	11	11
14	14	14
15	12	12
16	–	–
17	4	5
18	13	13
Calvus, 19	–	–
20	Calvus 9	Calvus 9
21	10	10
22	11	11
23	12	12
24	13	13
25	14	14
26	–	–
27	15	15
28	16	16
29	4	4
30	5	5
31	6	6
32	7	7
33	8	8
34	1	1
35	2	2
36	3	3
37	21	21
38	17	17
39	18	18
40	–	–
41	19	19
42	20	20

Hollis	Blänsdorf	Courtney
Egnatius, 43	Egnatius 1	Egnatius 1
43A	2	2
Memmius, 44	–	–
45	Memmius 1	Memmius 1
46	2	ad 1
Macer, 47	–	–
48	–	–
49	–	–
50	Macer 1	Macer 1
51	2	2
52	3	3
53	4	4
54	cf. 9	cf. 6
55	7	5
56	17	7
57	8	8
58	10	9
59	18	10
60	–	11
61	5	12
62	6	13
63	13	14
64	–	15
65	12	16
66	14	17
67	15	18
68	16	19
69	–	–
70	–	–
Bibaculus, 71	–	–
72	Bibaculus 7	Bibaculus 7
73	8	8
74	9	9
75	10	10
76	11	11
77	12	12
78	13	13
79	14	14
80	15	15
81	16	16
82	–	–
83	3	3
84	1	1
85	2	2
86	6	6
87	5	5
88	6a	–
89	4	4

Scaevola, 90	–	–
91	Scaevola 1	Scaevola 1
92	2	2
Cornificius, 93	–	–
94	–	–
95	Cornificius 1	Cornificius 1
96	2	2
97	3	3
Hortensius, 98	–	–
99	Hortensius 1	Hortensius 1
Ticida, 100	–	–
101	–	–
102	Ticida 1	Ticida 1
103	2	2
Volumnius, 104	Volumnius 1	Volumnius 1
Varro Atacinus 105	–	–
106	Varro Atacinus 23	Varro Atacinus 1
107	24	2
108	–	–
109	–	–
110	–	–
111	11	15
112	13	17
113	12	16
114	14	18
115	15	19
116	16	20
117	17	12
118	18	21
119	20	22
120	21	13
121	22	14
122	–	–
123	1	1
124	2	4
125	3	5
126	4	6
127	5	7
128	7	9
129	8	10
130	9	23
131	6	8
132	10	11
133	–	–
134	19	ad 21
Pollio, 135	–	–
136	Pollio 1	Pollio 1
137	–	–
Gallus, 138	–	–
139	–	–

Hollis	Blänsdorf	Courtney
140	–	–
141	–	–
142	–	–
143	–	–
144	Gallus 1	Gallus 1
145	2–5	2
Varius, 146	–	–
147	Varius 1	Varius 1
148	2	2
149	3	3
150	4	4
151	–	–
152	5	5
153	–	–
154	–	–
155	–	–
156	–	–
157	–	–
158	–	–
159	–	–
Octavian, 160	–	–
161	Octavian 1	Octavian 1
Valgius, 162	–	–
163	–	–
164	–	–
165	Valgius 1	Valgius 1
166	2	2
167	3	3
168	4	4
169	5	5
170	6	6
171	7	7
Marsus, 172	–	–
173	–	–
174	Marsus 1	Marsus 1
175	2	2
176	3	3
177	4	4
178	5	5
179	6	6
180	7	7
181	8	8
182	9	9
Maecenas, 183	–	–
184	Maecenas 1	Maecenas 1
185	2	2
186	3	3
187	4	4

188	5	cf. 5–6
189	6	cf. 5–6
190	7	7
191	8	8
192	9	9
193	11	10
Laurea, 194	Laurea 1	Laurea 1
Arbonius, 195	Arbonius 1	Arbonius 1
Dorcatius, 196	Dorcatius 1	Dorcatius 1
Gracchus, 197	–	–
198	–	–
199	–	–
200	–	–
201	–	–
Ena, 202	Ena 1	Ena 1
Severus, 203	–	–
204	–	–
205	Severus 1	Severus 1
206	–	–
207	–	–
208	2	2
209	3	3
210	4	4
211	5	5
212	6	6
213	7	7
214	8	8
215	9	9
216	10	10
217	11	11
218	12	12
219	13	13
220	14	14
Montanus, 221	–	–
222	Montanus 1	Montanus 1
223	2	2
224	–	–
Pedo, 225	–	–
226	–	–
227	–	–
228	Pedo 1	Pedo 1
Rabirius, 229	–	–
230	Rabirius 1	Rabirius 1
231	2	2
232	3	3
233	4	4
234	5	5
Adespota, 235	inc. 35	an. 10
236	in inc. 36–37	an. 14
237	Macer 11	an. 30
238	inc. 33	an. 8

Numbering of items: comparative table

Hollis	Blänsdorf	Courtney
239	inc. 34	an. 9
240	p. 196	–
241	inc. 32	an. 3
242	inc. 68	an. 6
243	inc. 63	an. 4
244	–	–
245	–	–
246	–	–
247	inc. 40	p. 145
248	inc. 70	–
249	inc. 82	an. 32
250	inc. 42	Maecenas 5–6
251	inc. 43	Maecenas 5–6
252	–	an. 25
253	inc. 52	an. 19
254	inc. 55	an. 12
255	inc. 57	–
256	inc. 64	an. 5
257	inc. 60	an. 15
258	inc. 58	–
259	inc. 54	an. 11
260	inc. 48	an. 24
261	inc. 65	–
262	inc. 46a	cf. p. 334

Introduction

Since there are introductory sections on almost every individual poet, I confine myself here to a few selected topics which involve several authors.

1. 'NEW' OR 'NEOTERIC' POETS

Among the copious discussions of this question see in particular R. O. A. M. Lyne, 'The Neoteric Poets', *CQ* NS 28 (1978), 167–87, Courtney 189–91, J. L. Lightfoot, *Parthenius of Nicaea* (Oxford, 1999), 54–7. Three passages of Cicero have aroused controversy.

(*a*) *Ad Atticum* 7.2.1 = 125 Shackleton Bailey (November 50 BC) 'ita belle nobis "flavit ab Epiro lenissimus Onchesmites". hunc σπονδειάζοντα si cui voles τῶν νεωτέρων pro tuo vendito.'

(*b*) *Orator* 161 (46 BC), on the elision of a final 's', regular in the time of Ennius and Lucilius, but avoided by 'poetae novi' as being 'subrusticum' ('somewhat uncultured'), 'ita non erat ea offensio in versibus quam nunc fugiunt poetae novi'.

(*c*) *Tusc. Disp.* 3.45 (45 BC), after quoting some tragic lines of Ennius, 'o poetam egregium! quamquam ab his cantoribus Euphorionis contemnitur.'

Note that none of these was written during the lifetime of Catullus and Calvus, though Helvius Cinna was still alive (and probably still active) in 45 BC. To start with (*b*), is 'poetae novi' purely a chronological indication, 'modern poets' (as argued by Courtney, p. 189, and Lightfoot, p. 55), or would 'modernist poets' be nearer the mark, suggesting a group with common aesthetic tastes, perhaps to be identified with the νεώτεροι of (*a*) (so Lyne)? In this matter I sympathize with Lyne. It would be surprising for Cicero to say that 'modern poets' avoided elision of a final 's'. Even if we disregard Egnatius (**43A**.1), as a minor figure, the statement would be contradicted by Lucretius (as much a 'modern poet' as Catullus or Calvus), who elides a final 's' 49

times (C. Bailey, Lucretius, *De Rerum Natura* (Oxford, 1947), i, 124). As for
(*a*), is the only significant point that 'flavit ab Epiro lenissimus Onchesmites'
has a spondaic fifth foot, or does the line have an aesthetic quality (Lyne 167),
similar to e.g. Catullus 64.28 'tene Thetis tenuit pulcherrima Nereine?'? More
probably the latter, in my view. Lucretius has some 26 σπονδειάζοντες (dis-
counting e.g. 1.223 where 'dissoluantur' should be scanned as five syllables),
but he does not seem to aim at any special elegance or distinction of style—I
cannot imagine a follower of Catullus paying hard cash for any one of them,
except conceivably 4.125 'habrotonique graves et tristia centaurea'.

It seems likely that Hellenistic influences (perhaps in a more extreme form)
continued to dominate Latin poetry in those mysterious ten years *c*.54–44 B C,
from the disappearance of Catullus down to the death of Cinna at Julius
Caesar's funeral. Cinna could have been the leading poet of that period, with
Cornelius Gallus (whose hero was Euphorion of Chalcis) beginning to make
his mark by 45 B C. One might also wonder about Valerius Cato (my Appen-
dix, p. 429). In Greek νεώτεροι was sometimes used to designate post-
Homeric hexameter poets, with a suggestion of inferiority to the master. The
implication (Courtney 189, cf. T. P. Wiseman, *Cinna the Poet* (Leicester, 1974),
51) is that Roman critics viewed Ennius as setting a norm for style and
language, which later poets failed to equal. Ennius certainly had his admirers
in the mid-first century B C (foremost among them Cicero), and we can see his
continuing influence (e.g. in Catullus 64); but his shortcomings did not
escape notice either. I doubt whether τῶν νεωτέρων in *Ad Att.* 7.2.1 (above) is
meant to imply inferiority to Ennius. Shackleton Bailey's 'avant-garde' (or
perhaps 'modernist') seems to catch the tone.

It would, however, be wrong to draw the boundaries between neoteric and
traditional poets too rigidly, as we can see from the cases of Furius Bibaculus
(**71–89**)—assuming that all the items under his name come from the same
poet—and Varro Atacinus (**105–34**). Both of these wrote traditional epics on
Julius Caesar's campaigns in Gaul (**72–81** and **106–7** respectively); Varro's
Satires (**108**) also suggest adherence to the old school of Latin poets. On the
other hand we have from Bibaculus some extremely elegant hendecasyllables
(**84–7** or **88**) which would not disgrace Catullus, and several poems by Varro
Atacinus breathe the atmosphere of Alexandria: a didactic *Chorographia*
(**109–19**) on astronomy and geography; another work of which the extant
lines (**120–1**) closely translate Aratus' *Phaenomena*, and, (Varro's masterpiece)
an *Argonauts* (**122–32**) based upon Apollonius Rhodius. Varro also wrote love
poetry (probably elegiac) for his Leucadia (**133**), perhaps inspired by
Cornelius Gallus.

2. LITERARY PATRONAGE

In the 50s BC Lucretius, Catullus and perhaps Cinna had attached themselves to the praetor Memmius in a relationship either obscure (Lucretius) or unsatisfying (Catullus); a decade later Pollio gathered to himself Cornelius Gallus (see my introduction to Gallus) as well as the young Virgil. We have plentiful evidence about Maecenas' group of poets: Virgil, Varius Rufus, Horace, and—a late-comer—Propertius. A surprising addition to the list is Domitius Marsus (**172–82**), chiefly an epigrammatist but also author of an epic *Amazonis* (**173**); his links to the regime are shown by some stiff funerary elegiacs on Atia, mother of Augustus (**181–2**).

The second most important patron of poets in this period was Messalla Corvinus, whose protégés included Tibullus (and the minor poets of the *Corpus Tibullianum*), Ovid (as we learn from the exile letters addressed to Messalla's sons), and Valgius Rufus (**163**). **171** raises the possibility that Messalla and Valgius were together in the Sicilian war, and sober scholars have approved the idea that 'Codrus' in **166** is none other than Valgius' patron. Cornelius Severus' presence in the household of Messalla is attested by the elder Seneca (**203***c*), and the subject-matter of the *Bellum Siculum* (**206–7**) would be welcome to Messalla and (after his death) to his sons. Perhaps we can trace Messalla's first steps towards literary patronage at a much earlier date: Suetonius (*De Gramm.* 4.2) quotes from a letter in which Messalla says that he 'has no dealings with' Furius Bibaculus (**71***b*), Ticida (**100**), or Valerius Cato (Appendix, p. 429). The expression 'non esse sibi . . . rem cum . . .' surely implies more than that he did not read their poetry—perhaps that he did not intend to become their patron. None of the three is known to have had another patron, and Cato at least suffered an impoverished old age. The poets mentioned could have formed something of a mini-group, since Bibaculus sympathized with Cato's financial plight (**84–5**) and Ticida praised Cato's *Lydia* (**103**).

One should stress that the groups under their patrons may have had a different ethos (Messalla's of higher social standing and politically less committed to Augustus), but there were no barriers between them: Horace valued the judgement of Valgius and Messalla (*Satires* 1.10.82 and 85); Ovid attended recitations by Propertius and Horace (*Tristia* 4.10.45 ff.) and Domitius Marsus lamented Tibullus as well as Virgil (**180**).

3. NAMING THE LADY

Catullus, Propertius, and Tibullus called their loves by a pseudonym (Lesbia, Cynthia, and Delia). So did Cornelius Gallus—indeed Lycoris (stage-name Cytheris, formal name Volumnia) appears in the first line of the new papyrus (**145**.1). On the other hand Licinius Calvus' most famous poem was a Lament for Quintilia (**26–8**), obviously her real name. Some have explained the difference by suggesting that Quintilia was Calvus' wife, not his mistress; that would have removed any need to conceal her identity. But Catullus 96.3–4 (= **26***a*) makes clear that Calvus' love for Quintilia was a thing of the past. More probably, therefore, she was the poet's mistress, and, in the time of Catullus and Calvus, no hard and fast convention had been established over this matter.

An interesting case, which could support the above hypothesis, is that of the noble Metella. She was apparently celebrated by more than one poet (Ovid, *Tristia* 2.437–8 'et quorum libris modo dissimulata Perillae / nomine nunc legitur dicta, Metelle, tuo'). 'Modo . . . nunc' could mean either 'previously . . . now', or 'at one time . . . at another'. See the detailed argument on Ticida, **101**, suggesting that Ticida used the pseudonym (as stated by Apuleius, *Apology* 10 = **101***b*) and that the poet who used her real name— which some might have considered brutal if the woman had a position in society—could have been the praetor Memmius.

These poetic pseudonyms mostly suggest Greek poetesses (Lesbia and Ovid's Corinna) or cult-titles of Apollo (Cynthia, Delia, and Gallus' Lycoris, appropriately more obscure, a title used by Callimachus and Euphorion). Varro Atacinus' Leucadia (Prop. 2.34.85–6 = **133***a*) ingeniously spans the two categories, with a hint both of Sappho and of Leucadian Apollo.

4. CHOICE OF GENRE AND SUBJECT MATTER

With the possible exception of comedy, allegedly patronized by Horace's friend Aristius Fuscus (see my Appendix for the *fabula trabeata* of Melissus), all the traditional genres were well employed in this period. Lyric cannot be considered traditional among the Romans; Horace ignores the eccentric Laevius (Courtney 118–43) and claims primacy for himself. According to Quintilian (10.1.96), the only other Latin lyric poet worth reading was Caesius Bassus (mid-first century A D).

Old-style Latin tragedy probably came to an end not with the death of Accius, but with the switch of Asinius Pollio from tragedy (**135**) to history in the 30s BC. Less than a decade later Varius Rufus staged his *Thyestes* (**154–6**), which, together with Ovid's *Medea* (e.g. Tac. *Dial.* 12.6 = **154**(*c*)) was judged to be of the highest quality; if **157** (perhaps not from *Thyestes*) is any guide, Varius may have replaced Pollio's old-fashioned manner with a style owing much to learned Hellenistic and Latin neoteric poetry. Minor Augustan tragedians include Gracchus (**197–201**) and Turranius (Appendix).

Ovid, *Ex Ponto* 4.16 (whence most of my Appendix) makes clear that every sort of epic retained its popularity. To start with poems centred on individual heroes, we find Diomedes (Antonius Iullus), Hercules (Carus), Perseus (Trinacrius), and Theseus (Albinovanus Pedo, **227**). Antenor (Largus) was an obvious plum, since it could be argued that he, rather than Aeneas, 'Troiae . . . primus ab oris / Italiam . . . venit'. Trojan themes without any Italian connection were no less favoured: events from the death of Hector (Camerinus), the return of Menelaus and Helen (Lupus), Ulysses among the Phaeacians (Tuticanus). Macer (not Aemilius) wrote on Troy (precise topic not specified). Ponticus (a friend of both Propertius and Ovid) may have written a *Thebaid*. In the mid-30s BC, Varius Rufus (**151**) had been the best writer of martial epic—we do not know of what sort.

The custom of writing epics on historical (rather than mythical) wars stemmed from Greek poets such as Choerilus of Samos and Rhianus of Crete. The earliest Latin example was the *Bellum Poenicum* (First Carthaginian War) of Naevius. In our period Varro Atacinus (**106–7**) and Furius Bibaculus (**72–81**) both celebrated Julius Caesar's Gallic campaigns. Obvious topics for an Augustan poet were the exploits of the Princeps—though perhaps not Philippi (too painful, and mainly Antony's victory). Indeed the poets of Maecenas' circle constantly promise such a work, but, interestingly, the fulfilment was left to poets not quite of the first class, who wrote near the end of Augustus' principate: Cornelius Severus, *Bellum Siculum* (**206–7**) and Rabirius (**231**, title unknown, sometimes guessed to have been *Bellum Actiacum*). Early in Tiberius' reign Albinovanus Pedo (**228**) wrote on the campaign of Germanicus in which he himself may have participated. More remote Roman history also had its appeal: Cornelius Severus, it seems, wrote about the regal period (**204**, something of a national treasure). *Ex Ponto* 4.16.23 (author not mentioned) probably dealt with the Carthaginian wars.

Besides the canon of four great elegists (Gallus, Tibullus, Propertius, Ovid), we find a number of lesser practitioners: Varro Atacinus (**133**), Montanus (**221***a*), Capella, Proculus, and Sabinus. Pastoral poets too were not deterred by Virgil; Ovid mentions Fontanus and Passer.

5. METRES

The close relationship in metre (as in subject matter) between Catullus and Calvus is very striking: they share hexameters, elegiacs, glyconics, hendeca-syllables, and choliambs. We can add to this list if I am right in thinking that Calvus, **37**, is not corrupt but an extract to be divided between two lines in the iambic metre of Catullus 25. Four of the above metres (not glyconics) are represented in the scanty remains of Helvius Cinna. Maece-nas, clearly a great admirer of Catullus, adds three more of his metres, the Priapean (**187**), the galliambic (**188–9**) and the iambic trimeter (**190**, as in Catullus 52).

It seems that the most characteristic metre of neoteric poets in the 50s BC was the Phalaecian hendecasyllable, followed by the choliamb (limping iam-bic). Bibaculus is also said to have written 'iambi' (**82**), but the precise metre does not emerge (**83** is a standard iambic trimeter). **84** and **85** show Furius Bibaculus continuing hendecasyllables, probably in the 20s BC (when Valerius Cato was well into old age). Both Bibaculus and Maecenas (like Catullus) do not demand a spondaic base to the hendecasyllable (contrast the practice of Martial a century later). Horace, who uses neither the hendecasyllable nor the choliamb, seems in this respect to distance himself from the poets of Catullus' generation.

6. THE FADING OF FRAGMENTARY POETS

It is interesting to consider for how long and how widely knowledge of the poets in this volume survived. Scepticism is in order. To take an extreme example, before discovery of the papyrus from Qaṣr Ibrîm our only line of Cornelius Gallus (**144**) was uniquely preserved by Vibius Sequester, who (perhaps about AD 500) compiled an alphabetical list of rivers, fountains, etc. mentioned by poets. Clearly there is no chance that Vibius, at such a date, had access to a complete text of Gallus. There is some slight reason to believe (see on **144**) that he derived the quotation from a commentary (more detailed than anything we now possess) on Virgil, *Georgics* 4 or Ovid, *Metamorphoses* 15. Another case of unlikely survival to later antiquity involves **244**. The Christian writer Lactantius (*c.*AD 300) probably would not have been able to tell us the identity of his second Epicurean poet (in addition to Lucretius) who used *animus* and *anima* indifferently. This looks like a nugget of infor-mation copied from an earlier source without full comprehension. There is, however, a plausible candidate for the second Epicurean poet: Varius Rufus in his *De Morte* (cf. **147–50**).

On the other hand it would be too sceptical to deny that Quintilian knew full texts of the poets on whom he passes critical judgement (even if his verdicts are conventional and derivative), and that he expected similar knowledge on the part of many readers. This applies to his judgements upon Varro Atacinus (**122***f*), Aemilius Macer (**48***b*), Rabirius and Pedo (**225***d*), Cornelius Gallus (**138***h*). Notable is Quintilian's familiarity with Varius Rufus' *Thyestes*. He quotes the only certain fragment of the play (**156**) and (anonymously) what may be its opening line (**245**.1) as well as making one or two possible allusions to this play (see on **154–6**).

There is even a faint chance that *Thyestes* survived until the early Middle Ages (see on **155**). By contrast Varius' hexameter poetry (from which we have just **147–50**), though admired by Virgil and Horace, seems to have faded quickly; note the remark in **154**(*d*), 'aliud nihil eius habetur', 'we possess nothing else of his [apart from *Thyestes*]'. The same is true of two epyllia by Catullus' friends, Cinna's *Smyrna* (**7–10**) and Calvus' *Io* (**20–5**). Without the quoting sources we would not know of *Io*'s existence, though it is certainly reflected in Virgil and Ovid (perhaps also in Propertius). *Smyrna* was kept in the public memory by Catullus 95 (= **7***a*), but people soon remembered only that the composition took nine years (e.g. **7***d*), and that the poem was obscure enough to need a commentary within a generation.

Among the Silver poets, Lucan is said to have borrowed the names of snakes from Aemilius Macer's *Theriaca* (**54***b*), and no doubt used his recent predecessors in military epic, Cornelius Severus and Albinovanus Pedo. I was surprised to find little or nothing of Varro Atacinus' *Argonauts* in Valerius Flaccus. The poet who shows most sign of knowing rare items from the mid-first century BC is another surprise: Silius Italicus. Particularly striking is the detailed and careful imitation of Cinna's *Propempticon Pollionis* (**6**) in *Punica* 13.86–9, and of Varius, *De Morte* (**150**) in 10.77–82; in both cases Silius takes the same number of lines as his model. The passages of Cinna and Varius are preserved for us via comments on Virgil; could Silius have known just these lines by a similar route? Possible, but not (I think) very likely. The context in Silius 13.86–9 (an ancient and wealthy shrine which inspires the utmost awe) raises the possibility that Pollio planned a visit to Delphi. Furthermore our source for **6** (Charisius) commits an egregious blunder in believing that Cinna's 'Belidis' (line 3) was genitive singular. More probably, therefore, Silius knew the full text and context of his model.

Certain grammatical and lexicographical sources are of particular interest, since they seem to have had access (if only indirect) to special rare texts. For example, some treatises classified metaphors according to transfer between, or within, the categories of 'animate' and 'inanimate'. In Charisius (and other grammarians) that is the ultimate source for **124** (Varro Atacinus, *Argonauts*). The same origin is obvious for **241–3** and **256** (all anonymous in Isidore, *Origines*), encouraging the hypothesis that **243** (conceivably also **241** and **242**) may belong to the same poem by Varro.

Finally, some persons of high culture and standing may have been able to lay their hands on rare texts as late as the fifth century. Thus Macrobius provides all our quotations from Varius Rufus, *De Morte* (**147–50**) and all but two of Furius Bibaculus, *Annales Belli Gallici* (**72–81**); he even ascribes the latter group to their individual book.

Text, Translation, and Commentary

C. Helvius Cinna

1

(*a*) Verg. *Buc.* 9.35–6: *nam neque adhuc Vario* [**146***b*] *videor nec dicere Cinna* / *digna, sed argutos inter strepere anser olores.* (Serv. ad loc. (p. 114 Thilo): *etiam Cinna poeta optimus fuit, qui scripsit Smyrnam* [v. **7***e*] . . .)

(*b*) Valgius Rufus, **166**.1–4: *Codrusque ille canit quali tu voce solebas* / *atque solet numeros dicere, Cinna, tuos,* / *dulcior ut numquam Pylio profluxerit ore* / *Nestoris aut docto pectore Demodoci.*

(*c*) Mart. 10.21: *scribere te quae vix intellegat ipse Modestus* / *et vix Claranus, quid, rogo, Sexte, iuvat?* / *non lectore tuis opus est sed Apolline libris;* / *iudice te maior Cinna Marone fuit.* / *sic tua laudentur sane; mea carmina, Sexte,* / *grammaticis placeant ut sine grammaticis.*

(*d*) Plut. *Brut.* 20.5: ἦν δέ τις Κίννας, ποιητικὸς ἀνήρ, οὐδὲν τῆς αἰτίας μετέχων, ἀλλὰ καὶ φίλος Καίσαρος γεγονώς . . . [de morte Cinnae, cf. **7***c*].

(*e*) Gell. *NA* 19.9.7: . . . *ecquis nostrorum poetarum tam fluentes carminum delicias fecisset, 'nisi Catullus' inquiunt* [sc. Graeci plusculi] *'forte pauca et Calvus* [**19***l*] *itidem pauca; nam Laevius implicata et Hortensius* [**98***c*] *invenusta et Cinna inlepida et Memmius* [**44***c*] *dura ac deinceps omnes rudia fecerunt atque absona.'*

(*f*) Gell. *NA* 19.13.5 [v. **11**]: . . . *Helvi Cinnae, non ignobilis neque indocti poetae.*

(*a*) 'For as yet I do not seem to utter verses worthy of Varius or Cinna, but to squawk like a goose among melodious swans.' Servius: Cinna too was an excellent poet who wrote the *Smyrna* . . .

(*b*) That Codrus sings with a voice like yours of old, Cinna, and utters verses such as you did, so that no sweeter tone ever issued from the Pylian mouth of Nestor or the wise heart of Demodocus.

(*c*) Sextus, what profit is there, pray, in writing poems which even Modestus and Claranus would be hard pressed to understand? Your compositions require not a reader but an Apollo; in your judgement Cinna was greater than

Virgil. I don't mind your poems being praised on such terms; let mine, Sextus, please commentators in so far as they can do so without commentators.

(*d*) There was a man called Cinna, a poet, who had no share of responsibility, but had actually been a friend of Caesar . . .

(*e*) [Some Greeks were considering] whether any of our Roman poets had written such fluent and charming pieces [as Anacreon]. 'Perhaps Catullus a few, and likewise Calvus; for those of Laevius were contorted, of Hortensius inelegant, those of Cinna lacking grace, of Memmius rough; and, beyond that, the compositions of all of them were crude and discordant.'

(*f*) . . . Helvius Cinna, a poet neither undistinguished nor unlearned.

2–6 *Propempticon Pollionis* (a send-off poem for Pollio)

2 (2 Blänsdorf, Courtney)

lucida quom fulgent alti carchesia mali

When the maintop of the lofty mast glows bright

Isid. *Orig.* 19.2.9: *carchesia sunt in cacumine arboris trochleae, quasi F littera, per qua funes trahuntur.* Cinna 'lucida–mali'. Non. Marc. p. 876 (vol. III) Lindsay (1903): *carchesia . . . alias summa pars mali, id est foramina quae summo mali funes recipiunt.* Lucilius [1309 Marx] . . . *Catullus Veronensis* 'lucida–mali'. Schol. Luc. 5.418 'hic utinam summi curvet carchesia mali', *Suppl. Adnot. super Luc.* I (1979), p. 322 Cavajoni: *sunt autem carchesia in cacumine arboris <trochleae> quasi F littera, per quae funes trahuntur.* Cinna 'lucida—mali'.

 quom fulgent *Lunelli (Aerius p. 66)*: cum fulgent *schol. Luc.*: confulgent *Isid.*: qua splendent *Non.* alti *Isid.*: summi *schol. Luc.*: *vocem om. Non.*

3 (3 Bl., C.)

atque anquina regat stabilem fortissima cursum

And may the strongest halyard guide a steady course

Isid. *Orig.* 19.4.7: *anquina* [funis] *quo ad malum antemna constringitur. de qua* Cinna 'atque–cursum'.

4 (5 Bl., 4 C.)

Charis., p. 171 Barwick[2] (1964) = GLK I p. 134 = Grammaticae Romanae Fragmenta I p. 527 Funaioli (1907): *'itiner' idem in eodem* [sc. Iulius Hyginus in Cinnae Propemptico<n>, v. **5**]. *'quaerunt' inquit 'etiam nonnulli quam ob rem a Corcura iubeat* [sc. Cinna] *Action navigare, quod est e regione traductionis Leucadiensis, et rursus ab Actio circa insulam moneat ire, quam a Corcura rectum itiner ad Leucatam.'*

The same writer in the same work [Iulius Hyginus in his commentary on Cinna's *Propempticon*, see **5**] used the form *itiner*. He said 'Some also ask why [Cinna] tells [Pollio] to sail from Corcyra to Actium, which is directly opposite the Leucadian Portage, and yet should advise him to sail from Actium around the island [Leucas], instead of taking the direct route from Corcyra to Leucata.'

5 (5 Bl., 4 C.)

Charis., p. 171 Barwick[2] = GLK I p. 134: *'iteris' Iulius Hyginus in Cinnae Propemptico<n>: 'ab Actio navigantes stad<ia circiter> LX veniunt ad Isthmum Leucadiensium. ibi solent iteris minuendi causa remulco, quem Graeci* πά<κτωνα> *dicunt, navem traducere'.* [deinde pergit Charis. 'Pacuvius quoque "iteris" . . . "itiner" idem in eodem' = **4**.]

Iulius Hyginus in his commentary on Cinna's *Propempticon* used the form *iteris*: 'Those who sail from Actium for about 60 stades come to the Isthmus of the Leucadians. There, in order to shorten the journey, they usually transport the ship by means of a tow-rope, which the Greeks call *pactōn*.'

6 (1 Bl., C.)

nec tam donorum ingenteis mirabere acervos
innumerabilibus congestos undique saeclis
iam inde a Belidis natalique urbis ab anno
Cecropis atque alta Tyriorum ab origine Cadmo

You will not marvel so much at the huge piles of offerings, heaped up from every source over countless centuries, continuously from the sons of Belus, from the natal year of Cecrops' city and from Cadmus, far-distant ancestor of the Thebans.

1–4 Charis., p. 158 B² = GLK I p. 124: *Belidis Cinna in Propemptico Pollionis* 'nec tam—Cadmi'. *patronymice dixit 'Belidis', ut 'urbis'. at vero Maro* (*Aen.* 2.82) *'Belidae Palamedis' ait.*

1 acerbos *cod. N*   2 congestos *ex* congestis *N*   4 Tyriorum *Keil:* Tyriū *vel* Tyriā *N:* Tyrii iam *L. Mueller*   Cadmo *Hollis:* Cadmi *N*

7–10 Smyrna

7

(*a*) Cat. 95 et 95b: *Smyrna mei Cinnae nonam post denique messem / quam coepta est nonamque edita post hiemem, / milia cum interea quingenta Hortensius* [nomen suspectum] *uno* [deest pcntameter] / *Smyrna cavas* [: *suas* coni. Nisbet] *Satrachi penitus mittetur ad undas, / Smyrnam cana diu saecula pervoluent. / at Volusi annales Paduam morientur ad ipsam / et laxas scombris saepe dabunt tunicas.* / [9–10 = 95b a praecedentibus seiunxit Statius, fort. recte] *Parva mei mihi sint cordi monumenta . . .* [deest finis hexametri] / *at populus tumido gaudeat Antimacho.*

(*b*) Suet. *De Gramm. et Rhet.* 18.1–2 (p. 22 ed. Kaster (1995)): *L. Crassicius . . . in pergula docuit, donec commentario 'Smyrnae' edito adeo inclaruit ut haec de eo scriberentur: 'uni Crassicio se credere Smyrna probavit: / desinite, indocti, coniugio hanc petere. / soli Crassicio se dixit nubere velle, / intima cui soli nota sua extiterint.'*

(*c*) Ov. *Ibis* 537–8: *conditor ut tardae, laesus cognomine, Myrrhae, / urbis in innumeris inveniare focis.*

(*d*) Quint. *Inst. Or.* 10.4.4: *nam quod Cinnae Smyrnam novem annis accepimus scriptam . . . ad oratorem nihil pertinet.*

(*e*) Serv. ad Verg. *Buc.* 9.35 [v. 1(*a*)]: *etiam Cinna poeta optimus fuit, qui scripsit Smyrnam; quem libellum decem annis elimavit.*

(*a*) The *Smyrna* of my dear Cinna has finally been published, nine harvests and nine winters after it was begun. Meanwhile Hortensius [the name is probably incorrect] <?spews forth> five hundred thousand <?verses> in a single <?year>. *Smyrna* will be sent as far as her own waters of the Satrachus; the greying centuries will for long unroll the *Smyrna*. But the *Annals* of Volusius will die by the mouth of the Po where they originated, and will often provide loose covers for mackerel. [The following couplet may belong to a different poem.] May I take pleasure in the small memorial of my <?friend>; but let the crowd rejoice in turgid Antimachus.

(*b*) L. Crassicius . . . taught in a building annexe, until, after the publication of his commentary on the *Smyrna*, he became so famous that the following was written about him: 'Smyrna has deigned to entrust herself to Crassicius alone; cease, you unlearned, from seeking a union with her. She has said that she will marry none but Crassicius, who alone is familiar with her intimate secrets.'

(*c*) Like the composer of slow-moving Myrrha, may you be found in countless parts of the City.

(*d*) The fact that Cinna's *Smyrna* (so we are told) was written over nine years has no relevance to the orator.

(*e*) Cinna too was an excellent poet who wrote the *Smyrna*, a piece which he polished over a period of ten years.

8 (8 Bl., C.)

tabis

Charis., p. 119 B² = GLK I p. 93 (fere eadem p. 184 B² = p. 145 K): *Cinna autem in Smyrna 'huius tabis' dixit nullo auctore.*

But Cinna in the *Smyrna* used the genitive, 'of wasting', which was not based on any previous authority.

9 (7 Bl., C)

at scelus incesto Smyrnae crescebat in alvo

But the wicked thing was growing in Smyrna's incestuous womb.

Prisc. GLK II p. 268: *'haec alvus, huius alvi', quod veteres frequenter masculino genere protulerunt . . . Cinna in Smyrna 'at scelus—alvo'.* Charis., p. 101 B² = GLK I p. 80: *alvum Vergilius feminino genere saepe dixit, sed masculino Calvus* [**25**] *et Helvius Cinna* 'at scelus—alvo'.

incesto Smyrnae *Burman ad Ov. Met. 10.298*: incesto cinnae *Prisc.*: incestum turpi *Charis.*

10 (6 Bl., C)

te matutinus flentem conspexit Eous,
te flentem paulo vidit post Hesperus idem.

You the early Morning Star caught sight of in tears; you the same saw in tears a little later as the Evening Star.

1–2 Serv. Dan. ad Verg. *Georg.* 1.288 'inrorat Eous' (p. 197 Thilo): *id est Lucifer, de quo etiam Cinna in Smyrna sic ait* 'te matutinus—idem'.

   1 matutinum *cod. V, corr. Guarinus Veronensis (v. Lunelli, Aerius, p. 156)*   2 te *Hollis:* et *V*

11–12 (carmina variis metris conscripta)

11 (9 Bl., C)

at nunc me Genumana per salicta
bigis raeda rapit citata nanis

But me a carriage, sped by a pair of ponies, is now rushing through the willow-groves of the Genumani.

1–2 Gell. *NA* 19.13.5: '*audio . . . respondere esse hoc verbum* [sc. nanos] *Latinum, scriptumque inveniri in poematis Helvi Cinnae, non ignobilis neque indocti poetae'; versusque eius ipsos dixit, quos, quoniam memoriae mihi forte aderant, adscripsi:* 'at nunc—nanis'.

   1 Genumana *codd.:* Cenumana *J. Gronovius*

12 (10 Bl., C)

somniculosam ut Poenus aspidem Psyllus

. . . as a Punic Psyllus [does to] a sleep-inducing asp

Gell. *NA* 9.12.12: *eadem ratione . . . Cinna in poematis* 'somniculosam—Psyllus'.

13–15 Epigrammata

13 (11 Bl., C.)

haec tibi Arateis multum vigilata lucernis
carmina, quis ignis novimus aerios,
levis in aridulo malvae descripta libello
Prusiaca vexi munera navicula.

This poem, which teaches us about the fiery bodies in the sky, the subject of
many sleepless nights with Aratus' lamplight, I have brought to you as a
present in a boat of Prusias, written on the dry bark of smooth mallow.

1–4 Isid. *Orig.* 6.12.1: *at vero historiae maiori modulo scribebantur, et non
solum in carta vel membranis, sed etiam in omentis elephantinis textilibusque
malvarum foliis atque palmarum. cuius generis Cinna sic meminit* 'haec—
navicula'.

  1 tibi *om. cod. K*   areteis *K*: aratis *BC*   vigilata *Scaliger (Lunelli, Aerius,
pp. 154–5):* invig- *codd.*   2 aerios *codd.*: aetherios *Basilius Zanchus (Lunelli,
p. 155)*

14 (14 Bl., C.)

saecula permaneat nostri Dictynna Catonis

May the *Dictynna* of my dear Cato last the centuries.

Suet. *Gramm.* 11.2, p. 16 ed. Kaster (1995): *meminit . . . Dianae* [sc. Valeri
Catonis carminis] *Cinna,* 'saecula—Catonis'.

15 (12 Bl., C.)

miseras audet galeare puellas

. . . has the audacity to helmet wretched girls

Non. Marc. p. 124 (vol. I) Lindsay: *clipeat . . . ita et galeare. Cinna in
Epigrammatis* 'miseras—puellas'.

16 (carmina amatoria)

Ov. *Tr.* 2.435: *Cinna quoque his* [v. ad Ticidam, **101**] *comes est, Cinnaque procacior Anser.*

Cinna too accompanies them, and Anser more licentious than Cinna.

17–18 (incertae sedis)

17 (4 Bl., 5 C.)

atque imitata nives lucens legitur crystallus

. . . and gleaming crystal, which resembles snow, is gathered

Schol. Iuv. 6.155 'grandia tolluntur crystallina' (p. 83 ed. Wessner, 1931): sic et Cinna dicit 'atque—crystallus'.

18 (13 Bl., C.)

Alpinaque cummis

. . . and Alpine gum

Non. Marc. p. 298 (vol. I) Lindsay: *cummi generis neutri, ut est usu, monoptoton; tamen feminino Cinna* 'Alpinaque gummis', *ut sit genetivus eius* 'huius cummis', *ut puppis febris pelvis.*

UNQUESTIONABLY the poet Cinna, friend of Catullus, is identical with the tribune Helvius Cinna, lynched by the Roman mob after Julius Caesar's murder because he was mistaken for Caesar's enemy Cornelius Cinna; this identification is argued, for example, by T. P. Wiseman, *Cinna the Poet and Other Roman Essays* (1974), 44–6, without mention of the strongest evidence in its favour (Ovid, *Ibis* 537–8 = 7c, see ad loc.). Valerius Maximus (9.9.1) gives the tribune's full name as C. Helvius Cinna, and that harmonizes with Catullus 10.30, where restoration of 'Cinna est Gaius' seems inevitable.

Cinna was probably born about 90 BC, a few years before Catullus, to whom he was a close neighbour. His home district seems to have been in the territory of the Cenomani, or—as Cinna himself called them (11.1)—the Genumani, which centred on Brixia, 'mother of Verona' (Cat. 67.34). We can trace his poetic career back at least to the mid-60s B C, when he began his nine-year stint on the epyllion *Smyrna* (Cat. 95 = 7a)—and it seems unlikely that *Smyrna* was his first composition. He probably remained an active poet until his death in 44 B C; otherwise Virgil in *Ecl.* 9.35–6 = 1a would not have spoken of him as virtually a contemporary figure. So, after the disappearance of Lucretius, Catullus, and Calvus (if the last-named lived significantly longer, he may have ceased to write verse), Cinna could have enjoyed almost a decade as the leading Roman poet; Nepos' evaluation of the otherwise unknown Julius Calidus (see Appendix) need not be taken too seriously. This pre-eminence may be reflected not only in Virgil, *Ecl.* 9.35–6 = 1a, but also in Cicero's outburst against the 'cantores Euphorionis' in 45 B C (*Tusc. Disp.* 3.45). Everything that we know about Cinna's poetic tastes, and the *Smyrna* in particular, would make him an ideal prime target for Cicero's attack, with the young Cornelius Gallus perhaps also coming into the sights.

Information about Cinna's life which is relevant to his poetry may be preserved in the Byzantine lexicon the Suda (Suidas), where we read s.v. Παρθένιος (III.58.10 ed. Adler = Parthenius, Test. 1 ed. Lightfoot) that Parthenius of Nicaea 'was taken by Cinna as a prize when the Romans defeated Mithridates (οὗτος ἐλήφθη ὑπὸ Κίννα λάφυρον ὅτε Μιθριδάτην Ῥωμαῖοι κατεπολέμησαν)'. Nicaea fell to Lucullus in 73 B C, but the reference here may be to Mithridates' final defeat—it would be rash to *demand* this sense from the verb, see Jane Lightfoot, *Parthenius of Nicaea* (Oxford, 1999), 11—which occurred in 66 B C. Suid. (or the ultimate source of the entry) seems to have felt that 'Cinna' was sufficiently well-known not to need further identification, and we do not know of a more plausible candidate than the poet; some, however, have thought of his father. Cinna's acquisition of Parthenius in 66 B C would go well enough with his commencement of the epyllion *Smyrna* (in the spirit of Parthenius and comparable Hellenistic poets) shortly after that date.

Certainly Helvius Cinna went to Bithynia at least once, since he mentions (**13**) bringing back from there a presentation copy of Aratus' *Phaenomena*. The date could be 66 B C, but it seems perverse to doubt that Cinna, like Catullus, accompanied the propraetor Memmius to Bithynia in 57–56 B C. That is much the most natural interpretation of the anecdote in Catullus 10—even though the litter with its bearers surely never existed (21 ff. 'at mi nullus erat neque hic neque illic' etc.) and 'it really belongs to my friend Gaius Cinna' (29–30) should be viewed as a mere evasion, aimed at explaining why Catullus cannot produce the litter on demand. If we believe that Cinna went to Bithynia in 57–56 B C, there are possible consequences for the *Propempticon Pollionis* (**2–6**, see introduction to that poem).

Cinna's two most influential works, in hexameters, were the *Propempticon*

Pollionis and the *Smyrna*, both of which attracted learned commentators. Above all *Smyrna* (see the testimonia in **7**) was the poem which makes him seem the Roman counterpart of Euphorion of Chalcis, even though that role was later appropriated by Cornelius Gallus. Probably these two works were issued separately. There may also have been a separate collection of Epigrams (**15** is quoted from 'Cinna in Epigrammatis'), or else the epigrams may have been joined to his polymetric poems (**11** is in hendecasyllables, **12** a choliamb). The spicy erotic material mentioned by Ovid (**16**) could have appeared equally well in epigram and polymetrics, as in the case of Catullus.

Although the supercilious Greeks in Aulus Gellius 19.9.7 = **1***e* denied to Cinna the small merit which they grudgingly allowed to Catullus and Calvus, it is possible that we have lost a major talent in Helvius Cinna. The scanty remnants of the *Propempticon Pollionis* (**2–6**) and *Smyrna* (**7–10**) are rather unprepossessing—Silius Italicus, however, thought **6** worthy of detailed imitation—but **11–12**, **17**, and, above all, **13** are in their different ways more attractive.

1

Only brief comment is required here on these items, to some of which we shall return. The favourable view of Cinna taken by Valgius Rufus (**1***b*= **166**.1–4) should be set alongside that of Virgil (**1***a*) and perhaps belongs to the same period (in Horace, *Sat.* 1.10.82, *c*.35 BC, Valgius is mentioned with Varius, Virgil, and others as a man whose critical approval Horace covets). **1***c* no doubt is particularly aimed at *Smyrna*, which needed the learned commentary of Crassicius (see **7***b*) in order to be intelligible. Martial's 'Modestus' (line 1) might be—although he must have died long before Martial's time— the freedman of Iulius Hyginus (Suet. *De Gramm.* 20.3, with Kaster ad loc.) who commented on the *Propempticon Pollionis* (see **4–5** for verbatim extracts). The Greeks in **1***e* were looking for sweet and sentimental short poems on love or drinking such as Anacreon composed; they admitted that a small number of pieces by Catullus and Calvus satisfied them, but judged Cinna's efforts in the same direction to be 'inlepida'. Bearing in mind the prominence of 'lepidus' and 'lepos' as a term of approval in Catullus (starting with 1.1 'lepidum novum libellum'), one might wonder whether the Greeks were denying Cinna success in the same terms in which he had claimed it for himself; presumably the reference is to erotic poems, in which, according to Ovid (*Tr.* 2.435 = **16**), Cinna was 'procax' though less so than Anser.

Attached to Philarg. on Virgil, *Ecl.* 9.35–6 (p. 172 Hagen) is a notice that picks up almost all the standard allusions to Cinna. Kaster, however, shows (Suet. *De Gramm.*, pp. 200–1) that this is not ancient, but derives from Politian or some other Italian of the same period.

2–6 *Propempticon Pollionis*

We have some slight evidence (Cicero, *Ad Fam.* 1.6 (= 17 SB).1) that Asinius Pollio planned a journey to Greece and the East in the spring of 56 BC when he was probably in his twentieth year (called 'puer' a few years earlier in Cat. 12.9). This was a normal age for young Romans to make such a tour, combining culture and education with sight-seeing (cf. G. W. Bowersock, *Augustus and the Greek World* (1965), 76 ff., Elizabeth Rawson, *Intellectual Life in the Late Roman Empire* (1985), 9 ff.); high points were visits to Athens and the cities of Asia (e.g. Prop. 1.6.13–14 'doctas cognoscere Athenas / et veteres Asiae cernere divitias', Ov. *Tr.* 1.2.77–8 'non peto quas quondam petii studiosus Athenas, / oppida non Asiae, non loca visa prius'). Absence from Rome in 56 BC might have had incidental advantages for Pollio, removing him from a slightly awkward political situation (J. André, *La Vie et l'œuvre de C. Asinius Pollion* (1949), 10–11). The consul of 57, P. Lentulus Spinther (proconsul of Cilicia in 56), had been entrusted by the senate with the task of restoring Ptolemy Auletes to the Egyptian throne, a commission which Pompey coveted and eventually obtained despite Pollio's vigorous support for Lentulus. Cicero's words to the latter, 'quae gerantur accipies ex Pollione, qui omnibus negotiis non interfuit solum sed praefuit' (*Ad Fam.* 1.6 (= 17 SB).1, perhaps March 56 BC) allow for the possibility that Pollio intended to visit Lentulus in his province, probably in conjunction with a tour round the cities of Asia.

Pollio's movements at this time interlock with those of the poet Cinna. It seems a natural deduction (above, p. 19) from Catullus 10.30 that Cinna had been with Memmius and Catullus in Bithynia in 57–56 BC. One would expect—but this is perhaps too literal-minded—the author to present a copy of his poem to Pollio in Rome before the latter's departure. 'To be in Rome and write a *Propempticon* for Pollio in February or March, Cinna would have to leave Bithynia in mid-winter' (Syme, *JRS* 51 (1961), 24). At the most pessimistic assessment (not wholly shared by L. herself), 'we know neither recipient, date, nor destination of Cinna's poem' (Jane Lightfoot, *Parthenius of Nicaea* (1999), 169). To judge from the *Smyrna*, Cinna was not a quick composer; it would not be surprising if, like many artistic works down the centuries, this poem was not completed until some considerable time after the occasion for which it was planned.

Elements of the Propempticon or 'send-off' poem (the main preoccupation of Francis Cairns, *Generic Composition in Greek and Roman Poetry* (1972)), are already present in early Greek lyric and elegy (Nisbet and Hubbard, Horace, *Odes*, I (1970), 41, more in McKeown on Ovid, *Am.* 2.11) and are taken up by the Hellenistic poets (e.g. Theocritus 7.52 ff., Callimachus fr. 400 Pf.—it is very doubtful whether *Suppl. Hell.* 404 was written by Erinna). The first poet whom we definitely know to have used the title *Propempticon* was Parthenius (fr. 26 Lightfoot = *SH* 639); the *SH* editors suggested that the name of a dedicatee may have dropped out from the title in the manuscripts of Steph. Byz., who records only that Parthenius mentions Corycos, a city of Cilicia (a curious coincidence in that Asinius Pollio may have been on his way to Cilicia). Fr. 36 L. = *SH* 647 Γλαύκῳ καὶ Νηρῆϊ καὶ εἰναλίῳ Μελικέρτῃ (? to whom sailors make offerings on their safe arrival, as in Virgil's imitation, *Georgics* 1.437 'Glauco et Panopeae et Inoo Melicertae') may also have belonged to this poem. It would not be surprising if Parthenius' poem exercised considerable influence on Cinna's, and that of Cinna on all Latin poems in the same genre down to Statius (*Silvae* 3.2). We shall see (on **2**) how the motif of St Elmo's fire is taken up by Horace and Statius; other items posited for the *Propempticon Pollionis* on the basis of recurrence in Horace (*Odes* 1.3), Ovid (*Am.* 2.11), or Statius are the rocks of Ceraunia/Acroceraunia, close to Corcyra which Cinna certainly mentioned (**4**, cf. N–H on Horace, *Odes* 1.3.20) and the injunction that only the friendly west wind should blow (N–H on *Odes* 1.3.4). Particularly interesting is the detailed imitation by Silius Italicus (13.86–9) of **6**, lines with which Ovid too may show familiarity— appropriate enough since he was a personal friend of Iulius Hyginus, commentator on Cinna's *Propempticon* (Suet. *De Gramm.* 20.2).

I would like to draw attention to Lucan 5.413 ff. Line 418 'hic [sc. Aquilo] utinam summi curvet carchesia mali' echoes Cinna **2** 'lucida quom fulgent alti carchesia mali' (the imitation would be even clearer if one preferred the variant 'summi' for 'alti' in Cinna). Lucan seems deliberately to reverse the normal motifs of a propempticon: e.g. it is customary to pray that only the west wind should blow (Horace, *Odes* 1.3.4, Ovid, *Am.* 2.11.41, Stat., *Silv.* 3.2.46), but Lucan's Caesar revels in the fact that he needs only ferocious Aquilo (5.417 'recti fluctus soloque Aquilone secandi'); the main-top will not be protected by St Elmo's fire (Cinna **2**) but bent by the north wind (5.418, quoted above). Caesar deliberately sails at the 'wrong' time (5.407, 413). Sometimes (Horace, *Epode* 10, Nonnus, *Dionysiaca* 47.357 ff.) the good wishes of a propempticon may be inverted to become a prayer for destruction; here, however, Caesar is challenging the elements to do their worst (cf. 423), confident in his own destiny (422).

Cinna's *Propempticon Pollionis* was the subject of a detailed commentary (from which **4** and **5** are verbatim extracts) by the Augustan scholar C. Iulius Hyginus (Suet. *De Gramm.* 20, see Kaster's edition, 205–14), which took the time to discuss criticisms of the poet made by earlier scholars (**4**, 'quaerunt etiam nonnulli . . .') and to mention an alternative route past the island of Leucas (**5**). Existence of such a commentary suggests that Cinna's poem was not too short—probably longer than the 143 lines of Statius' envoi for Maecius Celer (*Silv.* 3.2)—and that it appeared separately, like the *Smyrna* (**7a**) which also found at least one independent commentator (**7b**). See A. Perutelli, *Frustula Poetarum* (Bologna, 2002), 125–34.

Of the five surviving items, **2–3** refer to protection against rough weather at sea (in the Adriatic?); **4–5** (from the commentary of Hyginus) are concerned with the route from Corcyra around Leucas and into the Gulf of Corinth, while **6** almost certainly describes a visit to Delphi. I have ordered the items according to the sequence of the journey. No doubt Pollio would have continued to Athens, and thence—if indeed he was going to visit Lentulus Spinther in his province of Cilicia (see above)—across the Aegean.

2 (2 Blänsdorf, Courtney)

lucida quom fulgent alti carchesia mali: 'lucida' is predicative, 'gleams bright', and (together with 'fulgent') undoubtedly refers to the electrical discharge known as St Elmo's fire, which appears on the mast and rigging of ships and was thought to indicate the presence and protection of the Dioscuri, Castor and Pollux. See the full note of Nisbet and Hubbard on Horace, *Odes* 1.3.2 'fratres Helenae, lucida sidera'. This point was not appreciated by Lionel Casson (*Ships and Seamanship in the Ancient World* (1971), 233 n. 36). Perhaps through the example of Cinna it became customary in a propempticon to wish for St Elmo's fire to protect the voyager, cf. Stat. *Silv.* 3.2.8 ff.:

> proferte benigna
> sidera et antemnae gemino considite cornu,
> Oebalii fratres; vobis pontusque polusque
> luceat.

quom: the older spelling (Parsons in *JRS* 69 (1979), 132, on the Cornelius Gallus papyrus, **145**.2), which Cinna himself would very probably have used. Even after 'cum' began to replace it (in Cicero's time) many people still preferred to write 'quom' for the conjunction, thus distinguishing it from the preposition (Quint. 1.7.5). Here the variants '*con*fulgent' and '*qua* splendent' may be traces of the archaic form (cf. **6**.1 'ingenteis'), which I have retained.

alti: so Isidore, supported by A. Lunelli, *Aerius* (1969), 63 ff. Since Nonius omits the epithet, our only source for the variant 'summi' is the Lucan scholion, which may have been adapted to fit Lucan 5.418 'hic utinam summi curvet carchesia mali'. On the other hand Lucan may be deliberately recalling Cinna—that could still be the case even with 'alti' in the latter—and Cinna in turn may be imitating Lucilius 1309 Marx (cf. 619–20 Warmington) 'tertius [? sc. fluctus] hic mali superat carchesia summa'. Nonius' surrounding comment twice has a part of 'summus' (perhaps, however, from Lucilius 1309 M. which immediately follows). So, while 'alti' is probably to be preferred, 'summi' could yet be right.

carchesia: the main-top, cf. Casson, *Ships and Seamanship*, 233, 'On larger craft of both types [sc. galleys and sailing ships], the main mast was stout enough to support a main-top . . . girdled by a protective railing (*thorakion*).' For a specific connexion of St Elmo's fire with the καρχήσιον, cf. Lucian, *Navig.* 9 ἔφασκεν ὁ ναύκληρος . . . τινα λαμπρὸν ἀστέρα Διοσκούρων τὸν ἕτερον ἐπικαθίσαι τῷ καρχησίῳ καὶ κατευθῦναι τὴν ναῦν.

Nonius Marcellus, besides reading 'qua splendent', ascribes the fragment to 'Catullus Veronensis'. One or two older scholars tried to place it as 64.235b, while others have argued that the grammarians originally knew two quite separate fragments: (*a*) our line of Cinna, (*b*) a line of Catullus for which we are unable to find a home. More probably Nonius has made a simple mistake. Conversely Isidore (*Orig.* 19.33.3) credits Cinna with what is almost certainly a misquotation of Cat. 64.65.

3 (3 Bl., C.)

atque anquina regat stabilem fortissima cursum: when the wind becomes too strong for normal sailing, the halyard is loosened, in order to lower the sail and make the vessel ride on a more even keel (Casson, *Ships and Seamanship*, 262 n. 9, cf. 275).

anquina: 'the halyard' = Greek ἄγκοινα. The only other occurrence of the word in Latin literature comes from an (undoubtedly correct) emendation in Lucilius 1114 M. = 618 W. 'funis enim praecisus cito atque anquina [*so Junius for* anchora] soluta' (see Casson, 262 n. 9). After establishing the meaning 'halyard' for ἄγκοινα/anquina, Casson adds (262) that this suits the etymology (cognate with ἀγκάλη): 'A halyard is the one rope that is at all times "bent"; going up, as it does, to the mast-head and then down again, part of it bends, hairpin fashion, over the sheave in the block at the masthead.'

stabilem . . . cursum: see *OLD* 2 for *stabilis* = 'steady' of a ship.

fortissima: having to carry the weight of a vast spar nearly as long as the ship, the halyard would be the stoutest line of the running rigging (Casson, 262 n. 9).

4–5 (5 Bl., 4 C.)

Two verbatim extracts from the commentary on Cinna's *Propempticon* by Iulius Hyginus (see above on **2–6**), which incidentally show that H. was not the first scholar to expound the poem. Only **4** gives us information about Cinna; **5** explains what was the normal procedure ('solent') for those sailing from Actium, even though Cinna apparently did not mention or recommend it for Pollio. The grammarian's interest is limited to the forms 'itiner' (accusative) and 'iteris' (genitive) employed by Hyginus—there is no suggestion that Cinna used them. I have separated the two extracts and reversed their order, so that **4** (from Corcyra onwards) precedes **5** (from Actium onwards).

It seems that two criticisms ('quaerunt etiam nonnulli . . .') had been made of Cinna's proposed itinerary: (*a*) if he wished Pollio to sail round the west and south sides of the island of Leucas (Leucata is on the south-west tip), why should he make him put in at Actium instead of sailing directly from Corcyra around Leucas?; (*b*) if, on the other hand, he were prescribing a stop at Actium, it was customary to shorten the journey by proceeding from Actium for some 60 stades to the Leucadian Isthmus, between Leucas and Acarnania (see e.g. *Grosser Historischer Weltatlas*[2] (1954), 18–19), and having the boat hauled over (or towed through) the Isthmus. Courtney (217) thinks that Cinna wanted Pollio to visit temples at Actium (the cult of Actian Apollo was already established, though not as important as it became after 31 BC); but this cannot have been explicitly stated in the poem, or else there would have been nothing to argue about.

Leucas was connected to the mainland by a low neck of land, mostly silted sand (Gomme on Thuc. 3.81.1). Conditions in the area changed over the centuries. The Corinthians under Cypselus had dug a canal through the Isthmus (Strabo 10.2.8); Thuc. 3.81.1 ὑπερενεγκόντες τὸν Λευκαδίων ἰσθμὸν τὰς ναῦς clearly implies land transport, while in Arrian's time (*Indica* 41.2) there was a narrow navigable channel marked by stakes. I do not understand 'remulco, quem Graeci πάκτωνα dicunt', since a πάκτων is not a 'tow-rope' (*remulcum*, cf. Valgius Rufus **168.**1), but a shallow-draught boat associated with the Nile (see LSJ and Casson, *Ships and Seamanship*, 342), not—as far as I know—so-called elsewhere. Possibly πά<κτωνα> (Fabricius) is an incorrect

restoration; if the reference is to a small boat towing a larger one, the text of
Hyginus would seem to be lacunose. We are left in doubt whether Hyginus
has in mind dragging over land or towing over water (cf. H. Dahlmann, *Über
Helvius Cinna* (1977), 31–2; K. Deichgräber, *Hermes*, 99 (1971), 63), but the
former seems more likely. *OLD* s.v. *traductio* 1 notes that Hyginus uses the
noun in a 'quasi-concrete' sense, applied to a crossing place at an isthmus,
where boats are conveyed overland; I have translated this with 'Portage', to
which the same can apply. For 'e regione' + genitive = 'directly opposite . . .',
see *OLD* s.v. *regio* 2b. These problems do not immediately concern Cinna,
since nothing suggests that Cinna himself mentioned the alternative route
through the Leucadian Isthmus.

   One can confidently deduce that Cinna did prescribe for Pollio the some-
what paradoxical route from Corcyra to Actium and thence round Leucas
into the Gulf of Corinth. We do not know at which port he might have
disembarked, but **6** almost certainly finds Pollio at Delphi. Cinna seems to
have laid down the route quite dogmatically (*iubeat* and *moneat* are the
commentator's words), though this need not imply more than a second per-
son singular future indicative, like 'mirabere' in **6**.1. Compare Lucilius 102–4
M = 143–5 W (perhaps addressed to a friend who will accompany him to
Sicily) 'et, saepe quod ante / optasti, freta, Messanam, Regina videbis / moe-
nia, tum Liparas, Facelinae templa Dianae'. The rhetorician Menander
recommended that, in a *propempticon*, the writer should sketch out the
prospective journey and scenery, τὴν ὁδὸν καὶ τὴν γῆν δι’ ἧς πορεύεται
(398.30).

6 (1Bl., C.)

This fragment is closely and extensively imitated by Silius Italicus, in the same
number of lines (like his imitation of Varius Rufus, **150**). Silius describes the
grove of Feronia, whose treasures had been preserved inviolate through many
centuries simply by the religious awe which the place inspired (13.86–9):

> fama est intactas longaevi ab origine fani
> crevisse in medium congestis undique donis
> immensum per tempus opes lustrisque relictum
> innumeris, aurum solo servante pavore.

There may be other, more distant, echoes of the same model elsewhere in
Silius (2.49 'deductus origine Beli', 3.498 'longisque ab origine saeclis', 5.266
'congestis opibus donisque'). Whereas we depend for our knowledge of the

fragment upon an egregious blunder—not, one hopes, going back to Iulius Hyginus—of a grammarian (see on line 3 'Belidis'), Silius quite possibly knew Cinna's whole poem, and thus the context of our lines.

'Donorum' (1) above all suggests offerings made to a god, and 'congestis undique' (2) a great religious centre to which people come from all over Greece. It must be of high antiquity ('innumerabilibus . . . saeclis', 2) and the recipient of corporate dedications by Greek city-states (lines 3–4 clearly indicate Argos, Athens, and Thebes). The obvious candidate is Delphi, as seen by K. Deichgräber (*Hermes*, 99 (1971), 65). Rich shrines may have been a regular prospect in a propempticon—though not one that Helios can offer to Phaethon (Ov. *Met.* 2.76–8 'forsitan et lucos illic urbesque deorum / concipias animo delubraque ditia donis / esse: per insidias iter est formasque ferarum!'). Delphi fits well with what we can glean about Pollio's anticipated itinerary. We have pictured him (4–5) crossing the Adriatic to Corcyra, sailing to Actium, thence around the island of Leucas (and presumably into the Gulf of Corinth). We do not know where he might disembark, but his destination would almost certainly be Athens, the magnet of tourists and students (e.g. Prop. 1.6.13, 3.21.1), and an intermediate stop at Delphi would be both convenient and appropriate. One could also think of a fitting sentiment for the 'quam' clause implied by 'nec tam' in line 1. Morel quoted with approval the continuation given by Kiessling, 'quam in philosophorum scholis sapientiae et eloquentiae operam daturus es' (also in Courtney 215). Such no doubt would be Pollio's purpose in Athens, but the tenor of **6** suggests to me that the same place which contained abundant religious dedications ('donorum ingenteis . . . acervos', 1) also contained something at which Pollio would marvel even more. If that place was Delphi, then surely Pollio would marvel more at the oracle of Apollo and its atmosphere of religious awe. This idea may be supported from Silius (see above), who stresses the 'pavor' aroused by the Grove of Feronia (13.89).

1. nec tam donorum ingenteis mirabere acervos: the heavily spondaic line (cf. **10.**1–2 describing Smyrna's grief, where one might posit a special effect), with two elisions (cf. line 3 with three elisions) and no word-break in either the second or the third foot, is worthy of note. Catullus' hexameter poems (62 and 64) contain no line remotely like it, though one can find partial parallels in Cicero's *Aratea* (e.g. fr. 15.2 Buescu 'quod quasi temone adiunctam prae se quatit Arctum', cf. fr. 33.429) and Lucretius (e.g. 3.621 'membrorum ut numquam exsistat praeposterus ordo').

nec tam . . . mirabere: for the Roman not being overly impressed, cf. Horace, *Odes* 1.7.10–12 'me *nec tam* patiens Lacedaemon / *nec tam* Larisae percussit campus opimae / quam . . .'

donorum: offerings made at a shrine, ἀναθήματα (cf. Dahlmann, *Über Helvius Cinna*, 9–10).

ingenteis . . . acervos: a frequent collocation (Dahlmann, 10–11), particularly in Virgil (e.g. *Aen.* 4.402). Horace, *Odes* 2.2.23–4 'quisquis *ingentes* oculo irretorto / spectat *acervos*' (the ability to walk past piles of treasure) might be an echo of Cinna.

ingenteis: according to P. J. Parsons (*JRS* 69 (1979), 133 n. 56), 'The Gallus papyrus [145] may encourage us to believe that EI spellings in the MSS of Catullus [instances given ibid.] and Lucretius [see Lachmann on 4.602] are authorial, not simply scribal archaisms.' He gives an account (132–4) of the various systems used and recommended by the ancients, one of which would have written EIS to distinguish accusative plural *ingenteis* from genitive singular *ingentis*. See on **2** above for indications in the preserved variants that Cinna wrote 'quom'.

mirabere: appropriate of the traveller in a propempticon (cf. Ovid, *Am.* 2.11.11 'non illic [sc. at sea] urbes, non tu mirabere silvas'—for this poem see W. Görler, *Hermes*, 93 (1965), 338–47, with several references to Cinna, and now the full introduction and commentary by J. C. McKeown, *Ovid, Amores*, (1998), 222 ff.). But 'mirari' is also often used, with a certain disparagement, of the material possessions or honours which people hold in awe and strive for; e.g. Horace, *Epist.* 1.6.18 'cum gemmis Tyrios mirare colores', 1.1.47 'ne cures ea quae stulte miraris et optas', Cic. *Off.* 1.71 'despicere ea quae plerique mirentur, imperia et magistratus'. That sense may to some extent be felt here.

2. innumerabilibus . . . saeclis: nicely varied by Silius with 'lustris . . . / innumeris' (13.88–9), to which he adds, for good measure, 'immensum per tempus' (see above for that passage). Scaevola's tribute to the *Marius* of Cicero, 'canescet saeclis innumerabilibus' (**91**) might be a deliberate echo of this line, particularly since the 'canescet' motif is perhaps borrowed from Cinna's *Smyrna* (see on **7a**). 'Innumerabilibus' occupies the first half of a hexameter also in Lucr. 1.583.

Cinna refers to the centuries which had elapsed since the foundation of Argos, Athens, and Thebes (lines 3–4). Deichgräber (*Hermes* (1971), 65) points out that, according to one conventional chronology (the *Marmor Parium*, *FGH* 239), Cecrops became king of Attica in 1580 BC, Cadmus founded Thebes in 1518, and Danaus reached Greece in 1512. The foundation of cities was a topic of great interest in the Hellenistic age, becoming the subject of poems (e.g. several by Apollonius Rhodius, frs. 4–12 Powell).

congestos undique: cf. Silius 13.87 'congestis undique donis' (discussed above).

3–4. Although these lines contain nothing very testing, this is one of the few surviving fragments to give even a hint of the erudition and obscurity which enabled commentators, within a generation of Cinna's death, to make their reputation by elucidating his poems. It would be astonishing if Charisius' blunder over 'Belidis' (3, see below) came from Iulius Hyginus.

3. iam inde a: 'continuously from . . .' (*OLD iam* 2), as e.g. Virgil, *Georgics* 3.74 'iam inde a teneris'.

Belidis: ablative plural, referring to Danaus and Aegyptus ('Belidae fratres', Stat. *Theb.* 6.291). Charisius (who contrasts *Aen.* 2.82 'Belidae Palamedis') grotesquely believed that 'Belidis' was genitive singular, presumably corresponding to 'Cecropis'. Cinna no doubt introduces into Latin the patronymic 'Belides' with ī as if from Beleus. The only attested Greek occurrence is in *Et. Mag.* p. 165.41 Gaisford.

4. Cod. N of Charisius has Tyriū or Tyriā (which should be Tyrium or Tyriam). Keil emended this to 'Tyriorum', and Morel, Buechner, and Blänsdorf all print 'Tyriorum ab origine Cadmi'. If this is meant to be understood as '<from the natal year of the city> of Cadmus <who came> from the ancient origin of the Tyrians', the sense seems impossibly contorted. I have accepted 'Tyriorum', but emended 'Cadmi' to 'Cadmo', '. . . and from Cadmus, far-distant ancestor of the Thebans'. 'Cadmo' would be in apposition to 'origine', used of the founder of a race (*OLD* 5a), as in *Aen.* 12.166 'Aeneas, Romanae stirpis origo'. For 'Tyrii' used as a substantive = 'Thebans', cf. Stat. *Theb.* 11.430, though perhaps it is deliberately provocative to use 'Tyrians' for 'Thebans' in the context of the foundation of Thebes. One could make a case for emending 'alta' to 'alto'; cf. e.g. Horace, *Sat.* 2.5.62–3 'ab alto / demissum genus Aenea', Ovid, *Fasti* 4.305, Silius 8.405. It might be felt that 'origo' = 'founder of the race' would be better without an epithet. In either case the pattern of apposition would be intricate.

L. Mueller (endorsed by Dahlmann, 19) wished to read 'Tyrii iam ab origine Cadmi' (picking up the *iam* from line 3). This is printed by Courtney, and may well be right, perhaps gaining support from Stat. *Theb.* 2.613 'Chromis Tyrii demissus origine Cadmi'. 'Tyrii iam' is very close to one interpretation of N's reading (Tyriā). Kenney questions the elision of 'iam' in 4 (*CR* NS 29 (1979), 310); I am not sure how strong an objection this is.

7–10 *Smyrna*

I have throughout spelt the title of the poem and name of the heroine with Sm-, following Goold (1983 edition of Catullus, 261–2, cf. *HSCP* 69 (1965), 11), even though manuscript evidence overwhelmingly favours Zm-. The latter form was used well before Cinna's time for the great city, and R. Mer-kelbach (*Glotta*, 45 (1967), 39–40) showed that ζμήνεος and Ζμίνθος should be written in two epigrams from the Garland of Philip (*Anth. Pal.* 6.239 and 9.410 = Apollonius 3 and Sabinus 1 Gow–Page). But Priscian (GLK II, 41–2, cf. 23) insists on metrical grounds that the correct form is Sm-, not Zm-: 's quoque sequente m, ut "Smyrna", "smaragdus"; nam vitium faciunt qui zm scribunt'. Quoting Lucan 10.121, which ends 'distinctă smaragdo', he adds 'nisi esset s ante m, subtrahi in metro minime posset, nec staret versus'. The two cases are not wholly comparable. Without a previous short syllable 'smaragdus' would be unusable in dactylic verse, whereas difficulties over 'Smyrna' would arise only if a dactyl preceded the name. Although the Greeks show some interest in this spelling (*Anecdota Graeca Oxon.* III, 250 πολλοὶ ἁμαρτάνουσι γράφοντες διὰ τοῦ ζ, not based upon a metrical argument), I suspect that the discussion of 'Smyrna' in Priscian (from Crassicius' com-mentary, cf. 7*b*?) originally related to Cinna's poem. It seems to imply that Cinna himself allowed a dactyl to precede the name; this receives some sup-port from the epigram on Crassicius, where we read 'se crederĕ Smyrna probavit' (7*b*, line 4). Ovid, like Propertius (3.19.16), always calls the girl (and Cinna's poem in *Ibis* 537 = 7*c*) Myrrha; he would not have wished even to raise the problem discussed above, whereas in Cinna's contemporary Lucre-tius we find 'cederĕ squamigeris' (1.372) and other things even more surpris-ing. Finally, 'Smyrna' might seem to contemporaries a more 'literary', less commonplace spelling than 'Zmyrna', and hence was more likely to appeal to Helvius Cinna.

   Although only three complete lines and a single word survive from *Smyrna*, the poem has left a considerable afterglow. We can, with reasonable con-fidence, say quite a lot about the subject matter, style, probable sources, later imitations, and the impact upon ancient readers.

   The main action of Cinna's poem was clearly set in Cyprus (7*a* = Cat. 95.5 'Satrachi'). It would have reached its dénouement with Smyrna's transform-ation in Arabia. Ovid, although setting the scene in Cyprus, twice (*Met.* 10.307–10, 478) rather oddly writes as if the incestuous affair had occurred in Arabia (similarly [Virgil] *Ciris* 237–8, quoted below). The myth also had connections with Assyria and Cilicia. Thus the tale had a strongly Oriental flavour, such as can also be found in certain books (particularly 4 and 10) of Ovid's *Metamorphoses*. Eastern stories were no doubt collected by Greek prose-writers of the Hellenistic period. Some of the poets too had links with the East: Euphorion of Chalcis accepted Seleucid patronage; Nicander of Colophon (who possibly wrote of Smyrna in his *Heteroeumena*) praised an Attalid, and Parthenius of Nicaea, certainly an important model for Helvius Cinna, came to Rome from Bithynia.

In making Smyrna a Cyprian, daughter of King Cinyras (whom we first meet in *Iliad* 11.20), Cinna was probably choosing a rare version. More often (Panyassis fr. 27 Bernabé = 22ᴬ Davies, cf. V. J. Matthews, *Panyassis of Halikarnassus* (1974), 120–5, Ant. Lib. 34, perhaps from Nicander, *Heteroeumena*) she is daughter of Theias, usually a king of Assyria. In Antimachus of Colophon fr. 92 Matthews (probably *Lyde*, concerned with Adonis rather than Smyrna) Theias (? Thoas) rules Arabia as well as Assyria, but (if Matthews's restoration is correct) Antimachus may have been the first to make Cinyras father of Adonis. The predominant version of the myth is expressed some two centuries after Cinna's time by Oppian (*Hal.* 3.402 ff.):

$$\mu i \xi \epsilon \ \delta \epsilon \ \kappa o v \rho \eta s$$
δάκρυον Ἀσσυρίης Θειαντίδος, ἥν ποτέ φασι
πατρὸς ἐρασσαμένην δυσμήχανον ἔργον ἀνύσσαι
ἐλθεῖν τ’ ἐς φιλότητα χολωσαμένης Ἀφροδίτης·
ἀλλ’ ὅτε μιν καὶ δένδρον ἐπώνυμον ἐρρίζωσεν
αἶσα θεῶν, γοάει τε καὶ ἦν ὀλοφύρεται ἄτην
δάκρυσι δευομένη λέκτρου χάριν

Some conflation of the Cyprian and Assyrian traditions can be observed in Hyginus (not the commentator on the *Propempticon Pollionis*), *fab.* 58.1, 242.4, 270.1, 275.1), where Cinyras, though king of Assyria, is son of Paphos, and in schol. *Il.* 11.20, where Cinyras himself is son of Theias. The idea that Smyrna's passion was a punishment sent by Aphrodite (Oppian, *Hal.* 3.405 above) is explained by Hyginus *fab.* 58.1 (Smyrna's mother boasted that her daughter was more beautiful than the goddess).

A Greek poet who must be very important in the background to Cinna's *Smyrna* is Parthenius of Nicaea, whom Cinna himself (or else his father, see above) brought back as a prisoner of war from Bithynia. A brief verbatim fragment (29 Lightfoot = *Suppl. Hell.* 641) of Parthenius on this myth, with its surrounding comment (*Et. Gen.* s.v. Ἀῶιος), is of extraordinary complexity. The Aous was described as 'pouring from the Corycian [i.e. Cilician] mountains' (Κωρυκίων σεύμενος ἐξ ὀρέων). A possible interpretation (*SH*) is that the Aous rises in Cilicia, but disappears and flows underground, crossing the sea and re-emerging in Cyprus where it is called the Setrachus (Satrachus). Furthermore it is claimed that the daughter of Theias was called Aoa (rather than Smyrna), that her son Adonis was known as Aous, and that Cilicia used to be called Aoa. It seems unlikely that all these variant possibilities were mentioned by Parthenius, but Cinna clearly had a very rich tradition available to him. In view of Catullus 95.5 = 7*a* 'Smyrna cavas Satrachi penitus mittetur ad undas', Cinna must have mentioned the river Satrachus, named in the third century BC by Lycophron (*Alex.* 448), whose only other occurrence in surviving ancient poetry relates to the love affair of Aphrodite and Adonis (Nonnus, *Dion.* 13.458–60):

ἦχι θαλασσογόνου Παφίης νυμφήιον ὕδωρ
Σέτραχος ἱμερόεις, ὅθι πολλάκις εἷμα λαβοῦσα
Κύπρις ἀνεχλαίνωσε λελουμένον υἱέα Μύρρης.

We do not know whether Cinna dealt with events subsequent to the transformation of Smyrna and birth of her son Adonis.

Another poetic account of this myth lies behind Ant. Lib. 34. As has often been observed, Smyrna's prayer to the gods just before transformation, μήτε παρὰ ζῶσι μήτ’ ἐν νεκροῖς φανῆναι represents a Greek hexameter only lightly disguised: μήτε παρὰ ζώοις μήτ’ ἐν νεκύεσσι φανῆναι (or something very similar), which probably lies behind Ov. *Met.* 10.485–7 'ne violem vivosque superstes / mortuaque exstinctos, ambobus pellite regnis / mutataeque mihi vitamque necemque negate'. One can make quite a good case for Nicander's *Heteroeumena* as the unknown source, since (*a*) many stories in Ant. Lib. are stated to come from Nicander, (*b*) Ovid undoubtedly made wide use of the *Heteroeumena* when writing his *Metamorphoses*, (*c*) Nicander is known to have related the origin of the anemone from Adonis' blood (fr. 65 Gow–Scholfield). On the other hand a subsequent annotator of Ant. Lib.'s manuscript, who traced many stories to an origin in Nicander, was apparently unable to find a source for Ant. Lib. 34 (see Lightfoot, *Parthenius*, 253–6).

A version of the Smyrna myth which (as far as it goes) accords with what we can reasonably surmise about Cinna's *Smyrna* is ascribed to the *Metamorphoses* of Theodorus (*SH* 749). This Theodorus addressed a hexameter poem to Cleopatra (*SH* 752), and so must predate Ovid's *Metamorphoses* (*SH* 750 says that Ovid followed him); whether he would have been available to Cinna we do not know.

The extant verbatim fragments of Cinna's *Smyrna* refer to the wasting effects of the girl's passion (**8**), the growth in her womb of the incestuously conceived child (**9**) and her continual grief (**10**, perhaps shortly before her transformation). I will suggest that **7***b* wittily adapts an episode of the original in which the heroine is pressed by her father to choose a husband from among her many suitors (cf. Ant. Lib. 34.1, Ovid, *Met.* 10.315 ff., 356 ff.). Beyond that, we can only pick up hints from later versions which are likely to reflect Cinna's poem.

It seems likely that there was a detailed account of Smyrna's arboreal transformation, in a style which we would call Ovidian (cf. *Met.* 10.489 ff.) but may have been standard in neoteric epyllia (see p. 62 on Calvus' *Io*, cf. [Virgil], *Ciris* 80–2, 490–507). Particularly interesting (because it pre-dates Ovid) is

Propertius 3.19.16 'arboris in frondis condita Myrrha novae', a mode of description which is paralleled both in earlier Ovid (*AA* 1.286 'et nunc obducto cortice pressa latet', *Rem. Am.* 100 'non tegeres vultus cortice, Myrrha, tuos'), and in *Met.* 10.498 'mersitque suos in cortice vultus'. When Lucretius (2.702–3) numbers among impossibilities

> et altos
> interdum ramos egigni corpore vivo

Bailey writes 'Perhaps Lucretius is thinking of such metamorphoses as those of Daphne, Philemon and Baucis [a tale probably unknown to L.'s readers], or the sisters of Phaethon.' Is it too fanciful to suggest that Lucretius may be poking fun at Cinna's newly published poem (cf. Ov. *Met.* 10.493 'in magnos bracchia ramos')?

Almost certainly Smyrna's nurse played an important part in Cinna as the girl's helper and confidante; compare Ant. Lib. 34.2 (? from Nicander), Ov. *Met.* 10.382 ff., Lyne on *Ciris* 206–385 and (more generally on the nurse-figure) Lightfoot, *Parthenius*, 498. It is time to bring in the pseudo-Virgilian *Ciris*, a poem of uncertain date but probably later than Ovid's *Metamorphoses*. There, in the middle of the night, the nurse Carme intercepts Scylla as she is about to enter her father's bedchamber in order to cut off his magic lock of hair on which the city's safety depends. At first the old woman jumps to the wrong conclusion, thinking that Scylla has fallen in love with her father (237–8):

> ei mihi, ne furor ille tuos invaserit artus
> ille Arabae Myrrhae quondam qui cepit ocellos.

Although the poet uses the Ovidian form 'Myrrha', and makes the girl 'Arabian', it is reasonable to take this parallel reference as a literary signpost, indicating that Cinna's *Smyrna* is an important model at this point. Oliver Lyne, in his edition of the *Ciris* (Cambridge, 1978), 39 ff.), suggests that verbatim, or near-verbatim, adaptations of *Smyrna* by the *Ciris*-poet far exceeded those of Catullus 64, just as Cinna's subject matter was the more relevant. He even writes (p. 40) 'I think I have effectively isolated new fragments of Cinna', by identifying phrases which seem slightly ill at ease in the *Ciris* but could fit a plausible context in the *Smyrna*. Readers will probably find some of his examples more convincing than others, but they all merit careful attention (some discussed in detail, and others listed, with reference to the commentary, in Lyne 40–5).

The indebtedness of Ovid, *Met.* 10.298 ff. to Cinna's *Smyrna* would be overwhelmingly probable in any case, and we can see just about enough verbal imitation to confirm it: **9** 'at scelus incesto Smyrnae crescebat in alvo' is reflected in *Met.* 10.470 'conceptaque crimina portat' as well as 503 'at male conceptus sub robore creverat infans'. Ovid, *more suo*, insets the story of Atalanta, told by Venus to Adonis (*Met.* 10.560–707), to which he may have transferred one or two phrases and motifs from Cinna. Perhaps the most revealing piece of evidence about the *Smyrna* is the anonymous epigram, **7b** (see ad loc.); **1c**, which points in the same direction, is probably aimed primarily at the same poem. As well as emphasizing the difficulty of a poem which needed a learned commentary within a generation, the epigram probably parodies an episode from the *Smyrna* in which the girl's suitors unsuccessfully compete for her hand.

Although we have no evidence that the cult of Paphian Aphrodite figured in *Smyrna*, I would be surprised if Cinna missed the chance to include material so congenial to his tastes (cf. **6**, probably anticipating Pollio's visit to Delphi). It is worth transcribing the *locus classicus* in Tacitus, *Histories* 2.3.1–2:

Conditorem templi [sc. Paphiae Veneris] regem Aeriam vetus memoria, quidam ipsius deae nomen id perhibent. fama recentior tradit a Cinyra sacratum templum deamque ipsam conceptam mari huc adpulsam; sed scientiam artemque haruspicum accitam et Cilicem Tamiram intulisse, atque ita pactum ut familiae utriusque posteri caerimoniis praesiderent. mox, ne honore nullo regium genus peregrinam stirpem antecelleret, ipsa quam intulerunt scientia hospites cessere; tantum Cinyrades sacerdos consulitur. hostiae, ut quisque vovit, sed mares deliguntur; certissima fides haedorum fibris. sanguinem arae offundere vetitum; precibus et igne puro altaria adolentur, nec ullis imbribus quamquam in aperto madescunt. simulacrum deae non effigie humana, continuus orbis latiore initio tenuem in ambitum metae modo exsurgens, et ratio in obscuro.

Such material, while quite at home in a prose antiquarian like Varro, also breathes the atmosphere of learned poetry. For example, the distinction between 'vetus memoria' and 'fama recentior' (cf. e.g. πρεσβυτέρη φάτις and ὁπλοτέρη φάτις in Nonnus, *Dion.* 12.294, 41.155); the two families who share the inherited priesthood (cf. the two families who preside over the Roman cult of Hercules in *Aen.* 8.269–70); the withdrawal of one family (reminiscent of Callimachus, *Aetia*, cf. Pfeiffer on fr. 91 for the ending of rites); the 'marvel' of the altar on which rain never falls; the particular form of the cult object. A fairly recent papyrus find (*SH* 397) suggests that Eratosthenes near the end of his hexameter poem *Hermes* may have spoken of the foundation of the temple of Paphian Aphrodite by Smyrna's father Cinyras (a descendant of Hermes' union with Herse) and even mentioned the rainless altar.

To return to the general character of Cinna's *Smyrna*: the Greek poets whom we have encountered above as antecedents and possible sources (Panyassis, Antimachus, Lycophron, Eratosthenes, Nicander, Parthenius) very definitely represent the 'avia Pieridum loca', and for that reason would appeal to the *docti* of Cinna's own day. Within a generation of the poem's appearance the scholar Crassicius (see on **7***b*) wrote a commentary which won him glory and financial advancement because it explained the poem's obscurities in a way which rival scholars had failed to do. Of course one must allow for humorous exaggeration in the suggestion that *Smyrna* would be incomprehensible without Crassicius' commentary. I am reminded of the competitive rush to write commentaries on Tiberius' favourite Greek poets, Euphorion, Rhianus, and Parthenius (Suet. *Tib.* 70.2), and Clement of Alexandria's statement (*Strom.* 5.8.51) that Euphorion, Callimachus' *Aetia*, and Lycophron's *Alexandra* provided a γυμνάσιον εἰς ἐξήγησιν γραμματικῶν. The overall impression conveyed by ancient testimony is that Cinna's *Smyrna* would have been closest in spirit to the Greek poems of Euphorion in their obscurity and choice of sombre, not to say grotesque, themes. No doubt Cinna is foremost among the 'cantores Euphorionis' decried by Cicero (*Tusc. Disp.* 3.45) some ten years after *Smyrna*'s publication. We need not be surprised that nothing very difficult has survived among the verbatim fragments of *Smyrna* (**10**, on the identity of the Morning and Evening Star, would be child's play to the *docti*). The background of this myth, set out above, indicates what a rich field it offered to learned poet and commentator alike: the differing parentage of the heroine (daughter of Cinyras or Theias); the various settings (Cyprus, Assyria, Arabia, with links to Cilicia); the alternative names of the river Satrachus and the heroine herself, and (perhaps) the history of the cult of Paphian Aphrodite.

Catullus 95 (=**7***a*) indicates that *Smyrna* was published separately. We can only guess at the poem's length, but Catullus' contrast between its brief compass and the nine years for which Cinna laboured makes me think of some 500 lines—Catullus 64 has 408, and the pseudo-Virgilian *Ciris* 541. *Smyrna* is called a 'libellus' in **7***e*.

7*a*

Catullus 95, in the tradition of Hellenistic epigrams praising the work of a fellow poet (e.g. Callimachus, *Anth. Pal.* 9.507 = ep. 27 Pf. = 56 G–P on the *Phaenomena* of Aratus) is, together with **7***b* on Crassicius, the most valuable of our testimonia to Cinna's *Smyrna*. Some factual points emerge: that Cinna worked on the poem for nine years (? from the mid-60s BC), that it was of brief compass ('parva . . . monimenta', if Catullus' last couplet belongs to the same epigram). Mention of the Satrachus, elsewhere called Setrachus or Serachus, indicates that Cinna followed the Cyprian version of the myth, in which Smyrna's father is Cinyras, rather than the Assyrian which made her daughter of Theias. Incidentally, P. Chuvin, *Mythologie et Géographie Diony-siaques* (1991), 92, with reference to Lycophron, *Alex.* 448, believed that the Setrachus is a perfectly real and identifiable river, 'qui a gardé le nom de Sérakhis', but in his Addenda (321–2) he allows to O. Masson that the name might be a learned imposition of the eighteenth century rather than a sur-vivor from antiquity. Line 6 of Catullus probably reflects a prayer or boast by Cinna that his *Smyrna* will prove immortal (see below), in terms very similar to those which he himself used in praise of Valerius Cato's *Dictynna* (**14**, 'saecula permaneat nostri Dictynna Catonis').

From Catullus' epigram the nine years' labour almost passed into a proverb (Horace, *Ars Poetica* 388 'nonumque prematur in annum', cf. **7***c–e*). Horace (ibid.) ironically hints that the reason for so long a delay was that Cinna's first efforts proved unsatisfactory. I would guess that he has particularly in mind Catullus on Cinna (? with a glance at his own *Odes* 2.20) also in *AP* 345–6: the poet who 'miscuit utile dulci' (343) will succeed not only in terms of hard cash (345, 'hic meret aera liber Sosiis') but also in the scale of more lasting and intangible values (345–6) 'hic et mare transit [cf. Cinna's *Smyrna* travel-ling to Cyprus] / et longum noto scriptori prorogat aevum' (cf. Cat. line 6).

Lines 5–6 predict the wide diffusion (as far as the Satrachus) and long survival (until the centuries turn grey) of the epyllion. These are familiar enough motifs: e.g. in *Amores* 1.15.13 'Battiades semper toto cantabitur orbe' Ovid goes beyond Call. fr. 7.14 ἵνα μοι πουλὺ μένωσιν ἔτος, perhaps echoing some lost utterance of the master. Horace in *Odes* 2.20 catalogues the remote tribes who will read his poetry—see the abundant parallels in N–H, especially their reference to Alcman on p. 332. Probably both these motifs occurred in Cinna; at the end of his corresponding episode Ovid writes of myrrh, some-what oddly, 'nulloque tacebitur aevo' (*Met.* 10.502). This may be meant to recall a prayer for the immortality of his poem (or heroine) made by Cinna, perhaps likewise at the end of his epyllion. For the conceit 'cana . . . saecula' in a similar context, cf. **91** (Scaevola on Cicero's *Marius*) 'canescet saeclis innumerabilibus', *Ciris* 41 'senibus loqueretur pagina saeclis', Cat. 68.46 'charta loquatur anus'.

Catullus' mention of the Satrachus (alternatively Setrachus, see above) hints at the complexity of Cinna's poem and its sources. In all texts of Catul-lus the epithet applied to the river is printed as 'cavas', which Matthew Leigh (*MD* 33 (1994), 188 n. 20) defends as a reference to its subterranean journey (above, p. 31), comparing Ovid, *Ibis* 226 on the Styx. R. G. M. Nisbet (*Col-lected Papers*, 98–9) remarks that the reading of the archetype, 'canas', has clearly been influenced by 'cana' in the line below, and therefore one should not give undue weight to palaeographical considerations; also that the parallels for 'cavas' are less satisfactory than is generally supposed. He himself suggests 'suas'; the objection of J. B. Solodow, *CP* 84 (1989), 317 n. 15 (repeated by J. D. Morgan, *CQ* N S 41 (1991), 252–3, who conjectures 'sacras') that 'suas' does not sit well with the genitive 'Satrachi', lacks substance. I find this conjecture attractive for a reason which Nisbet does not make explicit. The Satrachus is Smyrna's personal river not only because they are both Cyprian; the pair also share a name. From the various comments of *Et. Gen.* relating to Parthenius fr. 29 Lightfoot = *Suppl. Hell.* 641 we learn that the Satrachus was also known as Aous, Smyrna as Aoa, and her son Adonis as another Aous.

7*b*

The anonymous epigram is very elegant—but J. Granarolo was not amused: 'cette épigramme . . . se veut spirituelle. En réalité, elle n'est pas de très bon goût' (*ANRW* I/3 (1973), 301 n. 28). Both Blänsdorf (223) and Courtney (306) include the poem in its own right. Kaster (Suetonius, *De Gramm.*, 200) thinks that Crassicius' commentary was written 'before the late 30s', and the epigram would well fit into the same period (note the polysyllabic pentameter endings):

> uni Crassicio se credere Smyrna probavit;
> > desinite, indocti, coniugio hanc petere.
> soli Crassicio se dixit nubere velle,
> > intima cui soli nota sua exstiterint.

It seems that several commentators had attempted to elucidate the *Smyrna* (cf. **4** on the *Propempticon Pollionis*), but, according to the epigram, only Crassicius succeeded. On one level this is obviously a parody of Catullus 10.1–2 'nulli se dicit mulier mea nubere malle / quam mihi, non si se Iuppiter ipse petat' and 72.1–2 'dicebas quondam solum te nosse Catullum, / Lesbia, nec prae me velle tenere Iovem'. But I suspect that the motif of Smyrna's disappointed suitors (i.e. the inferior grammatici) amusingly adapts a situation from Cinna's poem (this point taken by Peter Knox, *Ovid's Metamorphoses and the Traditions of Augustan Poetry* (1986), 63 n. 24). Almost certainly Smyrna in the epyllion was besieged by many suitors; cf. Ant. Lib. 34.1 (from an uncertain poetic source) ταύτην διὰ κάλλος πλείστοι ἐκ πόλεων πλείστων ἐμνήστευον, Ov. *Met.* 10.315–17 'undique lecti / te cupiunt proceres, totoque Oriente iuventa / ad thalami certamen adest' (*Met.* 10.358 'nominibus dictis' suggests a catalogue of names and cities), *Ciris* 412 (linked to Cinna by Lyne ad loc.).

One might expect that Smyrna's father Cinyras would choose her bride-groom, but, in Ovid at least, he is unable to make up his mind and passes the decision to his daughter, who (as in the epigram) must select one: 'at Cinyras, quem copia digna procorum / quid faciat dubitare facit, scitatur ab ipsa, / nominibus dictis, cuius velit esse mariti' (356–8, cf. 317–18 where the poet apostrophizes his heroine, 'ex omnibus unum / elige, Myrrha, virum'). What would be Smyrna's reaction? A point-blank refusal would be hard to maintain for ever. Obviously she would delay as long as possible (Ant. Lib. 34.1 ἡ δὲ πολλὰ ἐμηχανᾶτο πρὸς ἀπάτην τῶν γονέων καὶ ἀνάθεσιν τοῦ χρόνου). The way she evades the issue in *Met.* 10.364, telling her father that she longs for a husband 'similem tibi', seems quintessentially Ovidian. Perhaps Cinna made her set a condition which (she hoped) could never be fulfilled: 'I will marry only the man who . . .', as e.g. Atalanta decrees that she will marry only the man who can outrun her (*Met.* 10.568 ff.). In line 4 of the epigram, 'knowing her intimate parts' is not Crassicius' reward, but his qualification for marry-ing Smyrna: perhaps therefore in the epyllion Smyrna demanded that her suitors should solve a riddle or produce some particularly arcane piece of knowledge—both of them, of course, well-known ways of winning a princess in folktale.

A few points about the wording of the epigram. Note the prosody 'se crederĕ Smyrna', one reason why I have preferred 'Smyrna' to 'Zmyrna' (see above). In line 2 Blänsdorf (and his predecessors) printed 'coniugium hoc petere' rather than 'coniugio hanc'; if he were right, the phrase would be strikingly close to Ov. *Met.* 10.613 'coniugium petere hoc' in a similar context (many suitors seeking the hand of Atalanta). It would be characteristic of Ovid to transfer a phrase from Cinna's epyllion to an associated story in the *Metamorphoses*—the wooing of Atalanta, narrated by Venus to Myrrha's son Adonis, could be considered a kind of digression in Ovid's Myrrha.

7c tells us nothing extra about the *Smyrna* ('tardae . . . Myrrhae' no doubt reflects Cat. 95 = *7a*. 1–2 on the nine years of composition), but is interesting because it provides conclusive proof that Cinna the tribune, torn to pieces by the mob after Julius Caesar's funeral, was identical with Cinna the poet. Ovid's 'laesus cognomine' is quite precise: the poet/tribune and the enemy of Caesar for whom the mob mistook him shared the *cognomen* Cinna, but had different *nomina* (Helvius and Cornelius respectively). All this was seen by Housman (*Classical Papers*, p. 9 (vol. I)) and is forcefully restated by J. D. Morgan (*CQ* NS 40 (1990), 558–9). Ovid's couplet expresses a recognized literary theme, the paradoxical deaths of poets (surrounding lines of the *Ibis* contain many Greek examples). For the gruesome pentameter, cf. Prop. 3.15.40 (Dirce) 'in multis mortem habitura locis', Ov. *Tr.* 3.9.28.

8 (8 Bl., C.)

tabis: no doubt Myrrha is wasting away with passion for her father. We are told that Cinna was the first to use this genitive ('nullo auctore', Charisius), which remained rare; the only definite Augustan parallel is Livy 7.22.5. On the other hand, Charisius' view that this noun is confined to the nominative and ablative cases cannot be maintained, since the accusative appears in Cicero as well as Livy. Almost certainly the *Ciris*-poet borrowed from Cinna this rare genitive for the predicament of his Scylla (in love with her country's enemy Minos) in 254 'persequitur [sc. the nurse Carme] miserae causas exquirere tabis'. Lyne (ad loc.), comparing Ov. *Met.* 10.388 'laqueique requirere causam' and 394 'certa est exquirere nutrix' suggests that more of *Ciris* 254 than just 'tabis' may come from the *Smyrna*. One might also mention *Ciris* 182 'tabidulamque videt labi per viscera mortem'; could the unique epithet be owed to Cinna? Compare 'aridulus' (only Cinna, **13**.3 and Catullus until Ausonius).

9 (9 Bl., C.)

at scelus incesto Smyrnae crescebat in alvo: perhaps describing the stage of Smyrna's wanderings when her labour was drawing near, cf. Ov. *Met.* 10.481 'vixque uteri portabat onus'. The wording may be echoed in *Met.* 10.503, 'at male conceptus sub robore creverat infans' (after the transformation, but I would guess that Cinna's line describes the girl before her metamorphosis). 'scelus . . . crescebat' suggests that Smyrna's guilt grows together with the child (Adonis) in her womb.

    scelus: no close parallel presents itself for this usage, which may reflect (but is hardly to be classified under) the mainly colloquial application of *scelus* to a person 'whose very existence is a crime' (*OLD* 3). The slightly less audacious use of *crimen* (*OLD* 2*b*) in Ov. *Met.* 10.470 'conceptaque crimina portat' (cf. 3.268–9 'crimina pleno / fert utero') may derive from Cinna's *scelus.*

    incesto . . . alvo: as Priscian says, the masculine gender is common in older writers, e.g. Plautus, *Pseudolus* 823, Calvus, **25** 'partus gravido portabat in alvo' (more examples in *OLD*).

10 (6 Bl., C.)

Although Smyrna might weep at any stage, I suspect that this fragment describes her, exhausted by wanderings, shortly before her transformation. Thereafter her tears will become the exudation of myrrh; cf. *Met.* 10.500–1 'flet tamen et tepidae manant ex arbore guttae; / est honor et lacrimis'.

Both these lines are heavily spondaic (cf. **6.** 1, 3), a quality no doubt intended to suggest the grief of the heroine. But it must be said that the second line is by no means great poetry, particularly with the transmitted 'et', in which editors have acquiesced. The favourite conceit about the identity of the Morning and Evening Stars is not handled with the verve and elegance of Catullus 62.34–5, or even of *Ciris* 351–2. Several features of the fragment would be at home in a lament: the repeated 'te . . . / te' (with the emendation in line 2), as e.g. Virgil, *Georgics* 4.465–6 (Orpheus bewailing Eurydice) 'te, dulcis coniunx, te solo in litore secum, / te veniente die, te decedente canebat'. There is a hint of the Morning and Evening Star joining in the grief of Smyrna, as in the pathetic fallacy; cf. Prop. 1.16.23–4 'me [the excluded lover] mediae noctes, me sidera plena iacentem, / frigidaque Eoo me dolet aura gelu'. For grief stretching from morn to nightfall one can compare a lament for the fall of Adrianople to the Turks in AD 1362, '[the birds] weep late, weep early, weep at mid-day' (Margaret Alexiou, *The Ritual Lament in Greek Tradition* (1974), 93, cf. N–H on Horace, *Odes* 2.9.10). The mention of dawn and dusk also emphasizes that Smyrna has no respite from her sufferings, cf. Ov. *Met.* 5.440–1 'illam [Demeter seeking Persephone] non udis veniens Aurora capillis / cessantem vidit [? from Cinna], non Hesperus'.

1.   te: no doubt the poet apostrophizing his character; further parallels include Virgil, *Aen.* 7.759–60 'te nemus Angitiae, vitrea te Fucinus unda, / te liquidi flevere lacus', Ov. *Met.* 11.44 ff. (perhaps a little overdone) 'te maestae volucres, Orpheu, te turba ferarum, / te rigidi silices, te carmina saepe secutae / fleverunt silvae, positis te frondibus arbor / tonsa comas luxit'. Both the above have a bucolic air (cf. the repetition of the pronoun in Theocritus 1.71–2).

Eous: used as a noun = the Morning Star (*OLD* 1*b*).

2.   te: this emendation (for the lame 'et') occurred to me as a graduate student and was adopted by N–H on Horace, *Odes* 2.9.10 (though the text there is misprinted).

Hesperus idem: the popularity of this conceit among neoteric poets (cf. Catullus 62.34–5, *Ciris* 351–2) may be due to its appearance in Callimachus' *Hecale* (fr. 113 H. = 291 Pf.), the structure of which is clearly imitated in the *Ciris* lines. For further parallels and discussion see the notes of Pfeiffer and myself on the *Hecale* fragment (probably I should have avoided the astronomy, in view of Courtney 218), and H. Dahlmann, *Über Helvius Cinna*, 41–3; perhaps also Valgius Rufus, **164**.

It is conceivable that the unattached **17** belongs to the *Smyrna*.

11–12

11 (hendecasyllable) and **12** (choliamb) are both quoted by Aulus Gellius as from Cinna 'in poematis', and represent the tiny surviving counterpart (cf. Calvus, **34–7**) to Catullus' polymetric poems.

11 (9 Bl., C.)

We cannot be sure that 'me' in line 1 refers to the poet himself, but this lively hendecasyllablic fragment shows Cinna taking a keen delight in his home area (? contrasted with Rome). The Cenomani (in their most familiar form) were a Celtic people centred upon Brixia (Livy 32.30.6 'in vicos Cenomanorum Brixiamque, quod caput gentis erat'); their territory included Cremona and perhaps Verona. Polybius (2.17) calls them Γονομάνοι. Editors of Cicero and Livy restore the form 'Cenomani', but the manuscript readings, particularly in *Pro Balbo* 32 and to a lesser extent in Livy 5.35.1, rather favour Cinna's form. See A. Grilli, *Maia*, 37 (1985), 245–7. As T. P. Wiseman points out (*Cinna the Poet* (1974), 47), inscriptions show a concentration of Helvii in Brixia (*CIL* V. 4237, 4425–6, 4612, 4675; cf. 8865 from Verona).

bigis: a pair of horses (and thence a chariot drawn by two horses).

raeda: a four-wheeled Gallic travelling-carriage. Quintilian (1.5.57) observes 'plurima Gallica evaluerunt, ut "raeda" ac "petorritum"'. Another Gallic word which became naturalized in Latin was 'essedum'.

citata: 'made to travel quickly'. For application to horses, cf. Accius, 581–2 $R^2 = 585$–6 Warmington 'equis / . . . citatis', Virgil, *Aen.* 12.373. The participle is largely poetic, though also favoured by Livy.

nanis: Gellius (19.13) discusses whether 'nanus' is a respectable Latin word, and produces these lines in evidence. He tells us (19.13.4) that 'de mulis aut eculeis humilioribus vulgo dicitur'. *OLD* s.v. *bigae* states that the reference here is to mules. As a noun, 'nanus' is applied to dwarfs (cf. Greek νᾶνος).

12 (10 Bl., C.)

somniculosam ut Poenus aspidem Psyllus: an elegant choliamb. Morel noted 'sensus insequentis versus fuerit: "impune contrectat" vel sim' ('the next line began with something like <impune tractat>', Courtney 221). Gellius could indeed have quoted the *ut* clause without its verb because he is interested only in the adjective 'somniculosus'. But I suspect that this is the last line of the simile, with a verb (e.g. *mulceo*) to be supplied from what went before. Similarly, if Cat. 17.26 'ferream ut soleam tenaci in voragine mula' had been transmitted as a single-line fragment, we might wonder what followed — but that is the final line of the poem, and 'derelinquit' must be understood from 'derelinquere' in 25. In Cinna it seems that someone is stroking another person, animal, or object; the point of comparison might be the invulnerability of the Psylli to the snake's venom (e.g. Lucan 9.890 ff.), or simply the manner of stroking.

somniculosam: Gellius implies that the meaning here was 'sleep-inducing', though, on the fact of it, 'drowsy' (from the effects of stroking, as e.g. *Aen.* 7.753–4 of Umbro 'vipereo generi et graviter spirantibus hydris / spargere qui somnos cantuque manuque solebat') would be equally appropriate (cf. Pliny, *NH* 7.14).

Psyllus: the immunity to snake-bite of this African tribe (and their ability to help its victims) is mentioned in Nicander (fr. 32, from his elegiac *Ophiaca*). The Psylli purged Cato's camp during his famous march through Africa in 47 BC (Lucan 9.890–937, Plutarch, *Cato Minor* 56). One would like to know whether they appeared in Aemilius Macer's *Theriaca*, and, if so, what was the chronological relationship between that work and this mention in Cinna.

13 (11 Bl., C.)

Of all the surviving fragments of Cinna, these four lines make much the most positive impression, suggesting a talent which was indeed worthy to be set alongside that of Catullus. We may note the diminutives (*aridulo*, *libello*, *navicula*), of which Catullus too is very fond, the pentameters formed with a surer touch than many in Catullus, and the neat placing of words in line 3. Cinna dedicates to a friend a presentation copy of Aratus' *Phaenomena*, which he has brought back with him by ship from Bithynia (for the poet's contacts with that country, see above, p. 21). Speculation about the friend's identity —

some have fancied Catullus—is fruitless, but no doubt the recipient shared Cinna's tastes; we can gauge the popularity of Aratus at Rome from Cicero's early *Aratea* and a stream of subsequent translators or imitators (e.g. Varro Atacinus, **120–1**, Virgil, *Georgics* 1, the *Aratea* of Ovid and Germanicus, to go no further). Equally significant is the ringing testimonial to the poetic qualities of Aratus given by the *docti* in 55 BC (perhaps very soon after the composition of this epigram), 'constat inter doctos ... ornatissimis atque optimis versibus Aratum de caelo stellisque dixisse' (Cicero, *De Oratore* 1.69).

One could believe that the poem is complete but for the lack of a named addressee, which would be surprising since the lines suggest a gift lovingly chosen and brought home for a special friend. It might seem that line 1 makes a satisfying opening and line 4 just as satisfying a conclusion. But 'haec tibi' are particularly appropriate in the first words of such an epigram, as numerous little pieces in Martial (see the Index Epigrammaton in the OCT) make clear. So I suspect that the ending is deficient—perhaps by no more than one couplet, in which the recipient was named. This is the pattern in the closest parallel for this kind of presentation poem, written some 30 years later by Crinagoras (*Anth. Pal.* 9.545 = 11 Gow–Page), accompanying a gift of Callimachus' *Hecale* to Augustus' nephew Marcellus. First the author and the work are identified, with complimentary references to the poet's high craftsmanship. Then an indication is given of the subject matter; only in the third and final couplet of Crinagoras is the recipient named as Marcellus.

The phrase 'multum vigilata' (1) shows that Cinna was aware of Callimachus' famous epigram on Aratus (*Anth. Pal.* 9.507 = 27 Pf. = 56 Gow–Page), where in line 4 Ruhnken's emendation σύμβολον ἀγρυπνίης is almost universally adopted. Alan Cameron, *CR*, NS 22 (1972), 169, defends the manuscript reading σύντονος ἀγρυπνίη, 'intense wakefulness'. Could Cinna's 'multum' lend slight support to σύντονος in Callimachus?

1. Arateis ... lucernis: the noun indicates lucubration and midnight oil, cf. Juv. 1.51 'Venusina digna lucerna' (i.e. fit for satire in the tradition of Horace). It is not clear why Cinna uses the plural—perhaps each night's labour is represented by one *lucerna*. Alexander of Ephesus (*Suppl. Hell.* 19–38), a poet in the Aratean tradition, perhaps contemporary with Cinna, was nicknamed Λύχνος ('Lamplight'); it is particularly appropriate that astronomical poets should work at night when they can observe their subject matter.

multum vigilata: see above for the imitation of Callimachus' epigram on Aratus. I have adopted Scaliger's correction 'vigilata' for the manuscript's 'invigilata'. Although the latter might be defended (A. Lunelli, *Aerius* (1969), 59 n. 116), it seems much more plausible, with P. Sonnenburg (*Rh.M.* 66

(1911), 477–80), to regard 'multum vigilata' in [Virgil], *Ciris* 46 'accipe dona meo multum vigilata labore' (likewise presenting a poem), and Statius, *Theb.* 12.811, *Silv.* 4.6.25, as unchanged borrowings from Cinna, who also fathers the phrase 'vigilatum carmen' (Ovid, *AA* 2.285, *Fasti* 4.109). Horace makes a humorous variation on the theme in *Sat.* 2.1.7, where his excuse for composing poetry is 'nequeo dormire'.

2.   carmina: for the plural used of a single poem, cf. Cat. 65.16 'carmina Battiadae', Cicero, *DND* 2.104 'carminibus Arateis', Ovid, *Am.* 1.15.23 'carmina . . . Lucreti' (with McKeown's note). It seems very unlikely that the plural refers to various subdivisions of Aratus' *Phaenomena* made in antiquity (see the editions of J. Martin (1956), XXI ff. and D. Kidd (1997) on 733–57).

ignis: perhaps the earliest example of *ignis* = star (*OLD* 5, 'any luminous object in the sky'). One might look to Cicero's *Aratea* for the phrase 'ignis . . . aerios', but nothing like it occurs in the surviving parts.

novimus: suggesting, as well as the fame of the *Phaenomena*, the manner of a didactic poet who frequently stresses the benefit of his instruction to those previously ignorant: 'noscere' and 'cognoscere' between them occur ten times in Cicero's *Aratea.*

aerios: Lunelli (*Aerius*, 11–61) shows that there is no need to replace this with 'aetherios' (Zanchus).

3.   levis in aridulo malvae descripta libello: we are probably meant to gather that this is a special copy, and that the distinctive writing material which suits the distinctive quality of the verse, as in Catullus 1.1–2 'lepidum novum libellum / arida modo pumice expolitum' (the disparity between Suffenus' verse and his stationery is cause for comment in Catullus 22). Of the words used, only *levis* is transferable as a complimentary term of criticism (e.g. Horace, *Ars Poetica* 26 'sectantem levia', with Brink's note).

aridulo . . . libello: cf. Catullus 64.316 'aridulis . . . labellis', perhaps a subconscious echo by whichever poet wrote second. The adjective does not recur until Ausonius.

malvae . . . libello: Isidore, who quotes our fragment, thinks the reference is to writing on mallow leaves woven together ('textilibus . . . malvarum foliis'). He mentions also the use of palm-leaves, on which the Sibyl was supposed to have recorded her utterances (Servius on *Aen.* 3.444 cites Varro for this). But it seems more likely that 'libellus' is used here in the basic sense of 'liber' = inner bark (this meaning for the diminutive not recognized by *OLD*, though it can be found in LSJ and *TLL*). See Theodor Birt, *Kritik und Hermeneutik* (1913), 252–3. According to Pliny (*NH* 13.69) writing took place 'in palmarum foliis . . . dein quarundam arborum libris'. The *tilia* is most often mentioned in this connexion (Birt, *Kritik*, 253); no other reference to writing on *malva* has survived. Courtney (p. 222) informs us that '*Malva crispa* can grow to a height of 8 ft. (2.5 m.) and its stems can be 3 in. (7.5 mm.) wide at the base.'

4. **Prusiaca:** two kings called Prusias ruled Bithynia *c.*230–182 and 182–149 BC. The kingdom reached its highest prosperity under the former, with whom Hannibal sought refuge. The epithet *Προυσιακός* is applied to a tetradrachm in a second-century BC inscription (LSJ Supplement). Here it might mean 'Bithynian' generally, or derive from the sea-port Prusias, previously Cios, restored and renamed by the first king (Strabo 12.4.3). Cinna's ship could have been built there.

14 (14 Bl., C.)

saecula permaneat nostri Dictynna Catonis: a wish for the immortality of the *Diana* (presumably a hexameter epyllion) by P. Valerius Cato, in similar terms to the tribute paid by Catullus (95 = 7*a*) to the *Smyrna* of Cinna himself. Although quoting Cinna's line, Suetonius (*De Gramm.* 11.2) firmly calls the poem *Diana*. There may have been alternative titles given by the author, or perhaps *Dictynna* is Cinna's own more fanciful concoction. In either case it seems likely that Cato dealt with the myth of Britomartis who became Dictynna and was identified by some with Diana. Callimachus, *Hymn* 3.189–203 may have been among Cato's sources, and R. O. A. M. Lyne (*Ciris: A Poem Attributed to Vergil* (1978), p. 45, with further references there) argues plausibly that the *Diana/Dictynna* is reflected in *Ciris* 294–309; two anonymous hexameters (**235**) might conceivably come from this poem. For more on P. Valerius Cato, 'peridoneus praeceptor maxime ad poeticam tendentibus' (Suet. *De Gramm.* 11.1) see Appendix p. 429 and my commentary on the passages of other poets (listed there) which mention Cato.

    saecula permaneat: 'last the centuries'. If this is the first line of an epigram (or at least if there were no previous words which affected the syntax), this unparalleled use of *permanere*+ accusative seems more adventurous than a simple accusative of 'time how long' (of which there are examples in *TLL* X.1, fasc. X (1997), 1526.39 ff.). I do not find attractive the word-division 'saecula per maneat' (printed e.g. by Blänsdorf).

15 (12 Bl., C.)

miseras audet galeare puellas: 'galeare' is a back formation from 'galeatus', in which '-atus' is not really a past participle, but an adjectival suffix denoting possession or wearing (*OLD* -atus²). It would be nice to think that Q. Cornificius remembered his old poetic associate when he described the soldiers who deserted him as 'galeatos lepores' (see **93**). Non. Marc. quotes also 'clipeat' from Pacuvius. These verbs must have sounded very odd, 'galeare' perhaps a little less so, since the passive infinitive is found in [Caesar], *Bell. Afr.* 12.3 'milites in campo iubet galeari'.

Some have thought that this fragment refers to Amazons. Morel compared Prop. 4.3.44 (on Hippolyte) 'texit galea barbara molle caput', and hazarded a guess that the subject of 'audet' might be 'Themiscyra Amazonum sedes'. But 'miseras' hardly suits the Amazons, to whom warfare was meat and drink; it suggests rather the arming of girls against their custom and instincts. 'Audet' perhaps = 'has the audacity to', with the disparaging sense often borne by *audax*. Mythological instances of normally unwarlike women being armed include the daughters of Danaus (καὶ τότ' ἄρ' ὡπλίζοντο θοῶς Δαναοῖο θύγατρες / πρόσθεν ἐυρρεῖος ποταμοῦ Νείλοιο ἄνακτος, *Danais* fr. 1 Bernabé, Davies) and Heracles' wife Deianira against the Dryopians (schol. Ap. Rh. 1.1213 ff., cf. Pfeiffer on Call., *Aetia* fr. 23); the subject of 'audet' could then be Danaus or Heracles. But this would expect a lot from an epigram. Professor Donald Russell (ap. Courtney 223) ingeniously suggests a reference to a poet who traduces (*miseras*) women by representing them under arms; Courtney himself thinks of a context like Prop. 4.3.45 'Romanis utinam patuissent castra puellis'.

16

Ovid's coupling of Cinna with Anser is surprising, since in Virgil, *Ecl.* 9.35–6 (**1a**) the two represent opposite poles of poetic quality. We learn that Cinna was licentious (*procax*) in his erotic poems—but not to the same extent as Anser (for whom see App., p. 420). Presumably, like Catullus, he showed this *procacitas* both in polymetrics (**11–12**) and in elegiac epigrams (**13–15**). We do not know of any woman whom Cinna made famous (as Catullus Lesbia and Calvus Quintilia). Of what survives only **15** gives even the slightest hint of an erotic theme.

17 (4 Bl., 5 C.)

atque imitata nives lucens legitur crystallus: one may criticize the versifica-
tion of **6.**1 or **10.**2, but this line is as exquisite as anyone could desire, with its
alliteration and spondaic fifth foot. Not surprisingly, scholars have wished to
find it a home in one of the elaborate hexameter poems. Indeed, Morel,
Büchner, and Blänsdorf print the line among fragments of the *Propempticon
Pollionis* (the last two recording the doubts of Dahlmann, *Über Helvius Cinna*,
33). W. Göhrler (*Hermes*, 93 (1965), 343) saw a reflection of our line in Ovid's
propempticon, 'nec medius tenuis conchas pictosque lapillos / pontus habet;
bibuli litoris illa mora est' (*Am.* 2.11.13–14), but, as McKeown ad loc. notes,
the resemblance is very slight. Could Cinna have anticipated that Pollio would
visit a region (? in Asia Minor) which produced rock-crystal (cf. Pliny, *NH*
37.23 ff.)? But there is no positive reason to favour the *Propempticon Pollionis*.
One might well think of the *Smyrna*, and e.g. of costly gifts brought by the
girl's eastern suitors (cf. Ov. *Met.* 10.316–17 'totoque Oriente iuventa / ad
thalami certamen adest'). If this comes from a hexameter poem, and if 'atque'
links together two precious stones, 'iaspis' would suggest itself for the end of
the previous line. Both were thought of as primarily oriental (see Pliny, *NH*
37.115–18 for *iaspis*), and they are associated e.g. in Dionysius Periegetes 780–
2 κείνου δ᾽ ἂν ποταμοῖο [sc. the Thermodon in Pontus] περὶ κρυμώδεας ὄχθας
/ τέμνοις κρυστάλλου καθαρὸν λίθον, οἷά τε πάχνην / χειμερίην· δήεις δὲ καὶ
ὑδατόεσσαν ἴασπιν.

All the above suggestions are fantasy; while the style makes one think of an
elaborate and learned poem, the source of the fragment tends in a different
direction. Our line is quoted, with the introductory words 'sic et Cinna dicit',
by a scholiast on Juvenal 6.155 'grandia tolluntur crystallina', where the refer-
ence is to very expensive crystal vessels bought in Rome during the December
festival known as Sigillaria. Juvenal uses 'crystallina' and Cinna 'crystallus' of
rock-crystal or vessels made from it, but that seems an inadequate reason for
citing Cinna to illustrate Juvenal. The Juvenal scholia are capable of combin-
ing rare information with the oddest misunderstandings (witness the note on
'Agrippa' three lines later), but the quotation from Cinna would not make
much sense unless the context was similar, i.e. an expensive item bought at the
market (see my commentary on Ov. *AA* 1.407–8). 'Legitur' could mean 'is
selected' (for purchase), and the exquisite style might be ironical, somewhat
like Catullus 69.4 'aut perluciduli deliciis lapidis' (also of a costly gift, in a
poem of crude subject matter). If we could put sufficient trust in the Juvenal
scholiast, this line of argument would point to an elegiac epigram.

imitata nives: perhaps the earliest instance of *imitari* = 'to have the appearance of, resemble' (*OLD* 2*b*), with an inanimate subject (cf. e.g. Ov. *Met.* 2.2 'flammasque imitante pyropo'). The usage seems strongly poetic, particularly with a participle; it appears possible (however unexpected) that there is a recollection of Cinna in Pliny, *NH* 37.118 'iasponyx ... nives imitata'.

lucens legitur crystallus: the alliteration of 'l' and 'c' may be consciously reproduced in a fragment of Ovid (8 Bl., C.) 'currus crystallo lucidus albo'. This rhythm in the second half of a hexameter would not have appealed to Callimachus, who avoids having a word-break after the first syllable of both the fourth and the fifth foot in the same line, and (so far) produces only two examples of a σπονδειάζων ending in a three-syllable word (*Hymn* 1.41, *Hecale* fr. 166 H. = 756 Pf.). On the other hand Euphorion is more inclined to the final trisyllable (five examples from a smaller total) and has no objection to combining these word-breaks. The two phenomena come together in *Suppl. Hell.* 429.48 (= fr. 130 Powell) οὐδὲ κρυεροὶ καύηκες. Cinna's rhythm is paralleled also in Catullus 65.23 'praeceps agitur decursu'.

legitur: as noted above, this could mean, according to the (unknown) context, 'is selected' (for purchase at the Sigillaria) or 'is gathered' (from its place or origin, e.g. Tib. 2.4.27 'quicumque legit ... smaragdos', Prisc. *Per.* 1020 'legitur ... iaspis').

crystallus: in the sense 'ice', this word forms a trisyllabic hexameter ending from the time of Homer (*Il.* 22.152 ἢ ἐξ ὕδατος κρυστάλλωι, *Od.* 14.477), cf. Eratosthenes, *Hermes* fr. 16.16 Powell. For the feminine gender cf. Prop. 4.3.52 'crystallus ... aquosa'; the alternative is 'crystallum', neuter (an unambiguously masculine 'crystallus' is nowhere attested).

18 (13 Bl., C.)

Alpinaque cummis: sometimes we find an indeclinable neuter *cummi* (*gummi*) = gum, 'a viscid secretion from trees' (*OLD*), like κόμμι (in Greek too some inflected forms occur). The feminine 'c(g)ummis' appears first in Cato, *Agr.* 69.2 and is generally favoured by the best manuscripts of Pliny, *NH* (e.g. 13.66 'cummim optimam'). Obviously not a word for high poetry— perhaps from an epigram. There were Alps not far from Cinna's home region of Brixia (see on **11**), and so the reference here may be to a local product.

C. Licinius Calvus

19

(*a*) Cat. 50.1–5: *Hesterno, Licini, die otiosi / multum lusimus in meis tabellis / ut convenerat esse delicatos: / scribens versiculos uterque nostrum / ludebat numero modo hoc modo illoc.*

(*b*) Hor. *Serm.* 1.10.16–19: *illi scripta quibus comoedia prisca viris est / hoc stabant, hoc sunt imitandi; quos neque pulcher / Hermogenes unquam legit neque simius iste / nil praeter Calvum et doctus cantare Catullum.*

(*c*) Prop. 2.25.3–4: *ista* [sc. Cynthiae] *meis fiet notissima forma libellis, / Calve, tua venia, pace, Catulle, tua.*

(*d*) Prop. 2.34.89–90: *haec etiam docti confessa est pagina Calvi, / cum caneret miserae funera Quintiliae* [v. **26–8**].

(*e*) Ov. *Am.* 3.9.61–2: *obvius huic venies hedera iuvenalia cinctus / tempora cum Calvo, docte Catulle, tuo.*

(*f*) Ov. *Tr.* 2.431–2: *par* [sc. Catulli licentiae] *fuit exigui similisque licentia Calvi / detexit variis qui sua furta modis.*

(*g*) Sen. *Contr.* 7.4.7: *et carmina quoque eius* [sc. Calvi], *quamvis iocosa sint, plena sunt ingentis animi. dicit de Pompeio . . .* [**39**].

(*h*) Pliny, *Epist.* 1.16.5: *praeterea facit versus* [sc. Pompeius Saturninus] *quales Catullus meus aut Calvus . . . quantum illis leporis dulcedinis amaritudinis amoris! inserit sane, sed data opera, mollibus levibusque duriusculos quosdam; et hoc quasi Catullus aut Calvus.*

(*i*) Augurinus ap. Plin. *Epist.* 4.27.4 (vv. 1–3): *canto carmina versibus minutis, / his olim quibus et meus Catullus / et Calvus veteresque.*

(*j*) Pliny, *Epist.* 5.3.2: *facio non numquam versiculos severos parum . . .* (5) *sed ego verear ne me non satis deceat, quod decuit M. Tullium, C. Calvum . . . ?*

(*k*) Suet. *Div. Iul.* 49.1: *omitto Calvi Licini notissimos versus* [**38**]. ibid. 73 *Gaio Calvo post famosa epigrammata de reconciliatione per amicos agenti ultro ac prior scripsit.*

(*l*) Gell. *NA* 19.9.7 [v. 1*e*]: ... *ecquis nostrorum poetarum tam fluentes carminum delicias fecisset, 'nisi Catullus' inquiunt 'forte pauca et Calvus itidem pauca'.*

(*a*) Yesterday, Licinius, being at a loose end, we had much fun on my writing tablets, after agreeing to indulge ourselves: each of us wrote playful verses, first in one metre then another.

(*b*) In this respect the men who wrote Old Comedy succeeded, and in this they should be imitated—people who have never been read by pretty Hermogenes, or by that monkey trained to recite nothing but Calvus and Catullus.

(*c*) [to Cynthia] That beauty of yours will become most notorious through my books, with apologies to you, Calvus, and by your leave, Catullus.

(*d*) To such things [love affairs] the writings of skilful Calvus admitted, when he sang of poor Quintilia's death.

(*e*) You, erudite Catullus, will come to meet him [Cornelius Gallus], with ivy around your youthful temples, together with your dear friend Calvus.

(*f*) As great, and similar, was the licence of tiny Calvus, who disclosed his own secret affairs in a variety of metres.

(*g*) His poems too, though sportive, are full of enormous spirit. He says the following about Pompey ... [**39**].

(*h*) Furthermore [Pompeius Saturninus] composes verses like those of my Catullus or Calvus. How much charm and sweetness they contain, how much pungency and love! Admittedly he includes among the soft and smooth lines a few that are a trifle rough, but he does so deliberately—and in this too he resembles Catullus or Calvus.

(*i*) I [Augurinus] write poems in these little verses which my Catullus, Calvus, and the old poets used long ago.

(*j*) On occasion I [Pliny] compose little poems that are far from austere ... Ought I to be worried that what was appropriate to Cicero and Calvus might be judged inappropriate to me?

(*k*) I pass by those most notorious verses of Licinius Calvus [**38**] ... When, after the scandalous epigrams, Gaius Calvus negotiated through friends for a reconciliation, Caesar took the initiative and wrote to him first.

(*l*) [see 1*e*.]

20–25 *Io*

20 (9 Bl., C.)

a virgo infelix, herbis pasceris amaris

Ah, wretched girl, you will feed on bitter grasses.

Serv. Dan. ad Verg. *Buc.* 6.47 'a virgo infelix' (p. 74 Thilo): *Calvus in Io* 'a—amaris'.

21 (10 Bl., C.)

mens mea, dira sibi praedicens omnia, vecors

My distraught mind, foretelling everything dreadful for itself.

[Prob.] GLK IV p. 234: *sibi pronomen dativo casu utroque numero frequenter duabus brevibus constat, ut* . . . (*Aen.* 6.142), *interdum ex brevi et longa* . . . *ut Calvus in Io* 'mens—vecors'.

22 (11 Bl., C.)

cum gravis ingenti conivere pupula somno

When the pupil, heavy with overwhelming sleep, <? began> to close

Prisc. GLK II p. 479: *Calvus 'conivere' infinitum secundum tertiam coniugationem correpta paenultima protulit* 'cum—somno'.

urgenti *Heinsius*

23 (12 Bl., C.)

frigida iam celeri superatur Bistonis ora

Now in her haste she passes the chill Bistonian coastland.

[Prob.] GLK IV p. 226: *-is syllaba nominativi casus brevis est masculino sive feminino genere atque communi* . . . *feminino ut Calvus in Io* 'frigida—ora'.

celeri *Parrhasius*: celeris *cod. B*   superatur *Munro*: superata est *Baehrens*: peragratur *Lenchantin*: vergatar *B*   vistinis *B, corr. Munro*

24 (13 Bl., C.)

sol quoque perpetuos meminit requiescere cursus

Even the sun takes thought to rest his perpetual journeyings.

Serv. Dan. ad Verg. *Buc.* 8.4 'requierunt flumina cursus' (p. 92 Thilo): *cursus proprios retardarunt . . . quiesco enim duplicem habet significationem, et aliter dico 'quiesco ego', aliter 'quiesco servum', id est quiescere facio. Calvus in Io* 'sol—cursus'.

25 (15 Bl., C.)

partus gravido portabat in alvo

. . . was carrying the unborn child in her laden womb.

Charis., p. 101 B² = GLK I p. 80: *alvum Vergilius feminino genere saepe dixit, sed masculino Calvus* 'partus—alvo'.

26–28 (*Epicedion Quintiliae*)

26

(*a*) Cat. 96 *si quicquam mutis gratum acceptumve sepulcris* / *accidere a nostro, Calve, dolore potest,* / *quo desiderio veteres renovamus amores* / *atque olim missas flemus amicitias,* / *certe non tanto mors immatura dolori est* / *Quintiliae, quantum gaudet amore tuo.*

(*b*) Prop. 2.34.89–90 [= **19***d*]: *haec etiam docti confessa est pagina Calvi,* / *cum caneret miserae funera Quintiliae.*

(*a*) If anything, Calvus, that is pleasing and acceptable can reach the silent tomb from our grief and from the longing with which we renew old loves and weep for friendships long abandoned, then certainly Quintilia does not so much grieve at her early death as she rejoices in your love.

27 (15 Bl., C.)

cum iam fulva cinis fuero

At the time when I shall have become dark ash.

Charis., p. 128 B² = GLK I p. 101: *feminino genere dixit cinerem et Calvus in carminibus* 'cum—fuero'. Non. Marc. I p. 291 Lindsay: *cinis . . . feminino aput*

Caesarem et Catullum et Calvum lectum est, quorum vacillat auctoritas 'cum—
fueris'.

fulva] furva *L. Mueller*   fuero *Char. cod.* N (*et Cauchii ex deperdito codice
excerpta*): fueris *Non.* Bᴬ: fuerit *Char. cod. n.*

28 (16 Bl., C.)

forsitan hoc etiam gaudeat ipsa cinis

Perhaps your very ash feels pleasure at this.

Charis., p. 128 B² = GLK I p. 101 (post **27**): *item* 'forsitan—cinis'.

29–33 (*Epithalamia*)

29 (4 Bl., C.)

<‒ ◡ ‒> vaga candido
nympha quod secet ungui

<? a lily> for a wandering nymph to cut with her white fingernail.

1–2 Charis., p. 186 B² = GLK I p. 147: '*ungui*' *Licinius Calvus in poemate*
'vaga—ungui'.

1. <lilium> *suppl. Broukhusius ad Prop. 1.20.39*: <papaver ut / luteum> *Courtney,
praecedente Perutelli*

30 (5 Bl., C.)

Hesperium ante iubar quatiens

. . . before, brandishing its Hesperian radiance, . . .

Prisc. GLK II p. 170: '*iubar*' *quoque tam masculinum quam neutrum
proferebant . . . Calvus in epithalamio* 'Hesper<i>um—quatiens' '*hoc iubar*'
dixit.

Hesperium *ed. Ald.*: Hesperum *codd.* (*nisi quod* Vesperum *RG*): Vesper it *Baehrens*
quatiens *om.* RHLDGK

31 (6 Bl., C.)

et leges sanctas docuit et cara iugavit
corpora conubiis et magnas condidit urbes

She taught the solemn ratification of laws and joined together in marriage
loving couples and founded great cities.

1–2 Serv. Dan. ad Verg. *Aen.* 4.58 'legiferae Cereri' (III p. 274 ed. Harv. =
p. 474 Thilo): *alii dicunt favere nuptiis Cererem, quod prima nupserit Iovi et
condendis urbibus praesit, ut Calvus docet* 'et—urbes'.

1–2 et ... et ... / ... et] haec ... haec ... / ... haec *in marg. Ambros.*
1 sanctas docuit] docuit sanctas *Castorina*

32 (7 Bl., C.)

pollentemque deum Venerem

Venus who has power over the gods

Serv. ad Verg. *Aen.* 2.632 'ducente deo' (II p. 474 ed. Harv. = p. 311 Thilo):
*secundum eos qui dicunt utriusque sexus participationem habere numina. nam
Calvus in libro suo ait* 'pollentemque—Venerem'. Macrob. *Sat.* 3.8.2 (I p. 181
Willis): *... cum ille* [sc. Verg., *Aen.* 2.632] *doctissime dixerit* 'ducente deo', *non
'dea'. nam et apud Calvum Aterianus adfirmat legendum* 'pollentemque deum
Venerem', *non 'deam'*.

33 (8 Bl., C.)

hunc tanto munere digna

Deem this man worthy of so great a gift.

Serv. Dan. ad Verg. *Aen.* 11.169 'non alio digner te funere, Palla' (p. 496
Thilo): *alii 'dignem' legunt iuxta veteres ab eo quod est 'digno'. Calvus* 'hunc—
digna'.

huic ... magna *cod.* (*F, Paris. Lat.* 7929), *corr. Daniel.*

34–7 (*carmina variis metris conscripta*)

34 (1 Bl., C.)

et talis Curius pereruditus

And Curius, extremely well versed in gaming . . .

Asc., Cic. *In Toga Candida* fr. 28 Schoell (p. 93 Clark) 'Curium hominem quaestorium': *Curius hic notissimus fuit aleator, damnatusque postea est, in hunc est hendecasyllabus Calvi elegans* 'et—pereruditus'.

talis *Beroaldus*: talos *L. Mueller*: talus *codd. Asc.*   Curius pereruditus *ed. Ven.*: curios perud(ios)ius *codd.*

35 (2 Bl., C.)

durum rus fugit et laboriosum

. . . shuns the harsh and toilsome countryside.

Gell. *NA* 9.12.10: *item C. Calvus in poematis 'laboriosum' dicit, non, ut vulgo dicitur, qui laborat, sed in quo laboratur;* 'durum', *inquit,* 'rus—laboriosum'. Non. Marc. I p. 193 Lindsay: 'laboriosum', *in quo laboratur*. Calvus poematis 'durum—laboriosum'.

fugit et *Non. Marc. cod. Nic. Fabri*: fugite *Non. codd. plerique* fugi et *vel* fugi sed *codd. Gellii*: fugis et *ed. Par. 1536 Gellii*.

36 (3 Bl., C.)

Sardi Tigelli putidum caput venit

FOR SALE!, the disgusting person of Sardinian Tigellius.

Porph. ad Hor. *Serm.* 1.3.1 'omnibus hoc vitium est cantoribus' (p. 240 ed. Holder (1894)): *in eundem Tigellium Hermogenen et hic invehitur, eumque* 'Sardum' [ibid. 3] *dixit . . . adnotandum ergo et Sardum et Sardiniensem dici posse . . . Licinius Calvus de eodem Hermogene loquens 'Sardum' dixit,* 'Sardi— venit'. Cic. *Ad Fam.* 7.24 (= 260 SB).1: *id ego in lucris pono, non ferre hominem* [sc. Tigellium] *pestilentiorem patria sua, eumque addictum iam tum puto esse Calvi Licini Hipponacteo praeconio.*

37 (21 Bl., C.)

                <ᴗ _ ᴗ> lingua vino
temptantur et pedes <ᴗ _>

     . . . tongue and feet are affected by wine.

1–2 Schol. Bern. Verg. *Georg.* 2.94 'temptatura pedes olim vincturaque ling-
uam' (p. 223 ed. Hagen (1867)): *hos versus a Calvo poeta transtulit, ait enim
ille* 'lingua—pedes'.

   verba varie temptata, sed fortasse sana sunt; metrum idem esse potest quod in Cat.
25 invenimus.

38–39 (*Epigrammata*)

38 (17Bl., C.)

                Bithynia quicquid
et pedicator Caesaris unquam habuit.

     . . . all that Bithynia and Caesar's bugger ever possessed.

1–2 Suet. *Div. Iul.* 49.1: *pudicitiae eius famam nihil quidem praeter Nicomedis
contubernium laesit, gravi tamen et perenni obproprio et ad omnium convicia
exposito. omitto Calvi Licini notissimos versus* 'Bithynia—habuit'. Ibid. 73:
*Gaio Calvo post famosa epigrammata de reconciliatione per amicos agenti ultro
ac prior scripsit.*

39 (18 Bl., C.)

     Magnus, quem metuunt omnes, digito caput uno
        scalpit; quid dicas hunc sibi velle? virum.

Magnus, whom everyone fears, scratches his head with one finger. What
would you say he's after? A man!

1–2 Schol. Iuv. 9.133 'qui digito scalpunt uno caput' (p. 161 Wessner): *signum
infamium est uno digito caput scalpere; quod vitium habuit Magnus Pompeius,
ut de eo Martialis* [immo Calvus] *tale epigramma fecerit* 'magnus—virum'.
Schol. Luc. 7.726 'nunc tibi vera fides' codd. tres (Jocelyn, *Eikasmos*, 7 (1996),
247, cf. Wessner, Schol. Iuv. p. 275): . . . *unde Martialis de eo in epigrammate*
'Magnus—virum' . . . *ut Iuvenalis* (9.130–3). Sen. *Contr.* 7.4.7 *et carmina*

quoque eius [sc. Calvi], *quamvis iocosa sint, plena sunt ingentis animi'. dicit de Pompeio* 'digito—virum'.

1 omnes *Pithoeus*: homines *schol. Iuv. et Luc.*   2 quid dicas *schol. Iuv. et Luc.*: quo credas *Seneca*: quid credas *Pithoeus signum interrogationis post velle posuit Scaliger*: quid? dicas hunc sibi velle virum *malit Jocelyn*

40 (*carmina amatoria*)

(*a*) Prop. 2.25.3–4: *ista* [sc. Cynthiae] *meis fiet notissima forma libellis, | Calve, tua venia, pace, Catulle, tua* [=**19***c*].

(*b*) Ov. *Tr.* 2.431–2: *par* [sc. Catulli licentiae] *fuit exigui similisque licentia Calvi | detexit variis qui sua furta modis* [=**19***f*].

41–42 (*incertae sedis*)

41 (10 Bl., C.) *dub.*

ne triclinarius

. . . lest the <?> of the dining room

Charis., p. 97 B² = GLK I pp. 76–7: *cubicularius est custos cubiculi, cubicularis vero lectus cubiculo aptus . . . et balnearius fur, balnearis autem urceus et solea balnearis, unde perspicuum est Calvum ad amicos non recte dixisse* 'ne triclinarius', *cum* 'triclinaris' *dicere debuisset.*

triclinearius *Charis. cod. N*   *hoc frustulum fort. pedestri sermone conscriptum est.*

42 (20 Bl., C.)

Schol. Bern. Verg. *Georg.* 1.125 'ante Iovem nulli subigebant arva coloni' (p. 186 ed. Hagen (1867)): *dicunt Iovem commutasse omnia, cum bonus a malo non discerneretur terra omnia liberius ferente, quod Calvus canit.*

They say that Jupiter changed everything, because, at the time when the earth brought forth all things in greater abundance, there was no way of distinguishing between the good man and the bad, as Calvus says in one of his poems.

THE Elder Pliny tells us that Calvus was born on 28 May 82 BC, the same day as M. Caelius Rufus, whom Cicero defended (*NH* 7.165 'eadem die geniti sunt, oratores quidem ambo, sed tam dispari eventu'). Pliny may be right about Calvus, even if wrong about Caelius' birth date (doubts rejected by R. G. Austin, *Cicero, Pro Caelio*[3], app. I, sustained by R. Syme, *Latomus*, 39 (1980), 407 = *Roman Papers* III, p. 1224). Thus Calvus may have been a little younger than his great friend Catullus. His father, who died in 66 BC, was C. Licinius Macer, tribune of the plebs (73 BC), praetor (about 68 BC), historian (H. Peter, *Historicorum Romanorum Reliquiae*[2] (Leipzig, 1914), I, pp. cccl–ccclxv and 298–307) and orator (see E. Gruen, *HSCP* 71 (1967), 215–17; E. Malcovati, *Oratorum Romanorum Fragmenta*[2] (Paravia, 1955), 356–8). Sallust (*Hist.* 3.48) gives Macer a fiery tribunician speech.

As far as we know, Calvus neither held nor sought any political office, but his talent as an orator inevitably involved him in Roman politics. More than a century after Calvus' death, his series of speeches against Vatinius (cf. Catullus 53) was still read by all aspiring orators (Tacitus, *Dial.* 21.2 'at hercule in omnium studiosorum manibus versantur accusationes quae in Vatinium inscribuntur, ac praecipue secunda ex his oratio; est enim verbis ornata et sententiis, auribus iudicum accommodata . . .'). By that time Calvus' poetry may have faded from the public consciousness, with the exception of some notorious epigrams attacking Julius Caesar (**38**) and Pompey (**39**). After writing **38**, Calvus sought through intermediaries a reconciliation with Julius Caesar (Suetonius, *Div. Iul.* 73 = **19***k*), and one fruit of that reconciliation may have been Calvus' defence of a minor triumviral partisan, C. Porcius Cato (Gruen, *HSCP* 71 (1967), 222–4). Catullus too made his peace with Caesar (*Div. Iul.* 73), and even described him as 'great Caesar' in one of his last datable poems (11.10).

It appears that Calvus the orator was exceptionally active in the year 54 BC (see Gruen's article). Thereafter silence, until Cicero speaks of him in 46 BC in such a way as to make plain that he is dead (*Brutus* 279, 283, *Ad Fam.* 15.21 (= 207 SB). 4). Perhaps Calvus died late in 54 or 53 BC, not long before or after the death of Catullus. He would still have been in his twenties (called 'adulescens' in Cic. *Brut.* 279). For a book which covers the life, oratory, and poetry of Calvus, see E. Castorina, *Licinio Calvo* (Catania, 1946). There are also notes on the poetic fragments in L. Nosarti, *Filologia in Frammenti* (Bologna, 1999), 195–201.

19

These testimonia convey an overwhelming impression of Calvus' closeness to Catullus in poetry as well as personal friendship. The range of the two is almost identical. At the most elevated level both wrote a learned 'epyllion' in hexameters, Calvus' *Io* (**20**–**5**) corresponding to Catullus 64, and two marriage poems, one in glyconics (**29**, cf. Cat. 61) and one in hexameters (**30**–**3**, cf. Cat. 62). The few surviving fragments of Calvus' polymetrics are written in two of Catullus' favourite metres, hendecasyllables (**34**–**5**) and limping iambics (**36**); the puzzling **37**, which has generally been deemed corrupt (or even prose) may, I think, be explained satisfactorily by taking the transmitted text to be sound, and the metre that of Catullus 25 (iambic tetrameter catalectic). The targets of their verse were very similar: Caesar (**38**), Pompey (**39**), and a partisan of Caesar (**36**), as were their themes and vocabulary of personal and sexual invective (**36** 'putidum caput'; **38**.2 'paedicator'; **38** and **39** accusations of effeminacy). In the majority of Calvus' fragments some illuminating comparison can be made with Catullus. It would be rash to assume that Calvus was always the imitator just because he was slightly the younger; Catullus' poem (**50** = **19**a) about the pair's impromptu versifying (cf. Colin Macleod, *Collected Essays*, 171) implies their complete equality.

None of the judgements passed by later writers in **19** suggests that, as a poet, Calvus was in any way inferior to Catullus; for example, the supercilious Greeks of **19**l are prepared to allow merit to just 'a few' poems of each. I shall argue that, when Ovid wrote the *Metamorphoses*, everyone could be expected to know the *Io* of Calvus. Horace, however, indicates that the exclusive championing of Catullus and Calvus might, in the mid-30s BC, be regarded as an irksome affectation (*Sat.* 1.10.18–19 = **19**b; cf. Nisbet, *Collected Papers*, 396). In the 30s AD the elder Seneca praises the 'ingens animus' of Calvus' verse (**19**g, citing **39**); clearly he has in mind shorter poems like the epigram attacking Pompey. Perhaps Calvus' poetry, with the exception of **38** and **39** which would be kept alive in biographies of Caesar and Pompey, faded from the public consciousness more quickly than that of Catullus (still very much present in the epigrams of Martial). Part of the reason may have been that, in the Silver Age, Calvus was remembered more as an orator than as a poet. But the Younger Pliny had a friend (**19**h) who not only admired Catullus and Calvus, but tried to write poems in their style, full of 'lepor, dulcedo, amaritudo, amor'. He did slip in one or two which were 'a trifle harsh' (*duriusculos*, reminding one of Quintilian's description of Gallus as *durior*, [**138**h]), but in this too he was following Catullus and Calvus—and of course Pliny's friend did so deliberately, not because he could write no better.

20–25 *Io*

The *Io* of Calvus did not become notorious (like the *Smyrna* of Cinna) for its obscurity or the length of time which it took to compose. If, however, we possessed a complete text of Calvus' epyllion, we might find that it exercised as strong an influence as Catullus 64 on later Latin poetry at least until the death of Ovid, in whom one undeniable imitation can be seen, of **20** 'a virgo infelix, herbis pasceris amaris' at *Met.* 1.632–4 'frondibus arboreis et *amara pascitur herba,* / proque toro terrae non semper gramen habenti / incubat *infelix*'. Consider for a moment how little we would know of Catullus 64 if (as for the *Io* of Calvus) we had to rely on ancient grammarians, lexicographers, and Virgilian commentators. The total number of lines (counting parts as whole lines) would be eight, one of which (65) would have to be discounted because Isidore wrongly ascribed it to Cinna (Fordyce, *Catullus*, p. xxv, says to Calvus!). We could gather (from line 1) that Catullus wrote a stately poem on an Argonautic theme, to which lines 23–23b might tentatively be attributed. A minor poet also mentions a lament of Ariadne (Lygdamus = [Tibullus] 3.6.41–2 'sic cecinit pro te doctus, Minoi, Catullus / ingrati referens impia facta viri'), to which we could give 171–2 and perhaps 71–2. There would be no reason to connect the Argonautic poem with the Lament for Ariadne, and no need to ascribe 64.327 (the only other preserved line) to either.

Surviving fragments of Calvus' *Io* do not enable us to see the structure of that poem, or to answer detailed questions such as who (Jupiter or Juno) transformed Io and from what motive, or precisely how Argus was killed. Allusions to the Io myth in Latin poets from Virgil to Ovid may give us hints, though we must always remember (particularly with reference to Ovid, *Met.* 1.583 ff.) that a high-class poet will not be content to imitate slavishly even a famous predecessor; though expecting readers to remember the earlier version, he will introduce elements that are new and arresting. In Ovid's Io, Mercury finally puts Argus to sleep by telling him the tale of Pan and Syrinx; half way through the narration Mercury notices that all of Argus' eyes have closed, and the poet himself finishes the story in indirect speech. A charming and brilliant device, but it would seem sadly stale if there had been anything like it in Calvus. So, although Calvus almost certainly described Mercury putting Argus to sleep (**22**), this was probably effected in more orthodox fashion by means of the god's magic wand (see the discussion below of *Met.* 1.716). Ovid gives no details of Io's metamorphosis into a cow (610–11), but spreads himself on the much rarer opportunity to describe a reverse transformation from animal to human (738–46). This might be because Calvus had already written a detailed account of Io turning into a cow (cf. *Aen.* 7.790, mentioned below). Ovid may, for the most part, give prominence to what was *not* in Calvus, while playing down (by their absence or relative insignificance) elements which Calvus had emphasized. It is probably no coincidence that Ovid's Io episode, with its inset subsidiary myth, provides one of the most perfect examples in the *Metamorphoses* of the structure which may have characterized many Hellenistic and Latin epyllia. But we would be rash to assume that, in Calvus too, the inset was provided by Mercury's story-telling.

One of the few verbatim fragments of *Io* (**20** 'a virgo infelix, herbis pasceris amaris') is preserved by a commentator on *Ecl.* 6.47 'a virgo infelix'. I suspect that not only the one line of Virgil, but the whole passage on Pasiphae (*Ecl.* 6.45–60) conveys the atmosphere of Calvus' epyllion. The grasses which Io will eat are perfectly normal fodder for a cow—only when we think of Io in human terms do they become 'amarae', earning our sympathy for her. Pasiphae has not been transformed into a cow, but, having fallen in love with a bull, she too is caught between the human and the bovine. The words with which Virgil describes her beloved, 'ille latus niveum molli fultus hyacintho / ilice sub nigra pallentis ruminat herbas' (53–4), could appropriately be adapted to Io. The blend of pathos and irony with which the two heroines are addressed can be paralleled in later treatments of Io, and could well go back to Calvus.

The following passage of Propertius (2.33.7–12), occasioned by Cynthia's devotion to Isis (equated with Io), betrays a clear affinity of spirit to Virgil's lines on Pasiphae:

> tu certe Iovis occultis in in amoribus, Io,
>   sensisti multas quid sit inire vias,
> cum te iussit habere puellam cornua Iuno
>   et pecoris duro perdere verba sono.
> a quotiens quernis laesisti frondibus ora
>   mandisti et stabulis arbuta pasta tuis!

So does the digression on Io in Ovid, *Heroides* 14 (Hypermestra). The whole passage (85–108) is too long to quote, but here are lines 87–96:

> at satis est poenae teneram mugisse puellam,
>   nec, modo formosam, posse placere Iovi.
> adstitit in ripa liquidi nova vacca parentis
>   cornuaque in patriis non sua vidit aquis,
> conatoque queri mugitus edidit ore,
>   territaque est forma, territa voce sua.
> quid furis, infelix? quid te miraris in unda?
>   quid numeras factos ad nova membra pedes?
> illa Iovis magni paelex metuenda sorori
>   fronde levas nimiam caespitibusque famem.

The earliest reference to Io in Ovid is probably *Am.* 1.3.21 'carmine nomen habent exterrita cornibus Io'. One can reasonably press the detail 'exterrita cornibus': there was already in existence a famous poetic treatment of Io in which she saw her new horns reflected in the water and was terrified by them (as in *Her.* 14 above, and, later, in *Met.* 1.639–41). It seems quite likely that Ovid has in mind Calvus' *Io*. Other motifs (and sometimes even phrases) may plausibly be ascribed to Calvus on the basis of the passage mentioned above and a few others. Some examples:

(*a*) *The transformation of Io*: *Aen.* 7.789–90 (the shield of Turnus) 'at levem clipeum sublatis cornibus Io / auro insignibat, iam saetis obsita, iam bos'. As noted above, Ovid spends no time on Io's transformation into a cow (perhaps because Calvus had described it in detail), but when she turns back into human shape we read 'fugiunt e corpore saetae' (*Met.* 1.739). I wonder whether Virgil may have reversed the word order of a phrase 'obsita saetis' in Calvus. If we ask the point of 'sublatis cornibus', perhaps she raises her horns in supplication (cf. *Met.* 1.731 'tollens ad sidera vultus') because she can no longer raise her arms.

(*b*) *Io chewing the cud*: Prop. 2.33.12 'mandisti et stabulis arbuta pasta tuis'. Set alongside this *Ecl.* 6.54 'pallentes ruminat herbas' (in the passage on Pasiphae which borrows the phrase 'a virgo infelix' from **20**) and the so-called 'Somnium Ovidii', *Am.* 3.5.17–18 (not about Io) 'dum iacet et lente revocatas ruminat herbas / atque iterum pasto pascitur ante cibo'. Virgil and [Ovid] share the line-ending 'ruminat herbas', Propertius and [Ovid] the passive use of 'pastus' (not, I think, found elsewhere in the sense 'fed upon'). Perhaps we should postulate a common source in Calvus.

(*c*) *Io's gadfly*: It has long been suspected that [Virgil], *Ciris* 184 (on Scylla daughter of Nisus, see Lyne ad loc.) 'fertur et horribili praeceps impellitur oestro' is a close imitation—perhaps even a verbatim borrowing—of what Calvus wrote about Io. This idea may be supported by *Georgics* 3.152–3 (on the oestrus/asilus) 'hoc quondam monstro horribilis exercuit iras / Inachiae Iuno pestem meditata iuvencae'. Virgil would then have transferred the epithet 'horribilis' from the *oestrus* to the *irae*. Although Ovid does not mention the gadfly, perhaps he too means to recall Calvus by applying a compound epithet connected with 'horreo' to the Fury which drove Io on her wanderings: 'horriferamque [v.l. horrificamque] oculis animoque obiecit Erinyn' (*Met.* 1.725).

It is worth tabulating the motifs which can be ascribed to Calvus' *Io* with at least fair plausibility. Among the parallel texts I have included Valerius Flaccus 4.346–421, though uncertain to what extent Calvus' epyllion would still have been in the literary consciousness of Valerius' contemporaries. His account is strongly Ovidian—note even his amusing adoption of the Ovidian mannerism of -que outside direct speech when Mercury starts to address Argus, '"quo" que ait "hinc diversus abis?"' (4.387):

(*i*) Io sees her horns reflected in clear water (*Am.* 1.3.21, *Her.* 14.89–90, *Met.* 1.640–1).

(*ii*) She is terrified by her own appearance (*Am.* 1.3.21, *Her.* 14.92, *Met.* 1.641).

(*iii*) She tries vainly to speak (Prop. 2.33.10, *Her.* 14.91, *Met.* 1.637–8 (cf. 745–6), Val. Flacc. 4.372).

(*iv*) She endures many things natural to a cow but incongruous and distasteful for a young woman (**20**): Prop. 2.33.11, *Her.* 14.96, 99–100, *Met.* 1.631–4.

(*v*) She eats bovine fodder (**20**): Prop. 2.33.11–12, *Her.* 14.96, *Met.* 1.632, Val. Flacc. 4.379.

(*vi*) She is shut up in a stall (Prop. 1.33.12, *Met.* 1.631, cf. Statius, *Silvae* 3.2.101).

(*vii*) She chews cud: Prop. 2.33.12 (cf. Virgil, *Ecl.* 6.54, [Ovid], *Am.* 3.5.17–18).

(*viii*) She raises her horns in supplication (*Aen.* 7.790, *Met.* 1.731).

The search for Calvan motifs and phrases could be extended. For example, Nisbet and Hubbard on Horace, *Odes* 1.15.30 (cervus) 'graminis immemor' tentatively suggest a common source in Calvus for that phrase, Virg. *Ecl.* 8.2 'immemor herbarum . . . iuvenca' and *Georgics* 3.498 'immemor herbae'.

In one or two places Ovid seems deliberately to recreate the style of a neoteric epyllion for his own Io. Consider *Met.* 1.716:

languida permulcens medicata lumina virga.

The fabric of this hexameter (two nouns at the end, each preceded by an adjective, with a present participle holding the line together, and a word-break after a fourth-foot spondee) is characteristic of Catullus 64 (e.g. 7 'caerula verrentes abiegnis aequora palmis'), the pseudo-Virgilian *Ciris* (e.g. 3 'Cecropius suavis exspirans hortulus auras') and perhaps other neoteric epyllia such as Calvus' *Io* (**22** is similar but not identical). We may note that, for Ovid, use of the magic wand is only an extra precaution, since Argus has already been put to sleep by Mercury's story-telling. Even more striking is *Met.* 1.732:

et gemitu et lacrimis et luctisono mugitu.

The epithet 'luctisonus' is unique—one thinks of 'fluentisonus' (52), 'raucisonus' (263), and 'clarisonus' (320) in Catullus 64. Also the line exhibits not merely a spondaic fifth foot, but a rare subdivision of the σπονδειάζων: the final word is of three syllables (see on Helvius Cinna, **17**), and a Latin word (not, as much more often in Ovid, a Greek proper name). Compare Catullus 64.96 'quaeque Idalium frondosum', 297 'e verticibus praeruptis'. In these cases we cannot tell whether Ovid is echoing Calvus' actual words or merely suggesting his style.

Occasionally these texts may give us a glimpse of models used by Calvus. Richard Thomas suggests (*HSCP*, 86 (1982), 85 n. 17) that 'Inachiae . . . iuvencae' (*Georg.* 3.153, also Val. Flacc. 4.357) may be Calvan, but neither he nor Mynors points out the derivation of this phrase from Moschus, *Europa* 51 πόρτιος Ἰναχίης. The same poem may be reflected in *Aen.* 7.789–90 'Io / . . . iam saetis obsita, iam bos', cf. *Europa* 44–5 Ἰναχὶς Ἰὼ / εἰσέτι πόρτις ἐοῦσα, though εἰσέτι ('still a cow') looks forward to Io's resumption of human shape, whereas Virgil's 'iam bos' ('by now a cow') looks back to her original state. The echoes of Moschus may have been imported by Virgil, but it is by no means unlikely that Calvus admired and used the passage on Io in *Europa* 44–61. The double name of the gadfly (*Georgics* 3.147–8, there oestrus/ asilus) was a literary *topos* found in Callimachus (*Hecale* fr. 117 H.) and Apollonius Rhodius (3.276–7), poets who would have been to Calvus' taste. Callimachus also wrote a poem entitled Ἰοῦς ἄφιξις (the Arrival of Io). No identifiable fragment of that work survives (see Pfeiffer on fr. 472). Dr Nicholas Richardson long ago remarked to me that fr. 363 Pf. καὶ ἀγλαὰ πίσεα γαίης / βόσκεο has an Io-like ring to it, but those words are assigned to the *Hecale* (fr. 149 H.) by Hecker's Law. It seems likely that Callimachus' lost poem would have stressed the identification of Io with Isis, and the establishment of her cult in Egypt (cf. Prop. 2.33.3–4, 13–16, *Met.* 1.747–50, Val. Flacc. 4.417–18).

20 (9 Bl., C.)

a virgo infelix, herbis pasceris amaris: cf. Ovid, *Met.* 1.632–4 'amara pascitur herba / . . . / . . . infelix' (discussed above). The phrase 'a virgo infelix' occurs twice in the Virgil *Ecl.* 6 (47, 52), addressed by Silenus to Pasiphae (for *virgo* of a young married woman, see *OLD* 1). The present line might be addressed to Io by her father Inachus when he discovers her plight (cf. *Met.* 1.651 ff.), or even by Jupiter, but it seems most likely that the poet is apostrophizing his own character, a mannerism much beloved by Callimachus (e.g. *Hymn* 4.197 ff., 215 ff., fr. 75 Pf. 40, 44, 53, 74) and taken over, perhaps particularly from Callimachus, by Roman poets (cf. the apostrophe to Smyrna in Helvius Cinna, **10**, and to Phaethon, lacking from the Apollonius Rhodius model, in Varro Atacinus, **132**). Hypermestra apostrophizes Io at length in Ovid, *Her.* 14.93–106.

a: this highly emotional interjection may have been typical of neoteric poetry (cf. Catullus 64.71 'a misera', 135 'immemor a!'), as it is of elegy (Allan Kershaw, *CP* 75 (1980), 71–2, notes the particular frequency of 'a quotiens'). When Virgil puts a three fold 'a!' into the mouth of Cornelius Gallus (*Ecl.* 6.47–9), he must surely be emphasizing a real feature of Gallus' own poetry.

   virgo infelix: cf. the exclamation at *Ciris* 71 'infelix virgo' (with Lyne's note).

21 (10 Bl., C.)

mens mea, dira sibi praedicens omnia, vecors: probably spoken by Io (conceivably by her father Inachus, cf. *Met.* 1.587 'animo peiora veretur'). If so, perhaps by now she has become afflicted with madness, whether through the gadfly (cf. *Georgics* 3.152–3 and *Ciris* 184, quoted and discussed in the introduction to this poem) or the Fury (*Met.* 1.725–7, Val. Flacc. 4.393–4).

   vecors: 'frenzied'. The ve- (vae-) prefix denotes 'a fault either of excess or deficiency' (*OLD*); thus *vegrandis* can mean either 'undersized, puny' or 'morbidly large' (*OLD*). 'vecors' is attested in old Latin poetry (Pacuvius, Accius, Cicero, *Aratea*) and occurs twice in Catullus (15.14; 40.4). For the coupling with 'mens', Courtney mentions Cicero, *Pro Sestio* 117 'at cum ille furibundus incitata illa sua vaecordi mente venisset', Ovid, *Ibis* 343 'mens quoque sic furiis vecors agitetur'.

   The unique preservation of this fragment by [Probus] is puzzling. The grammarian has just quoted *Aen.* 6.142 to illustrate the scansion 'sibī'. He had the choice of half a dozen examples of 'sibī' in the *Aeneid*, but instead goes to Calvus for this triviality. Could the quotation from Calvus have originated from a time when the *Io* was a mainstream poem? Is he showing off his knowledge of a very rare text? Or could the line earlier have been cited by another grammarian for a different purpose, e.g. to illustrate *vecors* (cf. Festus p. 372 M 'vecors est turbati et mali cordis'). [Probus] is the unique source also of **23** (again, quoted for a triviality which might easily have been illustrated from elsewhere), and cites 'a virgo infelix' (GLK IV p. 219), perhaps conscious that Virgil had borrowed the phrase from Calvus' *Io*. So perhaps [Probus], *De Ultimis Syllabis* (or his source) was a genuine admirer of this poem.

22 (11 Bl., C.)

cum gravis ingenti conivere pupula somno: this line survives because of the apparently unique third conjugation 'conivĕre', 'to close', which is in the archaic manner (cf. e.g. Virgil, *Aen.* 8.677 'fervĕre Leucaten auroque effulgĕre fluctus'). Even the normal second conjugation of this verb is rare in poetry. Although not complete in sense, this line comes close to the pattern so common in Catullus 64: two nouns at the end, each with an epithet in the first half, and a verb in the middle (see the discussion of Ov. *Met.* 1.716 on p. 63 above).

    ingenti ... somno: Heinsius' conjecture 'urgenti' is unnecessary (cf. Martial 12.18.13 'ingenti fruor improboque somno'); he also suggested that the next line might have included 'coepit'.

    It seems highly probable that these words describe Argus being put to sleep by Mercury (cf. Ovid, *Met.* 1.714 'adopertaque lumina somno'). In Ovid the god achieves this by a combination of sweet music and story-telling (682 ff.), using his magic wand only as a final precaution (715–16, see introduction to this poem). For variant versions, see Apollodorus 2.1.3, Johansen and Whittle on Aeschylus, *Supplices* 305, *Lexicon Iconographicum Mythologiae Classicae* V/1, p. 662. Since Argus had 100 eyes, the single 'pupula' mentioned here may have been the last to close; perhaps this suggested to Ovid the amusing sequence in which Argus strives to keep a quorum of his eyes open (686–7 'et, quamvis sopor est oculorum parte receptus, / parte tamen vigilat') until, half way through the story of Pan and Syrinx, Mercury notices that they have all shut (713–14 'talia dicturus vidit Cyllenius omnes / succubuisse oculos').

    cum: Calvus himself would probably have written 'quom' (see on Cinna, **2**).

23 (12 Bl., C.)

frigida iam celeri superatur Bistonis ora: there can be little doubt that this fragment describes the wanderings of Io. 'Bistonis' (convincingly restored for the corrupt 'vistinis') indicates that she is in the region of Thrace, travelling towards the Thracian Bosporus (which she will cross). 'Celeri' (Parrhasius) could be (as Courtney says) a dative of the agent, or agree with e.g. 'cursu' in the following (or previous?) line. This fragment of Calvus is probably reflected in *Ciris* 165 'saeva velut gelidis Edonum Bistonis oris'.

    The words 'Bistonis ora' in our poet probably belong together, as in *Heroides* 16.346; Ovid has many similar collocations with 'ora' (Ausonis,

Illyris, Maenalis, Sarmatis, Taenaris). Lyne (on *Ciris* 165) doubts whether 'ora' should be taken with 'Bistonis' in Calvus. Presumably he would like to view 'orā' as ablative; if one could find a suitable epithet (instead of 'celeri') to agree with it, this hexameter would fall into the favourite neoteric pattern discussed above in connection with Ovid, *Met.* 1.716. But 'Bistonis' by itself = 'the Bistonian land' raises some doubts ('Achaeis' and 'Argolis' are occasionally so used). 'Frigida ... Bistonis orā', where the noun has two epithets (one of them descriptive, one possessive), is not infelicitous (Housman, *Classical Papers*, 1120); cf. **238**.2 'gelido de vertice Nonacrino', Cat. 4.9 'trucemve Ponticum sinum', Horace, *Odes* 1.4.17 'domus exilis Plutonia'.

iam: perhaps part of a sequence with repeated 'iam', to mark the stages of Io's journey, as in *Ciris* 468–71 (Scylla) 'iamque adeo ... / (470) iam ... / ... iam'.

Bistonis ora: the Βίστονες were a Thracian people (Hdt. 7.110), once ruled by Diomedes (the owner of the mares, not the son of Tydeus), whom Euripides calls τύραννον Βιστόνων (*Alcestis* 1022). Words connected with the Bistones are much favoured in Hellenistic, Roman, and late Greek poetry: Βιστονίς (with omega in Ap. Rh. 1.34 and Nonnus, *Dion.* 13.340), sometimes as a noun (e.g. Phanocles fr. 1.7 Powell Βιστονίδες and Horace, *Odes* 2.19.20 = 'Thracian women'). Pfeiffer thought that the reference in the damaged Call. fr. 114.21 is to Diomedes' mares. Here 'Bistonis ora' might refer specifically to the lake called Bistonia (Limni Vistonida).

Concerning the preservation of this fragment, see on **21**. Here too the trivial point about the short final syllable (Bistonis) could easily have been illustrated from Virgil (e.g. *Aen.* 2.787 'Dardanis').

24 (13 Bl., C.)

sol quoque perpetuos meminit requiescere cursus: perhaps making a contrast with the unceasing journeys of Io—even the sun takes a rest, but never Io. This could be narrative by the poet, a complaint by the heroine, advice or sympathy for someone else, etc. Or the emphasis could be on the time of day (cf. *Ciris* 232–3 'tempore quo ... / ... requiescunt flumina currus').

meminit: see on Varius Rufus, **150**.6 'nec serae meminit decedere nocti' (of the hunting dog). Here too there is no question of the sun 'remembering' (as opposed to 'forgetting') to still its course. Rather it 'turns its mind' to taking a rest, and would not allow anything to prevent it from doing so.

requiescere cursus: the fragment is quoted to illustrate the transitive use of 'requiescere' in Virgil, *Ecl.* 8.4 'et mutata suos requierunt flumina cursus', where, however, Clausen writes 'Virgil seems to have found the construction harsh . . . and to have modified it with *mutata*' (comparing *Aen.* 1.658 'faciem mutatus et ora Cupido'). The transitive use of this verb occurs also in Prop. 2.22.25, *Ciris* 233 (quoted above), and I am inclined to recognize it in *Ciris* 10 'requiescere Musas' ('to give my Muses a rest'), so that 'requiescere' is on a level with the transitive 'deponere' in the next line, and that one can understand 'mihi' with both infinitives.

25 (14 Bl., C.)

partus gravido portabat in alvo: very probably a reference to Epaphus, Io's son by Zeus (e.g. *Met.* 1.748). For the masculine 'alvus', compare Cinna, *Smyrna* 9 'at scelus incesto Smyrnae crescebat in alvo'. 'Gravido . . . in alvo' is also thus placed in Accius, or perhaps both go back to a common source, e.g. in Ennius, *Annales*. The verb 'portare' (discussed by B. Axelson, *Unpoetische Wörter* (1945), 30–1) suggests a great weight. It is twice applied by Ovid to another neoteric heroine, Myrrha/Smyrna (*Met.* 10.470 'conceptaque crimina portat', 481 'vixque uteri portabat onus').

26–28 (*Epicedion Quintiliae*)

The title (whether *Epicedion Quintiliae* or *Epicedion ad Quintiliam*) is nowhere attested. But we learn from Propertius 2.34.89–90 (**26b = 19d**) that Calvus wrote a famous poem lamenting the death of his beloved Quintilia. Once armed with this information, we may recognize Catullus 96 (=**26a**) as not only a consolation to his friend for Quintilia's death, but also a literary tribute to Calvus' poetic lament; Cat. 96 immediately follows another tribute to a notable poem by a friend (Cat. 95 on Cinna's *Smyrna*=**7a**). Just as the appearance of the Satrachus in Cat. 95.5 suggests that Cinna himself mentioned that river in the *Smyrna*, so we can hope that Cat. 96 will contain hints of the themes, and even the wording, of the poem praised. And that hope may be fulfilled, since Calvus **28** 'forsitan hoc etiam gaudeat ipsa cinis' (see ad loc.) could well lie behind Cat. 96.5–6. If that is right, then Calvus' poem is shown to be elegiac (as one would expect). Propertius' couplet (**26b**) suggests that Calvus' lament was quite a substantial poem, perhaps dominating Calvus' elegiac compositions at least as much as 68 stands out among the elegies of Catullus.

Many scholars (e.g. Pfeiffer, *CQ* 37 (1943), 32 = *Ausgewählte Schriften* (Munich, 1960), 146–7; Lyne, *CQ* NS 28 (1978), 178–9) have believed that Calvus' lament for Quintilia was in some way related to the lament for his wife Arete composed by Parthenius of Nicaea, who is connected with several Roman poets in this and the next generation (at least Helvius Cinna, Cornelius Gallus, and the young Virgil). That is entirely reasonable, though no proof exists. It has generally been thought that Parthenius wrote for Arete both an Encomium (*Suppl. Hell.* 607) and an Epicedion (*SH* 608–14). I am, however, inclined to agree with Jane Lightfoot (*Parthenius of Nicaea* (Oxford, 1999), 134, following Meineke) and to assign all the testimonia and fragments to a single poem (the source for *SH* 606 says merely Παρθένιος ἐν τῆι Ἀρήτηι), taking τῆς γαμετῆς Ἀρήτης ἐγκώμιον (Suid. s.v. Παρθένιος = Test. 1 Lightfoot) as a phrase in apposition: 'a Lament for Arete, being an encomium of his wife Arete in three books'. The parchment fragments (2–5 Lightfoot = *SH* 609–14), so brilliantly restored to the *Arete* by Pfeiffer, breathe the world of learned myth (Iris as husband of Zephyrus), history (the Athenian colonization of Cyzicus), and geography (the rivers of Bithynia); note that Propertius (**26b**) calls Calvus 'doctus' in the context of his Lament for Quintilia. In the next generation Prop. 4.7, which describes the ghost of Cynthia returning to the poet, may owe something to Calvus.

It has long been debated whether Quintilia should be thought of as Calvus' wife or his mistress. If—a questionable point—we can trust the entry in Diomedes, GLK I p. 376 'Calvus . . . ad uxorem', the poet was at least married. Some have felt, as Lyne (*CQ* (1978), 179 n. 36), that 'the fact that no pseudo-nym (apparently) is used for Quintilia points to her status as wife'. But perhaps the convention of a Greek pseudonym for the beloved (probably started by Catullus in poem 51, where 'Lesbia' is particularly appropriate to the translation from Sappho) had not yet become almost universal. Catullus (96.3–4 = **26a**) 'quo desiderio *veteres* renovamus *amores* / atque *olim missas* flemus *amicitias*' indicates pretty clearly that Calvus' love affair with Quintilia was a thing of the past, which the poet had broken off a considerable time before Quintilia's death. On balance it seems to be more likely that Quintilia was Calvus' mistress.

We can also deduce from Propertius (2.34.89–90 = **26b**) that, in the course of lamenting Quintilia ('cum caneret miserae funera Quintiliae'), Calvus admitted to other love affairs ('haec etiam docti confessa est pagina Calvi'), as he did elsewhere in his polymetric poems (Ov. *Tr.* 2.432 = **19f**) 'detexit variis qui sua furta modis'). Here Calvus probably blamed himself for these other loves, and 'told the sad story' (Cat. 96.4 'flemus') of how he abandoned

Quintilia. He may also have recalled happier times in their 'veteres . . . amores', as Cynthia's ghost does in Prop. 4.7.15–20 ('iamne tibi exciderant vigilacis furta Suburae / et mea nocturnis trita fenestra dolis?', etc.). Almost certainly Calvus said that Quintilia's death brought back his feelings of love for her (Cat. 96.2 'veteres renovamus amores') and hoped that, even in Hades, she might derive pleasure from such a thought (that may be the context of **28** 'forsitan hoc etiam gaudeat ipsa cinis').

Propertius 2.25.3–4 (=**19***c*) rather suggests that there was one woman whom Calvus immortalized by his verse. Certainly we do not know of any other name, but, if Quintilia played as large a part in Calvus as Lesbia in the poetry of Catullus, one would expect later authors to mention her more often. Lyne (who believes Quintilia to be Calvus' wife) thinks that Propertius has in mind only the *Epicedion,* and not any other poems addressed by Calvus to Quintilia. If, however, Quintilia were Calvus' mistress (as seems rather more probable), it would be surprising if he did not mention her until after her death. I suspect that Quintilia appeared as one of several women in Calvus' erotic poetry, but did not dominate that category; only the lament elevated her above his other loves.

The two verbatim quotations **27** and **28** are plausibly but not certainly attributed to this poem. I do not feel any desire to link them too closely (Courtney 209 suggests that they may belong to the same couplet). We may agree that the 'cinis' of **28** is Quintilia's; the speaker of **28** is most probably Calvus, and the line could be part of a final envoi (see ad loc., comparing Cat. 96.5–6). **27**, whether we read 'fuero' or 'fueris' (see below), is probably from the mouth of dead Quintilia. This poem was discussed in some detail by E. Fraenkel, 'Catulls Trostgedicht für Calvus', *WS* 69 (1956), 278–88 = *Kleine Beiträge zur klassischen Philologie* (Rome, 1964), ii. 103–13 and H. Tränkle, 'Neoterische Kleinigkeiten', *MH* 24 (1967), 87–103 (particularly 93–9).

27 (15 Bl., C.)

cum iam fulva cinis fuero: either the start of a hexameter or the end of a pentameter with final trisyllable (entirely acceptable, of course, in the time of Catullus and Calvus). If we read 'fuero', the speaker may be Quintilia, whether on her deathbed or at the time of their parting, saying e.g. that Calvus would regret his infidelities when she was dead: '<at flebis> cum iam fulva cinis fuero'. With 'fueris', the words might be spoken by Quintilia's ghost, looking forward to a reunion when Calvus too is dead, as the ghost of Cynthia does in Prop. 4.7.93 'nunc te possideant aliae; mox sola tenebo'.

fulva cinis: the noun is usually masculine. Nonius tells us that it was feminine in Caesar, Catullus, and Calvus, 'quorum vaccillat auctoritas'. It is not clear whether 'quorum' refers to all three authors or only to Catullus and Calvus; *cinis* appears nowhere in the surviving works of Julius Caesar (Courtney 187 thinks that feminine 'cinis' may have occurred in a poem by Caesar). But we can confirm that Catullus used both genders: masculine in 68.98, feminine in 68.90 and 101.4. So it is likely that Calvus somewhere else (in the same poem?) used *cinis* in the masculine—count that as a further fragment of Calvus if you will!

fulva: the epithet is applied to dust (e.g. Ennius, *Ann.* 315 Sk.) and sand. But there is something to be said for L. Mueller's conjecture 'furva', a rare archaic epithet equivalent to *ater* and *niger* (J. André, *Étude sur les termes de couleur dans la langue latine* (1949), 60), strongly associated with death (e.g. Horace, *Odes* 2.13.21 'furvae . . . Proserpinae').

28 (16 Bl., C.)

forsitan hoc etiam gaudeat ipsa cinis: this fragment is very plausibly linked to Catullus 96.5–6 'certe non tanto mors immatura dolori est / Quintiliae, quantum gaudet amore tuo'. We may suspect that Catullus' 'certe . . . / . . . gaudet' confirms Calvus' more tentative 'forsitan . . . gaudeat', and that the speaker is (surely) Calvus himself. 'Hoc' might then be the dead Quintilia's knowledge that Calvus still loves her, or the fact that he has written for her this poetic tribute. For the sentiment, cf. Martial 12.52.4 'cuius et ipse tui flagrat amore cinis'. Courtney well quotes Antipater of Sidon 13 G–P (= *Anth. Pal.* 7.23). 5–6 ὄφρα κέ τοι σποδιή τε καὶ ὀστέα τέρψιν ἄρηται / εἰ δή τις φθιμένοις χρίμπτεται εὐφροσύνα (the final couplet). Our line too might be the last of the poem. For another conclusion which sends joy to the dead (if only that is to be found in Hades), compare Euphorion's *Thrax* (*SH* 415.26) χαίροις, εἰ ἐτεόν τι πέλει καὶ ἐν Ἄϊδι χάρμα.

29–33 *Epithalamia*

Only **30** is explicitly attributed to such a work ('Calvus in Epithalamio'), but the subject matter of **29** ('Calvus in poemate') strongly suggests a marriage poem. One might take **31** as a straightforward list of Ceres' functions—'cara iugavit / corpora conubiis' does not seem to be emphasized more than the other items—but perhaps the surrounding context said more about Ceres favouring marriage. **32** and **33** are appropriate to an epithalamium, but both (particularly the latter) could be imagined in a great variety of contexts.

29 and **30** almost suffice to prove that Calvus wrote two marriage poems, one in the graceful glyconic/pherecratean metre, the other in stately hexameters (definitely the metre of **31**). These of course would correspond to Catullus 61 and 62—yet another indication that Catullus and Calvus were as closely linked by their poetic compositions as by personal friendship. Ticida also wrote a glyconic poem, from which **102** ('Ticida in hymenaeo') has survived.

Epithalamia were particularly associated with Sappho; the Alexandrian scholars made up a book of her poems in this genre (*Lyrica Graeca Selecta* 223–31, together with 222 = *P. Oxy.* 2294). From the Hellenistic period we have the mythical epithalamium for Menelaus and Helen (Theocritus 18), Callimachus' celebration of the actual wedding of Arsinoe to Ptolemy II Philadelphus (fr. 392 Pf.), an epithalamium ascribed to Eratosthenes (fr. 28 Powell) and hints of such a poem in Parthenius (fr. 37 Lightfoot = *Suppl. Hell.* 649, conceivably fr. 53 L. = *SH* 666). On 'Hymenaios' and 'Epithalamion' see R. Muth, *WS* 67 (1954), 5–45, and, for the conventional themes found in poems of this type, A. L. Wheeler, 'Tradition in the Epithalamium', *AJP* 51 (1930), 205–23.

29 (4 Bl., C.)

1–2. **< _ ‿ _ > vaga candido / nympha quod secet ungui:** the remains of a glyconic line followed by a complete pherecratean. Even these few words convey something of the same elegance and charm which pervade the marriage poem Catullus 61 (composed in stanzas of four glyconics plus one pherecratean). Comparison of an unmarried girl to a flower occurs in Cat. 61.87–9 'talis in vario solet / divitis domini hortulo / stare flos hyacinthinus'. In 62.39–44 the cutting of a flower represents the taking of a girl's virginity (lines sung by a chorus of girls hostile to marriage):

> ut flos in saeptis secretus nascitur hortis
> ignotus pecori, nullo convolsus aratro,
> quem mulcent aurae, firmat sol, educat imber;
> multi illum pueri, multae optavere puellae:
> idem cum *tenui carptus* defloruit *ungui*,
> nulli illum pueri, nullae optavere puellae.

In Sappho, *LGS* 225, the hyacinth which grows on the hills and is trodden underfoot by shepherds (οἴαν τὰν ὑάκινθον ἐν ὤρεσι ποίμενες ἄνδρες / πόσσι καταστείβοισι, χάμαι δέ τε πόρφυρον ἄνθος) may represent an unwanted girl. In our fragment of Calvus the details are unclear, but 'vaga' might imply that the flower, like Sappho's hyacinth, grows in an exposed place (contrast Cat. 62.39 'in saeptis . . . hortis') where it is vulnerable to any passer-by.

At the beginning of the line, Broukhusius supplied '<lilium>', based upon Prop. 1.20.37–9 'et circum irriguo surgebant lilia prato / candida purpureis mixta papaveribus, / quae modo decerptum [sc. Hylas] tenero pueriliter ungui . . .', etc.; this would fit excellently. Courtney (preceded by Perutelli, cf. *Frustula Poetarum* (Bologna, 2002), 113) suggests '<papaver ut / luteum>', thus providing the favourite colour contrast between white and some shade of red (e.g. Prop. 1.20.38 above), though perhaps not in a very effective form.

candido / . . . ungui: according to Courtney (p. 203) 'a strained phrase'— but it seems to me quite natural, since the whites of the finger-nails would be used for snipping the stem of the flower, as for tearing one's cheeks in Euripides, *Orestes* 961 τιθεῖσα λευκὸν ὄνυχα διὰ παρηίδων (though Hartung conjectured λευκῶν, which is adopted by West but not by Diggle or Willink).

30 (5 Bl., C.)

Hesperium ante iubar quatiens: the only fragment of **29–33** which is explicitly assigned to a marriage poem. Three preliminary matters:

(*a*) *The subject of the clause*: Heavenly bodies are said to 'shake' (*quatere*) their own light, perhaps an image from brandishing a torch. Lyne on *Ciris* 349 f. (discussed below) quotes Cicero, *Aratea* fr. 21.3 Buescu 'magnus Leo tremulam quatiens a corpore flammam' and [Virgil], *Culex* 43 (sol) 'aurato quatiebat lumina curru'. But Calvus can hardly have said that Hesperus shook his Hesperian radiance. So it seems more likely that a general word meaning 'star' agreed with 'quatiens' and formed the subject of the clause. Very appropriate would be 'ignis' (e.g. Cat. 62.26 'Hespere, quis caelo lucet iucundior ignis?').

(*b*) *The function of ante.* This could mean 'in front'. I suspect, however, that we have here part of *antequam* in tmesis. A natural sense would be that the formalizing of the marriage must await the appearance of Hesperus, as in Cat. 62.29 'nec iunxere [sc. the parents] *prius quam* se tuus [sc. of Hesperus] extulit ardor'.

(*c*) If Calvus said that the star shook its 'Hesperian' radiance, this would give him the opportunity to mention that the same star also had an 'Eoan' radiance, since the morning and evening stars were commonly identified (a favourite *topos* among the learned poets, see on Helvius Cinna, **10**.2).

Turn now to *Ciris* 349 ff. 'postera lux ubi laeta diem mortalibus almum / et gelida venientem *ignem quatiebat* ab Oeta / quem pavidae alternis fugitant optantque puellae / (Hesperium vitant, optant ardescere Eoum)', etc. In Cat. 62.7 'Oetaeos ostendit Noctifer ignis' and Virgil, *Ecl.* 8.30 'tibi deserit Hesperus Oetam', Oeta is associated with the evening star in an epithalamial context (the *Ciris* poet, of course, is describing the morning star). Although this passage of the *Ciris* seems clumsily constructed (see Lyne for difficulties), it contains in 351–2 a close and very elegant imitation of Callimachus' *Hecale* (fr. 113 H.=291 Pf., context unknown). The original liking for the evening star and dislike of the morning star has been reversed by the Latin poet to fit girls apprehensive about their wedding night (the same point arises from Catullus, 62.60 and 26, where the girls' 'Hespere, quis caelo fertur crudelior ignis?' contrasts with the young men's 'Hespere, quis caelo lucet iucundior ignis?'). Lyne (p. 252) suggests that *Ciris* 351–2 might be adapted from Cinna's *Smyrna* (though Call. *Hecale* fr. 113 H. is clearly more important than Cinna, **10** for *Ciris* 351–2). Taking into account the possible relationship of *Ciris* 350 'quatiebat' to 'quatiens' in our fragment, and the fact that Oeta (in the same line) was so often associated with marriage poetry, I wonder whether the *Ciris* poet may not have clumsily tried to adapt a longer passage from Calvus' hexameter *Epithalamium*, including perhaps even verbatim borrowing of 351–2. *Exempli gratia* I offer '<nec iuveni fas est sponsam donare puellam> / Hesperium ante iubar quatiens <quam surgat ab Oeta / ille Dionaeae Veneri gratissimus ignis> / quem pavidae alternis fugitant optantque puellae / —Hesperium vitant, optant ardescere Eoum.'

31 (6 Bl., C.)

1–2. et leges sanctas docuit et cara iugavit / corpora conubiis et magnas condidit urbes: note the alliteration of 'c' in both lines. It is conceivable that these lines describe Ceres' overall part in the advance of mankind from the primitive to the more civilized state. Laws, formal marriage (as opposed to casual unions), and cities had originally all been lacking, at least according to Lucretius book 5 (959 'nec legibus uti', 962 'Venus in silvis iungebat corpora amantum', 1108 'condere coeperunt urbis').

We owe this fragment to a dispute among ancient Virgilian commentators as to whether Dido made a wise selection of deities to honour when already in love with Aeneas. She included a sacrifice 'legiferae Cereri' (*Aen.* 4.58), who, according to some, had been the first wife of Jupiter, but was later abandoned by him; to the unmarried Apollo, and to the inconstant Bacchus. Some considered this a disastrous choice (Macrobius 3.12.10 'toto, ut aiunt, caelo errasse Vergilium cum Dido sua rem divinam pro nuptiis faceret'). On the other hand it was argued that Ceres, as the first wife of Jupiter, should be in favour of marriage (as well as having other attributes useful to a queen who is founding a new city). These two lines of Calvus are then quoted.

At first sight it seems that Ceres' interest in marriage is not being elevated above the other two attributes, and so one might question whether this fragment really belongs to an epithalamium. But all three items involve the socializing of mankind, which in itself creates conditions favourable to marriage. Servius (ad loc.) comments 'ante inventum a Cerere frumentum, passim homines sine lege vagabantur; quae feritas interrupta est invento usu frumentorum, postquam ex agrorum divisione nata sunt iura'. Calvus may well have mentioned Ceres' gift of crops to mankind (perhaps immediately before the quoted lines). Whether he also referred to the original marriage of Ceres and Jupiter (in Hesiod, *Theogony* 912–14 Demeter is one of Zeus's wives, but not the first) is quite unclear. Cicero (*In Verrem* 5.187) speaks of the *sacra* of Ceres and Libera as follows: 'a quibus initia vitae atque victus, morum, legum, mansuetudinis, humanitatis hominibus et civitatibus data ac dispertita esse dicuntur'.

1. leges sanctas: it is not clear whether 'sanctas' is felt more as an ordinary epithet ('sacred') or as the past participle of *sancio* ('solemnly ratified'); a similar doubt in Horace, *Sat.* 2.1.81 'sanctarum inscitia legum'. No doubt Calvus (like Virgil in *Aen.* 4.58 'legiferae Cereri') alludes to Demeter's title Θεσμοφόρος; perhaps he remembers Callimachus, *Hymn* 6.18 ὡς πολίεσσιν ἑαδότα τέθμια δῶκε, where ἑαδότα hints at a technicality (see Hopkinson ad loc.). Servius, after making the connection with Greek *thesmophoria*, asks tentatively 'an quia in aede Cereris aere incisae positae leges fuerunt?'.

docuit: the goddess's teaching role is stressed e.g. in Call., *Hymn* 6.21 ἐδιδάσκετο [sc. Triptolemus], Virgil, *Georgics* 1.148 'instituit'. We may wonder, with Courtney, why Calvus required the lengthening 'docuīt' when he could have written 'et leges docuit sanctas' (Castorina). The answer may be that occasional use of such a licence (even when there is no necessity for it) forms part of a poet's total armoury. Or Calvus may be reverting to an older custom, since final syllables in -t were originally long. For Ennius' practice, see O. Skutsch, *The Annals of Q. Ennius* (Oxford, 1985), 58–9 (we find voluīt in the same metrical position at *Ann.* 449). See further Austin on *Aen.* 4.64, Fordyce on 7.174, Nisbet and Hubbard on Horace, *Odes* 1.3.36. From a Hellenistic perspective, note that Euphorion has a particular tendency to lengthen short vowels before a single consonant (see van Groningen's (Amsterdam, 1977) edition, pp. 262–3).

1–2.   et cara iugavit / corpora conubiis: perhaps contrasting legitimate marriage with the more casual unions of primitive mankind (expressed in somewhat similar language by Lucretius, 5.962 'et Venus in silvis iungebat corpora amantum'). The goddess's connection with marriage is attested in both Greek and Latin (see Pease on *Aeneid* 4.58), although Farnell, *Cults of the Greek States*, iii (Oxford, 1907), 75–112, played down this aspect of Demeter Thesmophoros.

cara . . . / corpora: cf. Catullus 66.32 'caro corpore'.

2.   conubiis: in a number of places (e.g. Cat. 62.27, 64.141, 158, *Aen.* 3.319) the 'u' is unquestionably long. In cases like this (and e.g. *Aen.* 4.126) scholars dispute whether we should scan the word as three long syllables with synizesis (as recommended by Servius ad loc.) or regard the 'u' as short (cf. innuba, pronuba, subnuba). At the end of a long discussion on *Aen.* 4.126, Austin concludes that the true quantity is ŭ, with ū as a licence, adding, however, 'undoubtedly the word has something queer about it'.

et magnas condidit urbes: the founder-god par excellence was Apollo (Call. *Hymn* 2.56–7 Φοῖβος γὰρ ἀεὶ πολίεσσι φιληδεῖ / κτιζομένῃς'), one of whose titles was Archegetes (see C. Dougherty, *The Poetics of Colonization* (New York, 1993), index s.v. Apollo). Although Demeter promoted civilized life (above), she is not, as far as I know, specifically connected with the foundation of cities. Perhaps Calvus for the moment is conflating her with the Phrygian Great Mother, who was indeed closely associated with cities and wore a mural crown (Lucr. 2.606–7 'muralique caput summum cinxere corona / eximiis munita locis quia sustinet urbes', cf. *Aen.* 6.784–5 with Austin's notes). The two goddesses had much in common (see e.g. Homer A. Thompson, *Hesperia*, 6 (1937), 205–8), and the Magna Mater, like Ceres, was thought of as a civilizer.

32 (7 Bl., C.)

pollentemque deum Venerem: as a contribution to the long-running argument whether one should read 'deo' or 'dea' in *Aen.* 2.632 (see Austin ad loc., Goold, *HSCP* 74 (1970), 113–15 = *Oxford Readings in Vergil's Aeneid*, ed. Harrison (Oxford, 1990), 72–4), the Virgilian scholar (H)aterianus (who lived at latest in the third century and is cited five times in the *scholia Veronensia* to the *Aeneid*) adduced this phrase, noting that Calvus wrote 'deum' and not 'deam'. Obviously he took 'deum' to be accusative singular. That is not altogether impossible (see the discussion in A. Perutelli, *Frustula Poetarum* (2002), 114–22 and 124). Most modern scholars, however, suspect that Haterianus erred, and that 'deum' in Calvus was genitive plural, 'Venus who holds sway over the gods'. Even though an objective genitive is not elsewhere attested with *pollens*, it is common with *potens*, e.g. Horace, *Odes* 3.25.14 (Bacchus) 'Naiadum potens'. In Ovid, *Her.* 9.43 I would emend 'deo' to 'deum', producing 'deum . . . potenti', 'the ruler of the gods'.

33 (8 Bl., C.)

hunc tanto munere digna: while one cannot rule out the possibility that we have here the last syllable of a glyconic followed by a complete pherecratean (K. Deichgräber, *Hermes*, 99 (1971), 49), it seems much more likely that these words represent a hexameter ending. The active *digno* (here imperative) was recognized as archaic—hence in *Aen.* 11.169 some wished to read not *digner* but *dignem*, 'iuxta veteres'. *Dignatus*, coupled with an ablative, continued to be used as a passive, 'thought worthy of' (e.g. *Aen.* 3.475, Manilius 1.758, Silius 11.272). If the fragment belongs to an epithalamium, it could (as Courtney says) be addressed either to the bride's father (when the *munus* would be the bride) or to the bride herself (when the *munus* would be her virginity). In the latter case one might compare Ovid, *Her.* 14.123–4 'si . . . / quae . . . tibi tribui *munera dignus* habes' (Hypermestra refers, in my opinion, to her virginity which she gave to Lynceus on their wedding night).

    digna: the (deponent) verb is often used of a woman doing a man the honour of becoming his wife, e.g. Virgil, *Aen.* 4.192 'cui se pulchra viro dignetur iungere Dido' (cf. 3.475, *Ecl.* 4.63), Ovid, *Met.* 8.326–7 'o felix si quem dignabitur . . . / ista virum'.

34–37 (*carmina variis metris conscripta*)

Ovid speaks of Calvus' love poems (no doubt including short elegiac pieces which we might class as epigrams with **38–9**) as being composed 'variis . . . metris' (*Tr.* 2.432 = **19***f*). None of these four fragments is demonstrably concerned with love; two contain unfavourable comments on individuals (**34**, **36**), one an adverse judgement on the countryside (**35**, not necessarily the poet's own view), while **37** is sympotic. The metres of **34** and **35** (hendecasyllables) and **36** (choliambic) represent two of Catullus' favourites, also used by Helvius Cinna (**11** and **12**). **37** may be in the very rare metre of Catullus 25 (iambic tetrameter catalectic).

34 (1 Bl., C.)

et talis Curius pereruditus: Asconius (whose prosopographical identifications must be treated with respect) attaches this line to Q. Curius (*RE* Curius 7), of whom Sallust (*Cat.* 23.1) gives a damning account: 'natus haud obscuro loco, flagitiis atque facinoribus coopertus, quem censores senatu probri gratia moverant'; he conspired with Catiline and then betrayed his fellow conspirators. Elsewhere nothing is specifically said about his fondness for gambling, although that could have been a reason for his removal from the senate. Otherwise one might identify Calvus' target as Manius Curius, described by implication as a cheerful but disreputable character in Cicero, *Phil.* 5.13 'homo . . . festivus [sc. Lysiades Atheniensis], ut ei cum M'. Curio consessore eodemque conlusore facillime possit convenire'. He was indeed 'notissimus aleator' (Asconius' phrase); Quintilian (6.3.72) records how he employed a witticism to defend himself against a charge of gambling, 'cum eius accusator in sipario omnibus locis aut nudum eum in nervo aut ab amicis redemptum ex alea pinxisset, "ergo ego" inquit "numquam vici"' (Russell in the Loeb Quintilian prints Purcell's 'Quintus' for 'Manius').

talis: L. Mueller's 'talos' is an equally plausible emendation (cf. Horace, *Odes* 3.8.5 'docte sermones'); *erudio*, like *doceo*, can take an accusative of the subject taught.

pereruditus: also in Cicero, *Ad Atticum* 4.15. (= 90 S–B) 2 'homo pereruditus . . . et nunc quidem deditus Graecis litteris' (cf. *De Finibus* 2.12). The term would of course normally be applied to an honourable pursuit such as literature or philosophy; for its ironical extension one might compare Tacitus, *Ann.* 16.18 on Petronius, 'erudito luxu'. As a very long shot I wonder whether Curius could have written a treatise on gambling, of the sort described by Ovid (*Tr.* 2.471–4 'sunt aliis scriptae, quibus alea luditur, artes / (hoc erat ad nostros non leve crimen avos); / quid valeant tali, quos possis plurima iactu / figere, damnosos effugiasve canes.' This would give a special point to 'pereruditus'.

35 (2 Bl., C.)

durum rus fugit et laboriosum: there is a faint resemblance between this line and Cat. 1.7 'doctis, Iuppiter, et laboriosis'. One naturally sees here the dislike of the unsophisticated countryside which is prominent in Catullus (22.14 'idem infaceto est infacetior rure', 36.19 'pleni ruris et inficetiarum').

But these epithets may indicate the reasons why this unknown person leaves
(or shuns) the countryside, not the poet's own view; elsewhere (see on **42**)
Calvus may have endorsed (? tongue in cheek) the old Catonian view of
success in agriculture as the best measure of virtue. A link between **34** and **35**
is not out of the question ('et talis Curius pereruditus / durum rus fugit et
laboriosum'). Gambling and farming would represent (in traditional Roman
thought) morally opposite ways of supporting oneself.

fugit: in the Oxford text of Gellius, P. K. Marshall prints 'fugis', which is a
possible interpretation of the confused manuscripts but seems rather less
likely. The verb need not imply that the subject leaves the countryside—per-
haps he merely avoids going there (*OLD fugio* 11, 'shun', 'avoid'; *TLL* VI. 1.
1487.58 ff.).

laboriosum: Gellius' point about a special meaning here ('non … qui
laborat sed in quo laboratur') does not altogether carry conviction, since this
example could be grouped with others under the heading 'involving much
work or effort' (*OLD laboriosus* 1). The epithet is often connected with the life
of the countryside, e.g. Plautus, *Vidularia* 31 'laboriosa … vita est rustica',
Cicero, *In Verrem* 3.86 'aratoribus laboriosissimis'.

36 (3 Bl., C.)

Sardi Tigelli putidum caput venit: 'FOR SALE: the disgusting person of
Sardinian Tigellius'. Shackleton Bailey (*Cicero: Epistulae ad familiares* (Cam-
bridge, 1977), ii. 428) and (earlier) Palmer on Horace, *Sat.* 1.3.3 plausibly
suggest that this was the first line of Calvus' lampoon on Tigellius. Horace
(*Sat.* 1.3.3–4 'Sardus … / ille Tigellius') picks up the first two words, with
'ille' perhaps indicating the notoriety created by this poem. We can even
recover the outline of the whole poem with the aid of a remark which Cicero
made in August 45 B C (*Ad Fam.* 7.24 (= 260 SB). 1) at a time when he was on
bad terms with Tigellius: 'id ego in lucris pono, non ferre hominem pestilen-
tiorem patria sua [i.e. Sardinia], eumque addictum iam tum puto esse Calvi
Licini Hipponacteo praeconio'. Shackleton Bailey (*Ad Fam.*, vol. ii, p. 428)
translates the last clause with 'I regard him as knocked down to the highest
bidder all those years ago in Licinius Calvus' Hipponactean advertisement
[i.e. written in Hipponax's metre, the scazon or limping iambic].' 'Iam tum'
indicates a decade or more ago—Calvus seems to have left the scene about
54 B C.

The venality of Sardinians was proverbial (A. Otto, *Die Sprichwörter und
sprichwörtlichen Redensarten der Römer* (Leipzig, 1890; reprinted Hildesheim,

1962), 308–9 s.v. Sardus), as Cicero states in the same letter (*Ad Fam.* 7.24.2 'habes "Sardos venalis, alium alio nequiorem"'). Someone who is 'venal' is normally thought of as ready to sell himself. But Calvus, it seems, had the ingenious idea (cf. Horace, *Epist.* 2.2.2–16) of writing a poem in the form of an auction announcement ('praeconio' in Cicero), in which he himself took the part of the auctioneer and offered Tigellius for sale. The first duty would be to announce the fact of the sale and its contents, then to describe the quality of the merchandise on offer, and finally to suggest an appropriate price, whence Cicero's 'addictum' (*OLD addico* 2). See W. W. Buckland, *The Roman Law of Slavery* (Cambridge, 1908), 52 ff.

Sardi: 'The vendor must state the nationality of the slave . . . The reason assigned . . . is that nationality has a good deal to do with the desirability of slaves' (Buckland, *Law of Slavery*, 58). To come from Sardinia was not a recommendation (Cicero, *Ad Fam.* 7.24.2, quoted above). Sometimes a distinction was made (cf. Hispanus/Hispaniensis) between 'Sardus' = of Sardinian descent and 'Sardiniensis' = resident in Sardinia.

Tigelli: a friend of Caesar (as emerges from Cicero, *Ad Fam.* 7.24 = 260 SB, which includes the reference to Calvus' poem) and later of Octavian (Horace, *Sat.* 1.3.3–5); his bad relations with Cicero are also mentioned in *Ad Att.* 13.49–51 = 347–9 SB, all dating from August 45 BC (like *Ad Fam.* 7.24). This Tigellius is almost certainly to be distinguished from Tigellius Hermogenes (mentioned in Horace, *Sat.* 1.3.129; 1.4.72; 1.9.25; 1.10.17–18, 80, 90), although the pair shared a talent for singing. See E. Fraenkel, *Horace* (Oxford, 1957), 86 n. 2; Niall Rudd, *The Satires of Horace* (Cambridge, 1966), 292–3; Shackleton Bailey, *Cicero's Letters to Atticus*, vol. vii, p. 98 (correcting an earlier note). Since our Tigellius was a friend of Julius Caesar (above), Calvus' attacks on him may have been meant to discredit Caesar too (cf. **38**), like Catullus' attacks on Mamurra.

putidum caput: this might count as the vendor's acknowledgement of a defect (*vitium*), as in Buckland, *Law of Slavery*, 54–5. The phrase recurs in Virgil, *Catalepton* 6.2 'generque Noctuine, putidum caput' (cf. 12.1). In the *Catalepton*, however, the phrase is in apposition to the proper name, whereas here the name is in the genitive case (cf. Propertius 4.1.52 'longaevum . . . Priami . . . caput'). The latter construction is perhaps more grandiloquent (mockingly so in Calvus), since it would recall Greek tragic periphrases like Sophocles, *OT* 1207 κλεινὸν Οἰδίπου κάρα, *Antigone* 1 ὦ κοινὸν αὐτάδελφον Ἰσμήνης κάρα. Professor Nisbet, however, thinks that here the tone may not be grandiloquent, but that 'caput' would rather suggest a 'head' of cattle (*OLD* 8*b*). *Putidus* may have been a favoured word in the circle of Catullus and Calvus. The literal meaning, 'stinking', occurs in Cat. 17.10 'putidaeque paludis', and *OLD* sense 2 ('as a term of abuse indicating decrepitude or simply implying disgust') in 98.1 and four times in poem 42.

venit: 'FOR SALE', from vēneo. Such notice might be given in writing (e.g. Plautus, *Trinummus* 168 'aedis venalis hasce inscribit litteris'), but, since Cicero (*Ad Fam.* 7.24 = 260 SB. 1) speaks of 'Calvi Licini Hipponacteo praeconio', we should think here of a verbal announcement by the auctioneer (*praeco*), who is the poet himself. Among the graffiti from Pompeii I have found *CIL* IV Suppl. III (3) n. 8022 VINACIA VENIT (ASSIBUS) XXXII, also n. 7678 VASA FAECARIA VEN (either 'ven<eunt>' or 'ven<dit>' with the seller's name to follow), and 87776 a ('venal[i]s', the only word preserved).

37 (21 Bl., C.)

It seems almost certain that the Virgilian commentator means to quote a piece of Calvus' verse, which Virgil imitated ('hos versus a Calvo poeta transtulit') in *Georgics* 2.94 'temptatura pedes olim vincturaque linguam'. Courtney (p. 211) writes that the fragment 'looks like prose', but the intricate word order tells strongly against that possibility. And 'poeta' would be odd if the quote were prose. Scholars have almost universally (but note Donald Russell ap. Courtney) believed the citation to be corrupt. I see no need to question the transmitted text if one recognizes here the end of one line and beginning of the next, in the metre of Catullus 25 (iambic tetrameter catalectic). The quoted words would be preceded by an amphibrach ($\cup - \cup$) and followed by an iambus, to give the required word-break after the eighth syllable of each line. Most of the iambics in Cat. 25 are pure, but seven of the thirteen lines start with a spondee; so there would be no problem about 'tēmptantur' at the start of Calvus' second line. Common use of this very rare (in Latin) metre would be yet another link between Catullus and Calvus.

1–2. lingua vino / temptantur et pedes: 'temptantur' is plural by anticipation, the so-called *schema Alcmanicum* (see my note on Ovid, *Met.* 8.790 'Frigus iners illic habitant Pallorque Tremorque').

38–39 *Epigrammata*

Catullus attacked both Julius Caesar (in poems 29, 54, 57, 93) and Pompey (29, where surely Pompey, not Caesar, is called 'cinaede Romule' in line 5). We see here that the same applied to Calvus, whose side-swipe at Caesar (**38,** 'notissimos versus' according to Suetonius, *Div. Iul.* 49.1) became just as famous as Catullus' attack on Caesar through Mamurra, and was considered no less damaging. The reference to 'famosa epigrammata' in *Div. Iul.* 73 may indicate that Calvus wrote several poems against Caesar; like Catullus, Calvus was eventually reconciled with Caesar (Suetonius, ibid.).

38 (17 Bl., C.)

1–2. Bithynia quicquid / et pedicator Caesaris unquam habuit: this could be just a general description of a vast sum of money (as large as all the wealth of Bithynia and King Nicomedes). But it seems more likely that Calvus is attacking some individual who allegedly enriched himself from the breakup of the Bithynian kingdom and its subsequent take-over by Rome. For a similar exaggeration, in which a disreputable character is said to have acquired the total wealth of a conquered or tributary nation, compare Catullus 29.3–4 'Mamurram habere quod comata Gallia / habebat uncti et ultima Britannia'. Sallust's *Histories* contained a purported letter from King Mithradates VI Eupator of Pontus to the king of Parthia (Sinatruces or Phraates III ?), including complaints about the dismemberment of Bithynia: 'postremo Bithyniam Nicomede mortuo diripuere' (4.69.4). When Catullus went with Memmius to Bithynia in 57–56 BC, there was clearly still an expectation that such a trip would prove lucrative (10.6–8) 'quid esset / iam Bithynia, quo modo se haberet / et quonam mihi profuisset aere'). The identity of the profiteer has been forgotten, but everyone remembered the insult to Julius Caesar, which may even have been aggravated by the fact that it was merely a passing reference.

2. pedicator Caesaris: Nicomedes IV Philopator, the last king of Bithynia, who reigned c.94–74 BC and supposedly bequeathed his kingdom to the Roman People (though dark suspicions surrounded this bequest). See Richard D. Sullivan, *Near Eastern Royalty and Rome, 100–30 BC* (University of Toronto, 1990), 33–5, with associated notes. Nicomedes and his kingdom were things of the past when Calvus wrote (hence 'unquam'), and Julius Caesar's visit to the Bithynian court was even more distant in time (81–80 BC). According to Suetonius (*Div. Iul.* 2.1) 'stipendia prima in Asia fecit Marci Thermi praetoris contubernio; a quo ad accersendam classem in Bithyniam missus desedit apud Nicomeden, non sine rumore prostratae regi pudicitiae' (see p. 91 on Memmius). We do not know exactly when Calvus wrote these words, but perhaps at least twenty years later, bearing out the statement of Suetonius that the infamy of Caesar's alleged conduct was neither light nor short-lived ('gravi . . . et perenni obprobrio et ad omnium convicia exposito', *Div. Iul.* 49.1). We are given (ibid.) a selection of the insults called forth by this episode, culminating in the song of Caesar's soldiers at his Gallic triumph: 'Gallias Caesar subegit, Nicomedes Caesarem: / ecce Caesar nunc triumphat qui subegit Gallias, / Nicomedes non triumphat qui subegit Caesarem.'

pedicator: the verb *pedicare* is used three times by Catullus, but *pedicator* is paralleled only in *CIL* IV. 4008 (from Pompeii). A commoner noun form is *pedico* (*Priapea*, Martial, and graffiti). See J. N. Adam, *The Latin Sexual Vocabulary* (London, 1972), 123–5.

39 (18 Bl., C.)

These lines have been discussed by H. D. Jocelyn in *Eikasmos* (Quaderni Bolognesi di Filologia Classica), 7 (1996), 243–54. He examines in meticulous detail their social, historical, and political background, all relevant passages in other ancient authors, the transmission of the text and progress on it made by fifteenth- and sixteenth-century scholars (Politian, J. J. Scaliger, and P. Pithou), and the choices facing a modern editor. Jocelyn himself is not convinced that the couplet which we have represents a complete epigram, speculating (p. 249) that 'Calvus' lampoon struck not only at Pompey's nervous mannerism of scratching his head, but also at the leggings by means of which he concealed an unsightly sore, seeing in the former a sign of a desire for an active male sexual partner, and in the latter a sign of wanting to establish a Parthian-style kingship at Rome'. Compare Ammianus Marcellinus 17.11.4 (malicious criticisms of Pompey) 'quod ... caput digito uno scalpebat, quodque aliquamdiu tegundi ulceris causa deformis fasciola candida crus colligatum gestabat; quorum alterum factitare ut dissolutum, alterum ut novarum rerum cupidum adserebant'. The source of that passage (and others) is likely to be a biography of Pompey which cited Calvus' lampoon (Jocelyn p. 249). The Juvenal scholiast (misattributing to Martial, like the Lucan scholiast) clearly envisages a single-couplet epigram ('tale epigramma'), and that view seems to me the most plausible.

1. Magnus, quem metuunt omnes: suggesting, by contrast, that the poet has no such fears (as Catullus in poem 93, far from wishing to please Caesar, is totally indifferent to him). In place of 'omnes', the transmitted 'homines' might be retained, whether = 'people in general' (Plautus, *Capt.* 78, *Stich.* 606, 640) or 'ordinary men as opposed to gods', since 'Magnus' could indicate someone of superhuman strength and spirit: 'Calvus brings the semi-divine *Magnus quem metuunt homines* suddenly down to earth with *digito caput uno / scalpit*' (Jocelyn, p. 250).

1–2.   digito caput uno / scalpit: not, as some have thought, to avoid dis-arranging his hairstyle (Jocelyn, p. 244, points out that Pompey took little trouble with his hair). This nervous gesture was held to be a sign of passive homosexuality: 'impudicum et incessus ostendit . . . et relatus ad caput digi-tus' (Seneca, *Epist.* 52.12). Juvenal (9.133 'qui digito scalpunt uno caput') clearly imitates these words, whether he knew them from a text of Calvus or from a biography of Pompey.

3.   quid dicas hunc sibi velle? virum: for an epigram ending with a one-word reply to a question, compare Martial 1.10; 2.17, 56; 3.20; 9.4 (Jocelyn, p. 247 n. 23). The above punctuation is due to J. J. Scaliger, who was un-doubtedly influenced by a passage in Plutarch (*Pompey* 48.7) already cited by Politian. When in February 56 BC Clodius was prosecuting Milo *de vi*, and Pompey appeared in court to support the latter, Clodius gathered together a crowd, stationed himself in a conspicuous place, 'and put to them such ques-tions as these: "Who is an effeminate imperator?", "Which man is looking for a man?", "Who scratches his head with one finger?" And they, like a chorus trained in antiphonal singing, would answer each question, as he shook his toga, by shouting out "Pompey"' (Plut. *Pomp.* 48.7, cf. *Moralia* 89e, where the charge of effeminacy is said to be unjustified, and 800d). This humiliation for Pompey is mentioned also by Cicero, *Ad Fam.* 1.5b (= 16 SB). 1 'cum pro Milone diceret, clamore convicioque iactatus est' and, more fully, *Ad Quin-tum Fratrem* 2.3 (SB 7). 2, though Cicero does not repeat the worst insults. Compare Dio 39.19.1–2, Ammianus Marcellinus 17.11.4 (partly quoted above, apparently from the same source as Plut. *Mor.* 89e and 800d).

With the punctuation adopted, the form of Calvus' epigram may have been designed to recall Pompey's embarrassment at the trial of Milo. Jocelyn, how-ever, believes (p. 254) that an editor of Calvus should choose between 'quo credas' (thus Seneca, no doubt from memory) and 'quid? dicas hunc sibi velle virum?' ('quid dicas' more naturally go together (Nisbet)).

virum: from 'husband', the word is transferred to mean 'dominant homo-sexual partner', as in Cicero, *Red. Sen.* 12 'si eius [sc. of Gabinius] vir Catilina revixisset'. Pompey is represented as playing the passive role.

40

Calvus' love poems (like those of Catullus) were spread over different metres (Ov. *Tr.* 2.432 = **40***b*) and so did not form a separate category. They might have been felt to include his famous funeral lament for Quintilia (**26–8**). **40***a* = Prop. 2.25.3–4 suggests that there was one particular woman whom

Calvus celebrated above all, but (yet again) Propertius may refer to the lament for Quintilia. Certainly we do not know the name of any other woman loved by Calvus. Ovid speaks of him as 'revealing his *furta*' (*Tr.* 2.4.32). The term *furtum* (Adams, *Latin Sexual Vocabulary*, 167–8) denotes illicit sexual inter-course; it is glossed by Servius on *Aen.* 10.91 with 'adulterium'. This could be taken in a literal sense: Calvus was unfaithful to his wife (for whom see Diomedes, GLK I p. 376, discussed on p. 69 above) who was probably not Quintilia, or he had affairs with married women. But *furtum* can be used more loosely of surreptitious love; Catullus applies the word to Lesbia's infidelities to him, even though they were not married (68.135–6 'etsi uno non est contenta Catullo, / rara verecundae furta feremus erae'). That couplet seems to be reversed by Ovid in *Tr.* 2.429–30 'nec contentus ea [sc. Lesbia] multos vulgabat amores / in quibus ipse suum fassus adulterium est'. The lines on Calvus follow immediately; perhaps therefore Calvus' *furta* were affairs with women other than his main love (? Quintilia).

41 dub. (19 Bl., C.)

ne triclinarius: Charisius' point is that terminations in -*arius* should denote a person, those in -*aris* an object. So it appears that Calvus—wrongly, in the grammarian's view—applied 'triclinarius' (a form not recognized by *OLD* or Lewis and Short) to some object (e.g. a *lectus*) connected with the dining couch or dining-room. Courtney thinks, perhaps rightly, that 'Calvus ad ami-cos' (? cf. Cicero, *Ad Familiares*) points to a letter in prose (Diomedes, I p. 376 quotes from a letter of Calvus to his wife). On the other hand one can easily imagine a collective address to friends in a sympotic poem, as e.g. Horace, *Epodes* 13.3 'amici' (but see Mankin ad loc.), *Odes* 1.27.7 and 1.37.4 'sodales'. 'ne trīclīnarius' would fit a hexameter.

42 (20 Bl., C.)

The words 'terra omnia liberius ferente' (which immediately precede 'quod Calvus canit') seem to be merely a paraphrase of Virgil, *Georgics* 1.127–8 'ipsaque tellus / omnia liberius nullo poscente ferebat'. But one part of the scholion is not represented in *Georgics* 1.121 ff. (unless one remotely hinted at in 124 'nec torpere gravi passus sua regna veterno'), and may perhaps go back to Calvus: 'cum bonus a malo non discerneretur'. The Golden Age (reign of

Cronos/Saturn) was generally thought of as wholly admirable. But the quoted words point to a flaw in the situation: when Nature was equally generous to all, there was no way of distinguishing between the *bonus* (hard-working and efficient) and the *malus* (lazy and incompetent). We seem to have here an old Roman attitude famously expressed by Cato (*De Agri Cultura*, praef. 2): 'virum bonum quom laudabant, ita laudabant, bonum agricolam bonumque colonum. amplissime laudari existimabatur qui ita laudabatur'. One might be surprised if Calvus argued very seriously that for this reason the modern age was superior to the Golden Age, but he might have had his tongue in his cheek. **35** 'durum rus fugit et laboriosum' apparently describes someone who shrinks from the hard work of farming (see ad loc.).

Egnatius

43–43A *De Rerum Natura*, Liber I

43 (1 Bl., C.)

denique Mulciber ipse furens altissima caeli
contingit

Finally raging Mulciber himself touches the topmost heights of the sky.

1–2 Macr. 6.5.1–2 (I pp. 374–5 Willis): *multa quoque epitheta apud Vergilium sunt quae ab ipso ficta creduntur, sed et haec a veteribus tracta monstrabo . . . ut . . . Mulciber . . .* 'et discinctos Mulciber Afros' (*Aen.* 8.724) . . . *et Egnatius de rerum natura libro primo*: 'denique—†contingunt'.

1–2 furens . . . / contingit *Bergk*: ferens . . . / contingunt *codd.*

43A (2 Bl., C.)

roscida noctivagis astris labentibus Phoebe
pulsa loco cessit, concedens lucibus †altis

As the night-roving stars sank, dewy Phoebe, dislodged from her position, gave way, yielding the clear sky [?aethram] to daylight.

1–2 Macr. 6.5.12 (I p. 377 Willis) 'almaque curru / noctivago Phoebe' (*Aen.* 10.215–16): *Egnatius de rerum natura libro primo*: 'roscida—†altis'.

2 †altis] almis *Bergk*: albis *Frassinetti, Alfonsi*: fratris *Baehrens*: aethram *Hollis*

THE identity of this Egnatius is quite unknown—that he might be Catullus' friend of the flashing teeth and bushy beard is no more than fantasy. But the relationship of his work to Lucretius arouses interest. Egnatius had the same title, and his *De Rerum Natura* contained more than one book. Suppression of the final -s in **43A**.1 'labentibus Phoebe', considered 'subrusticum' by the *poetae novi* (Cicero, *Orator* 161, written in 46 BC) aligns him with Lucretius' generally old-fashioned style. It looks as though Virgil in *Aen.* 10.215–16 is definitely imitating **43A** (see ad loc.) since the resemblance is not confined to the compound epithet 'noctivagus'; for that reason one cannot make any chronological deduction from the fact that Macrobius illustrates 'noctivagus' from Egnatius rather than Lucretius (4.582, 5.1191). One naturally tends to believe that the greater poet wrote first, but the possibility that a lesser work provoked a greater one cannot be excluded.

43 (1 Bl., C.)

Bergk's emendation 'furens ... / contingit' for 'ferens ... / †contingunt' seems excellent. 'Furere' is regularly used of a raging fire (*OLD* 5(*b*), e.g. Lucr. 2.593 of Aetna); 'Mulciber' stands for 'fire' by a familiar metonymy. As Courtney says, the lines could well describe a volcanic eruption (e.g. Lucr. 1.725, again of Aetna 'ad caelumque ferat flammai fulgura rursum'), an appropriate subject in a scientific poem (cf. Lucr. 6.680–702).

1.   denique Mulciber ipse: a crude rhythm in Augustan terms (and there is nothing like it in Catullus 64), but quite acceptable in the older style. Ennius can start a hexameter 'fraxinus frangitur' (*Annals* 177 Skutsch), 'poste recumbite' (218), 'vicit Olympia' (523). Lucretius writes 'omnia denique sancta' (6.1270) and not infrequently fills the first two dactyls with a single word, e.g. 1.109 'religionibus', 468 'irrevocabilis'. It is worth remembering that Callimachus, the most refined writer of Greek hexameters, happily starts a line e.g. τλήσομαι εἴνεκα σεῖο or γείνεο, γείνεο, κοῦρε (*Hymn* 4.129, 214).

43A (2 Bl., C.)

1.   roscida: *OLD* 2(*b*), 'as epithet of the moon, stars, etc., associated with dew', e.g. Virgil, *Georgics* 3.337 'roscida Luna'.

noctivagis: there are many Greek compound epithets in νυκτι- or νυκτο- conveying this idea, but none with a special claim to be the model for 'noctivagus', which may have occurred in lost epic or tragedy before Lucretius (4.582, 5.1191) and Egnatius.

labentibus Phoebe: suppression of a final -s before initial consonant (see the introduction to Egnatius, above) is regular in Cicero's *Aratea* and Lucretius, but never found in Virgil. The one instance in Catullus (116.8 'tu dabis supplicium') is perhaps softened by the fact that in speech the two 's's would inevitably be run together.

2. The image is of withdrawal from the battlefield after a military defeat (contrast Cornelius Severus, **211**). Virgil's imitation (*Aen.* 10.215–16) is typically intricate:

> iamque dies caelo concesserat, almaque curru
> noctivago Phoebe medium pulsabat Olympum.

Virgil has changed the time from dawn to dusk. We expect that 'caelo concesserat' will correspond to 'concedens', but it turns out rather to reflect 'loco cessit', while 'pulsabat' very faintly recalls 'pulsa'.

†**altis:** this can hardly be sound. Of conjectures, 'albis' is quite uninteresting, 'almis' and 'fratris' (another suppression of final -s) a little better. In all the above 'concedens' is intransitive. It might, however, be transitive, with †'altis' concealing an object in the accusative. I suggest 'aethram', 'yielding the clear sky to daylight'. *Aethra* (used by Ennius, Lucretius, and Virgil), from Greek αἴθρη, particularly denotes a clear and brilliant sky. For the plural *luces* = 'daylight', cf. Lucretius 5.681 and 688 (with Bailey's note), Ovid, *Fasti* 6.39 (the daylight is longest in June); more examples in *TLL* VII. 2. 1911 s.v. lux (though not clearly differentiated from *luces* = 'days').

C. Memmius

44

(*a*) Ov. *Tr.* 2.433–4: *quid referam Ticidae* [**101***a*], *quid Memmi carmen, apud quos / rebus adest nomen, nominibusque pudor?*

    (*b*) Plin. *Epist.* 5.3.5 [v. **19***j*]: *ego verear ne me non satis deceat, quod decuit* . . . *C. Memmium* . . . ?

    (*c*) Gell. *NA* 19.9 [v. **1***e*]: . . . *Cinna* [**1***e*] *inlepida et Memmius dura* . . .

(*a*) Need I mention the poems of Ticida and Memmius, who call things by their names, and shame attaches to those names?

    (*b*) Should I fear that what was appropriate to . . . Gaius Memmius . . . is inappropriate to me?

    (*c*) . . . those of Cinna [see **1***e*] lacking grace, those of Memmius rough . . .

45 (1 Bl., C.)

ardua ne nitens fortunae scandere cliva

. . . lest, striving to climb the steep slope of Fortune . . .

Non. Marc. 194 (I p. 286 Lindsay): *clivus generis masculini, ut plerumque. neutri aput Memmium invenimus, cuius auctoritas dubia est:* '†ne ardua . . . cliva'.

    ardua ne *L. Mueller:* ne ardua *codd.*   scandere *Junius:* scendere *codd.*   fortunae escendere *Mercier*   virtus escendere *tempt. Courtney*

46 (2 Bl., ad 1 C.)

macella

Caper, GLK VII, p. 101: *hoc lutum atque macellum ἐνικῶς exire memento, / Memmius ista 'macella' licet, Caesar 'luta' dicat.*

Remember that *macellum* ('provision-market') has a singular termination, even though Memmius speaks of *macella* in the plural.

C. MEMMIUS (tr. pl. 66 BC, praetor 58 BC) is best known as the addressee of Lucretius' *De Rerum Natura* (whether he was ever an Epicurean is unclear) and the propraetor in whose *cohors* Catullus (and almost certainly Helvius Cinna, in view of Cat. 10.28–9) went to Bithynia in 57 BC. Catullus does not have a good word for him—though we may put it down to Memmius' credit that neither he nor his staff made any money from the governorship (Cat. 10.9–13). His general literary tastes should have made him sympathetic to the neoteric poets: 'perfectus litteris, sed Graecis, fastidiosus sane Latinarum' (Cicero, *Brutus* 247). Memmius' low regard for Latin literature may have been paralleled in his own reputation as a Latinist: he is a 'doubtful' authority for neuter *clivum* (**45**), and his use of plural *macella* is not sufficient to commend that form (**46**). The writing of poetry probably played a small part in Memmius' life; in this respect he may be more comparable with e.g. Mucius Scaevola (**90–2**) than e.g. Cornificius (**93–7**) who had as busy a public career but was a more significant poet. There is a possibility (depending on a transposition in Ovid, *Tristia* 2) that Memmius was one of the poets who celebrated Metella/Perilla; see on Ticida, **101***b*.

We can establish other links between Memmius, Catullus, and Calvus (there is no evidence that Memmius was Calvus' patron). Both Catullus (29, 54(*b*), 57, 93, cf. Suet. *Div. Iul.* 49.1 'perpetua stigmata') and Calvus (**38**, cf. *Div. Iul.* 49.1 and 73) made damaging attacks upon Julius Caesar: it was Memmius who had given details and named names from the episode at the court of King Nicomedes (*Div. Iul.* 49.2 'C. Memmius etiam ad cyathum et vinum Nicomedi stetisse obicit, cum reliquis exoletis, pleno convivio, accubantibus nonnullis urbicis negotiatoribus, quorum refert nomina'). Yet Suetonius (73) mentions together the reconciliation to Caesar of all three, which must have happened at about the same time, since Caesar was giving Memmius full support for the consulship in July 54 (Cic. *Ad Att.* 4.15 = 90 SB. 7 'Memmium Caesaris omnes opes confirmant'), in which year Catullus (11.9–12) speaks favourably about Caesar's exploits in Gaul and Britain.

Calvus made his reputation with speeches against Vatinius, whom Memmius, as praetor, had impeached (Cic. *In P. Vatinium Testem* 33).

Memmius' bid for the consulship was not successful—he soon lost the favour of Caesar following revelation of a corrupt electoral compact with the existing consuls. He was condemned for *ambitus* and exiled; in 50 B C he had hopes of restoration (Cic. *Ad Att.* 6.1 = 115 SB. 23). We do not know if these were fulfilled, but that 'is no wild supposition' (G. O. Hutchinson, *CQ* 51 (2001), 158). Presumably (in view of the notice in Cicero, *Brutus* 247) he was dead by the end of 47 B C.

45 (1 Bl., C.)

ardua ne nitens fortunae scandere cliva: Junius' 'fortunae scandere' is the simplest correction, avoiding elision of the diphthong (fortunae escendere); *scandere* is also more often used with direct accusative (e.g. Cat. 105.1 'Pipleium scandere montem') than *escendere*. Courtney, worried about the lack of a parallel for 'fortunae . . . cliva', tries 'virtus escendere cliva', but it seems to me that 'the steep path of Fortune' is readily comprehensible by analogy with the steep path of Virtue (see on Cornelius Severus, **208**). Nonius cites neuter *clivum* also from Cato.

This quotation by itself—but single lines can be deceptive—suggests a serious context. If the reference is to a search for wealth and political power, one might compare Lucretius 3.62–3 'noctes atque dies niti praestante labore / ad summas emergere opes', and the image of the disappointed politician as Sisyphus pushing his stone uphill (Lucr. 3.995–1002). Memmius himself had reverses in the public sphere (see above).

46 (2 Bl., ad 1 C.)

macella: we cannot even be sure that this is verse, though *macellum* occurs several times in comedy and satire. The grammarian insists on a singular termination (ἑνικῶς *exire memento*), but the plural is found also in Juvenal (11.64). This entry is expressed in hexameters, of a sort—presumably the other noun at issue was lŭtum rather than lūtum.

Aemilius Macer

47

(a) Schol. Bern. Verg. *Buc.* 5 praef. (p. 114, *Scholia Bernensia ad Vergilii Bucolica atque Georgica*, ed. H. Hagen, 1867): *Mopsus vero Aemilius Macer, Veronensis poeta, amicus Vergilii amantissimus, qui et ipse poeta fuit, accipitur.*

(b) Quint. 12.11.27: *si hanc cogitationem homines habuissent, ut nemo se meliorem fore eo qui optimus fuisset arbitraretur, ii ipsi qui sunt optimi non fuissent, nec post Lucretium ac Macrum Vergilius, nec post Crassum et Hortensium Cicero.*

(c) Ov. *Tr.* 4.10.43–4: *saepe suas volucres legit mihi grandior aevo, / quaeque nocet serpens, quae iuvat herba, Macer.*

(d) Hieronymi *Chronicon* (ed. Helm[2] (1956), p. 166) ann. Abr. 2001 = 16 a. Chr.: *Aemilius Macer Veronensis poeta in Asia moritur.*

(a) Mopsus is understood to be Aemilius Macer, the poet from Verona, who was a very close friend of Virgil and likewise a poet in his own right.

(b) If people had taken the following view, that no one thought he would surpass the man who had been best up to that point, those very people who currently are best would not have existed; there would have been no Virgil after Lucretius and Macer, and no Cicero after Crassus and Hortensius.

(c) Often in his old age Macer read to me his Birds [i.e. *Ornithogonia*], the serpent that harms [i.e. *Theriaca*], and the herb that brings relief.

(d) [16 BC] The poet Aemilius Macer, from Verona, dies in Asia.

48

(a) Quint. 10.1.56: *audire videor undique congerentis nomina plurimorum poetarum . . . quid? Nicandrum frustra secuti Macer atque Vergilius?*

(b) Quint. 10.1.86–7: *ceteri omnes longe sequuntur [sc. Vergilium]. nam Macer*

et Lucretius legendi quidem, sed non ut phrasin, id est corpus eloquentiae,
faciant. elegantes in sua quisque materia, sed alter [sc. Macer] *humilis, alter*
difficilis.

(*c*) Plinius Aemilium Macrum laudat inter auctores Nat. Hist. libr. IX, X, XI,
XVII, 'Licinium' Macrum (quem eundem esse apparet) inter auctores libr.
XIX, XXI, XXII, XXVIII, XXIX, XXXII.

(*a*) I seem to hear people throwing in the names of innumerable poets from
every side ... What? Did Macer and Virgil waste their efforts in following
Nicander?

   (*b*) All the others [sc. Latin hexameter poets] are left far behind [sc. Virgil].
For Macer and Lucretius are, admittedly, worth reading, but not to the end of
creating style, that is the solid substance of oratory. Each of them is elegant
within his own subject matter, but the one [Macer] is lacking in sublimity, the
other difficult.

(*c*) Aemilius Macer is mentioned among the sources for Pliny's *Natural*
History, bks 9, 10, 11, 17, and called 'Licinius' Macer in the sources for bks 19,
21, 22, 28, 29, 32.

49–53 *Ornithogonia*

49

Ov. *Tr.* 4.10.43–4: *saepe suas volucres legit mihi grandior aevo* / ... *Macer*
[=**47***c*].

50 (1 Bl., C.) *Liber I*

et nunc agrestis inter Picumnus habetur

Even to this day Picumnus is reckoned among <the gods of> the countryside.

Non. Marc. p. 834 Lindsay (vol. III): *Picumnus et avis est Marti dicata, quam*
picum vel picam vocant, et deus qui sacris Romanis adhibetur. Aemilius Macer
in Ornithogoniae [theogoniae *codd., corr. Bentinus*] *lib. I* 'et—habetur'.

   <deosque> *ante hunc versum suppl. Morel*

51 (2 Bl., C.) *Lib. II*

cum laude excelleat omni

seeing that it excels in every good quality

Diomedes, GLK I p. 374: *excello legimus crebro apud veteres, . . . verum tamen Macer Aemilius Ornithogoniae secundo* 'cum—omnis'.

excelleat (*vel* excellent) *Unger:* excellet *AM:* excellit *B:* excelleret *Scaliger* omni *Keil:* omnis *codd.*

52 (3 Bl., C.) *ex incerto libro*

Vulcani tosta vapore
cum virgis prosecta ferunt

Together with leafy twigs they bring portions which have been roasted in the heat of Vulcan.

1–2 Non. Marc. p. 325 Lindsay (vol. I): *prosecta, exta quae aris dantur ex fibris pecudum dissecta, sunt generis neutri. Aemilius* [Licinius *codd., corr.* Vossius] *Macer in Ornithogonia* 'Vulcani—ferunt'.

53 (4 Bl., C.)

(*a*)   cygnus in auspiciis semper laetissimus ales;
          hunc optant nautae, quia se non mergit in undas

(*a*) In auspices the swan is always the most propitious bird; this is what sailors long for, since it does not immerse itself in the water.

1–2 Isid. *Orig.* 12.7.19: *nautae vero sibi hunc* [sc. cygnum] *bonam prognosim facere dicunt, sicut Aemilius ait* 'cygnus—undas'.

(*b*)   cycnus in auguriis nautis gratissimus ales;
          hunc optant semper, quia numquam mergitur undis

(*b*) In auguries the swan is the bird most welcome to sailors; they always long for this, because it never sinks in the water.

1–2 Serv. ad Verg. *Aen.* 1.393 'bis senos cycnos' (p. 132 Thilo): *in auguriis autem considerandae sunt non solum aves, sed etiam volatus, ut in praepetibus, et cantus, ut in oscinibus, quia nec omnes nec omnibus dant auguria . . . item cycni nullis dant nisi nautis, sicut lectum est in Ornithogonia* 'cycnus—undis'.

54–66 *Theriaca*

54 (*b*=9 Bl., C.)

(*a*) Ov. *Tr.* 4.10.43–4: *saepe . . . legit mihi . . . / quaeque nocet serpens, quae iuvat herba, Macer* [=**47***c*].

 (*b*) Schol. Bern. ad Lucan. 9.701 'aspida somniferam tumida cervice levavit' (p. 308 ed. Usener, 1869): *serpentum nomina aut a Macro sumpsit de libris Theriacon—nam duos edidit—aut quaesita a Marsis posuit.*

(*b*) The names of the snakes he either took from Macer, from his books of *Theriaca*—for he produced two of them—or set down after discovering them from the Marsians.

55 (7 Bl., C.)

tumido resonantia sibila collo

. . . resounding hisses from its swollen neck

Charis., p. 102 Barwick² = GLK I p. 81: *sibilus dici oportet . . . sed et neutro genere quidam dixerunt, ut Ovidius . . . et Cornelius Severus* [**212**] *. . . et Macer* [<V> suppl. Barwick e Cauchii excerptis] *Theriacon* 'longo—collo'.

 tumido *Knaack*: tundo *N*: longo *A, excerpta Cauchii, Beda GLK VII p. 291*

56 (17 Bl., C.)

saucia naris

a wounded nostril

Charis., p. 136 Barwick² = GLK I p. 107: *naris singulariter, haec naris, dicimus, ut Aemilius Macer* 'saucia naris'.

57 (8 Bl., C.)

seu terga exspirant spumantia virus
seu tractus fumat qua taeter labitur anguis

whether its frothy skin exhales poison, or whether the path smokes where the foul snake glides

1–2 Isid. *Orig.* 12.4.24: *chelydrus serpens, qui et chersydros . . . per quam labitur terram fumare facit; quam sic Macer describit,* 'seu—anguis'.

1 fumantia *Courtney* (*errore typothetae*)   2 tractus *Nisbet*: terra *codd.*: tellus *Morel*   taeter] venter *Unger*

58 (10 Bl., 9 C.)

vepre occulta ruis

. . . concealed in a thorn-bush, you attack

Auctor de dubiis nominibus, GLK V p. 592: *vepres generis feminini . . . singularem non recipit, quamvis Aemilius* [*masculine* del. Baehrens] *dicat* 'veper—ruis'.

vepre *Baehrens*: veper *codd.*

59 (18 Bl., 10 C.)

maior ape, scrabrone minor

larger than a bee, smaller than a hornet

Serv. ad *Aen.* 1.435 'ignavum fucos pecus' (p. 143 Thilo): *proprie tamen apes vocantur ortae de bubus, fuci de equis, crabrones de mulis, vespae de asinis. fucus autem est secundum Aemilium Macrum* 'maior—minor'.

Isid. *Orig.* 12.8.3: *fugus est maior ape, scrabrone minor* [sine nomine poetae].

scrabrone *vel* crabrone *codd. Servii*: scrabrone *Isid.*: api, crabrone *Baehrens*: ape <at> crabrone *Unger*: [est] secundum Aemilium Macrum 'maior ape <est> . . .' *tempt. Courtney*

60 (11 C.)

Plin. *NH* 32.14: *Licinius* [errore Plinii, v. **48c**] *Macer murenas feminini tantum sexus esse tradit, et concipere a serpentibus, ut diximus* [9.76], *ob id sibilo a piscatoribus tamquam a serpentibus evocari et capi et pinguescere* [?], *iactato fusti non interimi, easdem ferula protinus.*

Licinius [*a mistake for* 'Aemilius'] Macer relates that morays are only of the female sex and that they conceive from serpents (as I said before); for which reason they are called forth by fishermen with a hiss like that of a snake, caught, and grow fat [? *something missing in the text round about here*]. He says that they are not killed by the throwing of a club, but killed straightaway by the giant fennel plant.

61 (5 Bl., 12 C.)

altis ex urbibus ibes

ibises from lofty cities

Charis., p. 170 Barwick[2] = GLK I p. 133: '*ibes, hae ibes*' *Aemilius Macer* [tum sacrae veniunt cultoribus id est *del. Keil*] 'altis—ibes'.

62 (6 Bl., 13 C.)

auxilium sacrae veniunt cultoribus ibes

sacred ibises come as assistance to the farmers

Charis. (post **61**): *item* 'auxilium—ibes'.

> **61** *et* **62** *Ornithogoniae dedit Baehrens, melius Theriacis Dahlmann*

63 (13 Bl., 14 C.)

o quales veget intubus herbas

O, what blades does the endive invigorate!

Charis., pp. 127–8 Barwick[2] = GLK I p. 100: *intiba neutro genere Vergilius* [*G.* 1.120] ... *sed et masculino genere frequenter a veteribus dictum est* ... *et Aemilius Macer masculino protulit* 'o—herbas'.

> protulit o *p: om. CN*   quales veget *Lachmann:* quale seges *N:* quales reges *C:* quales reget *p:* quales aget *Keil*

64 (15 C.)

Plin. *NH* 32.9: *homines quibus impactus est* [sc. lepus marinus] *piscem olent; hoc primo argumento veneficium id deprehenditur. cetero moriuntur totidem in diebus, quot vixerit lepus, incertique temporis veneficium id esse auctor est Licinius* [errore Plinii, cf. **48***c*] *Macer.*

People who are struck by it [the sea-hare] smell of fish; this is the first indication by which such poisoning is detected. For the rest, they die in as many days as the sea-hare has lived, and Licinius [*a mistake for Aemilius*] Macer is an authority for saying that this poisoning takes effect in a variable period of time.

> de lepore marino Nic. *Alex.* 465 sqq. itaque de *Alexipharmacis* Macri (**69** dub.) cogitare licet. sed haec *Theriacis* certe non absona.

65 (12 Bl., 16 C.)

inter praeteritas numerabitur ocimus herbas

Basil will be reckoned among omitted herbs.

Charis., p. 91 Barwick² = GLK I p. 72, eadem Beda GLK VII p. 282: *ocimum consuetudo neutraliter dicit, sed Aemilius Macer ait* 'inter—herbas'.

praeteritas] praetritas *Kessissoglu*: pertritas *vel* protritas *Courtney*

66 (14 Bl., 17 C.)

pallentesque crocos

. . . and pale crocuses

Auctor de dub. nom., GLK V p. 576: *crocum generis neutri; sed Macer Aemilius* 'pallentesque crocos'.

crocus *MV*: crocis *L, corr. Haupt*   *Theriacis dedit Dahlmann, pp. 23–4*

67–68 *incertae sedis*

67 (15 Bl., 18 C.)

illi multa lacus quem circum milia

There a lake around which many thousands <of ??> . . .

Schol. Bern. Verg. *Georg.* 2.160 'fluctibus et fremitu adsurgens Benace marino' (p. 229 ed. Hagen, 1867): *lacus circuitus stadia mille ut Aemilius Macer* 'illi—milia'.

illi *codd.*: illi<c> *Hagen*   <currunt> *vel* <curras> *suppl. Hagen*: <cingunt> *Pighi*

68 (16 Bl., 19 C.)

†flumant minu† margine summa

<??> at the topmost edge

Charis., pp. 81–2 Barwick² = GLK I p. 65: *margo feminino genere . . . ideoque et Aemilius Macer ait* '†flumant—summa'.

†flumant minu] fumant minu' *Barwick*: flumina *Lindemann*: fluitantem in *Unger*: fluvii nant nidi in *tempt. Courtney*

69 dub. (*De Herbis?*, *Alexipharmaca?*)

Disticha Catonis 2 praef. 2–3 (p. 90 ed. M. Boas, 1952): *quodsi mage nosse laboras / herbarum vires, Macer <haec> tibi carmina dicit.*

    Dubitare licet quantum fidei Distichis Catonis habeatur. Ov. Tr. 4.10.44=47c 'quae iuvat herba' ad Alexipharmaca Macri nonnulli rettulerunt. sed 'herbarum vires' Macer passim in Theriacis debuit dicere.

If you are more concerned to learn of the properties of herbs, Macer utters these verses for you.

70 dub. (*Tetrasticha?*)

Quint. 6.3.96: *adiuvant urbanitatem et versus commode positi, seu toti ut sunt (quod adeo facile est ut Ovidius* [fr. 14 Courtney] *ex tetrastichon Macri carmine librum in malos poetas composuit) . . . seu verbis ex parte mutatis.*

    Haec vel ad Aemilium Macrum vel ad Macrum iuniorem, Ovidi familiarem (Am. 2.18, Ex Ponto 2.10, v. App., p. 424), pertinere possunt.

Another aid to wit is the apt positioning of verses, whether quoted entire and as they stand (which is so easy that Ovid used the verse quatrains of Macer to compose a work *Against Bad Poets*) . . . or with the wording partly changed.

FOR a study of this poet see H. Dahlmann, *Über Aemilius Macer* (Mainz, 1981).

    The items collected under **47** establish that Aemilius Macer—we do not know his praenomen—came from Verona (*a* and *d*), that he was senior to Virgil and a personal friend (*a* and *b*), that in relative old age he lived in Rome and gave recitations at which the young Ovid (no doubt in the 20s BC) was a regular attender; finally (*d*) that he died in Asia in the year 16 BC when he might have been in his sixties.

    Macer may have been five to ten years younger than his fellow-countryman Catullus, coming to his full powers in that rather mysterious decade for Roman poetry (*c*.54–44 BC) between the disappearance of Lucretius and Catullus and the death of Helvius Cinna. One might question the evidence for a close friendship between Macer and Virgil (**47a**, and Philargyrius on the same eclogue, p. 90 ed. Hagen (1902)); as well as making Macer the Mopsus of *Ecl.* 5, some saw him as Thyrsis in *Ecl.* 7 (Schol. Bern. p. 136 Hagen (1867)). On the other hand he was not an obvious person to choose, and these fantasies may derive from a genuine tradition of personal friendship. It is disappointing that (unless Adesp. **237** is by Macer) we cannot point to any actual instances of the older poet's influence on Virgil—contrast the cases of Furius

Bibaculus, Varrro Atacinus, and Varius Rufus. But, when considering the relationship of *Georgics* 3.425 ff. to Nicander, *Theriaca* 411 ff., we should bear in mind that Virgil would have available a Latin intermediary, just as the Aratean weather signs in the First Georgic are mediated through Varro of Atax. In only one case do we possess two consecutive and complete lines of Macer (**53**, transmitted in two slightly different forms). **57** (almost two lines) effectively describes a monstrous and terrifying snake. But we are poorly placed to appreciate his 'elegance within his subject matter' (Quintilian, **47***b*), or the qualities which convinced young Ovid that he should persist in attending Macer's recitations (**47***c*).

Discussion of Aemilius Macer has been bedevilled by confusion with a younger Macer. Blänsdorf, although noting (p. 271) 'fortasse duo Macri', conflates their testimonia (pp. 272–3), as well as quoting (p. 273) Martial 8.55.21–4, a passage seemingly intended for his section on Domitius Marsus (p. 280) or Varius Rufus (p. 250). In almost all respects (only over **70**, the *Tetrasticha*, is there real doubt) the distinction is clear. The younger Macer (Appendix, p. 424) was a slightly older travelling companion of Ovid (cf. 'te duce' in *Ex Ponto* 2.10.21–2), probably a fellow member of Messalla Corvinus' circle (if, as seems most likely, the addressee of Tibullus 2.6) and the writer of epic poetry on Troy (*Am.* 2.18, cf. *Ex Ponto* 4.16.6 'Iliacusque Macer'). Scholars often call him 'Pompeius Macer', but that is almost certainly a mistake; see P. White, '"Pompeius Macer" and Ovid', *CQ* NS 42 (1992), 210–18.

48

On the reputation and survival of Macer's poetry. **48***a* is more concerned with the merits of Nicander: were Macer and Virgil wasting their time (cf. 'frustra') when they took him as a model? The implied answer is that they were not. In the 50s BC Nicander had a high reputation among the *docti* (Cic. *De Or.* 1.69, specifying the *Georgica*) and this continued at least until the time of Manilius (2.44–5). In *PLLS* 10 (1998), 169–84, I suggested that, in some respects, there is a definite affinity between Nicander and Lucretius. Quintilian (**48***b*) had no doubt that, as a writer of didactic verse (i.e. in the *Georgics*), Virgil far outstripped both Macer and Lucretius. We may be surprised that the grudging praise given to Macer puts him on the same level as Lucretius. This suggests that, on a more generous estimation, Aemilius Macer had quite a lot to be said for him. But the *communis opinio* found Lucretius 'difficilis', and that may have impeded a fair assessment. Macer's subject matter would have made it hard for him to achieve sublimity (cf. 'humilis'), but he may have deliberately eschewed it, in the Hellenistic manner.

It seems worth saying something about the books of Pliny's *Natural History* for which Macer is listed as a source (**48***c*). In almost all cases we can find something which appropriately could, or definitely did, appear in Macer—of course there may have been several items from Macer in the same book. When Macer is listed, so, for the most part, is Nicander (among the 'foreign sources'), with the result that we can not determine whether Pliny is using the Greek or the Latin poet, but in two places (**60** and **64**) Pliny actually names and paraphrases Macer, allowing an interesting comparison with Nicander. For *NH* 10 Boeus' *Ornithogonia* is listed, as well as Nicander and Macer, and it can be no coincidence that book 10 contains many transformations into birds.

In his first four appearances among the listed sources our poet is correctly called 'Aemilius Macer'; thereafter Pliny becomes forgetful, and always refers to him as 'Licinius Macer'. This confusion with the annalist and politician, father of the poet Licinius Calvus, is understandable, and not confined to Pliny (see **52**); the reverse mistake also occurs, e.g. Prisc. GLK II p. 525 'Aemilius Macer in XVI annalium'.

NH 9: In 9.76 Pliny mentions the impregnation of lampreys by snakes, which is explicitly attributed to Macer in 32.14 = **60**.

NH 10: A profusion of material. The battle of the eagle and the dracon (10.17) could derive either from Macer (see on **58**) or direct from Nicander (*Ther.* 448 ff.). The ibis coming to help Egyptians against winged serpents (10.75) does not appear in Nicander, so probably from Macer (**62**, *Theriaca* rather than *Ornithogonia*, since no transformation is involved). The coupling of snakes which proves fatal to both (10.169–70) appears in Nic. *Ther.* 128 ff. (not attested for Macer). It is noteworthy how many transformations into birds this book contains—all of them recurring in Ovid's *Metamorphoses*. Ovid probably knew the Greek Ὀρνιθογονία as well, but Aemilius Macer's recitations would surely have been a greater influence upon him. Thus *NH* 10.3–5 on the phoenix (*Met.* 15.392 ff.); 10.41 picus (*Met.* 14.386 ff., differing somewhat from the version implied in **50**); 10.74 Memnonides (*Met.* 13.600 ff.) and Meleagrides (8.542 ff.); 10.126 companions of Diomedes (*Met.* 14.497 ff.).

NH 11: Insects and spiders (cf. **59** and perhaps Adesp. **237**).

NH 17: On trees. Nothing obviously congenial to Macer, but the brief mention of Stercutus son of Faunus (17.50) takes us near to the myth of Picumnus/Picus (see on **50**).

NH 19: Grasses and plants. 19.89 mentions the *daucon* (cf. Nic. *Ther.* 859, 939), while 19.154 has a possibly significant verbal parallel with **65**.

NH 21: Flowers (including those used for garlands) and plants with medicinal effects. 21.40 (iris from Illyria) mentions the Drilon and Narona (as Nic. *Ther.* 607). Habrotonum (21.160–2, particularly useful against scorpions and spiders) appears several times in Nicander.

NH 22: Nicander named three times, 22.31 (referring to *Alex.* 201), 22.67 (*Ther.* 534 and 78–9) and 22.77 (*Ther.* 586). Many references to cures for bites of snakes, spiders, and scorpions.

NH 28: For this book Macer is listed as a source, but not Nicander (perhaps an inadvertent omission?). The subject is drugs obtained from animals, with special attention to snake-bite (28.149). 28.121 'super Saiticam praefecturam ... drachma ex aqua contra serpentes bibitur') recalls *Ther.* 566 (on the hippopotamus) ὑπὲρ Σάϊν αἰθαλόεσσαν ... 572–3 δραχμῆς βάρος ἰσοφαρίζειν / ὕδατι δ' ἐμπίσαιο, while 28.162 'papilio ... lucernarum luminibus advolans' is close to *Ther.* 760–1, 'the moth which the evening meal-time brings in to flutter round the lamps' (Gow–Scholfield). These passages on the hippopotamus and the fluttering moth are memorable in Nicander, and Macer would hardly omit them. Courtney (on his Macer fr. 6 = my **54***b*) suggests on the basis of *NH* 28.30 that Lucan 9.922 ff. (about the Psylli, mentioned by Nicander not in his *Theriaca* but in the elegiac *Ophiaca*, fr. 32) may come from Aemilius Macer.

NH 29: Much on snakes. In 29.65 asps 'torpore et somno necant' as Nic. *Ther.* 189 ὑπνηλὸν δ' ἐπὶ νῶκαρ ἄγει βιότοιο τελευτήν, while in 29.66 the basilisk puts other serpents to flight as in *Ther.* 402 φύζηι δὲ παλιντροπέες φορέονται.

NH 32: In this book Macer is twice named (32.9 and 14), and in both cases a substantial paraphrase of what he said is added. These passages (**64** and **60** respectively) show Macer going some way beyond his Nicandrean model.

49–53 *Ornithogonia*

Of the two major works by Aemilius Macer, we know much less about the *Ornithogonia*, though Ovid might have found it the more useful (as a source for his *Metamorphoses*). It had at least two books—perhaps just two, like the *Theriaca*. Macer's model would have been a Greek hexameter poem of the same name (also, it seems, in two books) ascribed to one Boeus or Boeo (if the latter, perhaps the legendary Pythian priestess). This may have been composed at the beginning of the Hellenistic age, since it was known to

Philochorus (*F. Gr. Hist.* 328 F 214, from Athenaeus 9.393e). No verbatim fragments of the Greek Ὀρνιθογονία survive—most of those adumbrated in Powell, *Coll. Alex.*, 24–5, would be disowned by any half-decent Greek poet— but the mythographer Antoninus Liberalis (second or third century A D?) in his *Metamorphoses* (the 1968 Budé edition by M. Papathomopoulos is very useful) provides prose paraphrases of ten transformations into birds which are credited, by notes accompanying the text, to the Ὀρνιθογονία of Boeus. In these stories we find a preoccupation with aetiology (explaining something which holds good 'to this very day') and with omens (birds of good or bad significance for humanity in general or for particular groups of people). These two features recur in Aemilius Macer (**50** and **53**).

Of the four fragments which definitely come from Macer's *Ornithogonia*, **50** is concerned with the woodpecker, and **53** (perhaps also **51** and conceivably **52**) with the swan. Boeus, who (according to Athenaeus 9.393 f.) asserted that every bird had originally been a human being, did not omit the woodpecker, relating how the craftsman Polytechnus became a πελεκᾶς (Ant. Lib. 11.10). But the woodpecker was not of as great mythological importance to the Greeks as it was to the Romans (D'Arcy W. Thompson, *A Glossary of Greek Birds*[2] (1936), 92), and Aemilius Macer tells quite a different, Italian, story. This free treatment of the model seems to characterize his *Theriaca* (with respect to Nicander) as well.

50 (1 B., C.)

et nunc agrestis inter Picumnus habetur: this line has been understood in two ways (Courtney 293): either (*a*) among peasants Picus is considered to be identical with Picumnus, or (*b*) Picumnus is counted among the gods of the countryside (Morel supplied e.g. <deosque> at the end of the previous line). The latter interpretation seems to me preferable. One would expect the quotation to illustrate the immediately preceding words in Nonius Marcellus, 'et deus qui sacris Romanis adhibetur'. And there may be an echo of Macer in Ovid, *Fasti* 3.315, where Faunus says of himself and Picus 'di sumus agrestes'. The deification of Picus/Picumnus is also hinted at in *Met.* 14.313–16, where we read of a statue of a young man with a woodpecker on his head, standing in a shrine in Circe's palace and adorned with garlands. Virgil speaks of Picus' transformation (*Aen.* 7.189–91), but not of his divinity.

et nunc: 'even today', the characteristic aetiological touch (e.g. Phanocles fr. 1.28 Powell εἰσέτι νῦν, Ap. Rh. 2.526 ἔτι νῦν) which is also standard in Ant.

Lib.'s paraphrase of Boeus (e.g. 7.8, 16.3). It would not be surprising if this were the final line of Macer's section on Picumnus.

Picumnus: a figure whose name and genealogy show many variations. Varro (Servius on *Aen.* 10.76, cf. on 9.4) recognized a pair of deities, Pilumnus and Pitumnus (*sic*). The former, in Virgil, is either grandfather (*Aen.* 10.76, see S. J. Harrison ad loc.) or great-great-grandfather (10.619) of Turnus, and one of the pair was also called Stercutus (or a similar name) as the originator of manuring the fields. In Pliny, *NH* 17.50 (a book for which Aemilius Macer is listed as a source) Stercutus is son of Faunus. Courtney (p. 293) distinguishes three strands: (*a*) *picus* = 'woodpecker', (*b*) Picus the prehistoric king in Latium, and (*c*) Picumnus (or Pilumnus), an agricultural deity—but see above on *Met.* 14.313–16.

51 (2 Bl., C.)

cum laude excelleat omni: the grammarian makes clear that Macer used a second-conjugation form ('*verum tamen* Aemilius Macer . . .', after giving third-conjugation examples). So Unger's 'excelleat' should be preferred to Scaliger's 'excellĕret'. *OLD* s.v. *excello* lists forms 'as from' [?] *excelleo*, without mentioning this fragment.

laude . . . omni: as *OLD laus* 3*b*, 'a cause of praise, praiseworthy thing, act or quality, virtue, good point, merit'. Dahlmann (p. 13) gives very convincing parallels for 'laude . . . omni', e.g. Cicero, *De Or.* 1.20 'omni laude cumulatus orator', 3.9 'virum omni laude praestantem'. He further suggests that the fragment may refer to the swan, which among birds had outstanding merits, such as its soft, snow-white plumage and the alleged sweetness of its song. It is even conceivable that **53** could follow immediately after **51**.

52 (3 Bl., C.)

1. Vulcani . . . vapore: 'Vulcanus' by itself = 'fire' is found in Plautus (*Amph.* 341) and Ennius (*Ann.* 509 Skutsch); cf. Egnatius, **43**.1 'Mulciber'. But coupling with a noun in the genitive seems rather different (though no less elevated), and I am not sure that this should be called 'metonymy'. Compare e.g. *Iliad* 17.88 φλογὶ . . . Ἡφαίστοιο, Pindar, *Pyth.* 3.39–40 σέλας / . . . Ἀφαίστου.

vapore: 'heat' rather than 'steam'. This sense is sometimes (as here) grandiose and archaic; for the link with *torreo*, cf. Martial 5.78.15 'lento castaneae vapore tostae'.

2.   virgis: Dahlmann (*Über Aemilius Macer*, p. 12) referred to Serv. Dan. on *Aen.* 10.270 'dicitur autem apex virga quae in summa pilleo flaminum lana circumdata et filo conligata erat' and Serv. on 2.683 'apex proprie dicitur in summo flaminis pilleo virga lanata'. But although an olive twig wrapped in wool formed part of the priests' cap (apex), it would be surprising to find 'virga' by itself denoting the whole headdress. And the collocation 'cum virgis prosecta ferunt' suggests that, like the *prosecta*, the *virgae* are carried by hand.

Courtney (comparing Virgil, *Georgics* 1.266) thinks that the 'virgae' are baskets made out of twigs. I wonder whether they could be 'verbenae', defined by *OLD* as leafy branches or twigs from any of various aromatic trees or shrubs, used especially for decorating altars. Thus Cicero, *In Verrem* 4.110 'praesto mihi sacerdotes Cereris cum infulis ac verbenis fuerunt' (more in Nisbet and Hubbard on Horace, *Odes* 1.19.4). '<sacerdotes>' might be supplied at the beginning of our fragment.

prosecta: severed portions (consisting of one of the major organs) of a sacrificial victim (*OLD*), cf. Varro, *De Lingua Latina* 5.110 'quod in extis nunc dicitur prosectum'. Ovid uses this technical term in his account of the sacrifices made by Achilles after his victory over Cygnus son of Poseidon (*Met.* 12.152 'ut imposuit prosecta calentibus aris'). This occurrence of the rare 'prosecta' (also *Fasti* 6.163 and Stat. *Theb.* 5.641) has suggested to some that our fragment, like **53** (and possibly **51**), may refer to the myth of Cygnus; but the argument is tenuous.

53 (4 Bl., C.)

Two versions of what are clearly the same lines; one, if not both, of the sources must be quoting from memory (an interesting example of the divergences which can arise from this habit). The original text might have been a mixture of the two versions, but, if one must express a preference for either as it stands, Isidore seems to have a slight advantage over Servius. That, as Courtney (p. 294) says, is a little surprising, since one would expect Servius to be Isidore's source, and the latter is generally less exact in his quotations. In particular 'laetissimus' seems preferable, as a technical term of augury (see below), and is supported by what looks like a definite imitation of Macer in Germanicus, *Aratea* 541 of the Twins, 'semper nautis laetissima signa' (Aratus, in the corresponding *Phaen.* 549, said nothing about good omens for sailors). So I take my lemmata from Isidore (version *a*).

Boeus had an account of Cygnus which (uniquely) we owe to Athenaeus (9.393e) rather than to Ant. Lib.; his Cygnus was a son of Ares killed by

Heracles (cf. Forbes Irving, *Metamorphosis in Greek Myths* (1990), 257–9). But Ovid has three different stories about a Cygnus (*Met.* 2.367 ff.; 7.371 ff., and 12.64 ff.). Among Hellenistic poets, Cygnus had figured also in Phanocles (fr. 6 Powell) and Nicander (fr. 52, from the *Heteroeumena*). And there is the splendid passage of Virgil (*Aen.* 10.185 ff.), mainly indebted (it would seem) to Phanocles, with a Ligurian setting as in Ovid, *Met.* 2.367 ff. It is impossible to say which of these variant myths of Cygnus (and the list is not complete) appeared in Aemilius Macer.

1. in auspiciis: one cannot argue that this is superior to Servius' 'in auguriis', since from an early date the two Latin words were virtually synonymous. See Skutsch on Ennius, *Annales* 73 'auspicio augurioque'.

semper: unlike birds which were sometimes of good omen, sometimes bad, according to the part of the sky in which they were seen. Servius (quoting version *b*) explains that swans did not give omens to anyone but sailors (for the bird of no significance, see Bulloch on Callimachus, *Hymn* 5.124); thus, whenever they were significant, swans were always favourable.

laetissimus: 'favourable, propitious' (*OLD laetus* 6, including this fragment). See above for the imitation in Germanicus, *Aratea* 541.

2. quia se non mergit in undas: so giving the sailors hope that their ship will not sink. Servius' alternative 'quia numquam mergitur undis' is not inferior (cf. Ovid, *Met.* 11.795 'quia mergitur').

This is the only fragment of Macer to give us two complete lines, and one may recognize here something of the *elegantia* which Quintilian (**48***b*) grudgingly allowed to Macer as to Lucretius. It seems to me conceivable that **51** (see ad loc.) might be joined to **53**: '<e.g. fitque ope Phoebea>, cum laude excelleat omni, / cygnus in auspiciis semper laetissimus ales; / hunc optant nautae, quia se non mergit in undas'. 'Semper laetissimus' could match 'laude excelleat omni', and the lines might provide an effective conclusion to the metamorphosis of Cygnus (as **50** for Picus/Picumnus).

54–66 *Theriaca*

It was probably on this poem (rather than the *Ornithogonia*) that Aemilius Macer's reputation mainly rested; sadly we do not possess any fragment of even two complete lines (**57** is the nearest) to help us form our own verdict. When Quintilian (10.1.56 = **48***a*) described Macer as a follower of Nicander, he obviously has the *Theriaca* in mind. Pliny no doubt read both poems for his *Natural History*, but drew much more material from the *Theriaca* (see above on **48**). We can only speculate on the extent to which Virgil used

Macer's *Theriaca* as a Latin intermediary for the Nicandrean material in the Third Georgic (414–39), but have explicit evidence (**54b**, discussed below) that Lucan borrowed at least the names of snakes from Macer for the horrifying passage in which Cato's men are bitten by a great variety of poisonous creatures (*Bellum Civile* 9.701 ff.). Traces of Macer may also be suspected in Calpurnius Siculus (probably of Neronian date), *Ecl.* 5.86–94.

The passage on snakes in Lucan's book 9 repays more detailed consideration. In all probability his debt to Macer stretched beyond the mere names of snakes (useful material in W. Morel, 'Iologica', *Philologus*, 83 (1927–8), 345–89, and I. Cazzaniga, 'L'episodio dei serpi libici in Lucano e la tradizione dei *Theriaca* Nicandrei', *Acme*, 10 (1957), 27–41) and started before line 700. We can make a firm connection between Macer, **57**.2 and Lucan 9.711 on the chelydrus which makes the earth smoke along its path—a detail absent from the corresponding passage of Nicander (*Ther.* 415 ff.).

Before starting his catalogue of snakes, Lucan provides a long mythological excursus (7.619–99) explaining why Libya teems with poisonous creatures. This is some way from Lucan's normal manner, but would be very appropriate to a learned Latin poet of the mid first century BC writing in the Hellenistic tradition. The myth is introduced with a typical note of scepticism: the poet himself does not credit it, but will persist nonetheless (621–3 'non cura laborque / noster scire valet, nisi quod vulgata per orbem / fabula pro vera decepit saecula causa'). One could compare e.g. Nicander, *Ther.* 309 εἰ ἔτυμον (the tale of Helen, Canobus, and the Blood-letter), Nonnus, *Dion.* 47.256–7; more widely, see T. C. W. Stinton, 'Si credere dignum est', in his *Collected Papers on Greek Tragedy* (1990), 236–64, especially 242–4.

Lucan's myth explains that the African serpents spring from drops of Medusa's blood which fell to the ground when Perseus flew over Libya carrying her severed head. This story is absent from Nicander's *Theriaca* (though it might be prompted by the different myth of Perseus in *Alexipharmaca* 100 ff.), but another Hellenistic poet, Apollonius Rhodius, treated it both in his *Argonautica* (4.1513 ff.) and in his lost *Foundation of Alexandria* (fr. 4 Powell), and it recurs in Ovid (*Met.* 4.614–20). In the Hellenistic manner, Lucan's narrative contains brief references to other myths: Orpheus charming Cerberus (643), Heracles overcoming the hydra (644), the transformation of Atlas (654–5), the battle of gods and giants at Phlegra (655–8). Learned curiosities abound, e.g. 660–1 (Perseus borrowed Hermes' wings to fly over Libya), 663–4 (the *harpe* was not employed for the first time against Medusa, since it had already been used to cut off the head of Argos). It would be rash to claim that Lucan found all this in Aemilius Macer, but reasonable to suspect that he is deliberately writing in the older poet's manner. Macer would surely have needed mythological diversions in order to give his poem variety.

Vestiges of Macer's style may also be discernible in Lucan's catalogue of snakes; e.g. the spondaic fifth foot (so popular in neoteric circles) in 719 'vergens caput amphisbaena' (cf. Nic. *Ther.* 384), 836 'victi decus Orionis', and 918 'et Thessala centaurea' (cf. Lucretius 4.125). Line 723 ending 'tabificus seps' suggests Macer for more than one reason. The monosyllabic ending was favoured by some Hellenistic poets, including Nicander (thus *Ther.* 147 ἐμβατέει σήψ), and even more prominent in the old Roman tradition of Ennius and Lucretius. One could well imagine Macer using the compound epithet 'tabificus', first in Lucretius 6.737 (cf. *PLLS* 10 (1998), 184). Sometimes we can compare Lucan with Nicander and wonder whether that tells us something about the intermediary. For example 716 'spinaque vagi torquente cerastae' could be set alongside *Ther.* 267 οἶμον ὁδοιπλανέων σκολιὴν τετρη-χότι νώτωι (also of the cerastes); 'vagi' corresponds to ὁδοιπλανέων, 'spina' to νώτωι, while 'torquente' conveys the sense of σκολιήν. Lucan 9.724 (the basilisk) 'sibilaque effundens cunctas terrentia pestes' is quite close to *Ther.* 399–400 οὐκ ἄρα δὴ κείνου σπειραχθέα κνώδαλα γαίης / ἰϋγὴν μίμνουσιν. And **57**.2 seems to show Macer interpreting Nicander in an odd way which is followed by Lucan.

55 (7 Bl., 5 C.)

tumido resonantia sibila collo: Knaack's conjecture 'tumido' (for 'longo') receives some support from the reading of N (tundo), and seems sufficiently convincing to stand in the text, particularly in view of Nicander, *Ther.* 179–80 ψαφαρὸς δ' ἀναπίμπραται αὐχήν / ἄκριτα ποιφύσσοντος ('and its dust-coloured neck *swells up* as it hisses continuously'). 'Sibila' as a neuter plural noun is by no means uncommon (e.g. Cornelius Severus, **212**, Lucan 9.724 'sibilaque effundens'). In our fragment '<effundens>' would be a possible supplement before or after the quoted words.

56 (17 Bl., 7 C.)

saucia naris: Virgil never uses the singular; when it does appear, the ablative (e.g. Silius 10.79, quoted on **150**) and genitive are commoner than the nominative case. But Ovid (four occurrences) has no objection to the nominative singular 'naris'. Blood flows from the nose of a victim of the haemorrhois in Nicander, *Ther.* 301 αἷμα διὲκ ῥινῶν and Lucan 9.812–13 'ora redundant / et patulae nares'.

57 (8 Bl., C.)

1–2. seu . . . / seu: the point might be that the snake is equally formidable in either case.

   1. terga: as Dahlmann (p. 20) says, 'terga' stands for the snake as a whole by synecdoche; Macer does not mean that the poison is exuded from the 'back'. Compare *OLD* tergum 7 (the animal's skin or hide).

   exspirant: this fragment may correspond to Nic. *Ther.* 421 τὸ δ' ἀπὸ χροὸς ἐχθρὸν ἄηται.

   2. tractus: the 'track' or 'trail' (*OLD* 5), of a serpent also in [Virgil], *Culex* 181 'manant sanguineae per tractus undique guttae'. I have adopted Nisbet's conjecture; Blänsdorf prints Morel's 'tellus', while Courtney leaves the transmitted 'terra' in cruces. It is a mystery what gave Macer the idea that the earth smokes (followed by Lucan 9.711 'tractique via fumante chelydri'). Nicander says no such thing. Courtney suggests (though it is a long shot) that Macer may have misunderstood the epithet αἰθαλόεις, applied to the chelydrus in *Ther.* 420. This can mean 'blazing', 'smoky', or 'sooty'. It may also refer to colour; the scholia and Eutecnius' Paraphrase of the *Theriaca* (p. 42 ed. I. Gualandri, 1968) both explain αἰθαλόεις here with μέλας.

   taeter: a word prominent in old Latin tragedy and epic, and particularly favoured by Lucretius.

58 (10 Bl., 9 C.)

vepre occulta ruis: since K. P. Schulze, *Rh. Mus.* 53 (1898), 543, scholars have compared Nicander, *Ther.* 418–19 (the chelydrus) ἔνθα κατὰ πρέμνον κοίλης ὑπεδύσατο φηγοῦ / ὀξὺς ἀλείς, κοῖτον δὲ βαθεῖ ἐνεδείματο θάμνωι. But 'ruis' is likely to mean 'you attack' (*OLD* 5 'to rush or descend (upon) in hostile or aggressive fashion, charge, swoop, etc.'). If the fragment is to be tied closely to anything in Nicander, a better parallel would be *Ther.* 455 θάμνου ὑπαΐξας ('darting out from under a thicket') of the dracon robbing the eagle of its prey—one of the most memorable passages in the *Theriaca*. The phrases even occupy the same part of the hexameter. The gender of 'occulta' (if applied to the dracon) is no problem, since it could well agree with *serpens*, which is usually feminine.

   vepre occulta: perhaps going with preceding words, e.g. '<when>, hidden in a thicket, <you see an eagle . . . >, you attack' (cf. Nic. *Ther.* 453 ff.).

vepre: for the rare singular, compare Ovid, *Met.* 5.628 'vepre latens' (of a hare trying to escape from dogs).

ruis: J. P. Nerandau, *ANRW* II. 30. 3, p. 1724 n. 100, questions the likelihood of an address to a serpent, on the ground that there are no examples in Nicander. Lucan, however, apostrophizes the dracones at some length (9.727–33)—in any case this device can be purely a metrical covenience.

59 (18 Bl., 10 C.)

maior ape, scrabrone minor: although the form 'scrabro' (rather than 'crabro') has no great authority elsewhere, it is well established in the manuscripts quoting this fragment. One may agree with Courtney that lengthening of 'apē' before 'crabrone' is unlikely; the commoner form could be combined with an (unattested) ablative 'api', or with 'ape <est>'.

The subject of this fragment is the *fucus*, which must have been mentioned in the text. Servius (see the sources for this fragment) is preoccupied by the question of which animals such insects spring from—variations of the βουγονία familar from the Fourth Georgic. This might suggest that Aemilius Macer had a more substantial passage on the lines of Nic. *Ther.* 741 ἵπποι γὰρ σφηκῶν γένεσις, ταῦροι δὲ μελισσῶν (cf. *Alex.* 446 ff.).

60 (11 C.)

A particularly interesting extract. Pliny states very definitely that the details which he gives were to be found in Macer (cf. **64**). They show our poet going far beyond Nicander, who made just a passing reference to the belief that muraenae mate with serpents on land (*Ther.* 826–7 εἰ ἔτυμον κείνην γε σὺν οὐλοβόροις ἐχίεσσι / θόρνυσθαι προλιποῦσαν ἁλὸς νομὸν ἠπείροισι). Oppian of Cilicia, writing about AD 180, vividly described the mating call of the serpent which, in Macer, the fisherman imitates. I quote *Halieutica* 1.563–7:

> στὰς δ' ἄρ' ἐπὶ ῥηγμῖνος ἑὸν νόμον ἐρροίζησε
> κικλήσκων φιλότητα, θοῶς δ' ἐσάκουσε κελαινή
> ἰϋγὴν μύραινα, καὶ ἔσσυτο θᾶσσον ὀϊστοῦ.
> ἡ μὲν ἄρ' ἐκ πόντοιο τιταίνεται, αὐτὰρ ὁ πόντου
> ἐκ γαίης πολιοῖσιν ἐπεμβαίνει ῥοθίοισιν.

The *ferula* which, according to Macer, brought instant death to the muraena (cf. *NH* 20.261, a mere touch will suffice) is the plant fennel-giant. Pliny uses the more archaic form of the ablative, 'fusti' (rather than *fuste*), which could be from Macer—perhaps the whole phrase 'iactato fusti'. On the muraena, see further D'Arcy Thompson, *A Glossary of Greek Fishes* (1947), 162–5.

61–62

These fragments were given to the *Ornithogonia* by Baehrens. But that poem was concerned with transformations. Although Hermes disguises himself as an ibis in Ant. Lib. 28.3 (from Nicander, *Heteroeumena*) and in Ovid, *Met.* 5.331, the conflict between ibises and winged snakes is not likely to have produced a transformation. Dahlmann (p. 17) much more plausibly gave the fragments to the *Theriaca*, even though Nicander does not tell of the battle between ibises and winged serpents.

61 (5 Bl., 12 C.)

altis ... urbibus: a standard collocation, e.g. Virgil, *Georgics* 1.485–6, Horace, *Odes* 1.16.18.

ibes: this plural form is found also in Cicero, *De Natura Deorum* 1.101 and 2.126, Pliny, *NH* 10.75 (quoted below).

62 (6 Bl., 13 C.)

auxilium sacrae veniunt cultoribus ibes: one could supply e.g. '<ferentes>' at the end of the previous line. But the sense may be complete. 'Auxilio [predicative dative] venire' is a much commoner phrase, but for 'auxilium [*OLD* 3, 'a thing or person affording help'] venire', in apposition to the helper ('ibes'), cf. Livy 3.5.15, Tac. *Hist.* 3.79.

The story of the flying snakes which enter Egypt from Arabia and are destroyed by the ibises starts in Herodotus (2.75, cf. 3.107); some have conjectured that he got it from Hecataeus. For a full presentation of the later ancient material, see Pease on Cicero, *DND* 1.101, and for critical discussion (attempting to find a kernel of truth), A. Lloyd, *Herodotus, Book II: Commentary 1–98* (1976), 326–30, D'Arcy Thompson, *A Glossary of Greek Birds*[2] (1936), 106–14. Pliny, *NH* 10.75 'invocant et Aegyptii ibes [note the form] suas contra serpentium adventum' may come from Aemilius Macer. A representation of the ibis attacking a winged snake can be seen on the coins of Juba II of Mauretania (J. Mazard, *Corpus Nummorum Numidae Mauretaniaeque* (1955), 116, no. 349)—no doubt that studious monarch discussed the phenomenon somewhere in his voluminous works on natural history.

63 (13 Bl., 14 C.)

o quales veget intubus herbas: C. Watkins, 'Etyma Enniana', *HSCP* 77 (1973), 195–206 at 195–201, without mentioning Macer, shows convincingly that *vegeo* is a causative-transitive verb, 'arouse, quicken, stir up'. In *OLD* a comma has unfortunately been misplaced: 'to impart vigour or activity, to enliven' should be 'to impart vigour or activity to, enliven' (cf. *OLD vegeto*, 'to impart energy to, invigorate'). 'Veget' is Lachmann's emendation, accepted by Courtney; most scholars had preferred Keil's 'aget', but (as Courtney notes) the future seems unlikely. *Vegeo* is found twice in Ennius (*Ann.* 509 Skutsch 'Volcanum ventus vegebat', *Scaen.* 367 Vahlen²), twice in Varro's *Satires*, once in Pomponius and once in Lucretius (5.532 'quae vegeant motum signis').

o: the interjection is preserved only in *p* (excerpts from the eighth-century cod. Par. 7530). Such enthusiasm for the intubus may surprise, and Nisbet would delete 'o'. For its placing in the hexameter, cf. Persius 1.1 (= Lucilius 9 Marx) 'o quantum est in rebus inane'. *Pace* Courtney p. 298, Nicander, *Alex.* 429 gives remedies not for snake-bite but for henbane (cf. 415).

64 (15 C.)

As in **60**, Pliny seems to ascribe to Macer a detailed version which goes far beyond Nicander. This time the parallel passage comes from the *Alexipharmaca* (465–82), not the *Theriaca*, giving some colour to the suggestion that Macer too may have written on *Alexipharmaca* (see on **69** dub.). But the material would have been quite appropriate to his *Theriaca*. The passage of Nicander does not say that the victims of the sea-hare develop a fishy smell, nor that they die in as many days as the sea-hare has lived. It might seem from Pliny that Macer regarded the poison of the sea-hare as inevitably fatal; elsewhere, however, Pliny mentions remedies for it (*NH* 28.158 ff., 32.58).

65 (12 Bl., 16 C.)

inter praeteritas numerabitur ocimus herbas: ocimum (not mentioned by Nicander) is useful against scorpion stings in Dioscorides 2.141. Some (see app. crit.) have wished to emend 'praeteritas'. Morel thought that a negative preceded—i.e. the ocimus will *not* be numbered among omitted herbs—comparing Virgil, *Georgics* 2.101–2 'non ego te, dis et mensis accepta secundis, / transierim, Rhodia, et tumidis, bumaste, racemis'. But the transmitted words could quite well mean that the ocimus (together with other herbs) will merely be mentioned in passing, not treated in detail. That is exactly what happens in Pliny, *NH* 19.154 'cetera in transcursu dici possunt. ocimum ... etc.'. And Virgil, after briefly mentioning some of the more attractive flowers and vegetables (*G.* 4.116 ff.), concludes (147–8) 'verum haec ... / ... praetereo'.

66 (14 Bl., 17 C.)

pallentesque crocos: probably the start of a line (as in Stat. *Theb.* 6.210 'pallentique croco'), though these words could span the feminine caesura. 'Pallentes' may represent κρόκος λευκός (Theophrastus), but the participle is often used as a poetic equivalent of χλωρός in Greek (e.g. Parthenius fr. 32 Lightfoot = *Suppl. Hell.* 644 χλωρὰ χελιδόνια). See J. André, *Étude sur les termes de couleur dans la langue latine* (Paris, 1949), 143–4. Neither in Pliny, *NH* 25.169 nor in 29.120 is crocus recommended for snake-bite, and 'Corycio ... croco' (Lucan 9.809, in a simile) does not help at all (these three passages cited by Dahlmann, p. 24).

67–68

Arguments for ascribing some of the recent items to the *Theriaca* have not been strong, and it seems best to categorize at least these two as 'incertae sedis'.

67 (15 Bl., 18 C.)

Aemilius Macer came from Verona (**47***a* and *d*), near Lake Garda (Benacus), which Virgil apostrophized memorably in *Georgics* 2.160. No doubt he could have found cause to mention the lake in either *Ornithogonia* or *Theriaca*; Courtney (p. 299), in mentioning the birds of Lake Garda, seems to lean towards the former.

This fragment baffles me. It is apparently quoted to establish the circumference of the lake as one thousand stades (twelve hundred in Serv. Dan. on the same line of Virgil, without mention of Macer). The originator of this comment (whether the Berne scholiast or an earlier source) would have known the full text and context in Macer, and so deserves a certain respect. No doubt the citation was originally longer, including at least a verb for the relative clause. With 'multa . . . milia' we could understand *passuum*. But it is hard to see how 'many [Roman] miles' could establish the precise 'one thousand stades' (8 stades = 1 Roman mile). One might suspect that 'multa' is corrupt. G. B. Pighi (in *Miscellanea di Studi Alessandri in memoria di Augusto Rostagni* (1963), 561) would emend to 'ille ducenta lacus quem circum milia <cingunt>'; the mathematics (200 Roman miles = 1600 stades) do not fit the figure in either Virgilian commentator but come close to the 143 kilometres = 214.5 Roman miles = 1716 stades for the road around Lake Garda in the Blue Guide, *North Italy* (1984), 211. It is surprising that readers of the Berne scholia should have been expected to engage in mental arithmetic (converting Roman miles to stades) instead of being given the circumference in the unit of measurement employed by Macer.

The quoted works, as they stand, do not particularly suggest a circumference. Courtney refers to the birds of Lake Garda (Claudian, *Carmina Minora* 25.107, cf. Blue Guide p. 211 'wildfowl abound'), and one might think of e.g. 'illi multa lacus quem circum milia <ludunt / alituum>'. But this would totally disregard the Berne scholiast.

illi: unlike Courtney, I feel that *illi*, an archaic form of the adverb 'there' (later *illic*) is not out of place in Aemilius Macer, whose fragments preserve a number of archaic features (notably 'veget' in **63**, if the restoration is correct). 'Illi' appears in Plautus and Terence (see *OLD*), and in a letter of Caelius to Cicero (*Ad Fam.* 8.15 = 149 SB. 2 'nobilem illi'). Housman printed it in Manilius 3.309, noting (Addenda, p. 72) that it has manuscript support in some passages of Ovid. One might, however, argue in favour of 'illi<c>' that it strengthens the alliteration (with 'la̲cus' and c̲ircum').

68 (16 Bl., 19 C.)

†flumant minu† margine summa: 'minu'' (i.e. 'minus' with the final 's' cut off, as often in Lucretius by only once in Catullus) is not impossible; compare Egnatius, 43A.1 'labentibus Phoebe'. Among emendations, R. Unger's 'fluitantem in' (*De Aemilio Macro Nicandri Imitatore* (1845), 14) deserves a mention—perhaps the cutting of a plant which moves gently in the current at the edge of a river. Nicander is fond of such pictures (e.g. *Ther.* 59–61); cf. Seneca, *Epist.* 51.12 'fluvitantem toto lacu rosam'. Courtney's suggestion is based upon a different fantasy, 'perhaps a nest or nests washed out of the riverbank by flood and floating at the level of the top of the bank' (p. 299). *Margo* is more often masculine; for the feminine, cf. Rabirius, 230, Juvenal 1.5.

69 dub.

It is tempting to connect 'herbarum vires' in the *Disticha Catonis* with 'quae iuvat herba' in Ovid, *Tr.* 4.10.44 (= 47c). Manilius (2.44–5) praises the *Theriaca* and *Alexipharmaca* of Nicander as follows:

> ille venenatos anguis [*Theriaca*] aconitaque [*Alex.* 12 ff.] et herbas
> fata refert vitamque sua radice ferentis.

Accordingly several scholars (including myself in *CR* N s 23 (1973), 11) have deduced that Aemilius Macer wrote *Alexipharmaca* as well as *Theriaca* (cf. Courtney 292; Nisbet, *Collected Papers*, 398). One or two fragments of Macer (notably 64) contain material covered by Nicander in his *Alexipharmaca*, and a few fragments on herbs or flowers (particularly 66) seem to have little, if any, connection with snake-bite. On the other hand, Nicander's *Theriaca* also included remedies (493 ff.). Courtney (p. 292) suggests that the first book of Macer's *Theriaca* dealt with snakes, and the second with cures. If so, the latter might have acquired a semi-independent status which could account for what we read in the *Disticha Catonis*.

70 dub.

There is at least an even chance that Quintilian refers not to Aemilius Macer but to the younger Macer (see above on 47 and below, Appendix, p. 424), travelling companion of Ovid and composer of epic poetry on Troy. Such a relationship between two near-contemporaries and friends might better suit the humorous activity which Quintilian describes.

From the time of the *Certamen Homeri et Hesiodi* to that of the *Christus Patiens* the Greeks and Romans enjoyed turning unaltered lines to unintended purposes. Nonetheless it is a little surprising that Ovid found it 'so easy' (Quintilian) to convert Macer's four-line poems into a book attacking bad poets. Ovid's version can hardly have contained nothing but unaltered lines of Macer. 'Tetrasticha' are recognized as a category in Martial 7.85.1. We have examples in Ausonius, *Caesares* 43 ff. (elegiacs), Prudentius, *Dittochaeon* (hexameters), and *Anth. Lat.* II. 555–90 ed. Riese, 1902 (hexameters and elegiacs). It may or may not be significant that the Qaṣr Ibrîm papyrus of Cornelius Gallus (**145**) presents a series of quatrains (Nisbet, *Collected Papers*, 120).

M. Furius Bibaculus

71

(*a*) Hieronymi *Chronicon* (p. 148 ed. Helm[2], 1956) ann. Abr. 1914 = 103 a. Chr.: *M. Furius poeta cognomento Bibaculus Cremonae nascitur.*

(*b*) Suet. *De Gramm. et Rhet.* 4.2 (pp. 6–8 ed. Kaster, 1995): *eosdem* [sc. grammaticos] *litteratores vocitatos Messalla Corvinus in quadam epistula ostendit, non esse sibi dicens rem cum Furio Bibaculo, ne cum Ticida* [**100**] *quidem aut litteratore Catone* [App., p. 429].

(*c*) Tac. *Ann.* 4.34.5: *carmina Bibaculi et Catulli referta contumeliis Caesarum leguntur; sed ipse divus Iulius, ipse divus Augustus et tulere ista et reliquere, haud facile dixerim moderatione magis an sapientia.*

(*d*) Hor. *Serm.* 1.10.36–7 '*turgidus Alpinus iugulat dum Memnona dumque / defingit* [vv. ll. diffingit, diffindit, defindit] *Rheni luteum caput, haec ego ludo*': Pseudacro ad loc. (II p. 110 ed. Keller, 1902) *Viva<cu>lum quendam poetam Gallum tangit.*

(*a*) 103 BC. The poet M. Furius, surnamed Bibaculus, is born at Cremona.

(*b*) The same people [i.e. *grammatici*] were called *litteratores*, as Messalla Corvinus reveals in one of his letters, when he says that he 'has no dealings with Furius Bibaculus, nor even with Ticida or the *litterator* Cato'.

(*c*) People read the poems of Bibaculus and Catullus which are crammed with insults against the Caesars; but the deified Julius and the deified Augustus themselves both endured those things and took no action against them—whether more through restraint or good sense is hard to say.

(*d*) 'While turgid Alpinus murders Memnon and [? moulds] the muddy head of the Rhine, I amuse myself with these trifles' [a commentator: his target is a Gaulish poet named Vivaculus].

72–81 *Annales Belli Gallici*

72–74 Liber I

72 (7 Bl., C.)

interea Oceani linquens Aurora cubile

Meanwhile Dawn, leaving the couch of Ocean . . .

Macr. *Sat.* 6.1.31 (I p. 351 ed. Willis, 1963) ad Verg. *Aen.* 4.585 'Tithoni croceum linquens Aurora cubile': *Furius in primo annali* 'interea—cubile'.

73 (8 Bl., C.)

ille gravi subito devictus volnere habenas
misit equi lapsusque in humum defluxit et armis
reddidit aeratis sonitum

He, suddenly overcome with a grievous wound, lost hold of his horse's reins and, after falling to the earth, sank down and gave out a sound from his bronze armour.

1–3 Macr. *Sat.* 6.4.10 (I p. 371 Willis) ad *Aen.* 11.500–1 'quam tota cohors imitata relictis / ad terram defluxit equis': *sic Furius in primo* 'ille—sonitum'.

74 (9 Bl., C.)

mitemque rigat per pectora somnum

. . . and diffuses gentle sleep through their breasts

Macr. *Sat.* 6.1.44 (I p. 353 Willis) ad *Aen.* 1.691–2 'placidam per membra quietem / inrigat': *Furius in primo* 'mitemque—somnum'.

75 (10 Bl., C.) Liber IV

pressatur pede pes, mucro mucrone, viro vir

Foot presses close upon foot, sword-point on sword-point, man on man.

Macr. *Sat.* 6.3.5 (I p. 367 Willis): *Homerus ait* [*Il.* 13.131]. *Furius in quarto annali* 'pressatur—vir'. *hinc Vergilius ait* 'haeret pede pes densusque viro vir [*Aen.* 10.361]'.

76 (11 Bl., C.) Liber VI

quod genus hoc hominum, Saturno sancte create?

Holy offspring of Saturn, what breed of men is this?

Macr. *Sat.* 6.1.32 (I p. 351 Willis) ad *Aen.* 1.539 'quod genus hoc hominum? quaeve hunc tam barbara morem . . .?': *Furius in sexto* 'quod—create?'

  hoc] hic *Courtney* (*errore typothetae*)

77 (12 Bl., C.) Liber X

rumoresque serunt varios et multa requirunt

They spread various rumours and ask many questions.

Macr. *Sat.* 6.1.33 (I p. 351 Willis) ad *Aen.* 12.228 'rumoresque serit varios ac talia fatur': *Furius in decimo* 'rumoresque—requirunt'.

78–79 Liber XI

78 (13 Bl., C.)

nomine quemque cict; dictorum tempus adesse
commemorat

He calls upon each by name; he reminds them that the time for words [? or 'deeds'] had arrived.

1–2 Macr. *Sat.* 6.1.34 (I pp. 351–2 Willis) ad *Aen.* 11.731 'nomine quemque vocans, reficitque ad [*Macr.:* in *Verg.*] proelia pulsos': *Furius in undecimo* 'nomine—commemorat'.

  1 dictorum] factorum *Hollis*   adesse] abisse *Nisbet*

79 (14 Bl., C.)

confirmat dictis simul atque exsuscitat acris
ad bellandum animos, reficitque ad proelia mentes

With his words he strengthens them and rouses their spirits to enthusiasm for fighting, and restores their minds for battle.

1–2 Macr. *Sat.* 6.1.34 (I p. 352 Willis) [post **78**] *deinde infra* 'confirmat—mentes'.

80–81 ex incertis libris

80 (15 Bl., C.)

Iuppiter hibernas cana nive conspuit Alpes

Jupiter spat with white snow all over the wintry Alps.

Porph. (p. 311 ed. Holder, 1894) ad Hor. *Serm.* 2.5.41 'Furius hibernas cana nive conspuet Alpes': *hic versus Furi Bibaculi est. ille enim cum vellet Alpes nivibus plenas describere, ait* 'Iuppiter—Alpes'. Pseudacro (II p. 171 ed. Keller, 1904) ad eundem locum: *Furius Vivaculus in pragmatia belli Gallici* 'Iuppiter—Alpes'. Quint. 8.6.17 *sunt et durae* [sc. tralationes], *id est a longinqua similitudine ductae, ut . . .* 'Iuppiter—Alpes'.

81 (16 Bl., C.)

hic qua ducebant vastae divortia fossae

Here, where a gap in the enormous ditch led [? them].

Schol. Veron. Verg. (Appendix Serviana, p. 441 ed. Hagen, 1902) ad *Aen.* 9.379 'obiciunt equites sese ad divortia nota': [post lacunam] *in annalibus belli Gallici* 'hic—fossae'.

82–89 carmina variis metris conscripta

82 (iambi)

(*a*) Quint. 10.1.96: *iambus non sane a Romanis celebratus est ut proprium opus, sed est a quibusdam interpositus; cuius acerbitas in Catullo, Bibaculo, Horatio (quamquam illi epodos intervenit) reperiatur.*

(*b*) Diomed. GLK I p. 485: *iambus est carmen maledicum plerumque trimetro versu et epodo sequente compositum, ut* [Hor. *Epod.* 10.1–2]. *appellatum est autem* παρὰ τὸ ἰαμβίζειν, *quod est maledicere. cuius carminis praecipui scriptores apud Graecos Archilochus et Hipponax, apud Romanos Lucilius et Catullus et Horatius et Bibaculus.*

(*a*) The Iambus has not much been practised by Romans as a distinct genre, but has been used by some in conjunction with other metres; its bitter quality may be found in Catullus, Bibaculus, and Horace (though in the last case a shorter line intervenes).

(*b*) [the Iambus] ... The most important writers of this kind of poetry were, among the Greeks, Archilochus and Hipponax, and, among the Romans, Lucilius, Catullus, Horace, and Bibaculus.

83 (3 Bl., C.)

Orbilius ubinam est, litterarum oblivio?

Where on earth is Orbilius, literature's forgotten man?

Suet. *De Gramm.* 9.6 (p. 14 Kaster): *vixit* [sc. Orbilius] *prope ad centesimum aetatis annum, amissa iam pridem memoria, ut versus Bibaculi docet* 'Orbilius—oblivio'.

84 (1 Bl., C.)

si quis forte mei domum Catonis,
depictas minio assulas, et illos
custodis videt hortulos Priapi,
miratur quibus ille disciplinis
tantam sit sapientiam assecutus,   5
quem tres cauliculi, selibra farris,
racemi duo tegula sub una
ad summam prope nutriant senectam.

Anyone who happens to see the house of my friend Cato, chips of wood painted with vermilion, and the little garden belonging to guardian Priapus, wonders by what training he has achieved wisdom so great that three cabbages, half a pound of grain, and two bunches of grapes under a single roof-tile can sustain him to the verge of extreme old age.

1–8 Suet. *De Gramm.* 11.3 (p. 16 ed. Kaster): *vixit* [sc. P. Valerius Cato] *ad extremam senectam, sed in summa pauperie et paene inopia, abditus modice gurgustio postquam Tusculana villa creditoribus cesserat, ut auctor est Bibaculus,* 'si quis—senectam'.

2 assulas *Beroaldus*: assyl(l)as *vel* as(s) illas *codd.*   3 custodis *Pontanus (in cod. Leid. Periz. Q 21)*: custodes *codd., Scaliger*   hortuli Priapos *Scaliger* 5 patientiam *Baehrens*   6 cauliculi *Pontanus (in cod. Leid.)*: calculi(s) *codd.* selibra *V*: et libra *codd. plerique*

85 (2 Bl., C.)

Catonis modo, Galle, Tusculanum
tota creditor urbe venditabat.
mirati sumus unicum magistrum,
summum grammaticum, optimum poetam
omnes solvere posse quaestiones,   5
unum deficere expedire nomen.
en cor Zenodoti, en iecur Cratetis!

Recently, Gallus, a creditor was offering Cato's Tusculan estate for sale all over the city. We wondered that this supreme teacher and excellent poet should be able to solve all conundrums, but fail to extricate just one name. See, the brains of Zenodotus, the heart of Crates!

1–7 Suet. *De Gramm.* 11.3 (p. 18 Kaster), post **84**: *et rursus* 'Catonis— Cratetis'.

7 Sacerdos, GLK VI p. 480: *Crates Cratetis . . . ut Bibaculus de Catone grammatico* 'en cor—Cratetis' (eadem Probus, GLK IV p. 29, 'iecur Cratetis').

6 deficere *Toup*: difficile *codd.*

86 (6 Bl., C.) dub.

Cato grammaticus, Latina Siren,
qui solus legit ac facit poetas

Cato the grammarian, the Latin Siren, who supremely chooses and makes poets.

1–2 Suet. *De Gramm.* 11.1 (p. 16 Kaster): *docuit* [sc. P. Valerius Cato] *multos et nobiles visusque est peridoneus praeceptor maxime ad poeticam tendentibus, ut quidem apparere vel his versiculis potest,* 'Cato—poetas'.

87 (5 Bl., C.)

nam meo grabato

for . . . my pallet

Auctor de dub. nom., GLK V p. 573: *crabatum antiqui; nunc grabatum generis neutri, ut Bibaculus* [babiculus *codd., corr. Clericus*] 'nam—grabato'.

88 (6a Bl.) dub.

duplici toga involutus

wrapped up in a double toga

Charis., p. 161 Barwick² = GLK I p. 127: *duplici Bibaculus;* 'duplici' *inquit* 'toga involutus', *non duplice.*

haec verba versui hendecasyllabo tribuit Lachmann ad Lucr. 3.954, plerique autem sermoni pedestri.

89 (4 Bl., C.)

Osce senex Catinaeque puer, Cu<ma>na meretrix

Oscan old man, boy of Catina, prostitute from Cumae

Schol. Iuv. 8.16 (p. 136 ed. Wessner, 1931) 'si tenerum attritus Catinensi pumice lumbum': *Catina oppidum Siciliae usque ad probra dissolutum notatur, ut et Bibaculus* (vibaculus *vel* vibalus *codd.*) 'Osce—meretrix'.

oste *codd., corr. Pithoeus*   Cu<ma>na *suppl. Pithoeus:* Campana *Nisbet*

In my opinion all the items gathered here probably belong to a single poet for whom we can construct a plausible life and literary career. Since, however, very different views have been taken, we may start with the names and titles given by our various ancient sources. The full name 'M. Furius ... cognomento Bibaculus' (according to Pliny, *NH* Praef. 24 'Bibaculus erat et vocabatur'), together with a birthplace (Cremona), and a date of birth (103 BC, probably some twenty years too early), appears only in Jerome (71*a*). 'Furius Bibaculus' is so called in a letter of Messalla Corvinus (71*b*, for which see also on Ticida, **100**) and in Horatian scholia discussing the unfortunate line about the Alps (**80**), which almost certainly came from a poem on the Gallic War. Our source for **81** (without mentioning the poet's name) gives a title *Annales Belli Gallici*, while scholia relating to **80** offer *Pragmatia Belli Gallici*; the former is more likely to be authentic (see below, p. 130). Macrobius has 'Furius in primo Annali' (**72**), 'Furius in quarto Annali' (**75**), elsewhere just a book number ('Furius in primo', etc.). See Kaster, *Suetonius, De Gramm.*, 96.

Horace gives indications that the writer of the epic on Gaul was himself a northerner: he describes Furius as 'pingui tentus omaso' (*Sat.* 2.5.40), using a Gallic word for ox-tripe (*Corpus Glossariorum Latinorum* ed. Goetz II. 138. 29) which suits the Cisalpine origin of Bibaculus. Also the nickname 'Alpinus' may hint at the writer's home region (Pseudacro on Hor. *Sat.* 1.10.36–7 =

71*d* 'poetam Gallum'), though it might refer only to the line about the Alps (Nisbet). So we have some reason to link Horace's Furius/Alpinus, a north-erner, with Jerome's M. Furius Bibaculus from Cremona. The epic poet is called just 'Furius' by Macrobius (quoting 72–9). It is undeniably strange that the writer of iambic poems (82), of lampoons against Julius Caesar and/or Augustus (71*c*), and of slight poems in various metres (83–9), is *never* called Furius by any ancient authority who quotes or mentions him, but always just 'Bibaculus'. I should add that Macrobius, our source for the 'Furius' epic fragments (72–9) once refers (*Sat.* 2.1.13) to a prose work by 'Furius Bibaculus'.

Some modern scholars have argued that the 'Furius' who wrote the very traditional epic on the Gallic War (anathema, it is thought, to Catullus and his friends) should be distinguished from the 'Bibaculus' of, in particular, the hendecasyllable poems (84–8) which seem to reflect the language, style, and literary outlook of Catullus. But not all poets divide neatly into 'parties'; the parallel of Varro Atacinus is relevant, even if Varro's poetic career was divided chronologically (see 105*a*) between 'traditional Roman' and 'Hellenistic/neoteric' phases.

One piece of evidence—though its interpretation is far from clear—provides a possible link between different literary styles in Furius Bibaculus (Hor. *Sat.* 1.10.36–7 = 71*d*):

> turgidus Alpinus *iugulat dum Memnona*, dumque
> defingit [vv. ll. diffingit, diffindit] Rheni luteum caput . . .

We can account for the Alps and the Rhine, but what about Memnon? J. Granarolo, *ANRW* I. 3. 305, thought of an excursus, devoted to Memnon, in the *Annales Belli Gallici*; that seems wildly unlikely. Courtney (p. 197) believes that the killing of Memnon occurred as a simile in the epic on Gaul; for such a comparison he quotes *Bell. Hisp.* 25.4 'hic, ut fertur Achillis Memnonisque congressus . . .' But I suspect that Horace has in his sights more than a mere simile. The myth of Memnon would be ideal material for a neoteric epyllion, with exotic eastern colouring (cf. Cinna's *Smyrna*), scope for learned debate (e.g. the location of Memnon's burial, cf. *Suppl. Hell.* 984.9–23), the pathos of the hero's death and grief of his mother Eos, a transformation and conclud-ing aetion (the yearly ritual immolation of the Memnonides). Nearly all of this can be seen from Ovid, *Met.* 13.576–622. When, in Virgil, Venus asks her husband to make arms for Aeneas, she says 'te filia Nerei, / te potuit lacrimis Tithonia flectere coniunx' (*Aen.* 8.383–4). Appeal to the precedent of Thetis and the arms of Achilles in the *Iliad* is entirely natural. But the parallel from Aurora and the arms of Memnon seems strangely remote—by Virgil's time the cyclic *Aethiopis* (Malcolm Davies, *Epicorum Graecorum Fragmenta*, 45–8) would have faded from the general consciousness. The existence of a recent literary treatment would give more substance to this allusion and also to *Aen.* 1.751, where Dido is keen to learn from Aeneas 'quibus Aurorae venisset filius armis'. A Shield of Memnon would provide the opportunity for a 'digression' with subsidiary myths (cf. the pseudo-Hesiodic *Shield of Heracles* and the scenes on the tapestry in Catullus 64). As we shall see, Catullus 11.9–12 may contain a reference to Furius Bibaculus' *Annales Belli Gallici*; it would be a nice touch if Propertius' imitation of that stanza were meant to recall another poem by Furius, 'cum quo Rhipaeos possim conscendere montis / ulteriusque domos vadere Memnonias' (1.6.3–4).

Courtney (p. 197) believes that, in describing the death of Memnon, Furius must have used the tasteless word *iugulare*. But the verb may be Horace's alone, condemning the quality of the poem (cf. Pseudacro, **71***d* cont. 'ipsum Memnona occidit describendo') as well as indicating its subject matter—somewhat similar is Juv. 7.151 'cum *perimit* saevos classis numerosa tyrannos', implying that the declamations on tyrannicide were themselves pretty gruesome. Horace's 'defingit [vv. ll. diffingit, diffindit, defindet]' clearly refers to a geographical set piece, but there is great uncertainty about reading and interpretation. See Courtney 197–8, and Nisbet, *Collected Papers*, 395, referring *luteum caput* to 'the silt-bearing waters of the Rhine before it enters Lake Constance', and commending the variant *diffingit*, 'remoulds' (? the transformation of water into ice). I shall return to the chronological implications for our poet of Horace, *Sat.* 1.10.36–7 = **71***d*.

Almost all scholars agree (an exception is J. Granarolo, *ANRW* I. 3. 305, following E. Castorina) that the birthdate of 103 BC which Jerome (**71***a*) gives for Furius Bibaculus is much too early, perhaps by twenty years: Valerius Cato (the subject of **84–6**) was born not before 96 BC, and it seems implausible that Bibaculus should have written as he does about Cato 'on the verge of extreme old age' (**84**.8 'ad summam prope nutriant senectam') if he himself were appreciably older. Both **84** and **85** could well come from a former pupil. Suppose that Cato's 'extreme old age' is something of an exaggeration, and that the old master was approaching 70 when Bibaculus wrote **84**: the poem would then be dated *c.*26 BC (note that the related **85** may be addressed to Cornelius Gallus, who died in 27 or 26 BC). If we lower the birthdate (103 BC) given by Jerome (**71***a*) by twenty years, Furius would have been in his late 50s when he composed **84**, and may have lived until at least 20 BC.

In that case Furius Bibaculus emerges as a little younger than Catullus. Many have wondered whether he might be the 'Furius' whom Catullus addresses, twice in conjunction with a certain Aurelius (poems 11 and 16) and twice by himself (23 and 26, with an anonymous but clear mention in 24). There is no obvious indication that this 'Furius' is a poet—indeed in 16 he and Aurelius are berated for their ignorance of poetic convention. But three points are worth bearing in mind.

(*a*) In 23.1 Catullus writes 'Furi, cui neque servus est neque arca', and an almost identical description of Furius recurs twice in poem 24 (lines 5 and 10). These words must have some special significance, and would be more amusing if Furius himself had written in similar terms about his own poverty.

(*b*) In poem 26 Catullus mocks Furius for his inability to service the mortgage on his family home ('Furi, villula vestra non ad Austri / flatus opposita est neque ad Favoni / nec saevi Boreae aut Apheliotae, / verum ad milia quindecim et ducentos, / o ventum horribilem atque pestilentem!'). Could Furius have written a poem praising the ideal location of his villa? Critics have also been reminded of **84** and **85** in which Bibaculus writes about the poverty of Valerius Cato and the loss of his Tusculan estate. But **84** certainly (and probably **85**) was composed long after the death of Catullus. The most that one can put forward is that the resemblance between Catullus 62 and **84–5** makes it likely that the 'Furius' is the same (even though the poems are separated by a long time-gap).

(*c*) If Catullus' Furius were the author of the *Annales Belli Gallici* (**72–81**), which no doubt eulogized Julius Caesar, there would be special point in Cat. 11.9–12 (see p. 126 above for Propertius' imitation) wherein Furius and Aurelius are prepared to go to the ends of the world with their friend Catullus, perhaps even to Gaul and Britain ('sive trans altas gradietur Alpes / Caesaris visens monimenta magni, / Gallicum Rhenum horribile aequor ulti- / mosque Britannos'). But Catullus cannot be traced after 54 BC; at the time when he wrote poem 11, Furius' *Annales Belli Gallici* (a large work in at least eleven books) is unlikely to have been much more than a future project. Nonetheless the identification of Catullus' Furius with the poet Furius Bibaculus remains quite possible, and has been accepted by Nisbet (*Collected Papers*, 393–4).

So Catullus may hint at the start of Furius Bibaculus' poetic career (Caesar's own commentaries on the war, published probably in 51 BC, would have been helpful). Did Furius also compose lampoons against Julius Caesar? Most scholars have deduced from Tac. *Ann.* 4.34.5 = **71***c* 'carmina Bibaculi et Catulli referta contumeliis Caesarum' that, since Catullus attacked only Julius Caesar, Bibaculus attacked only Octavian/Augustus, and I myself would incline to that view. Nisbet, however, remarks (*Collected Papers*, 394) that 'if his [Bibaculus'] lampoons had been aimed only at Augustus, one would expect Tacitus to have written "Catulli et Bibaculi"'. He adds that the enmities of the late Republic may have been intense but could be resolved very quickly—witness the reconciliation of Julius Caesar with both Catullus and Calvus. An alternative reason why Tacitus mentions Bibaculus before Catullus might be that the insults uttered by the former were more numerous and more damaging.

Tacitus (**71**c) proves beyond doubt that Furius Bibaculus attacked Octavian/Augustus. Praise of Julius Caesar (in the *Annales Belli Gallici*) would be entirely compatible with abuse of his adopted son, particularly if, after Caesar's death, Furius gravitated to the circle of Mark Antony, like Anser (Appendix). The decade of the 30s BC was marked by virulent personal attacks, in both prose and verse (Horace's *Epodes* are highly literary examples of the same tendency), and the lampoons of Bibaculus against Octavian would fit excellently into that period. It is strange that nothing of Bibaculus on Octavian has survived, since his poems were definitely available in the reign of Tiberius (**71**c 'carmina Bibaculi ... leguntur'), presumably in the time of Quintilian (10.1.96 = **82**a), perhaps still when Tacitus composed his *Annals*. One might have expected Suetonius to quote some choice specimens in his Life of Augustus (as he quotes Calvus, **28**, on Julius Caesar). Tacitus (*Ann.* 4.34.5) makes Cremutius Cordus speculate on the motives of Julius Caesar and Augustus in taking no action against Catullus, Bibaculus, or their poems. If Augustus' reason for tolerance was 'sapientia', one can say that his judgement has been vindicated by time. The elegiac epigram, Vers. Pop. 7 Courtney, p. 473, although firmly anonymous, might give us some idea of Bibaculus' manner.

Furius would have been wise to desist from attacking Octavian/Augustus after 30 BC, and three or four surviving pieces (**83–5**, perhaps also **86**), which can plausibly be dated to the 20s, show him in a gentler mood, commenting ironically but (at least in the case of Cato) affectionately on the old age of the scholars and teachers Orbilius and Valerius Cato. The style (and the hendecasyllable metre of **84–6**) might have seemed old-fashioned by then, but the craftsmanship is of a high order.

72–81 *Annales Belli Gallici*

These fragments, which comprise fourteen lines (part or whole), are interesting because, together with the *Bellum Sequanicum* of Varro Atacinus (**106–7**, only two lines), they give us an idea of that very traditional category, Roman military epic, in the middle of the first century BC. The style is what we might expect, showing strong influence from Homer (**72, 74, 75, 78**.1) and Ennius (**73, 75**, perhaps **74**). By this time the old epic tradition had fallen into some disrepute; everyone knows what Catullus (poem 36) said about the 'Annales

Volusi' (of which not a word survives!). To Horace, Furius' poetry, and especially his unhappy conceit about Jupiter 'spitting' snow over the Alps (**80**) seemed worthy of the utmost derision (*Sat.* 1.10.36–7 = 71*d* and 2.5.41). Possibly, however, Horace had a concealed political motive in disparaging Furius, since (probably in the period of the *Satires*) the latter was writing notorious lampoons (**71***c*) against Octavian. It might seem tactically astute for a protégé of Maecenas to ignore these and, instead, to try to destroy the reputation of their author on purely aesthetic grounds. 'Rheni luteum caput' (*Sat.* 1.10.37 = 71*d*) could recall Callimachus' Assyrian river which carries mud and débris (*Hymn* 2.108–9, cf. Hor. *Sat.* 1.4.11 'cum flueret lutulentus' of Lucilius); more clearly *Sat.* 2.5.40 'pingui tentus omaso' suggests the Greek παχύς which was a Callimachean term of disapprobation (fr. 398, cf. fr. 1.23–4). Virgil, on the other hand, took Furius' epic quite seriously—why else should he have made such close imitations of almost every surviving fragment?

There is no proof that Furius wrote about Julius Caesar's Gallic War (rather than one of the many earlier wars between Romans and Gauls), unless one believes that Catullus refers to this Furius and (prospectively) to this laudatory epic in poem 11. But in any case it seems most unlikely that, in this period, a poet would devote such a large epic (at least eleven books) to any other Gallic war. When exactly Furius composed his *Annales* remains a matter for dispute. Catullus 11.9–12 (55 or 54 BC) might be a reference to its first conception. An epic of this length could not be completed in a day—even allowing for the extraordinary speed of composition which Catullus ascribes to adherents of the old school. It would certainly have been convenient for Furius to use Caesar's own commentaries on the war, which may have been published in 51 BC; my notes on the fragments cite several passages from Caesar, but the parallels are all very speculative and may be illusory. No doubt there was a great amount of other source material available to the poet, both written (e.g. Caesar's *Epistulae* to the senate at the end of each campaigning year) and oral.

Furius would have been grievously disappointed if he had failed to present Caesar with at least part of the poem before the dictator's assassination in 44 BC, though even after then the *Annales Belli Gallici* could have found a distinguished and appreciative reader in Mark Antony, who played a part in the later stages of the war (C. B. R. Pelling, *Plutarch, Life of Antony*, 126), being mentioned by Caesar in *BG* 7.81, several times by Hirtius (who composed the final book 8) and perhaps therefore in Furius' text. This point is worth remembering in connection with Furius Bibaculus' subsequent attacks on Octavian (**71***c*). Horace's 'dumque' (*Sat.* 1.10.36 = 71*d*) seems to imply that Furius was still at work on the *Annales Belli Gallici* in the mid-30s BC; Nisbet (*Collected Papers*, 412) ingeniously speculates that, after finishing with

Caesar's war, Furius returned to the same theme in order to celebrate the exploits of Alfenus Varus (Virgil, *Ecl.* 6.6–7).

The title *Annales Belli Gallici* is provided by the Verona scholia on *Aeneid* 9.379 (=**81**), though without the poet's name; the alternative *Pragmatia* (i.e. πραγματεία, 'a systematic or scientific historical treatise', LSJ) is 'scholiastic jargon' (Courtney 198, cf. *TLL* X. 2. fasc. VII. 1119. 69 ff.).

72 (7 Bl., C.)

interea Oceani linquens Aurora cubile: Eos rises from Ocean in *Il.* 19.1–2 ἀπ' Ὠκεανοῖο ῥοάων / ὄρνυθ', cf. 22.197; for Homeric dawn-formulae see Kirk on *Il.* 2.48–9. But 'cubile' clearly comes from *Od.* 5.1 where the bed belongs to Tithonus (ἐκ λεχέων παρ' ἀγαυοῦ Τιθωνοῖο), and Furius' combination oddly suggests that Aurora has been sleeping with Oceanus.

Macrobius refers this line to *Aen.* 4.585 (= *Georgics* 1.447) 'Tithoni croceum linquens Aurora cubile', no doubt because the last three words are identical; he could have brought in Oceanus (and also 'interea') by citing *Aen.* 4.129 = 11.1 'Oceanum interea surgens Aurora reliquit'.

73 (8 Bl., C.)

1–3.   ille gravi subito devictus volnere habenas / misit equi lapsusque in humum defluxit et armis / reddidit aeratis sonitum: 'presumably a Gallic chieftain' (Courtney). If these lines reflect anything in Caesar, one might think of the brave deaths of two noble Gaulish brothers fighting on the Roman side: one of them, seeing his brother fall from his horse, 'incitato equo se hostibus obtulit atque interfectus est' (*BG* 4.12). But this fragment comes from the first book of Furius' epic, and so presumably from an earlier stage in the war. The context in Virgil's alleged imitation is quite different: Camilla's horsemen are not wounded but merely dismounting (*Aen.* 11.500–1); the verbal similarity lies between 'in humum defluxit' (Furius) and 'ad terram defluxit' (Virgil). In some ways closer would be *Aen.* 11.827–8 (the death of Camilla) 'linquebat habenas / ad terram non sponte fluens'. As Courtney says, Livy 2.20.3 'moribundus Romanus labentibus super corpus armis ad terram defluxit' may point to a passage (used by both Furius and Virgil?) in Ennius' *Annales.* Note also Horace, *Sat.* 2.1.15 'aut labentis equo describat vulnera Parthi' (did someone attempt a poem on Ventidius' Parthian victories?), which follows an apparently ironical mention of epic verse on a Gallic war (ibid. 14 'fracta pereuntis cuspide Gallos').

2–3. et armis / reddidit aeratis sonitum: cf. *Iliad* 4.504 etc. δούπησεν δὲ πεσών, ἀράβησε δὲ τεύχε᾿ ἐπ᾿ αὐτῶι, Ennius, *Annales* 411 Skutsch 'concidit et sonitum simul insuper arma dederunt', *Aen.* 10.488 'sonitum super arma dedere'.

74 (9 Bl., C.)

mitemque rigat per pectora somnum: the subject of 'rigat' might have been *nox*. This image of 'pouring' sleep over someone is common enough throughout the epic tradition, e.g. *Od.* 2.395 ἔνθα μνηστήρεσσιν ἐπὶ γλυκὺν ὕπνον ἔχευε [sc. Athena], Lucr. 4.907–8 'somnus per membra quietem / irriget', *Aen.* 1.692–3 'placidam per membra quietem / irrigat' (Skutsch on *Ann.* 499 postulates a similar line, probably containing 'irrigat', in Ennius). While both 'rigo' and 'irrigo' would naturally be followed by an accusative of the object watered (thus, metaphorically, *Aen.* 3.511 'fessos sopor irrigat artus'), the compound is occasionally used even in prose with an accusative of the liquid poured out (Cato, *De Agri Cultura* 36 'amurcam . . . inriges', 151.4 'aquam inrigato'). Such use of the simple verb may be slightly more audacious and poetical; Furius had a certain precedent in Cicero, *Aratea* fr. 33.173 Buescu 'propter Aquarius obscurum dextra rigat amnem'. Note also Livy 5.16.9 'aquam . . . rigabis' (paraphrasing an oracle).

mitem . . . somnum: no doubt from the Homeric γλυκὺν ὕπνον (e.g. *Od.* 2.395, quoted above). 'Mitis' can refer to the sweetness of ripe fruit.

75 (10 Bl., C.)

pressatur pede pes, mucro mucrone, viro vir: such descriptions of hand-to-hand fighting start with *Iliad* 13.130–1 φράξαντες δόρυ δουρί, σάκος σάκεϊ προθελύμνωι. / ἀσπὶς ἄρ᾿ ἀσπίδ᾿ ἔρειδε, κόρυς κόρυν, ἀνέρα δ᾿ ἀνήρ (the second line = *Il.* 16.215). 'Foot to foot' is added by Tyrtaeus (fr. 11.31 West καὶ πόδα παρ ποδὶ θείς, cf. Eur. *Heraclidae* 836 ποὺς ἐπαλλαχθεὶς ποδί). It is strange that Macrobius omits Ennius' version (*Ann.* 584 Skutsch 'premitur pede pes atque armis arma teruntur', though the text cannot be restored with certainty from the paraphrase of *Bell. Hispan.* 31.7); Skutsch (p. 725) considered it 'almost certain' (surely an overstatement) that Ennius had a second line ending 'viro vir', like those of Furius and Virgil (*Aen.* 10.361 'haeret pede pes, densusque viro vir'). S. J. Harrison (on *Aen.* 10.361, misquoting *Ann.* 584) points out that the ablative after 'haeret' is odd (one would expect a dative), perhaps influenced by Furius' 'pressatur'.

76 (11 Bl., C.)

quod genus hoc hominum, Saturno sancte create?: I have put a question mark at the end, although it is not entirely certain that the sense is completed with the line. In Virgil's imitation the question forms part of a protest at uncivilized behaviour: 'quod genus hoc hominum? quaeve hunc tam barbara morem / permittit patria?' (*Aen.* 1.539–40). If the same was true of Furius, one might think of a horrified Roman reaction to the infamous Gaulish practice of human sacrifice (Caesar, *BG* 6.16), cf. Cicero, *Pro Fonteio* 31 'quis enim ignorat eos usque ad hanc diem retinere illam immanem ac barbaram consuetudinem hominum immolandorum? quam ob rem quali fide, quali pietate existimatis esse eos qui etiam deos immortales arbitrentur hominum scelere et sanguine facillime posse placari?' See further Hunink on Lucan 3.405 'humanis ... cruoribus'. This would give point to the invocation of Roman Jupiter (and his epithet 'sancte'), so different from the gods whom the Gauls appease with human blood.

    Saturno sancte create: the first surviving example in Latin epic of the past participle of 'creo' + ablative of the parent's name (often corresponding to a Greek patronymic, as here to Κρονίδη, cf. Nisbet and Hubbard on Horace, *Odes* 1.12.50 'orte Saturno'). Earlier are the anonymous tragic fragment 'Erebo ... creata Nox' (Klotz, *Scaenicorum Romanorum Fragmenta*, I. 132 inc.) and (perhaps also tragic) Manilius fr. 2 Courtney (p. 110), 'Coe<o> creata Titano', on Lato. The ascription of 'Saturno sancte create' to Ennius (Spuria 11 Skutsch) is almost certainly a mistake. Ovid has 'creatus' + ablative of the parent a dozen times in the *Metamorphoses*, Virgil (surprisingly) only twice in the *Aeneid* (10.517, 543). 'Sanctus' is applied to deities in Latin epic from Livius Andronicus' *Odyssey* 12 Blänsdorf 'sancta puer Saturni filia regina'.

77 (12 Bl., C.)

rumoresque serunt varios et multa requirunt: 'serere' in such a context often implies deliberate mischief-making (*OLD sero*[1] 4, 'to sow the seeds of, foment'), and that is the object of the disguised Iuturna in *Aen.* 12.228 'rumoresque serit varios'. But that does not seem to fit 'multa requirunt' very well. So perhaps Furius describes a situation of general uncertainty. For the vulnerability of the Gauls to rumours, and their habit of questioning travellers, cf. Caesar, *BG* 4.5 and 6.20.

78–79

These two fragments must have been closely connected (Macrobius introduces **79** with 'deinde infra'). Perhaps they were separated by a short speech from Caesar, if (as I suspect) he is the subject of the verbs in both fragments. Then one might wonder whether **79** was preceded by a line such as 'talibus infractas adverso Marte cohortes' (cf. *Aen.* 11.730 'variisque instigat vocibus alas' of Tarchon trying to rally his Etruscans as they fly from Camilla). 'Reficitque ad proelia mentes' (**79**.2), coupled with Virgil's imitation 'reficitque in proelia *pulsos*' (*Aen.* 11.731), suggests that the soldiers have suffered a recent reverse and are in special need of encouragement from their general. Caesar describes such situations in *BG* 2.25 and 5.52.

78 (13 Bl., C.)

1. nomine quemque ciet: clearly echoing *Iliad* 22.415 ἐξ ὀνομακλήδην ὀνομάζων ἄνδρα ἕκαστον (Priam appeals to the Trojans to let him visit Achilles); the Latin preserves a hint of the Greek pleonasm, since, even without 'nomine', *cieo* can mean 'to call on by name'. If (as suggested above) **78** and **79** describe Caesar encouraging his troops after a setback, one might compare *BG* 2.25 'centurionibusque nominatim appellatis . . . redintegrato animo . . .' and 5.52.4. Valerius Flaccus has 'nomine quemque premens' (4.649).

1–2. dictorum tempus adesse / commemorat: puzzling, at least to me. A natural translation would be 'he recalls [whether to himself or to his hearers] that now is the time for words'; *tempus*= the proper time or due time can be coupled with either genitive or dative (*OLD* 8 b). If that means 'it occurs to me that now I ought to make a speech', the sentiment is feeble and jejune— even more so if 'commemorat'='he mentions'. J. Granorolo (*ANRW* I. 3. 350) translates 'il rappelle que le moment est venu de tenir les promesses qu'on a faites' (alternatively 'que le moment est venu de l'accomplissement des oracles'). Conington (on 11.731) was also troubled, offering 'nomine quemque ciet ductorum: tempus adesse . . .' (postulating that the sense of the second clause was incomplete).

I suggest emending 'dictorum' to 'factorum': 'he recalls to them that now is the time for glorious deeds' (*OLD factum* 2 a, 'a mighty deed, achievement, exploit'). The corruption could have been caused by 'dictis' in **79**.1 (quoted by Macrobius immediately after **78**). Or else it could be an example of 'polar' corruption into the opposite: 'deeds' and 'words' are often contrasted in such a context, e.g. Livy 7.32.12 ' "facta mea, non dicta vos, milites" inquit, "sequi volo" ' (parallels in S. P. Oakley ad loc.). Professor Nisbet thinks of an alternative remedy, 'abisse' ('the time for words has passed') in place of 'adesse'.

79 (14 Bl., C.)

1–2. **confirmat dictis simul atque exsuscitat acris / ad bellandum animos, reficitque ad proelia mentes:** if 'animos' is the object of 'confirmat' as well as of 'exsuscitat' (and indeed *confirmo* (*OLD* 2) is sometimes linked with 'animum' or 'animos'), then one must detach 'acris', which fits only 'exsuscitat' (proleptically) and not 'confirmat'. Alternatively there might have been an object for 'confirmat' in the previous line; above (on **78–9**) I suggest 'cohortes', taking a hint from *Aen.* 11.730 'alas'. In that case Macrobius' citation would be syntactically less complete, but he is only concerned with 'nomine quemque ciet' (**78**.1) and 'reficitque ad proelia mentes' (**79**.2) which Virgil combines to form *Aen.* 11.731 'nomine quemque vocans, reficitque in proelia pulsos'.

2. **ad bellandum animos:** note Caesar, *BG* 5.49 'eos . . . ad dimicandum animo confirmat' (sc. Caesar), from a situation of the sort mentioned on **78–9** above.

80 (15 Bl., C.)

Iuppiter hibernas cana nive conspuit Alpes: this was the notorious metaphor (Quintilian 8.6.17) which Horace derided so mercilessly, substituting 'Furius' for 'Iuppiter' in *Sat.* 2.5.41, and calling Furius 'Alpinus' (because of his unfortunate line about the Alps) in *Sat.* 1.10.36. English can (without offence) speak of the sky 'spitting' with rain or snow when there is only a light precipitation. Not so Greek or Latin; even if there were a similar expression (for which no evidence exists) in colloquial Latin, that would not justify Furius' use of it in epic poetry. One is almost reminded of Strepsiades' untutored explanation for the rain (Aristophanes, *Clouds* 373).

hibernas ... Alpes: such use of an adjective instead of an adverb expressing time is grandiose or mock-grandiose style (Nisbet, comparing e.g. 'hesternus', 'matutinus').

conspuit Alpes: the prefix suggests all over (Petronius 23.3 'immundissimo me basio conspuit').

81 (16 Bl., C.)

hic qua ducebant vastae divortia fessae: various interpretations are possible. *Divortium* is explained in *OLD* 1 as 'a point where a road, river, or sim. branches, parting of the ways, junction'; our fragment is quoted with a note that 'vastae ... fossae' is genitive. 'Ducebant' might then be intransitive (*OLD ducere* 9, 'to lead, run', of a road), or transitive with an object to follow or understood ('led <them>'). Interpreting 'divortia fossae' thus, I can only imagine a single ditch which then branches in a 'Y'. On the other hand, J. Granorolo takes 'vastae ... fossae' as nominative plural and 'divortia' as accusative: 'là où d'amples fossés formaient des lignes de démarcation'.

Perhaps a more promising meaning for *divortium* here is 'an intervening strip' (*OLD* 3); the word might then apply to a gap separating two parts of an incomplete ditch. In Caesar, *BG* 7.71 some Gallic horsemen escape from Alesia by night through a gap in the Roman circumvallation ('qua nostrum opus erat intermissum'). As elsewhere (cf. e.g. on **76**) Virgil's imitation may hint at the general context of the original. The Verona scholiast quotes our fragment on *Aen.* 9.379 'obiciunt equites sese ad divortia nota', where the reference is to cavalry at night—though the horsemen in Virgil are trying to prevent, rather than to effect, an escape.

82 (iambi)

From Quintilian we may deduce the following points about Bibaculus.

1.   Unlike Archilochus and Hipponax (and, from the Hellenistic age, e.g. Callimachus and Herodas), Bibaculus did not write a separate book containing only iambic poems; like Catullus he interspersed his iambics with poems in other metres. As M. Winterbottom says ('Problems in Quintilian', *BICS*

suppl. 25 (1970), 191), however we deal with 'quibusdam interpositus' (I follow Russell's Loeb), that surely was the sense intended.

2.   Unlike Horace (to whom Winterbottom, 'Problems', rightly refers 'illi') but (again) like Catullus, Bibaculus did not use an ἐπωιδός (in the technical sense, LSJ II b, of the shorter verse in an iambic couplet, exemplified in Horace, *Epodes* 1–10). As Catullus shows, Furius would still be able to display in his iambic poems metrical variation between the ordinary iambic trimeter (**83**, cf. Catullus 52), the pure iambic trimeter (Cat. 4 and probably 29), Catullus' favourite 'limping' iambic or choliamb (Cat. 8, etc.), and perhaps something more complex like Cat. 25.

It is natural to connect these references to Furius Bibaculus as an iambic poet who displayed 'acerbitas' with Tacitus, *Ann.* 4.34.5 (=**71c**) on Bibaculus' share in the poems 'crammed with insults against the Caesars'. But it seems probable that not all Furius' lampoons of Octavian were written in iambics. Consider the case of Catullus, cited in the same passage of Tacitus and linked with Bibaculus as a leading writer of Latin iambi by both Quintilian and Diomedes (**82a** and *b*). According to our present evidence Catullus insulted Julius Caesar once in iambics (29), twice in hendecasyllables (54, 57), and once in elegiacs (93). Catullus, at least, clearly uses the term *iambus* to indicate abusive content 'without reference to the metrical form which gave its name to the genre' (Fordyce on Cat. 40.2), awkward though this may have been for writers who were primarily concerned to classify works according to their metre. Furius may also have composed poems in iambic metre which (like Catullus 4 and 8) were not abusive; **83**, on Orbilius, need not have been hostile in tone.

83 (3 Bl., C.)

Orbilius ubinam est, litterarum oblivio?: Suetonius clearly regarded the phrase 'litterarum oblivio' as in apposition to Orbilius (though if he knew only this isolated line he might have been mistaken), indicating that the ferocious old schoolmaster lost all memory of the literature which he used to teach ('amissa iam pridem memoria, ut versus Bibaculi docet'). In that case 'ubinam est . . .?' might imply that Orbilius is no longer himself—absent in mind, present only in body. Other interpretations are possible. Kaster ('Suetonius, *De Grammaticis et Rhetoribus*' (1995), 136) commends the view of Hartmann (*Mnemosyne*, 29 (1901), 147) that Orbilius' brutal teaching methods produced forgetfulness of literature in his pupils, while Nisbet (*Collected Papers*, 393, following Schanz–Hosius, *Geschichte der römischen*

Literatur[4], I, p. 580) suggests that Orbilius in his old age was forgotten by literature, 'literature's forgotten man'. This last seems to cohere better with 'ubinam est . . .?' than Hartmann's interpretation. In any case the use of 'oblivio' appears idiosyncratic.

Presumably Suetonius knew from some other source that Orbilius lived to almost 100 (so that he would have died in 15 BC); according to *De Gramm.* 9.3 Orbilius himself, already in extreme old age (*praesenex*) complained in one of his writings about his own poverty ('pauperem se et habitare sub tegulis quodam scripto fatetur'). If Orbilius was then about 80 (as *praesenem* might suggest), he had not lost his memory—supposing that Suetonius understood this line correctly—*c.*33 BC. Perhaps therefore Bibaculus composed the poem in the 20s BC, when he also wrote sympathetically about the impoverished old age of Valerius Cato (**84–5** and perhaps **86**).

84–85

We have here, almost certainly, the luxury of two short but complete poems. Catullus too has many pieces of seven or eight lines written in Phalaecian hendecasyllables, the favourite metre of his circle. **84–5** at least do not suffer from comparison with Catullus. Their style is very elegant, and the subject matter would fit a member of Catullus' group: both poems express affectionate but ironical sympathy for P. Valerius Cato the poet, scholar, and teacher (see Appendix, p. 429). **84**.1 'mei . . . Catonis' suggests a personal friendship with Cato similar to that claimed by Helvius Cinna (**14** 'nostri . . . Catonis'). But Cato was still a *pupillus* (i.e. he had not yet reached puberty) during the time of Sulla (Suet. *De Gramm.* 11.1) and so he can hardly have been born earlier than 95 BC. One may allow for some exaggeration in **84**.8 'ad summam prope . . . senectam', but the phrase naturally suggests a date in the 20s BC. **85**, on the loss of Cato's Tusculan estate, could have been composed somewhat earlier; **84**.7 'tegula sub una' may refer to the more cramped accommodation which Cato took up after being evicted from his estate. If the Gallus of **85**.1 were Cornelius, we would have to date that poem before the elegist's disgrace and death (27 or 26 BC). It was probably also in the 20s BC that Bibaculus wrote on the old age of another famous *grammaticus*, Horace's teacher Orbilius (**83** above).

84 (1 Bl., C.)

Courtney (p. 193) compares this poem with an epigram by Leonidas of Tarentum (*Anth. Pal.* 6.226 = 87 Gow–Page) on the small property which supported Cleiton for 80 years (unfortunately the text is very corrupt).

From a material point of view Cato's academic career ended in failure (cf. **85**). Making a virtue out of necessity, Bibaculus humorously presents it as a philosophical triumph: *disciplinae* (4) and *sapientia* (5) suggest philosophy rather than literature, and *assecutus* (5) implies that Cato's present condition was deliberately sought and achieved. His longevity, too, was the product of a simple vegetarian diet (6–8), so often lauded by philosophers; see Nisbet and Hubbard's notes on Horace, *Odes* 1.31.15–16 'me pascunt olivae, / me cichorea levesque malvae' (followed by prayer for a healthy old age). N–H quote, among other passages, Cicero, *Tusc. Disp.* 5.89 'ipse [Epicurus] quam parvo est contentus! nemo de tenui victu plura dixit' and Jerome, *Adv. Iovin.* 2.11 'Epicurus . . . omnes libros suos replevit holeribus et pomis, et vilibus cibis dicit esse vivendum'.

2. depictas minio assulas: I follow Kaster in taking this phrase to be in apposition to 'domum' (1), 'mere splinters painted bright red'. *Assula* can apply to a splinter of wood or a chip of stone. Vitruvius laments the current fashion for daubing whole walls with *minium* (cinnabar): 'at nunc passim plerumque toti parietes inducuntur' (7.5.8); he adds (ibid.) that it was an expensive business, which (as Kaster says) goes against the impression of Cato's poverty—or at least creates an amusing paradox.

Nisbet, wishing to avoid any hint of luxury, wonders whether *assulas* could refer to the figure of Priapus (which was also painted red, cf. Lejay on Horace, *Sat.* 1.8.5), whether composed of bits of wood nailed together, or even daubed on a garden fence (he notes the drawing of *sopiones* on the façade of a tavern in Catullus 37.10). He would like a solution that concentrated on the garden ('the real subject of the poem') rather than the house.

3. custodis . . . hortulos Priapi: an alternative correction of the confused manuscript tradition is 'custodes . . . hortuli Priapos' (Scaliger), but it seems unlikely that a small garden would contain more than one figure of Priapus (for his role as protector of gardens, cf. e.g. Virg. *Ecl.* 7.34 'custos es pauperis horti'). Since Bibaculus is humorously presenting Cato in terms which suggest a philosopher rather than a literary scholar (see above), it is worth mentioning that *hortulus* (whether singular or plural, *OLD* 3) sometimes denotes the garden in which a philosopher teaches his disciples, e.g. [Virgil], *Ciris* 3 'Cecropius . . . hortulus'. Diminutives are, of course, much beloved by neoteric poets (e.g. Helvius Cinna, **13.**3–4); this one occurs in Catullus 61.88.

5.   sapientiam: at first sight not altogether appropriate (Baehrens conjectured 'patientiam'). But Bibaculus paradoxically presents Cato's financial embarrassment as a philosophical triumph of spirit over matter: by mental training (*disciplinis*, 4) Cato has reduced his physical needs to a bare minimum, and so attained (*assecutus*) true wisdom.

6–7.   The sequence of diminishing numerals (three little cabbages, two bunches of grapes, one roof-tile) seems deliberate, discouraging emendation of 'una'.

selibra: 'half a pound' (one would expect a long first syllable, but it is short in all poetic occurrences). The Twelve Tables (Warmington, *Remains of Old Latin*, vol. III, p. 438) had allowed a debtor held under constraint one pound of *far* (i.e. *puls*, cf. Maecenas, **184**) per day.

7.   racemi: like Catullus (e.g. 1.4 'meas esse aliquid putare nugas'), Bibaculus is prepared to start his hendecasyllable with an iamb (also **85.**1, 'Catonis', and **86.**1, 'Cato', if by the same poet). Later Roman taste rejected this licence: in Martial the spondee is invariable, and Pliny wished to rewrite Catullus 1.4 (above) as 'nugas esse aliquid meas putare', in order to make it less harsh ('ut obiter emolliam Catullum conterraneum meum', *NH* Praef. 1).

85 (2 Bl., C.)

Valerius Cato has defaulted on a loan and consequently been forced to hand over his Tusculan estate to a creditor, who then tries to sell it all over Rome. The very fact that Cato had owned a country estate in the fashionable and exclusive region of Tusculum suggests that he had once been prosperous; this poem shows an earlier stage of his financial decline than **84** (by which time he has taken far inferior lodgings). If the 'Gallus' of **85.**1 is Cornelius, we would have to date this little poem before 27 or 26 BC (the elegist's disgrace and death), and perhaps before 30 BC when Gallus participated in the final attack on Cleopatra's Egypt, staying on to become the first Roman governor.

The essence of the poem lies in Bibaculus' clever manipulation of the technical language of literary scholarship and money-lending. The perfectly balanced lines 5–6 are full of double (indeed multiple) meanings, whereby each activity is described in terms which are almost appropriate to the other. Critics have noted a certain resemblance between this poem and Catullus 26 (which is even shorter, at five lines). There a Furius is mocked because his small villa is 'exposed' (*opposita*, a technical term of finance), not to the winds of North, South, East, or West, but to a fearsome mortgage. That Furius may possibly be our poet (as in Cat. 11, which might allude to the *Annales Belli Gallici*); if so he could have taken from Catullus the idea of punning on financial terms. But it seems likely that Furius Bibaculus wrote this poem at least twenty years after the death of Catullus.

1.   Catonis: for the initial iambus, see on **84**.7 'racemi'.

Galle: too common a name for us to have any confidence in the hypothesis that this is Cornelius Gallus. But the elegist would certainly have been interested in Valerius Cato, and may have mentioned him (some years earlier?) as a stern critic of poetry (see **145**.9).

Tusculanum: neuter = an estate at Tusculum. 'Located on the *via Latina* in the cool hills of Latium *c.* 23 km SE of Rome, Tusculum in the late Republic was the favourite inland spot for the retreats of Roman notables and other wealthy persons' (Kaster on Suetonius, *De Gramm.* 11.3, with further material, pp. 159–60).

2.   tota creditor urbe venditabat: 'tota . . . urbe' and 'venditabat' might imply that the creditor is having some difficulty in finding a buyer (perhaps because of sympathy with the dispossessed), but also stress the public humiliation of Cato, whose financial problems are revealed to all and sundry. Cicero used the same verb when, in 61 BC, his brother had been in a hurry to sell his estate in the same region: 'Tusculanum venditat ut, si possit, emat Pacilianam domum' (*Ad Att.* 1.14 = 14 SB. 7).

3.   mirati sumus: Cato's practical problems cause astonishment also in **84**.4 'miratur'.

3–4.   unicum magistrum, / summum grammaticum, optimum poetam: Bibaculus distinguishes Cato's three spheres of activity, in all of which he excels: teacher, scholar, poet. This (and **86**.1) is almost the first occurrence of the term 'grammaticus' in Latin. With regard to the earlier (Cicero, *De Or.* 1.10 (55 BC) 'huic studio litterarum, quod profitentur ei qui grammatici vocantur'), Kaster (Suetonius, *De Gramm.* p. 87) remarks that 'ei qui . . . vocantur' may indicate Cicero's sense that he is using a term not yet fully naturalized in Latin. Probably some years before Bibaculus wrote this poem, the aristocratic Messalla Corvinus referred to Cato (with unmistakable disdain) by the Latin equivalent 'litterator' (**71***b* = Suet. *De Gramm.* 4.2).

5–6.   omnes solvere posse quaestiones, / unum deficere expedire nomen: these lines are beautifully balanced: 'omnes–unum', 'solvere–expedire', 'posse–deficere', 'quaestiones–nomen', with the corresponding words in the same order except for 'solvere posse–deficere expedire'. On the theme of an intellectual unable to cope with the practicalities of life, Kaster quotes Hermesianax fr. 7.93–4 Powell (Socrates in love) οὐδέ τι τέκμαρ / εὗρε, λόγων πολλὰς εὑρόμενος διόδους (in Propertius 2.34.28 'rerum dicere posse vias' will not help Lynceus).

5. **omnes solvere posse quaestiones:** 'The business of a *grammaticus* is λύειν ζητήματα' (Courtney). A selection will give an idea of these literary/mythological conundrums, which were often used to tease or upset scholars and teachers: (*a*) Suetonius, *Tib.* 70 'grammaticos ... eius modi fere quaestionibus experiebatur: quae mater Hecubae, quod Achilli nomen inter virgines fuisset, quid Sirenes cantare sint solitae?'; (*b*) even when off duty, the schoolmaster might be pursued by demands such as 'dicat / nutricem Anchisae, nomen patriamque novercae / Anchemoli, dicat quot Acestes vixerit annis, / quot Siculi Phrygibus vini donaverit urnas' (Juvenal 7.233–6, see Courtney's notes ad loc.); (*c*) the γραμματικοί took pleasure in enquiring εἰ κύνας εἶχε Κύκλωψ (Philip, *Anth. Pal.* 11.321.6 = 60 Gow–Page, who comment 'the silence of the *Odyssey* might be used as an argument on one side, Theocritus 6.9 on the other'). More material in W. J. Slater, 'Aristophanes of Byzantium and Problem-Solving in the Museum', *CQ* N S 32 (1982), 336–49, R. A. Kaster, 'A Schoolboy's Burlesque from Cyrene?', *Mnemosyne*, N S 37 (1984), 457–8.

solvere: as well as being the appropriate term (corresponding to λύειν) for *quaestiones* (ζητήματα), the verb can also mean 'to pay off a debt'—just what Cato cannot do in the next line.

6. **unum:** it is not as though Cato had a multiplicity of debts; a single one has sufficed to bring him down.

deficere: 'to be unable ... to accomplish a task, falter, fail' (*OLD* 9 (*c*), with infinitive, quoting this line). The verb can also be used absolutely, of a personal failing financially (Juv. 7.129 'Matho deficit').

expedire nomen: when Cicero asks Atticus to settle the debts standing against his name, he writes 'nomina mea, per deos, expedi, exsolve' (*Ad Att.* 16.6 = 414 SB .3). This use of *nomen* can be traced from *OLD* 22 'an entry (of a loan etc.) in a ledger (from the practice of writing the name of the creditor or the debtor at the head of the page)'. Thence the word comes to mean a debt or loan (*OLD* 23); sometimes the *nomen* seems to be that of the borrower (as 'nomina mea' in Cicero, above), sometimes of the lender (*In Verrem* 2.1.28 'nomina sua exegisse'). Perhaps *nomen* in this usage came to be thought of as simply 'a debt or a loan', without too much concern as to whether the 'name' was that of the lender or borrower. Kaster (p. 160) comments that Cato was unable 'to extract a single name' (viz. his own) from the creditor's ledger (citing Cicero, *Ad Att.* 13.29 = 300 SB. 2 'Dollabellae nomen iam expeditum videtur'), but I think that the dominant meaning of 'unum ... nomen' here is 'a single debt' (though my translation tries to keep something of the multiple meaning).

expedire: 'to settle (a debt)', *OLD* 3 (*b*). The verb could also be used of solving a *quaestio* (Seneca, *De Beneficiis* 6.7.2 'haec quaestio facile expedietur'), like *explicare* in Quintilian 1.2.14 'quaestiones explicet'. Furthermore *expedire* can mean 'to supply, provide' (*OLD* 6); since the solving of a *quaestio* often involved supplying a name (e.g. of Hecuba's mother or of Achilles on Scyros), that might be yet another secondary sense of 'expedire nomen' here.

7. **en cor Zenodoti, en iecur Cratetis:** for the ironical *en*, one might compare the comment of Augustus when he saw a group of Roman citizens not wearing their toga, 'en Romanos rerum dominos gentemque togatam' (Suet. *Div. Aug.* 40.5, quoting *Aen.* 1.282). We cannot tell whether Bibaculus thought of *cor* and *iecur* as nominative or accusative (either would be legitimate).

cor Zenodoti: 'the intelligence of Zenodotus', the great scholar who came from Ephesus to Alexandria where he worked under the first two Ptolemies (see Pfeiffer, *History of Classical Scholarship: From the Beginnings to the End of the Hellenistic Age* (Oxford, 1968), 105 ff.). He was known as the first διορθωτής of Homer (ibid. 94), and that may have suggested the comparison with Valerius Cato, since the latter (according to the spurious but interesting Adesp. **240**, lines prefixed to Hor. *Sat.* 1.10) performed the same office for Lucilius (line 3 'emendare', which would be a fair equivalent to διορθοῦν).

iecur Cratetis: 'iecur' is puzzling. The liver was associated with strong emotions—grief, frustrated love, and especially anger (see Nisbet and Hubbard on Horace, *Odes* 1.13.4 'fervens difficili bile tumet iecur'). Here, however, we expect something connected with intellectual prowess (akin to *cor*). Such a meaning for *iecur* is found very rarely, but it does occur in a punning attack on examiners of entrails, 'plusque ex alieno iecore sapiunt quam ex suo' (Pacuvius, *Chryses* 105 Warmington). See Kaster's discussion (*De Gramm.*, p. 161).

Crates of Mallos in Cilicia went to Pergamum in the reign of Eumenes II (197–158 BC); see Pfeiffer, *History of Classical Scholarship*, 235 ff. The Romans had a special reason to cherish his memory, since in 168 while participating in an Attalid embassy, he fell down a manhole on the Palatine Hill and broke his leg. During his enforced inactivity Crates gave lectures and held discussions (Suet. *De Gramm.* 2.1).

86 dub. (6 Bl., C.)

Subject matter, style, and metre (line 1 Căto, cf. **84**.7 and **85**.1) are all consistent with ascription of these lines to Furius Bibaculus. But it seems clear that

Suetonius, who quotes and attributes **84** and **85**, did not know the author-ship of **86**. There can be no question of these two lines forming a complete poem. But they do look like the opening of a poem, which perhaps contrasted Cato's artistic and intellectual eminence with his practical shortcomings (as **84** and **85**).

1. Cato grammaticus, Latina Siren: Latin and Greek are sharply juxta-posed in the first phrase no less than the second—perhaps another indication that 'grammaticus' was not yet wholly naturalized in Latin (see on **85**.3–4). This elegant balance is reminiscent of what we find in **85**.5–6.

Latina Siren: this phrase suggests the sweetness of Cato's poetry, and also (probably) the attractiveness of his teaching. Cicero (*De Fin.* 5.49) reflects on the thirst for knowledge which draws people to the Sirens, con-tinuing with his own translation of *Od.* 12.184–91 (Cicero, fr. 30 Blänsdorf). According to Christodorus (*Anth. Pal.* 2.305) Apuleius was nur-tured by the Αὐσονὶς ... Σειρήν. In Latin this kind of phrase often contains an amusing incongruity between the nationality and the name, e.g. Horace, *Odes* 2.16.38 'Graiae ... Camenae', 4.8.20 'Calabrae Pierides'—what could be less Greek than the Camena, less Calabrian than the Pierides? Compare e.g. 'the English Satie', 'the Australian Diaghilev'. On a more earthy level, Roman satire and invective revelled in expressions such as 'the Medea of the Palatine' (Cicero, *Pro Caelio* 18). See further Nisbet on Cicero, *In Pis-onem* 20 'barbaro Epicuro', Wankel on Demosthenes, *De Corona* 242 ἀρουραῖος Οἰνόμαος.

2. qui solus legit ac facit poetas: 'visusque est peridoneus praeceptor, maxime ad poeticam tendentibus' (Suet. *De Gramm.* 11.1, followed by quota-tion of these two lines from which the statement is seemingly derived). 'Legit' is usually (Courtney 195, Kaster p. 153 (who allows 'selects' as a secondary meaning)) understood as 'reads', equivalent to *praelegit*, i.e. he reads and expounds poetic texts to his pupils (cf. *De Gramm.* 16.3 where Suetonius almost certainly misinterprets Domitius Marsus, **176**). I would prefer to take it as = 'chooses', ἐγκρίνει; Cato 'could be said to have formed a new canon single-handed' (Nisbet, *Collected Papers*, 392, cf. Pfeiffer, *History of Classical Scholarship*, 206, N–H on Horace, *Odes* 1.1.35).

solus: 'above all others' (*OLD solus* 6 'having no equal', cf. *unus* 8).

facit: through Cato's encouraging criticism of younger poets (P. G. Brown *ap.* Nisbet, *Collected Papers*, 392 n. 8).

87 (5 Bl., C.)

nam meo grabato: as it stands, the quotation does not suffice to establish neuter *grabatum* (elsewhere always *-us,* masculine); cf. Maecenas, **192,** Rabirius, **233,** both from the same treatise. Perhaps the quote was originally longer (e.g. 'nam meo grabato / nullum vilius est'), and a later scribe or grammarian unintelligently thought to economize by stopping at the noun.

grabato: from the Greek κράβατος or κράβαττος (perhaps the original term for a Macedonian soldier's portable camp-bed) which became widely diffused in the Hellenistic and Roman periods. In *Mark* 2: 11 Christ says to the paralytic ἆρον τὸν κράβαττόν σου ('take up thy bed', AV). The first Latin occurrence, in the *Satires* of Lucilius (251 Marx 'tres a Deucalione grabati restibus tenti') shows that a *grabatus* is very much a poor man's bed; so too in Catullus 10.22 'fracti qui veteris pedem grabati'.

88 dub. (6a Bl.)

duplici toga involutus: Courtney (p. 199) does not include this fragment, suspecting that it comes from Bibaculus' prose *Lucubrationes* (mentioned by the Elder Pliny, *NH*, Praef. 24). On the other hand, the phrase could scan as part of a hendecasyllable, and is not obviously unpoetical. Charisius' confidence that Bibaculus wrote 'duplici' rather than 'duplice' would be more firmly based if the long 'i' were guaranteed by metre. In fact 'duplici' is almost invariable ('duplice' Hor. *Sat.* 2.2.122 and Ausonius).

89 (4 Bl., C.)

Osce senex Catinaeque puer, Cu<ma>na meretrix: the line is quoted by a scholiast on Juv. 8.16 'si tenerum attritus Catinensi pumice lumbum', where the pumice from Catina in Sicily is being used as a depilatory (cf. e.g. Pliny, *NH* 36.154 'ii pumices qui sunt in usu corporum levandorum feminis, iam quidem et viris'). That ought to provide some sort of context for 'Catinaeque puer'. 'Osce senex' could also have disreputable connotations, as shown by Porphyrio on Horace, *Sat.* 1.5.62 'Campanum in morbum': 'Campani, qui Osci dicebantur, ore immundi habiti sunt, unde etiam obscenos dictos putant quasi Oscenos' (see further J. N. Adams, *Latomus,* 42 (1983), 100). This line seems more likely to have come from an elegiac epigram than from a hexameter poem; although not iambic, it hints (more than any other surviving fragment of Bibaculus) at the 'acerbitas' which Quintilian (10.1.96=**82***a*) found in our poet.

Cu<ma>na meretrix: as an alternative emendation of the corrupt 'Cuna' Nisbet suggests 'Campana' = 'Capuan' (rather than 'Campanian'). Capua was more associated with luxury and loose living than Cumae. A. Otto, *Die Sprichwörter der Römer* (1890), 68, actually cites this line s.v. *Campanus*, though printing 'Cumana'.

Q. Mucius Scaevola

90

Plin. *Epist.* 5.3.5 (cf. **19j**, al.): *ego verear ne me non satis deceat* [sc. 'versiculos severos parum' (5.3.2) facere] *quod decuit ... L. Sullam, Q. Catulum, Q. Scaevolam, Servium Sulpicium ... ?*

... Ought I to fear that [the writing of saucy little poems] might be judged inappropriate to me—something which did not discredit ... L. Sulla, Q. Catulus, Q. Scaevola, Servius Sulpicius ... ?

91 (1 Bl., C.)

canescet saeclis innumerabilibus

It [sc. the *Marius* of M. Cicero] will grow white over countless centuries.

Cic. *De legibus* 1.2 (loquitur Q. Cicero): *dum Latinae loquentur litterae, quercus huic loco non deerit quae Mariana dicatur, eaque, ut ait Scaevola de fratris mei Mario,* 'canescet—innumerabilibus'.

92 (2 Bl., C.)

lassas clunes

exhausted buttocks

Charis., p. 128 B.² = GLK I p. 101: *clunes feminino genere dixit ... et Scaevola:* 'lassas clunes'. *sed Verrius Flaccus masculino genere dici probat.* Auctor de dub. nom. GLK V p. 575: *clunes generis feminini, ut Scaevola:* 'lassas clunes'.

90

There are two candidates for identification with Pliny's Scaevola the poet: (*a*) the augur (RE Mucius 21), son of the consul of 174 BC; he lived to a great age, and must have died not long after we last hear of him in 88–7 BC; (*b*) perhaps his grandson (RE Mucius 23), tribune of the people in 54 BC, on good terms with Q. Cicero in 59 BC (*Ad Quintum Fratrem* 1.2.13 = 2 Shackleton Bailey, who challenges the common opinion that Scaevola had been a member of Quintus' *cohors* in Asia), and with M. Cicero at Ephesus in 51 BC (*Ad Fam.* 3.5 = 68 SB. 5). It seems to me that **91** certainly belongs to the younger Scaevola, and the uninhibited sexual language of **92** (cf. Ovid, *Tr.* 2.434, discussed on Ticida, **101**) sits much more comfortably in the 50s or 40s BC than *c.*100 BC— though the fact that in Pliny's list (**90**) Scaevola is preceded by Q. Catulus (cos. 102 BC) might make one think of the augur (thus A. N. Sherwin-White, *The Letters of Pliny* (Oxford, 1966), 317, unaware of any verses ascribed to a Scaevola). Could Pliny be confused? Scaevola, it seems, was not significant enough as a poet to be worth mentioning among the 'nomina tanta' (442) who wrote naughty verses in the 50s and 40s BC (Ovid, *Tristia* 2.427–42). In the Garland of Philip there is a Greek epigram (Scaevola 1 Gow–Page = *Anth. Pal.* 9.217) attributed to a Mucius Scaevola, highly praised by Gow and Page who allow it to the *tribunus plebis* of 54 BC.

91 (1 Bl., C.)

canescet saeclis innumerabilibus: as the *De legibus* makes clear, Scaevola wrote this line with reference to M. Cicero's hexameter poem *Marius* (Courtney 174–8); in the Dialogue Quintus transfers it to the *quercus Mariana*. Since Scaevola was personally known to both brothers, he does not need further identification in the *De legibus*. This pentameter has all the appearance of coming from a neoteric-style epigram prophesying immortality for the *Marius*, such as Catullus (95 = Cinna 7*a*) wrote for the *Smyrna* of Helvius Cinna (**7–10**), and Cinna himself (**14**) for the *Dictynna* of Valerius Cato. The link with Cinna is amusing, since Cicero did not labour for nine years over his poems (which he composed with extraordinary speed), and they were not so obscure as to require a learned commentary. Scaevola seems to reinforce the parallel by turning around Cinna's phrase 'innumerabilibus . . . saeclis' from the *Propempticon Pollionis* (**6.2**); if this is a deliberate borrowing, Scaevola must have written after 56 BC.

canescet: sc. the *Marius* (contrast Petronius 2.8 of sickly poems not destined for a long life, 'non potuerunt usque ad senectutem canescere'), but also Marius himself. As e.g. in **7***b* (the anonymous epigram on the *Smyrna*), **103** (Ticida on Valerius Cato's *Lydia*) and *Anth. Pal.* 9.63 (= Asclepiades 32 G–P on the *Lyde* of Antimachus) the title of the poem also stands for its eponym. Ordinary people grow white over a single lifetime, but Marius much more slowly. 'Canescet' might conceivably also suggest the physical appearance of a volume containing the poem: cf. Lygdamus, [Tib.] 3.1.9–10 'niveum . . . libellum / . . . canas . . . comas'. Varying ways of describing a poem's longevity became an ingenious neoteric game. Sometimes the *saecula* are old (Cat. 95 = 7*a*.6 'cana . . . saecula', [Virgil], *Ciris* 41 'senibus loqueretur pagina saeclis'), sometimes the material on which the poem is written (Cat. 68.46 'charta loquatur anus'), sometimes—as here—the poem/its eponym.

innumerabilibus: for a single word occupying the second half of the pentameter, cf. Callinus fr. 1.2 West² ἀμφιπερικτίονας, *Theognidea* 1058, Catullus 68.112 (likewise a three-word pentameter) 'audit falsiparens Amphitryoniades' (no doubt there were Hellenistic precedents for a patronymic filling this space), Rutilius Namatianus 1.450 'Bellerophonteis sollicitudinibus' (the only two-word pentameter known to me). In the isopsephic *Anth. Pal.* 9.12 = Page, *FGE* 522–3 by Leonidas of Alexandria (first century A D) the two pentameters end ἀντερανιζόμενος and ἀντιπαρασχόμενοι.

92 (2 Bl., C.)

lassas clunes: see Adams, *Latin Sexual Vocabulary*, 196, for 'lassus' and 'lassare' of sexual exhaustion, and p. 115 for 'clunes'.

Q. Cornificius

93

Hieronymi *Chronicon* (ed. Helm² (1956), 159) ann. Abr. 1976 = 41 a. Chr.: *Cornificius poeta a militibus desertus interiit, quos saepe fugientes 'galeatos lepores' appellarat. huius soror Cornificia, cuius insignia extant epigrammata.*

Jerome on the year 41 BC: Cornificius the poet died after being deserted by his soldiers, whom he had called 'helmeted hares' when they repeatedly ran away.

94 (carmina amatoria)

Ov. *Tr.* 2.435–6: *Cinna* [**16**] *quoque his comes est* [sc. Catullo, Calvo, Ticidae, Memmio], *Cinnaque procacior Anser, / et leve Cornifici parque Catonis opus.*

. . . Cornificius' light work and the similar output of Cato.

95 (1 Bl., C.)

deducta mihi voce garrienti

. . . <? said> to me in a quiet voice as I chattered.

Macr. *Sat.* 6.4.12 (I p. 372 Willis): '*deductum*' [Verg. *Buc.* 6.5] *pro tenui et subtili eleganter positum est: sic autem et Afranius in Virgine* ['. . . *voce deducta . . .*'] . . . *item apud Cornificium:* '*deducta—garrienti*'.

96 (2 Bl., C.) *Glaucus*

Centauros foedare bimembris
… to stain with blood the two-formed centaurs.

Macr. *Sat.* 6.5.1 ff. (I pp. 374–7 Willis): *multa quoque epitheta apud Vergilium sunt quae ab ipso ficta creduntur. sed et haec a veteribus tracta monstrabo …* [6.5.13] '*tu nubigenas, invicte, bimembris*' [*Aen.* 8.293]. *Cornificius in Glauco:* 'Centauros—bimembris'.

97 (3 Bl., C.)

†ut folia quae frugibus arboreis tegmina gignuntur†

as leaves which are produced to be coverings for fruits of the trees. [*The text as transmitted is metrically impossible.*]

Serv. Dan. ad Verg. *Georg.* 1.55 'arborei fetus alibi' (p. 146 Thilo): *arboreum aliqui duobus modis accipiunt: aliter enim in Aeneide* [12.888] *de telo* 'ingens arboreum'. *Cornificius:* 'ut folia—gignuntur'.

> ut folia, arboreis quae frugibus <‿ ◡ ◡ ‿ ◡‿> / tegmina gignuntur *Courtney, alii alia.*

93

Q. CORNIFICIUS is a most interesting figure, who had a wide-ranging and (until its final phase) successful career. He is described as an 'adulescens' by Caelius (Cic. *Ad Fam.* 8.7 = 92 SB. 2) in 50 BC, when he became engaged to the daughter, probably by an earlier marriage, of Catiline's widow. But that may mean 'Cornificius the Younger', to differentiate him from his homonymous father (still living), and in any case *adulescens* can be applied to people as old as their early or mid thirties. So Cornificius could have been a close coeval of Catullus, who addressed to him the lugubrious 'malest, Cornifici, tuo Catullo' (38).

He was quaestor, pro praetore, in Illyricum in 48 BC (Sumner, *Phoenix*, 25 (1971), 258) and became an augur, probably in 47 BC (hence Cicero, *Ad Fam.* 12.17 = 204 SB, headed 'Cornificio collegae'). After governing Cilicia and seeing military action in Syria, he became praetor in 45 BC (Sumner, *Phoenix* (1971), 358). Hitherto Cornificius had served the interests of Julius Caesar, but in 44 BC, soon after the Dictator's assassination, he was given command of Africa Vetus by the senate, and, remaining loyal, held it despite the efforts of Antony to reinstate his predecessor Calvisius Sabinus (see Elizabeth Rawson, *CQ* NS 28 (1978), 188). Proscribed by the Second Triumvirate, Cornificius was embroiled in fighting with the governor of Africa Nova, T. Sextius, and (after initial success deserving an imperatorial salutation) was deserted by his troops (**93**) and killed near Utica late in 42 BC.

Cicero (see Shackleton Bailey's *Ad Fam.*, vol. II, p. 596 for a list of his letters = *Ad Fam.* 12.17–30 to Cornificius) clearly respected Cornificius as a man and as an orator of Atticist inclination. It seems unlikely that the rhetorical treatise of a 'Cornificius', often mentioned by Quintilian, is the extant *Rhetorica ad Herennium* (see H. Caplan's Introduction to the Loeb of that work, pp. ix–xiv); consequently there is no reason to attribute the *Rhetorica* to our (or any other) Cornificius. Although Jerome (**93**) styles him 'the poet', rather than e.g. 'the augur', Cornificius seems to us a very minor poet compared, say, with his fellow neoterics Cinna and Calvus. He left behind two more enduring monuments: a handsome coinage in gold and silver, struck probably at Utica and showing himself on the reverse, dressed as an augur and holding the *lituus*, being crowned by Juno Sospita, with the legend Q. CORNUFICI AUGUR. IMP. See E. Sydenham, *The Coinage of the Roman Republic* (rev. edn., London, 1952), 212, nos. 1352–5; J. R. Fears, *Historia*, 24 (1975), 592–602; D. Sear, *The History and Coinage of the Roman Imperators 49–27 BC* (London, 1998), 132–5 (illustrated). The other memorial has, sadly, been lost: according to T. P. Wiseman (*BICS* 23 (1976), 15) it adorned 'a convex marble plaque . . . presumably from a circular tomb like that of Caecilia Metella'. The inscription read CORNIFICIA Q. F. CAMERI / Q. CORNIFICIUS Q. F. FRATER / PR. AUGUR. Wiseman (p. 16) deduced—reasonably, despite the doubts of Rawson (*CQ* (1978), 191 n. 18)—that 'Cornificia was already dead when her brother's ashes were brought back from Africa'. Cornificia could well have been the lady who wrote 'insignia . . . epigrammata' (**93**, Jerome no doubt from Suetonius), and her husband Camerius (a rare name) perhaps the addressee of Catullus 55 and 58b. Cornificius' description of the soldiers who deserted him as 'galeatos lepores', 'helmeted hares', was bitter but memorable; could he possibly have remembered Helvius Cinna's verb 'galeare' (**15**, but see ad loc.)? I am not sure whether this should be considered 'the only surviving fragment of Cornificius' oratory' (Rawson, *CQ* (1978), 193); it looks more like an offhand remark. For unknown reasons, C.'s name becomes embroiled in the prosopographical fictions of ancient commentators on Virgil's *Eclogues* (Rawson 189–90).

94

The company which Cornificius keeps in this passage of Ovid suggests light erotic poetry in a variety of metres (as in Catullus); the hendecasyllable **95** could well come from such a poem.

95 (1 Bl., C.)

deducta mihi voce garrienti: we cannot tell whether 'deducta . . . voce' applies to the person (? the poet) who is chattering ('garrienti'), or to someone who breaks in upon the chatter (Rawson, *CQ* (1978), 189). The phrase does not seem to have any of the Callimachean resonances of Virgil, *Ecl.* 6.5 'deductum . . . carmen'; *deducere* here means to 'reduce' or 'attenuate', as shown by the passages of Afranius ('verbis pauculis / respondit, tristis voce deducta etc.') and Pomponius ('vocem deducas oportet ut mulieris videantur / verba, etc.').

garrienti: suggesting inconsequential and unimportant chatter. The verb is most at home in comedy and satire.

96 (2 Bl., C.)

The fisherman Glaucus, who became a sea-god after eating a wonderful herb, attracted a remarkable amount of interest from Hellenistic and Roman poets, having been treated by Alexander of Aetolia in his Ἁλιεύς (fr. 1 Powell, *Coll. Alex.* = fr. 1 E. Magnelli (Florence, 1999)), Callimachus (a lost *Glaucus*, Pfeiffer vol. II, p. xcv), Nicander (frs. 2 and 25) and many others mentioned by Athenaeus (7.296a–297c). He stands first in the list of sea-gods to whom sailors sacrifice in the line of Parthenius (fr. 36 Lightfoot = *Suppl. Hell.* 647) adapted by Virgil (*Georgics* 1.437) and might have cast an eye upon Cynthia (Prop. 2.26A.13–14, quoted on p. 232 below). Cicero wrote a *Pontius Glaucus* (see Courtney 152, a youthful work in trochaic tetrameters according to Plutarch, *Cicero* 2.3). Only this one reference to Cornificius' *Glaucus* has survived, but, since all the other known neoteric epyllia involving transformation are reflected in Ovid's *Metamorphoses*, it would not be surprising if the account of Glaucus in *Met.* 13.904–14.69 owed some debt to Cornificius. The love affairs of Glaucus were many and varied, as we can see from Athenaeus (above) and Servius on *Aen.* 3.420; in Ovid he vainly loves Scylla (thus too Hedyle, *SH* 456) and rebuffs Circe. The three gods mentioned together by Parthenius (fr. 36 Lightfoot) were linked by love, since Glaucus had been loved by Nereus and himself loved Melicertes (both from Athenaeus). So there was plenty of scope for a *poeta doctus.*

centauros foedare bimembris: probably a reference to Heracles, in view of Virgil's imitation (*Aen.* 8.293) 'tu nubigenas, invicte, bimembris' (sc. 'mactas'), although no mythological link between Glaucus (see Marie-Odile Jentel in *LIMC* s.v. Glaukos I) and Heracles slaying the centaurs is apparent— beyond the point that they too, like the half-fish Glaucus, were 'bimembres'.

centauros . . . bimembris: cf. Stat. *Theb.* 1.457–8 'bimembris / centauros', Silius 3.41–2. The compound epithet, which (to judge from Macrobius) Cornificius invented, reflects the Greek διφυής, and was probably inspired by Sophocles, *Trach.* 1090 ff., where Heracles addresses his own arms, which subdued (κατειργάσασθε, 1094), among other monsters, διφυᾶ τ' ἄμεικτον ἱπποβάμονα στρατόν / θηρῶν (1095–6). This passage of Sophocles was translated into Latin (iambics) also by Cicero (fr. 34 Blänsdorf) who borrowed (line 38) Naevius' *bicorpor* to represent διφυής.

foedare: Servius auct. on *Aen.* 3.241 'ferro foedare volucres' glosses with 'cruentare'. The verb is at home in epic and tragedy (first attested in Ennius ed. Jocelyn, *The Tragedies of Ennius* (Cambridge, 1967), 399, 'ferro foedati iacent'. Virgil and Ovid (*Met.*) are fond of it; note also Adesp. **259** 'tune Clytaemestrae foedasti viscera ferro?'

The rhythm of this line (with no word-break in the third foot) is not inelegant in neoteric terms, provided that there was a break after the first syllable of the second foot (as in Cat. 64.193 'Eumenides, quibus anguino redimita capillo'). Virgil has preserved it in *Aen.* 8.293 'tu nubigenas, invicte, bimembris', where (with *OLD*, against LSJ s.v. *bimembris*) I would take 'nubigenas' to function as the noun. There may have been an ancient difference of opinion on this last point; Ovid (*Met.*) sometimes uses *bimembris*, sometimes *nubigena* as a noun.

97 (3 Bl., C.)

†**ut folia quae frugibus arboreis tegmina gignuntur**†: very puzzling. The sequence looks dactylic, and Courtney produces hexameters (or elegiacs) with 'ut folia, arboreis quae frugibus ‿ ‿ ‿ ‿ ‿ / tegmina gignuntur', supposing only one scribal error ('an accidental omission of *arboreis* and its replacement in a position where it was taken to be a correction of a phrase

now consequently omitted'). One might look for a more exotic metre (Rawson, *CQ* (1978), 189, 'perhaps in catalectic dactylic trimeters') but nothing seems to work. Courtney (p. 227) entertains the idea of V. Tandoi that the leaves might be mentioned as a parallel to the shortness of human life (cf. *Iliad* 6.146, in the mouth of a Glaucus, οἵη περ φύλλων γενέη, τοίη δὲ καὶ ἀνδρῶν). But the detail about protecting the trees' fruits seems unnecessary, even pedantically unwelcome, in such a context.

(?Q.) Hortensius Hortalus

98

(*a*) Ov. *Tr.* 2.441–2: *nec minus Hortensi, nec sunt minus improba Servi / car-mina. quis dubitet nomina tanta sequi?*

(*b*) Plin. *Epist.* 5.3.5 [cf. **19j**, al.] *ego verear ne me non satis deceat quod decuit . . . M. Messalam, Q. Hortensium, M. Brutum . . . ?*

(*c*) Gell. *NA* 19.9.7: *Laevius implicata et Hortensius invenusta et Cinna* [**1e**] *inlepida et Memmius* [**44c**] *dura ac deinceps omnes rudia fecerunt atque absona.*

(*a*) And the poems of Hortensius and Servius are no less outrageous. Who would hesitate to follow such great names?

(*b*) [Compare **19j**, and references to several others of these poets in the same passage of Pliny.] Should I fear that I might be discredited by what did not discredit . . . M. Messala, Q. Hortensius, M. Brutus . . . ?

(*c*) . . . Hortensius wrote inelegant poems . . .

99 (1 Bl., C.)

cervix

neck

Varr. *Ling. Lat.* 8.14: *alii dicunt 'cervices' . . . Hortensius in poematis 'cervix'.* LL 10.78: *adiectum est 'non repugnante consuetudine communi', quod quaedam verba contra usum veterem inclinata patietur, ut passa Hortensium dicere pro 'cervices' 'cervix'.* Quint. 8.3.35: *'cervicem' videtur Hortensius primus dixisse.*

Quintilian: Hortensius seems to have been the first to use 'cervix' (neck) in the singular.

ALTHOUGH only one word of Hortensius' poetry survives, his identity has been hotly disputed; compare the cases of Mucius Scaevola (**90–2**) and Servius Sulpicius (Appendix), all three named by Pliny (*Epist.* 5.3.5, whence **98***b*) in his catalogue of distinguished men who wrote light erotic verse. Is Hortensius the poet Cicero's colleague and rival, the famous orator (114–49 B C), or the orator's son, born in (or shortly before) 82 B C, perhaps praetor in 45 (G. V. Sumner, *Phoenix,* 25 (1971), 358; T. R. S. Broughton, *The Magistrates of the Roman Republic,* vol. III, supplement (1986), 103)? We must bear in mind Catullus 65, expressing overwhelming grief at the loss of his brother, but nonetheless sending to Hortalus (lines 2 and 15) a translation (Cat. 66) of Callimachus' *Lock of Berenice.* On the other hand I agree with those (including Courtney 231) who find the presence of 'Hortensius' *qua* voluminous poet in Cat. 95.3 embarrassing; the name should be replaced by an adjective referring to Volusius ('Hatrianus <in>' Munro). I have not included Cat. 95.3 among the testimonies to Hortensius' poetry.

Gellius' placing (**98***c*) of Hortensius between Laevius and Cinna somewhat favours the father. Also one might expect Varro (**99**) to quote the father (his close coeval) rather than the son—in fact it is surprising that he should mention either, since nearly all the quotations in *LL* are from much older poets such as Plautus, Ennius, and Lucilius (with Accius the last to be quoted regularly). But Varro does cite Sueius (frs. 5–6 Courtney), whose reference to the actor Clodius Aesopus shows him to have been a contemporary of Cicero; and the unattributed 'Vesper adest' in *LL* 7.50 may well be from Catullus 62.1. Finally, one might question whether the younger Hortensius and Servius Sulpicius were distinguished enough to qualify as 'nomina tanta' in Ovid, *Tr.* 2.442 (**98***a*)—but the emphasis could be on the distinction of the family name rather than the individual bearer.

When we come to the addressee of Catullus 65, he seems much more likely to be the son (some five years younger than Catullus) rather than the father (Catullus' senior by perhaps twenty-seven years). We know nothing to suggest that Hortensius Senior was Catullus' kind of person, to whom the poet would entrust his deepest feelings. A taste for Callimachus' more difficult poems (*Lock of Berenice*) suits very well the generation which came to full maturity in the 50s and 40s B C, and it is natural that such a one should himself have written verses. See Shackleton Bailey, *Onomasticon to Cicero's Speeches* (Stuttgart, 1988), 55–6, strongly in favour of Hortensius Junior as the addressee of Cat. 65 and the poet, and against the argument (adopted by Courtney 230) that the addressee of Cat. 65 must be the orator because his son cannot be shown to have borne the cognomen Hortalus. It remains possible, however, that the addressee of Cat. 65 is the son, but Pliny's (? and Ovid's) writer of erotic verses his father (in the tradition of Q. Lutatius Catulus, cos. 102 B C, Courtney 75–8). Wiseman (*Cinna the Poet,* 190 n. 65) believes Pliny to have in mind the younger Hortensius but the elder Servius Sulpicius. Syme (*CQ* N S 31 (1981), 426–7 = *Roman Papers* (III), 1422) favours the older Hortensius (and Servius Sulpicius) for Pliny's erotic poets ('various attestation' no doubt includes Cat. 95.3, which should be discarded), but allows that Ovid may have thought of the younger Sulpicius.

After all this, Varro's statement (**99**, repeated by others) that Hortensius was the first to use singular *cervix* is simply incorrect; see Ennius, *Annals* 483 with Skutsch's note.

Ticida

100

Suet. *De Gramm. et Rhet.* 4.2 (pp. 6–7 Kaster): *eosdem* [sc. 'poetarum inter-pretes, qui a Graecis grammatici nominentur'] *litteratores vocitatos Messala Corvinus in quadam epistula ostendit, non esse sibi dicens rem cum Furio Bibaculo* [**71***b*], *ne cum Ticida quidem aut litteratore Catone* [=**71***b*].

101 (carmina amatoria)

(*a*) Ov. *Tr.* 2.433–4: *quid referam Ticidae, quid Memmi* [**44***a*] *carmen, apud quos / rebus adest nomen, nominibusque pudor?* [=**44***a*].

(*b*) Apul. *Apol.* 10: *eadem igitur opera accusent C. Catullum, quod Lesbiam pro Clodia nominarit, et Ticidam similiter, quod quae Metella erat Perillam scripserit.*

(*b*) By the same process they would accuse Gaius Catullus on the ground that he gave the name Lesbia for Clodia, and Ticida likewise, because in his writings he called Perilla the woman who was really Metella.

102 (1 Bl., C.) *Hymenaeus*

felix lectule talibus
sole amoribus

O couch, supremely happy through such love-making.

1–2 Prisc. GLK II p. 189: *'sole' quoque antiqui. Ticida* (L. Mueller: attiquidas *vel* atticidas *codd.*: Ticidas *Hertz*) *in hymenaeo*: '*felix—amoribus*'.

103 (2 Bl., C.)

Lydia doctorum maxima cura liber

The work *Lydia*, greatest preoccupation of scholars.

Suet. *De Gramm. et Rhet.* 11.2 (p. 16 Kaster): *Lydiae* [sc. Valeri Catonis] *Ticida meminit:* 'Lydia—liber'.

THE poet Ticida is usually identified with 'L. Ticida eques Romanus' who, when bringing supplies to Caesar's army in Africa early in 46 BC, was captured and (we must infer) executed by the Pompeian Q. Metellus Scipio ([Caesar], *Bellum Africum* 44.1–46.3). That could fit the chronology of his beloved Perilla if (as seems quite likely) she was the daughter of Q. Metellus Celer (cos. 60 BC) and Clodia; this Metella married P. Lentulus Spinther about 53 BC, and was divorced in 45 BC. *Ad Att.* 12.52 = 294 SB. 2 suggests that Clodia and Lentulus Spinther were somehow connected in Cicero's mind (as mother-in-law and son-in-law?). See the intricate argument in Shackleton Bailey, *Cicero's Letters to Atticus*, vol. V, pp. 412–13; also Wiseman, *Cinna the Poet*, 112 and 188 ff.

So Metella/Perilla could have inspired this Ticida *c.*50 BC. There is, however, a different chronological problem (noted by Kaster, Suet. *De Gramm.*, 95, and Nisbet, *Collected Papers*, 397). The extract from Messalla Corvinus' letter implies that Ticida is still alive, like Furius Bibaculus and Valerius Cato (who pretty certainly survived into the 20s BC). If Corvinus wrote this letter before the death of L. Ticida in Africa (46 BC), he himself could not have been more than 18 at the time; the tone of this extract (even allowing for aristocratic hauteur) suggests an older man. Perhaps, therefore, the poet was an otherwise unattested Ticida. If Messalla's letter dates from *c.*40 BC, Perilla/Metella would then still be hardly more than 30! Her notoriety continued—she is almost certainly the Metella of Horace, *Sat.* 2.3.239.

The three poets mentioned in **100** are linked in that both Furius Bibaculus (**84–6**) and Ticida (**103**) praised Valerius Cato. Messalla 'has no dealings' with them ('non esse sibi dicens rem cum . . .'). It is worth remembering that from about 40 BC Messalla (like Maecenas with Varius, Virgil, and Horace) was building up a circle of literary patronage, the fruits of which (*c.*35 BC) can be seen in Horace, *Sat.* 1.10.85 ff. (see Ceri Davies, 'Poetry in the "Circle" of Messalla', *Greece and Rome*, 20 (1973), 25–35). These three names may have represented poets who were available but whom Messalla did not wish to associate with himself—Valerius Cato found no rich patron for his old age (**84–5**). There seems to be a gradation in the list: Furius Bibaculus is quite beyond the pale (perhaps because of his abusive lampoons, **71***c*, **82**), the other two somewhat more plausible but still rejected.

Suetonius quotes **100** to prove that 'litterator', like 'litteratus', could be used as an equivalent to 'grammaticus'. Perhaps, however, Messalla is deliberately disparaging Valerius Cato by demoting him from the more honourable status of a scholar and encourager of poets (Furius Bibaculus, **86** 'Cato grammaticus . . . / qui solus legit ac facit poetas', **85**.4 'summum grammaticum, optimum poetam') to the less respected position of an elementary schoolmaster (e.g. Catullus 14.9 'Sulla litterator').

101

(*a*) Against the serious and elevated Latin poetry of Ennius and Lucretius (*Tr.* 2.423–6) Ovid has set the love poems of Catullus and Calvus, in which they admitted to illicit affairs—the 'adulterium' (430) of Catullus and the 'furta' (432) of Calvus. He now moves on to a rather different point, the sexually explicit language of Ticida and Memmius (**44***a*). That must be the meaning of 434 'rebus adest nomen nominibusque pudor'; *res* can be a euphemism for the sexual organs (male or female) or, more generally = 'sexual matters' (Adams, *Latin Sexual Vocabulary* (1982), 62, 203). It would seem that the language of Ticida and Memmius was even more uninhibited than that of Catullus (who is free enough) and Calvus (from whom we have **38**.2 'pedicator'). Such explicitness is not to be found in the elegies of Tibullus, Propertius, or Ovid (we do not know about Cornelius Gallus), but in a six-line epigram (**161**) which Octavian wrote at the time of the Perusine War (41–40 BC) we find 'futuere' (three times), 'pedicare', and 'mentula'.

(*b*) In the course of delivering his *Apology* (AD 158 or 159) Apuleius becomes our sole source for the real names of several heroines of Latin love poetry, all of which (with the odd exception of Hostia/Cynthia) are exact metrical equivalents of the pseudonym under which they were addressed in the poems. 'Perilla' is aberrant in that it suggests neither a title of Apollo, as do Delia, Cynthia, and—not mentioned by Apuleius—Lycoris (Cornelius Gallus, **145**.1) and Leucadia (Varro Atacinus, **133***a*), nor a Greek lyric poetess, as do Lesbia and (not in Apuleius) Leucadia (again) and Corinna. Marilyn Skinner in H. Jocelyn (ed.), *Tria Lustra: Liverpool Classical Papers*, 3 (1993) 303–4, and (independently) Nisbet, *Collected Papers*, 397 n. 27, ingeniously suggest that Perilla was so called because she roasted her victims, like Perillus/Perilaus who made the brazen bull for Phalaris (a story publicized particularly by Callimachus, frs. 45–7 Pf., *Suppl. Hell.* 252).

We must now extend the quotation from *Tristia* 2. After discussing Catullus and Calvus (427–32), Ovid (according to his manuscripts) continued:

> quid referam Ticidae, quid Memmi carmen, apud quos   433
>   rebus adest nomen nominibusque pudor?
> Cinna quoque his comes est, Cinnaque procacior Anser,   435
>   et leve Cornifici parque Catonis opus;
> et quorum libris modo dissimulata Perillae   437
>   nomine, nunc legitur dicta, Metelle, tuo.

Armed with the information provided by Apuleius (**101***b*), we may be surprised by Ovid's apparent disassociation of Ticida (433) from Perilla (437), and even more so by his failure to identify the poets who sang of Perilla/ Metella. Ovid's own interest lay very much in naming the earlier Latin poets, to show in what good company he had been; true, Varro Atacinus is not named in 439–40, but his identity is unmistakable ('is quoque Phasiacas Argon qui duxit in undas').

The solution to these difficulties was, in my opinion, found by Riese, who transposed 433–4 to follow 435–6:

> Cinna quoque his comes est, Cinnaque procacior Anser,   435
>   et leve Cornifici parque Catonis opus.
> quid referam Ticidae, quid Memmi carmen, apud quos   433
>   rebus adest nomen nominibusque pudor,
> et quorum libris modo dissimulata Perillae   437
>   nomine nunc legitur dicta, Metelle, tuo?

I would translate 437–8 '. . . and in whose works we read of a woman at one time concealed under the name of Perilla, at another called by your name, Metellus'. A minor advantage of the transposition is that 'Cinna quoque his comes est' now connects Cinna to his closest poetic associates, Catullus and Calvus (427–32). More important, Riese restores the link revealed by Apuleius (**101***b*) between Ticida and Metella/Perilla. A bonus would be the information that Memmius, as well as Ticida, wrote poems about Metella—whether shortly before his exile for *ambitus* in 52 BC, or in the early 40s if his hopes for restoration (Cic. *Ad Att.* 6.1 = 115 SB. 23, February 50 BC) were ever fulfilled (cf. Hutchinson, *CQ* NS 51 (2001), 158).

'Modo . . . nunc' (*Tr.* 2.437–8) could mean 'previously . . . now'. Thus Gordon Williams, *Tradition and Originality in Roman Poetry* (Oxford, 1968), 528: 'At the time when Ovid was writing (not more than 50 years later) there are copies of the poems going about with the real name substituted for the fictitious.' But the altered reissue of such minor love poetry does not seem very likely. I would prefer (with the Loeb) to interpret 'at one time . . . at another' (for the combination, cf. Bömer on *Met.* 8.290–1, *OLD modo* 6, *nunc* 8*b*), and to see here a distinction between Ticida and Memmius: the former called her Perilla (**101***b*), the latter used her real name (cf. **26**, Calvus and Quintilia).

S. G. Owen did in fact adopt Riese's transposition in his 1915 OCT (printing in 437 his own unhappy conjecture 'Perilla est'), but turned against it in his Oxford, 1924, edition with translation and commentary. His main reason was a belief that 'apud quos / . . . et quorum' is incorrect Latin (p. 237, 'the introduction of the connecting relative by *et* is not permissible'). But the objection is unfounded: Professor Nisbet refers to Kühner–Stegmann, *Ausführliche Grammatik der lateinischen Sprache* (1914), II. 2, p. 323, who quote Cic. *De Or.* 3.16 'nos enim *qui* ipsi sermoni non interfuissemus *et quibus* C. Cotta sententias huius disputationis tradidisset . . .', Caesar, *BG* 4.21.7 'Commium . . . *cuius* et virtutem et consilium probabat *et quem* sibi fidelem esse arbitrabatur . . .'

Some have been concerned to identify the Metellus addressed in 438; Wiseman, *Cinna the Poet*, 189, suggests Q. Metellus Creticus Silanus, cos. A D 7, Courtney (pp. 228–9) Q. Metellus Celer cos. 60 B C (Metella's father). The latter would certainly be preferable; one might also think of the putative ancestor of the *gens*, who first bore that name. But the apostrophe is purely a metrical convenience, and to seek a particular Metellus seems as unnecessary here as in *Aen.* 5.123 'genus unde tibi, Romane Cluenti'.

For the surprising reappearance of 'Perilla' as the name (probably a pseudonym) of a poetess who may have been Ovid's stepdaughter, see Appendix.

102 (1 Bl., C.)

After illustrating the vocative 'une' from Catullus (37.17) and Plautus, the grammarian goes on to this, apparently the one surviving instance of vocative 'sole'. It emerges that Ticida, like Catullus (61) and Calvus (**29**) wrote a marriage poem in glyconics. We can see from Cat. 61.199 ff. that it was quite acceptable to speak frankly about the love-making of the bridal couple in such a context. Ticida's μακαρισμός of the bed seems to be reflected in Propertius 2.15.1–2 'O me felicem! nox o mihi candida, et o tu / lectule, deliciis facte beate meis!', and may owe something to Philodemus (with whom Ticida could have been personally acquainted), *Anth. Pal.* 5.4 = 1 G–P. 5–6 σὺ δ', ὦ φιλεράστρια κοίτη, / ἤδη τῆς Παφίης ἴσθι τὰ λειπόμενα. In Catullus 61.107 ff. there was a stanza (unfortunately only the first and last lines survive)

addressed to the bed: 'o cubile, quod omnibus . . . / . . . candido pede lecti';
the apostrophe continued into the next stanza, 'quae tuo veniunt ero / quanta
gaudia' etc. (109 ff.).

1. **lectule:** this diminutive, though characteristically neoteric (Catullus
64.88), has a wider diffusion (see Lyne on [Virgil], *Ciris* 440).

2. **sole:** both 'unus' and 'solus' can describe not uniqueness but pre-
eminence in a field (e.g. Furius Bibaculus, **86.**2 'solus', Virgil, *Ecl.* 10.32–3 'soli
cantare periti / Arcades', Ovid, *AA* 1.131 'Romule, militibus scisti dare com-
moda solus'. Housman, *Classical Papers*, 695 (vol. II), wanted to fill up the
line with 'sole <conscie> amoribus', which would alter the sense of *solus*. But
there is no need to postulate a lacuna in Priscian's quotation.

103 (2 Bl., C.)

Lydia doctorum maxima cura liber: for the elaborate double apposition, cf.
Prop. 2.3.14 'oculi geminae sidera nostra faces'. Nearly, but not quite, the
pattern which becomes established from Virgil's *Eclogues* onwards: adjective–
phrase in apposition–noun (e.g. 1.57 'raucae, tua cura, palumbes'; see
J. Solodow, *HSCP* 90 (1986), 129 ff. 'Doctorum maxima cura' suggests that
Valerius Cato's *Lydia* may have needed (and received) learned exegesis, per-
haps a full scholarly commentary, like that of Crassicius on Cinna's *Smyrna*
(see **7b**, where the 'indocti' are warned off). Here, as in the epigram on
Crassicius, the scholars are represented as lovers of the girl after whom
the poem is called. For more on Valerius Cato, see Appendix. 'Lydia' might
have been the name/pseudonym of Cato's beloved, but we have no means of
confirming that.

Volumnius

104 (1 Bl., C.)

stridentis dabitur patella cymae
A dish of sizzling young cabbage will be given.

Auctor de dub. nom., GLK V p. 574: *cyma. alii cymam, ut Volumnius:* 'striden-
ti<s>—cymae'.

stridentis *Keil*: stridenti *codd.*

THE author is very probably P. Volumnius Eutrapelus, patron of the actress
Cytheris, who became Cornelius Gallus's Lycoris. That he wrote verses in a
Catullan manner (and in Catullus' favourite hendecasyllable metre) is not
attested elsewhere, but entirely credible—compare e.g. Maecenas (**185–6**).
This line certainly looks like an invitation to a simple meal (cf. Catullus 13
and e.g. Horace, *Epist.* 1.5.2 'nec modica cenare times holus omne patella').
Such an invitation could be made at any time (for the genre, see Courtney's
Introduction to Juvenal 11, and my edition of Callimachus, *Hecale*, Appendix
III), but would be particularly appropriate after Caesar's sumptuary law of
(probably) October 46 BC; see Cicero, *Ad Fam.* 9.26 = 197 SB. 4 (written at a
frugal dinner given by the same Volumnius Eutrapelus) and 7.26 = 210 SB. 2
(vegetables).

stridentis: the sizzling noise of crisp young vegetables in a hot pan.

cymae: from κῦμα (connected with κύω), 'young sprout' of plants, espe-
cially of a cabbage (LSJ II. 2); the first instance (later in Columella and the
elder Pliny) of the Greek neuter becoming a Latin feminine (cf. Cornelius
Severus, **220** 'syrma').

P. Terentius Varro Atacinus

105

(*a*) Hieronymi *Chronicon* (p. 151 ed. Helm[2], 1956) ann. Abr. 1935 = 82 a. Chr.:
P. Terentius Varro vico Atace in provincia Narbonensi nascitur. qui postea XXXV annum agens Graecas litteras cum summo studio didicit.

(*b*) Vell. Pat. 2.36.2, de consulatu Ciceronis (ann. 63 a. Chr.): *quis . . . ignorat diremptos gradibus aetatis floruisse hoc tempore . . . auctores . . . carminum Varronem* [Atacinum, credo, non Reatinum] *ac Lucretium neque ullo in suscepto carminis sui opere minorem Catullum?*

(*a*) [82 BC]. P. Terentius Varro is born in the village of Atax in the province of Narbonensis. Later, in the course of his thirty-fifth year, he learnt Greek literature with great enthusiasm.

(*b*) Who does not know that in this period (separated by the degrees of their ages) flourished . . . the poets Varro and Lucretius and Catullus?

106–107 *Bellum Sequanicum*

106 (23 Bl., 1 C.) Liber II

deinde ubi pellicuit dulcis levis unda saporis

Then, when the light water of a sweet taste enticed . . .

Prisc. GLK II pp. 496–7: *'pellicui' quoque pro 'pellexi' veteres protulerunt. Laevius in Laudamia* [fr. 18.6 C., *'pellicuit'*]. *sed Terentius in Phormione* [68, *'pellexit'*]. *invenitur etiam . . . 'pellicuit'. P. Varro belli Sequanici libro II* 'deinde—saporis'.

107 (24 Bl., 2 C.) ex incerto libro

semianimesque micant oculi lucemque requirunt

Half-alive eyes flicker and seek the light.

Serv. ad Verg. *Aen.* 10.396 (II p. 434 Thilo) 'semianimesque micant digiti ferrumque retractant': *Ennii est, ut 'oscitat in campis caput a cervice revulsum, / semianimesque micant oculi lucemque requirunt'* (*Ann.* 483–4 O. Skutsch), *quem versum ita ut fuit transtulit ad suum carmen Varro Atacinus.*
Bello Sequanico trib. F. Skutsch (*RE* V. 2616. 7), *Argonautis* Baehrens (fr. 10 *FPR*, coll. Ap. Rh. 4.1525).

108 *Saturae*

Hor. *Sat.* 1.10.46–7: '*hoc erat, experto frustra Varrone Atacino / atque quibusdam aliis, melius quod scribere possem*' (Porf. ad loc. (pp. 283–4, ed. Holder, 1894): *quoniam alii <alia> carminum genera consummate scriberent ... , sermonum autem frustra temptasse<t> Terentius Varro Narbonensis, qui Atacinus ab Atace fluvio dictus est ...*).

It was this [sc. satire] that I could write better, after Varro Atacinus and some others had tried in vain.

109–119 *Chorographia*

109 dub.

Comment. Bern. ad Luc. 9.411 'tertia pars rerum Libye' (p. 301 ed. Usener, 1869): *quidam diviserunt orbem in duas partes, ut Varro, id est Asiam et Europam, quidam in tris Asiam Europam et Africam, ut Alexander* [fort. Ephesius, *Suppl. Hell.* 23], *quidam in quattuor adiecta Aegypto ...*

Hoc Varroni Reatino satis bene, Atacino fortasse vel melius convenit. si ita, colligere possis Atacini carmen quoque in duas partes esse divisum, Europam scilicet (cf. **114** 'Varro in Europa') et Asiam.

Some, like Varro [Atacinus or Reatinus?], have divided the world into two parts, that is Asia and Europe.

110

Varro Atacinus (sc. *Chorographia*) inter fontes nominatur Plin. *Nat. Hist.* librorum III, IV, V, VI (pp. 15, 16, 18, 20 ed. Mayhoff, 1906).

[Varro Atacinus named among sources for Pliny, *Natural History*, books 3, 4, 5, and 6.]

111 (11 Bl., 15 C.)

> vidit et aetherio mundum torquerier axe
> et septem aeternis sonitum dare vocibus orbes
> nitentes aliis alios, quae maxima divis
> laetitia est. at tunc longe gratissima Phoebo
> dextera consimiles meditatur reddere voces.   5

He also saw the universe revolving on the celestial axis, and the seven spheres emitting a sound with everlasting voices, as they pressed onwards—different spheres with different notes, causing the greatest delight to the gods. But at that time the right hand by far most pleasing to Phoebus practised reproducing identical sounds.

1–5 Mar. Vict. GLK VI p. 60: *alii tradunt hoc sacrorum cantu concentum mundi cursumque ab hominibus imitari. namque in hoc quinque stellae quas erraticas vocant, sed et sol et luna, ut doctiores tradunt philosophorum, iucundissimos edunt sonos per orbes suos nitentes . . . de qua re Varius sic tradidit* [**157**], *item et Varro* 'vidit—voces'.

   4 laetitia est. at *edd.*: laetitia stat *codd.*   tunc *om.* B   Phoebo *Hollis (ut Mercurii sit dextera)*: Phoebi *codd.*

   Varronis Atacini *Chorographiae* trib. Scaliger

112 (13 Bl., 17 C.)

> ut quinque aetherius zonis accingitur orbis
> ac vastant imas hiemes mediamque calores,
> sic terrae extremas inter mediamque coluntur
> quas solis valido numquam †ut auferat† igne

Just as the heavenly sphere is girdled by five zones and cold ravages the outermost two, heat the middle one, so the lands between the outermost and the middle zone are inhabited, those which the sun's <? chariot> never <? parches> with powerful fire . . .

1–4 Isid. *De Natura Rerum* 10.2 (pp. 209–11 ed. Fontaine, 1960): *horum* [sc. circulorum mundi] *primus septentrionalis est, secundus solstitialis, tertius aequinoctialis, quartus hiemalis, quintus australis, de quibus Varro ita dicit* 'at—igne'. Salomonis episcopi Constantiensis (ob. ann. p. Chr. 919) glossarium (ap. H. Usener, *Kl. Schr.* II, p. 247) s.v. zona: *de quibus zonis Varro ita dicit* 'a—ignes'.

    1 ut *Hollis, coll. Ov., Met. 1.45–7:* at *Isid.:* a *Salom.*   aetherius *Isid. codd. AMS, Fontaine:* (a)etheriis *Isid. codd., VPEKL, Salom., edd. plerique*   2 hiemes *Isid.:* hiemis *Salom.*   4 quas *Grialius:* quam *codd. Isid., Salom.:* qua *Arevalus* valido] calido *Scaliger:* rabido *Baehrens*   numquam] non iam *D. A. Russell*   †ut *(om. Salom.)*] vis *La Bigne (1580):* rota *Scaliger*   auferat *Isid. codd. (nisi quod* adferat *V), sanum putat Kraggerud:* asserat *Salom.:* atterat *Wuellner:* vis hauriat *Nisbet*   igne *vel* ignem (igni *B) codd. Isid.:* ignes *Salom.*

113 (12 Bl., 16 C.)

    ergo inter solis stationem et sidera septem
    exporrecta iacet tellus; huic extima fluctu
    Oceani, interior Neptuno cingitur ora.

Thus the land lies stretched out between the tropic of Cancer and the Pole Star; its outer shore is surrounded by the stream of Oceanus, the inner by the Mediterranean sea.

1–3 Prisc. GLK II, p. 100: *'exterior extremus' vel 'extimus'. Varro in Chorographia (sic cod. D rec. man. in marg.: ort(h)ographia codd. plerique)* 'Ergo—ora'.

(**114** (+ **115**?) *Europa,* pars *Chorographiae,* ut videtur)

114 (14 Bl., 18 C.)

tutum sub sede fuissent

They would have been in safety [??] under the abode . . . [?].

Fest. p. 494 ed. Lindsay (1913): *'tutum'* [? 'tantum', v. Courtney] *frequenter dicitur 'maxime'. Varro in Europa* 'tutum [? 'tantum]—fuissent'.

115 (15 Bl., 19 C.)

munitus vicus Caralis

Caralis, a fortified village

Consent. GLK V, p. 349: *primum directum casum examinare debemus; quo invento et de genere ac numero certiores efficiemur, ut ecce ait <Ata>cinus* 'munitus—Caralis'.

<Varro Ata>cinus *vel* <Ata>cinus *suppl. Herz.* cinus *vel* cynus *codd.*

(116–119, *Asia,* pars *Chorographiae* ? sed titulus nusquam commemoratur)

116 (16 Bl., 20 C.)

cingitur Oceano, Libyco mare, flumine Nilo

. . . is surrounded by the Ocean, the Libyan sea and the river Nile.

Charis., pp. 75–6 Barwick² = GLK I, p. 61 (fere eadem p. 174 B² = 137 K): *ab hoc mare an ab hoc mari dici debeat quaeritur . . . Atacinus quoque* 'cingitur—Nilo'. Prisc. GLK II, p. 331: *vetustissimi tamen solebant huiuscemodi nominum ablativum etiam in e proferre . . . Atacinus quoque* 'cingitur—Nilo'.

117 (17 Bl., 12 C. (*Argonautae*, lib. IV))

feta feris Libye

Libya, teeming with wild beasts

Serv. Dan. ad Verg. *Georg.* 3.176 'fetae' (p. 292 Thilo): *antiqui . . . 'fetum' pro gravido solebant ponere, ut Varro Atacinus* 'feta—Libye'.
Chorographiae trib. Wernsdorf, *Argonautis* Ruhnken coll. Ap. Rh. 4.1561 (item Morel, qui tamen adnotat hoc fragmentum cum **116** posse coniungi).

118 (18 Bl., 21 C.)

Indica non magna minor arbore crescit harundo;
illius et lentis premitur radicibus humor,
dulcia cui nequeant suco contendere mella.

The Indian cane grows no smaller than a large tree, and from its tough roots is pressed a liquid which sweet honey could not rival in flavour.

1–3 Isid. *Orig.* 17.7.58 (vol. II ed. Lindsay, 1911): *in Indicis stagnis nasci arundines calamique dicuntur, ex quorum radicibus expressum suavissimum sucum bibunt; unde et Varro ait* 'Indica—mella'.

1–2 Comm. Bern. (p. 104 Usener) ad Luc. 3.237 'quique bibunt tenera dulcis ab harundine sucos': *de hoc Varro dixit* 'Indica—illius' [desunt plura]. 1, 3 Adnotationes super Lucanum (p. 97 ed. Endt, 1909) ad eundem locum: *de his ait Varro* 'Indica—mella' [om. v. 2].

   1 magna minor arbore *Comm. Bern.* (arbore *om. Adnot.*): magna (magnam, magnum) in arbore *Isid. codd.*   2 et] e *Arevalus*   3 contendere *vel* concedere *Isid. codd.*: contendere *Adnot.*

119 (20 Bl., 22 C.)

Prob. ad Verg. *Georg.* 2.126 'Media' (p. 369 Hagen): *pars Parthorum Media est appellata a Medo, filio Medeae et Aegei, ut existimat Varro, qui quattuor libros de Argonautis edidit.*

haec in *Argonautis* narravisse Varronem veri dissimile est, at *Chorographiae* bene conveniunt.

Part of the Parthians' territory is called Media, from Medus son of Medea and Aegeus, in the opinion of Varro who produced four books about the Argonauts.

120–121 (? *Epimenides*, vel *Epimenis*, vel *Ephemeris*)

120 (21 Bl., 13 C.)

nubes si ut vellera lanae

constabunt

If clouds like woolly fleeces collect together

1–2 Brev. Exp. Verg. *Georg.* 1.397 'tenuia nec lanae per caelum vellera ferri' (p. 265 Hagen): *item 'vellera' nubes dixit, 'tenuia' aranearum texturas, quae inminente tempestate per aera raptantur. Varro in Epimenide* [*sic cod. G*: epimedine *codd. cett.*: Ephemeride *coni. Bergk*] 'nubes—constabunt', *sicut et Aratus* [*Phaen.* 938–9].

   1 si ut *Buecu*: sicut *Brev. Exp.*: [sic] *Riese*: ceu *Baehrens*: nubesque *Tandoi*

121 (22 Bl., 14 C.)

tum liceat pelagi volucres tardaeque paludis
cernere inexpletas studio certare lavandi
et velut insolitum pennis infundere rorem;
aut arguta lacus circumvolitavit hirundo,
et bos suspiciens caelum—mirabile visu—   5
naribus aerium patulis decerpsit odorem;
nec tenuis formica cavis non evehit ova.

Then you might observe the birds of the sea and of the slow-moving marsh insatiably vie with each other in their enthusiasm for washing, or pour water over their feathers as if that was something unusual; or the tuneful swallow flew round the lake and the heifer, looking up to heaven—an extraordinary sight—with flared nostrils plucked down the scent of the air, and the delicate ant clears out its eggs from holes.

1–7 Serv. Dan. ad Verg. *Georg.* 1.375 sqq. 'aut bucula caelum' etc. (pp. 205–6 Thilo): *hic locus de Varrone est; ille enim sic:* 'tum—ova'.

   post v. 4 lacunam posuit Bergk

122–132 *Argonautae*

122

(*a*) Prob. ad Verg. *Georg.* 2.126 (p. 369 Hagen): . . . [v. **119**] *Varro, qui quattuor libros de Argonautis edidit* [=**119**].

   (*b*) Prop. 2.34.85: *haec quoque* [sc. carmina amatoria, v. **133***a*] *perfecto ludebat Iasone Varro.*

   (*c*) Ov. *Am.* 1.15.21–2: *Varronem primamque ratem quae nesciet aetas / aureaque Aesonio terga petita duci?*

   (*d*) Ov. *AA* 3.335–6: *dictaque Varroni fulvis insignia villis / vellera germanae, Phrixe, querenda tuae.*

   (*e*) Ov. *Tr.* 2.439–40: *is quoque Phasiacas Argon qui duxit in undas / non potuit Veneris furta tacere suae* [cf. **133***b*].

   (*f*) Quint. *Inst. Or.* 10.1.87: *Atacinus Varro in iis per quae nomen est adsecutus* [sc. *Argonautis*] *interpres operis alieni* [sc. Ap. Rh.], *non spernendus quidem, verum ad augendam facultatem dicendi parum locuples.*

   (*g*) Stat. *Silv.* 2.7.77: [cedet . . .] *et qui per freta duxit Argonautas.*

(*b*) Varro too wrote trifles like this after he had completed his Jason.

(*c*) What age will not know of Varro, the first ship, and the golden fleece sought under the leadership of Aeson's son?

(*d*) ... and the fleece of which Varro spoke, distinguished by its yellow-brown tufts, a cause of complaint to Phrixus' sister [Helle].

(*e*) And the man who led the Argo to the waters of the Phasis could not keep quiet about his illicit love affairs.

(*f*) Varro Atacinus, in the poem which won him his reputation, was the translator of someone else's work ...

(*g*) ... and he [Varr. At.] who led the Argonauts over the seas.

123–125 Liber I

123 (1 Bl., 3 C.)

> ecce venit Danai multis \<celebrata propago\>;
> namque satus Clytio, Lerni quem Naubolus ex se,
> Lernum Naupliades Proetus, sed Nauplion edit
> fil\<ia Amymone Europae\> Danaique superbi

See, there came \<Nauplius\> the descendant of Danaus, made famous by many; for he was the son of Clytius, whom Naubolus son of Lernus begat. Naubolus' father was Proetus son of Nauplius, while Nauplius' mother was Amymone, daughter of Europa and arrogant Danaus.

1–4 Schol. Verg. Veron. ad *Aen.* 2.82 'Belidae nomen Palamedis' (p. 418 Hagen): *Nauplii quidem filius Palamedes, sed longius repetita origine Belidis epitheton posuit et ad Belum refert. origo autem eius talis traditur. Epaphus ... genuit Libyam, ex qua et Neptuno Belus et Agenor nati sunt; ex Belo Danaus et Aegyptus, ex Danao Amymone, sororum L una, ex qua genuit Neptunus Nauplium; huius Proetus, et Proeti filius fuit L[a]ernus, cuius Naubolus filius et inde Clytius, ex quo Nauplius, et ex eo Palamedes, de quo nunc Sinon loquitur. Varro Argonautarum primo* 'ecce—superbi'.

 1 \<celebrata propago\> *suppl. Keil*   2–3 Laerni ... Laernum *schol. Veron.* 4 \<ia Amymone Europae\> *suppl. Keil*

124 (2 Bl., 4 C.)

> Tiphyn \<et\> aurigam celeris fecere carinae
> ... and they made Tiphys driver of the swift ship.

Charis., p. 358 Barwick[2] = GLK I, p. 272: *metaphora . . . ab animali ad animale, sicut* 'Tiphyn—carinae' *. . .* [p. 359 B[2]] *metaphorae quaedam sunt communes, quae a Graecis acoluthoe appellantur, ut* 'Tiphyn—carinae', *quia, quem ad modum in navi auriga dici potest, ita et in curru gubernator* (fere eadem Diom. GLK I, p. 457, Donat. GLK IV, p. 399 et Pomp. GLK V, p. 305 qui addit 'Tiphys gubernator fuerat navis Argus').

Typhin *ex* typho *Charis. cod. N (varie errant ceteri testes)*   <et> *suppl. Buechner coll. Ap. Rh. 1.400* (δ'): <at> *Unger.* aurigam Tiphyn *Morel* celeris] celeres *nonnulli omnium testium codices*

Varronis Atacini Argonautis dederunt Unger et Keil, coll. Ap. Rh. 1.400–1.

125 (3 Bl., 5 C.)

quos magno Anchiale partus adducta dolore
et geminis cupiens tellurem Oeaxida palmis
scindere Dicta<eo ⏑⏑ _ ⏑⏑ nympha sub antro>

[the Idaean Dactyls] whom <the nymph> Anchiale, tense with the great pain of child-birth and wanting to split the Cretan earth with her pair of hands, <discharged at the foot of> the Dictaean <cave>.

1–3 Serv. ad Verg. *Ecl.* 1.65 'et rapidum Cretae . . . Oaxen' (pp. 14–15 Thilo): . . . *Philistides* [Stiehle, coll. Plin. *NH* 4.58] *ait Apollinis et Anchiales filium; hunc Oaxen in Creta oppidum condidisse, quod suo nomine nominavit, ut Varro ait* 'quos—dicta' [inde Philarg. in Verg. *Ecl.* 1.65, p. 28 Hagen, pessime corrupta].

2 Vib. Seq. *De Fluminibus etc.* 114 (p. 20 ed. Gelsomino, 1967): *Oaxes, Cretae, a quo et civitas Oaxus. Varro hoc docet,* 'geminis—palmis'.

   2 cupiens *codd. Serv., Philarg., Vib. Seq. cod. V man. prim.:* capiens *Vib. cod. V corrector*   tellurem *Vib.:* dolorem *Serv., Philarg.*   Oaxi(d)a *Serv., Philarg., Vib., corr. Salmasius*   3 'pro dicta *scriptum fuit fortasse* Dictaeo *et totus Varronis versus, quem in* antro *exisse suspiceris, laudatus'* (Thilo). Dicta<eo . . . sub antro> *Traglia*   nympha *suppl. Hollis coll. Ap. Rh. 1.1129* νύμφη. *fort.* profudit nympha (prō- *ut* Cat. 64.202): quondam est enixa *Tandoi, Disiecti Membra Poetae I* (1984), p. IX (Ap. Rh. 1129 ποτε).

126–127 Liber II

126 (4 Bl., 6 C.)

Prob. ad Verg. *Georg.* 1.14–15 'et cultor nemorum, cui pinguia Ceae / ter centum nivei tondent dumeta iuvenci' (p. 351 Hagen): ibi [*sc. in insula Cea*] existimatur pestilentia fuisse pecorum et armentorum gravis propter interitum Actaeonis [: Icarii *coni. Hollis*]. Aristaeus monstrante Apolline patre profectus est in insulam Ceam et ibi sacrificio facto aram Iovi Icmaeo constituit, qui placatis flatibus et aestu, qui necabant pecora et armenta, liberavit ea. ipse autem post excessum vitae imperante oraculo Apollinis ab inhabitantibus eam insulam relatus in numerum deorum appellatus est Nomius et Agreus [*coni. Ruhnken*: Aegoros *Prob. cod. E*: Aegaros *MP*: Aegatos *V*], quod et agresti studio et cura pecorum armentorumque non mediocriter profuerat hominibus. *traditur haec historia de Aristaeo in corpore Argonautarum a Varrone Atacino.*

[On the island of Cea/Ceos] there is thought to have been a grievous plague affecting flocks and herds on account of the death of Actaeon [?: perhaps rather 'of Icarius']. At the indication of his father Apollo, Aristaeus set off for the island of Cea, and there (after making a sacrifice) he established an altar of Zeus the Moistener who, by calming the blasts and heat which were killing the flocks and herds, rescued them. Aristaeus himself, after his death, on the orders of Apollo's oracle, was numbered among the gods by the inhabitants of that island, and called Pastor and Countryman, because he had done outstanding service to mankind, through both his rural activities and his care of flocks and herds. This account of Aristaeus is recorded by Varro Atacinus in his *Argonauts*.

127 (5 Bl., 7 C.)

te tunc Coryciae tendentem spicula nymphae
hortantes 'o Phoebe' et 'ieie' conclamarunt

At that time, as you directed your arrows, the Corycian nymphs cried out in encouragement 'O Phoebus' and 'Ïëïë'.

1–2 Aud., GLK VII, p. 332: qui primum his observationibus in componendis carminibus usi sunt? Phemonoe dicitur, Apollinis vates, prima per insaniam ita locuta, cuius Hesiodus meminit. Varro vero in Argonautis nymphas hexametrum fecisse sic scripsit, 'te—(con)clamarunt'.

1 tunc (*vel* tum) *Hollis*: nunc *Aud.*   Coryciae *Wuellner*: Ortigiae *Aud. cod. B*:

elicona ortigie *M*   tendentem *Wuellner.* tenentem *B*: terentem *M*   specula *Aud.*
2 hortantes *Wuellner.* orantes *Aud.*   et ieie conclamarunt *Wuellner* (*qui tamen*
conclamarunt *'Graverti mei inventum' esse dicit*): et loliscona clamarunt *B*: et
locolicon aclamarunt *M*

128–130 Liber III

128 (7 Bl., 9 C.)

huic similis curis experdita lamentatur

Like her she lamented, utterly destroyed by cares.

[Serg.], GLK IV p. 564: *per praepositiones sic fiunt soloecismi, cum alia pro alia
aut supervacua ponitur aut necessaria subtrahitur:* ... *supervacua ponitur, ut
apud Varronem* 'huic—lamentatur'; *'ex' enim supervacua est.*
experdita *Buecheler* (*qui de tertio Argonautarum libro obiter cogitaverat*), *Morel*
(*qui contulit Ap. Rh. 3.664*): expedit alamentatur *[Serg.] cod. L*

129 (8 Bl., 10 C.)

desierant latrare canes, urbesque silebant;
omnia noctis erant placida composta quiete.

Dogs had ceased to bark and cities were silent; everything had been laid to
rest in the peaceful quiet of night.

1–2 Sen. *Contr.* 7.1.27: *nam in narratione, cum fratrem traditum sibi describ-
eret* [sc. Cestius], *placuit sibi in hac explicatione una et infelici: 'nox erat concu-
bia, et omnia, iudices, canentia <sub> sideribus muta erant'. Montanus Iulius,
qui comes fuit <Tiberii>, egregius poeta, aiebat illum imitari voluisse Vergili
descriptionem* [Aen. 8.26–7], *'nox erat et terras animalia fessa per omnis, /
alituum pecudumque genus, sopor altus habebat'; at Vergilio imitationem bene
cessisse, qui illos optimos versus Varronis expressisset in melius, 'desierant—
quiete'. solebat Ovidius dicere potuisse fieri longe meliores si secundi versus
ultima pars abscideretur et sic desineret: 'omnia—erant'. Varro quem voluit
sensum optime explicuit, Ovidius in illius versu suum sensum invenit; aliud
enim intercisus versus significaturus est, aliud totus significat.*
2 Sen. *Epist.* 55.5–6: *nam quid prodest totius regionis silentium, si adfectus
fremunt? 'omnia—quiete' falsum est; nulla placida est quies nisi quam ratio
composuit.*

   1 urbesque] orbesque *tempt. Nisbet*   2 placida] tacita *Sen. Epist., codd.* (*sed
ibid.* 'nulla *placida* est quies')

130 (9 Bl., 23 C. (*Chorographia*))

cuius ut aspexit torta caput angue revinctum

When <? he> saw <? her> head, bound with twisted snakes . . .

Charis., p. 114 Barwick[2] = GLK I, p. 90: *anguis cum sit masculini generis, dixerunt tamen et feminini, ut . . . Varro Atacinus* 'cuius—revinctum' (eadem sine Varronis verbis Beda, GLK VII, p. 264). Non. Marc. p. 281 Lindsay: *angues feminino . . . Varro Atacinus* 'cuius—devinctum' [sic].

hoc fragmentum *Argonautis* tribuerunt vv. dd. post Ruhnken (*Epist. Crit. ad Ernest.* (1751), 220), coll. Ap. Rh. 3.1214–15; abiudicat Zetzel (*Hermes*, 108 (1980), 501–2), de *Chorographia* cogitans.

131–132 Liber IV

131 (6 Bl., 8 C.)

frigidus et silvis Aquilo decussit honorem

. . . and chill Aquilo has shaken down from the woods their glory.

Serv. ad Verg. *Georg.* 2.404 'frigidus et silvis Aquilo decussit honorem' (p. 255 Thilo): *Varronis hic versus est.*

libro quarto dedit Hollis, coll. Ap. Rh. 4.216–17; secundo edd. priores, coll. Ap. Rh. 2.1098–1100.

132 (10 Bl., 11 C.)

tum te flagranti deiectum fulmine, Phaethon

Then you, Phaethon, struck down by a blazing thunderbolt.

Quint. *Inst. Or.* 1.5.17: *vitium, quod* συναίρεσιν *et* ἐπισυναλοιφὴν *Graeci vocant, nos complexionem dicimus, qualis est apud P. Varronem:* 'tum—Phaethon' (*versum bis laudat, omisso nomine poetae,* Mar. Vict. GLK VI, pp. 66, 147).

tum *Quint.*: cum *bis Vict.*   deiectum *Quint.*: deiecit *bis Vict.*

Varr. At. *Arg.* lib. IV fortasse tribuendum est **243** (cf. Ap. Rh. 4.225–6)

133 (carmina amatoria)

(*a*) Prop. 2.34.85–6 (cf. **122***b*): *haec quoque perfecto ludebat Iasone Varro, / Varro Leucadiae maxima flamma suae* [= **122***b*].

(*b*) Ov. *Tr.* 2.439–40 (cf. **122***e*): *is quoque, Phasiacas Argon qui duxit in undas, / non potuit Veneris furta tacere suae* [=**122***e*].

134 (19 Bl., ad 21 C.) incertae sedis

Comm. Bern. (p. 175 Usener, 1869) ad Luc. 5.517 'cannaque intexta palustri': *cum omnes 'harundinem' dicant, hic 'cannam' dixit secutus Varronem, sicut et Ovidium* [e.g. *Met.* 8.630]. Cf. Adnot. super Lucanum ad eundem locum (p. 184 Endt).
'haud scio an Atacinum' (Usener). *Chorographiae* dedit Morel (**118** cont. Baehrens).

Whereas others use the word 'harundo' ('reed'), Lucan spoke of 'canna', following Varro and Ovid.

VARRO 'Atacinus' was born in 82 BC (Jerome, **105***a*). His nickname (e.g. in Horace, *Sat.* 1.10.46 = **108**, perhaps written about 35 BC very soon after Varro's death) derives more probably from the Gallic river, now the Aude (Porf. on **108**) than from a *vicus* called Atax (Jerome, **105**). See the detailed discussion in Courtney 135–6. Perhaps initially disparaging of his provincial origin—though this area of Transalpine Gaul was highly Romanized— 'Atacinus' served to distinguish P. Terentius Varro from the polymath M. Terentius Varro of Reate. O. Brogan (*Roman Gaul* (1953), 10) speculates that the poet might have been the son of a Roman colonist of Narbo Martius (Narbonne), which had been founded in 118 BC. This is called by Pomponius Mela (2.5.75) 'Atacinorum Decimanorumque colonia' (see A. Silberman in the Budé Mela (1988), 213, n. 20).

We do not know when Varro made his way to Rome, but his earliest poem may have been the *Bellum Sequanicum* (**106–7**), celebrating Julius Caesar's campaign of 58 BC. Was this written in response to a commission, or designed by Varro as a piece of self-advertisement, with the object of attracting powerful Roman patrons? It would not be surprising if Varro came to Rome with hopes very similar to those entertained by the young Archias, who had reached the capital in 102 BC during the consulship of Marius and Catulus 'quorum alter res ad scribendum maximas, alter cum res gestas tum etiam studium atque auris adhibere posset' (Cicero, *Pro Archia* 5). Varro's *Satires* (**108**), which probably belong to his earlier period, would also most naturally fit the setting of metropolitan Rome.

Bellum Sequanicum and *Saturae* suggest adherence to an old Roman style of poetic composition, looking back to Ennius and Lucilius respectively. This did not rule out an interest in modernist techniques of the *poetae novi*; if the

fragments generally ascribed to Furius Bibaculus all belong to the same
author, we would find in him a poet who combined a very old-fashioned epic
on Julius Caesar's Gallic campaigns (**72–81**) with elegant hendecasyllables
not unworthy of Catullus (**84–6**). Yet if there is any truth in what Jerome says,
'postea XXXV annum agens Graecas litteras cum summo studio didicit'
(**105a**), Varro's poetic career took a different turn in 48 or 47 BC. One has to
be sceptical about this statement as it stands: would Varro really have
embarked on a martial epic, even of a traditional Roman cast, if he could not
read Homer in the original? Also, if we must divide Varro's career into two
parts, before and after 48–47 BC, the great majority of his poems, which
betray Hellenistic influence, would have to be crammed into the last dozen
years of his life. Nonetheless I feel that something genuine must lie behind
Jerome's words. In 48–47 BC Catullus and Calvus had disappeared from the
scene. The leading Roman poet was probably Helvius Cinna, who seems to
have written in a more obscure and Alexandrian manner than Catullus;
perhaps Varro's fellow-countryman Cornelius Gallus was already becoming
successful. Cicero's remark about the elision of final 's', 'quam nunc fugiunt
poetae novi' (*De Oratore* 161), belongs to 46 BC, and his outburst against the
'cantores Euphorionis' (*Tusc. Disp.* 3.45) to 45 or 44 BC. So it seems that these
years were marked by a continuance of neoteric ideals, and perhaps by a
stronger admiration for impenetrable Greek poetry than in the time of
Catullus.

In such a context it would not be surprising if Varro fell deeply under the
spell of the prevailing ethos. Perhaps he met a learned Greek like Parthenius
of Nicaea (see on **133** for a possible link between the two) and was fired with
enthusiasm, like Helvius Cinna, Cornelius Gallus, and the young Virgil.
Clausen (*Virgil's Aeneid and the Traditions of Hellenistic Poetry* (1987), 5)
suggests that Varro published his *Argonautae* when he was 35; that would ease
the congestion of his later years (see above), but there is no clear sign of
Varro's *Argonauts* in Virgil's *Eclogues* (the alleged connection between **125**
and *Ecl.* 1.65 is certainly bogus). Another poem, *Chorographia* (**109–19**),
seems to draw (at least for **111–13**) on Eratosthenes and Alexander of Ephe-
sus, Hellenistic poets more difficult than Apollonius Rhodius; **120** and **121**
closely follow Aratus, though it would be rash to infer that Varro made a
complete translation of the *Phaenomena*. Our only definite statement about
the order of Varro's compositions comes from Propertius (2.34.85 = **122b**),
according to whom the love-poems for Leucadia followed the *Argonauts*
('perfecto . . . Iasone')—perhaps in the late 40s or early 30s BC, under the
influence of Cornelius Gallus' elegies for Lycoris.

If we believe Ovid (*Am.* 1.15.21–2 = **122c**), time has robbed us of a major
talent in Varro; Quintilian (10.1.87 = **122f**) confirms the high repute of the

Argonauts ('in iis per quae nomen est adsecutus'), and we can find hints of quality in fragments such as **129** and **131**. When considering the links between Virgil and Apollonius, we should remember that a fine Latin version of the Argonautic legend had been published not long before the *Aeneid*. In all probability it would have played an intermediary part, as Varro's weather signs (**120–1**) did between Virgil and Aratus.

106–107 *Bellum Sequanicum*

The Roman fashion for writing epic poems on contemporary (or at least not too ancient) wars started with the *Bellum Poenicum* of Naevius; in the second century BC we can mention the *Bellum Histricum* of Hostius, describing events of 129 BC (Courtney 52–5). Another poem celebrating the Gallic campaigns of Julius Caesar was the substantial *Annales Belli Gallici* (if that is the correct title) by Furius Bibaculus (**72–81**). One suspects that the average quality of such works in the first century was not high—though Virgil may have had a better opinion of Furius Bibaculus than did Horace.

Varro's poem, in at least two books, was devoted to Caesar's campaign of 58 BC, not against the Sequani but in their territory (of which the chief town was Besontio, now Besançon) against the German Ariovistus, ruler of the Suebi (Caesar, *BG* 1.37–54). He had originally been invited by the Sequani, and stayed to subjugate them. If not written immediately after the event, the poem might have been prompted by Caesar's own *Bellum Gallicum*, generally thought to have been published in 52–51 BC (e.g. C. E. Stevens, *Latomus*, 11 (1952), 3–4). Note that the Sequani themselves could not be so-called in dactylic verse: the 'e' is long, the 'a' short (Lucan 1.425 'optima gens flexis in gyrum Sequana frenis', Martial 4.19.1 'Sequanicae pinguem textricis alumnam').

106 (23 Bl., 1 C.)

deinde ubi pellicuit dulcis levis unda saporis: we owe this fragment to the form *pellicuit* (rather than *pellexit*), which is not uncommon. Drinking from foreign rivers was a conventional heroic image of campaigning away from home, e.g. Tib. 2.6.8 'ipse levem galea qui sibi portet aquam', Prop. 3.12.8 'potabis galea fessus Araxis aquam' (cf. the story told of Alexander the Great in Arrian, *Anab.* 6.26.2–3 and of Cato in Lucan 9.500 ff.). The fetching of water (*aquatio*) was of course vitally important to an army. Description of rivers was probably a standard feature of military epics; Catullus 11.11 as well as Horace, *Sat.* 1.10.37 (**71***d*) may glance at Furius Bibaculus' poem on Caesar (**72–81**). *Bellum Sequanicum* would give Varro the opportunity to expatiate on the Rhône, Saône (Arar), Doubs (Dubis, flowing around Besontio, where Caesar spends a few days in *BG* 1.38), and no doubt others.

pellicuit: the verb suggests being lured into a dangerous situation (e.g. Lucr. 5.1005 'pellicere in fraudem ridentibus undis').

dulcis ... saporis: Nisbet compares Frontinus, *De Aquis* (e.g. 2.90–1) for Roman sensitivity to the differing taste and quality of water.

levis unda: perhaps of mountain water, not heavy or muddy (Nisbet, noting that Dubis rises in the Jura).

107 (24 Bl., 2 C.)

semianimesque micant oculi lucemque requirunt: Jocelyn (*CQ* NS 15 (1965), 141) is 'extremely suspicious' of this fragment, but the borrowing of a line unaltered from Ennius (*Ann.* 484 Skutsch) may not have been alien to the ethos of such epics; compare the very Ennian ring (not an exact quotation) of Furius Bibaculus **75**. Accordingly I have followed F. Skutsch in attributing this line to the *Bellum Sequanicum*. Others (including Baehrens and Morel) have given it to the *Argonauts*, comparing πολλὴ δὲ κατ᾿ ὀφθαλμῶν χέετ᾿ ἀχλύς (Ap. Rh. 4.1525, on the death of Mopsus from snake-bite). That remains possible but seems less likely.

108 *Saturae*

Horace, *Sat.* 1.10.46 (=**108**) provides our only evidence that Varro wrote *Satires*; one may suspect that they belong to his earlier, more traditionally Roman, phase which included the *Bellum Sequanicum* (describing events of 58 BC). Since Horace considered the Satires of Atacinus to be direct competitors which he could surpass, presumably they were written in hexameters (like most of Lucilius) and did not represent the medley of prose and verse known as 'Menippean' Satire, patronized by Varro of Reate.

There is a faint possibility that **240** (lines prefixed to Horace, *Satires* 1.10 in some manuscripts) come from Varro Atacinus or one of the others who attempted this genre (Hor. *Sat.* 1.10.47 = **108**).

109–119 *Chorographia*

One can draw quite a plausible picture of this poem, but all conclusions must be tentative. Varro's main model may have been a near-contemporary Greek poem by Alexander of Ephesus (*Suppl. Hell.* 19–38)—note, however, that the editors of *SH* condemn as mendacious the reference to an epic by Alexander on the Marsian War (*SH* 39), and so we lose this *terminus post quem* for dating the poet. Alexander of Ephesus, nicknamed Λύχνος, 'midnight-oil', whether because of his industry or his subject matter (cf. Helvius Cinna, **13**.1–2 'Aratea multum vigilata lucerna / carmina'), wrote hexameters in which he 'described the position of the heavenly bodies and gave a geographical account of the continents, producing a poem on each' (Strabo 14.1.25 = *SH* 19 ἔπη κατέλιπεν ἐν οἷς τά τε οὐράνια διατίθεται καὶ τὰς ἠπείρους γεωγραφεῖ, καθ' ἑκάστην ἐκδοὺς ποίημα). This suggests that he composed separate poems on astronomy and geography (Varro probably covered both subjects in a single poem). His astronomical poem may have been called Φαινόμενα (*SH* 20); if the geographical work had an overall title, we do not know it, since Alexander divided the world into three continents (see **109**), and ancient sources quote fragments as from his Εὐρώπη (*SH* 25–8), Ἀσία (*SH* 29–33 and perhaps 34–7), and, puzzlingly, Ἀσία καὶ Λιβύη (*SH* 37). If **109** refers to V. Atacinus, it would seem that he divided the world into just two continents; accordingly we find 'Varro in *Europa*' (**114**), though no mention of *Asia*.

Alexander's geographical poem was known in Italy during Varro's youth; in 59 BC Cicero borrowed a copy from his friend Atticus, had it transcribed and sent it back, each time with a disparaging comment: 'poeta ineptus, et tamen scit nihil; sed non est inutilis' (*Ad Att.* 2.20 (= 40 SB). 6), and 'neglegentis hominis et non boni poetae, sed tamen non inutilis' (*Ad Att.* 2.22 (= 42 SB). 7). At that time Cicero was himself contemplating a geographical work (*Ad Att.* 2.4 (= 24 SB). 3), perhaps represented by a fragment of 'Cicero in *Chorographia*' quoted by Priscian (GLK II, p. 267). Alexander's poem might also have been useful when, some five years later, Cicero composed the *Somnium Scipionis*.

Varro may have had another important source for at least part of his poem—one which combined geographical theory (the zones of heaven and earth, **112**) with Pythagorean/Platonic astronomical philosophy (the harmony of the spheres, **111**). This was the *Hermes* of Eratosthenes (Powell, *Collectanea Alexandrina*, 58–63, with *Suppl. Hell.* 397A supplementing the text of fr. 15.3 Powell), which also no doubt had influenced Alexander of Ephesus (*SH* 21 on the harmony of the spheres). It seems likely that

Alexander wrote separate poems on astronomy and geography (see above), but that Varro combined them in one, starting from 'a panoptic vision of the cosmos which then narrowed down to contemplation of the terrestrial globe' (Margaret Hubbard *per litteras*, comparing the *Somnium Scipionis*). Varro's lines on the harmony of the spheres apparently diverge in some details from both Eratosthenes and Alexander.

The tradition of geographical poetry is quite well illustrated by the Greek work of Dionysius Periegetes (time of Hadrian). Its geography may be confused or obsolete (decried e.g. by J. Oliver Thomson, *History of Ancient Geography* (1948), 228–9, etc.), but that is not really the point. Dionysius, like Varro, undoubtedly used Alexander of Ephesus, and material common to the two Greek poets will give an idea of the favourite kind of topics in this genre: the island Ogyris, tomb of the mythical king Erythras who gave his name to the Erythraean sea (Alexander, *SH* 33, cf. Dion. Per. 606–7); Taprobane (Ceylon) with its elephants (Alexander, *SH* 36, cf. Dion. Per. 593). Even in the scanty remains of Varro's poem we can find an interest in mythological origins (**119**, Media named after Medus, son of Medea, cf. Dion. Per. 1020 ff.) and the picturesque and paradoxical (**118**, the 'Indica . . . harundo' which grows to the height of a large tree and produces a liquid sweeter than honey). A reading of Dion. Per. may suggest possible links between Varro's *Chorographia* and other Latin poetry; e.g. Virgil's powerful and dramatic description of Scythia (*Georgics* 3.349 ff.) has a briefer and less vivid counterpart in Dion. Per. 652–78, and it would not be surprising if Varro too had a set piece on Scythia.

Varro's *Chorographia* by no means attained the glory of his *Argonauts*, but **112** on the five zones is reflected in Virgil's *Georgics*, perhaps also in the *Panegyricus Messallae*, Ovid's *Metamorphoses*, and Lucan. We cannot date it more closely; if one took literally (see p. 178 above) Jerome's statement (**105a**) that Varro 'learnt Greek with great enthusiasm at the age of 35' (i.e. about 47 BC), one would place the *Chorographia* in the last decade of Varro's life. Certainly Eratosthenes and Alexander of Ephesus would be more formidable propositions than Apollonius or even Aratus. The complete poem probably survived at least to the time of the Elder Pliny (**110**).

The title *Chorographia* is preserved by Priscian together with the text of **113**, and can be regarded as secure enough; the variants (e.g. ort(h)ographia) are very closely paralleled in Priscian's quotation from 'Cicero in *Chorographia*' (GLK II, p. 267). This was a conventional title, and may have been given e.g. by Pomponius Mela to his geographical work. Ptolemy (1.1) discusses a distinction between γεωγραφία and χωρογραφία which is probably not relevant to Varro Atacinus. For earlier discussion (besides Courtney) of this poem, see H. Dahlmann and W. Speyer, *Varronische Studien*, II (1959), 751–67.

109 dub.

In my opinion there is a better than even chance that the 'Varro' here cited is Atacinus. One can certainly make a good case for the polymath M. Terentius Varro of Reate, e.g. *De Lingua Latina* 5.31 '[divisa est] terra in Asiam et Europam' (cf. *De Re Rustica* 1.2.3 referring to Eratosthenes), but perhaps an even better one for Varr. At., since part of the *Chorographia* was actually entitled *Europa* (see **114**)—the corresponding title *Asia* is attested for Alexander of Ephesus (p. 181 above), but not for our poet. Two points somewhat favour Atacinus: (*a*) the linking with Alexander, who is very probably the Ephesian (*SH* 23), Varro's immediate model for this poem; (*b*) the source of this testimony in the Berne Commentary on Lucan, which also preserves **118** (and the unplaced **134**, perhaps likewise *Chorographia*) and generally is interested in out of the way Latin poetry (**67** (Aemilius Macer), **208** (Cornelius Severus)).

Another geographical work which divides the world into *Europa* and *Asia* is the *Periegesis* of pseudo-Scymnus, written *c*.100 BC in (very poor) Greek iambics.

110

The Elder Pliny used Varr. At. as a source for the geographical books 3–6 of his *Natural History*—not, it would seem, for book 2 which discusses astronomy, including the zones (cf. **111–12**). These books have an identical summary of contents: 'situs, gentes, maria, oppida, portus, montes, flumina, mensurae, populi qui sunt aut qui fuerunt'. So many other sources, Latin and Greek, are mentioned that it would be fruitless to try to identify what Pliny may owe to Varro Atacinus (e.g. *NH* 5.1 on the boundaries of Libya agrees with **116** but could have come from almost anywhere). If one so wishes, one might note certain interests shared with Alexander of Ephesus and/or Dionysius Periegetes (e.g. *NH* 6.33 Eous and Indicus, cf. Dion. Per. 36–7; 6.153 Ogyris, burial place of King Erythras, cf. Alexander *SH* 33, Dion. Per. 606–7) and other things which are in the spirit of this kind of poetry (e.g. *NH* 6.38, the Albani are descended from Jason, cf. Varr. At. **119**, the Medes descended from Medus).

111 (11 Bl., 15 C.)

A particularly difficult fragment (I am grateful to Dr M. J. Edwards of Christ Church, Oxford, for advice on the spheres), discussed also by L. Nosarti, *Filologia in Frammenti* (1999), 210–15. The subject of 'vidit' (1) is unclear. One naturally compares ἔτετμε, 'he [Mercury] found' in Eratosthenes' *Hermes* (fr. 16.1 Powell), where the infant god ascends to the heavens and is astonished to find that the music of the spheres exactly harmonizes with that of the lyre which he has just invented (see the texts quoted by Powell, *CA*, on Eratosthenes fr. 13). Alexander of Ephesus likewise speaks of Hermes as the inventor: τοίην τοι σειρῆνα Διὸς πάϊς ἥρμοσεν Ἑρμῆς / ἑπτάτονον κίθαριν, θεομήστορος εἰκόνα κόσμου (*Suppl. Hell.* 21.25–6). Lines 4–5 of our passage raise the possibility that he gave Apollo a part similar to that played by Hermes in Eratosthenes' poem, but I have preferred to emend 'Phoebi' (4) to 'Phoebo' ('by far the most pleasing to Phoebus'), so that the 'dextera' (5) can be that of Mercury, restoring normality.

1. aetherio mundum torquerier axe: I think that the 'mundus' here is not 'the world' but 'the universe' (as in Varius Rufus, **157**.4), and that Varro refers to the stars which are thought to be fixed in a revolving celestial sphere with the other seven spheres (Varro line 2) below them: cf. Cicero, *Somnium Scipionis* 17 'caelestis, extumus [sc. orbis], qui reliquos omnes complectitur ... in quo sunt infixi illi qui volvuntur stellarum cursus sempiterni; cui subiecti sunt septem qui versantur retro contrario motu atque caelum'. The Stoics identified this outer sphere with the aether (see Ronconi on the *Somnium Scipionis*, 94–6).

  aetherio ... axe: the axis on which the outer sphere revolves.

  torquerier: Wigodsky (*Virgil and Early Latin Poetry*, 43, 104) suggests that Varro may be responsible for 'torquet' in a Virgilian line otherwise indebted to Ennius, 'axem umero torquet stellis ardentibus aptum' (*Aen.* 4.482 = 6.797, cf. 9.93 'torquet qui sidera mundi'); the anonymous **257**.1 'Iuppiter omnipotens, caeli qui sidera torques' cannot be dated. The passive infinitive in -ier gives an old-fashioned flavour, suitable to a didactic poem (as in Virgil, *Georgics* 1.454 'inmiscerier'), though metrical convenience preserved the form until the time of Ausonius (cf. Austin on *Aen.* 4.493 'accingier').

  2. septem ... orbes: the five known planets (Mercury, Venus, Mars, Jupiter, Saturn) plus the Sun and Moon. For the Platonic idea of a musical note emitted by the spheres, cf. Alex. Eph., *SH* 21.9–10 πάντες δ' ἑπτατόνοιο λύρης φθόγγοισι συνωιδόν / ἁρμονίην προχέουσι, διαστάσει ἄλλος ἐπ' ἄλλῃ ('Together they all pour forth a harmony which matches the notes of a seven-stringed lyre, at intervals one above another'). See further M. Papathomopoulos, *Nouveaux fragments d'auteurs anciens* (1980), 44–7; F. Solmsen, *TAPA* 73 (1942), 199–201; W. Stahl, *TAPA* 73 (1942), 234; Pease on Cicero, *DND* 2.119 'concentus' and on 3.27 'ad harmoniam canere mundum'.

3. **nitentes:** 'as they press onwards', cf. *OLD nitor*[1] 6, e.g. Lucr. 1.372 'squamigeris ... nitentibus'. Our quoting source (Marius Victorinus) paraphrases 'per orbes suos [through their orbits] nitentes'.

aliis alios: 'different spheres with different notes', understanding 'vocibus' (from 2) with 'aliis' (thus Dr M. J. Edwards, *per litteras*). It is the harmony of different notes which causes so much pleasure to the gods (3–4).

3–4. **quae maxima divis / laetitia est:** perhaps suggesting θεοῖσι δὲ χάρμα τέτυκται, although that phrase does not occur in extant Greek poetry.

4–5. In Eratosthenes, *Hermes* (fr. 13, see the texts quoted by Powell ad loc.), the god, ascending to the heavenly regions, is astonished to find that his new invention, the lyre, exactly parallels the harmony of the celestial spheres. Here perhaps the notes of the instrument are made to copy those of the spheres (5).

longe gratissima Phoebo / dextera: the manuscripts have 'Phoebi'. I have emended to 'Phoebo' in order that the 'dextera' (5) can be that of Hermes, who could then be the subject of 'vidit' (all as in Eratosthenes). The dative with 'gratissima' is not unwelcome (cf. *Ciris* 473–4 'longe gratissima Delos / Nereidum matri et Neptuno Aegaeo', *Aen.* 3.73–4 without 'longe'). The *Homeric Hymn to Hermes* repeatedly stresses how much pleasure Apollo derives from Mercury's lyre (420–1 γέλασσε δὲ Φοῖβος Ἀπόλλων / γηθήσας, 443–6 θαυμασίην γὰρ τήνδε νεήφατον ὄσσαν ἀκούω, / ἣν οὔ πώ ποτέ φημι δαήμεναι οὔτε τιν' ἀνδρῶν, / οὔτε τιν' ἀθανάτων οἳ Ὀλύμπια δώματ' ἔχουσι, / νόσφι σέθεν, 453–5, 523–5).

5. **meditatur reddere:** 'practises reproducing' (see *OLD meditor* 5 for other examples with the infinitive).

112 (13 Bl., 17 C.)

This fragment of Varro (discussed by K. Buechner in *Hermes*, 105 (1977), 384) seems clearly indebted to the famous passage from Eratosthenes' *Hermes* (fr. 16 Powell) which we have already encountered (see Introduction to the *Chorographia*, and on **111**) and may in turn be imitated by Virgil (*Georgics* 1) and Ovid (*Met.* 1)—perhaps also by the author of the *Panegyricus Messallae* and Lucan.

The doctrine of the five zones (ζώνη literally = 'belt' or 'girdle') which embrace the sky, and of the corresponding five zones of the earth, is usually attributed to Pythagoras (Aëtius 3.13.1 in Diels, *Doxographi Graeci*[2] (1929), 378). See further T. L. Heath, *Aristarchus of Samos* (1913), 21, 65–6; J. Oliver Thomson, *History of Ancient Geography* (1948), index s.v. Zones, Strabo 2.2.2 ff. (there are useful notes in H. L. Jones's Loeb); W. H. Stahl, 'Astronomy and Geography in Macrobius', *TAPA* 73 (1942), 232–58 (a clear and helpful exposition); I. G. Kidd on Posidonius, Περὶ ὠκεανοῦ (fr. 49 Kidd, vol. II. 1, pp. 216–75). For the exact correspondence of celestial and terrestrial zones, cf. e.g. Achilles, Isagoga Excerpta 29 (Maass, Commentariorum in Aratum Reliquiae (1898), 62) εἰσὶ δὲ [sc. ζῶναι] καὶ ἐν οὐρανῶι καὶ ἐπὶ γῆς, αἳ κατὰ καθετόν εἰσι [are vertically below] τῶν ἐν τῶι οὐρανῶι, Strabo 2.5.3 πεντάζωνον μὲν γὰρ ὑποθέσθαι δεῖ τὸν οὐρανόν, πεντάζωνον δὲ καὶ τὴν γῆν, ὁμωνύμους δὲ καὶ τὰς ζώνας τὰς κάτω ταῖς ἄνω.

I do not understand the conventional punctuation of this fragment, with a full stop (Courtney) or semi-colon (Blänsdorf) after line 1 and a colon after 2.

1.   ut: my conjecture for the MSS 'at'. 'Ut' (coupled with 'aetherius' rather than 'aetheriis') gives real point to 'sic' (3), insisting on a precise correspondence between the celestial and terrestrial zones (see the Greek passages quoted above) and the climate of each pair. Ovid may reflect Varro's 'ut . . . / . . . / sic' (note the identical spacing) in *Met.* 1.45–8: '*ut*que duae dextra caelum totidemque sinistra / parte secant zonae, quinta est ardentior illis, / *sic* onus inclusum [sc. the Earth] numero distinxit eodem / cura dei, totidemque plagae tellure premuntur'. Stahl (*TAPA* (1942), 249) puts it clearly:

a belt on the celestial sphere lying directly over the zone bounded by these solstitial points [Cancer and Capricorn] is constantly scorched by the sun beneath it. Two belts about the celestial poles are always stiff with cold because they are furthest removed from the sun's path. In between are two temperate celestial belts, chilled on the one hand and warmed on the other. The upper air and atmosphere conduct to the earth the temperature of the region directly above in the sky.

aetherius: so three manuscripts of Isidore, *De Rerum Natura*, preferred to 'aetheriis' by the 1960 editor J. Fontaine (p. 345), though purely, it seems, on aesthetic grounds because of the more elegant word order *quinque (a) aetherius (b) zonis (a) . . . orbis (b)* (cf. T. E. V. Pearce, *CQ* ns 16 (1966), 167 and 302). Blänsdorf, Courtney, and others print 'aetheriis'. To my mind 'aetherius' is essential, making clear that Varro refers to the celestial (not the terrestrial) sphere, the orbis 'caelestis extumus' of Cic. *Rep.* 6.17—see above.

accingitur: glancing at the literal meaning of ζώνη ('belt' or 'girdle'). Cicero uses a Latin noun (*Somnium Scipionis* 21 'terram quasi quibusdam redimitam et circumdatam cingulis'); Varro is the first to borrow the Greek term for this astronomical sense.

2. **vastant:** 'ravage', cf. *Pan. Mess.* 153 'atque duae gelido vastantur frigore semper'. In this kind of passage we may find applied to the celestial sphere language which seems more appropriate to the terrestrial (cf. Mynors on *Georgics* 1.233, 'V. describes these [the celestial zones] in language more suited to their earthly counterparts').

imas: the plural, applying to both the northern and the southern outermost zone, is surprising—could it owe anything to the belief of some (discussed by Strabo, 2.3.3) that, on the Earth, the Equator was the 'highest' part of the globe? A similar but not identical problem arises in Lucan 4.106–7 (perhaps reflecting our fragment) 'sic mundi pars ima iacet, quam zona nivalis / perpetuaeque premunt hiemes', where Housman commented 'mundi partem imam non facile aliam esse posse quam plagam antarcticam . . . sed cur illa potius quam septentrionalis [to which Isidore, *Orig.* 3.41 and *DRN* 9.3 refer these lines of Lucan] commemoretur, non apparet'.

hiemes: 'extreme cold'.

3. **sic:** picking up 'ut' (line 1, see ad loc.).

extremas inter mediamque: sc. zonas. The similar anastrophe in *Georgics* 1.127 'has [referring back to 'extremae' in 235] inter mediamque' seems to confirm that Virgil did indeed have this fragment in mind (cf. R. F. Thomas, *HSCP* 90 (1986), 197).

coluntur: perhaps 'are inhabited' rather than 'are cultivated', though either would fit the general doctrine (e.g. Isidore, *DRN* 10.3 on the torrid zone, 'ut nec fruges ibi nascantur propter exustam terram, nec homines propter nimium ardorem habitare permittantur'). Eratosthenes stresses the fertility of the two temperate zones, ἄμφω ἐΰκρῆτοί τε καὶ ὄμπνιον ἀλδήισκουσαι / καρπὸν Ἐλευσίνης Δημήτερος (fr. 16.17–18 P.).

4. **quas:** sc. 'terrae' (3), Grial's emendation for the manuscripts' 'quam', which could only refer to 'mediamque'.

†ut auferat†: Grial's 'vis' has commended itself to many (cf. e.g. Lucr. 4.326), and 'valido . . . vis' would be somewhat in the Lucretian alliterative manner (e.g. 6.137 'validi vis . . . venti'). Some consider 'auferat' sound, taking it to mean either 'consume', 'destroy' (but see Skutsch on Ennius, *Annals* 244), or 'deny access to' (Kraggerud, comparing Lucr. 5.204–5). Courtney commends the latter sense, but remarks that it does not go well with 'numquam' (as if the torrid zone were sometimes habitable, sometimes not).

I am attracted by Scaliger's 'solis . . . rota' (cf. Cicero, *Aratea* fr. 33.281 Buescu 'rota fervida solis', Lucr. 5.432, 564, Seneca, *HO* 1439 'Phoebique tritam flammea zonam rota'), which might be followed by 'torreat' (almost the *vox propria* for the innermost zone, e.g. Cicero, *Somnium Scipionis* 21, Pliny, *NH* 2.172, cf. Virgil, *Georgics* 1.234 'torrida semper ab igni'). Nisbet suggests 'vis hauriat' (*OLD haurio* 7a). Probably Varro would have continued with a reference to the frozen zones, something like '<nec semper glacies adstringat frigore et imbri>' (cf. *Georgics* 1.236 'glacie concretae atque imbribus atris').

113 (12 Bl., 16 C.)

This fragment (discussed by Dahlmann and Speyer, *Varronische Studien*, II (1959), 751–6) seems clearly geographical rather than astronomical. On the hypothesis that Varro may have started from a vision of the whole cosmos, and thereafter turned to contemplation of our world (see above, Introduction to the *Chorographia*), I have, unlike Courtney and Blänsdorf, placed these lines after **112**.

1. solis stationem: not 'the position normally or properly occupied by' the sun (so *OLD statio* 2c), but a poetical variant for 'solstitium', designating the summer solstice = Tropic of Cancer. Isidore (*DRN* 8.2) writes 'solstitium autem dicitur quasi solis statio'.

    sidera septem: the 'septem triones' or 'septem stellae' of the Great Bear; *OLD* gets it right s.v. *septem*, wrong s.v. *sidus* 2a (quoting Varr. At. in both cases). Compare e.g. Accius, *Trag.* 566–7 R² 'sub axe posita ad stellas septem, unde horrifer / Aquilonis stridor gelidas molitur nives'.

    2. tellus: not 'the earth', but 'the land', i.e. the northern habitable zone (cf. **112**), which stretched from the Arctic Circle to the Tropic of Cancer (ἀπὸ ἀρκτικοῦ κύκλου μέχρι θερινοῦ τροπικοῦ, Achilles, *Isagoga Excerpta* (Maass, *Commentariorum in Aratum Reliquiae* (1898), 62). As time progressed, observation came to conflict with theory as to whether the 'torrid zone' was in fact inhabited (the dispute can be followed via Thomson, *History of Ancient Geography*, index s.v. zones).

    extima: we owe the preservation of the fragment to this form, which is not so rare (e.g. Lucr. 3.219, Cic. *Rep.* 6.17, and several times in Silver Latin prose).

    2. Although 'Neptunus' is often used by metonymy for the sea (like Nereus and Amphitrite), the particular antithesis between Oceanus and Neptunus is unusual: Catullus 31.3 'uterque Neptunus', i.e. salt and fresh water, may be similar in spirit, but is not a close parallel. Dionysius Periegetes opposes Ὠκεανός to Ἀμφιτρίτη and often gives the latter an epithet (e.g. 201 Τυρσηνίδος Ἀμφιτρίτης, 324 Προποντίδος Α.), as Nonnus does with Νηρεύς (*Dion.* 25.51 Λίβυς ... Νηρεύς, 32.194 Ἄραψ ... Ν.). Here 'Neptunus' = the Mediterranean sea.

114 (14 Bl., 18 C.)

tutum sub sede fuissent: quite baffling (see Courtney 251–2). Festus seems to say that 'tutum' was commonly used (? among older writers) for 'maxime', which is hard to credit. In his second edition of Festus, Lindsay wished to replace 'tutum' with 'tantum', which 'is at least in the semantic area of quantity' (Courtney), and would come closer to alphabetical order (the lemma is surrounded by words starting in *ta*-). Normal Latin for 'in security' (which might cohere with 'sub' in a protecting sense) was 'tuto' or 'in tuto'.

The citation 'Varro in *Europa*' is valuable, suggesting that parts of the *Chorographia* had separate titles—presumably there was a corresponding title *Asia* (see **109** dub. for the possibility that Varr. At. divided the world into just two parts), though it is nowhere attested. The idea of separate titles perhaps came from Alexander of Ephesus (see above, Introduction to the *Chorographia*).

115 (15 Bl., 19 C.)

munitus vicus Caralis: the manuscripts of the grammarian Consentius offer only 'cinus' or 'cynus' for the name of the author; Hertz made the supplement '<Ata>cinus', which suffices (cf. **116** for omission of 'Varro'). Caralis was a town in Sardinia (now Cagliari); see *TLL* Onomasticon II, col. 179, for other references. Claudian, at least, found something of poetic interest in Caralis: 'urbs Libyam contra Tyrio fundata potenti / tenditur in longum Caralis, tenuemque per undas / obvia dimittit fracturum flamina collem; / efficitur portus medium mare, tutaque ventis / omnibus ingenti mansuescunt stagna recursu' (*Bell. Gild.* 1.520–4). A geographical poet might have a special section on islands; Dion. Per. starts his with a new invocation (447 ff.), mentioning Sardinia very briefly (458).

116 (16 Bl., 20 C.)

There are obvious attractions in linking this fragment with **117** to produce 'cingitur Oceano, Libyco mare, flumine Nilo / feta feris Libye' (Morel), though Courtney considers 'Libyco mare . . . / . . . Libye' to be inelegant, and **117** may yet come from the *Argonauts*. In any case Libya must be the subject of **116**, and the line could well have opened the description of that land. If **109** dub. refers to our Varro, he would have considered Libya to be part of Asia; those who divided the world into three parts made the boundary between Libya and Asia either the Nile (e.g. Dion. Per. 230 ὅς ῥά τε καὶ Λιβύην ἀποτέμνεται Ἀσίδος αἴης) or the Red Sea. See I. G. Kidd, *Posidonius: The Commentary*, II. 1, p. 265.

   mare: the ablative in -e rather than -i is common enough (e.g. Lucr. 1.161, Ovid, *Tr.* 5.2.20, *Ex Ponto* 4.6.46).

<h2 style="text-align:center">117 (17 Bl., 12 C.)</h2>

feta feris Libye: as explained above, it is attractive to link this fragment to **116**. But Ruhnken could still have been right in ascribing the words to book 4 of the *Argonauts*, comparing Ap. Rh. 4.1561 Λιβύηι θηροτρόφωι. 'Feta' = 'teeming or abounding with' (*OLD fetus*¹ 3*b* of places, with ablative, cf. Solinus 17.4 'Hyrcani ... gens ... feta tigribus'), but keeping the word's associations with birth and pregnancy. Countries are regularly 'mother' or 'nurse' of the animals which they contain; see Nisbet and Hubbard on Horace, *Odes* 1.22.16 'arida nutrix', Vitruvius 8.3.24 'Africa parens et nutrix ferarum bestiarum', and e.g. Dion. Per. 593 'μητέρα Ταπροβάνην Ἀσιηγενέων ἐλεφάντων. 'Feta feris' is a nice alliterative phrase, cf. *Aen.* 1.51 'loca feta furentibus Austris'.

<h2 style="text-align:center">118 (18 Bl., 21 C.)</h2>

On the Indian sugar cane see R. J. Forbes, *Studies in Ancient Technology*, V (1966), 101–11, mentioning our passage of Isidore but not Varr. At. Western traditions are confused about this. Nearchus, Alexander the Great's admiral, commented on the 'honey-bearing reeds' of India (εἴρηκε δὲ καὶ περὶ τῶν καλάμων, ὅτι ποιοῦσι μέλι, Strabo 15.1.20), and Eratosthenes believed, like Varro, that the sweetness came from the roots (ibid., τὰς ῥίζας τῶν φυτῶν καὶ μάλιστα τῶν μεγάλων καλάμων γλυκείας καὶ φύσει καὶ ἑψήσει). Dion. Per. 1127 has burgeoning forests of sugar cane (ὕλαι τηλεθόωσιν Ἐρυθραίου καλάμοιο). Seneca reports a belief 'inveniri apud Indos mel in arundinum foliis' (*Epist.* 84.4), perhaps a motif from the Golden Age, e.g. Virgil, *Georgics* 1.131 'mellaque decussit foliis', while Nonnus is most fantastical (*Dion.* 26.183 ff.). More factually, *Periplus Maris Erythraei* 14 mentions among exports from Ariace and Barygaza (Broach) μέλι τὸ καλάμινον τὸ λεγόμενον.

The *Adnotationes super Lucanum* (p. 97 Endt, on 3.237) are surprisingly well informed: 'cannarum viridium caudicibus tunsis sive tritis dicuntur exprimere sucos'.

1. non magna minor arbore: 'non' goes with 'minor' (cf. Housman on Lucan 1.145). In fact the sugar cane grows to between six and twelve feet high. Exaggeration is rife: according to Solinus (I52.46, p. 192 Mommsen) 'Indorum nemora in tam proceram sublimantur excelsitatem ut transiaci ne sagittis quidem possint' (there follows a close paraphrase of Varr. At., quoted on line 2 below). Compare Virgil, *Georgics* 2.123–4 (on India) 'ubi aera vincere summum / arboris haud ullae iactu potuere sagittae'.

2. illius et lentis: Arévalo suggested 'e' for 'et'; one might consider deleting 'et' and scanning 'illīus', but Varro seems to like postponed 'et' (**111.1, 131**, perhaps **124**). Solinus 52.48 (see above, on line 1) 'e radicibus eius [sc. harundinis] umor dulcis exprimitur ad melleam suavitatem' seems a virtual paraphrase of Varr. At., perhaps originally taken from some commentary on Lucan 3.237 which quoted our fragment.

3. cui nequeant ... contendere: for such an implied contest between plants or products, cf. Horace, *Odes* 2.6.14–16 'ubi non Hymetto / mella decedunt, viridique certat baca Venafro', with Nisbet and Hubbard on 15 'decedunt'. Nonnus has a contest between Aristaeus' honey and Dionysus' wine (*Dion.* 19.227–62, cf. 13.271 ff.).

suco: probably ablative, 'in flavour', rather than dative agreeing with 'cui'; in the latter case 'suco' would be virtually redundant after 'umor' in the previous line.

contendere: in Greek ἐρίζω, e.g. Call. *Hecale* fr. 74.15 H. καὶ ἂν κύκνοισιν ἐρίζοι, Dion. Per. 757 κείνοις [sc. Chinese silks] οὔτι κεν ἔργον ἀραχνάων ἐρίσειεν.

119 (20 Bl., 22 C.)

The manner of citation ('ut existimat Varro, qui quattuor libros de Argonautis edidit') made Baehrens (fr. 11) and Morel (fr. 13) include this among fragments of the *Argonautae*, though they could not suggest an appropriate placc for it. Could Varro have expanded on the later history of Medea which (after her abandonment by Jason and the murder of her children) included her flight to Athens and marriage with Aegeus? That seems conceivable, but unlikely.

It will be noticed that the citation stops short of saying that this story came from the *Argonauts*; one may wonder whether 'qui quattuor libros de Argonautis edidit' (= **122a**, incidentally our only proof that Varro's epic had the same number of books as its model) is not a clumsy way of distinguishing Varro Atacinus from V. Reatinus. If Varro said not merely that the Medes descend from Medus, but also that Media was part of Parthia, one could even more confidently give this item to the *Chorographia*; Parthia had no mythological significance, but was of great concern to Romans in the 50s and 40s BC.

Ascription to the *Chorographia* gains slight support from Dionysius Periegetes, who described the flight of Medea from Athens to her ὁμώνυμον ... γαῖαν (1026)—he derives the name Media from the heroine, not her son—and then goes on to the Parthians (1040 ff.). There may be an element of mythological polemic involved. Some believed that Medea returned to Colchis and even helped the aged Aeetes to regain his throne (thus, probably, the *Medus* of Pacuvius, Warmington, *Remains of Old Latin*, II, pp. 248 ff.), but Dionysius insists that she could not go back home for fear of her father (1028, μῆνιν γὰρ ἑοῦ δειδίσσετο πατρός). Dion. Per. likes to digress on the mythical origin of peoples and places (e.g. 775 ff. on Sinope), and that was no doubt characteristic of learned geographical poetry as a whole (cf. on **110**). On this fragment see further Dahlmann and Speyer, *Varronische Studien*, II, pp. 765–6.

120–121 (? *Epimenides,* or *Epimenis* or *Ephemeris*)

The two surviving fragments of this work are closely based on the *Phaenomena* of Aratus and separated by only two lines (940–1) in the Greek original. But the title and overall nature of Varro's poem remain mysterious. Codd. N and P of the *Brevis Expositio* (which quotes **120**) have the nonsensical 'Varro in Epimedine'; cod. G offers 'in *Epimenide*'. One might make something of the latter. Morel noted that the word ἐπιμηνίς (? = 'monthly account'), though not attested, would be 'probe formata'; alternatively Varro might have chosen as his title the name of the Cretan sage and miracle-worker Epimenides (on Adesp. **238** I float the possibility of a poem with a double title, 'Epimenides sive Cretica'). Courtney (p. 246) argues forcefully for Bergk's conjecture 'in *Ephemeride*', which he translates 'weather-forecast' (cf. *OLD* 2 'calendar, almanac'). There is some evidence of Hellenistic poems entitled Ἐφημερίς or Ἐφημερίδες (see *Suppl. Hell.* 2–3 and 362), but their nature is quite obscure.

It would be rash to assume that the poem was a full version of Aratus' *Phaenomena* (in which case one might expect it to be cited more often by ancient commentators on Virgil's First Georgic). Perhaps the Aratean imitation was a set piece inserted in a poem of a different character; Virgil, though with greater freedom in imitation, inserts into his *Georgics* passages modelled upon Eratosthenes' *Hermes* (*G.* 1.233 ff.) and Nicander's *Theriaca* (3.425 ff.). We can see from **121** that Varro was acquainted with Cicero's *Aratea*; the use made of **121** by Virgil in *Georgics* 1.375 ff. provides one of the most notable examples of creative imitation in all Latin poetry.

120 (21 Bl., 13 C.)

1–2. **nubes si ut vellera lanae / constabunt:** the comparison of clouds with woolly fleeces goes back beyond Aratus (*Phaen.* 938–9 πολλάκι δ' ἐρχομένων ὑετῶν νέφεα προπάροιθεν / οἷα μάλιστα πόκοισιν ἐοικότα ἰνδάλλονται) to Aristophanes (*Clouds* 343) and pseudo-Theophrastus (*De Signis Tempestatum* 13), and was obviously popular. Compare in Latin Lucr. 6.504 'veluti pendentia vellera lanae', Virgil, *Georgics* 1.397 'tenuia nec lanae per caelum vellera ferri'.

1. **si ut:** I am convinced by the arguments of V. Buescu (*Problèmes de critique et d'histoire textuelles* (1942), 15–27), who deletes only one letter from the transmitted text ('*sicut* vellera' could easily be influenced by '*sicut* et Aratus*' immediately after the quotation). The elision of 'si' before 'u' is not common, but permissible (Virgil, *Ecl.* 7.27 'si ultra', *Aen.* 6.770 'si umquam'). Buescu (p. 19) points out that in Avienus' *Aratea* 1696–1705 ten signs of coming rain are introduced with 'si', including 1697 'vellera si caelo volitent'; on p. 26 he adds Pliny, *NH* 18.355 'si nubes ut vellera lanae spargentur' (a deliberate echo of Varro?). This solution of the textual problem seems far superior to those of Riese (delete 'sic') and Baehrens ('ceu' for 'sicut').

2. **constabunt:** as *OLD consto* 1b, 'to be collected in a mass', 'lie'. Courtney notes that the verb is a favourite of Lucretius.

121 (22 Bl., 14 C.)

This, our longest fragment of Varr. At., plays an important part in one of the most notable sequences of creative imitation in Latin poetry; we can see Cicero, Varro, and Virgil taking up the Greek model in Aratus' *Phaenomena*, and those later in the sequence commenting on and refining the work of their Latin predecessors. For discussion, see Gordon Williams, *Tradition and Originality in Roman Poetry* (1968), 255–9; R. F. Thomas' commentary on *Georgics* 1.374–87; G. Bocuto, 'I segni premonitori del tempo in Virgilio e in Arato', *Atene e Roma*, 30 (1985), 9–16.

The first four lines of Varro correspond to Aratus 942–5:

> πολλάκι λιμναῖαι ἢ εἰνάλιαι ὄρνιθες
> ἄπληστον κλύζονται ἐνιέμεναι ὑδάτεσσιν,
> ἢ λίμνην πέρι δηθὰ χελιδόνες ἀίσσονται
> γαστέρι τύπτουσαι αὔτως εἰλυμένον ὕδωρ.

the last three to Aratus 954–7:

> καὶ βόες ἤδη τοι πάρος ὕδατος ἐνδίοιο
> οὐρανὸν εἰσανιδόντες ἀπ' αἰθέρος ὠσφρήσαντο,
> καὶ κοίλης μύρμηκες ὀχῆς ἒξ ὤεα πάντα
> θᾶσσον ἀνηνέγκαντο.

Some scholars seem to have thought this fact sufficient in itself to establish a lacuna in Varro (Blänsdorf was very precise, 'lacuna novem versuum'). H. D. Jocelyn (*CQ* NS 15 (1965), 140), while not wishing to lay weight on that argument, wrote 'The verse *aut arguta lacus circumvolitavit hirundo* attaches neatly neither to the preceding three verses nor to the following two. I should therefore suppose that a collector of Virgil's *furta* set down a consecutive series of passages from Varro's work . . . and that some commentator ran two distinct passages relating to *G.* 1.383–7 and to *G.* 1.375–80 into what we now read in the Danieline scholium on *G.* 1.375, assimilating the text of the first verse of the second passage to that of *G.* 1.377.'

For the moment I leave on one side Jocelyn's suspicion that the text of Varro's fourth line (= **121**.4, see ad loc.) may have been altered. Aratus likes to introduce individual signs of impending rain with a repeated ἤ, first word of the line in 940–1, 944, 946, 948–9 (Virgil has 'aut' *not* at the line beginning in *G.* 1.374–5, at the line beginning in 377 = **121**.4), but another method of introduction is πολλάκι (first word in 938 and 942). It is hardly essential that 'aut' in **121**.4 should be part of a series with repeated 'aut'; the sequence 'tum liceat . . . / cernere . . . / aut . . . / et . . . / nec . . . non' does not seem to me sufficiently objectionable to demand a lacuna. As an argument against a lacuna one may note that Varro has incorporated in our surviving lines some elements from the intervening lines of Aratus (see on 2 and 3).

Virgil too felt free to omit, amplify, and alter the order of the weather signs. Where close verbal imitation occurs, he may change e.g. the part of speech ('certatim' for Varro's 'certare'), number ('rores' for 'rorem'), or metrical position ('_ ◡ ◡ _ patulis _ _ _ naribus' for 'naribus _ ◡ ◡ _ patulis'). His version of Varro's first three lines runs (*G.* 1.383–7 with an artful anacoluthon) 'iam variae pelagi volucres et quae Asia circum / dulcibus in stagnis rimantur prata Caystri—/ certatim largos umeris infundere rores, / nunc caput obiectare fretis, nunc currere in undas / et studio incassum videas gestire lavandi'. For Varro lines 4–6 Virgil produces (375–7) 'aut bucula caelum / suspiciens patulis captavit naribus auras / aut arguta lacus circumvolitavit hirundo'.

1. tum: i.e. 'when rain is impending'. We cannot be sure that this fragment was as close to **120** as suggested by the mere two-line interval in Aratus (from 938–9 to 942 ff.).

1–2. liceat . . . / cernere: not in Aratus, this touch invites a reader to share the observation (Williams, *Tradition and Originality*, 256–7); it becomes 'videas' in *G.* 1.387.

1. pelagi volucres tardaeque paludis: preserving the distinction of *Phaen.* 942 λιμναῖαι ἢ εἰνάλιαι ὄρνιθες, with addition of an epithet for the 'palus'. Virgil amplifies the birds of the lake by means of a Homeric simile (*Il.* 2.459 ff.), 'iam variae pelagi volucres et quae Asia circum / dulcibus in stagnis rimantur prata Caystri' (383–4).

2. inexpletas: from *Phaen.* 943 ἄπληστον (note the etymological link).

studio certare lavandi: the enthusiasm ('studio') and the competitive element ('certare') are Varro's own intensification. 'Lavandi' was perhaps suggested by ἐβάψατο in *Phaen.* 951 (though by then Aratus may have moved on to the crow). Virgil has the adverb 'certatim' (385), and in 387 'et studio incassum videas gestire lavandi' he echoes our line ending. Incidentally 'incassum' shows that Virgil took αὔτως in *Phaen.* 945 to mean 'vainly'.

3. et velut insolitum: 'The water is certainly not new to the birds, but [this phrase] nudges the reader into adopting for himself an impression that the poet feels as he watches' (Williams, *Tradition and Originality*, 256).

pennis infundere rorem: also probably from the description of the crow in *Phaen.* 951–2 ἐβάψατο μέχρι παρ' ἄκρους / ὤμους. Virgil has seen this, and returns more closely to the Greek model with '*umeris* infundere rores' (*G.* 1.385).

rorem: Lucretius (1.496, etc.) may have originated the poetical use of 'ros' for any liquid which falls in drops (cf. Cicero fr. 10.44 Courtney 'vitali rore' of the she-wolf's milk).

4. aut arguta lacus circumvolitavit hirundo: = *Georgics* 1.377. Jocelyn (*CQ* ns 15 (1965), 139–40) is suspicious of this line, as of others which Virgil is said by ancient commentators to have borrowed whole from earlier poets. I agree with him that Varius Rufus, **150**.6 has probably been tailored to make it identical with *Ecl.* 8.88, but see no need to question either this line or **131** from the *Argonauts* (= *Georgics* 2.404). Perhaps the weighty 'circumvolitavit' held Virgil's fancy.

5. et bos suspiciens caelum—mirabile visu—: here we can also compare lines of Cicero's *Aratea* (fr. 37.10–11 Buescu) 'mollipedesque boves, spectantes lumina caeli, / naribus umiferum duxere ex aere sucum'; these are heavily criticized by Gordon Williams (*Tradition and Originality*, p. 257).

bos: R. F. Thomas (on *G.* 1.375–6) notes that Virgil is not fond of the word 'bos', and so replaces it with the diminutive 'bucula'.

suspiciens caelum: cf. οὐρανὸν εἰσανιδόντες (*Phaen.* 955) 'caelum / suspiciens' (*G.* 1.375–6).

—mirabile visu—: 'really weak, an artificial and unconvincing piece of poetic posturing, especially attached, as it is, to a nicely observed description' (Williams, *Tradition and Originality*, p. 256). One must agree that the action is not sufficiently surprising to warrant the parenthesis; to my mind this is the only weakness in the fragment. As far as we know Varro first introduced 'mirabile visu', no doubt as an equivalent of the Greek θαῦμα ἰδέσθαι (*Il.* 5.725, etc.).

6. naribus aerium patulis decerpsit odorem: the beginning of the line shows that Varro was familiar with Cicero's version ('*naribus umiferum* dux-ere ex aere sucum', *Aratea* fr. 37.11 Buescu). The 'flared nostrils' are a nice touch, which Virgil clearly admired. R. F. Thomas is less than fair both to 'odorem', which represents in *Phaen.* 955 not αἰθέρος (covered by the adjec-tive 'aerium'), but the verb ὠσφρήσαντο, and to the humorous 'decerpsit' (adapted from *OLD decerpo* 1*b*, of a feeding animal).

7. nec . . . non: introduced to poetry by Varro. See Mynors on *Georgics I* 2.449.

evehit: unfavourably compared by Thomas with Virgil's 'extulit' (*G.* 1.379), but, again, perhaps unjustly. The verb suggests the owner of a house or shop 'clearing out' valuable property from the threat of an advancing flood.

122–132 *Argonautae*

This was the poem which, according to Quintilian (10.1.87 = **122***f*) 'won Varro his name'; Ovid (*Am.* 1.15.21 = **122***c*) even prophesied that it would be numbered among the immortal works of Latin literature. We can fairly deduce from Quintilian (**122***f*) and Statius (**122***g*) that people still read the *Argonauts* in the Flavian period (though few, if any, signs of its use by Valerius Flaccus can be detected), and oddities were preserved by grammarians. But time did not confirm Ovid's judgement.

Part of the reason for Quintilian's lukewarm praise ('non spernendus qui-dem') seems to be that he did not regard the *Argonauts* as an original work, but as a translation ('interpres operis alieni'). Clearly the poem was based upon Apollonius Rhodius much more closely than was the later epic of Valerius Flaccus. The number of books is the same (**122***a*), and almost all the surviving fragments can be put in their place by comparison with the Greek.

Sometimes Varro has taken care to recreate the rhythm and structure of Apollonius' hexameters (see **127**.2); **125** seems to show him using (and being misled by) a commentary on Ap. Rh. which expressed a view also found in the surviving scholia. On the other hand we may discover original touches of fine poetry (**131**) and learned mythology which was not in Apollonius (see on **123**.4 and **126**). Ovid nowhere betrays any consciousness that the *Argonauts* was other than a work of creative ability which deserved to be judged in its own right; he would hardly have praised e.g. a Latin version of Aratus' *Phaenomena* in the tone of **122***c*.

It is disappointing that the ancient commentators on Virgil's *Aeneid* do not seem to have used the *Argonauts* (only **123** is quoted, for a point of genealogy); one would expect them to pick up **129**.2 'placida composta quiete' as an ingredient of *Aen.* 1.249 'placida compostus pace quiescit'. The remark of Julius Montanus associated with **129** gives a tantalizing hint of what we may be missing. Everyone knows that the love story of Aeneas and Dido owes much to the love of Jason and Medea in Apollonius, *Arg.* 3, but we should not forget that there was a famous Latin account of Jason and Medea which Virgil must have consulted. The same consideration applies to the many similes deriving from Ap. Rh. which we find in the *Aeneid*.

Wendell Clausen (*Virgil's Aeneid and the Tradition of Hellenistic Poetry* (1987), 5) would date publication of the *Argonauts* c.47 BC, believing this to be the significance of Jerome's statement (**105***a*) that Varro learnt Greek with great enthusiasm in his thirty-fifth year. I suspect, however, that the poem appeared rather later. It has left no trace in Virgil's *Eclogues* (the alleged connection between **125** and *Ecl.* 1.65 is certainly bogus, and the reference to the Argo in *Ecl.* 4.34–5 inspired by Catullus 64), first making an impact on the *Georgics* (Virgil borrows **131** unaltered) and Horace's *Epodes* (**131** again, see ad loc.). That would be consistent with publication soon after 40 BC, leaving Varro's love poetry (? elegies) for Leucadia (**133**), which followed the *Argonauts* (**122***b*), to fit into the early 30s BC, in the wake of Cornelius Gallus' elegies for Lycoris.

The title always appears as *Argonautae*; this would not have distinguished Varro's poem from that of Apollonius. We call the latter *Argonautica*, but ancient authorities may write e.g. Ἀπολλώνιος ὁ τοὺς Ἀργοναύτας ποιήσας (Strabo 14.2.13) or Ἁ ἐν τοῖς Ἀργοναύταις ([Longinus] 33.4).

122

(*a*) Although the substance of this note on Virgil, *Georgics* 2.126 much more probably refers to the *Chorographia* (see **119**), we may rely on the statement that Varro (unlike Valerius Flaccus) followed the four-book scheme of Ap. Rh. Only **123** is ascribed to a particular book in our sources, but comparison with Ap. Rh. enables us to place almost all, if not all, the other items.

(*b*) See my introduction to the *Argonauts* (above) for the date at which Varro wrote (or published) his epic poem which, according to Propertius, preceded his love poetry for Leucadia.

(*c*) Many of Ovid's tributes to other poets in *Am.* 1.15 are coupled with verbal echoes of their own work (e.g. lines 24 on Lucretius and 27 on Tibullus). So Ovid may be playing the same game with Varr. At. McKeown in his *Amores* commentary (vol. II, p. 406) notes that 'quae nesciet aetas' might reflect Varro's version of Ap. Rh.'s prayer for his poem's future renown in the concluding 'seal' (4.1773–5 αἴδε δ' ἀοιδαί / εἰς ἔτος ἐξ ἔτεος γλυκερώτεραι εἶεν ἀείδειν / ἀνθρώποις). 'Aurea ... terga petita' probably glances at the Latin equivalent of Ap. Rh. 1.4 χρύσειον μετὰ κῶας ('in search of the golden fleece') and the grandiloquent 'Aesonio ... duci' (with the adjective used as a patronymic) is surely Varronian too (cf. Val. Flacc. 3.240 and 4.8–9). I am also interested in 'primam ... ratem': whatever the chronological difficulties, the Argo was thought to have been the first ship (e.g. Catullus 64.11). Ap. Rh. makes nothing of this in the opening to book 1, but it became customary for epic poems to stress at the outset that they are describing some 'first' occurrence (e.g. 'Troiae qui *primus* ab oris', 'Of man's *first* disobedience'). Val. Flacc. opens with 'Prima deum magnis canimus freta pervia natis', and it would not be surprising if some part of 'primus' stood at the beginning of Varro's epic.

(*d*) The phrase 'fulvis insignia villis' (cf. *Her.* 12.201 'villo spectabilis alto') might reflect Varro's version of Ap. Rh. 4.177 (when Jason actually takes the fleece) λήνεσσιν ἐπηρεφές, 'thickly clustered with flocks'.

(*e*) The Phasis is not mentioned in Ap. Rh. bk. 1; Varro may have introduced it at an earlier stage, or perhaps Ovid has in mind the Argonauts' arrival at their destination (cf. Ap. Rh. 2.1261, 1278). The adjective 'Phasiacus' (not attested before Ovid) could be Varro's coinage. 'Argon qui duxit' might reflect Ap. Rh. 1.4 εὔζυγον ἤλασαν Ἀργώ (of the heroes)—by a common figure the poet is said to do what he describes as happening.

(*f*) For discussion of Quintilian's verdict, see my introduction to the *Argonauts* (above).

(*g*) The same figure as in (*e*) recurs, but Statius has added a further twist, in that 'Argonautas' refers to the title of Varro's poem as well as to the heroes.

123 (1 Bl., 3 C.)

This fragment shows that Varro did not shirk the most intimidating part of his task, a full-blown Catalogue of Argonauts (occupying lines 23–227 in Ap. Rh. 1). Indeed he adds supererogatory detail—the learned touch 'multis celebrata' (line 1) and the mention of Amymone's mother as Europa (4), who appears in Apollodorus 2.1.5 but not in Ap. Rh. or his surviving scholia (note however that these parts of lines 1 and 4 have been restored by H. Keil). The Greek model (Ap. Rh. 1.133 ff.) runs τῷι δ' ἐπὶ δὴ θείοιο κίεν Δαναοῖο γενέθλη, / Ναύπλιος, ἦ γὰρ ἔην Κλυτονήου Ναυβολίδαο, / Ναύβολος αὖ Λέρνου, Λέρνον γε μὲν ἴδμεν ἐόντα / Προίτου Ναυπλιάδαο, Ποσειδάωνι δὲ κούρῃ / πρίν ποτ' Ἀμυμώνη Δαναῖς τέκεν εὐνηθεῖσα / Ναύπλιον ὃς περὶ πάντας ἐκαίνυτο ναυτιλίῃσιν. One can only speculate whether Varro had any counterpart to ὃς ... ναυτιλίῃσιν (138). If, at the beginning of his epic (see on **122c**), he stressed that Argo was the first ship, he may have thought it inappropriate that Nauplius should already be a skilled seaman.

The text comes from Virgilian scholia in a famous palimpsest, Verona XL (38), originally written in the fifth century; see E. A. Lowe, *Codices Latini Antiquiores*, IV (1947), no. 498, and Mynors's OCT of Virgil, p. vi (on the manuscript known as V). Several scholars have stated, or implied, that parts of this fragment could be read clearly by the first editor, A. Mai (1818), but subsequently became illegible. That is not so (see A. Lunelli, *Aerius* (Rome, 1969), 159–62). The quotation from Varr. At. occupies (not all of) three lines, of which the first ends with 'multis'; the second starts with 'namque' and ends with 'fil', the third starts with 'Danaique'. The loss of text in lines 1 and 4 of our fragment has been caused by trimming of the right-hand margin in the first two of the three lines in the palimpsest; the supplements '<celebrata propago>' and '<ia Amymone Europae>' are (very plausible) conjectures by H. Keil. The same palimpsest is the unique source of Furius Bibaculus, **81**, and Valgius Rufus, **166** (parts illegible).

1. The subject of the fragment is Nauplius (II), who probably was named in the preceding line; for postponement of 'ecce', cf. Virgil, *Ecl.* 2.46–7 'tibi lilia plenis / ecce ferunt Nymphae calathis'. In spite of the eight generations normally allowed between the Danaids and Heracles, some believed that the same Nauplius not only sailed in the Argo, but even wrecked the Greek fleet on the return voyage from Troy—as Strabo (8.6.2) reasonably asks, 'How can a son of Amymone still be alive at the time of the Trojan war?' Unconvincing attempts were made to give him preternatural longevity (Apollodorus 2.1.5 μακρόβιος). Ap. Rh.'s solution, followed by Varro, was to double the character

of Nauplius and insert four generations (Proetus, Lernus, Naubolus, and Clytoneüs or Clytius) between Nauplius I and Nauplius II. A Nauplius (II) who joined the Argo in his youth could still be alive as an embittered old man at the end of the Trojan war.

Danai multis <celebrata propago>: grandiose, as e.g. Lucr. 1.42 'Memmi clara propago', Manilius 1.795.

multis <celebrata: referring to the many writers who had made Nauplius famous, a piece of self-conscious erudition not in the Greek (but perhaps suggested by the different 'learned' touch in Ap. Rh. 1.135 ἴδμεν ἐόντα). This motif may descend from *Od.* 12.70 Ἀργὼ πασιμέλουσα, and is often used to indicate that a myth has become hackneyed through retelling (Virgil, *Georgics* 3.4 'omnia iam vulgata', cf. e.g. Ovid, *AA* 1.335). Nauplius' resentment at the death of his son Palamedes led him to a series of horrific actions (the best known was his luring of the Greek fleet to shipwreck by lighting deceptive beacons). These provided excellent material for tragedies: Sophocles probably wrote two plays bearing his name (*TrGF* IV, pp. 353 ff., cf. Pearson, *Fragments of Sophocles*, II, pp. 80 ff.) and we hear of others by Astydamas II, Philocles I, and Lycophron (*TrGF* I, pp. 141, 206, and 277 respectively).

2. Clytio: unless he has altered the name for metrical convenience, Varro may (as H. Fränkel suggested, not approved by Courtney 239) have read Κλυτίου τοῦ Ναυβολίδαο rather than Κλυτονήου N. in his text of Ap. Rh. 1.134.

4. fil<ia Amymone Europae>: this is Europa no. 7 in Roscher, a rare bird indeed (Apollodorus 2.1.5 lists her together with Danaus' other wives).

Danaique superbi: apparently corresponding to θείοιο . . . Δαναοῖο in Ap. Rh. 1.133. While the Greek epithet sounds conventionally eulogistic, the Latin hints at the tyrannical arrogance of Danaus, who induced all but one of his 50 daughters to murder their husbands on the wedding night.

124 (2 Bl., 4 C.)

Tiphyn <et> aurigam celeris fecere carinae: not ascribed to an author or work by the grammarians, but Unger and Keil convincingly found this line a home by comparison with Ap. Rh. 1.400–1 ἐπὶ δ' ἔτρεπον αἰνήσαντες / Τῖφυν ἐϋστείρης οἰήϊα νηὸς ἔρυσθαι.

Tiphyn <et> aurigam: I adopt Büchner's supplement; Varro seems fond of postponing 'et' to second word in the hexameter (**111**.1, **118**.2, **131**). Morel transposed, 'aurigam Tiphyn'. Courtney, however, is prepared to accept the false quantity 'Tiphyn [scanned as a spondee] aurigam', suggesting that

Varro's late acquisition of Greek caused him to misinterpret Τῖφυν ἐΰ-
[‒ ◡ ◡ ‒] as Τίφυν εὐ- [‒ ‒ ‒]. I find that very hard to believe: surely a
grammarian would have reprehended him for the error (cf. [Probus], GLK IV,
p. 227, contrasting Tethȳs with Capȳs), particularly since the line was quoted
by grammarians for another reason. Varro was not allowed to get away with
scanning 'Phaethon' (**132**) as a spondee—something in which Manilius
(1.736) followed him.

    aurigam ... carinae: quoted as an example of metaphor 'ab animali ad
animale', because 'et auriga et gubernator animam habent' (GLK IV, p. 399)
and 'quem in modum in navi auriga dici potest, ita et in curru gubernator'
(Charis. p. 359 B²). For 'auriga' of a steersman, cf. Ovid, *Tr.* 1.4.16. Compare
'currus' of a ship (e.g. Cat. 64.9), ὄχος and ὄχημα (e.g. *PV* 468).

    celeris ... carinae: Ap. Rh.'s ἐϋστείρης literally means 'having a good keel'.
Greek compounds often caused problems to Roman poets—e.g. Catullus
(66.53–4) entirely contracts out of 'violet-girdled' (ἰοζώνου) Arsinoe in his
Callimachean model (fr. 110.54 Pf.). Here Varro by no means does badly:
'carinae' represents the στεῖρα element in the compound, while 'celeris' indi-
cates the ship's effectiveness. Adesp. **243** 'alta carina' may also come from
Varr. At. on the Argo (see ad loc.).

125 (3 Bl., 5 C.)

We owe this fragment to a misunderstanding of Virgil, *Ecl.* 1.65 'rapidum
cretae veniemus Oaxen' (probably the Oxus) by ancient critics who read
'cretae' as 'Cretae' and looked for a comparable Cretan name (see Clausen ad
loc.). Varro in turn (abetted by a commentary on Apollonius reflected in the
surviving scholia) may have misunderstood his model; see F. Vian in the Budé
Ap. Rh., vol. I (1974), 264–5; H. Fränkel, *Einleitung zur kritischen Ausgabe der
Argonautika des Apollonius* (1964), 94–5. The Greek runs (*Arg.* 1.1129–31):

> Δάκτυλοι Ἰδαῖοι Κρηταιέες, οὕς ποτε νύμφη
> Ἀγχιάλη Δικταῖον ἀνὰ σπέος, ἀμφοτέρῃσιν
> δραξαμένη γαίης Οἰαξίδος ἐβλάστησεν.

Apollonius almost certainly meant that Anchiale made the Cretan dust run
through her fingers, and that from this the Idaean Dactyls ('Fingers', already
Latinized as Idaei Digiti by Cicero, *DND* 3.47) sprang up; ἐβλάστησεν = 'made
to grow', as of a gardener. But some in antiquity believed that Anchiale was
mother to the Dactyls, and that she 'grasped the Oeaxian land' in the agony of
childbirth. Thus schol. e on *Arg.* 1.1126–31 (p. 102 Wendel) δραξαμένη: ἔθος

ἐστί ταῖς κυούσαις τῶν παρακειμένων λαμβάνεσθαι καὶ ἀποκουφίζειν ἑαυτὰς τῶν ἀλγηδόνων. Varr. At. has enthusiastically taken up the latter interpretation, laying great stress on the nymph's birth-pains.

1. adducta: I have not found a close parallel, but *adducere* can mean to 'draw together' (e.g. of the brows in a frown) or 'tighten', and here seems to describe the tensing of the body.

2. geminis ... palmis: representing ἀμφοτέρηισιν. See *OLD* s.v. *geminus* 4*b* ('parts of the body occurring together in natural pairs'); the earliest surviving example is Catullus 63.75 'geminas ... aures' (see the note of Fordyce, who also favours Schrader's 'aures geminae' in Cat. 51.11).

cupiens: with 'scindere' in line 3, intensifying the impression of Anchiale's birth pangs (above). Some have preferred the variant 'capiens', as a counterpart to δραξαμένη, but, when the third line became truncated and unintelligible, there would be a temptation to make a sense-unit of line 2 by changing 'cupiens' to 'capiens'.

tellurem Oeaxida: 'the land of Crete' from Oaxus (*Oi*- and Oe- for metrical convenience), a town in the western central part of the island.

3. It seems almost certain that Servius originally quoted three full lines of Varro, and that 'dicta' conceals some part of 'Dictaeus'. 'Dictaeo ... sub antro' suggests itself, as in Virgil, *Georgics* 4.152 (though not identically placed) from a different Apollonian context (1.509). In Ap. Rh. 1.1129 ποτε (whence 'quondam', Thilo–Hagen) is less significant than νύμφη, and I would restore 'nympha' in Varro. That would leave us needing only a verb (probably a molossus, according to the pattern of Catullus 64) after the masculine caesura. To reinforce the picture of the nymph's painful and violent labour I suggest 'profudit', which is normally prŏ-, but prō- thus placed in Cat. 64.202 (for the variable quantity in verbs compounded with pro- see Bailey's 1947 Lucretius, vol. I, p. 130). Compare Lucilius 119 Marx, Lucretius 5.225 'nixibus ex alvo matris natura profudit'. So the complete line of Varro might have run 'scindere, Dictaeo profudit nympha sub antro'.

126 (4 Bl., 6 C.)

Although this item is only a prose summary of Varro given by a Virgilian scholiast, it contains much of interest. The paraphrase seems to correspond especially to Ap. Rh. 2.516–24:

ἦμος δ' οὐρανόθεν Μινωίδας ἔφλεγε νήσους
Σείριος, οὐδ' ἐπὶ δηρὸν ἔην ἄκος ἐνναέτηισιν,

τῆμος τόνγ᾽ ἐκάλεσσαν ἐφημοσύναις Ἑκάτοιο
λοιμοῦ ἀλεξητῆρα, λίπεν δ᾽ ὅγε πατρὸς ἐφετμῆι
Φθίην, ἐν δὲ Κέωι κατενάσσατο, λαὸν ἀγείρας
Παρράσιον, τοίπερ τε Λυκάονός εἰσι γενέθλης,
καὶ βωμὸν ποίησε μέγαν Διὸς Ἰκμαίοιο,
ἱερά τ᾽ εὖ ἔρρεξεν ἐν οὔρεσιν ἀστέρι κείνωι
Σειρίωι αὐτῶι τε Κρονίδηι Διί.

But when from heaven the Dog-star parched the Minoian isles, and for a long time the inhabitants had no remedy, then at the bidding of the Far-Shooter [Apollo] they summoned him [Aristaeus] to ward off the pestilence. He, on his father's instructions, left Phthia and settled in Ceos, gathering together the Parrhasian people who are sprung from Lycaon; and he constructed a great altar of Zeus the Moistener, and duly offered sacrifices on the mountains, to the Dog-Star and to Zeus son of Cronos himself.

The two titles of Aristaeus, however, Nomios and Agreus (I have little doubt that Varro too used the latter form, though our text of the Virgil scholion reads Aeguros) come a little earlier in Ap. Rh. (2.506–7):

ἔνθα δ᾽ Ἀρισταῖον Φοίβωι τέκεν, ὃν καλέουσιν
Ἀγρέα καὶ Νόμιον πολυλήιοι Αἱμονιῆες.

There to Phoebus she [Cyrene] bore Aristaeus, whom the Haemonians, rich in corn-land, call Hunter [or 'god of the countryside'] and Pastor.

Such a scholiastic summary always makes one wonder how much of it was actually in the poet named at the end. In the present case the text of Ap. Rh. provides at least a partial check—and some of the commentator's words cohere very closely with the Greek:

(*a*) 'monstrante patre profectus est in insulam Ceam', cf. Ap. Rh. 519–20 λίπεν δ᾽ ὅγε πατρὸς ἐφετμῆι / Φθίην, ἐν δὲ Κέωι κατενάσσατο.

(*b*) 'sacrificio facto aram Iovi Icmaeo constituit', cf. Ap. Rh. 522–3 καὶ βωμὸν ποίησε μέγαν Διὸς Ἰκμαίοιο / ἱερά τ᾽ εὖ ἔρρεξεν.

While it would be wrong to give any weight to the absence from the summary of elements present in Ap. Rh. (e.g. the 'Parrhasian people' which Aristaeus gathers in lines 520–1), we have every reason to notice features of the summary which were not in the Greek poem, since there is a good chance that they appeared in Varro:

(*i*) The summary gives a reason why the plague struck Ceos/Cea—as the text stands, 'propter interitum Actaeonis', though I find that hard to credit (see below).

(*ii*) In the summary, the deification of Aristaeus and establishment of his cult-titles is due not to the Thessalians ('Haemonians', Ap. Rh. 2.507) but to the Ceans, who obey an oracle given to them after Aristaeus' death. We can the more confidently ascribe this detail to Varro because it is also stressed in Virgil, *Georgics* 1.14–15 'cultor nemorum, cui pinguia Ceae / ter centum nivei tondent dumeta iuvenci'.

(*iii*) The two cult-titles of Aristaeus are carefully tied to different benefits which he conferred on mankind: Agreus for his devotion to the 'agreste studium' and Nomius for his services to shepherds and cowherds.

propter interitum Actaeonis: I find this almost incredible. Why should the Ceans be punished for the death of Actaeon, son of Aristaeus, who, according to the familiar story, died in Boeotia, torn to pieces by his own hunting-dogs (e.g. Ovid, *Met.* 3.138–252 with Bömer's commentary)? Granted that there were variant versions, none gives the slightest colour to what is alleged here; even if the Ceans were in some way culpable, a plague caused by the Dog-Star would be an incongruous punishment.

In place of 'Actaeonis' I conjecture 'Icarii', and would interpret in terms of Eratosthenes' famous elegiac poem *Erigone* (see now Alexandra Rosokoki, *Die Erigone des Eratosthenes* (Heidelberg, 1995)), the plot of which Hyginus (*Astr.* 2.4.2 ff.) summarizes. Then everything falls into place. The Ceans share the blame for the death of Icarius because they gave refuge to his murderers (*Astr.* 2.4.3). The Dog-Star is an appropriate agent of retribution because it represents the catasterized family dog of Icarius and Erigone; even the pestilence attacking the Cean flocks and herds fits the crime, because Icarius' killers were shepherds who believed that the old man was trying to steal their animals (*Astr.* 2.4.3). The change in our text of the Virgil scholion may be due to a reader or scribe whose mythological learning included the fact that Actaeon was son of Aristaeus but did not stretch to the more recondite connection between Aristaeus, Icarius, and the Ceans. If I am right, this would be notable evidence that Varro's Hellenistic erudition went far beyond his immediate model in Ap. Rh.

in insulam Ceam: the form 'Cea', also in Virgil (*Georgics* 1.14) and Ovid (e.g. *Her.* 20.222, cf. Bömer on *Met.* 7.368) was normal in Latin and no doubt used by Varro.

placatis flatibus: Varro may have employed the verb 'placare', which is suitable for 'pacifying' the angry Dog-Star; if so, he could have intended a reference to another famous piece of Hellenistic poetry on the placating of the Dog-Star, Callimachus, *Aetia* fr. 75.35 Pf. πρηΰνειν χαλεπὴν Μαῖραν ἀνερχομένην. Nonnus, who was familiar with all the Hellenistic treatments of the Aristaeus myth (including Euphorion, *Suppl. Hell.* 443.4 ff.), has an extravagant picture of the whole operation: οὐδὲ σιδηροχίτων δεδοκημένος ἀστέρος αἴγλην / Σείριον αἰθαλόεντος ἀναστέλλων πυρετοῖο / ἐννύχιος πρήυνε, τὸν εἰσέτι διψαλέον πῦρ / θερμὸν ἀκοντίζοντα δι᾽ αἰθέρος αἴθοπι λαιμῶι / ἄσθμασι λεπταλέοισι καταψύχουσιν ἀῆται (*Dion.* 13.281–5).

Nomius et Agreus, quod et agresti studio et cura pecorum armentorumque non mediocriter profuerat hominibus: Ruhnken was surely right to restore 'Agreus' as the second cult-title (cf. Ap. Rh. 2.507 Ἀγρέα). Probus cod. E has 'Aegoros'; Morel and successors print 'Aeguros' (intended to mean 'protector of goats'?). There is an obvious etymological play between Agreus and 'agresti studio' (as LSJ say, the reference to hunting in Ἀγρεύς is secondary). Aristaeus was thought to have instructed countrymen in all sorts of rural techniques (e.g. [Oppian], *Cyn.* 4.268 ff., Nonnus, *Dion.* 5.229 ff.).

127 (5 Bl., 7 C.)

These two lines come from a brief hymn to Apollo (Ap. Rh. 2.705–13, there reported in indirect speech) which Orpheus sang after an epiphany of the god. The subject is the slaying of a monstrous snake, called Delphyne(s) by Ap. Rh. (2.706) but better known as the Python. The Corycian nymphs encourage the young god by crying out ἴη ἴε (an exclamation suggesting 'shoot! shoot!') and this is held to be the origin of what became a ritual refrain (ἐφύμνιον, Ap. Rh. 2.713) in honour of Phoebus.

1. te: in the hymnic (or panegyric) style the pronoun is placed prominently (e.g. **256**.1, *Aen.* 8.293 'tu nubigenas, invicte, bimembris . . .', Ovid, *Met.* 7.433 'te, maxime Theseu . . .'); cf. E. Norden, *Agnostos Theos* (1923 reprint), 150 ff. The same applies to laments (see on Helvius Cinna, **10**). Apollonius, though reporting Orpheus' song in indirect speech, himself briefly intervenes to apostrophize the god (708 αἰεί τοι, ἄναξ, ἄτμητοι ἔθειραι).

tunc: my conjecture for the MSS 'nunc'. Ap. Rh. (2.711–13) explains that the original cry uttered *on that occasion* by the nymphs later became a refrain in the worship of Apollo. So 'tunc' rather than 'nunc' seems appropriate. Note the strong alliteration of 't' and 'c' in this line. Indeed 'tunc Coryciae' might seem too harsh a collision (for such sensitivities, cf. Cicero, *De Or.* 3.172, *Orat.* 150, Quint. 9.4.37, all quoted by Nisbet, *Collected Papers*, 318–19). So perhaps 'tum' (cf. **132**) rather than 'tunc'.

Coryciae . . . nymphae: these nymphs are also mentioned by Callimachus (fr. 75.56–7 Pf., later driven from Parnassus to the island of Ceos); for discussion, see Vian on Ap. Rh. 2.711, J. Fontenrose, *Python* (1959), 407–12.

tendentem spicula: Ap. Rh. has ὥς ποτε πετραίηι ὑπὸ δειράδι Παρνησοῖο /

Δελφύνην τόξοισι πελώριον ἐξενάριξεν (2.705–6). At this point the Latin seems closer to Callimachus' account of the same incident, τὸν μὲν σὺ κατήναρες ἄλλον ἐπ' ἄλλωι / βάλλων ὠκὺν ὀϊστόν, ἐπηΰτησε δὲ λαός (*Hymn* 2.101–2). As we have seen (on **126**), Varro's learning was by no means confined to his model in Ap. Rh. 'Tendere' should strictly apply to the bow, but is also used of arrows (*Aen.* 9.606 'spicula tendere cornu', Horace, *Odes* 1.29.9 'sagittas tendere'). [Virgil], *Ciris* 299 has 'contendens spicula'.

2. hortantes: cf. Ap. Rh. 2.712 θαρσύνεσκον ἔπεσσιν.

ieie conclamarunt: carefully preserving the rhythm (with spondaic fifth foot) of Ap. Rh. 2.712 ἴη ἴε κεκληγυῖαι. There is a faint resemblance to Cat. 64.255 'euhoe capita inflectentes'.

128 (7 Bl., 9 C.)

huic similis curis experdita lamentatur: F. Buecheler (*Jahrb. f. Phil.*, 93 (1866), 610 = *Kl. Schr.* I, pp. 624–5) first restored 'expe<r>dita' and thought of *Argonauts* 3 (without citing a precise parallel from Ap. Rh. 3). Morel (at that time unaware of Buecheler's suggestion) also proposed 'expe<r>dita', and convincingly compared Ap. Rh. 3.664 τῆι ἰκέλη Μήδεια κινύρετο. The clausula echoes Catullus 64.119 (see W. Clausen, *ICS* 2 (1977), 219–23), where we should probably read 'deperdita lamentata est' (Conington) or 'lamentatur' (Buecheler, above) rather than 'laetabatur' (Lachmann).

huic similis: with exactly the same metrical value, and in the same position (cf. **127.2**) as the Greek τῆι ἰκέλη. Ap. Rh. compared Medea to a virgin bride whose husband has perished (cf. M. Campbell, *Studies in the Third Book of Apollonius Rhodius' Argonautica* (1983), 39–40, with associated notes).

experdita: 'utterly destroyed'. The compound does not occur elsewhere in literary Latin, but Morel referred to C. Goetz, *Corpus Glossariorum Latinorum* (1892), III, pp. 447.64 and 481.5, where 'experdens' is glossed ληστής.

129 (8 Bl., 10 C.)

1–2. desierant latrare canes, urbesque silebant; / omnia noctis erant placida composta quiete: compare Ap. Rh. 3.749–50 οὐδὲ κυνῶν ὑλακὴ ἔτ' ἀνὰ πτόλιν, οὐ θρόος ἦεν / ἠχήεις· σιγὴ δὲ μελαινομένην ἔχεν ὄρφνην. These lines (our most interesting fragment of the *Argonauts*) were famous in antiquity, and hint at the likely quality of the whole poem. They come to us associated with anecdotes about two later poets, Ovid and Julius Montanus (see **221–3**); the latter is seemingly responsible for the value-judgement 'illos optimos versus Varronis'. There is also a tantalizing suggestion of the influence which Varro's third book might have exercised upon Virgil's *Aeneid*.

I have included in my text quite a lot of the surrounding material in the elder Seneca, who tells us (*Contr.* 7.1.27) that an unhappy 'vignette' (explicatio) of the declaimer Cestius Pius, 'nox erat concubia, et omnia, iudices, canentia <sub> sideribus muta erant' was (according to Julius Montanus) based upon *Aen.* 8.26–7 'nox erat et terras animalia fessa per omnis, / alituum pecudumque genus, sopor altus habebat'. Montanus added that Virgil (unlike Cestius) had been successful in his imitation, since the lines from *Aen.* 8 improved upon the already excellent lines of Varro.

We may be surprised that Montanus should have attached our fragment to *Aen.* 8.26–7 rather than to 4.522 ff. 'nox erat et placidum carpebant fessa soporem / corpora per terras', etc. (with 'pecudes pictaeque volucres' in 525). The latter would be, for us, the 'right' passage to compare with Varro, since the sleepless torment of Medea in *Arg.* 3 is best paralleled by that of Dido (and *Aen.* 4.527 'somno positae' could recall Varro's 'composta quiete'). But Seneca is reporting a piece of casual conversation, and Montanus may have been content with a brief Virgilian passage which included animals and birds—he would have had to quote more of *Aen.* 4 in order to achieve the same end.

Another puzzling question remains: how could Montanus be so sure that *Aen.* 8.26–7 were based upon our fragment? M. Wigodsky (*Virgil and Early Latin Poetry* (1972), 104) reasonably complains that there is no verbal resemblance. Seneca here combines two anecdotes, one involving Montanus, one Ovid. For the latter, only these two lines of Varro were required; Montanus, however, might have quoted some slightly earlier lines of Varro, corresponding not to Ap. Rh. 3.749–50, but to 3.744 ff. νὺξ μὲν ἔπειτ᾽ ἐπὶ γαῖαν ἄγεν κνέφας κτλ. If by chance Varro had opened his section 'nox erat, et terris (-as) . . .', there would be a clearer link between Varro and *Aen.* 8. As things stand, the earliest example of 'nox erat et . . .' is Horace, *Epodes* 15.1 (surprisingly absent from Pease's long list of parallels to *Aen.* 4.522). See further H. Mc. L. Currie in *LCM* 18 (1993), 92–5.

An equally tentative idea, incompatible with the previous one: Horace, *Satires* 1.5 (written at a time when Varro's *Argonauts* would have been quite recently published) contains a mock heroic description of the coming of night, 'iam nox inducere terris / umbras . . . parabat' (9–10) which closely resembles Ap. Rh. 3.744, quoted above (Lucr. 6.864 would offer a reasonable precedent in the Latin epic tradition if one adopted Marullus' 'umbris' for 'undis'). Continuing the same line of thought, I wonder how close Horace's 'tandem fessus dormire viator / incipit' (*Satires* 1.5.17–18) was to Varro's version of Ap. Rh. 3.746–7 ὕπνοιο δὲ καί τις ὁδίτης / ἤδη ... ἐέλδετο.

1. desierant latrare canes: as R. L. Hunter on Ap. Rh. 3.744–51 says, the Greek poet seems first to describe the onset of night (744 ff.) and then to move to a much later time in the dead hours. Ovid similarly mentions the silence of dogs during his last night in Rome, 'iamque quiescebant voces hominumque canumque' (*Tristia* 1.3.27, cf. *Fasti* 5.429–30). Note also *Met.* 7.185–6 (from the Medea episode) 'homines volucresque ferasque / solverat alta quies'.

urbesque silebant: Ap. Rh. (3.749) was already concentrating on the particular city of Colchis (ἀνὰ πτόλιν) in which Medea lived. Varro apparently has a generalizing plural referring to all cities. Also odd is the way in which 'canes' and 'urbes' seem to be put on the same level—unless the point is that the barking of dogs is the last noise to cease, and only then can the cities be truly silent.

In place of 'urbes', Professor Nisbet suggests 'orbes', 'wheels' (as e.g. *Georgics* 3.173 'iunctos temo trahat aereus orbis'), pointing to the sleeper who is wakened by wheeled traffic at daybreak in Callimachus, *Hecale* fr. 74.26–7 H. ἔγρει καί τιν' ἔχοντα παρὰ πλόον οἰκίον ἄξων / τετριγὼς ὑπ' ἄμαξαν. It may have been characteristic of Varro to combine Ap. Rh. with suggestions of other Hellenistic poets; cf. on **126** (the conjecture 'Icarii'), **127.1** 'tendentem spicula', **131**.

2. omnia noctis erant placida composta quiete: according to Ovid the verse would have been greatly improved if Varro had stopped at 'omnia noctis erant', 'night held all' (for a similar criticism of *Aen.* 11.188 ff. by Ovid's patron Messalla Corvinus, see Seneca, *Suas.* 2.20). That would be very Ovidian, but (as Seneca realized) 'placida composta quiete' is not mere padding. Ovid too must have seen this, and I would hesitate to deduce from an apparently light-hearted remark that O.'s admiration for Varro's *Argonauts* was not unreserved (so McKeown on *Amores* 1.15.21–2 = my **122c**, where we find Ovid's more serious judgement).

Lucretius has 'placidaque quiete' (1.463); we see traces of Varro's wording in *Aen.* 4.527 'somno positae' and 5.836 'placida laxabant membra quiete' (the adjective not identically placed). Most interesting is the way in which Virgil combines this fragment with Ennius, *Annals* 523 Skutsch 'nunc senio confectus quiescit' to produce *Aen.* 1.249 'nunc placida compostus pace quiescit'. See Austin ad loc. and Norden on *Aen.* 6.24 for the archaizing tone of syncopated forms like 'compostus' (noted also by Else Hofmann, *WS* 46 (1928), 163).

130 (9 Bl., 23 C.)

cuius ut aspexit torta caput angue revinctum: generally given to *Arg.* 3 on
the basis of Ap. Rh. 3.1214–15 πέριξ δέ μιν ἐστεφάνωντο / σμερδαλέοι δρυΐνοισι
μετὰ πτόρθοισι δράκοντες (Hecate coming to accept the sacrifice of Jason).
J. E. G. Zetzel (*Hermes*, 108 (1980), 501–2) objects that 'aspexit' does not fit
Ap. Rh.'s account: Medea has told him not to look round (3.1038 ff.) and he
obeys her instructions (1221–2), though terribly frightened by the shaking of
the earth, barking of dogs, and wailing of nymphs (1217–20). It was of course
dangerous if not disastrous for a mortal to gaze upon an infernal deity. Zetzel
would attribute this fragment to the *Chorographia* and to some petrification
caused by looking at Medusa's head. He notes that in a rare version (schol.
Lyc. *Alex.* 836 and Lucian, *De Domo* 22) Andromeda's monster is dealt with in
this manner, and that Ovid (*Met.* 4.631–62) makes Perseus turn Atlas from
Titan to mountain in the same way; so this kind of incident could figure in a
geographical poem.

Zetzel's objection is substantial; if this fragment belongs to the *Argonauts*,
Varro seems to have been careless. Nonetheless, the wording quite closely
recalls Ap. Rh. 3.1214–15 and so I have, hesitantly, retained the line in its
traditional place.

torta ... angue: cf. Catullus 64.258 'tortis serpentibus'. The feminine
gender of *anguis* (to which we owe the fragment) is by no means
uncommon—see *OLD.*

131 (6 Bl., 8 C.)

frigidus et silvis Aquilo decussit honorem: = Virgil, *Georgics* 2.404, where
Servius comments 'Varronis hic versus est'. H. D. Jocelyn (*CQ* N S 15 (1965),
142) feels that an editor of Varr. At. should do no more than print the Virgil
scholion as a testimonium to the *Argonauts*. His scepticism is partly a general
one (pp. 139 ff.) about whole verses which Virgil is alleged to have borrowed
from earlier poets, and partly rests on the vagueness of the comparison which
scholars customarily make with Ap. Rh. 2.1098 ff.: Ζεὺς δ' ἀνέμου Βορέαο
μένος κίνησεν ἀῆναι / ... / αὐτὰρ ὅ γ' ἡμάτιος μὲν ἐν οὔρεσι φύλλ' ἐτίνασσε /
τυτθὸν ἐπ' ἀκροτάτοισιν ἀήσυρος ἀκρεμόνεσσι. The North Wind is indeed
specified, but otherwise the parallel fails to satisfy: in Ap. Rh. Boreas blows
lightly and merely shakes the leaves, while in Varr. At. it knocks them off the
trees. Our line most naturally suggests a description of very late autumn or

early winter, as in *Georgics* 2.403–4 'seras posuit cum vinea frondes / frigidus et silvis Aquilo decussit honorem' and Horace, *Epodes* 11.5–6 (below).

I feel that a much more convincing parallel can be found in Ap. Rh. 4.216–17, where the Colchians gathering to pursue the escaping Argonauts are compared in number to the leaves of the forest which fall in autumn:

ἢ ὅσα φύλλα χαμᾶζε περικλαδέος πέσεν ὕλης
φυλλοχόωι ἐνὶ μηνί.

('or as many as the leaves which fall to the ground from a thickly-branched wood in the month of leaf-shedding'). On this basis I have reassigned our fragment, from book 2 (as previous editors) to book 4 of the *Argonauts*. Another interesting parallel occurs in Horace, *Epodes* 11.5–6:

hic tertius December, ex quo destiti
Inachia furere, silvis honorem decutit.

Scholars have debated whether Horace drew only on Virgil, or directly on Varr. At. In fact we cannot exclude the possibility that *Epode* 11 was written before this part of *Georgics* 2; be that as it may, I suspect that there is a link between Horace and Varro. In *Epode* 11 the subject of 'decutit' is not Aquilo but the personified December. Remembering that in Ap. Rh. 4.217 the month itself sheds leaves (φυλλοχόωι . . . μηνί), I wonder whether Varro too named and personified a particular month. Martial, at least, not infrequently personifies December (7.37.6, 95.1), sometimes in the same breath mentioning the North Wind (1.49.19–20 'at cum December canus et bruma impotens / Aquilone rauco mugiet', 7.36.5 'horridus ecce sonat Boreae stridore December'. For ἢ ὅσα φύλλα χαμᾶζε περικλαδέος πέσεν ὕλης / φυλλοχόωι ἐνὶ μηνί I offer (purely exempli gratia) '<aut quot humi densis foliorum milia ramis / lapsa iacent, cum iam rauco sonat ore December> / frigidus et silvis Aquilo decussit honorem'. *Aen.* 6.309–10 'quam multa in silvis autumni frigore primo / lapsa cadunt folia' could well owe something to Varr. At., since the context is similar (crowds gathering at a river bank).

For later passages in the same tradition, cf. Ovid, *AA* 3.162 (of *capilli*), 'ut Borea frondes excutiente cadunt', Seneca, *Hercules Oetaeus* 383 'et saeva totas bruma decussit comas', Nonnus, *Dion.* 11.514 (Autumn) φυλλοχόοις ἀνέμοις ἀπεκείρατο δενδράδα χαίτην.

Aquilo: not mentioned in the corresponding passage of Ap. Rh., but Varro may be reminding us of Apollonius' likely model in the *Hecale* of Callimachus (fr. 69.11–12 H. οὐχὶ νότος τόσσην γε χύσιν κατεχεύατο φύλλων / οὐ βορέης, οὐδ' αὐτὸς ὅτ' ἔπλετο φυλλοχόος μείς).

honorem: also not in Varro's model, and very elegant (probably what attracted Virgil to the line). One may compare the Greek ἀγλαΐα and ἀγλάισμα—both used of human hair, to which the leaves correspond (cf. Statius, *Silvae* 3.4.10–11 'comae . . . honorem / praemetet'). Note also Virgil, *Ecl.* 10.24 'agresti capitis Silvanus honore'.

132 (10 Bl., 11 C.)

tum te flagranti deiectum fulmine Phaethon: cf. Ap. Rh. 4.597–9 (Argo entering the Eridanus) ἔνθα ποτ' αἰθαλόεντι τυπεὶς πρὸς στέρνα κεραυνῶι / ἡμιδαὴς Φαέθων πέσεν ἅρματος Ἠελίοιο / λίμνης ἐς προχοὰς πολυβενθέος. I print the text as transmitted by Quintilian; the grammarian Victorinus gives 'cum . . . deiecit', variants which cannot be ruled out (the subject of 'deiecit' would be Jupiter), but seem less likely.

tum: if correct, this might correspond to ποτ' in Ap. Rh. 4.597: Phaethon's occurred at that time long ago, but the marsh still (599 ἔτι νῦν) belches forth clouds of steam. Alternatively 'tum' might indicate the progress of the Argo ('next she passed . . .').

te: the apostrophe is due to Varro, not Apollonius.

flagranti: the adjective αἰθαλόεις sometimes means 'sooty, smoky', sometimes 'blazing'; Varro takes up the latter sense.

deiectum fulmine: *Aen.* 6.581 'fulmine deiecti' (of the Titans) may be a deliberate imitation of Varro.

Phaethon: scanned as a spondee (_ _) rather than an anapaest (ᴗ ᴗ _). One might put this down to defective knowledge of Greek from a man who learnt the language relatively late (**105***a*), or—as I would prefer—to provocation of the *grammatici* by a sophisticated poet. Varro found a follower in Manilius (1.736 'Phaethontem patrio curru per signa volantem'), as noted by Bentley.

Adesp. **243** 'pontum pinus arat, sulcum premit alta carina' has, in my opinion, a good chance of belonging to *Arg.* 4 (cf. Ap. Rh. 4.225–6 πόντον ἔταμνε / νηῦς). **241** and **242** have a weaker claim on the *Argonauts*, **256** a barely existent one.

133 (carmina amatoria)

These poems were probably elegies, though they might have been written in varied metres, like those of Catullus and Calvus ('detexit variis qui sua furta modis', Ov. *Tr.* 2.432 = **40***b*). Propertius (**133***a*) says that Varro composed them after finishing the *Argonauts*, and we can probably accept this as sober fact, even though Propertius likes the figure of the epic or tragic poet who succumbs to love and has to change his style (e.g. Lynceus earlier in the same poem). We have seen that the *Argonauts* did not apparently make an impact until after 40 B C; perhaps therefore the love poems for Leucadia belong to the early 30s, which would be convenient enough, since then they could have been inspired by Cornelius Gallus' elegies addressed to Lycoris (see **145**). Francis Cairns's tentative suggestion that Varro's poems for Leucadia might even antedate those of Catullus for Lesbia (*Tibullus* (1979), 225) seems to me very unlikely.

We have only these two references to the love poems. If they were elegies, nonetheless Varro did not gain a place in the 'canon' of Roman elegists— whether because (like Catullus) he also confessed his love in other metres, or because the poems were judged inferior. Propertius apparently thought well of them; perhaps they simply formed too small a part of Varro's total output.

Varro gave his beloved the pseudonym Leucadia, probably a metrical equivalent of her real name (in Varro's time she could comfortably form a quadrisyllabic pentameter ending). These poetic pseudonyms mostly fall into one of two classes, suggesting either titles of Apollo, the patron god of poetry (so Gallus' Lycoris, Tibullus' Delia, and Propertius' Cynthia) or Greek poetesses (Catullus' Lesbia and Ovid's Corinna). 'Leucadia' cleverly combines both features. See R. D. Williams on *Aeneid* 3.274 f. for Leucadian Apollo; the second connection seems less well-omened, since Sappho was supposed to have jumped from the Leucadian rock to her death—this is hinted at *passim* in the Letter of Sappho to Phaon which may not be by Ovid (cf. Palmer on *Her.* 15.171). Interestingly, Parthenius of Nicaea, who influenced so many Roman neoteric poets, composed a poem entitled Λευκαδίαι (Meineke conjectured Λευκαδία). Its nature is unknown (see on *Suppl. Hell.* 625, and Lightfoot, *Parthenius of Nicaea* (1999), 156–7).

Ovid speaks of Varro as confessing his 'furta'; the noun may imply that Leucadia was represented as a married woman (cf. J. N. Adams, *The Latin Sexual Vocabulary* (1982), 167–8, quoting Servius on *Aen.* 10.91 'furtum est adulterium'), or at least as firmly in the charge of another lover—or else that the poet admitted to love affairs with other women besides Leucadia (cf. Cat. 68.136, where 'furta' = Lesbia's infidelities to Catullus and Ov. *Tr.* 2.432 = **40***b* on Calvus).

The wording of Prop. 2.34.86 'Varro, Leucadiae maxima flamma suae' deserves attention, since it may keep something of the original. 'Flamma' in the concrete sense, 'object of one's passion', did not establish itself in the regular language of Latin love poetry (there are a few instances of 'ardor' and 'ignis' so used). One can quote Horace, *Odes* 1.27.20 'digne puer meliore flamma', but the best parallel (and the only place where 'flamma' stands in apposition to a proper name) is, surprisingly, *Ilias Latina* 320 'venisti, mea flamma Paris' (Helen speaks). Also, while it was customary to describe the girl as the 'cura' (e.g. Virgil, *Ecl.* 10.22 'tua cura Lycoris') *vel sim.* of the man, according with the convention that he loves her more than is reciprocated, here the relationship seems to be reversed. Did Varro represent Leucadia as unusually devoted to him—or as more devoted to him than to other men (perhaps including her husband) who shared her favours?

134 (19 Bl., 21 C.) incertae sedis

The noun 'canna' is of Eastern origin; Columella (7.9.7, 'degeneris arundinis quam vulgus cannam vocant') seems to regard it as a 'low' word. This is the earliest known occurrence in Latin. The context of Lucan 5.517 'cannaque intexta palustri' suggests that the Berne Commentator, in mentioning Ovid, has in mind *Met.* 8.630 'canna tecta palustri', which is one of fourteen Ovidian instances (in *Met.* 8.337 'canna' is distinguished from 'harundo').

This fragment might belong to the *Chorographia*, perhaps in connection with **118** (Indian sugar cane). This ancient commentator on Lucan also preserves **118**.1–2 and **109** dub. (perhaps *Chorographia*).

One or two odds and ends before we leave Varro Atacinus.

(*a*) Older scholars gave to Atacinus a 'non invenustum Varronis epigramma' (schol. Pers. 2.36) which runs 'marmoreo Licinus tumulo iacet, at Cato nullo, / Pompeius parvo: credimus [quis putet Schol. Cruq. ad Hor. *AP* 301] esse deos?' That our Varro should have written epigrams with a political slant is of course entirely possible (cf. Catullus, Calvus), and the lost codex Bellovacensis of the *Anthologia Latina* added 'Attacini' (see Baehrens, *PLM* IV, p. 64) for what that is worth. 'Licinus' has generally been identified with a freedman of Augustus whose death occurred too late to be known to a poet who himself probably was dead by 35 BC. T. P. Wiseman, however, argues that 'Licinus' was a Caesarian senator, thus removing the chronological objection (*CQ* NS 14 (1964), 132–3). Blänsdorf (but not Courtney) prints the epigram (his Varr. At. 24a), but the short final 'o' in 'Catŏ' (line 1) seems unlikely in our poet.

(*b*) R. M. Ogilvie, *JThS* NS 26 (1975), 411–12, suggested that the second Epicurean poet (in addition to Lucretius) of Lactantius, *De Opificio Dei* 18.2 is probably Varro Atacinus. But we have no evidence that Atacinus was an

Epicurean, and the texts that Ogilvie relied on to show that a Varro wrote in verse *de rerum natura* more probably point to Varro of Reate (Dahlmann and Speyer, *Varronische Studien*, II (1960), 736–44). The second Epicurean poet, in my opinion, is likely to be Varius Rufus in his *De Morte* (see **244**).

C. Asinius Pollio

135 (tragoediae)

(*a*) Verg. *Buc.* 3.86–7: *Pollio et ipse facit nova carmina: pascite taurum / iam cornu petat et pedibus qui spargat harenam.*

(*b*) Verg. *Buc.* 8.9–10: *en erit ut liceat totum mihi ferre per orbem / sola Sophocleo tua carmina digna coturno?*

(*c*) Hor. *Sat.* 1.10.42–3: *Pollio regum / facta canit pede ter percusso.*

(*d*) Hor. *Carm.* 2.1.9–12: *paulum severae Musa tragoediae / desit theatris; mox ubi publicas / res ordinaris, grande munus / Cecropio repetes coturno.*

(*e*) Tac. *Dial.* 21.7: *Asinius ... videtur mihi inter Menenios et Appios studuisse; Pacuvium certe et Accium non solum tragoediis sed etiam orationibus suis expressit, adeo durus et siccus est.*

(*a*) Pollio himself is also writing new poems; fatten up a bull who already can butt with his horns and scatter the sand with his feet.

(*b*) O will the time ever come when I can broadcast to the world your poems, supremely worthy of Sophocles' tragic boot?

(*c*) Pollio sings of the deeds of kings in the metre of three beats [i.e. the trimeter].

(*d*) For a little while let the Muse of austere Tragedy be missing from the stage; when in due course you have set in order the affairs of state, you will resume your sublime role with the Attic buskin.

(*e*) Asinius seems to me to have been to school with people like Menenius and Appius. Certainly he reproduced Pacuvius and Accius in his speeches as well as his tragedies—so harsh and dry he is.

136 (1 Bl., C.)

Veneris antistita Cuprus
Cyprus, priestess of Venus

Charis., p. 127 Barwick² = GLK I p. 100: *hospes, cum sit communis generis, hospita quoque dicitur . . . et antistes habet antistitam, ut . . . et Polio* 'Veneris— Cuprus'.

Cuprus *N*: Cupra *Keil*
metrum non apparet

137 (carmina amatoria)

Pliny, *Epist.* 5.3.5 [inter 'doctissimos gravissimos sanctissimos homines' qui 'versiculos severos parum' fecerunt]: *ego verear ne me non satis deceat quod decuit M. Tullium, C. Calvum, Asinium Pollionem . . . ?*

[Compare **19j**.] Need I fear that what was appropriate to M. Tullius, C. Calvus, and Asinius Pollio should be judged inappropriate to me?

Asinius Pollio (born in 76–5 BC) had smart poetic connections from his early youth. He was described by Catullus as 'leporum / differtus puer ac facetiarum' (12.8–9). Helvius Cinna almost certainly addressed a *Propempticon* (**2–6**) to him, and Pollio seems to have been the first patron of both Cornelius Gallus (Cic. *Ad Fam.* 10.32 = 415 SB. 5) and Virgil (*Ecl.* 8.11–12 'a te principium, tibi desinam; accipe iussis / carmina coepta tuis'—I do not doubt that this passage is addressed to Pollio). Unquestionably he made his greatest contribution to Latin literature as a historian and orator (see J. André, *La Vie et l'œuvre d'Asinius Pollion* (Paris, 1949); Nisbet and Hubbard on Horace, *Odes* 2.1). But there was a period (perhaps *c.*45–35 BC) when he seemed a significant tragedian and indeed the leading Roman exponent of that genre— if Serv. Dan. on *Ecl.* 8.10 is to be believed, he wrote plays in Greek as well as Latin. Pollio may have moved from tragedy to history at just about the time that Varius Rufus migrated from epic to tragedy.

Accius, last of the dynasty of archaic Latin tragedians, died probably in 86 BC. Thereafter the old plays continued to be read and performed (as is clear from references and quotations in Cicero), but we do not hear of any outstanding new talents. Something of a curiosity was Q. Cicero's composition of four tragedies in sixteen days (Cic. *Ad Quintum fratrem* 3.5 = 25 SB. 7). One of these bore the title *Erigone*, and the jocular allusion—which has puzzled some—to Erigone's dog (*Ad Q. f.* 3.7(9) = 27 SB. 7) proves conclusively (SB ad loc.) that this dealt with Erigone daughter of Icarius, whose dog conducted her to her father's corpse. This was a myth which came to prominence in the Hellenistic age (Callimachus, *Aetia* fr. 178.3–4 Pf. and Eratosthenes, *Erigone*), and Quintus may have based his play on a Hellenistic model. Containing murder, mass suicide, pestilence, expiation, catasterism, and aetia, the story provided rich material for a tragedy. See on **126** for a suggestion that Varro Atacinus, in his *Argonauts*, may have expanded on this myth in so far as it concerned the island of Ceos/Cea.

Virgil and Horace praise Pollio's tragedies (**135a–d**). There is nothing mysterious about 'nova carmina' in *Ecl.* 3.86 (**135a**); this certainly does not mean 'neoteric' poetry, and I see no need for 'unprecedented', 'marvellous' (Courtney 255, following Servius). Mention of the bull suits tragedy through the link with Dionysus. We know nothing about Pollio's themes, and the play referred to in Cic. *Ad Fam.* 10.32 = 415 SB. 5 (see p. 219 on Cornelius Gallus) was probably not by Pollio. But Tacitus, *Dial.* 21.7 (**135e**) reveals an interesting fact: Pollio still wrote in the style and spirit of the old tragedians Pacuvius and Accius. Barely a decade separated the plays of Pollio from the *Thyestes* of Varius Rufus, but if **157** (perhaps not from *Thyestes*) is typical of the latter, that gap, rather than the death of Accius, may have marked the transition from old Latin tragedy to a modern style which led to the plays of Seneca. **135e** seems to tell against R. J. Tarrant's wish to connect Pollio with the birth of new-style Roman tragedy (*HSCP* 82 (1978), 258–60). Horace (**135d**) speaks of Pollio's *Histories* as an intermission in his true work as a tragedian, but the latter may never have returned to the Attic buskin.

136 (1 Bl., C.)

Veneris antistita Cuprus: this could be part of a hexameter, with lengthening (Venerīs) or omission (e.g. Veneris<que>), or else (as most have taken it) a lyric fragment from a tragedy—though the metre baffles me. 'Cuprus' (the old form) is seemingly in apposition to 'Veneris antistita'; i.e. the whole island is 'priestess of Venus'. Perhaps the nicest parallel for this religious expression is in the *Acts of the Apostles* 19: 35, where the town clerk reminds a restive crowd that the city of Ephesus is 'temple-warden' (*NEB*) of the great Diana (νεωκόρον ... τῆς μεγάλης Ἀρτέμιδος); see further LSJ s.v. νεωκόρος II. In poetry the tone will be grandiloquent, e.g. Pindar, *Nem.* 1.2–3 Ὀρτυγία / δέμνιον Ἀρτέμιδος, Euphorion fr. 51.11 Powell Αἴτνην ψολόεσσαν, ἐναύλιον

Ἀστερόποιο, or mock-grandiloquent (e.g. Cat. 36.15 'Dyrrhachium, Hadriae tabernam' or Nonnus, *Dion.* 41.143 ff., where a whole string of such appositional phrases is applied to Βερόη/Beirut).

antistita: cf. Plautus, *Rudens* 624 (again grandiose) 'Veneri Veneriaeque antistitae'. The form is indeed (cf. **135***e*) found in Accius (153 Warmington), and e.g. in Cornelius Severus, **210**.

137

Pollio's amatory trifles, mentioned by Pliny alone, were not thought worth including by Ovid in *Tristia* 2.

C. Cornelius Gallus

138

(*a*) Hieronymi *Chronicon* (ed. Helm² (1956), p. 164) ann. Abr. 1990=27 a. Chr.: *Cornelius Gallus Foroiuliensis poeta, a quo primum Aegyptum rectam supra* [p. 162 Helm²] *diximus, XLIII aetatis suae anno propria se manu interficit.*

(*b*) Asinius Pollio ap. Cic. *Ad Fam.* 10.32=415 SB. 5: *etiam praetextam si voles legere, Gallum Cornelium, familiarem meum, poscito.* Cf. 10.31=368 SB. 6: *quod familiarem meum tuorum numero habes, opinione tua mihi gratius est. invideo illi tamen quod ambulat et iocatur tecum.*

(*c*) Suet. *De Gramm. et Rhet.* 16.1 (ed. Kaster, 1995, p. 20): *Q. Caecilius Epirota* [cf. **176**] *... libertus Attici ... cum filiam patroni nuptam M. Agrippae doceret, suspectus in ea et ob hoc remotus ad Cornelium Gallum se contulit, vixitque una familiarissime; quod ipsi Gallo inter gravissima crimina ab Augusto obicitur.*

(*d*) Prop. 2.34.91–2: *et modo formosa quam multa Lycoride Gallus / mortuus inferna vulnera lavit aqua.*

(*e*) Ov. *Am.* 3.9.63–4: *tu quoque* [sc. Tibullo in Elysia valle obvius venies], *si falsum est temerati crimen amici, / sanguinis atque animae prodige Galle tuae.*

(*f*) Ov. *Tr.* 2.445–6: *non fuit opprobrio celebrasse Lycorida Gallo, / sed linguam nimio non tenuisse mero.*

(*g*) Ov. *Tr.* 4.10.53–4: *successor fuit hic* [sc. Tibullus] *tibi, Galle, Propertius illi, / quartus ab his serie temporis ipse fui.*

(*h*) Quint. 10.1.93: *Elegia quoque Graecos provocamus, cuius mihi tersus atque elegans maxime videtur auctor Tibullus; sunt qui Propertium malint. Ovidius utroque lascivior, sicut durior Gallus.*

(*a*) [The Chronicle of Jerome under 27 BC]: The poet Cornelius Gallus of Forum Iulium, who, as we have mentioned above, was the first governor of Egypt, killed himself with his own hand in the forty-third year of his life.

(*b*) [Asinius Pollio to Cicero]: If you want to read the Roman historical drama as well, ask my friend Cornelius Gallus for it . . . [from another letter] . . . The fact that you are including my friend in your circle is more welcome to me than you might have thought. And yet I envy him that he strolls and jokes with you.

(*c*) When Q. Caecilius Epirota . . . a freedman of Atticus . . . was teaching his patron's daughter after her marriage to M. Agrippa, he became suspected of improper conduct towards her, and for that reason was removed. He took himself to Cornelius Gallus, and lived with him as a very close friend; this is one of the most serious charges made against Gallus by Augustus.

(*d*) And recently how many wounds from fair Lycoris did Gallus after his death wash in the waters of the underworld.

(*e*) You too, Gallus, wasteful of your blood and life [will come to meet Tibullus in Elysium], if the charge of violating a friendship is false.

(*f*) The reproach against Gallus was not that he had celebrated Lycoris, but that he failed to hold his tongue after too much wine.

(*g*) Tibullus was the successor of Gallus, Propertius of Tibullus; after them I came fourth in chronological sequence.

(*h*) We challenge the Greeks in elegy too, of which Tibullus seems to me the most polished and elegant composer; some prefer Propertius. Ovid is more extravagant than either, as Gallus is more harsh.

139

(*a*) Serv. ad Verg. *Buc.* 10.1 (p. 118 Thilo): *Gallus . . . fuit poeta eximius; nam et Euphorionem . . . transtulit in latinum sermonem et amorum suorum de Cytheride scripsit libros quattuor.*

(*b*) Prob. ad Verg. *Buc.* 10.50 'Chalcidico . . . versu' (p. 348 Thilo): *Euphorion elegiarum scriptor Chalcidensis fuit, cuius in scribendo secutus colorem videtur Cornelius Gallus.*

(*a*) Gallus . . . was an outstanding poet; for he both translated Euphorion into Latin and wrote four books of love poems about Cytheris.

(*b*) [on 'Chalcidic verse']: The elegiac poet Euphorion came from Chalcis, and Cornelius Gallus in his writings seems to have followed the colouring of Euphorion.

140

(*a*) Ov. *Am.* 1.15.29–30: *Gallus et Hesperiis et Gallus notus Eois / et sua cum Gallo nota Lycoris erit.*

(*b*) Ov. *AA* 3.537: *Vesper et Eoae novere Lycorida terrae.*

(*c*) Ov. *AA* 3.333–4: *et teneri possis carmen legisse Properti / sive aliquid Galli sive, Tibulle, tuum.*

(*d*) Ov. *Rem. Am.* 765: *quis potuit lecto durus discedere Gallo?*

(*e*) Ov. *Tr.* 5.1.15–18: *delicias si quis lascivaque carmina quaerit, / praemoneo, non est scripta quod ista legat. / aptior huic Gallus blandique Propertius oris, / aptior, ingenium come, Tibullus erit.*

(*f*) Mart. 8.73.5–6: *Cynthia te vatem fecit, lascive Properti; / ingenium Galli pulchra Lycoris erat.*

(*a*) Gallus will be known both to Westerners and to Easterners; and his beloved Lycoris will share Gallus' notoriety.

(*b*) The west and eastern lands have come to know Lycoris.

(*c*) You might have read a poem of tender Propertius, or something by Gallus or Tibullus.

(*d*) Who could leave in a harsh frame of mind after reading Gallus?

(*e*) If anyone is looking for refinement or ornamental poetry, I give advance notice that he has no reason to read those poems. For such a one Gallus is more appropriate . . .

(*f*) . . . fair Lycoris was the talent of Gallus.

141

Verg. *Buc.* 10.42–61: *hic gelidi fontes, hic mollia prata, Lycori, / hic nemus; hic ipso tecum consumerer aevo. / nunc insanus amor duri te* [Heumann, Heyne: me *codd.*] *Martis in armis / (45) tela inter media atque adversos detinet hostes. / tu procul a patria (nec sit mihi credere tantum) / Alpinas, a, dura nives et frigora Rheni / me sine sola vides? a, te ne frigora laedant! / a, tibi ne teneras glacies secet aspera plantas! / (50) ibo et Chalcidico quae sunt mihi condita versu / carmina pastoris Siculi modulabor avena. / certum est in silvis inter spelaea ferarum / malle pati tenerisque meos incidere amores / arboribus; crescent illae, crescetis, amores. / (55) interea mixtis lustrabo Maenala nymphis / aut acres venabor apros. non me ulla vetabunt / frigora Parthenios canibus circumdare saltus. / iam mihi per rupes videor lucosque sonantes / ire, libet Partho torquere Cydonia cornu* / (60) *spicula—tamquam haec sit nostri medicina furoris* / *aut deus ille malis hominum mitescere discat.*

(*a*) Serv. ad v. 46 (p. 124 Thilo): *hi autem omnes versus Galli sunt, de ipsius translati carminibus.*

(*b*) Serv. ad vv. 50–1 (p. 125 Thilo): *Euboea insula est, in qua est Chalcis civitas, de qua fuit Euphorion, quem transtulit Gallus . . . et hoc dicit: 'ibo et Theocriteo stilo canam carmina Euphorionis'.*

[Virgil, *Ecl.* 10.42–61]: Here are cool springs, here soft meadows, Lycoris, here a grove; here, with you, I would be wasted away by time itself. But, as things are, mad passion keeps you [translating 'te'] away from me in the arms of cruel Mars (45) amid weapons and confronting enemies. Do you (ah, heartless one) far from your homeland (if only I could disbelieve it!) alone without me gaze upon Alpine snows and the frozen Rhine? Ah, may the cold not harm you! Ah, may the sharp ice not cut your delicate feet! (50) I will go and play on the pipe of a Sicilian shepherd the songs which I composed in Chalcidic verse. Rather it is my resolve to endure in the woods among the caves of wild beasts, and to carve my Loves upon the young trees; they will grow and so will my Loves. (55) Meanwhile I will range over Maenalus together with the Nymphs, or hunt fierce boars. Already I seem to myself to be passing through crags and echoing groves; it is my pleasure to shoot Cretan arrows from a Parthian bow (60)—as if this could be medicine for my madness, or that god would learn through human suffering to become gentle.

(*a*) [Servius on line 46] All these are lines of Gallus, transferred from his own poetry.

(*b*) [Servius on 50–5] Euboea is an island containing a city called Chalcis, from where came Euphorion whom Gallus translated . . . And he is saying 'I will go and sing the poems of Euphorion in the style of Theocritus'.

142

Verg. *Buc.* 6.64–73: *tum canit, errantem Permessi ad flumina Gallum* / (65) *Aonas in montis ut duxerit una sororum,* / *utque viro Phoebi chorus adsurrexerit omnis;* / *ut Linus haec illi divino carmine pastor* / *floribus atque apio crinis ornatus amaro* / *dixerit: 'hos tibi dant calamos (en accipe) Musae* / (70) *Ascraeo quos ante seni, quibus ille solebat* / *cantando rigidas deducere montibus ornos.* / *his tibi Grynei nemoris dicatur origo,* / *ne quis sit lucus qua se plus iactet Apollo.'*
Serv. ad v. 72 (p. 78 Thilo): *Gryneum nemus est in finibus Ioniis . . . in quo luco aliquando Calchas et Mopsus dicuntur de peritia divinandi inter se habuisse*

certamen: et cum de pomorum arboris cuiusdam contenderent numero, stetit gloria Mopso; cuius rei dolore Calchas interiit. hoc autem Euphorionis [fr. 97 Powell] *continent carmina, quae Gallus transtulit in sermonem Latinum.*

[Virgil, *Ecl.* 6.64–73] Then he [Silenus] sang how, as Gallus wandered by the stream of Permessus, one of the Sisters led him up into the Aonian mountains; how the whole choir of Phoebus rose to the great man, and how Linus, shepherd of divine song, his hair decorated with flowers and bitter parsley, said 'These pipes (come, take them) the Muses give to you, (70) which previously they gave to the old man of Ascra [Hesiod], with which he used to draw down stiff ash trees from the mountains. With these you must tell the origin of the Grynean wood, so that there is no grove in which Apollo takes more pride.' [Servius on line 72] The Grynean Grove is in the territory of Ionia . . . in which grove on one occasion Calchas and Mopsus are said to have held a competition for their skill in divining. And when they were contending about the number of apples on a particular tree, the glory ended up on Mopsus' side; in pain over this matter Calchas died. This story is to be found in the poetry of Euphorion, which Gallus translated into Latin.

143

Parthenius (p. 308 ed. Lightfoot, 1999), *Hist. Amat.*, praef.: Παρθένιος Κορνηλίωι Γάλλωι χαίρειν. Μάλιστα σοὶ δοκῶν ἁρμόττειν, Κορνήλιε Γάλλε, τὴν ἄθροισιν τῶν ἐρωτικῶν παθημάτων, ἀναλεξάμενος ὡς ὅτι μάλιστα ἐν βραχυτάτοις ἀπέσταλκα. τὰ γὰρ παρά τισι τῶν ποιητῶν κείμενα τούτων, μὴ αὐτοτελῶς λελεγμένα, κατανοήσεις ἐκ τῶνδε τὰ πλεῖστα· (2) αὐτῶι τέ σοι παρέσται εἰς ἔπη καὶ ἐλεγείας ἀνάγειν τὰ μάλιστα ἐξ αὐτῶν ἁρμόδια. <μηδὲ> διὰ τὸ μὴ παρεῖναι τὸ περιττὸν αὐτοῖς, ὃ δὴ σὺ μετέρχηι, χεῖρον περὶ αὐτῶν ἐννοηθῆις· οἱονεὶ γὰρ ὑπομνηματίων τρόπον αὐτὰ συνελεξάμεθα, καὶ σοὶ νυνὶ τὴν χρῆσιν ὁμοίαν, ὡς ἔοικε, παρέξεται.

Greetings from Parthenius to Cornelius Gallus. Thinking that the collection of Sufferings in Love is particularly appropriate to you, Cornelius Gallus, I have gathered them and sent them to you in the shortest possible form. For those of the present collection which occur in some of the poets, but are not told in their entirety, you will, for the most part, discover from what follows. And it will be open for you to render the most appropriate of them into hexameter and elegiac verse. You must not think the worse of them because they do not display that quality of refined elaboration which you make your objective. For I have collected them after the manner of a notebook, and they will, I trust, be of similar service to you.

144 (I Bl., C.)

uno tellures dividit amne duas

[The Scythian river Hypanis] divides two lands with its single stream.

Vibius Sequester, *De Fluminibus* etc. 77 (p. 14 ed. Gelsomino, 1967): *Hypanis Scythiae, qui, ut ait Gallus,* 'uno—duas'. *Asiam enim ab Europa separat.*

145 (2–5 Bl., 2 C.)

tristia nequit[ia fact]a, Lycori, tua.	1
Fata mihi, Caesar, tum erunt mea dulcia quom tu	2
maxima Romanae pars eri<s> historiae	3
postque tuum reditum multorum templa deorum	4
fixa legam spolieis deivitiora tueis.	5
. . . . .] . . . . . tandem fecerunt c[ar]mina Musae	6
quae possem domina deicere digna mea.	7
. . . .] . atur idem tibi, non ego, Visce,	8
. .] . . . . l . Kato, iudice te vereor.	9
] . . . [ ] .	10
] . . . [ ] . Tyria	11
] .	12

<? made> sad, Lycoris, by your wantonness

My fate, Caesar, will be sweet to me at that time when you become the greatest part of Roman History, and when, after your return, I survey the temples of many gods, richer for being fixed with your spoils.

. . . Finally the Muses have made <? these> poems <? for me> that I could call worthy of my mistress. <? And if she tells> you the same, I do not, Viscus, I do not, Cato, fear . . . with you as judge.

. . . Tyrian . . .

1–12 P Qaṣr Ibrîm inv. 78–3–11 (L1/2), col. i (ed. Anderson, Parsons, Nisbet, *JRS* 69 (1979), 125–55).

1 fact]a *Nisbet*   2 Caesar, tum erunt] tum, Caesar, erunt *Lyne*   3 erit *pap., corr. Nisbet et Parsons*   6 haec mih]i vix (*P. G. Brown*) *non excluditur*   9 *fort.* upla (*vel* uple) Kato   plakato (*i.e.* placato) *Hutchinson*

CORNELIUS Gallus, first Prefect of Roman Egypt and the missing member of the dynasty of four Latin elegiac poets, is a fascinating figure. In front of St Peter's in Rome stands an obelisk which originally bore an inscription of his, commemorating the foundation of a Forum Iulium, presumably in or near Alexandria (see J. P. Boucher, *Gaius Cornelius Gallus* (Paris, 1966), 33–8; P. M. Fraser, *Ptolemaic Alexandria* (Oxford, 1972), vol. II, pp. 97–8; R. G. M. Nisbet *et al.*, *JRS* 69 (1979), 154). On the island of Philae in the Nile near Aswan (the effective southern boundary of Cornelius Gallus' province) a trilingual inscription (*CIL* III. 14147, Boucher pp. 38–45 with photograph) was discovered in 1896, wherein Gallus claims to have carried his arms further south than the Ptolemaic kings of Egypt or the Roman people before him. Both monuments were damaged (presumably in consequence of Gallus' downfall) and shortly afterwards put to other uses—the obelisk for a dedication by Caligula, *CIL* VI. 882 (the original inscription was removed and has to be reconstructed from the nail-holes of the letters), and the trilingual stele for a temple of Augustus built by the prefect P. Rubrius Barbarus in 13 BC. Even more remarkably, in 1978 a papyrus (see **145**) containing lines of Latin elegiac verse, the very first of which names Gallus' girlfriend Lycoris, was found in Egyptian Nubia at Qaṣr Ibrîm, some 150 miles south of Cornelius Gallus' territory (L. P. Kirwan, 'Rome beyond the Southern Egyptian Frontier', *Proceedings of the British Academy*, 63 (1977), 13–31). The find-spot was a ruined fortress which—probably but not quite certainly (*JRS* (1979), 127)—the Romans of our period occupied only for some five years *c*.25–20 BC during the governorship of C. Petronius. So this papyrus apparently was written, if not during Gallus' lifetime, at least within very few years of his death.

Gallus was a close contemporary of Virgil—indeed, if we can trust Jerome (**138***a*), born in the same year, 70 BC. Some, however, by combining Jerome's figure for Gallus' age at death ('in his 43rd year') with Dio's date for Gallus' death (26 BC, Dio 53.23) have arrived at 69 or 68 for his birth (a procedure not approved by Syme, *CQ* 32 (1938), 40 n. 7). The name Forum Iulium (Courtney 260 fears confusion with Gallus' Alexandrian foundation, see above) would be anachronistic in 70 BC. Of the towns later bearing that name the most distinguished (and favoured for Gallus' birth place) was Fréjus in Narbonese Gaul, though Boucher (p. 11) prefers Forum Iulii Iriensium in Liguria (modern Voghera). Syme (p. 43) sees the poet as the son of a local dynast of Gallia Narbonensis: 'These men came from a class that was eminently presentable and highly civilized, Greek before they were Roman; they are the precursors of the famous Narbonensian senators of the first century of the Empire.' Probus' introduction to the *Eclogues* and *Georgics* (p. 328 Hagen) speaks of Gallus as Virgil's 'condiscipulus'—if so, one might wonder where (cf. Boucher, pp. 9–10). This would take the pair's acquaintance back to the mid-50s BC, but is probably just an inference from the introduction of Gallus into *Eclogues* 6 and 10; Probus also believed (p. 329 Hagen) that Meliboeus in the first eclogue is Cornelius Gallus. *Ecl.* 10.73–4 'Gallo, cuius amor tantum mihi crescit in horas …' etc. rather suggests a more recent friendship, probably arising from the shared patronage of Asinius Pollio.

The first literary recognition of Cornelius Gallus may well be in Cicero, *Tusc. Disp.* 3.45 'o poetam egregium [sc. Ennium]! quamquam ab his cantoribus Euphorionis contemnitur'. Although what we know of Helvius Cinna makes him a plausible 'cantor Euphorionis' (for 'cantor' Jane Lightfoot, *Parthenius of Nicaea* (Oxford, 1999), 57, suggests 'chanter'—see her discussion), the only Latin poet explicitly connected with Euphorion is Cornelius Gallus (see below on **139**). The date (July 45 BC) may be too early for complete books of elegies on Lycoris, but by then Gallus would have been approximately 25, quite old enough to have made a hit with poetry in the style of Euphorion unconnected to Lycoris (cf. Lightfoot, *Parthenius*, 64, 'nothing requires that Cytheris had anything to do with *all* Gallus' Euphorionic poetry'). Such poetry could well have been in hexameters, as—to our present knowledge—was all of Euphorion except for two epigrams (see on **139**). Indeed it would be easier for Gallus to establish a reputation as the Roman Euphorion (*Ecl.* 10.50 'Chalcidico … versu') if he started by writing in Euphorion's metre; this reputation could then be carried over into his elegies.

A definite reference to Cornelius Gallus occurs in **138b**, a letter from Asinius Pollio to Cicero (*Ad Fam.* 10.32 = 415 SB. 5) in June 43 BC, where the context is literary: Cicero can, if he wishes, ask Gallus ('familiarem meum') for the text of a Roman tragedy (by Balbus rather than Pollio himself, cf. F. Graf, *Gymnasium*, 89 (1982), 26 n. 18). Gallus may also be Pollio's unnamed 'familiaris' in another letter to Cicero (*Ad Fam.* 10.31 = 368 SB. 5 = **138b**). One might speculate that Cicero, after denouncing Gallus as one of the 'cantores Euphorionis' two years earlier, met Gallus for the first time in 43 BC and found him a surprisingly agreeable companion. If the 'Caesar' in **145**.2 is Julius, it follows that Gallus' poetry for Volumnia/Cytheris/Lycoris (**145**.1, cf. **140–1**) had started by 45–4 (see Nisbet, *JRS* (1979), 151–5 'The Historical Framework').

How long the relationship with Lycoris lasted (and the composition of poetry about her, which might have continued longer) we do not know, but according to Servius (**139a**) there were four books of love poems, perhaps (like Ovid's) entitled *Amores*. Hints survive of a public role for Gallus in the aftermath of Philippi, relating to land confiscations for the settlement of veteran soldiers. In general one must be extremely suspicious of biographical material in the ancient commentators on the *Eclogues*. But Servius auctus on

Ecl. 9.10 (p. 110 Thilo) preserves an item which looks more solid: a verbatim quotation by 'Cornelius', attacking Alfenus Varus for exceeding his instructions and taking too much land from the Mantuans: 'cum iussus tria milia passus a muro in diversa relinquere, vix octingentos passus aquae, quae circumdata est, admetireris, reliquisti'. The name Cornelius is of course enormously common (hence the scepticism of Nisbet, *Collected Papers* (Oxford, 1995), 408), but no more obvious Cornelius suggests himself, and it seems that speeches attributed to Gallus were known: 'in oratione Labieni (sive illa Cornelii Galli est) in Pollionem' (Quint. 1.5.8, though one would not expect Gallus to speak against his patron Pollio). If the extract is not genuine, where did the commentator find it? The precise measurements do not sound like an exercise from the rhetorical schools. See L. P. Wilkinson, *The Georgics of Virgil* (Cambridge, 1969), p. 31.

I doubt whether one can deduce anything about Gallus' real life from *Ecl.* 10.44–5 (perhaps we should emend 'me' to 'te' in line 44, see on **141** below). In the early to mid-30s Gallus may have lived for a while in Rome, thus gaining at least the opportunity to write more poetry. That period provides a likely context for **138c.** R. Kaster (Suetonius, *De Grammaticis et Rhetoribus* (Oxford, 1995), 183) dates the marriage of Attica to M. Agrippa either *c.*42 or in 37 BC. By taking in Caecilius Epirota, who was suspected of impropriety towards his married pupil (still no doubt in her teens), Gallus may have been showing robust independence and support for a friend whom he believed to have been unjustly accused, but there is a hint of the incaution which later ruined Gallus. Agrippa, and through him Octavian, must have been gravely offended. Kaster (p. 185) refers 'gravissima crimina' (**138c** ad fin.) to Augustus' *Commentarii de vita sua*, and this matter may have contributed to the charge against Gallus, 'ingratum et malevolum animum' (Suet. *Div. Aug.* 66.2). If so, the resentment was long-lasting, though it did not stop Octavian from employing Gallus as a commander in the attack upon Egypt (30 BC), or thereafter appointing him as first Prefect. Suetonius goes on to tell us that, after Gallus' death, Epirota opened a school and became the first grammarian to expound Virgil 'et alios poetas novos' (*De Gramm.* 16, cf. on Domitius Marsus, **176**). Did he include among the 'others' his former benefactor, Cornelius Gallus?

Syme (*The Roman Revolution* (Oxford, 1939), 252 n. 4) conjectured that Gallus served Asinius Pollio as *praefectus fabrum* in Cisalpina in 41 BC. The Vatican obelisk now reveals that he held that important office in Egypt, presumably in the final months of 30 or the very beginning of 29 (before he became Prefect). Perhaps in the same capacity, he had participated in the invasion which brought Antony and Cleopatra to their deaths. Dio (51.9) represents Gallus as playing a skilful part in winning over the forces of Pinarius Scarpus and capturing Paraetonium, while Plutarch (*Antony* 79) describes how he conversed with Cleopatra shortly before her death. The Philae stele records quick suppression of a revolt in the Thebaid and a diplomatic settlement on Philae with Ethiopian envoys.

As for Gallus' downfall, Dio (53.23) mentions wild and insulting talk about Augustus, erection of statues of himself all over Egypt, and even inscription of his own deeds upon the Pyramids; these items were apparently the basis of a denunciation by Valerius Largus, a former friend. The senate voted that Gallus should be convicted in the courts (a process rendered unnecessary by the victim's suicide), deprived of his property, and exiled, while Augustus specified that he should be banned from the imperial provinces. Suetonius' words 'domo et provinciis suis interdixit' (*Div. Aug.* 66.2) look like an adaptation to Empire of the Republican method of renouncing friendship by denying one's house.

It must be said that Gallus' two surviving Egyptian inscriptions do not go beyond the bounds of political acceptability: the Vatican obelisk records foundation of the Forum Iulium IVSSU IMP CAESARIS DIVI F, while on the Philae stele Gallus makes no mention of his own part in the defeat of Cleopatra, giving all the credit to Octavian (POST REGES A CAESARE DEIVI F DEVICTOS). Neither Suetonius nor Ovid refers to misconduct during Gallus' governorship, which may not have stretched beyond the year 29. So Boucher (pp. 50 ff.) may have been right in arguing that Gallus' disgrace stemmed from conduct after his return to Rome. Ovid defines the charge as 'temerati crimen amici' (*Am.* 3.9.63 = **138e**), adding (*Tr.* 2.446 = **138f**) 'linguam nimio non tenuisse mero'. These words stress the personal nature of the offence, as does Augustus' somewhat hypocritical plaint after Gallus' suicide, 'quod sibi soli non liceret amicis quatenus vellet irasci' (Suet. *Div. Aug.* 66.2).

A famous story alleges that Virgil removed 'laudes Galli' from the Fourth Georgic after Gallus' downfall. This occurs in two forms—though the ancient commentator does not seem aware of any discrepancy. In his introduction to *Eclogue* 10 (Thilo p. 118) Servius writes 'fuit autem [sc. Gallus] amicus Vergilii adeo ut quartus Georgicorum a medio usque ad finem eius laudes teneret: quas postea iubente Augusto in Aristaei fabulam commutavit', while in the introduction to *Georgics* 4 (Thilo p. 320) we read 'sane sciendum, ut supra diximus, ultimam partem huius libri esse mutatam; nam laudes Galli habuit locus ille qui nunc Orphei continet fabulam, quae inserta est postquam irato Augusto Gallus occisus est.' *Laudes Galli* on the scale of the Orpheus section (106 lines), let alone the whole Aristaeus/Orpheus epyllion (243 lines), would completely unbalance the poem by comparison with the 18 lines on Octavian at the beginning of *G.* 1 and the three lines at the end of *G.* 4. How would Octavian have taken such praise of Gallus when Virgil recited the whole of the *Georgics* to him in the summer of 29 BC? Some (e.g. Nisbet,

JRS (1979), 155 with n. 163) have allowed that just a few lines could have been excluded (perhaps round about *G.* 4.287 ff. where there is mention of Egypt), though that does not properly accord with either of Servius' statements. But chronology suggests that the original version of the *Georgics* should have circulated for at least a year before Gallus' disgrace, and an enforced alteration (however small) on political grounds would be likely to become notorious — we would expect to hear much more about it than we do. So I am inclined to reject the story, though its origin is mysterious (it seems unlikely that an earlier commentator said 'at the end of the *Georgics*' when he meant 'of the *Eclogues*' and that Servius was deceived).

There are two Greek epigrams ascribed to a Gallus (not necessarily, of course, the same Gallus) in the *Anthology* (*Anth. Pal.* 5.49 and *Anth. Plan.* 89, Page, *Further Greek Epigrams* (Cambridge, 1981), 60–2). The latter is about a cup with a figure of Tantalus. Lines 5–6 read ʽπῖνεʼ λέγει τὸ τόρευμα ʽκαὶ ὄργια μάνθανε σιγῆς· / οἱ γλώσσηι προπετεῖς ὧδε κολαζόμεθαʼ (for reasons unexplained Page prints τὸ γλύμμα and ταῦτα for τὸ τόρευμα and ὧδε). There is a striking coincidence with Ovid's version of Gallus' offence, 'linguam nimio non tenuisse mero' (*Tr.* 2.446 = **138f**), and several scholars since F. Jacobs have considered the possibility that 'Gallus' could be our Cornelius — most recently Lloyd-Jones, *Academic Papers*, vol. II, p. 205 (discovery of the first half of *Suppl. Hell.* 970, col. i, line 8 in *P. Brux. Inv. E 8934* makes it less likely that Gallus had that line in mind), and R. Aubreton in the Budé *Anthologie Grecque*, vol. XIII (Paris, 1980), 259.

138d, to which I shall return in connection with Gallus and Euphorion, describes (perhaps in 26 or 25 BC) Gallus' death as 'recent'; Propertius may be observing political correctness in attributing Gallus' death to his painful love for Lycoris rather than the wrath of Augustus. Ovid, however, *c.*19 BC in his lament for Tibullus (**138e**) ventures to suggest that the charge of violating a friendship may not have been justified — otherwise Gallus would be in a much less pleasant place than Elysium — and hints that suicide was an excessive reaction. Ovid clearly had a strong sense of the dynasty of four love-elegists starting with Gallus and ending with himself, to the exclusion of any lesser figures who may also have written love elegies (e.g. Varro Atacinus with his poems for Leucadia, **133**). Several of the items in **140** stress the dynasty of four. By the time of Quintilian (**138h**) each poet had a standard characterization (it being implied that some found Propertius even more 'tersus atque elegans' than Tibullus). Perhaps these were already established in Ovid's day. In *Rem. Am.* 765 (**140d**) he asks 'quis poterit lecto durus discedere Gallo?' — the very epithet, though in a different sense, applied to Gallus by Quintilian (**138h**). Perhaps Ovid is deliberately contradicting a current view that Gallus' elegiac poetry was 'harsh' (*durus*). It is not surprising that later generations found him technically less accomplished than Tibullus and Propertius; one may see some vindication of this view in the new papyrus (**145**). Gallus' _floruit_ was some twenty years earlier than that of the other elegists, and in the development of poetic technique twenty years can be a long time. A feeling that Gallus was technically inferior to his younger rivals may have contributed significantly to the loss of his poetry; there is no suggestion whatever that this loss was caused by the author's disgrace and violent death.

139

In **139**_a_ Servius gives us a piece of information not preserved elsewhere nor deducible from the text of Virgil, that Gallus wrote four books of love poems for Cytheris (whom he called Lycoris). Also we should probably infer that Gallus' poems were entitled _Amores_, like those of Ovid; there may be a special point when the word 'amores' occurs in the tenth _Eclogue_ (see on **141**). But my main concern at this juncture is to explore the relationship of Cornelius Gallus to Euphorion of Chalcis, the most formidable and obscure of the learned Hellenistic poets (with the exception of his fellow-citizen Lycophron).

It seems to me certain that _Ecl._ 10.50 'Chalcidico . . . versu' (quoted in **141**) refers to Euphorion, as understood by Quintilian (10.1.56) and the Virgilian commentators; Courtney's reference (_QUCC_ 34 (1990), 107–8) to Theocles of Chalcis (probably mentioned in Callimachus fr. 43.26 as founder of Sicilian Naxos) seems very far-fetched and has not carried conviction (see, most recently, Lightfoot, _Parthenius_, 60). The phrase shows the importance of Euphorion in the Rome of the 40s; besides _Tusc. Disp._ 3.45 on the 'cantores Euphorionis' (p. 226 above) compare Cic. _De Divinatione_ 2.133 'ille . . . Euphorion'. Perhaps Gallus himself had used the expression 'Chalcidic verse' of his poetry in the style of Euphorion, and even claimed to be the Roman Euphorion, as Virgil's 'Syracosio . . . versu' stakes a claim to be the Roman Theocritus (_Ecl._ 6.1).

But what precisely did Gallus owe to Euphorion? This question would be easier to answer if Euphorion had been a notable Greek elegist, and the Virgilian commentators say that he was (**139**_b_ and Philargyrius on _Ecl._ 10.50 (p. 185 Thilo), cf. Diomedes, GLK I, p. 484 [elegia] 'quod genus carminis praecipue scripserunt apud Romanos Propertius et Tibullus et Gallus imitati Graecos Callimachum et Euphoriona'). The possiblity that Euphorion wrote some elegiac poems remains open, but our knowledge of him has increased (37 more pages in _Supplementum Hellenisticum_) and there is still no sign of anything elegiac apart from two brief epigrams (_Anth. Pal._ 6.279 and 7.651 =

Euph. 140 and 141 Powell). Any notion that Euphorion was a *leading* Greek elegist, or *predominantly* an elegist, can be confidently dismissed. Athenaeus' regular term for him (e.g. 4.182e) is ἐποποιός (better 'hexameter poet' than 'epic poet'). Almost certainly the Latin commentators have deduced, reasonably but wrongly, that, since Gallus wrote elegies and imitated Euphorion, the latter too must have written elegies.

Euphorion and Gallus are brought together also in *Ecl.* 6.64–73 (**142**), where Gallus, wandering by the river Permessus, is conducted by a Muse higher up Helicon, there to be presented with the pipes which the Muses had previously given to Hesiod. With these he is urged to sing of the grove of Grynean Apollo. Servius ad loc. speaks of a contest in divination at this grove between Mopsus and Calchas in which the former is victorious and the latter dies of chagrin, concluding 'hoc autem [this should refer to the contest, not to the foundation of the grove, though both could have been combined in a single poem] Euphorionis (fr. 97 Powell) continent carmina, quae Gallus transtulit in sermonem Latinum'. Unlike Barigazzi (*SIFC* NS 26 (1952), 149 ff.) I do not see sufficient reason for thinking that *Suppl. Hell.* 429 preserves remnants of the contest between Mopsus and Calchas (though Τιτα]ρήσιος might be restored in col. I, line 21, and referred to Mopsus). Note that Euph. fr. 98 describes the death of Mopsus in a dispute with Amphilochus over the city of Mallos. We cannot rule out the possibility that Gallus somewhere 'translated Euphorion into Latin', as Catullus (66) did for Callimachus' *Lock of Berenice* (fr. 110). But Latin commentators regularly overstate the dependence of Latin upon Greek poets, and it seems more likely that Gallus was felt in some way to have caught the spirit and essence of Euphorion, his 'color' as Probus puts it (**139***b*), in Latin.

When we compare *Ecl.* 6.64 (**142**) 'errantem Permessi ad flumina Gallum' with Propertius 2.10.25–6 'nondum etiam Ascraeos norunt mea carmina fontis, / sed modo Permessi flumine lavit Amor' (surely from Gallus), it is natural to think that 'wandering by the streams of Permessus' represents a lower genre such as love poetry, while going up into the mountains and meeting the Muses suggests higher inspiration and more learned subject matter (e.g. the Grynean grove), perhaps written in hexameters rather than elegiacs, and that Euphorion was relevant only to Gallus' more learned poetry, which furthermore was written later than his love elegies. But most, if not all, of these natural assumptions may need to be modified. For example, Gallus' diversion from a lower to a higher genre may reflect not the chronological order in which he composed his poems but the supposedly higher esteem attaching to the loftier genres. We have seen that Gallus' poetry in the style of Euphorion may already have become well known by the summer of 45 BC (Cicero, *Tusc. Disp.* 3.45).

Virgil's reference to the Grynean Grove (a topic of interest also to Gallus' friend Parthenius, cf. fr. 10 Lightfoot = *Suppl. Hell.* 620 Γρύνειος Ἀπόλλων) is more likely to be praise of a poem already written than encouragement of a future project. David Ross (*Backgrounds to Augustan Poetry* (Cambridge, 1975), 79–80) adventurously suggested that the *locus amoenus* described by Servius auctus on *Ecl.* 6.72 (not unlike that in Propertius 1.20) might be derived from Gallus on the Grynean Grove. *Ecl.* 10.50–1 ('ibo et Chalcidico . . .' etc.) seem to warn us not to divorce the *color* of Euphorion from the elegies for Lycoris.

Remarkably, we may be able to substantiate the conjunction of Gallus and Euphorion from Propertius 2.34.91–2 'et modo formosa quam multa Lycoride Gallus / mortuus inferna vulnera lavit aqua' (*vulnera* suggests the infidelities of Lycoris as well as the passion which she inspired). The pentameter bears an unmistakable resemblance to Euphorion fr. 43, printed by Powell (and others) as Κώκυτός <τοι> μοῦνος ἀφ' ἕλκεα νίψεν Ἄδωνιν. We can surely forget about the alleged doctor called Κώκυτος; and I suspect that the relative pronoun ὅς has coalesced with the name of the river in some other case (-ος in three out of four syllables might be excessive), e.g. Κώκυτόν <θ'> ὅς μοῦνος ἀφ' ἕλκεα νίψεν Ἄδωνιν (? in a list of underworld rivers). For the motif, cf. Ovid, *Met.* 15.532 (of Hippolytus) 'et lacerum fovi Phlegethontide corpus in unda'. Perhaps Gallus, like Euphorion, applied the figure to Adonis, and Propertius transferred it to Gallus' love affair.

One may still wonder what an elegy reflecting the *color* of Euphorion might be like; there are two poems in the other elegists which could offer a clue. Propertius 2.26A is, in my view, correctly reckoned as a separate poem, and deserves to be quoted in full:

> Vidi te in somnis fracta, mea vita, carina
>   Ionio lassas ducere rore manus,
> et quaecunque in me fueras mentita fateri,
>   nec iam umore gravis tollere posse comas,
> qualem purpureis agitatam fluctibus Hellen,   5
>   aurea quam molli tergore vexit ovis.
> quam timui, ne forte tuum mare nomen haberet,
>   teque tua labens navita fleret aqua!
> quae tum ego Neptuno, quae tum cum Castore fratri,
>   quaeque tibi excepi, iam dea, Leucothoe!   10
> at tu vix primas extollens gurgite palmas
>   saepe meum nomen iam peritura vocas.
> quod si forte tuos vidisset Glaucus ocellos,
>   esses Ionii facta puella maris,

et tibi ob invidiam Nereides increpitarent,   15
    candida Nesaee, caerula Cymothoe.
sed tibi subsidio delphinum currere vidi,
    qui, puto, Arioniam vexerat ante lyram.
iamque ego conabar summo me mittere saxo,
    cum mihi discussit talia visa metus.   20

The *color* of Euphorion, one imagines, would be sombre and melancholy, with more stress on the sufferings than the happiness of love. In this spirit we could count the *vulnera* inflicted by Lycoris on Gallus (**138***d*) and the sadness of his life due to her *nequitia* (**145**.1, cf. Prop. 2.26A.3 above). Nearly all the stories in Parthenius' Ἐρωτικὰ Παθήματα (**143**) are of unhappy love and (like many of the myths ascribed to Euphorion) come to a gruesome and disastrous end. Propertius 2.26A also contains a number of motifs characteristic of Euphorion. Above all, the description of drowning—compare Euph. fr. 44 Powell:

> τὸν δ᾽ ἐκάλυψε θάλασσα λιλαιόμενον βιότοιο,
> καί οἱ πήχεες ἄκρον ὑπερφαίνοντο ταθέντες
> ἀχρεῖ᾽ ἀσπαίροντος ἅλις Δολοπιονίδαο
> δυστήνου· ζωὴν δὲ μεθ᾽ ὕδατος ἔκβαλε πᾶσαν
> χεῖρας ὑπερπλάζων, ἅλμη δ᾽ ἔκλυσσεν ὀδόντας.

'Him did the sea cover, though he longed for life, and his outstretched arms were visible above the surface as the wretched offspring of Dolopion struggled abundantly but in vain; and he expelled all his life together with the water, waving his hands above his head, and the brine washed over his teeth.'

Note particularly lines 2 and 11 of Prop. 2.26A. The damaged *Suppl. Hell.* 442.7 includes soaked hair (βρεκτῶν τε κομάων, cf. Prop. line 4), while the dolphin who comes to the rescue (Prop. 17) may be paralleled by *SH* 415.16 δελφῖνες πηγοῖο δι᾽ ὕδατος ἐγκονέεσκον, and the jump into the sea (Prop. 19, apparently to commit suicide) by *SH* 415.14 εἰς ἅλα δειμήνασα κατ᾽ αἰγίλιπος θόρε πέτρης. The dream by a cliff-top is paralleled in Euph. fr. 75 P. χθιζόν μοι κνώσσοντι παρ᾽ Ἀργανθώνιον αἶπος. Propertius combines all this with learned but not too taxing mythology—Helle who gave her name to the Hellespont, the vicissitudes of Ino/Leucothoe, Glaucus the amorous sea-god (a favourite subject of Hellenistic and neoteric verse, cf. on Cornificius, **96**), named Nereids and finally Arion. The elegy as a whole, despite its sombre atmosphere, is strikingly beautiful.

The other poem, too long to quote, is *Amores* 3.6, which seems noticeably different from Ovid's usual manner. The poet, parted from his mistress by a river in spate, argues that rivers should help young men in love, since they themselves had felt the effects of passion. There follows (25–82) an extended catalogue of the loves of river-gods; some of the examples are little-known or even otherwise unattested. While most are confined to a single couplet, one (the Anio and Ilia) is dealt with at much greater length (45–82), in a manner distinctly reminiscent of Virgil's sixth *Eclogue*, where Pasiphae has the lion's share (16 lines out of 51 in the song of Silenus). And *Ecl.* 6 is the nearest thing in Latin to the 'catalogue' or 'collective' poetry much favoured by Euphorion (fr. 9 Powell, *SH* 413–15, 429, 443, and perhaps other *SH* papyri), passing a great number of myths in brief review. *Amores* 3.6 may give a hint as to how Gallus could have used Parthenius' Ἐρωτικὰ Παθήματα for his own elegies.

140

In this section I pick up a few allusions to Gallus' poetry from which we can discern motifs almost certainly used by Gallus himself, a procedure to be followed in more detail with regard to the tenth *Eclogue* (**141**). In the passages surrounding all these extracts (apart from (*a*) where Ovid is concerned only with dead poets, hence omitting Propertius) the four elegists are mentioned together. For this sense of a dynasty, cf. **138***g* and **138***h* above.

The 'furthest East and furthest West' motif, applied to a poet and his work, may go back to Alcman (a list of foreign peoples who will read him, see Nisbet and Hubbard on Horace, *Odes* 2.20.14 and McKeown on Ovid, *Amores* 1.15.29–30). Like Ovid in **140***b*, Propertius (2.3.33–4, surely from Gallus) applies it just to the beloved girl: 'sive illam Hesperiis sive illam ostendit Eois, / uret et Eoos, uret et Hesperios'. When Ovid says (**140***a*) that Lycoris will be 'nota', we must remember that the word can also mean 'notorious' in a bad sense (*OLD* 7, e.g. Cicero, *Pro Caelio* 31 'muliere non solum nobili verum etiam nota') and that Lycoris was noted for her infidelity and *nequitia* (**145**.1). A poet could immortalize his subject for ill as well as good, e.g. Catullus 40, Ovid, *Tristia* 4.9.21 ff. (to a false friend), 'ibit ad occasum quicquid dicemus ab ortu, / testis et Hesperiae vocis Eous erit . . . / (25) nec tua te sontem tantummodo saecula norint: / perpetuae crimen posteritatis eris'.

140 *f* recalls Propertius 2.1.3–4 'non haec Calliope, non haec mihi cantat Apollo; / ingenium nobis ipsa puella facit'. It is possible that Gallus too somewhere rejected the conventional Callimachean sources of inspiration (Apollo and the Muses) in favour of his mistress.

141

Virgil's tenth *Eclogue*, with great ingenuity, recasts the pastoral lament for Daphnis of Theocritus, *Idyll* 1 as a tribute to the love poems of his friend Cornelius Gallus. These were probably entitled *Amores* (see **139a**), and we should look out for a special point whenever that word appears in Virgil's text. For example, when Gallus says to the Arcadians 'o mihi tum quam molliter ossa quiescent / vestra meos olim si fistula dicat amores' (33–4), the words might be reinterpreted to mean 'How happy I would be to think that my *Amores* will be read by future generations after my death' (cf. e.g. Prop. 3.1.21 ff., Ovid, *Am.* 1.15.41–2). 'Tenerisque meos incidere amores / arboribus' (53–4) suggests that Gallus will inscribe not merely the beloved's name (as Acontius does in Callimachus fr. 73 'Cydippe is fair', and the poet himself in Prop. 1.18.22), but lines from his *Amores* (cf. Ovid, *Her.* 5.29–30 and Calpurnius Siculus 1.33 ff., where a poem of 56 lines is inscribed on a beech tree!). In line 54 'crescetis, amores', the verb suggests that his love poems will become ever more famous (cf. Prop. 3.1.33–4 'Homerus / posteritate suum crescere sensit opus', Horace, *Odes* 3.30.8). Individual words in *Ecl.* 10 have been tentatively attributed to Gallus, e.g. 'spelaea' (52, elsewhere in Latin poetry only at *Ciris* 467 until the time of Claudian). Likewise with phrases: when Tragoedia asks Ovid 'ecquis erit . . . tibi finis amandi?' (*Am.* 3.1.15), one may wonder about the relationship to *Ecl.* 10.28 'ecquis erit modus?' (Pan to Gallus).

David Ross (*Backgrounds to Augustan Poetry*, 85 ff.) follows F. Skutsch (*Aus Vergils Frühzeit* (Leipzig, 1901), 2–27, particularly 15, and *Gallus und Vergil* (Leipzig/Berlin, 1906), 155–92) in comparing Gallus' hunting among 'Parthenios . . . saltus' (*Ecl.* 10.57) with Milanion hunting 'Partheniis . . . in antris' (Prop. 1.1.11). Propertius 2.19.17 ff. (from a poem not discussed by Ross, but mentioned by Skutsch and, earlier, Jacoby) may comment humorously on a poem of Gallus underlying *Ecl.* 10.55 ff. Gallus hunts the boar, 'acris venabor apros' (56), but Propertius' bravery does not stretch beyond hares and birds (2.29.17–24):

> ipse ego venabor . . .
> incipiam captare feras et reddere pinu   19
>   cornua, et audacis ipse monere canes;
> non tamen ut vastos ausim temptare leones
>   aut celer agrestis comminus ire sues.
> haec igitur mihi sit lepores audacia mollis
>   excipere et structo figere avem calamo.

In Ovid, *Met.* 10.535 ff. Venus hunts with Adonis, but avoids dangerous animals and urges him to do the same.

We can with some confidence recover from *Ecl.* 10 the outlines of an elegy (or series of elegies, as Prop. 1.8B continues 1.8A) describing how Gallus' beloved Lycoris left him for a soldier rival, with whom she went to Gaul or Germany. The soldier as a rival in love to the hero is to be found in comedy. He is the Pyrgopolinices ('Conqueror of many fortresses') of Plautus' *Miles Gloriosus* (and its Greek model *Alazon*) who takes Philocomasium against her will from Athens to Ephesus (99–113). This figure appears in Propertius 1.8 and 2.16 (where he is said to be a praetor). Verbal similarities between *Ecl.* 10 and Prop. 1.8 (see below) strongly suggest that Propertius is drawing on the lost poem(s) of Gallus, but he has made several changes—the rival is serving in Illyricum, not Gaul or Germany, and (at the last moment) Cynthia decides not to go with him (1.8B.1 'Hic erit! hic iurata manet!'). Ovid gives a sinister twist to the soldier rival; he is clearly a profiteer from the recent civil wars, 'sanguine pastus eques' (*Am.* 3.8.10). In a different genre, compare the senator's wife who goes off with a gladiator (Juvenal 6.82–113), cheerfully enduring the discomforts of shipboard (90, 92–4), which would be too much for Propertius' Cynthia (1.8A.5–6), and even giving the sailors a hand with the rigging (102).

Servius (Intr. to *Ecl.* 10, p. 118 Thilo) tells us that the lover for whom Lycoris abandoned Gallus was none other than Mark Antony. Certainly Volumnia/Cytheris/Lycoris (see on **145**.1) was, as a matter of historical fact, attached to him, but that liaison preceded her affair with Cornelius Gallus. One might think it unnecessary to seek a real identity for the stock literary type of Gallus' soldier rival, but Nisbet (*JRS* (1979), 153) wonders about D. Brutus or Lycoris' patron Volumnius Eutrapelus. He is also concerned (ibid.) to find a plausible background for the military operations in Gaul or Germany, but we are not well informed about this area in the mid to late 40s BC.

On line 46 ('tu procul a patria . . .') Servius makes his famous comment 'hi autem omnes versus Galli sunt, de ipsius translati carminibus'. We have already noted (p. 231 on Gallus and Euphorion) the tendency of ancient commentators to exaggerate the dependence of their poet on a predecessor. Here one must make the obvious qualification that Gallus wrote his *Amores* in elegiacs. But in this case it seems likely that not only the theme but also the wording closely follows the model. For example 'me sine sola vides?' (48) could well end a pentameter, as observed by Coleman and Clausen in their commentaries. 'Tu procul a patria'—note that Servius makes his comment precisely at this point—might begin a new poem; several Propertian elegies open with an emphatic pronoun, including 1.8A.1 'Tune igitur demens . . .?' It seems highly probable that Prop. 1.8A.7–8 'tu pedibus teneris positas fulcire pruinas, / tu potes insolitas, Cynthia, ferre nives?' imitate a lost elegy of Gallus rather than the tenth *Eclogue*. Virgil's threefold 'a!' might be a mannerism of Gallus' elegy (as of neoteric epyllion, Cat. 64.135, Calvus, *Io*, **20**, *Ciris* 185, cf. Virgil, *Georgics* 4.526), humorously overdone. For 'a!' in the elegists, see A. Kershaw, *CP* 75 (1980), 71–2.

A few miscellaneous points. (*a*) A curious parallel to speculation about the effects of the harsh climate may be found in Cicero, *In Catilinam* 2.23 'quo autem pacto illi [the 'pueri . . . delicati' who follow Catiline] 'Appenninum atque illas pruinas ac nivis perferent?' (*b*) I would be inclined to put a question mark after 'me sine sola vides' (*Ecl.* 10.48). (*c*) *Ecl.* 10.44–5 'nunc insanus amor duri me Martis in armis / tela inter media atque adversos detinet hostis' are explained by Servius as referring to Gallus' thoughts, which are constantly with Lycoris in the soldier's camp (cf. Prop. 4.8.48 'Lanuvii ad portas, ei mihi, solus eram'). If that interpretation is rejected, as by Nisbet (p. 154 n. 146) and, seemingly, Clausen, I do not see how the lines are to be understood satisfactorily. Clausen writes (p. 104) 'Gallus seems to have forgotten for the moment that he is in Arcadia'—a short memory indeed! In my opinion there is much to be said for the emendation 'te' (Heumann, Heyne) in 44. Gallus would like to be with Lycoris in his present surroundings ('hic' (43), i.e. in Arcadia), but, as things are ('nunc', 44), mad love (Lycoris' love for the soldier) keeps her away from him. Coleman objects to the emendation that an officer's mistress should not be so close to the front line (recognizing that this is not a strong objection since there could be deliberate hyperbole), that the emphatic 'tu' (46) implies a contrast with the person referred to in the previous lines—that could, but surely need not, be so—and that elsewhere in the poem *Gallus'* madness is emphasized—but Cynthia is 'demens' in Prop. 1.8A.1. It is only Lycoris' crazy infatuation that keeps the couple apart. We know that in real life Gallus was a soldier, but that fact is best kept out of the tenth *Eclogue*.

Professor Nisbet (*per litteras*) had thought that Gallus was in 'Arcadia' only in imagination, and that with 'nunc' (44) he returns to reality. But he now acknowledges the case for 'te' in 44, noting in its favour that Gallus remains in his dream-world for the rest of the poem.

142

This passage has already been discussed (on **139**) with regard to Gallus and Euphorion; here I add some details. The Permessus is mentioned (but given no special significance) in Hesiod's invocation which precedes his encounter with the Muses (*Theog.* 5). Callimachus almost certainly wrote in his *Aetia*-prologue Ἀγανίππη / <‿ ⏑⏑> Περμησσοῦ παρθένος Ἀονίου (lemmata from fr. 2a, in Pfeiffer vol. II, pp. 102–3); the spring is 'daughter' of the river from which it draws its water. Nicander (*Ther.* 12) speaks of Hesiod παρ᾽ ὕδασι Περμησσοῖο. Although mentioned by Gallus, Virgil, and Propertius (2.10.26, see above on **139**), the Permessus did not become part of the standard vocabulary of poetic initiation (never, for example, in Ovid or Statius), unlike Ἀόνιος (Aonius), 'Boeotian' (e.g. Cornelius Severus, **209**), which may have been inaugurated by Callimachus (above), cf. Euphorion, *SH* 442.1 Ἀονίοιο (probably agreeing with a lost noun). Virgil's 'Aonas in montis' comes from Aon, the name of a Boeotian hero (Stat. *Theb.* 8.475). That form, as an adjective, must have occurred somewhere in lost Hellenistic poetry (cf. Steph. Byz. s.v. Ἄονες . . . καὶ Ἄων τὸ ἐθνικὸν καὶ Ἀόνιος, Nonnus, *Dion.* 5.37 Ἄονι . . . λαῶι). Latin 'Aonius' is found first in Catullus 61.28, linked to Aganippe. In *Ecl.* 10.12 we read 'Aonie Aganippe'; it would not be surprising if (as Clausen suggests) both the adjective and the name of the spring occurred in Gallus.

For speculation about the ancestry of the role which Virgil gave to Linus as 'divino carmine pastor' (67, cf. *Ecl.* 4.56–7, Prop. 2.13.8) see Ross, *Backgrounds to Augustan Poetry*, 21–3, 34–6, 118–20. We have noticed (on **139**) that Grynean Apollo was of interest to Parthenius (fr. 10 Lightfoot = *SH* 620) as well as Euphorion. This cult-title appeared in Parthenius' *Delos* (perhaps part of the reason why 'Latonia Delos' is called a commonplace theme in Virgil, *Georgics* 3.6). So it may be significant that *Ecl.* 6.73 is quite close to Callimachus, *Hymn* 4.269–70 (Delos herself speaks) οὐδέ τις ἄλλη / γαιάων τοσσόνδε θεῶι πεφιλήσεται ἄλλωι.

143

The collection of Parthenius' Ἐρωτικὰ Παθήματα ('Sufferings in Love', Lightfoot), with its dedication to Cornelius Gallus, is a fascinating document, now admirably edited (together with Parthenius' poetic fragments) by Jane Lightfoot, *Parthenius of Nicaea* (Oxford, 1999). As well as her commentary on the Preface (pp. 367–71), see her pages (50–76) on Parthenius in Rome, with much on Euphorion and Gallus. A dedicatory preface will always contain flattery of the addressee. Nonetheless there are some points which we can make with fair confidence: (*a*) at the time of writing Gallus had already established his reputation as a poet, and remained active; (*b*) he was associated with the kind of subject matter which the Ἐρωτικὰ Παθήματα contains (unhappy love, often with something monstrous attached and ending in total disaster), such as Helvius Cinna too had chosen for his epyllion *Smyrna* (7–10); (*c*) in poetic craftsmanship Gallus aimed at, and achieved, τὸ περιττόν ('refined elaboration', Lightfoot), a quality associated with Gallus' admired model, Euphorion of Chalcis, in an epigram by Theodoridas, *Anth. Pal.* 7.406 = 14 Gow–Page, 1. Although the epigram is hostile and full of obscene double meanings, τὸ περιττόν would normally be commendable (cf. Lightfoot, p. 370). Thus it seems that, at the time when Parthenius wrote this dedication (? early to mid 40s B C, but see Lightfoot p. 217), Gallus' reputation for style and technique was distinctly different from Quintilian's 'durior Gallus' (**138**h).

Jane Lightfoot (p. 367) notes that τὴν ἄθροισιν strictly ought to mean 'the collecting' rather than 'the Collection'; and the strict sense could be particularly appropriate to Gallus if he had patronized the kind of 'collective' or 'catalogue' poetry typical of Euphorion (see on **139**). Probably no one would argue nowadays that *Ecl.* 6 contains a list of subjects treated by Gallus, but it may give us an idea of Euphorion's manner in Latin; if so, the intrusion of Gallus into this poem would not be out of place. Parthenius stresses that 'in certain of the poets' (παρά τισι τῶν ποιητῶν) his myths may not be 'told in their entirety' (αὐτοτελῶς λελεγμένα). Although he does not name these poets, his words would suit Euphorion well.

Without doubt the 'manchettes' (Lightfoot, p. 247 n. 121) attached to most of the Ἐρωτικὰ Παθήματα, giving sources for the myths, do not go back to Parthenius himself (Lightfoot, pp. 247–56). They represent considerable effort and learning, but sometimes the annotator had to admit defeat. Even when he names a source, we cannot be sure that this was the one used by Parthenius; for example it looks as though the conclusion of 16 (Laodice) was drawn from Euphorion (fr. 58 P.) and perhaps Lycophron (*Alexandra* 494–505), but neither is mentioned in the manchettes at this point. While Parthenius' Preface speaks of poets handling these myths, the manchettes mostly cite prose writers (Lightfoot, p. 248).

Parthenius anticipates that Gallus will use the most convenient parts εἰς ἔπη καὶ ἐλεγείας, 'for hexameter and elegiac verse' (Clausen, *Virgil: Eclogues*, 204, slightly misrepresents with 'for either hexameter or elegiac verse'). We know that Gallus wrote elegies. These words do not prove that he wrote hexameter poems, but show at least that Parthenius expected him to do so, and are consistent with the hypothesis that he had done so already. Parthenius himself employed both metres in Greek (frs. 1–14 and 27–32 Lightfoot definitely elegiac, frs. 33–4 definitely hexametric). Of the Latin neoteric poets, at least Catullus (64 and 68) and Calvus (*Io* and *Lament for Quintilia*) wrote substantial poems in hexameters and in elegiacs; Cinna too showed metrical versatility, though his one certain elegiac fragment (**13**) looks to come from an epigram. Finally, some have argued that the omission of Ovid in

Diomedes, GLK I p. 484 ('Elegia . . . quod genus carminis praecipue scripse-runt apud Romanos Propertius et Tibullus et Gallus, imitati Graecos Callimachum et Euphoriona') is due to the fact that Ovid wrote non-elegiac poems—it follows (so runs the argument) that Gallus, like Propertius and Tibullus, wrote nothing but elegies. That, however, would put far too much weight on Diomedes, who is almost certainly wrong in stating that Euphorion was an elegist (see on **139**). On this point I agree with J. E. G. Zetzel (*CP* 72 (1977), 250), against David Ross (*Backgrounds to Augustan Poetry*, 44).

<h1 style="text-align:center">144 (1 Bl., C.)</h1>

uno tellures dividit amne duas: Vibius Sequester (? *c.*AD 500) compiled an alphabetical list of rivers, fountains, etc., mentioned by certain poets. It seems enormously unlikely that Vibius had access to a complete text of Cornelius Gallus; we have to take it on trust from whoever originally made the quotation that Gallus referred to the Hypanis rather than e.g. the Tanais (see below). The probable source is a commentary (fuller than anything we now possess) on either Virgil, *Georgics* 4.370 'saxosusque sonans Hypanis' or—note the mention of Scythia—Ovid, *Met.* 15.285 'Scythicis Hypanis de montibus ortus'. If the latter, this would be an addendum to my paper 'Traces of Ancient Commentaries on Ovid's *Metamorphoses*', *PLLS* 9 (1996), 159–74. Vibius must have been proud of this rare item, since (unusually) he both names the poet and quotes verbatim, as he does for Varro (Atacinus) in **125**.2, where we can see that his source is a commentary on the *Eclogues*. Another item surviving uniquely in Vibius (83) is a reference to Stesichorus on the Himera, possibly (see Gelsomino, *Vibius Sequester*, p. xlvii) from a commentary on Silius Italicus 8.233 ff.

There is nothing 'durum' about Gallus' pentameter; on the contrary, his word-patterning is highly artistic. Two numbers span the line ('uno . . . duas'); 'uno tellures . . . amne duas' produces both an ABAB arrangement (ablative–accusative–ablative–accusative) and a chiasmus (number–noun–noun–number). 'Dividit' appropriately stands at the mid-point of the line (with two words on either side) and the word 'amne' splits 'tellures . . . duas' just as the river itself splits the continents.

Most commonly (as indeed in Vibius 148) the river which divides Europe from Asia is the Tanais (Don), e.g. in Manilius 4.677, Lucan 3.273–6, Dion. Per. 660–1, cf. J. O. Thomson, *History of Ancient Geography* (Cambridge, 1948), 254. No other authority makes Hypanis (Bug) the boundary. Proper-tius uses the Hypanis to illustrate the width of his separation from Cynthia

(1.12.3–4 'tam multa illa meo divisa est milia lecto / quantum Hypanis Veneto dissidet Eridano') and elsewhere suggests ways in which a faraway river might have functioned in love poetry: e.g. to show the impossibility of escape (2.30.1–2 'tu licet usque / ad Tanain fugias, usque sequetur Amor'), or the extent of the poet's and his beloved's fame (2.7.17–18 'hinc etiam tantum meruit mea gloria nomen, / gloria ad hibernos lata Borysthenidas', cf. Catullus 95.5 = 7(*a*) on Cinna's *Smyrna* and the Satrachus).

Ovid expands Gallus' pentameter into a whole couplet in *Ex Ponto* 4.10.55– 6 'quique duas terras, Asiam Cadmique sororem, / separat et cursus inter utramque facit', but he must have in mind the Tanais, since the Hypanis has just been mentioned (47). Gallus may have named the Hypanis in his preceding hexameter. Finally, note Ovid, *Heroides* 19.142 (on the Dardanelles) 'seducit terras haec brevis unda duas', perhaps a more distant echo of Gallus.

145 (2–5 Bl., 2 C.)

First intimations of the papyrus discovery, from a fortress in Egyptian Nubia (above, p. 225), were given by R. D. Anderson (*JEA* 64 (1978), 2, 'a Latin poem probably in honour of Augustus'). Publication followed in *JRS* 69 (1979), 125–55, by R. D. Anderson ('The Archaeological Context'), P. J. Parsons ('The Papyrus', and 'Text, Translation and Commentary' jointly with Nisbet), and R. G. M. Nisbet ('The Poet, Metre and Style', 'The Literary Framework, and the Historical Context') with actual size and enlarged photographs. Nisbet's contribution was reprinted in his *Collected Papers on Latin Literature*, ed. S. J. Harrison (Oxford, 1995), 101–31, but I refer to the original *JRS* publication because it contains the other sections.

For more on the papyrus, see G. Ballaira, *Esempi di scrittura latina dell' età romana*, I (Alessandria, 1993), 31–42. His bibliography takes into account the view put forward by F. Brunhölzl (*Codices Manuscripti*, 10 (1984), 33–7) that the writing on the papyrus is a modern forgery (an idea entertained by one or two others). On this topic I have also seen an unpublished paper by P. J. Parsons, rebutting Professor Brunhölzl's papyrological arguments. The great majority of scholars have accepted the fragments as genuine and by Gallus (G. Giangrande, *QUCC* N s 5 (1980), 141–52, believed that they were ancient, but written by a poet other than Gallus who could have addressed Gallus' Lycoris in the vocative). The alleged forger, who would have needed at least the complicity of the excavation team, also must have possessed a mixture of learning, incompetence, cunning, and sheer good luck that stretches credulity to breaking point. Presumably a test on the ink would be decisive, if it were thought worth destroying a portion of the writing for this purpose.

As Parsons explains (*JRS* (1979), 129), 'The text is articulated, after col. i. 1, 5 and 9, and col. ii. 4, by wide spacing (some three times the normal line-spacing) and by H-shaped signs placed towards the left and right margins in these spaces (so after i. 1 and 5; after i. 9 only the right-hand sign survives, after ii. 4 only the left-hand sign).' These signs are naturally taken to mark an important break between col. i. lines 1 and 2, 5 and 6, 9 and 10, and col. ii. 4 and 5 (the only letters in col. ii which can be read certainly are Qui at the start of line 5). Ballaira (p. 33) thought that the symbol represents Hic desinit and Hic incipit; J. B. Hall, *CR* ns 47 (1997), 227, is not totally convinced. On the face of it we seem to have a sequence of separate four-line epigrams, but see the further discussion at the end of commentary on this item. We do not know how much is lost at the foot of column i (Parsons, *JHS* (1979), 127). I will not discuss in detail the orthography of the papyrus (which may be Gallus' own); see *JHS* (1979), 132–4. It is interesting that Gallus' Philae inscription has 'deivi' (genitive singular) and 'dieis patrieis' among many spellings in simple 'i' (*JHS* (1979), 134 n. 67), whereas the Vatican obelisk had 'divi'.

1.   In this pentameter [. . fact]a (Nisbet) would be good, [. . fat]a perhaps (but not certainly) on the short side. Nisbet (140) supplied as the preceding hexameter (purely *exempli gratia*) 'tempora sic nostrae perierunt grata iuventae'.

   nequitia: both Propertius (1.15.38; 2.5.2) and Ovid (*Am.* 3.11.37) ascribe *nequitia* to their mistress, and stand accused of it themselves (Prop. 2.24.6; Ov. *Am.* 2.1.2 and 3.1.17). The word is not to be found in Tibullus.

   Lycori: it is indeed fortunate that this very first line contains the beloved's name, thus pointing to the authorship of the text. Horace chooses the name Lycoris in a poem addressed to another elegist, Tibullus (*Odes* 1.33.5 'insignem tenui fronte Lycorida').

   The lady's proper name, as a freedwoman of P. Volumnius Eutrapelus, was Volumnia (the identification already in Servius' introduction to *Ecl.* 10, p. 118 Thilo, 'Cytheridem meretricem, libertam Volumnii'). That was how respectable townspeople had to address her in May 49 bc (Cic. *Phil.* 2.58, written some five years later): 'inter quos aperta lectica mima portabatur, quam ex oppidis municipales homines honesti, obviam necessario prodeuntes, non noto illo et mimico nomine [sc. Cytheris] sed Volumniam consalutabant' (cf. *Ad Att.* 10.10 = 201 SB. 5 and 10.16 = 208 SB. 5, both written at the time). So too Cicero calls her in a letter to his wife (*Ad Fam.* 14.16 = 163 SB, January 47 bc), 'Volumnia debuit in te officiosior esse quam fuit, et id ipsum quod fecit potuit diligentius facere et cautius'—evidently an unsatisfactory episode for Terentia! On stage she was Cytheris, and late in 46 BC Cicero found himself at dinner with her and her patron (*Ad Fam.* 9.26 = 197 SB. 2): 'infra Eutrapelum Cytheris accubuit ... non mehercule suspicatus sum illam adfore', but he seems to have enjoyed the occasion well enough.

'Lycoris' was thus an exact metrical equivalent of the stage name Cytheris; this principle applies to all the poetic pseudonyms for which we know the real names (Lesbia/Clodia, Delia/Plania, Perilla/Metella (see on Ticida, **101**)) with the odd exception of Cynthia/Hostia where the real name would sometimes cause a hiatus or fail to lengthen a preceding syllable. Most of these pseudonyms suggest either a Greek lyric poetess (Lesbia, Corinna) or a title of Apollo (Cynthia, Delia); Varro Atacinus' Leucadia (**133***a*) did both. It is appropriate that Gallus drew on a more obscure cult-title (as he did with 'Grynean' Apollo), Λυκωρεύς, used by his hero Euphorion (fr. 80.3 Powell Λυκωρέος οἰκία Φοίβου) and, earlier, by Callimachus (*Hymn* 2.19). Ap. Rh. (4.1490) has Λυκώρειος.

2–5. The identification of 'Caesar', and of his anticipated military campaign, has been much debated without producing general agreement. If he is Octavian, we could think of operations in Illyria in the mid-30s (favoured by Hutchinson, *ZPE* 41 (1981), 37–42 at 40) or the attack upon Egypt in 30 BC— David West, *LCM* 8 (1983), 92–3, thinks that Gallus is remaining in Egypt and sending Octavian off homewards. Both these possibilities were considered by Nisbet (*JRS* (1979), 152). Even allowing for the exaggerations of panegyric (Hutchinson), the Illyrian campaign would hardly make Octavian 'maxima Romanae pars ... historiae', and, if Gallus were in Alexandria bidding farewell to Octavian in the summer of 30 BC, 'it seems tactless to imply in the aftermath of victory that he will be sad till he reads of the triumph in the histories' (Nisbet p. 152, though I would understand 'legam' (5) differently). Thus I am inclined (with Nisbet, ibid.) to go back to Julius Caesar and to his planned invasion of Parthia which was only three days away when the Dictator was assassinated. Victory in this would have made Caesar a second Alexander and 'the greatest part of Roman history', greater even than the Scipios who defeated and destroyed Carthage. In favour of Octavian, Hutchinson (*ZPE* 41 (1981), 38) urges the 'extreme warmth' with which Gallus addresses 'Caesar', better suited (in real terms) to Gallus' relationship with Octavian. But the expression of what sounds like personal devotion to a ruler, even when there is no personal link to justify it, can be paralleled down the ages.

There are two other poems which seem considerably indebted to these lines of Gallus. The first is Propertius 3.4, predicting an (unrealized) invasion of Parthia by Augustus in the mid to late 20s BC—this slightly supports reference of Gallus' words to the Dictator's Parthian project. Links between the poems, recognized by Nisbet, were usefully stressed by C. J. Putnam, 'Propertius and the New Gallus Fragment', *ZPE* 39 (1980), 49–56. Propertius sends the expeditionary force on its way to be of service to Roman history by avenging the Crassi (9–10):

> Crassos clademque piate!
> ite et Romanae consulite historiae!

He looks forward to the time when he will witness Caesar's triumph and the wagons laden with spoil (12 ff.):

> ante meos obitus sit precor illa dies
> qua videam spoliis oneratos Caesaris axis ... etc.

A third parallel may be delusive: Propertius will read the placards bearing the names of captured towns as the floats go by (16 'titulis oppida capta legam'). No problem there, but it is by no means certain that this helps us to understand 'legam' in Gallus, line 5 (see ad loc.).

The other relevant poem is surprising: the pseudo-Ovidian *Consolatio ad Liviam*, a poor composition supposedly marking the death of Drusus in 9 B C but perhaps written in the principate of Tiberius (J. Richmond, *ANRW* II.31.4 (1981), 2768–83). This poem was adduced by H. Schoonhoven, *ZPE* 53 (1983), 73–8. Livia's son did not return in triumph, but (267–8)

> *pars erit historiae,* totoque *legetur* in aevo,
> seque opus ingeniis carminibusque dabit.

It seems highly probable that the minor poet borrowed 'pars erit historiae', and something of the surrounding context, from Gallus, even though the situation which he described was very different.

2 fata ... mea: *pace* Nisbet (p. 141), who remains unconvinced, I think that this phrase means 'my death'; the plural is often used for the death of one individual (e.g. *Aen.* 4.20 'fata Sychaei'). There was an established *topos*, 'May I die as soon as I receive some particularly welcome news / witness or experience something particularly pleasurable.' Thus Euripides, *Electra* 663 (of Clytemnestra's death) εἰ γὰρ θάνοιμι τοῦτ' ἰδὼν ἐγώ ποτε. See further my note on Callimachus, *Hecale* fr. 161 τεθναίην ὅτ' ἐκεῖνον ἀποπνεύσαντα πυθοίμην and Kost on Musaeus 79 αὐτίκα τεθναίην λεχέων ἐπιβήμενος Ἡροῦς (a moment of felicity which could never be bettered). This interpretation of 'fata ... mea' would go with 'survey' or 'read the inscriptions on' (rather than 'read in the history books') for 'legam' (5). If there is meant to be an artistic contrast between 'dulcia' (2) and 'tristia' (1)—as seems likely, though not certain—the quatrain (?) which ended with line 1 could have contained a suggestion that Lycoris' *nequitia* would be the death of the poet (*Ecl.* 10.10

'indigno cum Gallus amore peribat', perhaps **138***d*, cf. Prop. 2.1.78 'huic misero fatum dura puella fuit').

tum erunt: this (and other examples with final 'm') should perhaps be considered not a 'hiatus' but rather the survival of an old licence whereby -m was not always disregarded before an open vowel (Priscian, GLK, II p. 30 'vetustissimi non semper eam subtrahebant', quoting Ennius, *Annals* 330 Skutsch 'milia militum octo'). Other examples are *Ann.* 514 'quidem unus', Lucilius 4 Warmington 'quam homo', Lucretius 2.681 'cum odore', 3.394 'quam in his', 3.1082 'dum abest', 6.276 'cum eo', Horace, *Sat.* 2.2.28 'num adest'. There is also the remarkable *Ecl.* 8.11 'a te principium, tibi desinam. accipe iussis', which is facilitated by the heavy pause at the bucolic diaeresis (likewise the complete hiatus at *Aen.* 1.405 'patuit dea. ille ubi matrem'). If allowing metrical force to -m before an open vowel was an old-fashioned feature, like cutting off a final 's' (see introduction to Egnatius, p. 87 above), that too might be considered 'subrusticum' and a sign of Gallus' less than perfect technique. There is no parallel for 'tum erunt' in elegy; Courtney compares Catullus 97.1 'di ament' but such correption (shortening) of a long vowel or diphthong is surely quite different. Lyne (ap. Nisbet, *JRS* (1979), 141) would remove the anomaly by rearrangement ('tum, Caesar, erunt') but I prefer to keep the transmitted order.

quom: *cum* began to replace *quom* in Cicero's time, but Quintilian (1.7.5) tells us that many people still maintained a distinction between *quom* (conjunction) and *cum* (preposition). See Parsons, *JRS* (1979), 132, and Helvius Cinna, **2**, where manuscript variants may point to an original 'quom'.

3. maxima Romanae pars eris historiae: in fact the scribe wrote 'erit', which one or two have tried to defend, in vain. For 'Romanae . . . historiae' (or another case) thus placed, cf. Propertius 3.4.10 (quoted above), [Virgil], *Catalepton* 11.6, Martial 14.191.2).

historiae: I would understand this, with M. C. J. Putnam (*ZPE* 39 (1980), 51) 'not as written record but as *res gestae*, as the chain of events whose accounting constitutes that record' (cf. *OLD*, *historia* 3). According to Nisbet (p. 141) '*historiae* refers to historiography, not to the events themselves'; this goes with his interpretation of *legam* (5). 'The greatest part of Roman History' would be an appropriate designation for a leader who could conquer the Parthian Empire (see above on lines 2–5).

4–5. An extraordinarily contorted couplet, of which the interpretation remains far from clear.

4. postque tuum reditum: as Nisbet says (p. 141), the -que indicates that 4–5 are still under 'quom' (2).

5. fixa . . . spolieis: normal would be 'spolia in templis [or 'templis'] figere', but Gallus' phrase extends normal usage in the kind of way which one expects from a poet. Courtney (p. 266) compares Lucr. 5.1205 'stellisque micantibus aethera fixum'. The precise attachment of 'deivitiora' is uncertain—perhaps 'the richer for being hung with your trophies' (Nisbet, p. 143, admitting that the word-order is very artificial).

legam: perhaps the most puzzling of all the difficulties. Without great confidence I take this to mean 'scan', 'survey', a rare sense of the verb (*Aen.* 6.755, Silius 12.569); see Putnam, *ZPE* 39 (1980), 52 with n. 10. Courtney follows Schoonhoven (*ZPE* 53 (1983), 77) in understanding 'templa legere' as 'to read the dedicatory inscriptions on the temples' (a 'concentrated sense', Courtney 266). Nisbet, in accord with his interpretation of 'historiae' (3), takes 'legam' as 'I will read about [in the history books]'. He speaks (p. 141) of Eastern wars as a subject for 'instant historiography'. But Caesar's triumph would surely anticipate even the most energetic historian, and so the impact of Gallus' words would be curiously weakened. As David West says (*LCM* 8 (1983), 92), Gallus could see the enrichment of the temples just by walking down the street—Nisbet's remarks (p. 142) about Gallus' isolation from Caesar's victories were designed to counter such an objection. Things would be different if Gallus had made clear that he faced a prolonged absence from Rome, and West (*LCM* 8 (1983), 92) dates the epigram to 30 BC, at the beginning of his governorship of Egypt, but that is less attractive for other reasons (Nisbet, p. 152).

6–9. A quatrain on Gallus' inspiration and the quality of his verse. Since it comes from the Muses and [perhaps] has the approval of Lycoris herself, he need not fear the adverse judgement of critics.

6.   tandem: an appropriate word to express satisfaction as a work nears completion. So there may be implications for our overall view of the papyrus (to be discussed below). We need not take 'tandem' literally as referring to a lengthy period of composition (like the *Smyrna* of Cinna) or to any previously unsuccessful efforts. Before 'tandem' Peter Brown suggested 'haec mih]i vix', and Parsons (*JRS* (1979), 144) judges 'vix' to be 'possible, except that the highest traces at the end must be taken as stray ink'. Alternatively one might think of an epithet for the Muses (e.g. 'Castaliae', 'Aonides'), but neither -es nor -ae fits the traces at all well (*JRS* (1979), 143).

fecerunt carmina Musae: it was not uncommon to represent the Muses as co-authors with the poet, as does Euphorion, fr. 118 Powell Μοῦσαι ἐποιήσαντο καὶ ἀπροτίμαστος Ὅμηρος (the object may be the *Iliad* and/or *Odyssey*, or part(s) thereof). That fragment was adduced by D. E. Keefe in *CQ* NS 32 (1982), 237–8. I would not put too much weight on the fact that the author is Gallus' model, since the *topos* is found elsewhere, e.g. in Asclepiades, *Anth. Pal.* 9.63 = 32 G–P, 4 τὸ ξυνὸν Μουσῶν γράμμα καὶ Ἀντιμάχου (on the *Lyde*), Crinagoras, *Anth. Pal.* 9.513 = 49 G–P, 2 ἔγραφεν ἢ Μουσέων σὺν μιῆι ἢ

Χαρίτων (sc. the plays of Menander), Lucr. 1.24 (to Venus) 'te sociam studeo scribendis versibus esse'. From such joint composition it is but a short step to representing the deity as responsible for everything (thus, of course, guaranteeing the quality) as in Horace, *Epist.* 2.2.92 'caelatumque novem Musis opus' (of an elegiac poet), Prop. 4.1.133 'tum tibi pauca suo de carmine dictat Apollo'.

7. **quae possem domina dicere digna mea:** 'that I could call worthy of my mistress'; Courtney's interpretation (p. 267), now accepted by Nisbet (who in *JRS* (1979), 144 had offered 'utter as worthy of my mistress'). This suits 'idem' (apparently a critical judgement) in 8. The poems are 'worthy of Lycoris' perhaps not only because of her beauty but also because she was a discriminating critic (cf. *Ecl.* 10.2 'quae legat ipsa Lycoris), like Propertius' Cynthia (2.13.12 'auribus et puris scripta probasse mea').

domina: though it is found in Lucilius (738 Warmington), Gallus introduced to elegy this term for the beloved. In Catullus 68.68 we should retain the manuscripts' 'dominam', referring to the châtelaine of Allius' house (see L. P. Wilkinson, *CR* N s 20 (1970), 290).

digna mea: Stephen Hinds, 'Carmina Digna . . .' (*PLLS* 4 (1983), 43–54) collects many examples of that combination, one or two of which may be deliberate echoes of Gallus (e.g. Ovid, *Amores* 1.3.20 'provenient causa carmina digna sua', cf. *CQ* N s 30 (1980), 542).

].**atur:** as possible patterns for the beginning of the hexameter, Nisbet (pp. 144–5) offers 'quodsi iam videatur', 'quae si iam testatur (or "confiteatur")', describing the latter as 'more pointed' but finally preferring the former, because 'though Gallus can address both Lycoris and the critics, Lycoris does not so naturally address the critics'. That seems an unnecessary worry: Lycoris could be imagined as a *testis*, appearing before Viscus as *iudex* to give evidence for the quality of Gallus' verse.

8–9. **non ego, Visce, / . . . iudice te vereor:** one can hardly doubt that there is deliberate reminiscence between these lines and Virgil, *Ecl.* 2.26–7 'non ego Daphnin / iudice te metuam'. Nisbet (p. 144), followed by Courtney, is inclined to give priority to Virgil, and several small indicators point that way. Virgil's words have some warrant (*Id.* 6.37, ὡς παρ' ἐμὶν κέκριται) in the Theocritan model for this passage of *Ecl.* 2 (Courtney 267); also (Nisbet p. 144) 'non ego Daphnin' after the bucolic diaeresis is characteristic of the *Eclogues* (cf. 7.7 'atque ego Daphnin', 8.102 'his ego Daphnin').

If Gallus is the imitator, there are chronological implications. Nisbet (p. 144 with n. 109) takes up C. G. Hardie's dating of *Ecl.* 2 as early as 45 BC ('Octavian and *Eclogue* 1', in *The Ancient Historian and his Materials: Essays in Honour of C. E. Stevens* (1975), 111). I doubt, however, the force of Hardie's argument that Pollio must have been in Italy to encourage Virgil to start the

Eclogues (cf. 8.11–12 'iussis / carmina coepta tuis') and that 45 BC was the only convenient gap in Pollio's absences from Italy. Pollio could well have made the request by letter. Courtney (p. 267) maintains the traditional date (*c.*42 BC) for *Eclogue* 2, and welcomes the conclusion that lines 6–9 of **145** were written some two years after **145.**2–5 (if the 'Caesar' is Julius), because he believes that this papyrus contains an anthology of extracts from Gallus' poetry. I myself would not regard the arguments for Virgil's priority as decisive.

8. Visce: Horace in *Satires* 1.10.83 mentions two Visci whose judgement he values ('et haec utinam Viscorum laudet uterque'). According to [Acro] ad loc. they were brothers, whose father had been a friend of Augustus (when Augustus was still Octavian?) but remained an *eques* after his sons had become senators. If the information can be trusted (a considerable doubt), this reference would suit the 30s BC rather better than the 40s—a point conceded by Nisbet, p. 145. A single Viscus appears also in Horace, *Sat.* 1.9.22 and 2.8.20 (cf. F. Verducci, *QUCC* NS 16 (1984), 127 n. 16).

9. A baffling and most frustrating line. With what we can read, and traces of some preceding letters, it ought to be possible (one feels) to suggest plausible restorations. Particularly puzzling is KATO. Is this a proper name? The initial K might possibly indicate so, but the evidence is murky (Parsons, *JRS* (1979), 134 with n. 77). In that case there should be a preceding interpunct, and the traces before K could indeed suggest an interpunct preceded by a very narrow letter (I or E); if, however, A (not impossible and apparently more promising) preceded K, any interpunct must have stood higher up, in an area where the surface of the papyrus is now damaged.

Almost everyone has taken 'Kato' to be a proper name here, and a suitable candidate presents himself in the person of the scholar-poet P. Valerius Cato (Appendix, p. 429, where I list references to him and his works in several other writers). There is no problem (*pace* Hutchinson, *ZPE* 41 (1981), 41) in linking this Cato with Viscus, since the former probably lived on till the 20s BC, and even a positive inducement to recognize him here since the 'Gallus' who is informed about Cato's financial plight in Furius Bibaculus **85.**1 could quite well be Cornelius. For his activity as a severe critic we can compare the spurious lines (**240**) prefixed to Horace, *Satires* 1.10 in which Cato is said to 'correct' (*emendare*) inferior verses of Lucilius. Nisbet and the great majority of scholars take 'Kato' to be vocative case. If so, 'te' (9) must cover both 'Visce' and 'Kato', which has caused some concern (e.g. to Courtney 267–8 and myself in *CQ* NS 30 (1980), 541–2). Hutchinson (*ZPE* 41 (1981), 41) compares Catullus 4.13–15 'Amastri Pontica et Cytore buxifer, / tibi haec fuisse et esse cognitissima / ait phaselus'. He notes, however, that the conditional clause, as well as 'te', would have to apply also to Cato, concluding 'The total result feels to me exceedingly uncomfortable in its compression.'

Before KATO the traces could represent ṾPḶA or ṾPḶE (*JRS* (1979), 139, 145); before Ṿ apparently 'a short oblique, descending from left to right, a little above base-level', perhaps an interpunct or part of the right side of A, K, M, R, X, though W. S. Barrett suggested to me (*CQ* (1980), 541 n. 1, in connection with the possibility of ḍupḷa, mentioned below) that the apparent 'short oblique' might conceivably be a cross-section from the thick base of a D. If there is a word-break before KATO, the only Latin words consonant with the preceding traces are quad]rupla (or -e) and perhaps dupla (or -e). F. Verducci (*QUCC* 16 (1984), 123 n. 8), starting from Nisbet p. 145, wonders whether Viscus might have been addressed as 'quadruple Kato', i.e. a critic four times as severe as Valerius Cato (one might alternatively think of Cato the severe Censor). C. Murgia (ap. Verducci) compared Sentius Augurinus (Courtney 365–6) quoted by Pliny, *Epist.* 4.27.4, line 7, 'ille o Plinius, ille quot Catones'—i.e. Pliny is the equivalent of any number of Catos. A repeated 'non' could then have begun the line. This interpretation would remove the problem (if it is one) of the double address.

Although 'vereor' could stand absolutely ('non ... vereor' = 'I have no fears'), one naturally looks for an object (cf. 'Daphnin' in *Ecl.* 2.26). Nisbet (pp. 145–6) considers 'quadrupla', 'four-fold penalties'. In *CQ* ns 30 (1980), 541, I suggested that 'Kato' might be nominative rather than vocative (a notion entertained also by Courtney 267–8), offering 'quae volt dupla Kato', 'the double punishment which Cato recommends', with one eye on the Censor's *De agri cultura* 1 'furem dupli condemnari' (though this is the prescription of the ancestors, not Cato's own). Nisbet (p. 146) also played with the idea of literary theft. If the sequence of thought were that Gallus has stolen his poems from their true authors, the Muses (line 6 above), but defends himself on the ground that nothing else would be good enough for Lycoris, that would seem a very whimsical argument. Another Cato (the father of Uticensis) recommended a double penalty for those who failed to mention defects of which they were aware in goods offered for sale (Cicero, *De officiis* 3.65, cf. Val. Max. 8.2.1). This case may have attained some celebrity as a singular instance of a *iudex* giving a reason for his judgement. Finally (a complete shot in the dark), on the analogy of stories about Choerilus of Iasus (see on *Suppl. Hell.* 333), one might imagine that Valerius Cato had jokingly proposed to reward every good line of verse but to exact twice as big a penalty from every bad line.

Nothing in the above paragraphs provides an easy solution. In *ZPE* 41 (1981), 37–42, Gregory Hutchinson gently returned to his suggestion, considered but rejected by Nisbet (p. 146), that we should obliterate Cato and interpret the letters as PLAKATO (the past participle). He did not wish to detach 'te' from 'iudice' ('plakato iudice, te vereor'), but rather to take 'plakato iudice te' together, starting the line (*exempli gratia*) 'haec dare'. This was most ingenious; there is indeed a trace before PLA which could represent an interpunct. But the word-order in Hutchinson's suggestion seems strained and improbable. One naturally views 'iudice te' as a self-contained phrase (cf. *Ecl.* 2.27). So I leave this line with the melancholy reflection of Professor Nisbet (p. 146) 'Since none of these approaches gives a satisfactory solution, there is a strong possibility that the traces should be read in some other way.'

Let us now consider the papyrus as a whole. These fragments have been viewed as (*a*) a series of separate four-line epigrams, with certain thematic connections between them (so e.g. the first editors); (*b*) continuous lines from a single elegy, despite the marking of quatrains (cf. Parsons, *JRS* (1979), 129, J. E. Miller, *ZPE* 44 (1981), 173–6, opposed by S. J. Heyworth, *LCM* 9 (1984), 63); (*c*) an amoebean poem with two speakers competing against each other (Janet Fairweather, *CQ* NS 34 (1984), 167–74); (*d*) an anthology of extracts from different poems by Gallus (Heyworth, *LCM* 9 (1984), 63–4). Courtney (p. 264) somewhat unenthusiastically acquiesces in (*d*). It seems to me (*pace* Courtney) that lines 2–5, interpreted as I have suggested above, make quite a satisfactory epigram; likewise 6–9. After 9 another quatrain may have followed, though the papyrus breaks off after three lines (we cannot tell how much is missing at the foot of col. i), and the only legible word is 'Tyria' at the end of 11 (clearly a pentameter). Col. ii. 1–4 (nothing legible) may represent yet another quatrain, since a dividing mark stands between lines 4 and 5; of the latter we can read the opening Qui.[.

Although the evidence is not wholly clear, such uniformity of four-line pieces would be surprising (in Catullus 69–116 there are only eleven four-line poems) and might be used as an argument by those who believe that the papyrus contains extracts—i.e. the anthologist was looking for four-line extracts. Nonetheless it is worth considering whether we might have here remnants not of a book of Gallus' *Amores* but of a collection of his epigrams. Two fragments of other poets are said to have occurred not 'in an epigram', which could have been a one-off piece, but 'in Epigrammatis', rather suggesting a collection of epigrams: Cinna **15** (part of a hexameter) 'in Epigrammatis', likewise Ovid, fr. 3 Blänsdorf, Courtney 'Larte ferox caeso Cossus opima tulit'. Ovid, fr. 4 Bl., C. 'cur ego non dicam, Furia, te furiam?' ('apud Ovidium ludentem') also seems to indicate that he recognized epigram as a genre with less strict technical requirements, in which he could end his pentameter with a trisyllable. It would be rash to put too much weight on a citation 'in Epigrammatis', but Catullus 69–116 could be part of such a collection. As we learn primarily from Martial, certain poets (Catullus, Furius

Bibaculus, Domitius Marsus, Albinovanus Pedo) won a recognized place in the tradition of Latin epigram, but others may also have contributed to this genre.

Lines 6–9 perhaps point in a different direction. The poet speaks with satisfaction of a task completed, and with confidence about the quality of his achievement. These lines suggest that the preceding poems have been at least predominantly about Gallus' beloved Lycoris. 'Fecerunt carmina Musae' (6) could pick up something which occurred near the beginning of the same book—an appeal to the Muses for help or even an initiation scene in the tradition of Hesiod and Callimachus (cf. **142**). In fact 6–9 could, in themselves, quite well be the concluding lines of a book, and Nisbet (*JRS* (1979), 149–51) suspects that the fragments, at least of col. i, belong near the end of a book of elegies, perhaps (p. 151) Gallus' very first book. Unfortunately the mysterious H signs at the beginning and end of quatrains give no hint that the break after col. i. 9 is any more significant than other breaks.

Certain features of the new verses are much as we might have expected. The metre most resembles that of Propertius I, particularly in the pentameter endings: one quadrisyllable ('historiae') and two trisyllables ('vereor' and 'Tyria'—though if Gallus wrote e.g. 'in Tyria' that would become in effect a quadrisyllable) match three disyllables ('tua', 'tueis', 'mea'). Propertius would not have written 'tum erunt' (2). Two molossic words ('multorum' and 'fecerunt') after the hexameter's masculine caesura, such a prominent feature of Catullus 64, 'give a heavy and slightly old-fashioned effect' (Nisbet, p. 148). On the other hand the subject matter differs from what we might have predicted. There is no learned and obscure mythology in the style of Euphorion (a parallel from Euphorion for **145.6** has been drawn, but seems not especially significant). And we would not have expected a series of four-line poems (if that is what they are).

In the first publication Nisbet was not uncomplimentary, but widespread disappointment has been expressed about the quality of these lines, e.g. by Stephen Heyworth, *LCM* 9 (1984), 64, 'the unbalanced and jejune group of verses' (due, he believes, to the selection made by an anthologist), Duncan Kennedy, *CQ* NS 32 (1982), 371, 'those wretched lines from Qaṣr Ibrîm'. Conferences which had arranged sessions on the new fragments found their initial eagerness abating (J. Van Sickle, *QUCC* NS 9 (1981), 122–3, on the Americal Philological Association meeting in December 1979). Some have gone further, arguing that the new fragments expose Gallus' reputation as a fraud, based upon Virgil's personal friendship for him.

This last reaction seems to me quite excessive. Suppose that we had lost all the poems of Catullus, having to judge him wholly on later testimonia, and then recovered a papyrus (of the same length as the new Gallus) from

Catullus' elegiac epigrams near the end of his book. Would we be any less disappointed? I conducted this imaginary exercise in *Collecting Fragments*, ed. Glenn Most, *Aporemata*, 1 (Göttingen, 1997), 116–17, choosing Catullus 92.1–95.1 (nine continuous lines). This was partly in response to a colleague who suspected forgery and had challenged his audience to find a passage of the same length which contains so many pointers to the identity of the author. The sensible reaction, in my view, is that these are not the bits of Cornelius Gallus which we would have chosen to recover, though they do (in a number of ways) illustrate his position midway between the generation of Catullus and the Augustan elegists. Assertions of Gallus' quality do not depend on Virgil alone, but are reinforced by Propertius (**138***d*) and particularly Ovid (**140**). Such testimonies from great poets are the most valuable evidence; in this I agree with Duncan Kennedy (*CQ* N S 32 (1982), 371), though his hunt for Gallus in the pseudo-Virgilian *Culex* seems to me chimerical.

Finally, I continue to doubt (with Syme, *History in Ovid*, 99 ff.) whether any of the Galli in Propertius I are to be identified with the poet Cornelius Gallus, though there has been a definite movement of scholarly opinion in that direction, at least with regard to Prop. 1.20 (see Francis Cairns, *PLLL* 4 (1983), 83 ff.).

Postscript: For a very detailed discussion of the Gallus Papyrus, together with enlarged photographs of col. i, see now M. Capasso, *Il retorno di Cornelio Gallo: il papiro di Qaṣr Ibrîm venticinque anni dopo* (Napoli, 2003). I am grateful to Professor Gregory Hutchinson for bringing this book to my attention in 2006.

L. Varius Rufus

146

(*a*) Hieronymi *Chronicon* (ed. Helm[2] (1956), p. 166) ann. Abr. 2000 = 17 a. Chr.: *Varius et Tucca, Vergilii et Horatii contubernales, poetae habentur inlustres. qui Aeneidum postea libros emendarunt sub lege ea, ut nihil adderent.*

(*b*) Verg. *Ecl.* 9.35–6: *nam neque adhuc Vario videor nec dicere Cinna* [**1***a*] / *digna, sed argutos inter strepere anser olores* [=**1***a*].

(*c*) Hor. *Epist.* 2.1.245–7 [ad Augustum]: *at neque dedecorant tua de se iudicia atque* / *munera, quae multa dantis cum laude tulerunt* / *dilecti tibi Vergilius Variusque poetae.*

(*d*) Hor. *AP* 53–5: *quid autem* / *Caecilio Plautoque dabit Romanus ademptum* / *Vergilio Varioque?*

(*e*) Mart. 8.55.21–2: *quid Varios Marsosque* [**172***j*] *loquar, ditataque vatum* / *nomina?*

(*a*) [Jerome on 17 BC]. Varius and Tucca, close friends of Virgil and Horace, are considered poets of renown. Later they revised the books of the *Aeneid*, on condition that they should add nothing.

(*c*) [Horace to Augustus] But those beloved poets of yours, Virgil and Varius, do not disgrace your judgement of them and the gifts which they received, together with great praise from the donor.

(*d*) [Horace] Why will the Roman people grant to Caecilius and Plautus what they deny to Virgil and Varius?

(*e*) [Martial] Need I mention people like Varius and Marsus [**172***j*] and the names of poets who have been enriched?

147–150 *De Morte*

147 (1 Bl., C.)

vendidit hic Latium populis, agrosque Quiritum
eripuit; fixit leges pretio atque refixit.

This man sold Latin rights to the nations and seized estates belonging to
Roman citizens; he made and unmade laws for profit.

1–2 Macrob. *Sat.* 6.1.39 (I p. 352 ed. Willis) ad Verg. *Aen.* 6.621–2 'vendidit
hic auro patriam, dominumque potentem / imposuit; fixit leges pretio atque
refixit': *Varius De Morte* 'vendidit—refixit'.

148 (2 Bl., C.)

incubet ut Tyriis atque ex solido bibat auro

. . . so that he may recline on coverlets of Tyrian purple and drink from cups
of solid gold.

Macrob. *Sat.* 6.1.40 (I p. 352 Willis) ad Verg. *Georg.* 2.506 'ut gemma bibat et
Sarrano dormiat ostro'. *Varius De Morte* 'incubet—auro'.

149 (3 Bl., C.)

quem non ille sinit lentae moderator habenae
qua velit ire, sed angusto prius orbe coercens
insultare docet campis, fingitque morando.

[a horse] whom that holder of the pliant rein does not allow to go where he
would, but, first confining him within a tight circle, teaches to prance upon
the plain and moulds by restraint.

1–3 Macrob. *Sat.* 6.2.19 (I p. 362 Willis) ad Verg. *Georg.* 3.115–17 'frena
Pelethronii Lapithae gyrosque dedere / imposti dorso atque equitem docuere
sub armis / insultare solo et gressus glomerare superbos': *Varius De Morte*
'quem—morando'.

2 orbe *Torrentius*: ore *codd.*

150 (4 Bl., C.)

ceu canis umbrosam lustrans Gortynia vallem,
si veteris potuit cervae comprendere lustra,
saevit in absentem et, circum vestigia latrans,
aethera per nitidum tenues sectatur odores;
non amnes illam medii, non ardua tardant   5
†perdita†, nec serae meminit decedere nocti.

Just as a Gortynian hound traversing a shady valley, if it has been able to come upon the haunts of a long-lived deer, exercises its savagery upon it in absence, and, barking around the tracks, follows the fine scent through the bright air. Rivers in the way and <? rocky> heights do not slow it down, and it does not think to give way to far-advanced night.

1–6 Macrob. *Sat.* 6.2.20 (I p. 362 Willis) ad Verg. *Buc.* 8.85–8 'talis amor Daphnin qualis cum fessa iuvencum / per nemora atque altos quaerendo bucula lucos / propter aquae rivum viridi procumbit in ulva / perdita, nec serae meminit decedere nocti'. *Varius De Morte* 'ceu—nocti'.

   2 comprendere *N*: deprendere *Baehrens* (*coll.* Sil. 10.82)   3 lustrans *codd.*, *corr. Ulitius*   6 perdita *codd.*: 'culmina *vel tale aliquid libenter reponam*' *Willis*: scrupea *Hollis*

151 (epica)

(*a*) Hor. *Sat.* 1.10.43–4: *forte epos acer / ut nemo Varius ducit.*

   (*b*) Hor. *Carm.* 1.6.1–2 [ad Agrippam]: *scriberis Vario fortis et hostium / victor Maeonii carminis alite* (Porf. ad loc., p. 11 ed. Holder, 1894): fuit autem L. Varius et epici carminis et tragoediarum et elegiorum auctor, Vergilii contubernalis).

(*a*) [Horace] Spirited Varius composes forceful epic like no one else.

   (*b*) [Horace to Agrippa] You will be written of by Varius, that bird of Homeric song, as a brave man and conqueror of your enemies. (Porphyrio on these lines: Lucius Varius, a close friend of Virgil, was a composer of epic poems, tragedies, and elegies.)

152 *Panegyricus Augusti* dub. (5 dub. Bl., C.)

> tene magis salvum populus velit an populum tu
> servet in ambiguo qui consulit et tibi et urbi
> Iuppiter.

Whether the people wishes more for your well-being, or you for theirs, let
Jupiter, who looks after both you and the City, allow to remain in doubt.
(Porphyrio: These lines come from a very famous panegyric of Augustus.
Acro: Varius had written this about Augustus.)

1–3 Hor. *Epist.* 1.16.25–9 'si quis bella tibi terra pugnata marique / dicat, et his
verbis vacuas permulceat auris: / "tene—Iuppiter", Augusti laudes agnoscere
possis': Porf. ad loc. (pp. 338–9 ed. Holder, 1894): *si quis pro tuis laudibus tibi
dicat Caesaris laudes et addat hos versus:* 'tene—Iuppiter', *qui sunt notissimo ex
panegyrico Augusti,* etc.; Pseudacro ad loc. (II p. 259 ed. Keller, 1902): *haec
enim Var<i>us de Augusto scripserat.*

153–158 tragica

153

(*a*) Ov. *Ex Ponto* 4.16.31: *cum Varius Gracchusque* [**197**] *darent fera dicta
tyrannis . . .*

(*b*) Incerti auctoris, *Laus Pisonis* 238–9: *Maecenas tragico quatientem
pulpita gestu / erexit Varium.*

(*c*) Mart. 8.18.7–8: *et Vario cessit* [sc. Vergilius] *Romani laude cothurni /
cum posset tragico fortius ore loqui.*

(*d*) Porf. ad Hor. *Carm.* 1.6.1–2 (v. **151***b*): *fuit . . . L. Varius . . . tragoedi-
arum . . . auctor* [=**151***b*].

(*e*) Macr. *Sat.* 2.4.2 (I p. 143 Willis): *postea L. Varius tragoediarum scriptor
interrogabat eum* [sc. Augustum Caesarem] *quid ageret Aiax suus . . .* [**160***b*].

(*a*) [Ovid] When Varius and Gracchus were giving ferocious utterances to
tyrants . . .

(*b*) [from an anonymous panegyric of Piso] Maecenas raised up Varius,
who made the platform shake with his tragic gestures.

(*c*) [Martial] And he [Virgil] gave place to Varius in glory for Roman
tragedy, even though he himself was capable of speaking more forcefully with
tragic delivery.

(*e*) [Macrobius] Later Lucius Varius, the writer of tragedies, asked him [Augustus] how his *Ajax* was getting on . . .

154–156 *Thyestes*

154

(*a*) Pseudacro ad Hor. *Carm.* 1.6.8 'nec saevam Pelopis domum' (I p. 39 ed. Keller): *propter Atreum et Thiestem, a quibus diis epulae humanae carnis appositae sunt, unde et tragoediam Var<i>us scripsit.*

(*b*) Quint. *Inst. or.* 10.1.98: *iam Varii Thyestes cuilibet Graecarum comparari potest.*

(*c*) Tac. *Dial. de or.* 12.6: *plures hodie reperies qui Ciceronis gloriam quam qui Vergili detrectent, nec ullus Asini aut Messalae liber tam inlustris est quam Medea Ovidi aut Varii Thyestes.*

(*d*) Iun. Philarg. ad Verg. *Buc.* 8.6 'tu mihi . . .' (p. 144 Hagen): *eiusdem autem Vari* [sc. Alfeni] *est tragoedia Thyestes omnibus tragicis praeferenda: aliud nihil eius habetur* [*legitur* Schol. Bern.].

(*a*) [Acro on Horace, 'the cruel house of Pelops']. On account of Atreus and Thyestes, who, at a banquet, served up to the gods food consisting of human flesh. On this subject Varius wrote a tragedy.

(*b*) [Quintilian] Now the Thyestes of Varius can be compared to any of the Greek plays.

(*c*) [Tacitus] Today you will find more people who disparage the glory of Cicero than that of Virgil, and there is no work of Asinius [Pollio] or Messalla [Corvinus] so famous as the *Medea* of Ovid or the *Thyestes* of Varius.

(*d*) [Philargyrius on Virgil] There is a tragedy *Thyestes* written by the same Varus [he means Alfenus Varus] which should be placed ahead of all tragedies; we possess no other work of this author.

155

Cod. Paris. Bibl. Nat. Lat. 7530, fol. 28ʳ.1–5 et cod. Rom. Bibl. Casanatens. Lat. 1086, fol. 64ᵛ, col. b, 17.14–18 (v. H. D. Jocelyn, *CQ* ɴs 30 (1980), 387):
INCIPIT THUESTES VARII. Lucius Varius cognomento Rufus Thyesten tragoediam magna cura absolutam [*Quicherat*: absoluto *codd.*] post Actiacam victoriam Augusti [*Mommsen*: aug . . . *Par.*¹: augusto *Par.*², *Casan.*] ludis eius in scaena edidit, pro qua fabula sestertium deciens accepit.

HERE BEGINS VARIUS' THYESTES. Lucius Varius, surnamed Rufus, produced on stage his tragedy *Thyestes*, which had been completed with great care, at Augustus' Games after his victory at Actium. In return for this play he received one million sesterces.

156 (Klotz, Scaen. Rom. Frag. I (1953), p. 309)

ATREUS
iam fero infandissima,
iam facere cogor.

1–2 Quint. *Inst. or.* 3.8.45: *neque enim quisquam est tam malus ut videri velit. sic Catilina apud Sallustium* [*Cat.* 20] *loquitur ut rem scelestissimam non malitia sed indignatione videatur audere, sic Atreus apud Varium* 'iam fero' *inquit* 'infandissima, iam facere cogor'.

[Quintilian] No one is so evil that he wishes to be seen to be such. Thus Catiline in Sallust [*Cat.* 20] speaks in a way to make it appear that he is daring to do a most evil deed not out of wickedness but out of indignation. Thus Atreus says in Varius 'Now I endure the most unspeakable things; now I am compelled to do the same.'

157–158 ex incertis fabulis

157 (Klotz, *SRF* I, p. 309)

primum huic
nervis septem est intenta fides
variique apti vocum moduli,
ad quos mundi resonat canor in
sua se vestigia volventis   5

He [Mercury] was the first to stretch the lyre with seven strings, and to fit on it the different intervals of sound, in harmony with which the tuneful Universe re-echoes as it revolves backwards over its own path.

1–5 Mar. Vict. GLK VI p. 60: *alii tradunt* [v. ad Varr. At., **111**] *hoc sacrorum cantu concentum mundi cursumque ab hominibus imitari. namque in hoc quinque stellae quas erraticas vocant, sed et sol et luna, ut doctiores tradunt philosophorum, iucundissimos edunt sonos per orbes suos nitentes. igitur concentum mundi cursumque imitans chorus canebat dextrorsumque primo tripudiando ibat, quia caelum dextrorsum ab ortu ad occasum volvitur; dehinc sinistrorsum redibat, quia sol lunaque et cetera erratica sidera, quae Graeci* πλανῆτας *vocant, sinistrorsum ab occasu ad ortum feruntur. tertio consistebant canentes, quia terra, circa quam caelum rotatur, immobilis medio stat mundo. de qua re Varius sic tradit* 'primum—volventis'. *item et Varro* (**111**).

[Victorinus] Some say that in this ritual song mortals imitate the harmony and course of the Universe. For in this the five stars which they call planets ['wanderers'] and also the sun and moon (as the more learned of the philosophers tell us) emit sounds of the greatest sweetness as they press onwards through their orbits. Thus the chorus sang in imitation of the harmony and movement of the Universe, first by dancing from left to right, because the heavens revolve to the right from east to west. Then it came back to the left, because the sun and moon and the other wandering stars, which the Greeks call 'planets', travel leftwards from west to east. Thirdly they halted while singing because the earth, around which the heavens revolve, stands motionless at the centre of the Universe. On this subject Varius writes as follows (**157**) . . . Also Varro (**111**) . . .

3 *apti Schneidewinus*: *addita codd. AB*: *additi* ς: *dati Bothius*   *moduli Bothius*: *modi AB*ς   *post v. 3 propter hiatum lacunam posuit Ribbeck*   4–5 *sic Schneidewinus*: resonat canor [tenor ς] sua se volventis in vestigia *AB*ς
5 vestigia se sua volventis *Buecheler*

158 dub. (Klotz, *SRF* I p. 310)

et frondosam et
semiputatam queritur vitem

1–2 Philarg. ad Verg. *Buc.* 2.70 'semiputata tibi frondosa vitis in ulmo est' (p. 46 Hagen): '*frondosa vitis*', *idest de qua si quis biberit, furit. sic avarus* [: *Varius* coni. Weichert] 'et frondosam—vitem'.

[Philargyrius on Virgil] 'A leafy vine', that is one which sends mad anybody who has drunk from it. Thus Varius [the name is particularly uncertain], ' . . . complains that the vine was both leafy and half-pruned'.

159 dub. (elegi)

Porf. ad Hor. *Carm.* 1.6.1–2 (v. ad **151**b): *L. Varius . . . et elegiorum auctor* [=**151**b].

There is a book on this poet by P. Cova, *Il poeta Vario* (Milan, 1989); I wrote an account of him in 'Virgil's Friend Varius Rufus', *Proceedings of the Virgil Society*, 22 (1996), 19–33.

THE life and literary career of Varius Rufus, Virgil's first poetic associate and perhaps his closest friend, make a fascinating study. Most of our surviving information is in some way entwined with Virgil. During the 40s BC the pair belonged to the same south Italian Epicurean community: 'vixit [sc. Vergilius] pluribus annis . . . liberali in otio secutus Epicuri sectam, insigni concordia et familiaritate usus Quintili, Tuccae et Vari' (*Vita Probiana* 12, in *Vitae Vergilianae Antiquae*, ed. C. Hardie (Oxford, 1966), 27). This community seems to have enjoyed the guidance of two Greek Epicurean teachers, Siro and Philodemus. The former appears twice in the *Appendix Vergiliana* (*Catalepton* 5.9 and 8.1, poems which may well be genuine Virgil—note that the more dubious *Catalepton* 7 apostrophizes 'Vari dulcissime' in the first line), while in philosophical papyri found at Herculaneum the latter actually addresses Plotius Tucca, Varius Rufus, Virgil, and Quintilius Varus. It is nice now to have definite confirmation of all four names, together with a photograph of the text, from M. Gigante and M. Capasso in *SIFC* 82 (1989), 3–6. A quarter of a century later Varius and Tucca were entrusted with publication of the *Aeneid* after Virgil's death (e.g. **146a**). No doubt Varius, himself a poet of quality, took the leading, perhaps even the sole part (G. P. Goold, *HSCP* 74 (1970), 124 = *Oxford Readings in Vergil's Aeneid*, ed. S. J. Harrison (1990), 83); our only evidence that Tucca was a poet comes from a questionable statement in **146a**. They seem to have fulfilled the task with fidelity, discretion, and good taste (Goold in *Oxford Readings*, 87, 'No carping critics ever rose to accuse [Varius] of a less than satisfactory performance; and if no devotee of Virgil has ever said "Well done", why, that in itself is the consummation of praise'). Varius also passed on some personal information about Virgil (Quintilian 10.3.8 'Vergilium quoque paucissimos die composuisse versus auctor est Varius'). Later the name of Varius was drawn into wild biographical fantasy about Virgil, involving plagiarism, sexual favours, and even murder (see J. Hubaux, 'La "Maîtresse" de Virgile', *REL* 12 (1934), 343–59). That debased tradition regularly confuses Varius Rufus with Alfenus Varus (e.g. **154d**) or Quintilius Varus; when Martial (8.18.7–8 = **153c**) says that Virgil was capable of writing better tragedies than Varius, he may have known a story that Virgil actually wrote a tragedy which Varius passed off as his own (Hubaux, pp. 343–6).

We do not know the relative age of the two poets, but, in the service of the Muses, Virgil counted himself the junior (*Ecl.* 9.35–6 = **146b**). References to the land confiscations suggest a date of 41 BC for the ninth *Eclogue*; Virgil's admiration at that time for Varius' poetry was most likely based on the *De morte*, which would be all the more congenial because it was on an Epicurean theme and expressed a philosophical doctrine to which they would both have subscribed. Certainly *De morte* was written by 39 BC at latest, since in the eighth *Eclogue*, dated by its reference to Pollio's campaigns, Virgil (lines 85–8) adapts a Varian simile (**150**)–I am inclined to think that he did *not* borrow a complete line unaltered.

Until 39 BC Virgil was still under the patronage of Pollio; there is no Maecenas in the *Eclogues*, and, although the *iuvenis* in *Ecl.* 1 is surely Octavian, the poem as a whole seems at best a double-edged compliment to Caesar's heir. Varius, on the other hand, is not connected with any patron before Maecenas. Perhaps he was the first member of the 'Maecenas circle', and even introduced Virgil, just as he and Virgil subsequently introduced Horace (*Sat.* 1.6.55); *Sat.* 1.5 (particularly lines 39–44) reveals Horace's joy at being admitted to the friendship of the men whom he must already have admired as poets. About 35 BC Horace praises 'acer / . . . Varius' as the unrivalled contemporary master of 'forte epos' (*Sat.* 1.10.43–4 = **151***a*). It is unclear to what extent, if at all, this eulogy reflects *De morte*, but both epithets rather suggest that, between the completion of *De morte* and 35 BC, Varius wrote other hexameter poems, perhaps with a military flavour, whether drawn from Greek mythology, remoter Roman history, or near-contemporary events.

This notion of a single acknowledged master in each branch of poetry may have influenced a change of genre by Varius in the second half of the 30s. At the time of the *Eclogues* the Roman tragedian was unquestionably Asinius Pollio (8.10 'sola Sophocleo tua carmina digna cothurno' = **135***b*), and that is still the case about 35 BC (Hor. *Sat.* 1.10.42–3 'Pollio regum / facta canit pede ter percusso' = **135***c*). Soon afterwards, however, Pollio took himself to history—a move perhaps not unconnected with the death of Sallust, whose assistant, Ateius Philologus, Pollio acquired (Suet. *De gramm.* 10.6). Although Horace implies (*Odes* 2.1.9–12 = **135***d*) that Pollio would soon return to tragedy, he subsequently became more interested in forensic oratory and declamation. Thus in a sense Pollio left a vacancy for another poet to become 'the' Roman tragedian—just as Horace claims in *Sat.* 1.10.46–7 = Varr. At., **108** (it is hard to say how seriously) that the lack of a master satirist led him to choose that genre—and Varius filled the gap. His most enduring work, the tragedy *Thyestes*, was produced at celebrations after the battle of Actium (**155**), probably in the year of Octavian's triple triumph (29 BC). I suspect that the fine anapaestic fragment **157** comes from a different play, also written between about 35 and 30 BC (the fifth line is closely paralleled in Virgil, *Georg.* 2.402).

Horace, *Odes* 1.6 (surely more gratifying to Varius than to Agrippa), written perhaps about 28 BC, encapsulates our poet's career. Although his pre-eminence as an epic poet was by now a thing of the past, he is still 'the bird of Maeonian song' (line 2) and best qualified to sing of Agrippa's victories; Varius may have used the image of himself, since he is a swan also in Virgil, *Ecl.* 9.36 = **146***b*). The *Thyestes* is present too ('saevam Pelopis domum', 8) and there may even be a glance forward to what became a *Panegyricus Augusti* (**152**) in line 11 'laudes egregii Caesaris', although (as we shall see) that work is surrounded by doubt.

After the death of Virgil, Varius might have contended with Horace for the position of greatest living poet; perhaps that is why **146***a* was attached to the year 17 BC (with the name of Tucca added because of his share in editing the *Aeneid*). Preparing Virgil's epic for publication must have taken considerable time and effort. Whether Varius continued to write poetry himself, and how many years he still had to live, cannot be determined. Ovid, *Ex Ponto* 4.16.31 = **153***a* 'cum Varius Gracchusque darent fera dicta tyrannis', written about AD 17, is curious; except for Domitius Marsus (line 5 = **172***a*) and Sabinus who is said already to have died (lines 13–16), the poets in *EP* 4.16 seem to belong to the final years of Augustus and the beginning of Tiberius' reign (e.g. Albinovanus Pedo, Cornelius Severus, Rabirius). It is surprising to find among them a poet whose career began before 40 BC; if, however, this is our Varius (see on **153***a*), one might deduce that he lived on and continued to write tragedies for some years after Virgil's death.

There is a possibility that Silius Italicus had access to a text of *De morte* (see on **150**), but the hexameter poems of Varius do not rate a mention in Quintilian or any other survey of Roman literature (cf. **154***d* 'aliud nihil eius habetur/ legitur'). *Thyestes*, on the other hand, was still read and greatly admired in the time of Quintilian and Tacitus (**154***b* and *c*); many have believed that a copy of the play survived into the eighth century, but that is open to question (see on **155**).

As noted above, some sources from late antiquity confuse Varius Rufus with Alfenus Varus (or even Quintilius Varus), a process no doubt aided by the fact that contemporaries of the poet would have written his genitive case as 'Vari', not 'Varii' (see H. D. Jocelyn, *CQ* NS 30 (1980), 393 n. 37 and 398–9). Housman (*CQ* 11 (1917), 45 = *Classical Papers* (1972), III, p. 945) in his demolition of an unfortunate piece by H. W. Garrod (*CQ* 10 (1916), 206–21), wrote 'Where MSS give *Varius*, we must hesitate before changing it to *Varus*, but ... where they give *Varus* we may change it to *Varius* without much scruple.'

147–150 *De morte*

We would not know even the existence of this poem but for the fact that Macrobius (*Sat.* 6.1.39–40 and 6.2.19–20) quotes four fragments; the first two (**147–8**) in a chapter containing 'quos ab aliis [sc. Vergilius] vel ex dimidio sui versus vel paene solidos' (6.1), the second pair (**149–50**) from a section where Macrobius sets himself 'locos locis componere' (6.2.1). None of these fragments is to be found in the surviving Virgil scholia—Jocelyn (*CQ* N S 15 (1965), 138) explains that, whereas Macrobius selected material which he considered unfamiliar at the time of writing, Servius and Philargyrius were apparently compiling manuals for the general reader. There are also other Virgilian parallels for these same fragments of Varius (e.g. *Georg.* 3.253–4 for **150.5–6**) to which Macrobius does not draw attention.

J. H. Voss (on Virgil, *Ecl.* 8.85, 9.35, and *Georg.* 2.506) conjectured that the main theme of the poem was the death of Julius Caesar; some scholars have even expanded Macrobius' title to *De morte Caesaris*, and others, while confining themselves to *De morte*, still hanker after the same idea (e.g. W. Wimmel, *ANRW* II.30.3 (1983), 1581–2). There may have been other contemporary allusions besides those to Mark Antony which can be detected in **147–8**, but there is no evidence that the death of Caesar played an important part in Varius' poem—or indeed occurred at all. On the other hand, several indications converge to commend the idea of A. Rostagni (*RFIC* N S 37 (1959), 380–94), which I took up in *CQ* N S 27 (1977), 187 ff., that *De morte* was an Epicurean poem dealing with the fear of death, inspired by Lucretius 3 and the contemporary Greek prose treatise Περὶ θανάτου of Varius' Epicurean mentor Philodemus (edited by T. Kuiper, *Philodemus over den Dood* (Amsterdam, 1925), cf. M. Gigante, *Ricerche filodemee* (1969), 63–122).

Varius' Epicurean leanings are sufficiently established by the Proban *Life of Virgil* and the Herculaneum papyri (see above, p. 260), but there is no reason to disallow the confirmation in Quintilian 6.3.78 'L. Var<i>o [: Vareo A: Varo a corrector of T and most editors] Epicureo, Caesaris amico' (R. Syme, *AC* 28 (1985), 43–4), *pace* C. E. Murgia, *CQ* N S 41 (1991), 189 ff. The desire to free mankind from the fear of death stands at the centre of Lucretius' *De rerum natura*, and Philodemus' Περὶ θανάτου seems to have influenced other Augustan poets too (e.g. Horace, *Odes* 1.9.14 and 2.14.22–4). It is most significant that Virgil interweaves imitation of Varius Rufus, *De morte* with imitation of Lucretius in *Ecl.* 8.85–8 and, above all, *Georg.* 2.505 ff.

There may be an unnoticed allusion to Varius, *De morte* in Adesp. **244** (from Lactantius). Of the two Epicurean poets who used 'animus' and 'anima' indifferently, one is unquestionably Lucretius; for the other there is no candidate as plausible as Varius Rufus, and *De morte* would offer many opportunities to discuss 'animus' and 'anima' (terms especially prominent in Lucretius 3).

147 and **148** contain scornful contemporary allusions, the first certainly and the second quite probably to M. Antonius. These could fit into a passage not unlike Lucretius 3.59–86; 'hic' (**147**.1) might suggest that Antony was only one of a series of individuals, more or less recognizable, whose behaviour was censured (cf. the repeated 'hic' in Virgil, *Georg.* 2.505 ff. where 506 imitates **148**, and *Aen.* 6.621 ff. where the second half of 622 is borrowed unaltered from **147**.2). We must now consider the historical context in which such attacks on Antony might occur, and hence the dating of Varius, *De morte.* On this point I would part company from Rostagni (*RFIC* 37 (1959), 380–3, followed by Wimmel, *ANRW* II.30.3 (1983), 1573 n. 24), who believed that the poem was written after the formation of the Second Triumvirate in November 43 B C—apparently holding that **148** could only describe Antony's conduct as a triumvir (whereas charges of luxurious living were hurled against him throughout his life).

The specific accusations in **147** clearly refer to Antony's behaviour as consul in the months after Julius Caesar's murder (March 44 B C). On 1 August of the same year Piso, Philodemus' patron, attacked Antony in the senate (Cicero, *Ad Att.* 16. 7 (= 415 SB). 7, *Ad Fam.* 12. 2 (= 344 SB). 1, *Phil.* 1.14), and Momigliano put in that context the unfavourable reference to Antony in Philodemus, Περὶ θεῶν (*JRS* 31 (1941), 154). Poems, of course, are not produced overnight, and 43 B C (rather than 44) may have been the year which saw the completion of *De morte*; Kuiper (*Philodemus over den Dood*, 96) dated Περὶ θανάτου to 43 B C—'approximately right' according to Momigliano (*JRS* (1941), 154), but I cannot see why 44 B C is not equally possible. The important point (accepted by Syme in *AC* 28 (1985), 44) is that Varius, *De morte* surely belongs before, rather than after, the formation of the Second Triumvirate. After November 43 B C it would be rash indeed for Varius to revive the language of Cicero's *Philippics* against Antony, until the time of the Perusine War (41–40) when Antony again became vulnerable (Octavian lampooned him in **161**) and Varius might already have been protected by the patronage of Maecenas. But an attack on Antony for his sponsorship of land confiscations in 44 B C (**147**.1–2) seems unlikely at a time when Octavian incurred greater unpopularity for the similar confiscations which followed the battle of Philippi (42 B C).

Some have felt that **149** (breaking in of a horse) and **150** (simile from a Cretan hound) tell against the view of *De morte* as a didactic poem and point to a full-blown epic. But both of these fragments could well illustrate a philosophical lesson; a hunting dog is put to just such a purpose in Lucretius 1.404 ff. (perhaps even Varius' model), and a horse in Horace (*Epist.* 1.2.64–5, where more than one scholar has seen traces of Varius). Since there is no evidence that *De morte* was split into books, some have thought that a didactic poem in a single book is unlikely; but, to take the most relevant parallel (the individual books of Lucretius, *De Rerum Natura*), we could envisage a poem of significantly more than a thousand lines.

147 (1 Bl., C.)

This fragment is replete with the themes and terminology of Cicero's attacks on Antony in the *Philippics.*

1–2. vendidit hic Latium populis, agrosque Quiritum / eripuit; fixit leges pretio atque refixit: Virgil's imitation (*Aen.* 6.621–2) runs 'vendidit hic auro patriam, dominumque potentem / imposuit; fixit leges pretio atque refixit'. Servius remarks on 622 'possumus Antonium accipere'; in Varius' two lines the allusion to Antony is much more clear and specific. Varius, however, may not have named Antony; 'hic' (line 1) could have been part of a series of pronouns, 'one man . . . another', from a catalogue of malefactors (like *Georg.* 2.505 ff. as well as *Aen.* 6.621 ff.). The Epicureans believed that men commit such injustices, and indulge in a frenzied struggle for power and wealth, in order to fence themselves against their fellow men—and that such actions were basically motivated by a fear of death (Lucr. 3.63–4 'haec vulnera vitae / haud minimam partem mortis formidine aluntur', cf. Bailey on Lucr. 3.31–93).

1. vendidit hic Latium populis: 'he sold Latin rights to the nations'. P. Cova (*Il poeta Vario* (1989), 63 n. 99) well compared Tac. *Hist.* 3.55 on Vitellius, 'Latium externis dilargiri'. No doubt 'Latium' here = 'Latin rights' (sometimes 'ius Latii', sometimes just 'Latium', see *OLD* s.v. *Latium* 2); there is also a hint of 'selling his country', taken up in Virgil's 'vendidit hic auro patriam' (*Aen.* 6.621).

vendidit: a constant motif in Cicero's *Philippics*, e.g. 3.10 'vendidit', 3.30 'vendiderit immunitates', 12.12 'immunitates ab eo [sc. Antonio] civitatibus, sacerdotia, regna venierunt' (cf. 2.92 and 97, 5.11).

Latium: a lower status than, but sometimes a stepping-stone to, full citizenship. See A. N. Sherwin-White, *The Roman Citizenship*[2] (1973), index s.v. *ius Latii.* No other source accuses Antony of malpractice specifically over Latin rights, though Cicero claims that he sold the Roman citizenship (*Phil.* 1.24 and *Ad Att.* 14.12.1, both quoted below).

populis: 'to the nations' (*OLD* 1(*b*), *populi*='the peoples of the world', though citing our fragment under 1(*a*)), as in *Aen.* 6.851 'tu regere imperio populos, Romane, memento', Mart. 12.2.1. By a typical exaggeration (like Sen. *Apocol.* 3.3 on Claudius, 'constituerat enim omnes Graecos, Gallos, Hispanos, Britannos togatos videre') it is suggested that Antony sold Latin rights to the whole world. The main (? sole) basis in fact may have been the treatment of Sicily. Cicero's letter of 22 April 44 B C to Atticus reveals that Caesar had conferred Latin rights on at least some Sicilians. Cicero, for all his good will, could not approve—now Antony is going much further, and (in return for a large bribe) proposing to make them full Roman citizens (*Ad Att.* 14. 12 = 366 SB. 1): 'multa illis [the Sicilians] Caesar, neque me invito (etsi Latinitas erat non ferenda. verum tamen). ecce autem Antonius *accepta grandi pecunia fixit legem* "a dictatore comitiis latam" qua Siculi cives Romani; cuius rei vivo illo mentio nulla.' On the question whether Antony's grant of citizenship was later rescinded, see Sherwin-White, *Roman Citizenship*[2], 230, 341 (differing in emphasis). In the *Philippics* Antony's corrupt grants of citizenship are often linked to corrupt tax exemptions (*immunitates*) whereby Roman revenues were diminished (see on 'vendidit' above).

It would be rhetorically less effective to understand 'populis' as 'to whole communities [as opposed to individuals]', though that too was a complaint which Cicero made against Antony, e.g. 'civitas data non solum singulis sed nationibus et provinciis' (*Phil.* 1.24, cf. 2.92).

1–2. agrosque Quiritum / eripuit: Antony's corrupt generosity to foreigners (*populi*) contrasts with his harsh treatment of those who rightfully possessed the Roman citizenship (*Quirites*) and were entitled to protection. The basic discussion of Antony's agrarian legislation was by W. Sternkopf (*Hermes*, 47 (1912), 146–51). In *Phil.* 5.7 Cicero writes 'hic [M. Antonius] omnem Italiam moderato homini [sarcastic!] L. Antonio dividendam dedit'. It seems that the consular Lex Antonia Cornelia Agraria dated from early June 44 B C. Antony's brother Lucius took the leading part on the Board of Seven (septemviri), and Cicero heaps the odium on him in *Phil.* 5.20: 'dividebat agros quibus et quos volebat; nullus aditus erat privato, nulla aequitatis deprecatio, tantum quisque habebat possessor quantum reliquerat divisor Antonius'. This law was annulled at the beginning of 43 B C (*Phil.* 6.14—Cicero remarks that the new owners would depart without too great distress, because they had not been put to any expense). One argument for dating Varius, *De morte*, before the formation of the Second Triumvirate (November 43 B C) and not in 41–40 B C (the time of the Perusine War) is that such an attack on Antony for his short-lived agrarian legislation is unlikely in 41–40 B C when Octavian was incurring greater unpopularity because of the confiscation after Philippi. On the latter occasion (by an irony of fate) L. Antonius did indeed play the man of moderation, sympathizing with the dispossessed (contrast *Phil.* 5.7 quoted above). See further on Octavian, **161**.

2. fixit leges pretio atque refixit: repeated verbatim in *Aen.* 6.622. 'Fixit leges' refers to the legislation passed by Antony in 44 B C, allegedly representing the wishes of the murdered Dictator; e.g. *Phil.* 3.30 'falsas leges C. Caesaris nomine et falsa decreta in aes incidenda et in Capitolio figenda curaverit'. Already on 23 April 44 B C (*Ad Att.* 14.12.1, quoted on line 1 'populis') Cicero wrote in connection with the enfranchisement of Sicily 'Antonius accepta grandi pecunia fixit legem'. But 'refixit' applied to Antony is not so easy. Cicero twice uses the verb of the senate annulling Antony's acts (*Phil.* 12.12 'num figentur rursus eae tabulae quas vos decretis refixistis?' and 13.5 'acta M. Antoni rescidistis; leges refixistis'). Perhaps, in Antony's case, the literal meaning should not be pressed; he would accept money either to pin up laws or to refrain from pinning them up. Cicero also remarks that Antony was much less keen on those laws which Caesar had actually passed during his lifetime: 'It seems that those contained in scraps of memoranda and holographs and papers produced on Antonius' sole authority, or not so much as produced but merely alleged, are to stand; whereas those which Caesar inscribed on bronze, as legislative acts of the people and permanently valid statutes, are to be treated as of no account' (*Phil.* 1.16 tr. Shackleton Bailey).

148 (2 Bl., C.)

incubet ut Tyriis atque ex solido bibat auro: for the luxurious combination of purple and gold, see Pease on *Aen.* 4.134 'ostroque insignis et auro'. Virgil (*Georg.* 2.506) reverses the order of the two halves: 'ut gemma bibat et Sarrano [Phoenician] dormiat ostro'. He also slightly changes the meaning, since in Varius 'incubet' clearly refers to reclining at a banquet rather than sleeping. With Courtney (p. 272) one wonders whether Sen. *Thy.* 909 'purpurae atque auro incubat' could be influenced by something in Varius' *Thyestes*. Characteristically, Virgil includes both 'incubat' and 'auro' (but in a different sense) in his very next line (*Georg.* 2.507 'condit opes alius defossoque incubat auro'), which takes us on to *Aen.* 6.610 'divitiis . . . incubuere', quite close to Virgil's imitation of **147**.

Macrobius' citation of **148** after **147** provides some ground for thinking that this was the order in Varius Rufus' poem (Jocelyn, *CQ* N S 14 (1964), 290). Morel suggested that **148** might immediately follow **147** ('si poeta consecutione temporum liberius usus est; *incubaret* poetae dactylico negatum') to produce

> vendidit hic Latium populis, agrosque Quiritum
> eripuit, fixit leges pretio atque refixit,
> incubet ut Tyriis atque ex solido bibat auro.

The run of the passage would then be closely similar to Virgil, *Georg.* 2.505–6

> hic petit excidiis urbem miserosque penatis,
> ut gemma bibat et Sarrano dormiat ostro.

Both poets would then speak of the acts of injustice and cruelty which men commit in order to obtain wealth and a life of empty luxury. On grounds of sense the idea is distinctly attractive (commended also by M. Wigodsky, *Virgil and Early Latin Poetry* (1972), 103). H. Dahlmann, *Zu Fragmenten römischer Dichter* (1983), 27–8, felt that 'Tyriis' in Varius requires a noun at or near the end of the previous line, thus ruling out Morel's join. *OLD* quotes only this fragment for the neuter plural 'Tyria' = fabrics of Tyrian purple, but I would so interpret also Ov. *AA* 2.297, taking 'Tyriis' as neuter, to balance the neuter 'Cois' in the next line ('sive erit in Tyriis, Tyrios laudabis amictus, / sive erit in Cois, Coa decere puta'), the masculine 'Tyrios . . . amictus' being dictated by metrical convenience. Courtney (p. 272), however, is unable to accept the change of sequence to present subjunctives ('incubet . . . bibat') which Morel's idea would involve.

For the luxurious lifestyle of Antony (long before his Alexandrian days) one can quote e.g. Cic. *Phil.* 2.62 'in urbe auri argenti maximeque vini foeda direptio'. When he took over the possessions of Pompey, 'conchyliatis Cn. Pompeii peristromatis servorum in cellis lectos stratos videres' (*Phil.* 2.67, cf. 2.73).

atque ex solido bibat auro: the adjective emphasizes that the gold is neither alloyed nor hollow. Varius' 'drinking from gold' may have been remembered by Lucan (4.380 'non auro murraque bibunt'); Plutarch (*Ant.* 9.8, during Caesar's lifetime) described how people were offended at the sight of golden drinking vessels being carried out for Antony's picnics (χρυσῶν ἐκπωμάτων ὥσπερ ἐν πομπαῖς ταῖς ἀποδημίαις διαφερομένων). C. B. R. Pelling in his 1988 edition (p. 137) notes that these details do not appear in the *Philippics*, and that Plutarch may have supplemented Cicero from a second source. In Varius 'bibat' probably has no pejorative associations, but of course drinking was an activity which Antony carried to notorious excess, eventually having to compose a treatise *De ebrietate sua*.

The hexameter ending of two disyllables ('bibat auro'), not preceded by a 'protecting' monosyllable, represents a slight infelicity, which may have moved Virgil to a deliberate slight infelicity in the caesura of *Georg.* 2.506 ('ut gemma bibat et . . .').

149 (3 Bl., C.)

On the training of a spirited horse. We cannot know to what use Varius put
this illustration, but Dahlmann (*Zu Fragmenten römischer Dichter*, 29, cf.
Cova, *Il poeta Vario*, 73) drew attention to resemblances between our frag-
ment and Hor. *Epist.* 1.2.62–5 'animum rege, qui, nisi paret, / imperat; hunc
frenis, hunc tu compesce catena. / fingit equum tenera docilem cervice
magister / ire viam qua monstrat eques'. It is by no means impossible that
Horace has our lines of Varius in mind, and that the original context was not
dissimilar (e.g. training the mind to face the prospect of death).

1. ille: for this deictic use of the pronoun in a simile, see S. J. Harrison on
Aen. 10.707–8.

moderator habenae: Bömer on Ov. *Met.* 6.223 (where we should probably
read 'moderantur habenas') collects parallels for this association of words;
this seems to be the earliest instance. For 'lentae . . . habenae' cf. e.g. Ov. *AA*
1.5, *Tr.* 4.6.3.

2. qua velit ire, sed angusto prius orbe coercens: the rhythm of the line
is extremely unusual—sense-break after the second trochee together with no
word-break in the third foot. The closest parallel which I have found is *Aen.*
12.910 (itself based on Lucr. 4.456) 'velle videmur, et in mediis conatibus
aegri' where 'in mediis' cohere so that there is virtually no third-foot caesura.
It might not be too fanciful to see a special effect: the eccentric distribution of
the first two dactyls representing the horse's desire to go where it will, which
is slowed down and put under tight constraint by the spondaic 'angusto'
which blocks the third foot.

orbe: Torrentius' emendation for 'ore' (vainly defended by Morel). Per-
haps the most cogent parallel is Ov. *Her.* 4.79–80 (Phaedra to Hippolytus)
'sive ferocis equi luctantia colla recurvas / exiguo flexos miror in orbe pedes'
(note also Manilius 1.299 'angusto . . . in orbe' of a heavenly body). The skill
of the rider is shown by the smallness of the circle in which he wheels his
horse. This training exercise is often described by the noun 'gyrus', e.g. in Ov.
AA 3.384 'in gyros ire coactus equus', while the Greeks used the word πέδη
('fetter') for a 'figure-of-eight' manœuvre (Xen. Περὶ ἱππικῆς 3.5 and 7.14);
cf. Aelian, *HA* 13.9 (of Indian horsemen) περιδινεῖσθαι ἐς ταὐτὸν
στρεφομένους.

3. insultare docet campis: compare Virg. *Georg.* 3.117 'insultare solo et
gressus glomerare superbos'. One is tempted to think of a 'dressage' move-
ment, but probably should not press the parallel too far (cf. J. K. Anderson,
Xenophon (1974), 190–1, *Ancient Greek Horsemanship* (1961), ch. 10

'Advanced Equitation'). Varius may have in mind the moment, described by Xenophon (*Περὶ ἱππικῆς* 10.15) when the horse, coming out of his turns (cf. line 2 'prius') is urged forward and simultaneously checked: 'We are to suppose the horse springing forward, but held by the bit from galloping, and so developing a vigorous trot, with his head held high, and high leg action, but stiff and constrained' (Anderson, *Ancient Greek Horsemanship*, 121, without reference to our fragment).

fingitque morando: cf. *Aen.* 6.80 'fingitque premendo' (Apollo taming the Sibyl like a horse, no doubt a deliberate imitation of Varius) and the more remote *Georg.* 2.407 'fingitque putando' (pruning vines). *Fingere* can be a technical term (*OLD* 5) for moulding the behaviour or a person or animal, e.g. Hor. *Epist.* 1.2.64 'fingit equum' (perhaps from Varius, see the introduction to this item).

150 (4 Bl., C.)

This six-line simile of the Cretan hunting dog (discussed also by A. Perutelli, *Frustula Poetarum*, 135–44) gives us perhaps the best chance of appreciating why the young Virgil admired Varius so much (*Ecl.* 9.35–6 = **146***b*), and why *De morte* remained in Virgil's consciousness throughout his career. I would say that these lines are fully up to Virgil's own standard. Some have argued from the elevated style that *De morte* was a full-blown epic, rather than didactic poem. But, as with the training of a spirited horse (**149**), this illustration could have conveyed a philosophical message, e.g. a determination to pursue an enquiry until the truth is discovered. One might even suspect that Varius had a model in Lucretius 1.404 ff. (Merrill ad loc. quoted our fragment):

> namque canes ut montivagae persaepe ferarum
> naribus inveniunt intectas fronde quietes
> cum semel institerunt vestigia certa viai,
> sic alid ex alio per te tute ipse videre
> talibus in rebus poteris, caecasque latebras
> insinuare omnes et verum protrahere inde.

Several comparable passages are found in later poetry, e.g. *Aen.* 12.749 ff., Lucan 4.437 ff., Seneca, *Thyestes* 497 ff., Oppian, *Hal.* 4.274 ff., [Oppian], *Cyn.* 1.506 ff. Particularly attention is due to Silius 10.77–82:

> ut canis occultos agitat cum Belgicus apros
> erroresque ferae sollers per devia mersa

> nare legit, tacitoque premens vestigia rostro
> lustrat inaccessos venantum indagine saltus,
> nec sistit nisi, conceptum sectatus odorem,
> deprendit spissis arcana cubilia dumis.

Both Varius and Silius have a six-line simile, and one can hardly doubt that the latter consciously imitates the former: note particularly Silius 81 'sectatus odorem' with Varius 4 'sectatur odores', Silius 80 'lustrat . . . saltus' with Varius 1 'lustrans . . . vallem' and Silius 82 'deprendit . . . cubilia' with Varius 2 'comprendere lustra'. It would be interesting to know whether Silius had a complete text of *De morte*, or whether he found just these lines quoted by some Virgilian commentator in connection with the Eighth Eclogue. A detailed imitation of Cinna's *Propempticon for Pollio* (**6**, see ad loc.) gives reason to think that Silius had access to some texts which, by his day, had faded from the general literary consciousness.

1.   ceu: a word mostly belonging to the high poetic style (also five times in Lucretius).

canis . . . Gortynia: a trace of the Greek convention (also observed in Lucr. 1.404 'canes . . . montivagae') whereby κύων, when denoting a hunting dog, is ordinarily feminine (see W. S. Barrett on Euripides, *Hippolytus* 18 κυσὶν ταχείαις). Contrast Silius 10.77 'canis . . . Belgicus'.

Gortynia: simply 'Cretan', not denoting a distinct breed from Gortyn any more than Oppian, *Hal.* 4.275 refers to a distinctively 'Cnosian' hound.

2.   veteris: the deer proverbially lived as long as four crows ([Hesiod], fr. 304.2), i.e. thirty-six generations of men! Solinus (19.18) would have us believe that Alexander the Great fastened collars on deer, and that the animals were observed wearing them 100 years later; in fact the red deer has a potential life span of about nineteen years (D. B. Hull, *Hounds and Hunting in Ancient Greece* (1964), 81). It was also proverbial that an old deer was a more wily antagonist (Ov. *AA* 1.766 'longius insidias cerva videbit anus').

comprendere: Baehrens conjectured 'deprendere', comparing Silius 10.82 'deprendit . . . cubilia' (see above), and he is followed by Courtney. But there is no objection to 'comprendere' (*OLD* 6); Silius may deliberately vary his model.

3.   saevit in absentem et, circum vestigia latrans: the build of this hexameter may strike us as markedly 'Virgilian': 'et' causes an elision at the masculine caesura, after which the expected continuation of the main clause is delayed until the next line by an interposed clause with a present participle. Thus *Georg.* 1.513 'addunt in spatia et, frustra retinacula tendens', 3.433 'exsilit in siccum et, flammantia lumina torquens'.

saevit in absentem: compare *Aen.* 9.63 'saevit in absentes' (in a simile of a wolf raging against lambs who are safe with their mothers inside the sheep-fold). Philip Hardie in his *Aeneid* commentary (p. 85) writes that the expression 'is the more striking in that *saevire in* is normally used of the actual performance of violence'.

latrans: this correction of the manuscripts' 'lustrans' was made by Ulitius (also independently by Willis, see *Rh. M.* 100 (1957), 162), and is unquestionably right. 'Lustrans' would be intolerable after 'lustrans' (1) and 'lustra' (2), though, surprisingly, championed by Dahlmann and Shackleton Bailey (*Gnomon*, 56 (1984), 179)—given short shrift by S. J. Harrison, *CR* N s 40 (1990), 487 (reviewing Cova) and Courtney. Compare Xenophon, *Cyn.* 3.5 ὑλάκτουσι περὶ τὰ ἴχνη.

4. aethera per nitidum tenues sectatur odores: Macrobius quotes our fragment for its similarity to Virgil, *Ecl.* 8.85–8. But in some respects there is a closer parallel with *Georg.* 3.251 ff. (see below on 5 and 5–6), where the Varian imitation is introduced by the idea of a scent carried on the breeze (251 'si tantum notas odor attulit auras'). See further Philip Hardie, *Virgil's Aeneid: Cosmos and Imperium* (1986), 159–60.

sectatur odores: cf. Silius 10.81 'sectatus odorem' (the whole passage quoted in the introduction to **150**).

5. amnes . . . medii: 'rivers in the way', i.e. forming an obstacle between the dog and its quarry (like 'obiecta . . . flumina' in *Georg.* 3.253–4).

illam: such an emphatic pronoun in a simile (e.g. *Aen.* 4.72) often marks a shift from subject to object (as here) or vice versa; see Austin on *Aen.* 2.628.

5–6. non ardua tardant / †perdita†,: in thus punctuating, and obelizing, 'perdita', I indicate agreement with Willis (*Rh. M.*, 100 (1957), 162) and Jocelyn (*CQ* N s 15 (1965), 139) that Virgil in *Ecl.* 8.88 did not borrow a whole line unaltered from Varius—though I am prepared to accept that Virgil did occasionally make such a borrowing (Varro Atacinus **121**.4 and **131**). Here the text of Virgil has corrupted the fragment: 'perdita' is entirely appropriate to the 'desperate' heifer who has lost her calf in *Ecl.* 8.88 (a picture partly inspired by Lucretius 2.355 ff.), much less so to the hunting dog in Varius. Also lines 5–6 of Varius would produce a more artistic tricolon (each limb longer than its predecessor) if the first foot of line 6 cohered with line 5. This point draws some support from Virgil's imitation in *Georg.* 3.253–4:

> non scopuli rupesve cavae atque obiecta retardant
> flumina

Although Virgil has reversed the order of Varius' rivers and mountains, 'obiecta retardant / flumina' is an exact metrical equivalent to 'non ardua tardant / <‿ ◡ ◡>'; Virgil thereafter goes his own way ('correptosque unda torquentia montis').

6. †perdita†: as Willis says, in such a case of intrusion the *ductus litterarum* of the manuscript reading may not offer much help. He himself suggested 'culmina' ('too high up', Nisbet), inviting alternatives. It is natural to look for a noun, but 'ardua' could equally well function as a noun (cf. *Georg.* 3.291 'deserta per ardua', Val. Flacc. 2.516 'Rhiphaea per ardua'), leaving us in need of an adjective. *Georg.* 3.253 'non scopuli rupesve cavae' stresses rockiness; accordingly in *PVS* 22 (1996), 27, I proposed 'scrupea' ('composed of sharp rocks or projections of rock', *OLD*). The adjective comes from archaic high-flown poetry (attested in the tragic fragments of Ennius, Pacuvius, and Accius). Virgil writes 'spelunca ... / scrupea' in *Aen.* 6.237–8, and Servius' comment ad loc. shows that 'scrupea' would go excellently with 'tardant' in Varius, since the literal reference of *scrupus* is to a sharp stone which impedes progress ('qui incedentibus impedimento est').

nec serae meminit decedere nocti: very fine, as Virgil obviously thought (he repeats 'serae ... decedere nocti' in *Georg.* 3.467). Varius is not merely indulging his poetic fantasy, since the Cretan (cf. line 1) hounds known as 'Workers' (διάπονοι) 'spend the nights as well as the days in the battle against the beasts, and often, after sleeping beside the beasts, begin the battle after it is day' (Pollux 5.41, tr. D. B. Hull, *Hounds and Hunting in Ancient Greece* (1964), 149). Several bits of Greek poetry float in the background, particularly *Iliad* 8.502 (= 9.65 = *Od.* 12.291) πειθώμεθα νυκτὶ μελαίνηι.

nec ... meminit: the verb does not imply that the hound 'forgets' to end its hunting, but rather that it does not 'turn its mind' to doing so, because it will not be diverted from the more important task of tracking down the deer.

decedere nocti: with a touch of personification. *Decedere* + dative may be used of giving way to e.g. superior force or superior social status.

152 (5 dub. Bl., C.) dub. *Panegyricus Augusti*

Although the positive evidence is slight, one can believe that Varius wrote such a poem. In Horace, *Sat.* 2.1.11 (*c*.30 BC) a suitable theme is 'Caesaris invicti res dicere'; his military achievements would be prominent, but other virtues should not be overlooked (ibid. 16 'et iustum poteras et dicere fortem'). The language in which Hellenistic court poets had praised their rulers (reflected particularly in Virgil, *Georg.* 1.24 ff., 3.46–8, 4.560–2, *Aen.* 6.791 ff., 8.720 ff., Horace, *Odes* 3.3.9 ff.) offered an enticing, if perilous, model; in Horace's later poems all aspects of Augustus' policy are included (*Epist.* 2.1.5 ff., *Odes* 4.5, 4.14, and particularly 4.15). Ovid claims that he tried the theme, but found it too great for him (*Tr.* 2.335–6 'divitis ingenii est immania Caesaris acta / condere', cf. 73 ff.).

One might see an anticipation of Varius' *Panegyric* in Horace, *Odes* 1.6.11 'laudes egregii Caesaris' (Varius could express them better than Horace), and an acknowledgement of the material rewards which accrued to the panegyrist in Hor. *Epist.* 2.1.245–7 (= **146***c*). If any weight can be put on 'Augusti' in the title, we would date the poem not earlier than 27 BC; this is our only evidence that Varius was still active in the 20s BC, though he may have continued writing tragedies (**153***a*). The surviving *Panegyricus Messallae* ([Tibullus] 4.1) ostensibly dates from 31 BC; Courtney (p. 275) suggests that the original title, in both cases, was *Laudes* rather than *Panegyricus*.

1–3.   tene magis salvum populus velit an populum tu / servet in ambiguo qui consulit et tibi et urbi / Iuppiter: E. Fraenkel described the content of these lines as a 'scornful parody', adding 'It is well known that anything even remotely reminiscent of a panegyric was utterly distasteful to Horace' (*Horace* (1957), 430 and n. 2). But the sentiments are entirely appropriate to the genre (and less absurd than much of the *Panegyricus Messallae*); no topic was more conventional than the reciprocal goodwill (εὔνοια) existing between the beneficent ruler and his subjects (see E. Doblhofer, *Die Augustuspanegyrik des Horaz in formalhistorischer Sicht* (1966), discussing this passage on pp. 52–66). For the people's unselfish prayers to Jupiter on behalf of their Emperor, compare the acclamation quoted by Tertullian (*Apol.* 35.7) 'de nostris annis tibi Iuppiter augeat annos'. This formula, which occurs with a small transposition of words among the proceedings of the Arval Brethren in Tertullian's time (e.g. W. Henzen, *Acta Fratrum Arvalium* (1874), p. ccvii, lines 37–8, from AD 218) may already have been official, or semi-official, during the principate of Augustus, to judge from Ovid, *Fasti* 1.613 'augeat imperium nostri ducis, augeat annos [sc. Iuppiter]' (see Bömer ad loc.). The health of Augustus was fragile: he himself records that 'vota pro valetudine mea suscipi per consules et sacerdotes quinto quoque anno senatus decrevit' (*Res Gestae* 9.1). These started in 28 BC. Perhaps even earlier (30 BC) began the annual 'nuncupatio votorum pro salute imperatoris' (see Lloyd W. Daly, *TAPA* 81 (1950), 164–8).

Nonetheless I find it hard to believe that Horace is making a verbatim quotation from Varius. The rhythm of the two line-endings 'an populum tu' and 'et tibi et urbi' is of the rough and ready sort deliberately cultivated in Horace's *Epistles* (and *Satires*), but certainly quite unlike the very accomplished metrical technique exhibited by our longest specimen of Varian hexameters (**150**). One would expect a *Panegyric* to be written in the most careful and elaborate style. Perhaps, therefore, Horace has borrowed the sentiment from Varius but changed the wording. It is, of course, possible to disbelieve the ancient commentators, and to argue that the lines were composed by Horace unaided, as a specimen of what a typical panegyric would be like.

153

I have suggested (in connection with **135***e*) that the ending of old-style Latin tragedy should be placed not at the death of Accius but at the withdrawal of Asinius Pollio in the mid-30s BC, leaving a very brief interval before the emergence, with Varius Rufus, of a smarter and more sophisticated style (an aesthetic judgement based upon **157**) which led to the plays of Seneca. Some of the items in **153** suggest that Varius wrote several tragedies; we should not put any weight on these (they could all refer to *Thyestes*), but it is not obvious how **157** would fit into the myth of the horrid brothers.

153*a* is problematical (see p. 262 above), in that the great majority of poets named in Ovid, *Ex Ponto* 4.16 flourished in the late Augustan/early Tiberian period. Perhaps indeed this is evidence that Varius continued as a tragedian and wrote other plays after *Thyestes*. Martin Helzle in his 1989 commentary on *Ex Ponto* IV (p. 190), following Housman (*Classical Papers*, III, p. 946), questions whether the reference is to Varius Rufus (Housman would not have approved of his apparent doubts whether Varius even wrote a *Thyestes*). Helzle's hesitations over the name (Varius/Varus) are unnecessary (see above, p. 262), and, unfortunately, he gets himself entangled with the biographical fictions of later antiquity (p. 260 above).

154–156 *Thyestes*

Varius' own form was probably *Thuesta* (Jocelyn, *CQ* NS 30 (1980), 393). In the Flavian period the *Thyestes* of Varius and *Medea* of Ovid were coupled together as the glories of the Roman stage (**154***c* = Tac. *Dial.* 12.6), much as Cicero (*De fin.* 1.4) had selected the *Medea* of Ennius and *Antiope* of Pacuvius; Quintilian asserts proudly that *Thyestes* 'can be compared with any Greek play' (10.1.98 = **154***b*). **154***d*, though a confused note stitched together from earlier commentaries, supports the impression that before too long no work of Varius other than *Thyestes* was generally known. Some have thought that a complete text of the play survived as late as *c.*AD 800 (but see on **155**).

The myth of Atreus and Thyestes was handled by many Greek tragedians, and particularly appealed to Roman writers (cf. Jocelyn, *The Tragedies of Ennius* (1967), 412–19, and S. G. Owen on Ovid, *Trist.* 2.391); we hear e.g. of an *Atreus* by Accius, and another by Gracchus (**200**). The story contained elements which the Romans thought quintessentially tragic—deeds of incredible wickedness and arrogant princes who indulge in ferocious rhetoric. When Ovid wishes to characterize Varius and Gracchus, both of whom treated this myth, he writes 'darent fera dicta tyrannis' (*EP* 4.16.31 = **153***a*).

Our only certain verbatim quotation seems to indicate that Varius described the fearful revenge which Atreus took upon his brother Thyestes for the latter's seduction of his sister-in-law Aerope; having enticed Thyestes to a banquet, Atreus there served up to him the flesh of the children resulting from this adulterous union. This was of course the most notorious part of the myth; the sun turned back in horror at the cannibal feast.

E. Lefèvre, *Der Thyestes des Lucius Varius Rufus* (1976), reconstructed the play along quite different lines, arguing that it covered a period of some twenty years, and culminated in the murder of Atreus by Thyestes' son Aegisthus and the installation of Thyestes upon the throne. Furthermore, Lefèvre believed that the strife of the two brothers was meant to mirror the recent Roman civil war; as Jocelyn says (*Gnomon*, 50 (1978), 780), 'No similarity between Mycenae under the rule of Thyestes and his son and the Rome of 29 BC could be indicated which was entirely comforting to Octavian.' The basic flaw seems to be Lefèvre's conviction that the subject matter of a play probably produced in connection with Octavian's Triple Triumph, for which the author received one million sesterces (**155**), must have related to contemporary Roman politics. In my opinion the fact that the play was hailed as an artistic masterpiece would be quite sufficient cause for Octavian's pleasure. No doubt he was also gratified to think that people would remember the circumstances of its first production.

Since Varius' play became so famous, one may reasonably ask whether any anonymous allusions to it, or even verbatim fragments, can be recovered. Perhaps the most plausible case is Quintilian (who quotes **156**) 11.3.73 'itaque in iis quae ad scaenam componuntur fabulis artifices pronuntiandi a personis quoque adfectus mutuantur, *ut sit Aerope in tragoedia tristis*, atrox Medea, attonitus Aiax, truculentus Hercules'. Wilamowitz (*Hermes*, 34 (1899), 226) was surprisingly confident that this must be a specific allusion to Varius Rufus on the ground that Aerope was not a typical tragic character in the same way as the others mentioned. He may have been right, but Aerope seems to have been a protagonist at least in Euripides' *Cretan Women* (to which play Webster, *Tragedies of Euripides* (1967), 39, would refer these words of Quintilian). Another hint that Quintilian kept Varius' play in his mind may be drawn from the phrase 'tragoedia Thyestes' (1.5.52). Ovid also names

Aerope in *Tristia* 2.391–2 'si non Aeropen frater sceleratus amasset / aversos Solis non legeremus equos'—could there be a special point in 'legeremus', directing thoughts towards a play which was currently much read? In *AA* 1.327–30 (probably following Euripides, cf. Webster, *Tragedies*, 38) Aerope, rather than Thyestes, is singled out for blame.

Our play also has some claim on two anonymous fragments: particularly Adesp. **245** (first words of Atreus, from Seneca with, significantly, one line quoted by Quintilian) and, more remotely, Adesp. **246**.

155

On the basis of this note (incidentally our only source for the poet's cognomen Rufus), found in Cod. Paris. Bibl. Nat. Lat. 7530 (written at Monte Cassino between AD 779 and 796) and Cod. Rom. Bibl. Casan. Lat. 1086 (written at Benevento towards the middle of the ninth century), it has been generally believed that a complete text of Varius' *Thyestes* survived until almost AD 800. Housman wrote as follows (*CQ* 11 (1917), 42 = *Classical Papers* III, p. 941): 'One day towards the end of the eighth century the scribe of Cod. Paris. Lat. 7530 . . . began to copy out for us . . . the *Thyestes* of Varius. He inscribed the title and the prefatory title . . . Then he changed his mind; he proceeded with a list of *notae* employed by Probus and Aristarchus, and the masterpiece of Roman tragedy has rejoined its author in the shades.'

Other scholars have lamented the loss in more emotional terms (see H. D. Jocelyn, *CQ* NS 30 (1980), 393–4). Jocelyn, in his painstaking investigation of the possibility 'that a complete text of the famous Augustan tragedy lay in a library like that of the Abbey on Monte Cassino through the eighth century unread and uncopied except for its title' (*CQ* (1980), 395), comes to the conclusion that it is only a possibility, with no degree of real probability, though he allows that during the eighth century there were undoubtedly to be found in Southern Italy a number of literary and semi-literary works absent from the libraries of the rest of Europe. He ends (pp. 399–400):

Copies of Varius' tragedy, like other rarities, could have survived a long time in the odd library, little consulted and gradually rotting away. I suggest that the surviving parchment of one such copy was at some stage washed along with bits of unused or unusable ancient books in order to provide material for copying a collection of works on grammar, and title and its explanatory note, because of their position either at the bottom or at the top of a relatively unused page, escaped the wash, and that the first copier of an account of the critical signs used by Aristarchus and Probus let the unwashed (or perhaps only lightly washed) words stand. A subsequent copier either wrote out the title of the account of the signs in the same style of script as that in which he copied out the note on the first performance of the *Thyestes* or omitted it altogether, leaving INCIPIT THYESTES VARII to head the curious amalgam of material which survives in the two South-Italian codices.

Jocelyn also discusses, producing parallels from notes associated with Greek and Latin drama, the aesthetic judgement on the play (*magna cura absolutam*) and the details about the first performance and payment made to the author, arguing (pp. 392–3) that 'there is little positive to show that anyone consciously designing an edition of the *Thyestes* might have set the note between the title and the text'. He suggests that a note (perhaps taken from Suetonius' biography of Varius) was added by a reader 'anxious to penetrate an opaque title' (p. 393).

As to the contents of the note, F. W. Schneidewin (*Rh. M.* 1 (1842), 110) thought that the *ludi* at which *Thyestes* was performed were those celebrated by Octavian in connection with his Triple Triumph of 29 BC (Dio 51.21.7). Jocelyn (*Gnomon*, 50 (1978), 780) suggests that *ludi* accompanying the dedication of the Palatine temple of Apollo in 28 BC (*Res Gestae* 19) might have been a more appropriate occasion. As for the sum of one million sesterces (two and a half times the equestrian property qualification) received by Varius, Jocelyn urges caution, citing discrepant accounts of Virgil receiving ten million sesterces (*CQ* (1980), 393 n. 40).

156

The 'infandissima' which Atreus suffered from Thyestes were the seduction of his wife Aerope and (with her help) the theft of the golden sheep which guaranteed Atreus' rule (cf. Accius, *Atreus* 169–77 Warmington, Seneca, *Thyestes* 222–35), and the 'infandissima' which he is forced to perpetrate in revenge are the killing of Thyestes' children and serving of their flesh to Thyestes at the banquet. Atreus' determination to inflict abnormal punishment on his brother is expressed with powerful alliteration by Accius (*Atreus* 163–6 Warmington, 'iterum Thyestes Atreum adtrectatum advenit, / iterum iam adgreditur et quietum exsuscitat. / maior mihi moles, maius miscendumst malum, / qui illius acerbum cor contundam et comprimam'. The closest parallel to our fragment in Seneca's *Thyestes* would be 193–5 'aliquod audendum est nefas / atrox, cruentum, tale quod frater meus / suum esse mallet'.

1.   **infandissima:** we do not know any other example of this superlative.

157

Could this fine anapaestic fragment be accommodated in the *Thyestes*? The last line, describing the ordered movement of the heavenly bodies, might make one think of the celestial disarray which followed the abominable crime of Atreus (cf. Seneca, *Thyestes* 789–874), or, in a rarer version, confirmed Atreus' claim to the throne (cf. Frazer's notes in the Loeb Apollodorus, vol. II, pp. 164–6), but the opening line, describing Mercury's invention of the lyre, seems to rule this out. In variant forms of the legend Mercury does intervene in a small way, either providing the golden sheep (schol. Eur. *Orestes* 812) or taking a message to Atreus (Apollodorus, *Epit.* 2.12).

None of these possibilities seems plausible. The fragment looks like an encomium of Mercury with special reference to his inventions (or, less probably, an encomium of music). I suspect that it comes from a different play; it would be surprising if Varius' tragic reputation rested solely upon *Thyestes*. If so, this unknown play was probably also written in the later 30s BC, since line 5 is closely paralleled in *Georgics* 2.402—of course Virgilian priority is possible.

These lines provide the only clear sign of Varius' interest in Hellenistic learning (some scholars, without good cause, have seen neoteric tendencies in *De morte*). Here we are in the world of Eratosthenes' *Hermes*, Alexander of Ephesus, and Varro Atacinus' *Chorographia* (**109–19**). This fragment is quoted by the grammarian Marius Victorinus together with Varr. At. **111**. If my conjecture 'Phoebo' for 'Phoebi' in **111**.4 is correct, Mercury would be the subject of both pieces. It is clear that Marius Victorinus is mainly interested in the last two lines of the Varius fragment.

The metre is anapaestic dimeter. Hiatus occurs between lines 3 and 4; some scholars have postulated a lacuna at that point, unnecessarily in my opinion.

1.   huic: clearly Mercury, 'curvaeque lyrae parentem' (Hor. *Odes* 1.10.6; cf. Alexander of Ephesus τοίην τοι σειρῆνα Διὸς πάϊς ἥρμοσεν Ἑρμῆς / ἑπτάτονον κίθαριν (*Suppl. Hell.* 21.25–6). The pronoun 'huic' seems very emphatic, suggesting that the fragment may have belonged to a more extended eulogy of Mercury, with special reference to his ἀρεταί or inventions ('primum', cf. Nisbet and Hubbard on Hor. *Odes* 1.3.12 'primus').

2.   intenta: cf. *OLD* s.v. *intendere* 2(*b*), 'to bring into a state of tension', of a lyre, quoting also Virg. *Aen.* 9.776 'numerosque intendere nervis'.

3.   apti: here used as a past participle (from the obsolete *apire*) rather than an adjective, suggesting the Greek ἁρμόζειν (cf. ἥρμοσε in Alex. Ephes. quoted above) and ἁρμονία. 'Aptari' often has the same associations (see

Nisbet and Hubbard on Hor. *Odes* 2.12.4 'aptari citharae modis'). So Schneidewin's emendation for the manuscripts' 'addita' or 'additi' is more appropriate than 'dati' (Bothius).

moduli: 'a sequence of intervals forming a scale or tune' (*OLD* 3(*b*)).

3–4. After line 3 Ribbeck (*Tragicorum Romanorum Fragmenta*³ (1897), I, p. 265) placed a lacuna 'propter hiatum', in which 'motus chori memorari poterant' (cf. Marius Victorinus, partly quoted as a source for this fragment and more fully as a source for Varr. At. **111**). But I am far from convinced that we should expect Varius to have described the movements of the dance. As for the hiatus, we seem to have no clear example of hiatus between lines in the anapaests of archaic Latin tragedy, but hiatus between anapaestic lines is not infrequent in Seneca (cf. R. J. Tarrant, *Seneca's 'Agamemnon'* (Cambridge University Press, 1976), 369), and may well have been acceptable to Varius, particularly when, as here, there is an appreciable sense-break.

4.   ad quos: 'in harmony with which'. The notes emitted by the heavenly bodies (according to the Platonists) exactly match those of the seven-stringed lyre; cf. Varr. At. **111**.5 'consimiles . . . voces', Alex. Ephes., *SH* 21.9–10 πάντες δ' ἑπτατόνοιο λύρης φθόγγοισι συνωιδόν / ἁρμονίην προχέουσι (see on **111**.2), F. Solmsen, *TAPA* 73 (1942), 199–201.

5. sua se vestigia volventis: so Schneidewin. The order of words in the manuscripts is unmetrical; an equally good rearrangement would be 'vestigia se sua volventis' (Buecheler). The notion, as explained by Mar. Vict., is that 'caelum dextrorsum ab ortu ad occasum volvitur; dehinc sinistrorsum redibat, quia sol lunaque et cetera erratica sidera . . . sinistrorsum ab occasu ad ortum feruntur'. Compare W. H. Stahl, *TAPA* 73 (1942), 234 'The celestial sphere makes a complete rotation from east to west every twenty-four hours, dragging along with it the seven planets lying beneath, but the planets have independent revolutions from west to east.'

Virgil (if, as seems likely but not certain, he is the adapter) transforms this nice line of Varius into a picture of the farmer's recurring annual tasks: 'redit agricolis labor actus in orbem, / atque in se sua per vestigia volvitur annus' (*Georg.* 2.401–2). R. F. Thomas ad loc. admires Virgil but seems unaware of Varius; Mynors quotes Varius in an unmetrical form.

158 dub.

1–2.   et frondosam et / semiputatam queritur vitem: this quotation might be in anapaestic metre; 'Varius' for the manuscripts' 'avarus' was not an unreasonable conjecture by Weichert ('Varus' could have been an intermedi ate stage of the corruption). Philargyrius adds that to drink from a 'frondosa vitis' sent one mad, which ought to be relevant to the quotation. Some scholars have been prepared to consider attribution to Varius' *Thyestes*, perhaps in connection with the banquet (cf. Cova, *Il poeta Vario*, 29, Lefèvre, *Der Thyestes des Lucius Varius Rufus*, 12 n. 34). An almost inevitable consequence would be that this time Varius is imitating Virgil (*Ecl.* 2.70 'semiputata tibi frondosa vitis in ulmo est', from one of the earliest *Eclogues*). Such a borrowing from the love-sick Corydon for a tragedy would be peculiar, and the sentiment is barely credible. Like Jocelyn (*CQ* ns 30 (1980), 399 n. 77) I am extremely suspicious of this item.

159 dub. (elegi)

One must be cautious about his unsupported statement that Varius also wrote elegies, but the possibility cannot be ruled out.

Before we leave Varius Rufus, it is worth mentioning the idea of J.-P. Boucher in *REA* 60 (1958), 307–22, that he might be concealed under the pseudonym Lynceus in Propertius 2.34 (lynxes are 'variae' in Virgil, *Georg.* 3.264). The use of pseudonyms for Roman poets and literary figures in this period is well established (see on Valgius Rufus, **166**.1 for Codrus, and Appendix for Trinacrius and Demophoon/Tuscus). The poetic interests ascribed to Lynceus in Prop. 2.34 (scientific philosophy, epic, and tragedy) suit Varius Rufus; the recommendation that he should turn to love-elegy (Prop. 2.34.43–4) might even be linked to **159** dub.

C. Caesar Octavianus (Imp. Augustus)

160

(*a*) Suet. *Div. Aug.* 85.2: *poetica summatim attigit. unus liber exstat scriptus ab eo hexametris versibus, cuius et argumentum et titulus est Sicilia. exstat alter aeque modicus epigrammatum, quae fere tempore balinei meditabatur. nam tragoediam magno impetu exorsus, non succedenti stilo, abolevit, quaerentibusque amicis quidnam Aiax ageret, respondit Aiacem suum in spongiam incubuisse.*

(*b*) Macr. 2.4.2 (I p. 143 Willis): *Aiacem tragoediam scripserat eandemque quod sibi displicuisset deleverat. postea L. Varius tragoediarum scriptor* [**153***e*] *interrogabat eum quid ageret Aiax suus, et ille 'in spongiam' inquit 'incubuit.'*

(*c*) Macr. 2.4.21 (I p. 146 Willis): *temporibus triumviralibus Pollio, cum Fescenninos in eum Augustus scripsisset, ait 'at ego taceo. non est enim facile in eum scribere qui potest proscribere.'*

(*d*) Plin. *Epist.* 5.3.5 [inter eos qui versiculos severos parum fecerunt, cf. **19***j*]: *et, si non sufficiunt exempla privata, divum Iulium, divum Augustum* . . .

(*a*) [Suetonius] His contacts with poetry were superficial. One volume of his written in hexameters has survived, of which both the subject and the title is Sicily; also an equally brief book of epigrams, most of which he thought up at bathtime. He started with great enthusiasm on a tragedy, but, since the style did not go well, he wiped it out, and, when his friends asked him how Ajax was doing, he replied that his Ajax had fallen on the sponge.

(*b*) [Macrobius] He had written a tragedy, *Ajax*, but had destroyed the same because it had failed to please him. Later the tragedian Lucius Varius asked him how his Ajax was doing, and he replied 'He has fallen on the sponge.'

(*c*) [Macrobius] In the triumviral period, after Augustus had written Fescennine verses against him, Pollio said 'But I am going to hold my tongue, since it isn't easy to write (*scribere*) against someone who has the power to proscribe (*proscribere*).'

(*d*) [Pliny on distinguished men who wrote risky verses] . . . and, if private examples do not suffice, the deified emperors Julius and Augustus.

161 (1 Bl., C.) *Epigrammata*

Quod futuit Glaphyran Antonius, hanc mihi poenam
    Fulvia constituit, se quoque uti futuam.
Fulviam ego ut futuam? quid si me Manius oret
    pedicem? faciam? non, puto, si sapiam.
'aut futue aut pugnemus' ait. quid quod mihi vita   5
    carior est ipsa mentula? signa canant!

Because Antony is fucking Glaphyra, Fulvia decrees the following penalty for me, that I should fuck her too. I fuck Fulvia? What if Manius begged me to bugger him? Should I do it? Not, I think, if I had any sense. 'Either fuck or fight', she says. What of the fact that my penis is dearer to me than life itself? Let the trumpets sound!

1–6 Mart. 11.20.1 ff.: *Caesaris Augusti lascivos, livide, versus / sex lege, qui tristis verba Latina legis: / (3–8) 'quod futuit—canant!' / (9–10) absolvis lepidos nimirum, Auguste, libellos, / qui scis Romana simplicitate loqui.*

160

Of the poems attributed to Octavian/Augustus by Suetonius (**160***a*), the shortish piece in hexameters entitled (and about) Sicily perhaps described— though not at epic length—the Sicilian War of 38–36 B C against Sextus Pompeius. The existence of this work might have deterred subsequent poets from treating the same theme until Cornelius Severus (**206–7**, *Bellum Siculum*) at the end of Augustus' or even the beginning of Tiberius' reign. We learn that Octavian published a slim volume of epigrams (which no doubt included **161**). The tragedy, according to Johannes Lydus (*De mensibus* 4.112), would have been a version of Sophocles, *Ajax*—Lydus attributes to Cicero the question which Macrobius (**160***b*) gives to Varius Rufus. Macrobius, unlike Suetonius, implies that the tragedy was completed. We may note that, when defending himself in *Tristia* II, Ovid did not consider it a good idea to include the Emperor among those 'apud quos / rebus adest nomen nominibusque pudor' (*Tr.* 2.433–4 = Memmius **44***a* and Ticida **101***a*).

161 (1 Bl., C.)

There is no cause to doubt the authenticity of these six lines—surely a complete poem—preserved in Martial 11.20 (see N. M. Kay's (London, 1985) commentary on Martial XI). The versification, with two trisyllabic pentameter endings and consecutive elisions in line 3 'Fulvi(am) eg(o) ut' suits the late 40s BC. The general style, enlivened by the series of questions and final exclamation, still recalls Catullus, as does the presence in every line of a rude word—four times the verb *futuo*, which in line 5 is put into the mouth of a woman (a particular breach of decorum).

More important, the historical context is very precisely defined. Not, I think, during the siege of Perusia (autumn 41 BC to the beginning of spring 40) but in the summer of 41, a period of unsuccessful negotiations which preceded the outbreak of the bellum Perusinum. In this epigram Octavian transfers the series of complaints, demands, and refusals (Dio 48.4–12) from the military and political to the sexual plane, marking the imminence of actual fighting with the final words 'signa canant'. Another indication that the poem predates the siege of Perusia is that the scandal about Antony's infidelity involves the Cappadocian Glaphyra; not yet Cleopatra, whom Antony met at Tarsus in late summer 41 (see Pelling on Plutarch, *Antony* 30.4).

The trouble was provoked by a political necessity of confiscating land for the veterans of Philippi. Mark Antony himself was absent in the East; to what extent he supported (or even had instigated) the actions of his wife and brother remains unclear (E. Gabba, *HSCP* 75 (1971), 149). But he must have derived some quiet satisfaction from the difficulties of his junior partner, Octavian, since only three years earlier both he and his brother Lucius had become no less unpopular for their programme of land redistribution (see on Varius Rufus, **147**.1–2 'agrosque Quiritum / eripuit'). Now, in a remarkable turnabout, L. Antonius and Fulvia were gaining popularity by sympathizing with the dispossessed—though the settlement of veterans remained a joint policy of Antony and Octavian (Pelling in *CAH* X² (1996), 15). The epigram makes no mention of L. Antonius; as in the later propaganda against Cleopatra all the odium is heaped upon Fulvia, who is portrayed as domineering, unfeminine, yet sexually voracious. By implication the whole affair is blamed not on any political argument, but on Fulvia's sexual jealousy. Depiction of the Perusine war in terms of sexual assault was continued (by both sides) on some of the lead sling bullets found at, or near, Perusia; see Judith P. Hallett, 'Perusinae Glandes', *AJAH* 2 (1977), 151–71.

As things turned out, the terrible aftermath of Perusia's capture (Suet. *Div. Aug.* 14–15, cf. Propertius 1.21 and 22) became the worst blot on Octavian's reputation in the civil wars. Fulvia died soon afterwards; in retrospect it suited all parties (even Mark Antony) to blame her for the trouble, thus facilitating a reconciliation of the two triumvirs (and the marriage of Antony to Octavia in the autumn of 40). N. M. Kay (*Martial, Book XI: A Commentary*, 111) describes Octavian's poem as 'an effectively unpleasant piece of propaganda'. It may have been typical of its time; see K. Scott, 'The Political Propaganda of 44–30 BC', *Memoirs of the American Academy in Rome*, 11 (1933), 7–49 (pp. 25–8 on this poem). One can imagine that the poems of Furius Bibaculus, 'crammed with insults' (Tac. *Ann.* 4.34.5 = **71***c* 'referta contumeliis') against Octavian were not dissimilar.

1.   Glaphyran: Dio (49.32.3) describes her as a hetaera. The name, which suggests neatness and elegance (LSJ s.v. γλαφυρός) was judged not unsuitable for a queen, since it passed on to her granddaughter, who married two princes of Herod's dynasty and, in between, Juba II of Mauretania (Josephus, *AJ* 17.349, cf. Richard D. Sullivan, *Near Eastern Royalty and Rome, 100–30 BC* (Toronto, 1990), 185). Antony's Glaphyra cannot have been in her first youth, since, not long afterwards, her good looks induced him to make her son king of Cappadocia as Archelaus I Philopatris Ktistes, who proved remarkably durable (36 BC to AD 17) and successful (Sullivan, pp. 182–5). See on Domitius Marsus, **174**, for possible involvement of the *curator* (and bad poet) Bavius in Cappadocia. Glaphyra herself was honoured at Magnesia ad Maeandrum as queen and mother of King Archelaus (*OGIS* 361); a woman's statue, part of which was found near the inscription, may have been hers.

hanc mihi poenam: Fulvia should have addressed complaints about her husband's infidelity to Antony himself; instead she takes out her resentment on Octavian. It is implied that making love to Fulvia would be a pain rather than a pleasure.

1–2.   poenam / ... constituit: as if she were a magistrate authorized to determine penalties.

2.   Fulvia: it is a shock to realize that the woman traduced in this epigram had quite recently been Octavian's mother-in-law, though the party line was that his marriage to Clodia, daughter of Fulvia and the tribune P. Clodius (none other!) was never consummated and the bride returned home 'simultate cum Fulvia socru orta' (Suet. *Div. Aug.* 62). If first readers of the epigram were aware of this background, the hurt to Fulvia would be increased: after declining sexual relations with the daughter, Octavian pretends to do the same with the mother. For the career of the remarkable Fulvia, married successively to P. Clodius Pulcher, C. Scribonius Curio, and M. Antonius, see Diana Delia, 'Fulvia Reconsidered', in Sarah B. Pomeroy (ed.), *Women's History and Ancient History* (Chapel Hill, NC, 1991), 197–217. After the fall of

Perusia Fulvia was allowed to leave Italy (Velleius 2.76.2) and met her husband in Athens (Appian, *BC* 5.52.217), but was rebuffed by him and died soon afterwards at Sicyon (Plutarch, *Antony* 30.5).

3. **Manius:** Antony's *procurator* (Appian, *BC* 5.14.54 ὁ τῆς ἀποδημίας ἐπιτροπεύων τῶι Ἀντωνίωι Μάνιος), several times mentioned by Appian as playing an active part, together with L. Antonius and Fulvia, in the events of 41 BC. Manius is normally a *praenomen*, but occasionally a *nomen*. Syme (*Historia*, 13 (1964), 119 = *Roman Papers*, II, p. 597) notes that the triumvir's father had a legate called Manius in 73 BC.

3–4. **oret / pedicem:** for *oro* + subjunctive, without *ut*, see *OLD* 1(*b*). One might expect Manius to request the active role, but it is the other way round, perhaps in response to accusations of passive homosexuality made against Octavian by both L. and M. Antonius (Suet. *Div. Aug.* 68.1).

4. **faciam?:** deliberative, 'Ought I to do it?'

non, puto, si sapiam: 'not if I had any sense'. The implication (and again in line 6) is that he would be exposing himself to some unpleasant disease.

5. **'aut futue aut pugnemus':** as Judith Hallett points out (*AJAH* 2 (1977), 170 n. 66), *futuo* clearly belonged to 'male parlance', and was not used by respectable women (a slight qualification in Adams, *Latin Sexual Vocabulary*, 121). So the ascription to Fulvia in direct speech is meant to portray her as particularly unladylike.

6. **mentula:** 'the archetypal obscenity' (Adams, *Latin Sexual Vocabulary*, 9), occurring eight times in Catullus (including use as a pseudonym for Mamurra), eighteen times in the Pompeian graffiti. It was eschewed by Cicero in his discussion of obscenity (*Ad fam.* 9.22 = 189 SB) but clearly had been used by his correspondent (9.22.2 'id verbum quo tu usus es').

signa canant!: grandiose (as e.g. *Aen.* 10.310 'signa canunt').

C. Valgius Rufus

162

Hor. *Sat.* 1.10.81–3: *Plotius et Varius, Maecenas Vergiliusque, / Valgius et probet haec Octavius optimus atque / Fuscus, et haec utinam Viscorum laudet uterque.*

[Horace] May . . . Valgius . . . approve these poems.

163 (epica)

Pan. Mess. (= [Tib.] 3.7.) 179–80: *est tibi qui possit magnis se accingere rebus, / Valgius; aeterno propior non alter Homero.*

[to Messalla] You have Valgius, a person who can gird himself to great achievements; no one else is closer to immortal Homer.

164 (carmina amatoria)

Hor. *Carm.* 2.9.9–12: *tu semper urges flebilibus modis / Mysten ademptum, nec tibi Vespero / surgente decedunt amores / nec rapidum fugiente solem.* (Porph. ad 2.9.1, p. 66 ed. Holder (1894): hac ὠ<ι>δῇ<ι> Valgium consularem amicum suum solatur morte delicati pueri graviter adfectum).

[Horace to Valgius] You with your mournful strains never leave dead Mystes in peace, and your loves do not depart when the Evening Star rises or when it escapes from the swift sun.

165 (1 Bl., C.) *Epigrammata*

†situ† rugosa rutunda margarita

Spherical pearls <? become> wrinkled

Charis., p. 138 Barwick[2] = GLK I p. 108: *margarita feminini generis est . . . ergo neutraliter dicere vitiosum est; et tamen multi dixerunt, ut Valgius in epigrammate* 'situ—margarita'.

situ *codd.*: si tu *Dahlmann*: si [tu] *Courtney*: sint *vel* sunt *Nisbet*: in epigrammatis 'tu . . .' *L. Mueller, alii* metrum non apparet; 'situ rugosa, rutunda / margārita *Morel (alii hendecasyllabum fingunt)*

166–168 Elegi

166 (2 Bl., C.)

Codrusquẹ ille canit quali tu voce solebas,
    atque solet numeros dicere, Cinna, tuos,
dulcior ut numquam Pylio profluxerit ore
    Nestoris aut dọcto pectore Demọdọci
. . . . tra . . . . llam credis mihi sen . . vitam   5
    noctem, non hilarum posse t . . . . e d<iem>
falleris insanus quantum si gurgite nauta
    Crisaeo quaerat flumina Castaliae.

The famous Codrus sings with a voice like that of yours in the past, and writes poems such as you, Cinna, used to write; so that no sweeter utterance ever flowed from the Pylian mouth of Nestor or the wise heart of Demodocus. <If> you think that . . . [lines 5–6 unintelligible] . . . you are in your folly making as big a mistake as a sailor who looked for the stream of Castalia in the Bay of Crisa.

1–8 Schol. Verg. Veron. ad *Buc.* 7.22 'quale meo Codro' (p. 399 Hagen): *Codrum plerique Vergilium accipiunt, alii Cornificium, nonnulli Helvium Cinnam putant, de quo bene sentit. similiter autem hunc Codrum in elegiis Valgius honorifice appellat et quadam in ecloga de eo ait* 'Codrusquẹ—Castaliae'. Serv. Dan. ad eundem locum (p. 85 Thilo): *Codrus poeta eiusdem temporis fuit, ut Valgius in elegis suis refert.*

punctis subnotantur eae litterae quae Keilio verisimiliores quam certiores videbantur.

3 '*fort.* dulcius' *Courtney*   4 *suppl. Keil*   6 d<iem> *suppl. Unger*
8 Crisaeo *Markland, Hollis:* Crisaeae *cod.*

167 (3 Bl., C.)

et placidam fossae qua iungunt ora Padusam
navigat Alpini flumina magna Padi

Where the mouth of the canal links peaceful Padusa, [the ship] sails the great stream of Alpine Po.

1–2 Serv. Dan. ad Verg. *Aen.* 11.457 'piscosoque amne Padusae' (p. 534 Thilo–Hagen): *alii Padum tribus fontibus nasci dicunt, ex quibus uni sit vocabulum Padusa . . . alii partem fluminis Padi, in quam descenditur fossa. Valgius in elegis* 'et—Padi'.

168 (4 Bl., C.)

hic mea me longo succedens prora remulco
laetantem gratis sistit in hospitiis

Here my ship, following a long tow-rope, set me down rejoicing in a delightful place of hospitality.

1–2 Isid. *Orig.* 19.4.8: *remulcum funis quo deligata navis trahitur vice remi. de quo Valgius* 'hic—hospitiis'.

169 (5 Bl., C.)

sed nos ante casam tepidi mulgaria lactis
et sinum bimi cessamus ponere Bacchi?

But are we slow to set down in front of the cottage pails of warm milk and a bowl of two-year-old wine?

1–2 Serv. Dan. ad Verg. *Georg.* 3.177 'mulctraria' (p. 292 Thilo): *legitur et* 'mulgaria', *ut Valgius ait* 'sed—Bacchi'.

2 bimi *Unger:* vini *codd. (quo retento* Baccho *Broukhusius)*

170 (6 Bl., C.)

perfusam pelvem

... (?) a drenched basin

Auctor de dub. nom., GLK V p. 586: *pelves generis feminini, ut Valgius* [*Haupt:*
Vallius codd.] 'perfusam pelvem'.

perfusam] profusam *vel* percussam *Unger:* pertusam *Hollis*

171 (7 Bl., C.) dub.

Sen. *Epist.* 51.1: *tu istic habes Aetnam, †et illuc† nobilissimum Siciliae montem*
(quem quare dixerit Messala 'unicum', sive Valgius—apud utrumque enim
legi—non reperio, cum plurima loca evomant ignem, non tantum edita, quod
crebrius evenit, videlicet quia ignis in altissimum effertur, sed etiam iacentia).

[Seneca in a letter] You have there Aetna, ... a Sicilian mountain of the
greatest renown. Why Messalla should have called it 'unique'—or Valgius, if it
was he (for I have read it in both authors), I cannot discover ...

We do not know either the date or the place of Valgius' birth. But Horace
seems to treat him as an equal, both as a friend (*Odes* 2.9) and as a critic (*Sat.*
1.10.82) and Valgius may have been quite a close contemporary (i.e. born
about 65 BC). He achieved one distinction not shared with any fellow poet in
the circles of Maecenas or Messalla Corvinus, by becoming suffect consul. At
a relatively advanced age Valgius succeeded the defunct Messalla Appianus
in 12 BC and served for a few months before giving way to Caninius Rebilus
(R. Syme, *The Augustan Aristocracy* (Oxford, 1986), 55–6). Although Syme
describes the name Valgius as 'not prepossessing' (ibid.), he conjectures
(p. 395) a senatorial origin, noting *Bell. Hisp.* 13.2 'A. Valgius senatoris filius'.

There is no reason to reject the evidence of *Pan. Mess.* 179–80 (= **163**) that
Valgius was a protégé of the great Messalla Corvinus, and at that time (31 BC,
the year of Messalla's consulship) inclined towards epic poetry. The poets
gathered around Messalla were generally of higher social status than those
associated with Maecenas. Although the linking of Messalla and Valgius in
171 may be a coincidence—and the two appear in slightly different contexts
in Horace, *Sat.* 1.10, lines 82 (see **162**) and 85—it is quite possible that Valgius,
like Virgil in the seventh *Eclogue*, praised Messalla Corvinus under the
pseudonym Codrus in **166**.

Horace in *Odes* 2.9, which we have reason to date to 27 BC (Nisbet and
Hubbard, *A Commentary on Horace, Odes II*, 138), presents Valgius as cur-
rently writing love poems. Ovid, however, another protégé of Messalla, who
started reciting his own *Amores* probably about 25 BC, nowhere mentions
Valgius. So the latter's period of poetic activity may have stretched from the
early 30s to the mid 20s BC. Three of the six surviving elegiac pentameters
end in quadrisyllabic words, suggesting a date in the thirties or early twenties.
166, on Codrus, is connected with Virgil's seventh *Eclogue* (Valgius is prob-
ably the follower) and **165** perhaps with Horace's Eighth Epode, while the
journey poem (**167–8**) makes one think of Horace, *Satires* 1.5.

We must take Valgius' epic (**163**) and erotic (**164**) poetry on trust (**169** is
written in hexameters, but has a pastoral air). Elegy seems to predominate;
166, the most substantial and interesting fragment (but also the most frustrat-
ing) deals with literary matters. Overall the preserved lines make quite a
favourable impression, without suggesting that Valgius, as a poet, approached
the stature of his near namesake Varius Rufus. I have found no imitations in
Silver Latin poetry of Valgius' fragments—but they are too few for this to be
significant—and he did not find a place in conventional surveys of Roman
poetry (e.g. by Quintilian). Valgius also had wider interests, writing in prose
on grammar and rhetoric. And there was an unfinished volume on the prop-
erties of herbs, with a 'religiosa praefatio' addressed to Augustus, including
the prayer 'ut omnibus malis humanis illius potissimum principis mederetur
maiestas' (Pliny, *NH* 25.4). Such political correctness may have gone some
way towards earning Valgius his brief consulship.

162

As Nisbet and Hubbard point out (Horace, *Odes*, II, p. 134), Valgius here is
listed among the inner circle of critics, who are distinguished from the 'more
remote grandees', including Valgius' patron Messalla, mentioned by Horace a
few lines later (*Sat.* 1.10.85 ff.).

163

If the purported date of the *Panegyricus Messallae* (31 BC) is indeed the true
date, Horace would seem to have imitated these lines (by an unknown poet)
in his Ode to Agrippa, 'Scriberis Vario fortis et hostium / victor Maeonii

carminis alite' (1.6.1–2), though Nisbet feels resistance to the idea of Horace being indebted to such a third-rate work.

164

Critics (including Nisbet and Hubbard and Courtney) have naturally deduced that Valgius in his elegies ('flebilibus modis' probably glances at the popular derivation of ἔλεγος from ἒ ἒ λέγειν, as does 'miserabiles / . . . elegos' of Tibullus' poetry in *Odes* 1.33.2–3) lamented the death of a *puer delicatus* called Mystes. Perhaps—but caution is in order. If we had lost the poems of Tibullus, one might have deduced with no less confidence from *Odes* 1.33 that Tibullus had written elegies lamenting the loss of Glycera to a younger rival. In both cases Horace's primary concern may be to convey the mournful and sentimental ethos of elegy in general. There can be little doubt that, for the purposes of Horace's poem, Mystes is dead (witness the *exempla* in 13 ff.) and not merely lost to a rival (as argued by, among others, P. Murgatroyd, *Mnemosyne* NS 28 (1975), 69–71).

Lines 11–12 suggest that Valgius might have used the poetic cliché about the identity of the Morning Star and the Evening Star (see on Helvius Cinna, **10**.2). His perpetual lamentation recalls that of Orpheus for Eurydice in Virgil, *Georg.* 4.465–6 (quoted on **10**). It is possible that *'Amores'* was the title of a collection by Valgius, like that of Ovid and, perhaps, Cornelius Gallus (see **139***a* and on **141**).

165 (1 Bl., C.)

†situ† rugosa rutunda margarita: I have not felt able to mark a line division; it is probable, but not entirely certain, that 'situ' is corrupt. The noun could go with 'rugosa', but the only metrical way to accommodate the quotation as it stands would be to end a hexameter with 'rutunda' and start a pentameter (or a second hexameter) with 'margārita' (thus Morel). Such a lengthening (contrast Maecenas' hendecasyllable, **185**.3 'nec percandida margărita quaero') could not be paralleled before Prudentius, *Psych.* 873 'margaritum ingens' until the appearance of μαργᾶρῖτις in the new Posidippus col. II.19 (p. 35 Bastianini/Gallazzi, Milan, 2001). The grammarian's citation of this fragment as 'in epigrammate' creates a slight presumption in favour of elegiac metre. Otherwise one might reduce 'situ' to a monosyllable so as to make a hendecasyllable line.

'Rugosa' could agree with 'margarita', or else be nominative singular. The former seems more likely; as R. Unger pointed out, the epithet might be used of pearls which are past their best (Pliny, *NH* 9.109 'flavescunt tamen et illae rugisque torpescunt'). Since 'rutunda' describes a feature much admired in pearls, their perfect spherical shape (*NH* 9.112 'dos omnis in candore, magnitudine, orbe'), 'rugosa' would be predicative (Courtney): pearls which had previously been 'rutunda' become wrinkled. Some comparison might be made between the pearls and their wearer; cf. Horace, *Epodes* 8.3–4 'cum sit tibi dens ater et *rugis* vetus / frontem senectus exaret' (3–4) but 'nec sit marita quae *rotundioribus* / onusta bacis ambulat' (13–14).

166 (2 Bl., C.)

Although D. Servius on Virgil, *Ecl.* 7.22 notes that Valgius said something about Codrus, the text of this fragment is owed solely to the Verona palimpsest which is the unique source of Furius Bibaculus, **81** and Varro Atacinus, **123** (see ad loc.). In this case the condition of the manuscript seems to have deteriorated since the nineteenth century, and there is apparently little hope of establishing a more reliable text, especially of lines 5–6.

1. **Codrus:** highly praised by the victorious Corydon in Virg. *Ecl.* 7.21–3, 'Nymphae noster amor Libethrides, aut mihi carmen / quale meo Codro concedite (proxima Phoebi / versus ille facit)', criticized by the defeated Thyrsis, ibid. 26–8, and by Menalcas in *Ecl.* 5.11 'iurgia Codri'. The ancient commentators on the seventh *Eclogue* are confident, in their normal manner, that Virgil uses Codrus of a real Roman poet, and the Verona scholiast on *Ecl.* 7.22 'quale meo Codro' offers alternatives: Virgil himself (the majority view), Cornificius, and Helvius Cinna (praised in *Ecl.* 9.35). Clausen (on *Ecl.* 7.21–2) is prepared to allow that Virgil has a real person in mind. Courtney, however, while admitting (p. 288) that Valgius certainly took 'Codrus' to be a covername, thinks that our poet has misunderstood Virgil; he calls this the earliest trace of the allegorizing approach to the *Eclogues* which later gained so firm a hold. In this instance Courtney may be over-sceptical. It seems indubitable that in the 30s and 20s BC some Roman literary figures did adopt Greek pseudonyms: thus Lynceus in Propertius 2.34 (perhaps Varius Rufus, see p. 281 above) and probably Demophoon in Prop. 2.22 (see Appendix s.v. Tuscus).

Of the candidates suggested by the Verona scholiast, Cornificius has nothing to commend him, and Cinna (who died in 44 BC) would not do for Valgius' fragment—there would be no point in comparing Cinna to himself.

That Valgius' Codrus might be Virgil has at least one attraction: putting Virgil on a par with Cinna could be a response to the diffident *Ecl.* 9.35–6 'nam neque adhuc Vario videor nec dicere Cinna / digna'. But there are several points in favour of Rostagni's idea (in *Studi in onore di Luigi Castiglioni* (Florence, 1960), II, pp. 809–33 = *Virgilio minore*² (Rome, 1961), 405–27), taken up by Nisbet (*Collected Papers*, 401–2), that Codrus stands for Valgius' patron (see **163**), Messalla Corvinus. Codrus' Attic origin would suit Messalla, who wrote bucolic poems 'cum lingua, tum sale Cecropio' ([Virgil], *Catalepton* 9.14); and there was a proverb εὐγενέστερος Κόδρου, which might recall the much-vaunted *nobilitas* of a Corvinus. 'Quali tu voce' (1) could include Codrus' speaking voice as well as the quality of his verse (which is adequately covered by line 2); this too would suit Messalla, whose recitation of Ovid's poetry was praised by its author (*Tr.* 4.4.31–2 'deque meis illo referebat versibus ore / in quo pars magnae nobilitatis erat'). Finally, comparison with Nestor (Valgius, lines 3–4) is more to be expected for a sweetly persuasive orator (as e.g. Callimachus frs. 80 + 82.20–1 in Pfeiffer, vol. II, p. 113, Silius 15.456, cf. Quintilian 12.10.64) than for a poet. Some felt that Messalla's oratory pre-eminently possessed this sweetness (Tac. *Dial.* 18.2 'Cicerone mitior Corvinus et dulcior') and its effect is praised in similar terms (including a comparison with Nestor) at *Pan. Mess.* 46 ff. 'seu iudicis ira / sit placanda, tuis poterit mitescere verbis. / non Pylos aut Ithace tantos genuisse feruntur' etc. So Valgius might be hinting at another sphere of Messalla's activity besides his poetry.

quali tu voce solebas: perhaps one should bear in mind the faint possibility that 'tu' refers not to Cinna but to another poet who has been addressed before the extract starts, so that Codrus would be compared to two of his predecessors. But that seems much less likely.

2. atque solet: Valgius here violates the convention that -que of 'atque' should be elided—a convention almost completely observed by Augustan elegists (M. Platnauer, *Latin Elegiac Verse* (Cambridge, 1951), 78–82), and to a large extent by other poets of the first century BC and AD, except for Lucretius and Horace (see Platnauer, *CQ* 42 (1948), 91–3).

numeros . . . Cinna, tuos: this could mean 'the metres of Cinna'. But we know of nothing which distinguishes Cinna's metres from those of e.g. Catullus and Calvus. In Ovid, *Rem. Am.* 381 'Callimachi numeris non est dicendus Achilles', the reference may in part be to the elegiac metre of which Callimachus was the acknowledged master, but probably stretches beyond that to the whole personal style of Callimachus. Here it seems unlikely that Codrus is being praised for writing in the formidably obscure style of Cinna's *Smyrna* (**7–10**). Probably this is a general and unspecific tribute to the quality of Cinna's verse, following on from Virgil, *Ecl.* 9.35–6.

3. recalling *Iliad* 1.247–9 (Nestor striving to reconcile Agamemnon and Achilles) τοῖσι δὲ Νέστωρ / ἡδυεπὴς ἀνόρουσε, λιγὺς Πυλίων ἀγορητής, / τοῦ καὶ ἀπὸ γλώσσης μέλιτος γλυκίων ῥέεν αὐδή.

dulcior: probably understand 'vox' from line 1. This is not altogether straightforward (Courtney suggested 'dulcius'), because in this line *vox* would have a slightly different sense (*OLD* 5 'sound produced by the voice', 'utterance'), but perhaps is made easier by recollection of αὐδή in the Homeric model (above).

4. Nestoris: if Codrus were indeed Messalla Corvinus (see above), it might be worth adding that Nestor is mentioned in connection with Messalla's poems in [Virgil], *Catalepton* 9.16 'carmina quae Pylium vincere digna senem', but for the different and unexpected point that Messalla's poetry will outlast the three *saecula* conventionally given to Nestor. Messalla also outdoes Nestor (and Ulysses) as an orator in *Pan. Mess.* 45 ff.

docto pectore Demodoci: the epithet (applied elsewhere to Catullus and Calvus) would particularly well suit Cinna, who of all the neoteric poets was most famed for obscure learning. It may also have been suggested by Odysseus' tribute to Demodocus in *Od.* 8.488 ἢ σέ γε Μοῦσ᾽ ἐδίδαξε, Διὸς πάϊς, ἢ σέ γ᾽ Ἀπόλλων (J. O'Hara, *CP* 89 (1994), 390).

5–6. The faint text of the palimpsest allows us to say hardly anything about this couplet, except that the connection of thought with lines 7–8 appears to be 'If you think that . . . you are making as big a mistake as a sailor who . . .' We do not know the subject of 'credis' (5) and 'falleris' (7); it can hardly be Codrus, who was third-person subject of 'canit' and 'solet' in the first couplet. Line 5 may have started 'c̣ọntra'; this might make us expect an unfavourable literary judgement contrasting with the praise of Codrus, but that idea receives no support from what can dimly be read of the couplet. On the other hand, lines 5–8 should still be relevant to Codrus—otherwise the scholiast could conveniently have finished his quotation with line 4. For various attempts to restore 5–6, none of which seems to pay much attention to the reported spaces and traces, see Blänsdorf, p. 268.

6. d<iem>: Unger's restoration is plausible in view of 'noctem' at the start of the line. For 'hilarum . . . diem' cf. Catullus 61.11 'hilari die', Juv. 15.41.

7–8. falleris insanus quantum si gurgite nauta / Crisaeo quaerat flumina Castaliae: in place of the manscript's 'Crisaeae', I have printed the conjecture 'Crisaeo' (I thought it my own, but was anticipated by Markland). 'Gurgite', which by itself can refer to almost any kind of water, seems more in need than 'Castaliae' of a supporting and defining adjective (e.g. Cicero, *Aratea* fr. 33.422 Buescu 'Aegaeo . . . gurgite', Virgil, *Georg.* 4.387 'Carpathio . . . gurgite'). 'Crisaeo' also improves the couplet's balance, with 'gurgite . . . /

Crisaeo' matching 'flumina Castaliae'. The reference is to the Bay of Crisa, κόλπος Κρισαῖος (e.g. Thucydides 1.107, cf. *HH Apollo* 431 Κρίσης . . . κόλπος ἀπείρων), in Latin 'Crisaeus sinus' (Pliny, *NH* 4.7), a term sometimes applied more widely to the Gulf of Corinth. Water which arose from the Castalian spring (near Delphi) did indeed flow into the Bay of Crisa, via the river Pleistus; see Frazer on Pausanias 10.8.6 (V (1898), 248, with adjoining map). By then, however, the sweet stream of Castalia would have been dissipated and spoiled by the sea-salt, unless miraculously preserved like the stream of Arethusa (Virgil, *Ecl.* 10.5 'Doris amara suam non intermisceat undam'). So the mistake of the *nauta* seems to be that he looks too late and in the wrong place; how this relates to the mistake of the addressee ('falleris', 7) is entirely unclear. Courtney (p. 289) quotes Propertius 1.9.16 'insanus medio flumine ["gurgite" in C. is just a slip] quaeris aquam' (of a failure to recognize that what one seeks is at hand and readily available).

Since Castalia is connected with poetic inspiration (see McKeown on Ovid, *Amores* 1.15.35–6), some might see here the contrast between the small, pure spring and the large, polluted stream found in Callimachus, *Hymn* 2.108 ff. (and innumerable imitations). This could provide a link between 1–4 and 7–8, but would leave 5–6 inscrutable. The praise of Helvius Cinna in 1–2 raises the possibility that 7–8 allude to the *Propempticon Pollionis*: after sailing into the Gulf of Corinth (**4–5**), Pollio might conveniently disembark at Crisa and proceed overland to Delphi (**6**), where he would see the Castalian spring.

167–168

These two well-written couplets clearly belong to an elegiac journey-poem, probably relating the poet's own experiences (**168**.1 'me'). For this literary tradition, see C. Hosius, 'Die literarische Stellung von Ausons Mosellied', *Philologus*, 81 (1926), 192–201 (Ausonius does not sustain the impression of a journey, unlike his near-contemporary Rutilius Namatianus in *De reditu suo*). Julius Caesar wrote a poem entitled *Iter* (Suetonius, *Div. Jul.* 56.5, cf. Courtney 187). There was a famous satire in book 3 of Lucilius (97–147 Marx; 94–148 Warmington, Loeb *Remains of Old Latin*, III; I, pp. 122–31, in the Budé Lucilius ed. F. Charpin), describing the poet's journey to the Sicilian Strait, which must to some extent have inspired Horace, *Sat.* 1.5 (the journey to Brundisium). Also it is worth mentioning that in a propempticon the poet might prescribe and describe the traveller's route; Helvius Cinna clearly did that in his *Propempticon Pollionis* (see **4**, from the commentary of Iulius Hyginus).

Courtney (p. 467) suggests that a fragmentary line in a Tunisian mosaic, which he restores e.g. 'quae me sub<bla>xis quondam portantia <celsae / funibus>', with e.g. 'flamina' as antecedent to 'quae', might conceivably belong to this poem. The mosaic depicts various types of boat, together with quotations from old Latin (the latest from Cicero's *Marius*, 18 Courtney).

167 (3 Bl., C.)

1–2. et placidam fossae qua iungunt ora Padusam / navigat Alpini flumina magna Padi: Valgius' boat is sailing from the Adriatic up the Po. These lines describe the point where the mouth of the canal (*fossa*, later called Fossa Augusta, cf. Pliny, *NH* 3.119 'Augusta Fossa Ravennam trahitur [sc. Padus], ubi Padusa vocatur') joins the Padusa to the Po. See R. Chevallier in *REL* 40 (1962), 142–3, and, for a map, H. Philipp in Pauly-Wissowa XVIII, cols. 2183 and 2184 s.v. Padus.

2. Alpini . . . Padi: compare Pliny, *NH* 3.117 on the source of the Po, 'e gremio Vesuli montis celsissimum in cacumen Alpium elati finibus Ligurum Vagiennorum visendo fonte profluens'.

168 (4 Bl., C.)

1. longo succedens prora remulco: *remulcum* = 'tow-rope' does not recur in verse until the time of Ausonius (*Mosella* 41, *Pater ad filium* 9 (p. 20 Green)). Compare Cinna, **5** (from the commentary of Hyginus).

2. laetantem gratis sistit in hospitiis: perhaps this line would have been followed by a tribute to his generous host by name, as often in Rutilius Namatianus, *De reditu suo*, cf. Horace, *Sat.* 1.5.50 'hinc nos Coccei recipit plenissima villa'.

169 (5 Bl., C.)

This fragment has a strongly bucolic air, with three words of no great dignity (*casa, mulgaria, sinum*) in the space of two lines. But it would be rash to infer that Valgius systematically practised the pastoral genre. The milk and wine are probably offerings to rustic deities (cf. Virgil, *Ecl.* 5.67 ff.).

1–2.   sed nos ... / ... cessamus ...?: for the self-reproachful question designed to produce immediate action, cf. *Aen.* 6.806 'et dubitamus adhuc virtutem extendere factis?' (delicately expressed, because in fact Anchises is reproaching Aeneas, not himself).

1.   mulgaria: the lines are quoted by a Virgilian commentator to illustrate a variant reading 'mulgaria' (also given by Nonius Marcellus 312.13, vol. II, p. 487 Lindsay) for 'mulctraria' in *Georgics* 3.177. Both forms (whether regarded as from a singular *-are* or *-arium*) are very rare, 'mulctrum' or 'mulctra' (feminine) more common. Of course the object itself is generally below the notice of smart Latin authors.

2.   sinum: compare Virgil, *Ecl.* 7.33 'sinum lactis' (an offering for Priapus); the noun, here indeterminate, is more often neuter than masculine. 'Sinum lactis' recurs in Columella 7.8.2, but the word is mainly archaic. Varro (*De lingua Latina* 5.123) defines the object as 'vas vinarium grandius', deriving it from *sĭnus*, 'quod sinum maiorem cavationem quam pocula habebant'. In *LL* 9.21 he speaks of the old-fashioned forms of *sina* being driven out by vessels of different shapes imported from Greece.

bimi ... Bacchi: cf. Horace, *Odes* 1.19.15 'bimi cum patera meri' with Nisbet and Hubbard's note.

170 (6 Bl., C.)

perfusam pelvem: there is no evidence that this noun is anything but feminine elsewhere in Latin. One expects the object of 'perfundo' to be the person or thing which is drenched, rather than the vessel itself. Unger conjectured 'profusam' or 'percussam'; I thought of 'pertusam', a basin with a hole in it (cf. Lucretius 3.1009 'pertusum ... vas' with reference to the Danaids).

171 (7 Bl., C.) dub.

Rostagni suggested that Messalla and Valgius may have used the word 'unicus' because Aetna was supposed to be the source (via underground channels) of material for other volcanoes (Strabo 5.4.9, Diodorus 5.7.4, cf. [Virgil], *Aetna* 444 ff.).

Valgius Rufus was a protégé of Messalla Corvinus (see **163** and p. 290 above). Their coupling here may be coincidental, but it is a nice fancy that Valgius accompanied Messalla on his Sicilian campaign (Nisbet), like Tibullus on his Aquitanian. Nisbet and Hubbard (Horace, *Odes* II, p. 135) suggest that Valgius composed a didactic poem on Aetna; Courtney (p. 290) writes 'no doubt prose'. Seneca implies that both described Aetna as 'unicus' (the Loeb that Seneca has been reading both, and cannot remember which of them used the word, but that is not a natural understanding of the Latin). Perhaps the point at issue is which of them wrote first, and which was merely following the other.

The reference to Messalla is not to be found among his historical (H. Peter, *Historicorum Romanorum Reliquiae*, II, pp. 65–7), grammatical (H. Funaioli, *Grammaticae Romanae Fragmenta* I, pp. 503–7) or rhetorical (H. Malcovati, *Oratorum Romanorum Fragmenta*[2], pp. 529–34) fragments. Perhaps it comes from his own account of military service in Sicily during the war against Sextus Pompeius. Another client of Messalla, the poet Cornelius Severus, later wrote a set piece on Aetna in his epic *Bellum Siculum* (**206–7**). It is odd that the *Pan. Mess.* does not mention Messalla's service in Sicily, unless we should see an oblique allusion to it in 195–6 'pro te vel densis solus subsistere turmis [sc. 'ausim'] / vel parvum Aetnaeae corpus committere flammae' (cf. 56 on Ulysses' victory over the Cyclops).

Domitius Marsus

172

(*a*) Ov. *Ex Ponto* 4.16.5–6: *cumque foret Marsus magnique Rabirius* [**229***a*] *oris,* / *Iliacusque Macer sidereusque Pedo* [**225***a*].

(*b*) Plinius Marsum poetam laudat inter auctores Nat. Hist. lib. XXXIV.

(*c*) Mart. 1, praef.: *lascivam verborum veritatem, id est epigrammaton linguam, excusarem, si meum esset exemplum; sic scribit Catullus, sic Marsus, sic Pedo* [**226***a*], *sic Gaetulicus, sic quicumque perlegitur.*

(*d*) Mart. 2.71.2–5: *si quando ex nostris disticha pauca lego,* / *protinus aut Marsi recitas aut scripta Catulli.* / *hoc mihi das, tanquam deteriora legas,* / *ut collata magis placeant mea?*

(*e*) Mart. 2.77.1–6: *Cosconi, qui longa putas epigrammata nostra,* / . . . (5) *disce quod ignoras: Marsi doctique Pedonis* [**226***b*] / *saepe duplex unum pagina tractat opus.*

(*f*) Mart. 4.29.7–8: *saepius in libro numeratur Persius uno* / *quam levis in tota Marsus Amazonide.*

(*g*) Mart. 5.5.1–6: *Sexte, Palatinae cultor facunde Minervae,* / . . . (5) *sit locus et nostris aliqua tibi parte libellis,* / *qua Pedo* [**226***c*], *qua Marsus, quaque Catullus erit.*

(*h*) Mart. 7.29.1–8: *Thestyle, Victoris tormentum dulce Voconi,* / *quo nemo est toto notior orbe puer,* / . . . (5) *paulisper domini doctos sepone libellos,* / *carmina Victori dum lego parva tuo.* / *et Maecenati, Maro cum cantaret Alexin,* / *nota tamen Marsi fusca Melaenis erat.*

(*i*) Mart. 7.99.3–8: *carmina Parrhasia si nostra legentur in aula* / —*namque solent sacra Caesaris aure frui*— / *dicere de nobis, ut lector candidus, aude:* / '*temporibus praestat non nihil iste tuis,* / *nec Marso nimium minor est doctoque Catullo.*' / *hoc satis est; ipsi cetera mando deo.*

(*j*) Mart. 8.55.21–4: *quid Varios* [**146***e*] *Marsosque loquar ditataque vatum* / *nomina, magnus erit quos numerare labor?* / *ergo ero Vergilius, si munera Maecenatis* / *des mihi? Vergilius non ero, Marsus ero.*

(*a*) When there was Marsus and grandiloquent Rabirius, Trojan Macer and starry Pedo . . .

(*b*) (Domitius Marsus among the sources for Pliny, *Nat. Hist.* Bk. 34).

(*c*) I would make excuse for the playful realism of my words, that is the language of epigrams, if the example were set by myself. But that is how Catullus writes and Marsus, Pedo and Gaetulicus—indeed any poet who is read through to the end.

(*d*) If I ever read a few couplets from my own work, you immediately recite something written by Marsus or Catullus. Do you do this as a service to me, as if you were reading inferior works so that, by comparison, mine should be more attractive?

(*e*) Cosconius, you who think that my epigrams are long, learn something which you don't know: often two pages of Marsus and skilful Pedo deal with a single poem.

(*f*) Persius in one book scores more often than lightweight Marsus in the whole of his *Amazonis*.

(*g*) Sextus, eloquent worshipper of Palatine Minerva, . . . please find a place for my little books too, somewhere near Pedo, Marsus, and Catullus.

(*h*) Thestylus, sweet torment of Voconius Victor, as well-known as any boy in the whole world, lay aside your master's accomplished books while I read my little poems to your Victor. Maecenas too, when Virgil sang of Alexis, was familiar with Marsus' dark Melaenis.

(*i*) If my poems will be read in the Parrhasian court—for they often enjoy Caesar's sacred ear—be bold to say of me, as a candid reader, 'That fellow makes some contribution to your age; he is not vastly inferior to Marsus and learned Catullus.' That is enough—I leave the rest to the god himself.

(*j*) Do I need to mention men like Varius and Marsus, and the names of poets who were enriched? To count them would be a great labour. So shall I be Virgil if you were to give me the gifts of Maecenas? I shall not be Virgil, but I will be Marsus.

173 *Amazonis*

Mart. 4.29.7–8 [= **172***f*].

174 *Cicuta* (1 Bl., C.)

omnia cum Bavio communia frater habebat,
    unanimi fratres sicut habere solent,
rura domum nummos atque omnia; denique, ut aiunt,
    corporibus geminis spiritus unus erat.
sed postquam alterius mulier concumbere <fratri>   5
    non vult, deposuit alter amicitiam.
omnia tunc ira, tunc omnia lite soluta,
    <et> nova regna duos accipiunt <dominos>.

His brother held everything in common with Bavius, as is the custom between single-minded brothers: country estates, town house, ready cash and all—in short (as they say) there was one spirit in two bodies. But after the wife of one of them refused to sleep with her brother-in-law, the other one abandoned the friendship. Then everything was dissolved in anger and a court-case, and the new kingdom has acquired two masters.

1–8 Philarg. ad Verg. *Buc.* 3.90 'qui Bavium non odit, amet tua carmina, Maevi' (p. 65 Hagen): *ex quibus Bavius curator fuit, de quibus* [?quo] *Domitius in Cicuta refert* 'omnia—accipiunt'.

   3 atque omnia denique *Pithoeus*: at denique omnia *codd.*   5–6 concubitum novit *codd.*   5 concumbere <fratri> *scripsi* (concumbere *iam Unger, alii*): conubia <fratris> *Fogazza*: <sibi> concubitum <ire> *Courtney, alii alia.*   6 non vult *Buecheler*: novit *codd.* (*v. supra ad 5–6*)   deposuit<que> *Thilo*   7 et omnia *in initio codd.* (*et ad initium v. 8 transposuit Duebner*)   omnia <lite> soluta *Courtney* (<fraude> soluta *iam Peiper*), *alii alia*: desoluta omnia *codd.*   8 <et> *v. supra ad 7*   <dominos> *suppl. Duebner*

175 (2 Bl., C.) *Fabellae*, Liber IX

callum sibi pectore quendam

a kind of callus upon one's heart

Charis., p. 91 Barwick[2] = GLK I, p. 72: *callum neutro genere dicitur . . . sed Marsus fabellarum VIIII masculino sic*: 'callum—quendam'.

176–182 ex incertis carminibus

176 (3 Bl., C.)

Epirota tenellorum nutricula vatum

Epirota, wet-nurse of delicate young bards

Suet. *De gramm. et rhet.* 16.3 (pp. 20–2 ed. Kaster, 1995): *primus dicitur* [sc. Q. Caecilius Epirota] *Latine ex tempore disputasse, primusque Vergilium et alios poetas novos praelegere coepisse; quod etiam Domiti Marsi versiculus indicat:* 'Epirota—vatum'.

177 (4 Bl., C.)

si quos Orbilius ferula scuticaque cecidit

all those whom Orbilius has beaten with rod and strap

Suet. *De gramm. et rhet.* 9.4 (p. 12 ed. Kaster): *fuit autem* [sc. L. Orbilius Pupillus] *naturae acerbae, non modo in antisophistas . . . sed etiam in discipulos, ut et Horatius significat* [*Epist.* 2.1.70] *. . . et Domitius Marsus, scribens* 'si quos—cecidit'.

178 (5 Bl., C.)

hircum et alumen olens

smelling of goat and alum

Diomedes, GLK I, p. 319: *oleo unguentum, ut Cicero in Antonium* [*Phil.* 2.63] '*frustis esculentis vinum redolentibus*', *et Marsus* 'hircum—olens'.

179 (6 Bl., C.)

adipis pondo bis dena vetustae

twice ten pounds of old lard

Prisc. *GLK* II, p. 168: *quae vero supra syllabam sunt, si sint propria vel in* '*ps*' *desinentia, masculina sunt: . . .* '*adeps*' *. . . quae tamen veteres etiam feminino genere protulerunt . . . Marsus* 'adipis—vetustae'.

bis dena *Bahrens:* viginti (veginti *G¹*) *codd.*

180 (7 Bl., C.)

te quoque Vergilio comitem non aequa, Tibullo,
  mors iuvenem campos misit ad Elysios,
ne foret aut elegis molles qui fleret amores
  aut caneret forti regia bella pede.

You too, Tibullus, a companion to Virgil, unfair Death sent as a young man to the Elysian Fields, so that there should not be anyone to bewail soft loves in elegiacs or to sing of the wars of kings in heroic metre.

1–4 Tibulli codd. in fine (*Domitio Marso tribuerunt fragmentum Cuiacianum Scaligeri et excerpta Perrei sive Petrei*).

181 (8 Bl., C.)

ante omnes alias felix tamen hoc ego dicor,
  sive hominum peperi femina sive deum.

. . . yet I am called in this respect a mortal woman happy beyond all others, whether I gave birth to a human being or to a god.

1–2 *Epigrammata Bobiensia* 39 (ed. W. Speyer (1963), 49), *suprascripto* 'Domitii Marsi de matre Augusti'. *eadem* 'de matre Augusti' *sine nomine poetae, Ausonii Opuscula* (ed. R. Peiper (1886), 417).

  1 tamen] Atia *O. Skutsch* (*ap. Morel, Gymn.* 66 (1959), 318) dicor] dicar *ed. Lugd.* 1558, *Scaliger* 2 hominem] deum *Lugd., Vinetus* deum] virum *A, edd.*

182 (9 Bl., C.)

hic Atiae cinis est; genetrix hic Caesaris, hospes,
  condita; Romani sic voluere patres.

Here is the ash of Atia; here, stranger, is laid to rest the mother of Caesar. Such was the wish of the Roman Senate.

1–2 *Epigrammata Bobiensia* 40 (ed. Speyer, p. 50), *suprascripto* 'eiusdem in eandem' (cf. *ad* **181**).

INFORMATION about the life and dates of Domitius Marsus is in short supply. He wrote at least one funerary epigram (**181–2**) on Atia, mother of Augustus, who died in 43 BC—but Marsus' poems could have been composed some years later. On the other hand **180**, on the deaths of Virgil (19 BC) and Tibullus (shortly afterwards) looks like a more immediate response. Marsus enjoyed the patronage of Maecenas (see **172***h* and *j*), though he is not mentioned by any of the great man's other protégés. **174** (the Bavius brothers) joins the attack on one of Virgil's adversaries (*Ecl.* 3.90), while **176** refers to the school for promising young literary talents opened by Q. Caecilius Epirota after the death of Cornelius Gallus (27 or 26 BC). So Marsus' period of poetic activity seems to stretch from at least the 30s to beyond 20 BC, and **172***a* may suggest that it continued for some appreciable time thereafter, since Ovid links Marsus (as an epic poet) with Rabirius and Albinovanus Pedo, whose floruit was in the late Augustan and early Tiberian period.

Outside poetry, we hear of Marsus receiving a letter from the rhetorician Apollodorus of Pergamum (Quint. 3.1.18), who had numbered among his pupils the poet Valgius Rufus (Quint., 3.1.18) and the young Octavian (Suet. *Div. Aug.* 89). Quintilian speaks of Marsus with considerable respect (6.3.108 'hominis eruditissimi') as the author of a treatise *De urbanitate* of which he gives quite a lengthy account (6.3.102–12). It is reasonable to suggest a connection between that work and the epigrams of Marsus, which may have cultivated 'point' to a greater degree than those of Catullus; if so, Domitius Marsus could have represented an important step in the development of Latin epigram towards Martial. See E. S. Ramage, 'The *De Urbanitate* of Domitius Marsus', *CP* 54 (1959), 250–5; id., *Urbanitas* (Univ. of Oklahoma, 1973), 102–6.

Martial clearly considered Marsus to have been a valued predecessor in his own genre, whom he several times compared to himself (**172***c, e, g, h, i, j*); incidentally he reveals (**172***e*) that the epigrams of Marsus, like those of Albinovanus Pedo, were often quite substantial poems. Of what survives, **174** and **180** hint at real quality. Ovid, on the other hand (**172***a*) clearly thought of Marsus as primarily an epic poet, mentioning him in the same couplet as 'magni . . . Rabirius oris' ('magni . . . oris' perhaps meant to cover Marsus too), 'Iliacus . . . Macer' (not Aemilius Macer but the addressee of *Am.* 2.18 and, probably, Tibullus 2.6) and 'sidereus . . . Pedo'. We must presume that Ovid had in mind Marsus' *Amazonis* (**173**), even though that poem did not please Martial. Domitius Marsus may have turned from epigram to epic relatively late in life. This rather unexpected combination of genre was paralleled by Albinovanus Pedo (**225–8**); in the former's case nothing epic has survived, in the latter's nothing epigrammatic.

173

We hear just once of a Greek Ἀμαζονία (one might have expected Ἀμαζονίς), in the Suda s.v. Ὅμηρος (III.526.4 ed. Adler). This may have been another name for the Αἰθιοπίς (attributed by some to Arctinus of Miletus), a poem in five books which could be attached to the *Iliad* by substitution of ἦλθε δ' Ἀμαζών for ἱπποδάμοιο in the last line (see Bernabé, *Poetae Epici Graeci* (Leipzig, 1988), 65–71). As well as the death of Penthesilea, the Greek poem contained the story of Memnon; if Marsus followed suit, he would have answered a question which Virgil attributed to Dido, 'quibus Aurorae venisset filius armis' (*Aen.* 1.751, cf. 8.384). Even when there were no Italian connections, material from the epic cycle continued to attract Latin poets of Augustan Rome, as we can see from *Amores* 2.18 (Ovid's friend Macer, called 'Iliacus' in **172a**) and *Ex Ponto* 4.16 (several examples in my Appendix).

Martial did not think much of the *Amazonis*, remarking (**172f**) that Persius 'scored' (so Shackleton Bailey for 'numeratur', a metaphor from games) more often in his single book than Marsus in all the length of his epic. As an epigrammatist, Martial rated Domitius Marsus highly; so 'levis' here, as well as indicating a lack of epic 'gravitas', shows what Marsus did better, perhaps referring specifically to the *Cicuta* (**174**), for which this epithet would be appropriate (Calpurnius Siculus 4.20 'levibus . . . cicutis'). Martial's pentameter takes us into the territory of Callimachus' *Aetia* prologue, in which the long poems of Mimnermus were represented by a large woman (fr. 1.12 ἡ μεγάλη . . . γυνή) and compared unfavourably with his short poems. For a recent discussion of that vexed passage, see Alan Cameron, *Callimachus and his Critics* (Princeton, 1995), 310–12, who brings in Domitius Marsus (I would not accept Cameron's view that 'there was no epic *Amazonis*'). Ovid apparently thought better of Marsus *qua* epic poet. Any notion that the infamous parenthesis in Horace, *Odes* 4.4.18 ff. 'quibus / mos unde deductus per omne / tempus Amazonia securi / dextras obarmet . . .' etc. might be a hit at Marsus' *Amazonis* seems to me far-fetched.

174 (1 Bl., C.) *Cicuta*

'The Cicuta seems to have been a work as venomous as hemlock' (Courtney 301). Alternatively the title may refer to a rustic pipe made of hemlock-stalks, representing a (no doubt hypocritical) claim to artless simplicity. We are not told that the *Cicuta* was divided into books; perhaps therefore the bulk of

Marsus' epigrams belonged to the *Fabellae* (175), which contained at least nine books. In one or the other collection there must have been a significant number of poems about 'fusca Melaenis' (172*h*)—though Cameron (*Callimachus and his Critics*, 312 n. 52) thinks of elegies rather than epigrams. Clearly one can put no weight on the synchronization of Marsus' poems for Melaenis with Virgil's *Eclogues* in 172*h*; like others before and after him, Martial is confused about the chronology of Virgil's patrons.

Bavius is described by the quoting source as a 'curator'. Jerome's Chronicle under 35 BC (p. 159 ed. Helm²) has 'M. Bavius poeta, quem Vergilius in Bucolicis notat, in Cappadocia moritur'. Scepticism is in order, but Bavius could have been acting for Mark Antony, helping to supervise the kingdom which in the previous year Antony had entrusted to young Archelaus Philopatris Ctistes, who proved a remarkably successful and long-lasting monarch (see R. D. Sullivan, *Near Eastern Royalty and Rome, 100–30 BC* (Toronto, 1990), particularly pp. 182–5); the Glaphyra mentioned by Octavian (161.1) was his mother. While Marsus could have attacked Bavius posthumously, a date in the early to mid-30s BC would also suit the polysyllabic pentameter endings (lines 6 and 8). The text of lines 5–8 is sadly deformed (Blänsdorf obelizes), but this looks like a complete poem of eight lines, a common length in Martial.

1. omnia . . . communia: compare e.g. Euripides, *Orestes* 735 κοινὰ γὰρ τὰ τῶν φίλων, Terence, *Adelphoe* 803–4 'nam vetus verbum hoc quidem est / communia esse amicorum inter se omnia'. When, however, it came to brothers, everyone knew that no less proverbial was 'discordia fratrum' (e.g. Ovid, *Met.* 1.60, Tacitus, *Ann.* 13.17.2 'antiquas fratrum discordias et insociabile regnum aestimantes', cf. *Ann.* 4.60.5 'solita fratribus odia'), exemplified in mythology by Eteocles and Polynices, Atreus and Thyestes. So we may suspect that this wonderful harmony between the Bavius brothers will not last.

2. unanimi fratres: a grandiose phrase (cf. *Aen.* 7.335, Stat. *Theb.* 8.669). The epithet (perhaps modelled on Greek ὁμόφρων) is quite rare and strongly poetical.

3. rura, domum: the family is prosperous, with country estates and a town house.

nummos: 'cash', 'ready money'.

denique: *OLD* 3, 'in fine', 'in short', 'to sum up'.

4. corporibus geminis spiritus unus erat: cf. Ovid, *Tr.* 4.4.72 (Orestes and Pylades) 'qui duo corporibus, mentibus unus erant', Otto, *Sprichwörter der Römer* (1890), 111 s.v. animus.

5 ff. Propertius too felt that κοινὰ τὰ τῶν φίλων should not extend to the bedroom: 'te socium vitae, te corporis esse licebit, / te dominum admitto rebus, amice, meis: / lecto te solum, lecto te deprecor uno' (2.34.15–17). Perhaps we are meant to infer that one wife was content with the ménage à quatre, the other not.

5.   **mulier:** often opposed to *virgo*; a regular word for a wife, though it need not (e.g. Cat. 70.1 'mulier mea') imply legal marriage.

concumbere <fratri>: the manuscripts have 'concubitum novit' (the latter almost certainly a corrupt intruder from the next line). Courtney retains 'concubitum' as a supine, '<sibi> concubitum <ire>', remarking that 'sibi' should strictly be 'ei'. For many other conjectures, see Blänsdorf's app. crit.

<fratri>: the reference would be clear in the context. 'Levir', the technical term for a husband's brother, seems to have been little used except by grammarians and lawyers.

6.   **deposuīt:** this lengthening at the diaeresis of a pentameter is questionable, but perhaps sound. Compare 'apposuīt' at the masculine caesura of a hexameter in [Virgil], *Ciris* 532. If (a lot to ask) the anonymous quotation 'subposuīt humeros' in Auctor de Dub. Nom. (GLK V, p. 593.23) were genuine, uncorrupt, and poetical (? Hercules lifting the sky), that would be another example with a compound of *pono*. The lengthening might seem archaic (O. Skutsch, *Annals of Ennius*, 58–9). Calvus, **31**.1 has 'docuīt' before a vowel. Note 'Oceanūs' in **256**.3 (anon.).

7.   The text is again very uncertain (see Blänsdorf for other attempts). I follow Courtney (*BICS* 31 (1984), 134), agreeing with him that 'soluta' should be retained.

nova regna: I would take the plural to be merely poetical. Previously there had been a state of ideal communism (line 1, 'omnia . . . communia'), now a monarchy with two rival claimants to the throne and inevitable trouble ahead (e.g. Tac. *Ann.* 13.17.2 'insociabile regnum'). As a very long shot indeed, I wonder whether 'nova regna' might contain a secondary and incidental allusion to Bavius' sojourn in Cappadocia, if he helped to supervise the establishment of Archelaus' new dynasty (see introduction to this item).

175 (2 Bl., C.)

Fabellae, 'Tales', like *Cicuta*, is a modest title, but the former seems to have been an ample work (in at least nine books).

callum . . . quendam: 'a kind of callus' (literally 'hard skin'). The qualification indicates metaphorical use of the noun, as in Cicero, *Tusc. Disp.* 2.36 'ipse labor quasi callum quoddam obducit dolori'. For application to the *pectus*, cf. Prudentius, *Peristephanon* 5.177–8 'si tanta callum pectoris / prae-durat obstinatio'. *Callum* neuter is commoner than *callus* masculine, but the latter is found several times, starting in Naevius (*TLL* III. 176. 28 ff.).

176 (3 Bl., C.)

Epirota tenellorum nutricula vatum: perhaps an address in the vocative, and perhaps the first line of a poem. The two diminutives, followed by the high-flown 'vatum', suggest a humorous and slightly patronizing tone. For 'nutricula' in apposition to a male person, cf. Cicero, *In Vat.* 2.4 'Gellius nutricula seditiosorum'. The rhythm of this line (with no word-break in the third foot and only a trochaic caesura in the second) would not have satisfied Ovid, unless rougher versification was tolerated in an epigram. 'Tenellus' is rare, but attested in Laevius (Courtney 124), who also has 'tenellulus' (fr. 4.2 Courtney), as does Catullus (17.15).

We have already met Q. Caecilius Epirota in connection with Cornelius Gallus, whose house he shared (**138***c*). Suetonius may be right in saying that Caecilius read and discussed modern Latin poets with his pupils, but (on the face of it) he errs in quoting this line as proof, since the hexameter seems rather to describe the teaching and encouragement of young poets. Similarly Suetonius writes of Valerius Cato 'visusque est peridoneus praeceptor, max-ime ad poeticam tendentibus' (*De gramm. et rhet.* 11.1, p. 16 Kaster). Sueto-nius adds (16.2, p. 20 Kaster) that Caecilius set up his school after the death of Cornelius Gallus (27 or 26 BC), that he accepted few pupils and hardly anyone who had not yet taken the *toga virilis* (usually at the age of 16). This raises the intriguing possibility that Ovid might have been among the first 'tenelli vates' nurtured by Caecilius. Chronology fits exactly, since Ovid was 16 in 27 BC, and began to recite his poems in public 'when my beard had been cut once or twice' (*Tr.* 4.10.57–8), perhaps about 25 BC when he was 18. Ovid never had the chance to meet Gallus; if he was taught by Gallus' close friend, that might partly explain his first choice of poetic genre. As well as praising Gallus' poetry (**140**, particularly *a, b, d*), Ovid has the temerity to suggest that the charge against him may have been false (**138***e*).

177 (4 Bl., C.)

si quos Orbilius ferula scuticaque cecidit: these could have included Marsus himself. The ferocious schoolmaster was given a kind of immortality when Horace (apparently) coined the epithet 'plagosus' (*Epist.* 2.1.70). Mentioned by Furius Bibaculus (**83**), he is surely the 'grammaticorum equitum doctissimus' in the anonymous passage (**240**) attached to the beginning of Horace, *Sat.* 1.10. There, and in *Epist.* 2.1.70–1, he is portrayed as a champion of old Latin poetry.

ferula: a cane—Juvenal's way of saying that he too had a standard education is 'et nos ergo manum ferulae subduximus' (1.15).

scuticaque: a strap (see Headlam on Herodas 3.68).

178 (5 Bl., C.)

hircum et alumen olens: perhaps the beginning of a hexameter rather than half of a pentameter. The phrase is quoted to illustrate *oleo* + accusative = 'to smell of . . .' It is a nice fancy (no more) that the target might be 'olens Maevius' of Horace's Tenth Epode, in which case Marsus would have attacked both the bad poets pilloried in Virgil, *Ecl.* 3.90 (for Bavius, see **174** above).

alumen: alum (for its pungent smell, cf. Varro, *De lingua Latina* 5.25 'putidus odoribus saepe ex sulphure et alumine'). Probably here used for some medicinal purpose. Pliny in *NH* 34 (for which book he names Marsus among his sources, **172***b*) mentions *alumen* as an ingredient of an emetic (106).

179 (6 Bl., C.)

adipis pondo bis dena vetustae: 'twice ten pounds of old lard', perhaps also medicinal (e.g. Pliny, *NH* 34.168), though the amount seems large. It is often specified that the *adeps* should be 'recens' or 'vetustus (-a)' (*TLL* I, 631.2 ff., cited by Courtney). 'Pondo' is originally an ablative form, but used in effect as an indeclinable neuter noun. Note that Priscian classifies Marsus among the 'veteres'.

180 (7 Bl., C.)

Beautiful lines on the death of Tibullus, which (we learn) followed soon after that of Virgil (21 September 19 BC). See M. J. McGann in *Latomus*, 29 (1970), 774–80. This could well be a complete poem. 'Te quoque' does not prove it to be an extract from a longer list; Courtney compares 'Anacreon', *Anth. Pal.* 7. 263, which starts καὶ σέ, Κλεηνορίδη. Here 'te quoque' carries some implication of 'you as well as Virgil' and an element of consolation ('even you, Tibullus, were not exempt from death'). See further Horsfall on *Aeneid* 7.1.

campos misit ad Elysios: picking up Tib. 1.3.58 (the poet lying sick in Corcyra) 'ipsa Venus campos ducet in Elysios', as does Ovid with *Am.* 3.9.60 'in Elysia valle Tibullus erit'. Marsus (unlike Ovid) preserves Tibullus' polysyllabic pentameter ending, though by 19 or 18 BC taste had turned against it.

3. ne foret: Death is represented as having a particular spite against Latin poetry, deliberately removing the leaders of two genres at opposite ends of the stylistic spectrum. This kind of final clause has something in common with passages cited by R. G. Nisbet, 'Voluntas Fati in Latin Syntax', *AJP* 44 (1923), 27–43, though here we are told whose the purpose was (Death's). It was conventional in such a context to speak as if the literary genre had been totally wiped out by the death of the great man, even if there were others still alive and active. See on Sextilius Ena, **202** 'Deflendus Cicero Latiaeque silentia linguae' (at which Asinius Pollio took unnecessary offence) and Cornelius Severus, **219**.11 'conticuit Latiae tristis facundia linguae'. In the case of elegy, Propertius was still writing (though on rather different themes in book 4), and the young Ovid would certainly have made a hit by 19–18 BC. It is true that we have more difficulty in naming epic poets at that particular time. If Varius Rufus still composed, he was more probably engaged with tragedies; people like Cornelius Severus, Rabirius, and Albinovanus Pedo were still some way in the future. There may have been some degree of self-effacement on Marsus' part if his own *Amazonis* already existed. In any case the literary *topos* is unaffected.

fleret amores: 'tell the sad story of . . .', since elegy mainly concentrated on unhappy aspects of love.

4. forti . . . pede: the heroic hexameter, suitable to its subject matter.

regia bella: cf. Virgil, *Ecl.* 6.3 'reges et proelia', Propertius 3.3.3 (an epic theme) 'reges, Alba, tuos, et regum facta tuorum'. Such passages owe something to the 'kings' (in my view contemporary Hellenistic kings) of Callimachus, fr. 1.3.

181–182

Two funerary couplets on Atia, the mother of Augustus, who died between August and November 43 BC. She was the daughter of M. Atius Balbus and Julia, sister of Julius Caesar. This family name accounts for the Trojan boy Atys, who is a particular friend of Iulus and ancestor of the Atii in Virgil, *Aen.* 5.568–9 'alter Atys, genus unde Atii duxere Latini, / parvus Atys pueroque puer dilectus Iulo'. Dio (47.17.6) tells us that Atia was honoured with a public funeral, but we hear nothing about the deposition of her remains. One might wonder whether she was later transferred to the Mausoleum of Augustus, there eventually to be reunited with her son and daughter. But there is no evidence for Atia among the fifteen 'great ones' (down to the Emperor Nerva) whom we know to have been in the Mausoleum; see Cordingley and Richmond, *PBSR* 10 (1927), 23 (with n. 5, where they omit Octavia). Some inscriptions from the monument have been recovered—brief, stating their relationship to the princeps, e.g. MARCELLUS C. F. GENER AUGUSTI CAESARIS and OCTAVIA C. F. SOROR AUGUSTI (D. R. Dudley, *Urbs Roma* (1967), 196–9 and pls. 65–6). Wherever the bones of Atia lay (**182**.1 'hic'), it seems unlikely that either of these couplets was actually inscribed, though **182** is suitably stiff and formal, and the address to the passing stranger ('hospes') can be paralleled from real monuments as well as from literary epitaphs. As to the date, it seems inconceivable that Marsus could have written 'sive hominem peperi femina sive deum' (**181**.2) of the young Octavian in 43 BC; in **182** omission of the title Augustus might, but need not, be of significance for dating.

The order in which the *Epigrammata Bobiensia* present these couplets (**181** before **182**) is probably not important. **182** might be a complete poem, or else the beginning of a longer piece. I agree with Courtney that **181** cannot possibly be complete as it stands; the two obstacles are 'tamen' (O. Skutsch's emendation to 'Atia' would solve this but leave the other problem) and 'hoc'. Both of these could be accounted for if we envisaged some preceding lines: perhaps Atia had bewailed her early death, but nonetheless (*tamen*) pronounced herself *felix* in this respect (*hoc*), that she had produced such an extraordinary son. **181** could not well follow immediately after **182**; that might suit 'hoc' (picking up 'genetrix . . . Caesaris') but would leave 'tamen' insufficiently motivated. Also Atia is the speaker in **181**; it is far from clear (though not impossible) that she speaks in **182**. If **181** and **182** belong together, the latter must surely precede, and there must be a lacuna between the couplets. On the other hand the two couplets may be quite separate, in which case **182** (but not **181**) might be complete in itself.

181 (8 Bl., C.)

1. **dicor:** 'dicar' might be right—future generations will call her *felix.*

2. **sive hominem peperi femina sive deum:** for this ambiguity of status, compare the oracle on the Spartan lawgiver Lycurgus in Herodotus 1.65.3, lines 3–4 δίζω ἤ σε θεὸν μαντεύσομαι ἤ ἄνθρωπον, / ἀλλ᾽ ἔτι καὶ μᾶλλον θεὸν ἔλπομαι, a pattern curiously replicated in Lygdamus, [Tib.], 3.1.26–7 'sive sibi coniunx, sive futura soror, / sed potius coniunx'. It was alleged that Augustus' real father was not Octavius but Apollo (Suetonius, *Div. Aug.* 94.4, Dio 45.1.2). Similar stories were told about Alexander the Great (Plutarch, *Alexander* 2), but perhaps the closest parallels are with Seleucus I (see Robert Hadley, 'Hieronymus of Cardia and Early Seleucid Mythology', *Historia,* 18 (1969), 142–52). Compare particularly Justin 15.4 with *Div. Aug.* 94.4: in both the woman dreams that she has been impregnated by Apollo; this is later confirmed by an indelible mark upon the body (whether of the mother or the child). Octavian's claimed connection with Apollo arouses intense hostility in an anonymous lampoon (Courtney 473, Vers. Pop. 7, from Suet. *Div. Aug.* 70.1).

S. Weinstock, *Divus Julius* (Oxford, 1971), does not consider this couplet of Marsus to be funerary, and is prepared to date its composition even to the lifetime of the Dictator. Some time in the 30s BC seems much more likely to me.

182 (9 Bl., C.)

1. **hic:** we have no evidence that the remains of Atia ever rested in the Mausoleum of Augustus (see above, on **181–2**). The reference here could be to the tomb of the Octavii, the family of Atia's husband (cf. Tac. *Ann.* 4.44, quoted on line 2 below).

hospes: the usual equivalent of ξεῖνε in an address from the tomb to a passer-by (in a non-funerary context, cf. Prop. 4.1.1). 'Viator' is also common; see Richard Lattimore, *Themes in Greek and Latin Epitaphs* (Univ. of Illinois, 1942), 232–3.

2. **Romani sic voluere patres:** this may allude just to the honour of a public funeral (Dio 47.17.6). For a case of the Senate interesting itself in the last resting place of a more remote relative of the imperial family (L. Antonius, grandson of Augustus' sister), cf. Tac. *Ann.* 4.44 (AD 25) 'ossaque tumulo Octaviorum [*pace* Syme, surely not the Mausoleum of Augustus, see above on line 1 "hic"] inlata per decretum senatus'. Ovid, *Fasti* 4.950 'sic iusti constituere patres' and 6.216 'sic voluere Cures' might echo this line.

C. Maecenas

183

(*a*) *Elegiae in Maecenatem* 1.17–18: *Pallade cum docta Phoebus donaverat artes: | tu decus et laudes huius et huius eras.*

(*b*) Sen. *Epist.* 92.35: *diserte Maecenas ait* [**191**]. *alte cinctum putes dixisse; habuit enim ingenium et grande et virile, nisi illud secunda discinxissent.*

(*c*) Serv. ad Verg. *Georg.* 2.41 'pelagoque volans da vela patenti' (p. 221 Thilo): *constat Maecenatem fuisse litterarum peritum et plura composuisse carmina—nam etiam Augusti Caesaris gesta descripsit, quod testatur Horatius dicens 'tuque pedestribus | dices historiis proelia Caesaris, | Maecenas, melius ductaque per vias | regum colla minacium'* (*Carm.* 2.12.9–12).

(*a*) Phoebus together with learned Pallas had given you their arts; you were the glory and renown of both of these.

(*b*) Maecenas expressed it well [**191**]. You might have thought that he was stripped for action when he said that, for he had a talent that was both exalted and masculine—if only prosperity had not robbed it of its strength.

(*c*) It is established that Maecenas was well versed in literature and had composed several poems—for he even described the deeds of Augustus Caesar, something to which Horace bears witness when he says [*Odes* 2.12.9–12].

184 (1 Bl., C.)

ingeritur fumans calido cum farre catinus

A pot steaming with hot emmer is poured in.

Charis. ed. Barwick² p. 100 = GLK I, pp. 79–80: *catinus masculino genere dicitur, ut Maecenas in X* 'ingeritur', *ait,* 'fumans—catinus'. Cf. Auctor de dub. nom., GLK V, p. 575.

ingeritur fumans ... catinus *Paldamus*: ingeribus fumans ... catinus *N*: et
fumantes ... catinos *Dub. Nom. codd. MV*: ingere et fumantes ... catinos *Dub. Nom.*
L: ingere fumantes ... catinos *Le Clerc*

185 (2 Bl., C.)

lucentes, mea vita, nec smaragdos,
beryllos mihi, Flacce, nec nitentes,
<nec> percandida margarita quaero,
nec quos Thynia lima perpolivit
anellos, nec iaspios lapillos   5

Flaccus, my life, I ask for myself neither sparkling emeralds nor radiant beryls,
nor pure white pearls, nor finger-rings which a Thynian file has polished to
the uttermost, nor pebbles of jasper.

1–5 Isid. *Or.* 19.32.5–6: *inter genera anulorum sunt ungulus, Samothracius,*
Thynius [tinius *codd. BCK*: tinctus *T*] ... *Thynius* [Tinius *codd.*] *purus est, in*
Bithynia fabricatus, quam olim Thyn<i>am vocabant. <Maecenas ad> Flaccum
[*Lunderstedt*: Flaccus *codd.*] 'lucente<s>—lapillos'.

  1 lucentes *Alciatus*: lugente *vel* lucente *codd.*   2 beryllos mihi, Flacce, nec
Alciatus: beryllos neque, Flacce mi, *Torrentius, Courtney*: berillusque mi flacce nec *vel*
sim. codd.   3 <nec> *add. editores*   praecandida *coni. Alciatus*   4 Thynia
scripsi: Thynica *Avallone*: tinica *codd.*   5 anel(l)os *UVF*: anellus *KMNP* anulos
DE

186 (3 Bl., C.)

ni te visceribus meis, Horati,
plus iam diligo, tu tuum sodalem
hinnulo videas strigosiorem.

Horace, if I do not love you now more than my innermost self, may you see
your friend leaner than a young hinny.

1–3 Suet. *Vita Horati* (p. 45 ed. A. Reifferschied, *C. Suetoni Tranquilli praeter*
Caesarum libros Reliquiae, 1860): *Maecenas quantopere eum dilexerit satis*
testatur illo epigrammate: 'ni te—strigosiorem'.

  2 tu tuum *Muretus*: tutum *ACDE*   3 hinnulo *Oudendorp* (innulo *Roth*):
nimio *AC*: ninio *D*: ninno *vel* mimo *E*: ninnio *P. Pithoeus*: simio *Sudhaus, alii alia*

187 (4 Bl., C.)

debilem facito manu, debilem pede coxo,
tuber adstrue gibberum, lubricos quate dentes:
vita dum superest, benest; hanc mihi vel acuta
si sedeam cruce sustine.

Make me crippled in my hand, crippled in my lame foot; build a humped swelling upon my back, rattle my teeth till they are fit to fall out. As long as life remains, that's OK; preserve my life even if I should be impaled on a sharp cross.

1–4 Sen. *Epist.* 101.10–11: *inde illud Maecenatis turpissimum votum quo et debilitatem non recusat et deformitatem et novissime acutam crucem, dummodo inter haec mala spiritus prorogetur.* 'debilem—sustine'.

1 coxo *BQ¹DR*: coxa *Q²E¹*   2 gibberam *D*: gipperum *QE*: gypperum *R*
3 benest *B¹*: bene est *Bᶜφψ*   4 sedeam] sidam *dubitanter Buecheler*

188 (5 Bl., cf. 5–6 C.)

'ades', inquit, 'o Cybebe, fera montium dea,
ades et sonante typano quate flexibile caput.'

'Come here, Cybebe', he said, 'cruel goddess of the mountains, come here and shake your supple head to the beat of the resounding drum.'

1–2 [Caesius Bassus], GLK VI, pp. 261–2: *ex hoc nascitur galliambus repetito hoc metro, sed una syllaba detracta, ut habeat semipedem clausulam, quale est hoc,* 'mea Vatiena, amabo' [Laevius 28 Bl., C.] *ut faciat* 'mea Vatiena amabo, mea Vatiena ama' . . . *huic pares sunt apud Maecenatem:* ' "ades", inquit—caput" '. 1 Diom. GLK I, p. 514: *Galliambum metrum apud Maecenatem tale est:* ' "ades", inquit—dea" '.

2 tympano *ABS, corr. H. Grotius*

189 (6 Bl., cf. 5–6 C.)

latus horreat flagello, comitum chorus ululet
Let your side bristle with the scourge, let your band of companions yell.

[Caes. Bass.], GLK VI, p. 262: *proximum ab ultimo pedem brachysyllabon fecerunt et Graeci et hic ipse Maecenas iis quos modo rettuli* [sc. **188**] *proximum sic:* 'latus—ululet'. Diom., GLK I, p. 515 [sine nomine auctoris].

190 (7 Bl., C.)

hic nympha cingit omnis Acheloum senem

Here every nymph makes a circle around old Achelous.

[Caes. Bass.], GLK VI, pp. 262–3: *si quis . . . quaesierit quid ita, cum sit galliambicus versus, iambici quoque nomen acceperit, hoc versu, qui est apud Maecenatem, lecto intelleget eum ex iambico quoque trimetro nasci:* 'hic—senem'. *adice syllabam* 'Acheloo', *fiet galliambicus sic:* 'hic nympha cingit omnis Acheloïum senem'.

191 (8 Bl., C.)

nec tumulum curo; sepelit natura relictos

I am not concerned about a tomb; Nature buries those who are abandoned.

Sen. *Epist.* 92.35: 'non conterret' *inquit* 'me nec uncus nec proiecti ad contumeliam cadaveris laceratio foeda visuris. neminem de supremo officio rogo, nulli reliquias meas commendo, ne quis insepultus esset rerum natura prospexit: quem saevitia proiecerit dies condet.' *diserte Maecenas ait,* 'nec tumulum—relictos' . . . [see **183**b].

192 (9 Bl., C.)

cardine tornos

on a pivot . . . lathes [?]

Auctor de dub. nom., GLK V, p. 591: *tornum* [? tornus] *generis masculini, ut Maecenas* 'cardine turno'.

tornos *coni. R. Unger:* turno *codd. MV*

193 dub. (11 Bl., 10 C.)

Auctor de dub. nom., GLK V, p. 588: *Quirites singularem numerum non habet;*
nam Maecenas dixit 'Quiritem', sed non recipitur.

'Quirites' ['citizens'] does not have a singular, for Maecenas [? a mistake for
Horace (*Odes* 2.7.3)] wrote 'Quiritem', but that is not admitted.

Maecenas] *fort.* Horatius, *cf.* Cledon., GLK V, p. 42, *semper pluralia, ut manes,*
Quirites; licet Horatius [*carm.* 2.7.3] *singulari numero 'Quiritem' dixerit; sed usurpative*
usus est.

MAECENAS' protégés praised him to the skies for his loyalty to Augustus, his
restraint in not seeking political office, his financial generosity, the quality of
his friendship, and his appreciation of literature. One thing for which they did
not praise him was his own poetry. As E. Fraenkel put it (*Horace*, p. 17,
commenting on **186**), 'There is very little to enjoy. As a hopeless epigone he
keeps on sailing in the wake of the masters whom he admired when he was
young.' The influence of Catullus is almost overwhelming, in Maecenas'
metres (hendecasyllables in **185** and **186**, Priapean in **187**, galliambics in **188**
and **189**), subject matter (**188** and **189**, the Magna Mater), and phraseology
(note how, in the three lines of **186**, he combines two of Catullus' most
famous poems). It is not clear how extensively Maecenas wrote in verse; **183***a*
and **183***c* are vague and unspecific, and should be viewed with caution. In
particular Servius (**183***c*) has no justification for deducing from Horace, *Odes*
2.12.9–12 that Maecenas celebrated Augustus' achievements in verse. The
project (as yet unrealized) is for prose history—and (as Nisbet and Hubbard
point out) 'melius' means 'more appropriately', not 'with greater skill'. **184** is
cited by the grammarian as from 'Book Ten' of Maecenas. Has a title fallen
out? It is hard to believe that Maecenas wrote a single poem of such length.
Was this a collection of miscellaneous verse, or perhaps of Maecenas' writings
in verse and prose (Courtney)?

In *Epist.* 114 the younger Seneca makes a sustained attack on Maecenas'
literary style and lifestyle, which had much in common (114.4 'non oratio
eius aeque soluta est quam ipse discinctus?'). Several prose extracts—some
very hard to understand, some almost certainly corrupt—are there quoted.
Seneca does allow (ibid.) that Maecenas potentially had a *magnum ingenium*
(similarly *Epist.* 92.35 = **183***b*). No verse extracts are condemned in *Epist.* 114,
but in 101.10 particular contempt (on moral, not stylistic, grounds) is
expressed for **187** and its doctrine that life should be prolonged to the last
possible moment in whatever circumstances. From the other surviving verse

fragments one may single out **185** as showing particular preciosity of style, with the artificial word-order of lines 1–2, a fault ascribed to Maecenas' prose by Quintilian (9.4.28) as well as Seneca (*Epist.* 114.7 'verba ... tam contra consuetudinem omnium posita').

184 (1 Bl., C.)

ingeritur fumans calido cum farre catinus: not a grand banquet, but more like Juvenal's picture of the old times when 'grandes fumabant pultibus ollae' (14.171). 'Catinus', a dish or pot, is numbered among the vessels of the eating-table (*vasa in mensa escaria*) by Varro, *LL* 5.120, as a receptacle for *puls* (here 'calido ... farre'), a kind of porridge which preceded bread in the Italian diet—hence a Roman is 'pultiphagus' in Plautus, *Mostellaria* 828. See J. André, *L'Alimentation et la cuisine à Rome* (Paris, 1961), particularly pp. 62–3; he remarks that the attention paid to *puls* by the elder Pliny shows it still to have been important. The noun *catinus* is at home in satire (several times in Horace, also in Lucilius, Persius, and Juvenal). For 'emmer' (a word, I confess, previously not in my vocabulary), see Jasper Griffin, 'Horace in the Thirties', in Niall Rudd (ed.), *Horace 2000* (London, 1993), 9 with n. 30 (discussing our fragment); all made clear by L. A. Moritz, *Grain-Mills and Flour in Classical Antiquity* (Oxford, 1958), pp. xxii ff. and index s.v. 'emmer' and 'far'.

185 (2 Bl., C.)

This could be a preference for the simple life (however much at variance with reality) or a statement that Maecenas values Horace's friendship more highly than all the jewels listed here. Maecenas may have had a special interest in gemstones, since Augustus in a letter (*ap.* Macrob. 2.4.12) jokingly addresses him as (among other things) 'Tiberinum margaritum, Cilniorum smaragde, iaspi Iguvinorum, berulle Porsenae'—all jewels mentioned here, but probably without specific reference to Maecenas' poem. According to Pliny the first Roman who owned a collection of gemstones was Sulla's stepson Scaurus; after Pompey's defeat of Mithradates this fashion greatly increased (*NH* 37.11). For Pliny on jewels, and much more recent lore, see Sidney H. Ball, *A Roman Book on Precious Stones* (Los Angeles, 1950), including p. 46 on Maecenas as a collector.

1–2. lucentes, mea vita, nec smaragdos, / beryllos mihi, Flacce, nec

nitentes: the word-order is extraordinarily artificial. If one read 'beryllos neque, Flacce mi, nitentes', the order of corresponding items would be exactly reversed in the second line (Courtney). But it seems to me that after 'mea vita' we want only 'Flacce', not 'Flacce mi', and that 'mihi' does some work with 'quaero' in line 3 (*OLD quaero* 4 has examples with the dative pronoun, 'to want for oneself'). Also there are attractions (if that is the right word) in having 'nec' identically placed in the two lines. For ancient complaints about Maecenas' contorted word-order, see the introductory section above. The Greek poet most notable for his hyperbata is Callimachus, who may postpone ἀλλά to as late as the fifth word (fr. 110.61), but no parallel to what we have here comes to mind (there is a modest trajection of a first οὐδέ in fr. 178.1).

1.   mea vita: for this phrase applied by a man to a man, Courtney compares Cicero, *In Verrem* 2.3.27 (where a note of irony is apparent) 'ut te praetore videlicet aequo iure Apronium, delicias ac vitam tuam, iudicio reciperatorio persequantur'.

smaragdos: Pliny (*NH* 37.62) ranks jewels in order of esteem as *adamas— margaritum—smaragdus*.

2.   beryllos: cf. Pliny, *NH* 37.76 ff. and now the New Posidippus, col. I.26 τοῦτο τὸ μαρμαῖρον βηρύλλιον.

3.   percandida margarita: 'candor' is mentioned first among the desirable qualities of pearls (*NH* 9.112), shortly followed by a perfect spherical shape (cf. on Valgius Rufus, **165**). For *percandidus*, cf. Solinus 37.20 'solis gemma percandida'; here the conjecture 'praecandida' would be possible but not superior. The phrase, with its intensifying prefix, is faintly reminiscent of Catullus 69.4 'perluciduli . . . lapidis'.

4.   nec quos Thynia lima perpolivit: with some hesitation I print 'Thynia', otherwise unattested (the normal adjective is 'Thynus'). In the quotation, Isidore's manuscripts point to 'Thynica' (likewise unparalleled, though 'Bithynicus' is found, sometimes as a personal name or title) but twice in the preceding comment they definitely favour 'Thynius', and there seems no reason why Isidore should use that unique form if it was not in his text of Maecenas. 'Thynius' might sound more exquisite than 'Thynicus'. Strictly, the Thyni occupied the eastern side of the Sea of Marmora. Bithynia, which had ceased to be an independent kingdom with the death of Nicomedes IV in 74 BC, continued to appeal to Romans for its wealth and commercial opportunities; cf. Catullus 10 (disappointed hopes), Licinius Calvus, **38.1**, Horace, *Odes* 3.7.3 'Thyna merce beatum', *Epist.* 1.6.33 'ne Bithyna negotia perdas'.

lima: on the smoothing of jewels with a file (*lima*), cf. Pliny, *NH* 37.109, Ball, *A Roman Book on Precious Stones*, 40–1.

5.   anellos: the diminutive, balancing 'lapillos' at the end of the line, is appropriate in an admirer of Catullus, though not required by metre (almost

certainly Maecenas allowed a trochaic base to his hendecasyllables, cf. **186**.3).
Pliny (*NH* 33.8 ff.) discusses Roman practice in the wearing of rings.
A document sealed with Maecenas' own signet ring and its emblem of a
frog could cause alarm to the recipient, since it probably contained a
financial demand (*NH* 37.10). Nisbet writes, 'I picture Maecenas as wearing
ostentatious rings, like vulgarians in Juvenal.'

iaspios lapillos: jasper (*NH* 37.115–18).

186 (3 Bl., C.)

1–2.   ni te visceribus meis, Horati, / plus iam diligo: the parallel which leaps
at one is Catullus 14.1 'ni te plus oculis meis amarem', but that is to some
extent delusive. Catullus says to Calvus 'If I did not love you so much, I would
hate you violently.' Maecenas, on the other hand, employs the *topos* of guar-
anteeing the truth of a statement by wishing something unpleasant on oneself
should it not be true: 'if I do not love you . . . may you see your friend . . .' The
basic form (clearly colloquial) is 'peream (dispeream) nisi' + indicative, e.g. in
Catullus 92.2–4 'Lesbia me dispeream nisi amat / . . . illam . . . dispeream nisi
amo.' Maecenas surely had in mind the more elaborate wish of an ill fate on
oneself in Catullus 45.3 ff. 'ni te perdite amo . . . / (6) solus in Libya Indiaque
tosta / caesio veniam obvius leoni.'

1.   visceribus meis: representing the innermost self (cf. Lygdamus, [Tib.]
3.1.25 'teque suis iurat caram magis esse medullis'), but also relevant is that
the *viscera* are the seat of emotions such as love and affection.

2.   diligŏ: G. P. Goold (*HSCP*, 69 (1965), 21) notes that this and all other
trisyllabic verbs of which the final -o is shortened by the end of the Augustan
period are compounds of iambic verbs (in which -o could be shortened more
easily).

tuum sodalem: for describing oneself as 'your friend', cf. e.g. Catullus 30.2
'tui dulcis amiculi'. *Sodalis* is a favourite word of Catullus.

3.   hinnulo videas strigosiorem: the epithet 'strigosus' = 'lean', 'scraggy',
quite the opposite of how we might imagine Maecenas' normal appearance
(more like Horace's Epicurean self-portrait, 'pinguem et nitidum bene curata
cute', *Epist.* 1.4.15).

hinnulo: the text is uncertain, and some editors (including Courtney)
have preferred to obelize. *Strigosus* is used elsewhere of undernourished or
uncared-for horses (Livy 27.47.1, Masurius Sabinus *ap.* Gellius 4.20.11, con-
trasting 'equum nimis strigosum et male habitum' with 'equitem eius uber-
rimum et habitissimum'). It could also apply to inherited characteristics:

Columella (6.37.4) says of the offspring of a male ass and a mare 'strigosum ... patris praefert habitum'. Furthermore (6.37.5) he gives 'hinnus' as the term for the foal of a stallion and a she-ass. Pliny (*NH* 8.172) uses a diminutive: 'equo et asina genitos mares hinnulos antiqui vocabant', and 'hinnulo' (which I adopt from Oudendorp) or 'innulo' (Roth) seem the most likely restorations. Closer to the manuscripts' 'nimio' would be 'ninnio', commended by Fraenkel (*Horace*, p. 16 n. 4, comparing Plautus, *Poen.* 371 'ninnium' and Hesych. νίννον· τὸν καβάλλην ἵππον), or 'simio' (Sudhaus, but the wrinkled skin of an old monkey seems a less appropriate comparison). All the emendations considered above would imply that Maecenas, like Catullus and Furius Bibaculus (**84.**7, **85.**1, **86.**1) but unlike Martial, did not demand a spondaic base for his hendecasyllables.

187 (4 Bl., C.)

This fragment is written in Priapean metre, wherein each line consists of a glyconic followed by a Pherecratean; the metre of Catullus 17 ('O Colonia, quae cupis ponte ludere longo') and also—illustrating its proper use for a hymn to Priapus—of Catullus fr. 1 'hunc lucum tibi dedico consecroque, Priape'. Our lines contain words not normally encountered in higher literature (the adjectives *coxus* and *gibber*) and the tone is colloquial (3, 'benest', 'it's OK', contrast Cat. 38.1–2 'malest .../ malest').

Seneca stigmatizes Maecenas' desire to prolong life at all costs as 'turpissimum votum'; indeed the Stoics approved even of suicide in some circumstances. But in attacking Maecenas because 'debilitatem non recusat', the philosopher might seem on weaker ground, since his own school argued (in the words of Cicero, *Pro Murena* 61) 'solos sapientes esse, si distortissimi sint, formosos'. In *Epist.* 92 Seneca provides something of a counterblast (from Antipater of Tarsus), describing such things as 'crus solidum et lacertus et dentes et horum sanitas' as 'vilia', and the life of physical weakness as 'nec adpetenda ... nec fugienda' (19–20); the addition of 'debilitas' does not make a man 'miser' (22), and Epicurus is commended for being able, 'in summis cruciatibus', to say 'beatus sum' (25).

1. For 'debilis' + ablative = 'crippled in ...', cf. Cicero, *Pro Rabirio Perduellionis Reo* 21 'membris omnibus captus et debilis', Juv. 10.227 'ille humero, hic lumbis, hic coxa debilis'.

pede coxo: the epithet 'coxus' appears only here and in a gloss where it is explained χωλός, 'lame' (*TLL*). It survives in Spanish and Portuguese descendants (see Courtney), and was vindicated—against the variant 'coxa', 'in my hip'—by F. Buecheler in *Rh. M.*, 48 (1893), 88.

2. gibberum: 'humped', the adjective (there is also a noun *gibber*).

lubricos: 'liable to slip', here used proleptically.

3–4. On the kind of cross envisaged (involving impalement), see Courtney.

4. sedeam: Buecheler (see on line 1) suggested but did not approve 'sidam'. In Greek at least a dactylic base to the glyconic would be possible, and 'sessuro' in Seneca's following paraphrase (*Epist.* 101.12) supports 'sedeam' in the quotation for Maecenas.

188 (5 Bl., cf. 5–6 C.)

These lines, followed (perhaps immediately) by **189**, exhibit the technically difficult galliambic metre, so called because it went with poems in honour of the Phrygian Great Mother Cybele (or Cybebe) and her eunuch priests the Galli (often called Gallae in the feminine). For a detailed account of the metre with its permitted variations, see D. F. S. Thomson in his (Toronto, 1997), edition with commentary of Catullus, pp. 375–7. Apart from Catullus (63) and Maecenas, the only Latin poet whom we know to have written in galliambics was Varro in his Menippean Satire entitled *Eumenides* (frs. 131–2 Buecheler[3] = Varron, *Satires Ménippées*, ed. J. P. Cèbe (Rome, 1977, vol. IV, frs. 139–40). There are also two anonymous fragments which Courtney prints among his frs. 5–6 of Maecenas—perhaps rightly, but the way in which Diomedes quotes the former causes hesitation, and I have included both in the anonymous section (**250–1**).

1. o Cybebe: the alternative forms of the goddess's name are Cybĕle ($Kv\beta\acute\epsilon\lambda\eta$) and Cybēbe ($Kv\beta\acute\eta\beta\eta$), to be employed as the metre requires. The speaker is perhaps Attis, the lover/worshipper/priest of the goddess; this line looks like the start of a cletic address, summoning her to be present with her entourage and all her attributes.

2. typano: the correction (for 'tympano') necessitated by metre, as in Cat. 63.8–9.

quate flexibile caput: the wild tossing of the head (cf. Dodds on Euripides, *Bacchae* 862–5, in the related cult of Dionysus, Cat. 63.23 'ubi capita Maenades vi iaciunt hederigerae') is here attributed to the goddess herself.

189 (6 Bl., cf. 5–6 C.)

[Caesius Bassus] describes this line as 'iis quos modo rettuli [sc. **188**] proximum', making it probable that this was the very next line. In that case the 'flagellum' would be carried by Cybele herself, as on a relief from the Villa Albani, where she uses it to control the pair of lions which drive her chariot; see Margarete Bieber, *The Statue of Cybele in the J. Paul Getty Museum* (J. Paul Getty Museum Publications, 3 (1968), pl. 11. She also reproduces (pl. 12 = *LIMC* Kybele 122) a relief on which Archigallus carries the flagellum. In Apuleius, *Met.* 8.28 the *semiviri* scourge themselves.

latus horret flagello: 'let your side bristle with the scourge'. *Horreo* can be used of anything 'covered with protruding points or sim.' (*OLD* 2).

    comitum chorus ululet: Catullan vocabulary (63.28 'thiasus . . . ululat', 27 'comitibus', 30 'chorus').

190 (7 Bl., C.)

hic nympha cingit omnis Acheloum senem: an ordinary iambic line, as in Catullus 52 (nearly all Catullus' iambic poems are either choliambic or pure iambic); Maecenas could have alternated this with some other metrical form, as in Horace's *Epodes*. The line certainly looks like a representation of *Iliad* 24.616 νυμφάων αἵ τ' ἀμφ' Ἀχελώϊον ἐρρώσαντο, where the reference is to Sipylus in Lydia and the myth of Niobe (perhaps also in Maecenas). So, with Courtney, we should probably take Achelous to be the Lydian river of that name (Pausanias 8.38.9), not the famous one in western Greece. For more on the setting, see Nicholas Richardson in the Cambridge *Iliad* commentary, vol. VI, p. 342, and, for ring-dances around water, Martin West on Hesiod, *Theogony* 3–4.

    senem: river-gods are thought of, and depicted, as venerable figures (e.g. the Tiber is 'senior' in *Aen.* 8.32).

191 (8 Bl., C.)

nec tumulum curo; sepelit natura relictos: Seneca quotes this with the comment 'diserte Maecenas' (a far cry from his tone in *Epist.* 101, for which see **187**), after summarizing the views of the Stoic Antipater of Tarsus. 'Sepelit natura relictos' is a fine *sententia*. For indifference to the fate of one's body, cf. Cicero, *Tusc. Disp.*, 1.102 ff. Socrates showed 'se ... nihil laborare' (103) on this subject; Diogenes went further, and 'proici se iussit inhumatum' (104). According to Lucretius (3.870 ff.) the prospect of cremation, embalming, or inhumation could be considered as fearsome as being torn to pieces by wild beasts—if one made the mistake of imagining oneself as a spectator. To illustrate the particular fear of wild beasts and vultures, Cicero quotes the dramatic words of the ghost in Pacuvius' *Iliona* (209–10 Warmington) 'neu reliquias quaeso meas sieris denudatis ossibus / per terram sanie delibutas foede divexarier'. Philosophical unconcern about a body lying unburied was not, of course, typical of the ancients.

192 (9 Bl., C.)

cardine tornos: puzzling for more than one reason. 'Tornos' (Unger, for 'turno' codd.) does at least establish the gender, but 'tornus', as far as we know, is always masculine; the two nouns ('pivot' and 'lathe') together do not form a sense-unit. Something has gone badly wrong with this entry. One might wonder whether it has become displaced: perhaps an original, longer, quotation discussed the gender not of *tornus* (but what to do with that?) but of *cardo*, which is nearly always masculine but feminine in the tragedian Gracchus (**199**). If so, 'cardine' could have been preceded by an adjective which clarified the gender as between masculine and feminine. Similar problems several times arise with this source.

193 dub. (11 Bl., 10 C.)

To say that the singular of Quirites 'is not admitted' ('non recipitur') somewhat misrepresents the position in poetry; the singular occurs twice in Horace and four times in Ovid (see McKeown on *Amores* 1.7.29). If, however, Maecenas used the singular in prose, that would indeed be unique. Some have suspected that the grammarian confused Maecenas with Horace, since 'Quiritem' (from *Odes* 2.7.3) occurs elsewhere in the grammatical tradition (see app. crit.).

Diomedes (GLK I, p. 369) attributes 'nexisti retia lecto' to Maecenas (10 Bl.). Probably a simple mistake for Propertius (3.8.37), though a genuine quotation from Maecenas could have fallen out.

M. Tullius Laurea

194 (1 Bl., C.)

Quo tua, Romanae vindex clarissime linguae,
  silva loco melius surgere iussa viret
atque Academiae celebratam nomine villam
  nunc reparat cultu sub potiore Vetus,
hoc etiam apparent lymphae non ante repertae,   5
  languida quae infuso lumina rore levant.
nimirum locus ipse sui Ciceronis honori
  hoc dedit, hac fontes cum patefecit ope,
ut, quoniam totum legitur sine fine per orbem,
  sint plures oculis quae medeantur aquae.   10

O most glorious champion of the Latin language, in the place where your
wood was ordered to rise and flourishes more exuberantly, and where Vetus
restores with care of higher quality the villa dignified with the name of Academy,
there too previously undiscovered waters reveal themselves, which
relieve tired eyes by the instillation of drops. No doubt the site itself gave this
as a gift to honour its Cicero, when it brought to light springs with this
beneficial power, so that, since he is being read unceasingly throughout the
whole world, there may be more springs to heal the eyes.

1–10 Plin. *NH* 31.6–8: *oculis vero* [sc. *medentur*] *Ciceronianae* [sc. *aquae*].
dignum memoratu, villa est ab Averno lacu Puteolos tendentibus inposita litori,
celebrata porticu ac nemore, quam vocabat M. Cicero Academiam ab exemplo
Athenarum; ibi compositis voluminibus eiusdem nominis, in qua et monumenta
sibi instauraverat, ceu vero non in toto terrarum orbe fecisset. huius in parte
prima exiguo post obitum ipsius Antistio Vetere possidente eruperunt fontes
calidi perquam salubres oculis, celebrati carmine Laureae Tulli, qui fuit e libertis
eius, ut protinus noscatur etiam ministeriorum haustus ex illa maiestate ingenii.
ponam enim ipsum carmen, ubique et non ibi tantum legi dignum: 'quo tua—
aquae'.

... but the Ciceronian waters heal the eyes. There is a villa (something worthy of record) perched above the shore as one goes from Lake Avernus to Puteoli, made famous by a portico and grove, which Cicero (in imitation of Athens) called the Academy. In the front part of this estate, a short while after the death of Cicero himself when Antistius Vetus owned the property, hot springs broke out which were extremely beneficial to the eyes. They were made famous by a poem of Tullius Laurea, one of his freedmen, which makes it immediately obvious that even his servants drew inspiration from that grand genius.

5 ante] arte *Courtney (errore typothetae)*   6 languida quae] languidaque *Heinsius*

LAUREA, as Pliny tells us, was a freedman of Cicero; perhaps he acted as procurator of Cicero's Cumanum when it belonged to Antistius Vetus, and had the poem inscribed there (cf. 'non ibi tantum legi'). There are three Greek epigrams in the Garland of Philip (*Anth. Pal.* 7.17 and 294, 12.24 = Gow–Page 3909–30) ascribed to Tullius Laurea; the first of these is on the immortal fame of Sappho, and contains a sophisticated conceit (lines 5–6) not dissimilar in spirit to the ending of the Latin poem. Our epigram is very well written, and has a distinctly Ovidian air—not just the disyllabic pentameter endings (see on 8 'ope') and the expression of line 9, but also the intricate word-order of 1–2 ('quo ... loco', 'melius ... viret'). The poem consists of two long sentences (of six and four lines), but the couplets are perfectly controlled, with a clause complete at the end of each. I would be quite prepared to date this poem to the second half of the 20s BC, by which time Antistius Vetus may have finished his military career, and had leisure to attend to Cicero's villa.

The new owner is probably C. Antistius Vetus, suffect consul (for two or three months) in 30 BC. We hear of him fighting against the Salassi in 35–34 BC (Appian, *Illyr.* 17) and, as consular legate, taking over part of Augustus' unfinished business in Spain (26–25 BC, e.g. Velleius 2.90, cf. Syme, *Augustan Aristocracy*, 38, 393). All of this suggests a trusted lieutenant of Octavian/Augustus. Tracing him further back raises problems: can this really be the man, highly praised by Brutus, who 'would have been one of the assassins [of Caesar] if he had been in Rome' (Shackleton Bailey, *Cicero, Epistulae ad Quintum fratrem et M. Brutum*, 240), listed by Syme among the 'hopeless or irreconcilable' after Philippi? If so, the speed and extent of forgiveness on Octavian's part seems greater than in the case of e.g. L. Sestius (dedicatee of Horace, *Odes* 1.4). For an indication of the difficulties in disentangling Antistii Veteres, see Shackleton Bailey, *Two Studies in Roman Nomenclature*[2] (1991), 8–9.

1. Romanae vindex clarissime linguae: cf. Cornelius Severus, **219**.13–14 'ille senatus / vindex, ille fori', and, for the loss to Roman oratory when Cicero died, **219**.11, Sextilius Ena, **202**.

2.   melius . . . viret: perhaps a hint of empathy with Nature—the trees flourish more under the benevolent ownership of Antistius Vetus. The implied comparison in 'melius' (and line 4 'cultu sub potiore') might be with an unnamed and unknown person who took possession of the estate immediately after the proscription and murder of Cicero in 43 BC. Or perhaps the point is that the discovery of the springs ('lymphae non ante repertae', 5) has actually improved Cicero's property. Llewelyn Morgan (see below on line 10) suggests that the estate, until taken over by Vetus, may have been left unoccupied and deteriorating for a decade or more.

surgere iussa: sc. by Cicero himself (whether or not he actually planted the trees), it being assumed that any Academy would have shady walks like the Athenian original (Cicero, fr. 6 Bl. = 10 C. 73 'inque Academia umbrifera'). The Romans liked to recreate favourite sites from abroad: witness Hadrian's villa (Nisbet compares the replica of Troy in *Aen.* 3.349–50 'parvam Troiam, simulataque magnis / Pergama').

4.   reparat . . . Vetus: there is perhaps some irony in renewals carried out by a man called Old (so Nisbet).

5.   apparent: 'come into view', 'show themselves'.

6.   quae: there is nothing objectionable in this elision of the relative pronoun (Platnauer, *Latin Elegiac Verse*, 78).

8.   patefecit: the verb could be used literally of removing obstacles to the flow of water (Cato, *Agr.* 155 'sicubi aliquid aquae obstat . . . patefieri removerique oportet', cf. Lucr. 5.597–8 'patefactum . . . / . . . fontem' of a stream of light); compare the metaphorical use of *recludo* in Virgil, *Georg.* 2.175 'sanctos ausus recludere fontis'. There is also a suggestion of the First Inventor (πρῶτος εὑρετής) who reveals something to mankind; in Greek δείκνυμι, φαίνω, φράζω (e.g. Callimachus, fr. 110.49–50 γειόθεν ἀντέλλοντα, κακὸν φυτόν, οἵ μιν ἔφηναν / πρῶτοι, καὶ τυπίδων ἔφρασαν ἐργασίην), in Latin *monstro* (Virgil, *Georg.* 1.19 'puer monstrator aratri'). Often it seems that the invention already existed and only needed someone to draw attention to it.

ope: with 'fontes', of the springs' curative power. When ending a pentameter with a short open vowel, Ovid (quite unlike Propertius) shows a marked preference for -ĕ over -ă (Platnauer, *Latin Elegiac Verse*, 64); more than twenty Ovidian pentameters end in 'ope' (ibid. 65).

9.   totum legitur sine fine per orbem: with special reference to the *Academica*, which were written at this villa (see Pliny's words preceding the quotation). Of these we possess *Lucullus* and *Academica Posteriora*. The wording closely resembles Ovid's hopes for himself (*Am.* 1.15.8 'in toto semper ut orbe canar') and prophecy about Callimachus (ibid. 13 'semper toto cantabitur orbe').

10. **sint plures oculis quae medeantur aquae:** more springs with similar properties will have to be discovered to cure the eye-strain of all those who read Cicero's *Academica*. An artificial conceit, but not much more so than in Laurea's Greek epigram (*Anth. Pal.* 7.17 = 1 G–P 5–6) on Sappho, where he draws an analogy between the number of books in the current edition of Sappho (as if she herself had arranged it thus) and the number of Muses.

There is a fascinating postscript to this poem, for which I am indebted to Dr Llewelyn Morgan (see his paper 'Natura Narratur', in S. J. Harrison and S. J. Heyworth (eds.), *Classical Constructions: Papers in Memory of Don Fowler, Classicist and Epicurean* (Oxford, forthcoming 2007). In the spring of 1452 Flavio Biondo (1392–1463) visited Cumae, Baiae, and the area. He not only saw what was called the Bath of Cicero, but even identified broken fragments of Tullius Laurea's inscribed poem: 'balneum . . . nedum aedificii structuram sed et picturam quoque aliqua ex parte integram conservans, in quo versuum pars pictorum extat, ex quorum verbis carptim lectis coniicere licet id fuisse Ciceronis balneum, cui id carmen libertum eius adscripsisse Plinius asserit'. Morgan comments 'Biondo's proto-archaeological method . . . had rediscovered not only the bath of Cicero but also the inscribed poem of Tullius Laurea which Pliny had seen and copied there fourteen hundred years previously.'

Arbonius Silo

195 (1 Bl., C.)

ite agite, <o> Danai, magnum paeana canentes,
ite triumphantes; belli mora concidit Hector.

Go on, o Danaans, singing a great paean. Go on in triumph; Hector, the check
of war, has fallen.

1–2 Sen. *Suas.* 2.19–20: *Latro in hac suasoria* [de Laconibus ad Thermopylas]
*... illam sententiam adiecit: 'si nihil aliud, erimus certe belli mora'. postea
memini auditorem Latronis Arbonium* [Knoche, *Gnomon*, 4 (1928), 691:
arbronum *AB*: abronum *V*: Arbronium *Bursian*] *Silonem ... recitare carmen
in quo agnovimus sensum Latronis in his versibus: 'ite agite—Hector' ... (20)
sed ut sciatis sensum bene dictum dici tamen posse melius, notate prae ceteris
quanto decentius Vergilius* [*Aen.* 11.288–90] *dixerit hoc quod valde erat celebre
'belli mora concidit Hector'*.

Latro in this suasoria [about the Spartans at Thermopylae] added the epigram 'We shall be, if nothing else, a check on the war.' I remember Arbonius
Silo, a pupil of Latro, later reciting a poem in which we recognized the idea in
the following lines: 'Go on—has fallen.' To show you that a well-expressed
saying can nonetheless be expressed better, mark especially the greater propriety with which Virgil (*Aen.* 11.288–90) expressed the sentiment of 'Go
on—has fallen', which was extremely famous.

MUCH uncertainty surrounds this figure, with regard to his name (Courtney
judges Arbonius most plausible, while Blänsdorf and others prefer Arbonius), date, and poetic composition. One could deduce from Seneca's comment that Arbonius wrote before Virgil, and that the latter, in *Aen.* 11.288–90
('quidquid apud durae cessatum est moenia Troiae, / Hectoris Aeneaeque
manu victoria Graium / haesit et in decimum vestigia rettulit annum') deliberately set out to improve on an already famous epigram of Arbonius.
Chronologically that is not impossible, since Porcius Latro taught in Rome in

the early to mid-20s BC (R. Kaster, Suetonius, *De grammaticis et rhetoribus*, 330). But, apart from the implausibility of Virgil competing with such a minor figure, *Aen.* 11.288–90 are not close to Arbonius' wording. It is more likely that Virgil wrote first.

These two lines (particularly the first) are based on *Iliad* 22.391–3 (Achilles speaks) νῦν δ' ἄγ' ἀείδοντες παιήονα κοῦροι Ἀχαιῶν / νηυσὶν ἔπι γλαφυρῆισι νεώμεθα, τόν δε δ' ἄγωμεν. / ἠράμεθα μέγα κῦδος· ἐπέφνομεν Ἕκτορα δῖον. They could come from a full-blown epic poem, e.g. an *Achilleid.* There is plenty of evidence that Troy (not only because of its connection with Rome) continued to attract epic poets—e.g. Domitius Marsus with his *Amazonis* (**173**) and several in *Ex Ponto* 4.16 (see Appendix). But Arbonius is mentioned nowhere else, and these lines perhaps belonged to a relatively short piece written for recitation.

1. magnum paeana canentes: cf. *Aen.* 6.657 'laetumque choro paeana canentes'.

belli mora . . . Hector: as pointed out by D. A. Russell (ap. Courtney), there is a play between the two languages, since Hector's name means 'he who stays the battle'. 'Mora' can be a physical obstacle (*OLD* 10), e.g. a projection on a tool or blade to prevent movement beyond a certain point. Of people (*OLD* 9) we find *Aen.* 10.428 'pugnae nodumque moramque', Lucan 1.100 'Crassus erat belli medius mora' (further examples from prose as well as poetry in H. Dahlmann, *Cornelius Severus* (Mainz, 1975), 142–4). Homer has (of Achilles) *Il.* 1.283–4 (ὃς μέγα πᾶσιν / ἕρκος Ἀχαιοῖσιν πέλεται πολέμοιο κακοῖο and (rather different) *Il.* 7.211 ἕρκος Ἀχαιῶν of Ajax.

Dorcatius

196 (1 Bl., C.)

neu tu parce pilos vivacis condere cervi,
uncia donec erit geminam super addita libram

. . . and you must not fail to put in hairs of a long-lived stag, until you have
added one ounce above two pounds.

1–2 Isid. *Orig.* 18.69: *pila proprie dicitur quod sit pilis plena. haec et sfera a
ferendo vel feriendo dicta. de quarum genere et pondere Dorcatius sic tradit:* 'neu
tu—libram'.

A ball (*pila*) is so called properly because it is full of hairs (*pili*). It is also
known as a sphere (*sfera*), from carrying (*ferendo*) or striking (*feriendo*).
Dorcatius gives information on the type and weight of balls as follows . . .

THE two lines of this otherwise unknown poet are given interest by the very
convincing conjecture of M. Haupt (*Hermes*, 7 (1873), 11) that this work is
referred to by Ovid in *Tristia* 2.485 'ecce canit formas alius iactusque
pilarum', from a passage (471–92) listing didactic poems on trivial subjects
which never did any harm to their author. Certainly Dorcatius has caught the
mannerisms of the genre: the pompous admonitory tone ('neu tu parce . . .'),
insistence on the precise amount of an ingredient (as often in Nicander), and
just a touch—borrowed from Virgil—of poetical colour ('vivacis . . . cervi').
All of these find close parallels in Ovid's *Medicamina faciei femineae*, which
predates at least book 3 (see lines 205–6) of the *Ars amatoria*. One would like
to know the chronological relationship between Dorcatius and *Med. fac.*; if
Ovid wrote first, that would date Dorcatius' poem within quite a narrow
range of years (say 5 BC–AD 8). Like most (but not quite all) didactic poets
Dorcatius wrote in hexameters rather than elegiacs, giving his work a greater
appearance of solemnity.

For the *pila*, and different kinds of ball games, see H. A. Harris, *Sport in
Greece and Rome* (London, 1972), 75–111, with pp. 109–11 on this chapter of

Isidore ('a strange ragbag of sense and nonsense'). It seems likely that Dorcatius included the 'learned' etymological point (not ruled out by *OLD*) that the *pila* was so called because it contained *pili*.

1. **neu tu parce:** for the emphatic and admonitory pronoun, cf. Ovid, *Med. fac.* 69 'nec tu . . . dubita', E. J. Kenney in *Ovidiana*, ed. Herescu (Paris, 1958), 202. This is common in Nicander, whether expressed positively (*Alex.* 230, 239 καί τε σύ . . .) or, as here, negatively (*Ther.* 574 μηδὲ σύ γ᾽ . . . ἐπιλήθεο, 583 μηδὲ σέ . . . λάθοι).

vivacis . . . cervi: from Virgil, *Ecl.* 7.30 'et ramosa Micon vivacis condere cervi'. Ovid (preserving 'cornua') uses exactly the same line for the same purpose (part of a recipe) in *Med. fac.* 59–60 'et quae prima cadent vivaci cornua cervo / contere'.

condere: to insert (stuff) the hair inside the ball's cover.

2. At $2\frac{1}{12}$ Roman pounds (almost $1\frac{1}{2}$ of ours), Dorcatius' ball would have been remarkably large and heavy (Harris, *Sport in Greece and Rome*, p. 79). In *Med. fac.* 51–100 lists and amounts of ingredients are very much to the fore (e.g. 76 'sed iustum tritis uncia pondus erit', 92 'quinque parent marathi scripula, murrha novem'). One wonders how long Ovid could have sustained interest in this poem; we have only 100 lines, but *Med. fac.* was completed (cf. *AA* 3.205–6).

Gracchus

197

Ov. *Ex Ponto* 4.16.31: *cum Varius* [153*a*] *Gracchusque darent fera dicta tyrannis.*

While Varius and Gracchus were giving ferocious speeches to tyrants . . .

198 (Klotz, SRF I, p. 310) *Atalanta*

o grata cardo, regium egressum indicans

O welcome hinge, which indicates a royal exit.

Prisc. GLK II, p. 206: *hic cardo cardinis. quidam tamen veterum etiam feminino genere hoc protulerunt. Gracchus in Atalanta:* 'o grata—indicans'.

199 (Klotz, SRF I, p. 310) *Peliades*

sonat impulsu regia cardo

The royal hinge rings out at the impact.

Non. Marc. I, pp. 297–8 Lindsay: *cardo generis masculini. Vergilius* [*Aen.* 2.493]. *feminino Gracchus in Peliadibus:* 'sonat—cardo'.

impulsa *codd., corr. Delrio*

200 (Klotz, SRF I, p. 310) *Thyestes*

mersit sequentis umidum plantas humum

Following feet sank into the moist earth.

Prisc. GLK II, p. 269: *humus humi. hoc etiam neutrum in 'um' desinens inven-itur apud veteres, secundum quod oportune hanc declinationem servavit Laevius in Adone* [fr. 6 Courtney]. *Gracchus in Thyeste:* 'mersit—humum'.

plantis *codd., corr. Bentley*

201 (Klotz, SRF I, p. 311) ex incerta fabula

purpuram et diadema

Purple cloth and a diadem

Auctor de Dub. Nom., GLK V, p. 577: *diadema generis neutri, ut Gracchus:* 'purpura<m>—diadema'.

purpuram *Haupt:* purpura *codd.*

197

MANY scholars have thought that Ovid's tragedian is none other than the Sempronius Gracchus, lover of Augustus' daughter Julia, who was banished in 2 BC and killed on the orders of Tiberius in AD 14 (PIR III, p. 265 s.v. Sempronius Gracchus and IV, p. 38 s.v. Gracchus, poeta tragicus). Tacitus (*Ann.* 1.53) has a lengthy obituary notice and a devastating assessment: 'familia nobili, sollers ingenio et prave facundus ... constantia mortis haud indignus Sempronio nomine; vita degeneraverat.' He was thought (ibid.) to have composed the letter which Julia wrote to her father Augustus complaining about her husband Tiberius. If the identification is correct ('nothing forbids', Syme, *Augustan Aristocracy*, 91 n. 67—but one would have liked some positive evidence), Ovid must have known about Gracchus' exile. I wonder if he was aware of Gracchus' death when writing *Ex Ponto* 4.16.

With so few verbatim fragments, we are lucky to have three titles. One of these may surprise. The myth of Atreus and Thyestes was perhaps even more popular with Latin tragedians than with Greek; see Jocelyn, *The Tragedies of Ennius*, 412–19, R. J. Tarrant, *Seneca's Thyestes* (1985), 40–3. We know of seven poets who wrote an *Atreus* or a *Thyestes*, including Mamercus Aemilius

Scaurus (Dio 58.24.3–4, offensive to Tiberius) and Pomponius Secundus (cos. AD 44, Klotz, *SRF* I, pp. 312–14). But it was enterprising, if not rash, for Gracchus to choose (not long afterwards) the theme and title of Varius Rufus' *Thyestes* (**154–6**) which had been produced amid such celebration and official favour in 29 BC. When Ovid linked Varius and Gracchus as poets who 'darent fera dicta tyrannis' (*Ex Ponto* 4.16.31 = **197**), he may have been thinking particularly about those horrid brothers. We should also remember that Ovid himself had written a tragedy (*Medea, SRF* I, pp. 311–12) which could be mentioned in the same breath as Varius Rufus' *Thyestes* (Tacitus, *Dial.* 12.6 = **154***c*).

<h2 style="text-align:center">198</h2>

o grata cardo, regium egressum indicans: both **198** and **199** draw attention (here with pleasure) to the imminent arrival of someone from the palace door at the back of the stage. For this dramatic convention, cf. O. Taplin, *The Stagecraft of Aeschylus* (Oxford, 1977), 71 with n. 3, Jocelyn, *The Tragedies of Ennius*, p. 248 with notes 2–4, and C. D. N. Costa on Seneca, *Medea* 177 'sed cuius ictu regius cardo strepit?'.

Greek plays about Atalanta are listed by S. Radt in *Tr. G. F.* V (Aeschylus), 136. In Latin there was an *Atalanta* by Pacuvius; for the (controversial) satyr play by L. Pomponius (flor. 89 BC) mentioned by Porph. on Horace, *Ars poetica* 221, see Wiseman, *JRS* 78 (1988), 2–3. A tragedy on Atalanta (see Boardman in *LIMC* II. 1, pp. 940 ff.) could have dealt with her participation in the Calydonian Boarhunt—but the main figure in that was Meleager (hence the *Meleager* of Euripides and Accius). Perhaps a more promising theme, touching Atalanta more closely, would be the story of her son Parthenopaeus (named in Pacuvius, *Atalanta* 69 W), whose death is so movingly narrated by Statius at the end of *Theb.* 9.

grata cardo: feminine apparently only here and in **199**; contrast Maecenas, **192** (corrupt) and e.g. Seneca, *Medea* 177 (above). The speaker here welcomes the emergence of a royal personage.

regium egressum: use of the adjective ('a kingly/queenly egress') instead of a genitive singular is high-flown.

199

sonat impulsu regia cardo: compare Seneca, *Thyestes* 177 (above). The metre is anapaestic. A play entitled *Peliades* would tell how Medea tricked the daughters of Pelias into dismembering their father, in the hope that she would rejuvenate him by boiling in a cauldron (*LIMC* VII. 1, pp. 270 ff.). This myth was apparently the subject of Sophocles' *Rhizotomoi.*

200

mersit sequentis umidum plantas humum: the only indubitable occurrence of neuter *humum* (in Laevius fr. 6 C. it could be masculine). These words might describe the marshy district of Lerna (? Thyestes approaching Argos followed by his children (cf. Seneca, *Thyestes* 404 ff.), or a messenger explaining why he could not pursue any further). 'Sequentis' could be either gen. sing. or acc. plur.

201

purpuram et diadema: perhaps from the *Thyestes*, indicating the matters of dispute between the brothers. The metre is not clear.

Sextilius Ena

202 (1 Bl., C.)

Deflendus Cicero est Latiaeque silentia linguae
I must weep for Cicero and the silence of the Latin tongue.

Sen. *Suas.* 6.27: *Sextilius Ena fuit homo ingeniosus magis quam eruditus, inae-qualis poeta et plane quibusdam locis talis quales esse Cicero* [Pro Archia 26] *Cordubenses poetas ait, '<pingue> quiddam sonantis atque peregrinum'. is hanc ipsam proscriptionem recitaturus in domo Messalae Corvini Pollionem Asinium advocaverat et in principio hunc versum non sine assensu recitavit: 'Deflen-dus—linguae'. Pollio Asinius non aequo animo tulit et ait: 'Messala, tu quid tibi liberum sit in domo tua videris; ego istum auditurus non sum, cui mutus videor', atque ita consurrexit. Enae interfuisse recitationi Severum quoque Cornelium scio, cui non aeque displicuisse hunc versum quam Pollioni apparet, quod meliorem quidem* [**219**.11] *sed non dissimilem illi et ipse conposuit.*

Sextilius Ena was a man of talent rather than learning, a variable poet and in places altogether like the poets of Corduba whom Cicero described as 'having something thick and foreign in their tone'. When he was due to give a recita-tion on this same proscription in the house of Messalla Corvinus, he had invited Asinius Pollio to be among the audience, and started his recital with the following line, which won a degree of approval: 'I must weep—Latin tongue'. This was too much for Asinius Pollio, who said, 'Messalla, it's up to you to decide what is permissible in your own house, but I am not going to listen to a fellow who thinks that I am dumb'—and with these words he got up. I know that Cornelius Severus was also present at Ena's recitation; it is clear that he did not think so ill as Pollio of the line in question, since he himself composed one [**219**.11] that was admittedly better, but not unlike the other.

WE probably would not have heard of Sextilius Ena but for a passage of arms in Messalla Corvinus' house, involving Asinius Pollio (thus not later than

A D 4), and for the fact that he shared a home town (Corduba in Spain) with the elder Seneca. The last-named, whose judgements of poetry were not the most rigorous—contrast his verdict on Julius Montanus (**221***b*) with that of his son (**221***c*)—apparently knew a wider range of Ena's poetry, but can give him only faint praise. Martial 5.69.7 (on the death of Cicero) 'quid prosunt sacrae pretiosa silentia linguae?' looks like a combination of Ena ('silentia linguae') with Cornelius Severus (**219**.8–9 'quid . . . / profuerant?' and 'sacris', though both with different applications). If so, probably from Martial's reading of the elder Seneca.

202 (1 Bl., C.)

Deflendus Cicero est Latiaeque silentia linguae: it was customary, when lamenting the death of a great artist, to speak as if he had left no living successors and his branch of the art were totally extinct (e.g. 'Tallis is dead and Music dies'). Thus [Moschus], *Lament for Bion* 11–12 ὅττι σὺν αὐτῶι / καὶ τὸ μέλος τέθνακε καὶ ὤλετο Δωρὶς ἀοιδά, and Domitius Marsus on the death of Tibullus and Virgil (when Propertius, Ovid, and Varius Rufus were still alive), **180**.3–4 'ne foret aut elegis molles qui fleret amores / aut caneret forti regia bella pede'. The consequences of Naevius' death were even more drastic: 'itaque postquam est Orcho traditus thesauro, / obliti sunt Romae loquier lingua Latina' (lines 3–4 of the epigram in Gellius, *NA* 1.24). See further on **219**.11 (the corresponding line of Cornelius Severus).

Asinius Pollio's excessive reaction to this line was no doubt partly due to his well-known antipathy towards Cicero (Sen. *Suas.* 6.14 'infestissimus famae Ciceronis').

Cornelius Severus

203

(*a*) Ov. *Ex Ponto* 4.2.1–2: *Quod legis, o vates magnorum maxime regum, / venit ab intonsis usque, Severe, Getis. / . . .* (11) *fertile pectus habes, interque Helicona colentes / uberius nulli provenit ista seges. / . . .* (47) *at tu, cui bibitur felicius Aonius fons, / utiliter studium quod tibi cedit ama, / sacraque Musarum merito cole, quodque legamus / huc aliquod curae mitte recentis opus.*

(*b*) Ov. *Ex Ponto* 4.16.9: *quique dedit Latio carmen regale Severus.*

(*c*) Sen. *Suas.* 6.25–6: *nemo tamen ex disertissimis viris melius Ciceronis mortem deploravit quam Severus Cornelius* [sequitur **219**]. (27) *non fraudabo municipem nostrum* [sc. Sextilium Enam] *bono versu* [**202**], *ex quo hic multo melior Severi Cornelii processit:* [**219**.11] . . . *Enae interfuisse recitationi Severum quoque Cornelium scio . . . etc.* [v. **202**].

(*d*) Sen. *Epist.* 79.5: *quid tibi do ne Aetnam describas in tuo carmine, ne hunc sollemnem omnibus poetis locum adtingas? quem quominus Ovidius* [Met. 15.340–55] *tractaret, nihil obstitit quod iam Vergilius* [Aen. 3.571–87] *impleverat; ne Severum quidem Cornelium uterque deterruit. omnibus praeterea feliciter hic locus se dedit, et qui praecesserant non praeripuisse mihi videntur quae dici poterant, sed aperuisse.*

(*e*) Quint. 10.1.89: *Cornelius autem Severus, etiam si est versificator quam poeta melior, si tamen (ut est dictum) ad exemplar primi libri bellum Siculum perscripsisset, vindicaret sibi iure secundum locum* [sc. post Vergilium].

(*f*) Charis., p. 134 Barwick[2] = GLK I, p. 105, cf. Auctor de dub. nom., GLK V, p. 588. lacunam supplevit A. Mazzarino, Grammaticae Romanae Fragmenta aetatis Caesareae I (1955), p. 239: < '*pampinus*' *masculino genere dicitur. sed Cornelius Severus in . . .* [deest carminis titulus] *feminino dixit>:* [v. **214**], *cuius moveremur, inquit Plinius* [fr. 9 Mazzarino], *auctoritate si quicquam eo carmine puerilius dixisset.*

(*a*) What you are reading, mightiest bard of mighty kings, comes, Severus, right from the unshaven Getae . . . (11) You have a fertile mind, and among the cultivators of Helicon nobody's crop grows more fruitfully . . . (47) But you, who drink from the Aonian spring with happier results, cherish the pursuit which goes well for you; rightly cultivate the worship of the Muses, and send me some specimen of your recent work for me to read.

(*b*) . . . and Severus who presented to Latium a royal poem . . .

(*c*) But none of these extremely eloquent men lamented the death of Cicero better than Cornelius Severus . . . [**219**]. I will not cheat my fellow townsman [Sextilius Ena] of a good line [**202**], which gave rise to this much better line [**219**.11] of Cornelius Severus . . . I know that Cornelius Severus was also present . . . [as **202**].

(*d*) What could I give you not to describe Etna in your poem—not to touch on this theme which is traditional for every poet? The fact that Virgil had already treated it in full was no obstacle to Ovid handling it, and the pair of them did not put off Cornelius Severus. Furthermore this topic has offered itself successfully to every poet; those who preceded do not seem to me to have pre-empted what could be said, but rather to have opened up the way.

(*e*) Even if Cornelius Severus is a better versifier than a poet, yet he would justly claim for himself the second place [after Virgil] if (as has been said) he had completed his Sicilian War to the standard to the first book.

(*f*) 'Pampinus' is masculine, but Cornelius Severus made it feminine in . . . [the title of the poem is lost]. We would (says Pliny) be moved by his authority if he had uttered anything more childish in [or 'than'?] that poem.

204 *Reges Romani* (?)

(*a*) Ov. *Ex Ponto* 4.2.1–2: *o vates magnorum maxime regum / . . . Severe . . .*

(*b*) Ov. *Ex Ponto* 4.16.9: *quique dedit Latio carmen regale Severus.*

(*a*) . . . mightiest bard of mighty kings . . . Severus . . . [see **203***a*].

(*b*) . . . and Severus who presented to Latium a royal poem . . .

205 (1 Bl., C.) *Res Romanae* (Liber I)

pelagum pontumque moveri

stirring of the water and sea

Prob. GLK IV, p. 208: *inveniuntur tamen duo nomina, id est pelagus et vulgus, quae apud poetas masculino genere ponuntur . . . vulgus . . . melius . . . inter masculina poneretur; quamquam Vergilius et masculino* [*Aen.* 2.99] *et neutro* [*Aen.* 1.190] *dixerit . . . Cornelius Severus rerum Romanarum libro I dixit* 'pelagum—moveri'.

206–207 *Bellum Siculum*

206 (Liber I)

Quint. 10.1.89: *Cornelius . . . Severus . . . si . . . ad exemplar primi libri bellum Siculum perscripsisset, vindicaret sibi iure secundum locum* [=203*e*].

207

Sen. *Epist.* 79.5: *quid tibi do ne Aetnam describas in tuo carmine . . . ? . . . ne Severum quidem Cornelium uterque* [sc. Vergilius et Ovidius] *deterruit* [=203*d*].

208–220 incertae sedis fragmenta

208 (2 Bl., C.)

ardua virtuti longoque per aspera nisu
eluctanda via est; labor obiacet omnis honori.

For virtue there is a steep path and one that must be struggled over with long effort through rough ground.

1–2 Schol. Bern. ad Lucan. 9.402–3 'serpens sitis ardor harenae / dulcia virtuti' (p. 300 ed. Usener, 1869): *. . . ergo cum dicit gaudere asperis virtutem, Hesiodi sententiam explicat* [*Op.* 289–90]. *quam Severus ita scripsit:* 'ardua— honori'.

. . . so when [Lucan] says that virtue delights in difficulties, he is setting forth Hesiod's idea, which Severus put as follows . . .

1 longo . . . nisu *Usener:* longe . . . niu *cod.:* longe . . . cliva *Kiessling ap. Usener:* longo . . . clivo *Dahlmann*

209 (3 Bl., C.)

huc ades Aonia crinem circumdata serta

Come hither, your hair wreathed with an Aonian garland.

Charis., p. 137 Barwick² = GLK I, p. 107, cf. Auctor de dub. nom. GLK V, p. 590: *serta neutro genere, ut Vergilius* [*Buc.* 6.16], *sed Propertius feminine extulit sic* [2.33.37], *et Cornelius Severus* 'huc ades—serta'.

210 (4 Bl., C.)

stabat apud sacras antistita numinis aras

The deity's priestess was standing at the consecrated altars.

Charis., p. 127 Barwick² = GLK I, p. 100: *antistes habet antistitam, ut . . . et Polio* [**136**]; *sed et Cornelius Severus* 'stabat—aras'.

211 (5 Bl., C.)

ignea iam caelo ducebat sidera Phoebe
fraternis successor equis

By now Phoebe was leading the fiery constellations over the sky, relieving her brother's horses.

1–2 Charis., p. 108 Barwick² = GLK I, p. 86: *successor cum masculino genere proferatur, Cornelius Severus etiam feminine dixit* 'ignea—equis'.

  1 iam] naco *N*   1–2   Phoebe / fraternis] phoebei pater paternis *N, corr. n¹*

212 (6 Bl., C.)

et sua concordes dant sibila clara dracones

. . . and as like-minded snakes they emit their characteristic piercing hisses.

Charis., p. 102 Barwick² = GLK I, p. 81 (cf. Beda, GLK VII, p. 291): *sibilus dici oportet, ut Vergilius* [*Buc.* 5.82], *sed et neutro genere quidam dixerunt, ut Ovidius* [*Met.* 4.494] *et Cornelius Severus* 'et sua—dracones'.

  clara] saeva *Beda*

213 (7 Bl., C.)

flavo protexerat ora galero

. . . had protected his face with a pale yellow cap.

Charis., p. 101 Barwick² = GLK I, p. 80: *galeros Vergilius masculino genere dixit* [*Aen.* 7.688 'fulvosque lupi de pelle galeros'] *et Cornelius Severus* 'flavo— galero'.

214 (8 Bl., C.)

†therua† purpureis gemmavit pampinus uvis

[? Three times] the new vine-shoots budded with purple grapes.

Charis., p. 134 Barwick² = GLK I, p. 105 (post lacunam): '†therua†—uvis'; cf. Auctor de dub. nom., GLK V, p. 588: *pampinus generis feminini, ut Cornelius* 'purpureis—uvis' . . . [v. supra, **203**f].

†therua†] helvola *vel* helvaque *G. Hermann*: ter nova *vel* ter sua *Courtney*: tertia *Hollis, alii alia*   gemmavit] geminata Auctor de dub. nom.: gemmata est *Baehrens*

215 (9 Bl., C.)

pomosa lentos servabat in arbore ramos

. . . was watching the pliant branches on the fruitful tree.

Auctor de dub. nom., GLK V, p. 588: *ramus generis masculini, ut Cornelius Severus* 'pomosa—ramos'.

216 (10 Bl., C.)

pinea frondosi coma murmurat Appennini

the pine-wood hair of leafy Appennine murmurs

Schol. Pers. 1.95 (p. 270 ed. O. Jahn, 1843) 'costam longo subduximus Appen- nino': *omnia epicorum carmina ita fere sunt composita, ut proximus pes ab ultimo dactylus sit, exceptis admodum paucis quos spondaizontas appellant, ut apud Cornelium Severum* 'pinea—Appennini'.

217 (11 Bl., C.)

stratique per herbam
'hic meus est' dixere 'dies'

. . . and, stretched out over the grass, they said 'this day is mine'.

1–2 Sen. *Suas.* 2.12: *occurrit mihi sensus in eiusmodi materia a Severo Cornelio dictus tamquam de Romanis nescio an parum fortiter. edicta in posterum diem pugna epulantes milites inducit et ait* 'stratique—"dies"' . *elegantissime quidem adfectum animorum incerta sorte pendentium expressit, sed parum Romani animi servata est magnitudo; cenant enim tamquam crastinum desperent.*

1–2 strati . . . / . . . *codd. dett.*: grati . . . / . . . dixisse *ABV*

218 (12 Bl., C.)

luxuriantur opes atque otia longa gravantur

Wealth runs riot and finds long inactivity irksome.

Diomedes, GLK I, p. 378: '*luxurior' in crimine est, ut Cornelius Severus ait* 'luxuriantur—gravantur'; '*luxurio' autem in laude, ut Vergilius* [G. 3.81] 'luxuriantque toris'. *significat enim non lasciviam mentis sed habitudinem.*

otia *J. Caesarius 1533*: o(r)dia *codd.*   gravantur]: gratantur *ABM*

219 (13 Bl., C.)

oraque magnanimum spirantia paene virorum
in rostris iacuere suis, sed enim abstulit omnis,
tamquam sola foret, rapti Ciceronis imago.
tunc redeunt animis ingentia consulis acta
iurataeque manus deprensaque foedera noxae   5
patriciumque nefas exstinctum; poena Cethegi
deiectusque redit votis Catilina nefandis.
quid favor aut coetus, pleni quid honoribus anni

profuerant, sacris exculta quid artibus aetas?
abstulit una dies aevi decus, ictaque luctu   10
conticuit Latiae tristis facundia linguae.
unica sollicitis quondam tutela salusque,
egregium semper patriae caput, ille senatus
vindex, ille fori, legum ritusque togaeque
publica vox saevis aeternum obmutuit armis.   15
informes vultus sparsamque cruore nefando
canitiem sacrasque manus operumque ministras
tantorum pedibus civis proiecta superbis
proculcavit ovans nec lubrica fata deosque
respexit. nullo luet hoc Antonius aevo.
hoc nec in Emathio mitis victoria Perse
nec te, dire Syphax, non fecit <in> hoste Philippo,
inque triumphato ludibria cuncta Iugurtha
afuerunt, nostraeque cadens ferus Hannibal irae
membra tamen Stygias tulit inviolata sub umbras.   25

The heads of great-hearted men, still almost breathing, lay on the rostra which had been theirs, but the sight of ravaged Cicero, as if he were the only one, drew away the attention of all. Then the mighty deeds which he performed as consul come back to their minds: (5) the bands of conspirators, the detection of criminal compacts and the blotting out of aristocratic wickedness; they remember too Cethegus' punishment and Catiline cast down from his abominable ambitions. What good had the people's support and his public meetings done to him, or the sacred arts with which he adorned his life? (10) A single day snatched away the glory of the age, and, struck by grief, the eloquence of the Latin tongue sadly fell silent. He who was previously the supreme protector and saviour of the distressed, always the outstanding head of his country, he the champion of the Senate, (15) the public mouthpiece of the laws, religion, and civil life, for ever grew dumb through cruel arms. A fellow citizen cast down and joyfully trampled with arrogant feet the disfigured face, the white hair foully spattered with blood, those sacred hands which had helped to produce such great works, taking no thought for the slippery fates or the gods. (20) No amount of time will suffice for Antony to expiate this deed. Our gentle victory did not behave thus in the case of Macedonian Perseus or in yours, dread Syphax, nor in dealing with our enemy Philip; when we triumphed over Jugurtha no humiliation occurred, and when cruel Hannibal succumbed to our wrath, (25) nonetheless he took down his limbs unmutilated to the Stygian shades.

1–25 Sen. *Suas.* 6.26: *nemo tamen ex tot disertissimis viris melius Ciceronis mortem deploravit quam Severus Cornelius* 'oraque—sub umbras'.

11 Sen. *Suas.* 6.27: *non fraudabo municipem nostrum* [sc. Sextilium Enam] *bono versu* [sc. **202**], *ex quo hic multo melior Severi Cornelii processit* 'conticuit—linguae'.

6 exstinctum] est hunc *codd.*: exstincti *Håkanson*: exstinctum et *Gronovius* (et *ante* poena *cod. D.*)   9 profuerunt *D*   exculta *Kiessling*: etuita *ABVD*: exacta *Pithoeus*: devota *Gertz*   14 ritusque] iurisque *Heinsius*   15 evis *AB*: eius *VD²*: aevis *D¹, corr. Scaliger*   18 civis *V*: avis *D¹*: vices *AB*   22 fecit <in> *ed. Ven. 1490–1503*: fecerat *Kiessling*   24 afuerunt *Heinsius*: -at *codd.*: afuerant *Kiessling*

220 (14 Bl., C.)

tragica syrma

with tragic robe

Auctor de dub. nom., GLK V, p. 590: *syrma generis neutri; priores feminini, ut Cornelius* 'tragica syrma'.

tria greca syrma *V*: tragrema casyr *M, corr. Haupt*

203

THERE is a detailed linguistic study of this poet (covering also Albinovanus Pedo, Julius Montanus, Dorcatius, and Arbronius Silo) by H. Dahlmann, *Cornelius Severus* (Mainz, 1975).

Cornelius Severus belongs to a group of epic poets whose activity spanned the principates of Augustus and Tiberius. Their subject matter, for the most part, seems to have been Roman history of the not too distant past. Other members of this group were Rabirius and Albinovanus Pedo; perhaps we should add the unknown author (both Severus and Rabirius have been suggested, though the (mediocre) poem may be somewhat later) of the Herculaneum epic conventionally known as 'De Bello Actiaco' (Courtney 334–40). Like the anonymous epic, the fragments of Severus and Pedo betray very strong rhetorical influence; the only long extracts which we possess are quoted to show how poets could compete with, and even outdo, declaimers and prose historians. It is reasonable to see these authors as stepping stones on the way to the much more individual epic talent of Lucan.

All three poets receive a mention, and half-hearted commendation, from Quintilian: Rabirius and Pedo were 'non indigni cognitione, si vacet' (10.1.90) and Severus 'versificator quam poeta melior' (10.1.89). But Quintilian does link this somewhat disparaging remark with warmer praise for Cornelius Severus: if he had written the whole of his *Bellum Siculum* to the standard of the first book—we are left in doubt whether the epic was unfinished or completed to an inferior standard—Severus would deserve to be called the second-best Latin hexameter poet (**203***e*), behind only Virgil. And the younger Seneca, a more exacting critic of poetry than his father (compare their verdicts on Julius Montanus, **221***b* and *c*) indicates that, when it came to describing Etna, Severus (**203***d*) fully held his own against both Virgil and Ovid. **203***f* is corrupt and very puzzling; it seems that the elder Pliny would, in general, have granted 'auctoritas' to Cornelius Severus, but withheld it in this particular case because of the 'puerilitas' either of the line quoted (**214**, it is hard to see why) or of the whole poem from which the quotation derived. There may be a hint here of uneven quality, as, perhaps, in the *Bellum Siculum* (above).

The anecdote attached to **219** (from Seneca, *Suasoriae* 6.27) sets Cornelius Severus at a literary gathering in the house of Messalla Corvinus at some date before the death of Asinius Pollio (A D 4). Presumably Seneca himself was present; perhaps Ovid too, since *Ex Ponto* 2.3.75 seems to allude to Severus **219**.11 (see ad loc.) and through it to the line of Sextilius Ena (**202**) at which Pollio took somewhat unnecessary offence. In *Ex Ponto* 4.2.3–4 Ovid apologizes for the fact that this is the first poetic epistle addressed to Cornelius Severus by name—strong evidence that the Severus of *Ex Ponto* 1.8 is someone different. At the same time, however, Ovid reveals (4.2.5–6) that the two have been conducting a regular correspondence in prose. So it seems clear that they were personal friends as well as fellow poets; this friendship could well have arisen from a shared connection with the family of Messalla Corvinus. Although the great man was probably dead (Syme, *History in Ovid* (Oxford, 1978), 122 ff. for the date) before Severus embarked on his *Bellum Siculum*, that subject offered scope for praising Messalla which could have pleased his sons Messallinus and Cotta.

Ovid describes Severus as unusually prolific (*Ex Ponto* 4.2.11–12 = **203***a*). Two titles are preserved, *Res Romanae* (**205**) and *Bellum Siculum* (**206–7**). A title was probably cited for **214**, but has perished in the lacuna (see **203***f*). References in Ovid (**204**) suggest that Severus also wrote on kings; since that poem was something of a national monument (**204***b*), it almost certainly dealt with Roman (or conceivably Alban) rather than Greek kings, and I have provisionally labelled it *Reges Romani*. The only long fragment of Severus (**219**) probably belongs to *Res Romanae*; there seems no point in trying to link this either with the poem about kings (which would then have to cover an enormous span of Roman history) or with the *Bellum Siculum* (which we know to have had its own book numeration).

204 *Reges Romani* (?)

Ovid's 'quique dedit Latio carmen regale Severus' (*Ex Ponto* 4.16.9) suggests that this poem was on a national theme (cf. *AA* 3.338 on the *Aeneid* 'qua nullum Latio clarius extat opus') and that the style matched the subject matter (cf. *Tristia* 2.553 on his own *Medea*, 'dedimus tragicis scriptum regale coturnis'). The kings of Rome seem to offer more scope than those of Alba Longa, though the latter constitute an epic theme in a Propertian *recusatio* (3.3.3–4 'reges, Alba, tuos, et regum facta tuorum, / tantum operis, nervis hiscere posse meis'). Servius on Virgil, *Ecl.* 6.3 'cum canerem reges et proelia' has a nice fancy, not to be taken seriously, that Virgil attempted to write the deeds of Alban kings, 'quae coepta omisit nominum asperitate deterritus' (Ovid has no problem with their names in *Met.* 14.609–22).

'Vates magnorum maxime regum' (*Ex Ponto* 4.2.1) would inevitably recall the kings about whom Callimachus failed to write (fr. 1.3–4, perhaps βασιλ[ήων / πρήξι]ας); when lamenting the death of Virgil, Domitius Marsus (**180**.4) speaks of 'regia bella' as the typical subject matter of epic. Severus sets his sights high, and (if we are to believe Ovid) achieved success.

At least **213** might come from this poem, since use of a *galerus* as a protective helmet in warfare would suit the primitive age (cf. *Aen.* 7.688, Prop. 4.1.29).

205 (1 Bl., C.) *Res Romanae*

pelagum pontumque moveri: the masculine accusative 'pelagum' is paralleled only in Vitruvius 2.8.14 (v.l. 'pelagus'). No doubt the analogy is with *vulgus*, but 'vulgum' (*Aen.* 2.99) has more justification than 'pelagum' because the latter is derived from a Greek neuter noun. 'Pontumque moveri' = Virgil, *Georg.* 1.130; it seems unlikely that Severus is making any distinction of sense between 'pelagus' and 'pontus'. This citation may, like several other fragments of Severus, derive from Caper's *De Latinitate*, compiled in the second century (A. C. Dionisotti, *JRS* 74 (1984), 205–6).

Res Romanae (for the phrase, cf. Virgil, *Georg.* 2.498) may be meant to parallel Greek epic titles in the neuter plural, e.g. Μηδικά/Περσικά (Choerilus of Samos, *SH* **314**), Μεσσηνιακά (Rhianus, fr. 49 ff. Powell) and several other similar titles. The long fragment on the death of Cicero (**219**) could belong to this poem.

206–207 *Bellum Siculum*

To write poems on particular wars had been a long-standing Roman tradition, going back to the *Bellum Poenicum* of Naevius; from the late Republican and triumviral periods we hear of Varro Atacinus' *Bellum Sequanicum* (**106–7**) and the *Annales Belli Gallici* by Furius Bibaculus (**72–81**), both celebrating Julius Caesar's campaigns. But the Sicilian war against Sextus Pompeius would have caused certain problems to any poet. Although another Propertian *recusatio* mentions 'Siculae classica bella fugae' (2.1.28) in a list containing the even more double-edged example of Perusia (29, 'eversosque focos antiquae gentis Etruscae'), no poet, as far as we know, attempted a *Bellum Siculum* before Cornelius Severus at the very end of Augustus' reign or even after Augustus' death (at any rate after Ovid's *Metamorphoses*, as shown by **207**).

Octavian's own propaganda had presented the war as a piratical and servile uprising (*Res Gestae* 5.25, cf. Horace, *Epodes* 4.19 'contra latrones atque servilem manum', Velleius Paterculus 2.73, Lucan 1.43 'ardenti servilia bella sub Aetna'). This would inevitably diminish the glory of victory. Furthermore, Octavian had not had great personal success, becoming the target of an epigram: 'postquam bis classe victus navem perdidit, / aliquando ut vincat, ludit assidue aleam' (Courtney 475, from Suetonius, *Div. Aug.* 70.2). It would be interesting to know how much credit Cornelius Severus allowed to Agrippa.

Although the Sicilian war did not bring great glory to Octavian, Messalla Corvinus (who may have been Severus' patron) played a notable part in the final year of the war, if we are to believe Appian (*BC* 5.102–13, probably from Messalla's own memoirs, cf. Syme, *History in Ovid*, 132). There would even be scope for extolling Messalla at Octavian's expense, as we can see from Appian 5.113 where the historian, after relating Messalla's proscription, his escape to Brutus and Cassius, and his surrender to Antony, launches into a eulogy of the way Corvinus saved from dire distress the man who had proscribed him: καί μοι τοῦτο ἀναμνῆσαι νῦν ἔδοξεν ἐς ζήλωμα τῆς Ῥωμαίων ἀρετῆς, ὅπου Μεσσάλας, μόνον ἔχων ἐν τοσῆιδε συμφορᾶι τὸν προγράψαντα ἐθεράπευεν ὡς αὐτοκράτορα καὶ περιέσωιζεν. The *Panegyricus Messallae* is reticent about Sicily (likewise Tibullus 1.7), but it may be more than coincidence that we read there at line 56 'cessit et Aetnaeae Neptunius incola rupis' of Odysseus, outdone by Messalla who helped to defeat another son of Neptune (Horace, *Epod.* 9.7–8 'Neptunius / dux') in Sicily, and that the author would be prepared for Messalla's sake 'vel densis solus subsistere turmis / vel parvum Aetnaeae corpus committere flammae' (195–6).

We shall see (**207**) that Cornelius Severus' epic included a set piece (of which the younger Seneca approved) on Mount Aetna. Much more tentatively, one may be able to identify another set piece from this poem. In Lucan 6.813–14 the soldier's ghost refuses to tell Sextus Pompeius of his own fate, because

> tibi certior omnia vates
> ipse canet Siculis genitor Pompeius in arvis.

These words do not cohere with anything in our text of Lucan. Morford (*The Poet Lucan,* 72) wrote 'Evidently Pompey's ghost would have appeared in the later part of the poem which Lucan did not live to complete.' But it is hard to believe that Lucan would have extended his epic to the Sicilian war, necessitating either a poem of inordinate length or a somewhat ludicrous acceleration in the pace of the narrative. And Cornelia does in fact pass on posthumous advice from Pompey to his sons, with a hint of naval warfare (93 ff.), in Lucan 9.87 ff. P. Grenade in *REA* 52 (1950), 52–3, suggested (the same idea occurred to me independently) that Lucan in 6.813–14 is making a literary allusion to Cornelius Severus' epic. The *Adnotationes super Lucanum* (p. 245 Endt, on 6.814), though almost certainly just an imaginative expansion of Lucan's text, indicates what one might expect: 'mox enim in Sicilia hic somniaturus est patrem suum Pompeium ad se venientem et suadentem sibi ut fugiat; unde fatum, quod sibi immineat, recognoscet'. Such a scene would recall the appearance of Hector to Aeneas (*Aen.* 2.270 ff.) and of Dido to Anna (Ovid, *Fasti* 3.639 ff.).

207

At the head of his list of Latin poets who wrote of Etna, Seneca could have placed Lucretius (6.639–702, cf. 1.722–5). Without much doubt the mention of Cornelius Severus refers to the *Bellum Siculum* (cf. Lucan 1.43 'ardenti servilia bella sub Aetna', which might also recall Severus). Appian describes spectacular volcanic activity in the last year of the war, ἐγένοντο δὲ καὶ βρόμοι τῆς Αἴτνης σκληροὶ καὶ μυκήματα μακρὰ καὶ σέλα περιλάμποντα τὴν στρατιάν (5.117, 36 bc). This might suggest that the passage on Etna did not belong to the most celebrated (**206**) first book. But of course the poet could have prefaced his account of the war with a general account of Sicily, including Etna. It may be coincidence that Messalla and (? another) protégé of his, Valgius Rufus, are linked with regard to Etna in **171**.

The poem entitled *Aetna* in the Appendix Vergiliana (which some used to give to Cornelius Severus) may be of late Neronian or Vespasianic date (H. M. Hine in the *OCD*³, p. 31).

208 (2 Bl., C.)

1–2. Nisbet, while agreeing that 'longo . . . nisu' (so Usener) goes with 'eluctanda', doubts whether, to ancient feeling, there would be a pause after 'eluctanda': 'Modern punctuation underlines the syntax; ancient colometry emphasized the rhetorical phrasing.'

As the quoting source perceived, Severus imitates the famous lines of Hesiod on the paths of κακότης and ἀρετή (*Works and Days* 287 ff.), Rzach in his 1902 edition of Hesiod, ad loc., collects much material which no doubt could be augmented (e.g. with Prudentius, *Contra Symmachum* 2.149–50 'luctantem summis conatibus, inter acerba / sectandum virtutis iter'). Silius (4.603–4) might be imitating our passage: 'perque aspera duro / nititur ad laudem virtus interrita clivo'.

1.   longo . . . nisu: Usener's restoration seems the nicest, stressing both the time and the effort required. 'Longo . . . clivo' (Dahlmann) is possible— Silius (above) could be recruited either by Usener ('nititur') or by Dahlmann ('clivo')—but 'ardua' has already indicated the upward incline. 'Longo . . . cliva' (Kiessling) would be less attractive: although 'cliva' could indeed be neuter plural (cf. Memmius, **45**), agreeing with 'aspera', the more elegant poets generally avoided a hexameter ending such as 'aspera cliva'.

2.   eluctanda via: = Val. Flacc. 8.184.

labor . . . omnis: 'every kind of labour', as e.g. in Ovid, *AA* 2.236.

obiacet: 'lies in the way of', 'blocks the path to', like a boulder obstructing a road.

honori: for the dative, cf. Stat. *Theb.* 4.61–2 'obiacet alto / Isthmos'. Since 'honor' can mean (high) public or political office, or the holding of such office (*OLD* 5), one might wonder whether the context is political as well as moral. Lucretius uses somewhat similar language for a more cynical view of aspirants to power at Rome: 'noctes atque dies *niti* praestante *labore* / ad summas emergere* opes' (3.62–3).

209 (3 Bl., C.)

huc ades Aonia crinem circumdata serta: clearly the invocation of a Muse, probably near the beginning of a poem.

Aonia: 'Boeotian'. The epithet Ἀόνιος may have been invented by Callimachus; Pfeiffer guessed plausibly that, in the course of his dream at the beginning of the *Aetia,* he described Aganippe (a fountain of poetic inspiration) as Περμησσοῦ παρθένος Ἀονίου, 'daughter of Aonian Permessus' (Call. fr. 2a.15 ff. in Pfeiffer, vol. II, pp. 102–3, cf. G. Massimilla, *Callimaco, Aetia, Libri Primo e Secondo* (Pisa, 1996), 238 ff.). Euphorion followed (*Suppl. Hell.* 442.1 Ἀονίοιο) and Nonnus is fond of the epithet. In Latin it is very often used in connection with poetic inspiration; both Catullus (61.28–30) and Virgil (*Ecl.* 10.12) maintain the Callimachean link with Aganippe. See R. Mayer, *Greece and Rome,* 33 (1986), 48.

It is worth noting that Ovid writes to Cornelius Severus 'at tu, cui bibitur felicius Aonius fons' (**203**a= *Ex Ponto* 4.2.47), i.e. Aganippe. Did he know that Severus had used this epithet? The monosyllabic line-ending 'Aonius fons' is alien to the hexameters of elegy ('unique', Platnauer, *Latin Elegiac Verse,* 13), but appropriate to the grand epic style of Cornelius Severus.

serta: as well as in Propertius 2.33.37 (quoted by the grammarian) some have wished to restore feminine 'serta' in Prop. 4.6.3.

210 (4 Bl., C.)

stabat apud sacras antistita numinis aras: the preposition is regularly used with regard to gods or their altars (*OLD* 8c, *TLL* II, 336.77 ff.).

antistita: 'priestess'. This feminine form (first attested in an elevated context in Plautus, *Rudens* 624 'Veneri Veneriaeque antistitae', then in Accius 153 Warmington, cf. Asinius Pollio, **136**) has a more solemn and archaic tone (cf. Lyne on [Virgil], *Ciris* **166**) than 'antistes' (which can be either masculine or feminine). Gellius (13.21.22) comments 'sacerdotes quoque feminas M. Cicero "antistitas" dicit, non secundum grammaticam legem "antistites", nam cum insolentias verborum a veteribus dictorum plerumque respueret, huius tamen verbi in ea parte sonitu delectatus "sacerdotes" inquit "Cereris atque illius fani antistitas [*In Verrem* 4.99]"'.

211 (5 Bl., C.)

1–2. A description of the coming of night. Such passages become increasingly elaborate in Silver Latin poetry; this one shows no particular individuality apart from the feminine use of 'successor', but perhaps 'fraternis successor equis' is meant to suggest one military commander taking over from another (an image which might be helped a little by 'ducebat').

1. caelo ducebat: ablative, 'in the sky', or 'over the sky' rather than dative 'to the sky', which would be inappropriate (Nisbet).

212 (6 Bl., C.)

et sua concordes dant sibila clara dracones: 'If this is related to something in Roman history, the only pair of serpents acting in unison is that which killed Laocoon and his sons' (Courtney 322). 'Concordes . . . dracones' brings to my mind (also to Dahlmann, p. 40) Cadmus and Harmonia, for whose continuing affection and harmlessness to mankind see Ovid, *Met.* 4.595–603 (rather different from Nicander, *Theriaca* 609 δύω δασπλῆτε . . . δράκοντε). They were transformed in Illyria, and might have been mentioned in connection with Roman military operations in that part of the world during the 30s B C. 'Concordes' could even play on the name Harmonia. Outside Roman history one might think of a chariot drawn by a pair of dragons in unison (e.g. Ovid, *Met.* 8.794–5).

sua: typical, characteristic of snakes (*OLD suus* 11).

sibila: the neuter is common, being found in Aemilius Macer (**55**), Lucan, Valerius Flaccus, Statius, and Silius Italicus.

213 (7 Bl., C.)

flavo protexerat ora galero: perhaps only against the heat of the sun (cf. Calpurnius Siculus 1.7 'torrida cur solo defendimus ora galero?'). If, however, the *galerus* is being used as a helmet in warfare, one thinks of the primitive age, as in Virgil, *Aen.* 7.688 'fulvosque lupi de pelle galeros' and Propertius 4.1.29 'prima galeritus posuit praetoria Lycmon'; possibly therefore from Severus' poem on kings, whether Alban or Roman (**204**). The *galerus*, though also worn by pontifices and flamines, is normal peasant headgear (worn by

Simylus in [Virgil], *Moretum* 120, called 'Arcadian' in Stat. *Theb.* 4.303).
'Flavo ... galero' is thus placed in Juv. 6.120 'nigrum flavo crinem
abscondente galero' (referring to a wig), where the tone seems mock-epic and
there might be a deliberate allusion to Severus.

One may wonder—a common problem—how the grammarian knows that
Severus intended the masculine rather than the neuter (Nisbet suggests 'fla-
vus ... galerus', which would make the gender clear). The answer (though
unsatisfactory) is probably that Charisius is setting *galerus* not against neuter
galerum (credited to Fronto by Servius on *Aen.* 7.688) but against neuter
galear (illustrated by quotations from C. Gracchus and Varro).

214 (8 Bl., C.)

†therua†: G. Hermann's 'helvola', which Courtney describes as 'the best
emendation so far', does not attract me; this would be a technical term, 'sunt
et helvolae, quas non nulli varias appellant, neque purpureae neque nigrae'
(Columella 3.2.23, cf. Pliny, *NH* 14.29), which does not sit well with 'pur-
pureis' unless it were a case of grafting. More promising seems Courtney's
own 'ter nova', or perhaps simply 'tertia' (though the corruption would be
less explicable), marking the passage of time (e.g. the third and final year's
campaigning in the Sicilian war?), as in Ovid, *Fasti* 3.557–8 'tertia nudandas
acceperat area messes / inque cavas ierant tertia musta lacus'.

gemmavit: 'budded', cf. Cicero, *De oratore* 3.155 'gemmare vitis ... rustici
dicunt'.

pampinus: feminine also in Lucilius 1270 Marx 'purpureamque uvam
facit albam pampinum habere' (where M. thinks that the subject is autumn)
and several times in Varro (according to Servius on Virgil, *Ecl.* 7.58). For
Pliny's puzzling accusation of 'puerility' against this line (or the whole poem
in which it stood) see my introduction to Cornelius above, on **203f.** There is
certainly nothing puerile about the gender of 'pampinus' or the use of
'gemmare'.

215 (9 Bl., C.)

pomosa lentos servabat in arbore ramos: Dahlmann (pp. 51–3) plausibly
suggests that the subject is the snake which guarded the apples of the
Hesperides (e.g. Lucretius 5.32–3 'aureaque Hesperidum servans fulgentia

mala / asper, acerba tuens, immani corpore serpens'); the line-ending 'serva-bat in arbore ramos' is applied by Virgil (*Aen.* 4.485) to the priestess who fed the snake. This need not imply an extended treatment of the myth of Heracles and the apples; it could be a brief geographical reference in a historical poem.

pomosa: this adjective, first found in Tibullus 1.1.17 and Propertius 4.2.17, remained rare. It suggests the world of agriculture rather than high poetry; see P. E. Knox, 'Adjectives in -osus and Latin Poetic Diction', *Glotta*, 64 (1986), 90–101, especially 92 ff.

servabat: if the subject was the snake, 'servabat', as well as meaning 'guarded', might have a hint of 'continued to occupy' (*OLD* 3). In art the snake is regularly represented as entwined around the tree-trunk and some of the branches (*LIMC* s.v. Hesperides).

The grammarian's concern with the gender of 'ramus' seems superfluous; perhaps he was tacitly comparing it with neuter 'ramale' (as Servius on *Georg.* 4.303 'dicimus autem et "hic ramus" et "hoc ramale"'), cf. on **213**.

216 (10 Bl., C.)

pinea frondosi coma murmurat Appennini: I suspect that this was part of a simile. If there was an element of correspondence between the simile and the main narrative (see S. J. Harrison on *Aen.* 10.98–9 'caeca volutant / mur-mura'), 'murmurat' would suit a crowd (cf. *OLD murmur* 2 and *murmuro* 3). A possible model would be Ovid, *Met.* 15.603–4 (after Cipus had threatened the Romans with a king) 'qualia succinctis, ubi trux insibilat Eurus, / mur-mura pinetis fiunt'. It becomes a convention in Latin poetry, perhaps under Hellenistic influence (e.g. Callimachus, *Hymn* 6.51 ὤρεσιν ἐν Τμαρίοισιν, Euphorion, fr. 51.8 ἤ που Μελιγουνίδι) that a simile should be given a particu-lar geographical context. In *Aen.* 12.701–3 Aeneas, rousing himself to pursue Turnus, is compared to the Appennine: 'ipse, coruscis / cum fremit ilicibus, quantus, gaudetque nivali / vertice se attollens pater Appenninus ad auras'.

frondosi: the epithet gains a certain distinction from having been used by Ennius (*Ann.* 179 Skutsch 'silvai frondosai'), but lacks a close analogue in Homer or later Greek poetry (πολύφυλλος does not have a strong poetic resonance). A significant number of epithets in -osus are at home in the countryside (see above on **215** 'pomosa').

coma: cf. *Od.* 23.195 κόμην τανυφύλλον ἐλαίης, and Richardson on *HH Dem.* 454. In Latin we find 'coma' used of foliage first in an anonymous fragment, 'velatas frondentis comas' (*Trag. inc.* 120 Warmington), then in Catullus 4.12, *Aen.* 2.629, Ovid, *Am.* 1.7.54. See also on Varr. At., **131**.

Appennini: the σπονδειάζων is completed by a four-syllable proper name, but an Italian name, not (as so often in Catullus 64) Greek (e.g. Nonacrinae in the anonymous neoteric fragment, **238**.2). We can see from Persius 1.95 'subduximus Appennino' that ending a hexameter with some part of 'Appenninus' came to be considered a mannerism. Thus too Quintilian 9.4.65 'etiam in carminibus est praemolle . . . cum versus cluditur "Appennino"'. The first known example is Horace, *Epod.* 16.29 'in mare seu celsus procurrerit Appenninus'; Ovid, *Met.* 2.226 'et nubifer Appenninus' may also predate Severus. Later examples (not to mention Persius) can be found in Lucan, Petronius, Silius (twice), Rutilius Namatianus, and Sidonius Apollinaris (see Dahlmann, p. 58).

217 (11 Bl., C.)

The context is irretrievable; one might surmise that the Romans ('de Romanis', Seneca) were fighting against non-Romans (i.e. not in a civil war), and that those who said 'hic meus est dies' were not destined to fare well in the morrow's battle. But neither point is secure.

1.   stratique per herbam: like the Rutulians in *Aen.* 9.164–5 'fusique per herbam / indulgent vino et vertunt crateras aënos'. 'Fusique per herbam' ends a hexameter also in *Aen.* 1.214, 5.102.

2.   hic meus est . . . dies: in the course of confuting a pedantic grammarian who complained that Severus should have said 'noster' rather than 'meus', the elder Seneca (*Suas.* 2.13) notes the quasi-proverbial nature of these words. In Sen. *Medea* 1017 'meus dies est' the point is that Medea need not hurry because Creon has granted her a whole day in Corinth. Perhaps in Severus there was a strong antithesis between today, which belongs to the speaker, and tomorrow, as in Horace, *Odes* 3.29.42 ff. 'cui licet in dies / dixisse "vixi. cras vel atra / nube polum pater occupato / vel sole puro . . ."' etc.

dixere: in fact 'dixisse' has better manuscript authority, and might be accommodated if one supplied e.g. <narrantur>, but that would blunt the force of the saying.

218 (12 Bl., C.)

luxuriantur opes atque otia longa gravantur: puzzling. Courtney translates 'Abundance runs riot and is oppressed by long idleness', leaving me in doubt how he understands the grammar—*otia longa* nominative, *gravantur* deponent, with an accusative *opes* understood as an object of *gravantur*? The usual sense of deponent 'gravari' is 'bear unwillingly', 'find irksome', 'make difficulties over', with accusative first in Plautus, *Rudens* 438 'cur tu aquam gravare?', cf. Horace, *Odes* 4.11.27–8 'Pegasus terrenum equitem gravatus / Bellerophontem'. It seems likely that 'opes' (with an element of personification) is the subject of 'gravantur' as of 'luxuriantur': 'wealth runs riot and finds long inactivity irksome'. It was a Hellenistic commonplace (material in E. Fraenkel, *Horace* (Oxford, 1957), 211–13) that prolonged peace and freedom from fear accustomed citizens to luxury and led to ruin. This theory is applied to Rome in Sallust, *Jugurtha* 41 'mos partium et factionum ac deinde omnium malarum artium . . . ortus est otio atque abundantia earum rerum quae prima mortales ducunt'. Perhaps the closest parallel for the apparent situation in our fragment (the rich are not content with *otium*) may be found in Sallust, *Catiline* 17.6, on the young men (mostly nobles) who favoured Catiline, 'quibus in otio vel magnifice vel molliter vivere copia erat, incerta pro certis, bellum quam pacem malebant'.

Dahlmann (pp. 67 ff.), citing Servius on *Aen.* 8.171 (opibusque iuvabo), 'opes antiqui milites dicebant' (cf. *OLD ops*[1] 1(c), quasi-concrete, 'forces', 'troops') interprets 'luxuriantur opes' here as 'the soldiers run riot'. That seems to me hardly possible. Alternatively he wonders whether 'gravantur' might be passive in sense, 'are weighed down'. Perhaps one should leave open the possibility that Diomedes (whose distinction between pejorative *luxurior* and positive *luxurio* does not always hold good) is not quoting a complete sense-unit: e.g. '<inter avitas> / luxuriantur opes . . .' etc., with the subject stated previously (cf. Petronius, *Anth. Lat.* 470 SB = Courtney, *The Poems of Petronius* (Atlanta, GA, 1991), p. 55 line 4 'inter tam crassas luxuriantur opes').

luxuriantur opes: cf. Martial 10.96.6 'tenues luxuriantur opes' (in the simpler ambience of the poet's native Spain).

219 (13 Bl., C.)

In *Suasoriae* 6 the elder Seneca gives specimens of what declaimers had said when advising Cicero whether or not to beg Antony for mercy. This leads him on to consider (sections 15–25) how Roman historians had treated the memory of Cicero, with verbatim quotations from Asinius Pollio, Livy, Aufidius Bassus, Cremutius Cordus, and Bruttedius Niger. See Lewis A. Sussman, *The Elder Seneca* (*Mnemosyne*, suppl. 51 (1978), 72–3; generally for historians' obituaries Woodman and Martin on Tacitus, *Ann.* 3.30.1; A. J. Pomeroy, *The Appropriate Comment: Death Notices in the Ancient Historians* (1991). At the end of these extracts Seneca adds 'nemo tamen ex tot disertissimis viris melius Ciceronis mortem deploravit quam Severus Cornelius' and reproduces this, much our longest surviving fragment of the epic poet. Seneca adopts a similar procedure in *Suas.* 1, asserting that none of the Latin declaimers who imagined Alexander's fleet sailing on the Oceanus could equal Albinovanus Pedo's account of Germanicus at sea (**228**).

Seneca notes that historians, when relating the death of a great man, often add a kind of funeral eulogy. That of Cremutius Cordus (whose own death in A D 25 is related by Tacitus, *Ann.* 4.34–5) contained 'nihil . . . Cicerone dignum' (*Suas.* 6.23), but Cordus' account (*Suas.* 6.19) of Antony's and the people's reaction to Cicero's death has much in common with our passage of Cornelius Severus, and may have been influenced by the poet:

Quibus visis laetus Antonius, cum peractam proscriptionem suam dixisset esse, quippe non satiatus modo caedendis civibus sed differtus quoque, super rostra exponit. itaque, quo saepius ille ingenti circumfusus turba processerat, quam paulo ante coluerat piis contionibus, quibus multorum capita servaverat, eo tum per artus sublatus aliter ac solitus erat a civibus suis conspectus est, praependenti capiti orique eius inspersa sanie, brevi ante princeps senatus Romanique nominis titulus, tum pretium interfectoris sui. praecipue tamen solvit pectora omnium in lacrimas gemitusque visa ad caput eius deligata manus dextera, divinae eloquentiae ministra; ceterorumque caedes privatos luctus excitaverunt, illa una communem.

A close contemporary of Cremutius Cordus was the historian Velleius Paterculus, whom we can see changing into declamatory mode to lament the death of Cicero (2.66.2–3):

Abscisa . . . scelere Antonii vox publica est, cum eius salutem nemo defendisset qui per tot annos et publicam civitatis et privatam civium defenderat. nihil tamen egisti, M. Antoni—cogit enim excedere proposita formam operis erumpens animo ac pectore indignatio—nihil (inquam) egisti mercedem caelestissimi oris et clarissimi capitis abscisi numerando auctoramentoque funebri ad conservatoris quondam rei publicae tantique consulis incitando necem. rapuisti tu M. Ciceroni lucem sollicitam et aetatem senilem et vitam miseriorem te principe quam sub te triumviro mortem; famam vero gloriamque factorum atque dictorum adeo non abstulisti ut auxeris. vivit vivetque per omnem saeculorum memoriam, dumque hoc vel forte vel providentia vel utcunque constitutum naturae corpus—quod ille paene solus Romanorum animo vidit, ingenio complexus est, eloquentia inluminavit—manebit incolume, comitem aevi sui laudem Ciceronis trahet; omnisque posteritas illius in te scripta mirabitur, tuum in eum factum execrabitur; citiusque mundo genus hominum quam M. Cicero cedet.

Another indication that Cicero's death became a favourite theme for declaimers can be found in Martial 5.69.7–8 (addressed to Antony) 'quid prosunt sacrae pretiosa silentia linguae? [cf. Sextilius Ena, **202**] / incipient omnes pro Cicerone loqui'. Even the elder Pliny slips into this style (*NH* 7.116–17). Severus seems to allude several times to Cicero's own writings—particularly the Catilinarian orations, but note also imitation of the *Brutus* in lines 10–11.

We have here a unique opportunity to observe the style and metrical technique of Severus in a substantial and continuous passage. His dislike of elision—only lines 2 'en(im)' and 15 'aetern(um)'—was probably not uncommon in the first century A D; the most extreme example would be Calpurnius Siculus if, as seems likely, he should be dated to the reign of Nero. Courtney (p. 326) describes the versification as 'not quite as polished as the other fragments . . . would have led us to expect'. He mentions the successive trochaic caesurae in feet 4 and 5 (lines 16 'sparsamque cruore nefando' and 22 'non fecit in hoste Philippo'), but occasional use of this rhythm in a hexameter poem need not be regarded as infelicitous: in *Aeneid* 1–2 it occurs once every 74 lines, in *Met.* 1–2 (which we might expect to be the most significant parallel) once every 138 lines. Severus, like Ovid in the *Metamorphoses*, shows a marked preference for the dactyl over the spondee—the average number of syllables per line is above 15.00. Another predilection of Severus is the *tricolon crescens* (lines 5–6, 8–9, 16–17). Sense-pauses are tastefully varied, according to the example set by Virgil and followed by Ovid.

1. magnanimum . . . virorum: metrical convenience dictates the coupling of the old form of the adjective with the modern form of the noun; thus too (with identical placing) *Aen.* 3.704 'magnanimum . . . equorum', Stat. *Theb.* 3.349 'magnanimum . . . avorum'. The form 'magnanimorum' (found in Cicero, *Tusc. Disp.* 2.43) would be unwieldy in classical verse, necessitating either a five-syllable hexameter ending or an awkward elision. The adjective occurs first in Plautus, *Amphitryo* 212 'magnanimi viri' (grandiloquent); it would not be surprising if Ennius used it as an equivalent of Homer's μεγάθυμος.

Appian (*BC* 4.65 ff.) names magistrates who were the first victims of the proscriptions in November—December 43 B C together with Cicero: a tribune Salvius, praetors Minucius and Annalis, an ex-praetor Turranius. See Alain M. Gowing, *The Triumviral Narratives of Appian and Cassius Dio* (Ann Arbor, 1992), ch. 14, *CAH*[2] vol. IX (1994), ch. 12. Of course the others were minor figures compared with Cicero.

spirantia paene: increasing the horror, cf. Lucan 8.670 (Septimius about to behead Pompey) 'spirantiaque occupat ora'.

2. in rostris iacuere suis: compare Florus 2.16.5 'Romae capita caesorum proponere in rostris iam usitatum erat; verum sic quoque civitas lacrimas tenere non potuit, cum recisum Ciceronis caput in illis suis rostris videret nec aliter ad videndum eum quam solebat ad audiendum concurreretur.'

abstulit omnis: 'drew everyone's gaze' (*OLD aufero* 4(c)).

4. tunc redeunt animis ingentia consulis acta: perhaps an echo of Cicero's own words, *In Cat.* 3.26 'in animis ego vestris omnis triumphos meos, omnia ornamenta honoris, monumenta gloriae, laudis insignia condi et conlocari volo'. 'Tunc redeunt' might suggest that the Roman people's temporary forgetfulness of Cicero's past services to the state had exposed him to the fatal danger, cf. *In Cat.* 2.23 'nihil a vobis nisi huius temporis totiusque mei consulatus memoriam postulo; quae dum erit in vestris fixa mentibus, tutissimo me muro saeptum esse arbitrabor'.

5. iurataeque manus: cf. *In Cat.* 3.3 'coniuratorum manum', Sallust, *Cat.* 22.1 'quom ad ius iurandum popularis sceleris sui adigeret [sc. Catilina]'.

deprensaque: a verb used often by Cicero of all aspects of the conspiracy (e.g. *In Cat.* 3.11 'sceleris manifesti atque deprensi').

foedera noxae: Cicero has the phrase 'scelerum foedere' (*In Cat.* 1.33) and 'sceleris foedus' (2.8). 'Noxa' (not Ciceronian, though he occasionally uses the noun 'noxia') is equally at home in prose and verse, and can be used as a legal technical term.

6. patriciumque nefas exstinctum: as well as Catiline himself, two prominent conspirators were patricians, C. Cornelius Cethegus (*RE* Cornelius 89, Mayor on Juvenal 10.288) and P. Cornelius Lentulus Sura (*RE* Cornelius 240). This rank made their treachery all the more disgraceful (thus Sallust, *Cat.* 55.6 on the latter, 'ita ille patricius ex gente clarissuma Corneliorum, qui consulare imperium Romae habuerat, dignum moribus factisque exitum vitae invenit'), and contrasted strikingly with the *novus homo* Cicero. In Sallust, *Cat.* 31.7 Catiline attempts to benefit from this contrast between himself, 'patricio homini' and the consul, 'inquilinus civis urbis Romae'.

exstinctum: this restoration completes a *tricolon crescens*, balancing 'deprensa' (15), with chiasmus. It involves the slight infelicity of a strong sense-pause after fourth-foot spondee, which would be avoided by Håkanson's 'exstincti' (punctuating after 'nefas'), or Gronovius' 'exstinctum, et'. In any case the verb would allude to the conspirators' plans to burn Rome (e.g. Cic. fr. 10.64 C. 'clades patriae flamma ferroque parata', *In Cat.* 3.15 'quod urbem incendiis . . . liberassem' and other passages cited by Mayor on Juvenal 8.233 'flammas . . . paratis').

poena Cethegi: singled out because he was a patrician (above) and perhaps also because he had been given the task of killing Cicero (*In Cat.* 4.13, Sallust, *Cat.* 43.2), in which he was less successful than Antony. His punishment was to be strangled in the Tullianum (Sallust, *Cat.* 55.5–6); in *Pro Sulla*

70 Cicero asks 'cui non ad illius [sc. Cethegi] poenam carcer aedificatus esse videatur?' Cethegus was one of the most active and dangerous conspirators (*In Cat.* 3.16, *Cat.* 43.4).

7. deiectus ... votis ... nefandis: 'cast down from his abominable ambitions'. *Deici*+ablative sometimes means to be robbed of one's hope of obtaining a political office, e.g. Cicero, *Pro Murena* 76 'praetura deiectus est' (i.e. he was not elected). 'Spe deici' is common, e.g. Caesar, *BG* 1.8.4 'Helvetii ea spe deiecti', Silius 10.380 'tum spe deiectus iuvenis'.

8–9. 'What did it profit him . . .?' is a favourite motif in laments for the dead, e.g. Horace, *Odes* 1.28.4 ff. (Archytas), Propertius 3.18.11–12 (Marcellus), 4.11.11–12 (Cornelia); extended to an ox in Virgil, *Georg.* 3.525–6, to Corinna's parrot in Ovid, *Am.* 2.6.17–20. Repetition of 'quid . . .?' is a regular feature, e.g. Ovid, *Am.* 3.9.21–2 (in the course of his lament for Tibullus) 'quid pater Ismario, quid mater profuit Orpheo? / carmine quid victas obstupuisse feras?'

8. 'Favor' and 'coetus' form something of a hendiadys—the enthusiasm shown for Cicero in public meetings. Cremutius Cordus (*ap.* Sen. *Suas.* 6.19, quoted above) wrote 'turba . . . quam paulo ante coluerat piis contionibus'.

9. profuerant: here (unlike line 24 'afŭerunt') we may accept the pluperfect (rather than the variant 'profuerunt'), which is often found in manuscripts through scribes' failure to recognize the third person plural of the perfect with shortened penultimate.

sacris ... artibus: the liberal arts (bonae, ingenuae, liberales); Severus' adjective points especially to oratory (Courtney refers to Sen. *Contr.* 1 praef. 10 'sacerrimam eloquentiam', Tac. *Dial.* 10.5 'omnem eloquentiam omnesque eius partes sacras et venerabiles puto'), but the phrase would include all the arts to which 'exculta' was appropriate—in Cicero's case particularly philosophy.

exculta: cf. Cicero, *De officiis* 2.15 'artes . . . quibus rebus exculta hominum vita tantum distat a victu et cultu bestiarum', *De legibus* 2.36. Severus would remember Virgil, *Aen.* 6.663 'inventas aut qui vitam excoluere per artes', on which R. G. Austin quotes from an anonymous papyrus fragment (R. Merkelbach, *Mus. Helv.* 8 (1951), 1–11), fol. iii recto, line 7, αἳ δὲ [souls in the underworld] βίον σοφίῃσιν ἐκόσμεον.

10. abstulit una dies aevi decus: it is the work of a moment to destroy something which had held good for many years. This hemiepes recurs in Silius 2.5, probably from Ovid, *Ex Ponto* 1.2.4 (both on the Fabii); the most notable instance of the 'una dies' motif comes in Lucretius 5.95–6 (the eventual collapse of the universe) 'una dies dabit exitio, multosque per annos / sustentata ruet moles et machina mundi'. Compare Cicero, *Pro Sulla* 73 'haec diu multumque et multo labore quaesita una eripuit hora [sc. on Sulla's conviction]'.

aevi decus: cf. Ovid, *Ex Ponto* 2.8.25 (Augustus) 'saecli decus', *Ep. Sapph.* (*Her.* 15). 94 'o decus atque aevi gloria magna tui'.

ictaque luctu: it was a convention that, on the death of a great artist, the personification of his Art should grieve for him. Thus the epigrams (from Aulus Gellius, *NA* 1.24, see Courtney 47–9) on Naevius, lines 1–2 'immortales mortales si foret fas flere, / flerent divae Camenae Naevium poetam', and on Plautus (Aulus Gellius, *NA* 1.24) 'postquam est mortem aptus Plautus, Comoedia luget, / scaena est deserta; dein Risus Ludus iocusque / et Numeri innumeri simul omnes conlacrimarunt', Ovid, *Am.* 3.9.3 (on the death of Tibullus) 'flebilis indignos, Elegeia, solve capillos'.

11. conticuit Latiae tristis facundia linguae: this, as the elder Seneca tells us, is an improvement on the line 'deflendus Cicero Latiaeque silentia linguae' which Severus heard Sextilius Ena (**202**) recite in the house of Messalla Corvinus, thus causing offence to Asinius Pollio. History does not record whether Pollio was any less offended by Severus' variation—perhaps he had died by then! Severus has cleverly incorporated echoes of Cicero's own *Brutus*, a work lamenting the death of Hortensius and written at a time when Cicero himself had virtually withdrawn from public life: 5.19 (Atticus to Cicero) 'iam pridem enim conticuerunt tuae litterae', 6.22 (Cicero speaks) 'ea ipsa . . . eloquentia obmutuit' (for the verb cf. Severus line 15 below), 94.324 'hoc studium . . . nostrum conticuit subito et obmutuit'.

It seems to me that Ovid, who (as a protégé of Messalla) could well have been present at Ena's recitation, shows himself aware both of Severus' line and of the incident in Messalla's house when he writes to Cotta Maximus, younger son of his old patron (*Ex Ponto* 2.3.75–6):

> me tuus ille pater, *Latiae facundia linguae*
> quoi non inferior nobilitate fuit . . .

'Quoi' (i.e. 'cui') is Housman's emendation (*CR* 16 (1902), 445 = *Collected Papers*, 581–2), which seems unquestionably right and brings the expression into line with Severus. Those who read 'quae' in 76 and understand 'facundia' (75) as 'eloquent person', cannot explain the relative clause. Pollio and Messalla were acknowledged as the leading Augustan orators, and, by his echo of Severus, Ovid indicates that in Messalla (at least) Latin eloquence continued to speak after the death of Cicero.

12. unica sollicitis quondam tutela salusque: part of a standard eulogy of the public-spirited orator; compare Horace, *Odes* 2.1.13 (Asinius Pollio) 'insigne maestis praesidium reis', 4.1.14 (Fabius Maximus) 'et pro sollicitis non tacitus reis', Ovid, *AA* 1.459–62 (with a characteristic twist) 'disce bonas artes, moneo, Romana iuventus, / non tantum trepidos ut tueare reos; / quam populus iudexque gravis lectusque senatus, / tam dabit eloquio victa puella manus'. In all the above, our sympathy is engaged for the defendants; Nisbet and Hubbard on *Odes* 2.1.13 note of Asinius Pollio that 'in true Republican tradition' eight of his nine speeches of which we know the title were for the defence. Four hundred years later in Prudentius' account of his career (*Praef.* 18, from a poem with strong links to Horace, *Odes* 4.1), the balance has shifted: 'ius civile bonis reddidimus, terruimus reos'.

13.   egregium patriae semper caput: no doubt a reference to the time when Cicero was hailed as 'parens patriae' by Catulus in the Senate (*In Pisonem* 6) and by Cato in the popular assembly (Plutarch, *Cicero* 23). 'Semper' makes the point that not only then did Cicero deserve such a title.

13–15.   I would take 'vindex' with 'senatus' and 'fori', 'publica vox' with 'legum ritusque togaeque'. Winterbottom (in the Loeb Elder Seneca) takes all the genitives in 14 with 'vindex'; a third possibility would be to take 'vindex' only with 'senatus', attaching 'ille fori . . .' etc. to 'publica vox'. Near the end of his life Cicero summarized his preoccupations as follows: 'omne enim curriculum industriae nostrae in foro, in curia, in amicorum periculis propulsandis elaboratum est' (*Phil.* 7.7).

13–14.   senatus / vindex: cf. Lucan 8.554 'vindexque senatus' (of Pompey).

14.   legum ritusque togaeque: perhaps referring as much to Cicero's written works on these subjects as to his spoken utterances. 'Legum' could cover *De legibus*, 'ritusque' such works as *De divinatione* and the lost *De auguriis* (Cicero himself became an augur), 'togaeque' *De officiis*. General support for the continuation of traditional religious rites is expressed in statements like *De div.* 2.148 'maiorum instituta tueri sacris caerimoniisque retinendis sapientis est', *De natura deorum* 2.5 (Cotta speaks) 'quod eo, credo, valebat ut opiniones quas a maioribus accepimus de dis immortalibus, sacra caerimonias religionesque defenderem'. 'Togaeque' (contrasting with 'armis' in 15) may also allude to Cicero's notorious line (fr. 12 Courtney) 'cedant arma togae, concedat laurea laudi'; it seems from *Phil.* 2.20 that Antony (like some others) had mocked this line. Cicero has to admit that on a later occasion Antony's *arma* had the better of the argument ('at postea tuis armis cessit toga').

ritusque: Heinsius conjectured 'iurisque', which was adopted by Courtney and may be right. But 'ritusque' seems unobjectionable and extends the range of Cicero's listed Roman interests.

15.   publica vox: probably with 'legum ritusque togaeque' (14), 'the communal mouthpiece of the laws, religion, and civil life'. The phrase 'publica vox' does not seem a standard one (in Lucan 1.270 Curio is called 'vox . . . populi'), but recurs in Velleius 2.66.2 (quoted above), also of Cicero and probably from Severus.

16–17. sparsamque cruore nefando / canitiem: (cf. Silius 9.652 'spar-sosque cruore meorum', with the same rhythm) a particularly gruesome specimen of the contrast between red and white, so beloved of Hellenistic and Roman poets. Compare Cremutius Cordus *ap.* Sen. *Suas.* 6.19 'orique eius inspersa sanie'.

17–18. sacrasque manus operumque ministras / tantorum: one thinks naturally of the *Philippics*, which brought about Cicero's death, but there may be a wider application to the whole range of Cicero's writings. Here, more clearly, Cremutius Cordus (*ap.* Sen. *Suas.* 6.19) has our poet in mind: 'manus dextera, divinae eloquentiae ministra'.

18. civis: 'a fellow-citizen'. Cicero had asked Antony to keep his enmity within those bounds (*Phil.* 1.27 'peto ut sic irascatur ut civi') and claims to treat Antony on the same basis (*Phil.* 2.9 'quod scribam tanquam ad civem').

proiecta: the neuter participle covering the masculine (voltus) and feminine (canitiem, manus).

19. proculcavit: Cicero himself was fond of the synonym *conculcare*.

lubrica fata: *OLD* 5 (of fortunes, hopes, etc.), 'not to be relied on', 'shift-ing', 'inconstant'. After 'cruore', pedibus', and 'proculcavit', we are also perhaps meant to think of a surface made slippery by blood (as *Aen.* 5.335 'per lubrica surgens').

20. nullo luet hoc Antonius aevo: piling all the odium for Cicero's death on to Antony. The Augustan line was that the proscription of Cicero was demanded by Antony and Lepidus, 'repugnante Caesare sed frustra adversus duos' (Velleius 2.66.1, see Woodman ad loc.). The historian adds (2.66.2) 'nihil tam indignum illo tempore fuit quam quod aut Caesar aliquem proscribere coactus est aut ab ullo Cicero proscriptus est'.

21–5. In contrast to Antony's treatment of his fellow-citizen, the poet lists five defeated foreign enemies of Rome, three of whom (Perse<u>s, Syphax, and Philip V) were allowed to live on, whereas the two who lost their lives (Jugurtha and Hannibal) suffered no bodily disfigurement. The cases of Syphax and Perse<u>s king of Macedonia were linked by Severus' close contemporary Valerius Maximus (5.1.1):

illud quoque non parvum humanitatis senatus indicium est. Syphacem enim, quondam opulentissimum Numidiae regem, captivum in custodia Tiburi, mortuum publico funere censuit efferendum, ut vitae dono honorem sepulturae adiceret. con-similique clementia in Persa usus est. nam cum Albae, in quam custodiae causa relegatus erat, decessisset, quaestorem misit qui eum publico funere efferret, ne regias reliquias iacere inhonoratas pateretur.

In response to a demand that Philip V should be killed or dethroned, T. Quinctius Flamininus, the victor of Cynoscephalae, replied 'Romanos, praeter vetustissimum morem victis parcendi, praecipuum clementiae documentum dedisse pace Hannibali et Carthaginiensibus data ... cum armato hoste infestis animis concurri debere; adversus victos mitissimum quemque animum maximum habere' (Livy 33.12.7–9).

21.   Emathio: 'Macedonian'. Ἡμαθίη as a region appears first in *Iliad* 14.226, 'Emathia' in Catullus 64.324, Virgil, *Georg.* 1.492, 4.390. The adjective 'Emathian' is (surprisingly) not attested in Greek; in Latin first in Ovid, *Met.* 15.824 etc.—unless this passage and/or [Virgil], *Ciris* 34 are earlier.

Perse: Perses or Perseus (the latter on his coins) was a son of Philip V. He ruled Macedon 179–168 BC, and was defeated by L. Aemilius Paullus at Pydna (168). For his relegation to Alba Fucens, see Val. Max. quoted on lines 21–5 above.

22.   te: understand 'in' from the previous line.

dire Syphax: an epithet commonly applied to Syphax's ally Hannibal (e.g. Horace, *Odes* 3.6.36, cf. Nisbet and Hubbard on 2.12.2). After wavering between the Romans and Carthaginians, Syphax was defeated by Scipio Africanus and died in Tibur—not such an unpleasant place of exile!—in 201 BC (cf. Val. Max. above).

nec fecit <in> hoste Philippo: the clemency shown to Philip V consisted in the fact that, though defeated by the Romans at Cynoscephalae (197 BC), he was allowed to remain king until the end of his life (179 BC). See Livy quoted on 21–5 above. For 'in hoste Philippo', compare *Aen.* 2.541 'talis in hoste fuit Priamo' with Austin's note. One feels the need to supply '<in>' (omitted by the manuscripts) since it has to be understood with 'te' earlier in the line; thus 'fecit <in>' is preferable to Kiessling's 'fecerat'.

23–5.   Jugurtha and Hannibal both lost their lives, but were not mutilated. The idea that disfigurements suffered in this life persisted in the underworld may be illustrated by the case of Deiphobus (*Aen.* 6.494 ff.). Juvenal contrasts the beheading of Pompey with the death of the Catilinarian conspirators (*Sat.* 10.286–8): 'hoc cruciatu / Lentulus, hac poena caruit ceciditque Cethegus / integer, et iacuit Catilina cadavere toto'. He probably has in mind our passage of Severus (cf. lines 6–7 above).

23–4.   Jugurtha was either strangled or starved to death after Marius' triumph (104 BC).

23.   triumphato ... Iugurtha: this passive use, particularly of the past participle, is very common (see McKeown on Ovid, *Am.* 1.14.46).

ludibria: see *OLD* 3(b) for this application to humiliating treatment of a body.

24.   afuerunt: this time (unlike line 9) the perfect with short penultimate may confidently be restored, though Kiessling preferred 'afuerant' (to go with his 'fecerat' in 22). See Housman, *Classical Papers*, 1068–9.

nostraeque cadens ferus Hannibal irae: 'falling to our anger'. Such a dative with *cado* is not common (Dahlmann cites Sen. *Contr.* 9.2.8 and 10.3.16), and Manilius 4.41 'Hannibalem nostris cecidisse catenis' looks like a deliberate imitation by one poet or the other. In fact Hannibal died by poisoning himself (cf. most famously Juvenal 10.160–6), though he was facing extradition to Rome from his refuge with the king of Bithynia.

25. inviolata: Dahlmann compares Silius 11.383–4 'deinde quieto / accepit tellus ossa inviolata sepulcro'.

220 (14 Bl., C.)

tragica surma: we have no knowledge that Severus wrote in any metre which might allow three consecutive short syllables. Most likely seems 'tragicā syrmā' before the masculine caesura of a hexameter; if the words are not continuous, 'syrma' could have ended a hexameter. Use of a Greek neuter noun like σύρμα (the long tragic robe) as a first-declension feminine can be found in Petronius, but is not just a late (or uneducated) feature; the grammarians offer feminine *syrma* also from 'Valerius in Phormione' (Priscian, GLK II, p. 200), and 'Afranius Divortio' (Non. Marc. I, p. 273 Lindsay).

Blänsdorf adds as his fragments 15 and 16 entries from Diomedes, GLK I, p. 375 (Severus: 'distractos atque sallitos') and Priscian, GLK II, p. 546 (Cornelius Severus in VIII de statu suo 'ad quem salliti pumiliones afferebantur'). The text of both quotations is very uncertain—more probably prose than verse (attempts to make the words scan are inevitably gruesome). 'VIII de statu suo' is mystifying. Ovid conducted a prose correspondence with Cornelius Severus (*Ex Ponto* 4.2.5–6), but there is no indication that it was published.

Iulius Montanus

221

(*a*) Ov. *Ex Ponto* 4.16.11–12: *quique vel imparibus numeris, Montane, vel aequis / sufficis et gemino carmine nomen habes.*

(*b*) Sen. *Contr.* 7.1.27: *Montanus Iulius, qui comes <Tiberii> fuit, egregius poeta, aiebat illum* [sc. Cestium Pium] *imitari voluisse Vergili descriptionem* [*Aen.* 8.26–7], *at Vergilio imitationem bene cessisse, qui illos optimos versus Varronis* [**129**] *expressisset in melius.*

(*c*) Sen. *Epist.* 122.11–13: *recitabat Montanus Iulius carmen, tolerabilis poeta et amicitia Tiberii notus et frigore. ortus et occasus libentissime inserebat; itaque cum indignaretur quidam illum toto die recitasse et negaret accedendum ad recitationes eius, Natta Pinarius ait: 'numquid possum liberalius agere? paratus sum illum audire ab ortu ad occasum.' cum hos versus recitasset* [**222** 'incipit— ministrat'] *Varus eques Romanus, M. Vinicii comes, cenarum bonarum adsectator, quas improbitate linguae merebatur, exclamavit: 'incipit Buta dormire'. deinde cum subinde recitasset* [**223** 'iam sua—incipit'] *idem Varus inquit: 'quid dicis? iam nox est? ibo et Butam salutabo'.*

(*d*) *Vita Donati* 29 (*Vitae Vergilianae Antiquae*, ed. Hardie (1966), p. 12): *Seneca tradit Iulium Montanum poetam solitum dicere involaturum se Vergilio quaedam, si et vocem posset et os et hypocrisin; eosdem enim versus ipso pronuntiante bene sonare, sine illo inanes esse mutosque.*

(*a*) . . . and you, Montanus, who are capable of writing either elegiacs or hexameters, and have won a reputation in two kinds of poetry.

(*b*) Julius Montanus, a member of Tiberius' circle and an outstanding poet, used to say that he [the declaimer Cestius Pius] had wanted to imitate Virgil's description [*Aen.* 8.26–7], but that Virgil's imitation was successful, seeing that he improved on those excellent lines of Varro [**129**].

(*c*) Julius Montanus, a passable poet who was known both for his friendship with Tiberius and their estrangement, was reciting a poem. He used at every opportunity to insert descriptions of dawn and dusk; thus when someone complained that he had recited all day and said that one should steer clear of his recitations, Natta Pinarius said, 'Could I possibly make a more generous offer? I'm prepared to listen to him from dawn to dusk.' When he had recited the following lines [**222**], the Roman knight Varus, a companion of M. Vinicius, always on the lookout for good dinners which he earned by his outrageous wit, exclaimed 'Buta is beginning to drop off.' Then, shortly afterwards, when he had recited [**223**], that same Varus said, 'What? Night already? I will go and pay Buta a wake-up call.'

(*d*) According to Seneca, the poet Julius Montanus used to say that he would steal some things from Virgil if he could also steal his voice, delivery, and histrionic power; for the selfsame lines sounded well in the mouth of their author, but without him were empty and lacking in resonance.

222 (1 Bl., C.)

> incipit ardentes Phoebus producere flammas,
> spargere <se> rubicunda dies; iam tristis hirundo
> argutis reditura cibos inmittere nidis
> incipit et molli partitos ore ministrat.

Phoebus begins to extend his burning flames, and roseate day to spread herself out; now the mournful swallow, on the first of her journeys, begins to put food into her shrill nestlings and, after dividing it up, serves it with her soft mouth.

1–4 Sen *Epist.* 122.12 [v. supra, **221***c*]: 'incipit—ministrat'.

   2 <se> suppl. p²: spargier et *Baehrens*

223 (2 Bl., C.)

> iam sua pastores stabulis armenta locarunt,
> iam dare sopitis nox pigra silentia terris
> incipit

Now the cowmen have settled their herds in stalls, now inactive night begins to give silence to the lands overcome by sleep.

1–3 Sen. *Epist.* 122.13 [v. supra, **221***c*]: 'iam sua—incipit'.

224 (Elegi)

Ov. *Ex Ponto* 4.16.11–12 [=**221***a*, supra].

221

221*d*—we do not know which Seneca is referred to (see Miriam Griffin, *JRS* 62 (1972), 10)—strongly suggests that Montanus had heard Virgil recite; for the latter's policy, cf. *Vita Donati* 33 'recitavit et pluribus, sed neque frequenter et ea fere de quibus ambigebat'. In that respect he was more privileged than the young Ovid (*Tr.* 4.10.51 'Vergilium vidi tantum'). If the restoration 'comes <Tiberii>' is correct in (*b*) (compare (*c*) 'et amicitia Tiberii notus et frigore') perhaps Montanus was with the future emperor during the latter's withdrawal to Rhodes (6 BC–AD 2); cf. Tac. *Ann.* 4.15.1 on Lucilius Longus, 'unus . . . e senatoribus Rhodii secessus comes'.

It is amusing that Montanus was 'egregius poeta' to the elder Seneca, but only 'tolerabilis' to the younger. When it came to judging poets, the son probably had higher critical standards. But Ovid's 'gemino carmine nomen habes' (*Ex Ponto* 4.16.12 = **221***a*) confirms that Montanus' reputation among contemporaries was quite high, for elegiacs as well as hexameters. His versification is competent and very smooth (note the absence of any elision from the six preserved lines). Half a century later the style might have seemed more commonplace (Calpurnius Siculus is equally smooth, and avoids elision almost completely), and ever more elaborate descriptions of dawn, dusk, and other hours of the clock had proliferated. Witness Seneca, *Apocol.* 2.3 '<adeo his> adquiescunt omnes poetae, non contenti ortus et occasum describere, ut etiam medium diem inquietent'. It would be unkind to point out that three out of seven lines of Montanus start with 'incipit', and that there are three examples of the 'iam . . .' motif. But 'subinde' and 'iam nox est?' in **221***c* suggest that the gap between **222** and **223** was not very wide.

222 (1 Bl., C.)

Description of times of day (with accompanying animal and/or human activity) start modestly in early Greek epic and are embellished by the Hellenistic poets, e.g. daybreak in Callimachus, *Hecale* fr. 74.22 ff. H. or the coming of night in Ap. Rh. 3.744 ff. (the source of Varro Atacinus, **129**, which Montanus described as 'illos optimos versus Varronis').

2. **spargere <se>:** *OLD spargo* 2(c), to emit in all directions, scatter (light or other physical phenomena). 'Spargier et' (Baehrens) is also possible; the old form of the passive infinitive has a long life, due to its metrical convenience.

tristis hirundo: still mourning Itys.

3. **argutis ... nidis:** 'shrill nestlings'. This metonymy occurs first in Virgil's *Georgics* (see Mynors on 2.210), cf. *Aen.* 12.475 'nidisque loquacibus escas'.

reditura: she will have to make several journeys to satisfy her young. The future participle is a refined predilection, e.g. 'ablatura' and 'flexura' in the exquisite lines mocked by Persius (*Sat.* 1.100–1).

inmittere: inserting the food into the fledglings' mouths.

3–4. In a familiar Virgilian 'theme and variation' (e.g. *Aen.* 2.230–1 'sacrum qui cuspide robur / laeserit et tergo sceleratam intorserit hastam'), the poet restates the action, emphasizing different aspects (the softness of the mother's mouth, and division of the food into appropriately sized pieces).

223 (2 Bl., C.)

1. **stabulis armenta:** thus placed in Virgil, *Georg.* 1.355 and 3.352.
locarunt: 'settled'.
2. **nox pigra:** because it is a time of inactivity.

Albinovanus Pedo

225

(a) Ov. *Ex Ponto* 4.16.5–6: *cumque foret Marsus* [**172a**] *magnique Rabirius* [**229a**] *oris, / Iliacusque Macer sidereusque Pedo.*

  (b) Ov. *Ex Ponto* 4.10.71–6: *at tu* [sc. Pedo], *non dubito, cum Thesea carmine laudes, / materiae titulos quin tueare tuae / . . .* (75) *qui quamquam est factis ingens et conditur a te / vir tanto quanto debuit ore cani . . .*

  (c) Sen. *Suas.* 1.15: *nemo illorum* [sc. qui Latine declamabant] *potuit tanto spiritu dicere quanto Pedo qui in navigante Germanico dicit* [**228**].

  (d) Quint. 10.1.90: *Rabirius* [**229c**] *ac Pedo non indigni cognitione, si vacet.*

(b) I do not doubt that, when you praise Theseus in your poem, you are preserving the glory of your subject . . . (75) Although he is great in his deeds, and you write of him with a grandeur that the hero requires . . .

  (c) None [of the Latin declaimers] was capable of speaking with the spirit which Pedo showed on the subject of Germanicus at sea [**228**].

  (d) Rabirius and Pedo are worth investigating, if you can spare the time.

226 Epigrammata

(a) Mart. Lib. I, praef.: *lascivam verborum veritatem, id est epigrammaton linguam, excusarem, si meum esset exemplum: sic scribit Catullus, sic Marsus* [**172c**], *sic Pedo, sic Gaetulicus, sic quicumque perlegitur* [=**172c**].

  (b) Mart. 2.77.1–6: *Cosconi, qui longa putas epigrammata nostra, / . . .* (5) *disce quod ignoras: Marsi* [**172e**] *doctique Pedonis / saepe duplex unum pagina tractat opus* [=**172e**].

  (c) Mart. 5.5.1–6: *Sexte, Palatinae cultor facunde Minervae, / . . .* (5) *sit locus et nostris aliqua tibi parte libellis, / qua Pedo, qua Marsus* [**172g**], *quaque Catullus erit* [=**172g**].

227 *Theseis*

Ov. *Ex Ponto* 4.10.71–6 [= **225***b*, v. supra].

228 (1 Bl., C.), de Germanici expeditione

iam pridem post terga diem solemque relictum
†iam quidem†, notis extorres finibus orbis,
per non concessas audaces ire tenebras
ad rerum metas extremaque litora mundi.
hunc illum, pigris immania monstra sub undis   5
qui ferat, Oceanum, qui saevas undique pristis
aequoreosque canes, ratibus consurgere prensis
(accumulat fragor ipse metus); iam sidere limo
navigia et rapido desertam flamine classem,
seque feris credunt per inertia fata marinis   10
iam non felici laniandos sorte relinqui.
atque aliquis prora caecum sublimis ab alta
aera pugnaci luctatus rumpere visu,
ut nihil erepto valuit dinoscere mundo,
obstructa in talis effundit pectora voces: 15
'quo ferimur? fugit ipse dies, orbemque relictum
ultima perpetuis claudit natura tenebris.
anne alio positas ultra sub cardine gentes
atque alium bellis intactum quaerimus orbem,
di revocant rerumque vetant cognoscere finem   20
mortales oculos? aliena quid aequora remis
et sacras violamus aquas divumque quietas
turbamus sedes?'

For a long time now they <? look in vain> for the daylight and the sun which
they had left behind them, banished from the known boundaries of the earth,
daring to pass through unpermitted darkness to the limits of Nature and the
outermost shores of the world. (5) This, then, was that Ocean which below its
sluggish surface breeds huge monsters, everywhere savage beasts and dogs of
the sea, the one which rose and carried away their ships (the very crashing
adds to their fears); at another time the vessels were sinking in mud and the
fleet had been deserted by the swift wind, (10) and they think that they are

being abandoned by a miserable fate, to be torn to pieces by wild beasts of the sea in a passive death. Someone high up on the prow, struggling with his combative gaze to break through the impenetrable mist, when he lacked the strength to distinguish anything—for the world had been snatched away—(15) poured out his choking heart in words such as this: 'Where are we being carried? Day itself is in retreat and outermost Nature shuts off the world which we have left in perpetual darkness. Are we seeking races beyond, who live under another pole, and another world untouched by war, (20) and do the gods call us back, forbidding mortal eyes to learn of Creation's end? Why do we violate seas that belong to others and holy waters with our oars, disturbing the peaceful abodes of the gods?'

Sen. *Suas.* 1.15: *nemo illorum* [sc. qui Latine declamabant] *potuit tanto spiritu dicere quanto Pedo qui in navigante Germanico dicit.*

1 iam pridem] iamque vident *Kent*   relictum] relincunt *Haupt*   2 iam quidem *BV*: iam quidam *A*: iam pridem *D*: iamque vident *Withof*: seque vident *Goodyear*   notis] natis *ABV*: noti se *Baehrens*   3 <se> audaces *susp. Buechner* 4 ad rerum *Haupt*: asperum *AB*: hesperii *VD*   5 hunc *Pithoeus*: nunc *codd.* 6 ferat] fert *Gertz*   11 iam *Schott*: tam *codd.*: quam *Heinsius*: a<h> *Gertz* 12 caecum *Haase*: cedunt *AB*: cedat *corr. ex* cedunt *V*: sedat *D*: densum *Bramble* 13 pugnaci] pungenti *tempt. Nisbet*   visu (*corr. ex.* visum) *V*: visum *AB*: nisu *D, Scaliger*   15 obstructa in . . . pectora *Bursian*: obstructo *D, Scaliger*: obstructum *ABV*   16 fugit *Gronovius*: rugit *ABD*: ruit *corr. ex.* rugit *V*   19 bellis *Meyer*: liberis *AB*: libris *V*: nobis *Burman*: flabris *Haupt*: alii alia

ALBINOVANUS Pedo, renowned as a story-teller and wit (Seneca, *Epist.* 122.15–16, Quintilian 6.3.61), was a younger friend of Ovid—the recipient of *Ex Ponto* 4.10 (with thanks for loyalty but a plea for positive proof of affection) and an eyewitness of the famous occasion when Ovid was asked to delete three lines of his poetry (Sen. *Contr.* 2.2.12). He may have been related to Horace's friend Albinovanus Celsus (*Epist.* 1.8, conceivably the Celsus lamented in Ovid, *Ex Ponto* 1.9). Martial (10.20.10) mentions 'parva . . . domus Pedonis' on the Esquiline by the Lacus Orphei; no doubt he cherished the house as having belonged to a fellow epigrammatist.

Pedo's literary fame rested mainly on his epic verse. Quintilian (**225***d*) seems to rate him a little below Cornelius Severus (who could have reached the heights) and on a par with Rabirius as worth reading 'if you have the leisure' (*si vacet*). This comparative ranking of Severus and Pedo seems not unfair, to judge from the single long fragment of each poet (**219** and **228** respectively) which we possess—with the reservation that our text of Pedo may be considerably the more corrupt. Ovid (**225***a*), it is true, calls Pedo 'sidereus', an epithet applied to Virgil by Columella (10.434), but when writing of a personal friend in a poem where the judgements are generous throughout. Unless Ovid in **225b = 227** refers to aspirations which remain unfulfilled, Pedo also wrote a mythological poem on Theseus. And he is several times (**226**) mentioned by Martial as an epigrammatist, linked particularly to Domitius Marsus who likewise cultivated two genres (epic and epigram) at opposite ends of the literary spectrum. We learn from **226b** that the epigrams of both poets were sometimes of considerable length.

228 (1 Bl., C.)

Lucan was to write a Roman epic on events of a century before his own time; Cornelius Severus and Rabirius treated those of nearly half a century ago. Albinovanus Pedo, however, chose the campaign of Germanicus in which he himself participated, if (as seems likely) he is the Pedo of Tacitus, *Ann.* 1.60.2 'equitem Pedo praefectus finibus Frisiorum ducit'. The disaster which overtook Germanicus' fleet in the summer of A D 16 is described in Tacitus, *Ann.* 2.23–4; some have thought (see Goodyear, *The Annals of Tacitus*, II (Cambridge, 1981), 243–5) that Pedo may here refer to those ships, hastily repaired after a storm, which Germanicus 'misit ut scrutarentur insulas' (in order to rescue survivors). For the purpose of writing this passage Pedo hardly needed to set foot outside the schools of rhetoric in Rome, since most of the themes were already familiar from declamations on Alexander the Great (cf. Curtius Rufus 9.3.8, 9.4.18, and 9.6.20). I quote the closer parallels in my commentary below, but it is worth reading the whole of Seneca, *Suas.* 1 (which includes our fragment).

Seneca admires the 'spiritus' of Pedo—a desirable quality in an epic poet (see Nisbet and Hubbard on Horace, *Odes* 2.16.38). Technically the versification is very competent, more spondaic than the long fragment of Cornelius Severus (one might ascribe that in part to the solemn subject matter). For independent texts of this fragment, see (besides Blänsdorf and Courtney) Winterbottom in the elder Seneca Loeb, Bramble in the *Cambridge History of Classical Literature*, II (1982), 489–90, Goodyear, *Annals of Tacitus*, II (1981), 456–7 (Appendix 2). Linguistic parallels are collected by V. Tandoi, *SIFC* 36 (1964), 129–68 and 39 (1967), 5–66; H. Dahlmann, *Cornelius Severus*, 128–37 (with a text on p. 137).

1 ff. The opening lines of the passage present structural problems (in my opinion not insoluble). Courtney (p. 316) characterizes the first sentence (which he would extend to 11 lines) as 'lumbering'. Restoring 'iamque vident' in 2, 'hunc' in 5, and punctuating with a comma after line 4, he sees the 'skeleton' (p. 317) of the construction as *iam vident diem solemque relictum iamque (hunc) illum Oceanum consurgere, iam sidere navigia et desertam classem.* I have punctuated more heavily after 4 and (following Nisbet) take the infinitives 'consurgere' (7), 'sidere' (8), and 'desertam' (9, understanding 'esse') as parts of accusative + infinitive without main verb, 'of the sort which one meets in historians and at *Aen.* 7.255–6 "hunc illum ... / portendi generum"'. We return to a finite verb in line 10, 'credunt'.

1.   There is perhaps a faint echo of this line and its context in Lucan 1.369–70 'haec manus, ut victum post terga relinqueret orbem, / Oceani tumidas remo conpescuit undas'.

diem solemque relictum: a favourite theme in the Alexander declamations, e.g. Sen. *Suas.* 1.1 'satis sit hactenus Alexandro vicisse qua mundo lucere satis est' and 'confusa lux alta caligine et interceptus tenebris dies', 1.2 'vicimus qua lucet'. Compare line 16 'fugit ipse dies'.

2.   **†iam quidem†:** obviously there has been some intrusion from line 1. Nisbet would like to see a verb with the sense of 'quaerunt', 'look in vain for', but doubts whether 'anquirunt' would be appropriate. 'seque vident' (Goodyear) would convert 'extorres' and 'audaces' (2–3) into accusatives; for 'iamque vident' (adopted by Courtney) see above on 1 ff.

extorres finibus orbis: banished not merely from their homeland (cf. *Aen.* 4.616 'finibus extorris') but from the whole world (Sallust, *Hist.* 2.14 M. 'orbe terrarum extorres'). The adjective is not applied objectively to exile, but enlists the reader's sympathy (see Ogilvie on Livy 2.6.2).

2–3.   Pedo combines the idea of an outcast with that of a trespasser on forbidden ground.

3.   **non concessas:** the gods and Nature object (cf. 17, 20).

audaces ire: the infinitive depends on the adjective, a favourite Horatian construction (e.g. *Odes* 1.3.25 'audax omnia perpeti').

4.   **rerum metas:** not a regular expression (*Aen.* 1.278 is clearly not comparable), although 'meta' is often used of the limit of the world. Quite close are Sen. *Suas.* 1.10 'rerum naturae terminos', *Pan. Lat.* 2.23.1 (Pacatus to Theodosius) 'dum ultra terminos rerum metasque naturae regna Orientis extendis'. A declaimer might question whether in fact there was such a boundary, 'nec usquam rerum naturam desinere, sed semper inde ubi desisse videatur novam exsurgere' (*Suas.* 1.1). Horace writes about the end of the world almost in terms of Lucretius' argument about the infinity of the Universe, and what would happen to a weapon thrown outwards from its apparent limit: 'quicumque mundo terminus obstitit, / hunc tanget armis' (*Odes* 3.3.53–4, cf. Lucr. 1.968 ff.). 'Res' (plural) = 'things combining to form the physical world' (*OLD res* 4) may first have been used as the title of Lucretius' poem.

5. hunc illum: like Courtney I print Pithoeus' conjecture 'hunc' (for the manuscripts' 'nunc', which many, including Bramble and Winterbottom, retain). As Courtney says, 'hic ille est' (which, as here, can be put into oblique cases) is used 'when one identifies something before one's eyes as something previously vaguely apprehended'. Much the best parallel is *Aen.* 7.255–6 'hunc illum . . . / portendi generum'; the infinitives 'portendi' and 'consurgere' (7) correspond, giving the thoughts, in Virgil of Latinus as he hears about Aeneas and connects him with Faunus' prophecy, in Pedo of the sailors as they experience in reality what they had been told about the Oceanus. Compare also *Aen.* 7.272 'hunc illum poscere fata', Tac. *Ann.* 14.22 'hunc illum numine deum destinari', and see Fordyce on *Aen.* 7.128 'haec erat illa fames'.

pigris . . . sub undis: as if Nature loses her strength at the edge of the world—a recurring motif, e.g. *Suas.* 1.1 'stat immotum mare, quasi deficientis in suo fine naturae pigra moles . . . ipsum vero grave et defixum mare', 1.2 'inmobile profundum', Curtius Rufus 9.4.18 'inmobiles undae, in quibus emoriens natura defecerit', Tac. *Agr.* 10.6, *Germ.* 45.1.

immania monstra: cf. Curtius Rufus 9.4.18 'repletum immanium beluarum gregibus fretum'. Alexander's admiral, Nearchus, claimed that his men had measured a whale 90 cubits long (Arrian, *Indica* 39.4, cf. E. Badian, *YCS* 24 (1975), 148). Not, of course, absent from the Elder Seneca: *Suas.* 1.1 'novae ac terribiles figurae, magna etiam Oceano portenta, quae profunda ista vastitas nutrit', 1.2 'foeda beluarum magnitudo', 1.4 'immanes propone beluas'. See Tandoi, *SIFC* 39 (1967), 29–30. Horace calls the Oceanus 'beluosus' (*Odes* 4.14.47–8). According to Tacitus (*Ann.* 2.24) survivors from Germanicus' expedition 'miracula narrabant, vim turbinum et inauditas volucris, monstra maris, ambiguas hominum et beluarum formas, visa sive ex metu credita'.

6. ferat: subjunctive because it conveys the sailors' thoughts (Courtney 317).

pristis: alternatively *pistris* or *pistrix*, in Greek πίστρις or πρίστις (the latter suggesting a link with πρίω/πρίζω, 'I saw', and hence identification with the sawfish). The word's first Latin occurrence is in Cicero's *Aratea* (fr. 33.140 Buescu), representing the constellation Cetus. Sometimes perhaps = the whale, but often (as here) a fabulous sea monster.

7. aequoreosque canes: κύων (ἡ θαλαττία), a dogfish or smaller shark (sometimes connected with the 'dogs' of the sea monster Scylla). See D'Arcy W. Thompson, *A Glossary of Greek Fishes* (London, 1947), 136–7.

consurgere: the rise and fall (cf. 8 'sidere') of tides could cause trouble and consternation to Romans, e.g. *Suas.* 1.2 'litora modo saeviente fluctu inquieta, modo fugiente deserta', Tac. *Ann.* 2.23.4 'postquam mutabat aestus . . . , non adhaerere ancoris'.

prensis: cf. Lucretius 6.429–30, Catullus 25.12–13 'velut minuta magno /

deprensa navis in mari'. After 'aequoreosque canes' there may also be a hint of teeth fastening upon the ships.

8.   (accumulat fragor ipse metus): cf. Val. Flacc. 3.404 'Oceani praeceps fragor', Sen. *Suas.* 1.11 'fremit Oceanus, quasi indignetur quod terras relinquas'.

sidere: 'settle' (*OLD* sido 2), as e.g. Prop. 2.14.30 'mediis sidat onusta vadis'.

9.   desertam: the correct term (e.g. Ovid, *Ex Ponto* 4.12.42 'ne sperata meam deserat unda ratem') but, here as often (*OLD* desero 2(b)), with a touch of personification (a companion abandoned in need).

10.   per inertia fata: 'in a passive death' (*per* as *OLD* 16, of an attendant circumstance). Instead of going out to attack the enemy, they must wait, marooned, until the monsters come to chew them up. Compare Ovid, *Met.* 7.544 (a spirited horse succumbing to plague in its stable) 'leto moriturus inerti', and, with *ignavus*, 8.518 (Meleager) 'ignavo . . . et sine vulnere leto'.

11.   iam non felici: they had escaped the rising tide (7), but now good fortune deserts them. The interjection 'a!' (Gertz, for 'iam', cf. Virgil, *Ecl.* 6.77) seems stylistically out of place here.

12 ff.   atque aliquis . . .: an unnamed member of the crowd, voicing the general opinion. Dahlmann, *Cornelius Severus*, 129–30, illustrates this motif in Greek epic from Homer (*Il.* 4.81 etc., ὧδε δέ τις εἴπεσκεν ἰδὼν ἐς πλησίον ἄλλον) to Nonnus (e.g. *Dion.* 29.49 ff. καί τις ἰδὼν Διόνυσον . . . / (51) τοῖον ἔπος κατέλεξε). See also McKeown on Ovid, *Am.* 2.1.7 'atque aliquis iuvenum'. This pattern does not occur in the *Aeneid*, Valerius Flaccus, or Silius, but is found in the *Metamorphoses* (3.404 ff.) and Statius, *Theb.* (1.171 ff., 4.825 ff.).

12.   caecum: *OLD* 5 (of night, clouds, etc.), 'opaque', 'dark', 'black', 'impenetrable' (e.g. Lucr. 2.746 'caecis . . . tenebris'). This is some way from the transmitted text, and Bramble's 'densum' deserves equal consideration.

13.   pugnaci . . . visu: the variant 'nisu' (D, favoured by Heinsius) has some attraction, and would sit more easily with 'pugnaci', but the idea of strenuous effort is sufficiently conveyed by 'luctatus'. 'Pugnaci . . . visu' is an awkward phrase; *Aen.* 10.447 'truci . . . visu' (Pallas not afraid to confront Turnus) does not provide a very good parallel. Nisbet thought of 'pungenti . . . visu', 'with piercing gaze'. One might compare Lucretius 2.460 (of atoms) 'pungere uti possint corpus penetrareque saxa'.

rumpere: perhaps suggesting a bolt of lightning which forces its way through the clouds. Compare Val. Flacc. 1.463–4 (of Lynceus) 'possit qui rumpere terras / et Styga transmisso tacitam deprendere visu'.

15.   obstructa in talis effundit pectora voces: 'obstructa in' and 'pectora' are due to Bursian in his 1857 edition of the elder Seneca, followed by

Morel, W. A. Edward (in his (Cambridge, 1928) elder Seneca), Winterbottom ('he pours his frustrated heart into words') and Bramble ('he chokes [sc. the spoken words] from his tightened lungs'). All manuscripts have 'pectore', and D 'obstructo' (ABV 'obstructum'). Without doubt 'obstructo . . . pectore' (Dahlmann, *Cornelius Severus*, 131, Courtney, Blänsdorf) is the easier expression; in fact 'talis effundit pectore voces' would be identical with *Aen.* 5.482 and can be taken back to Ennius, *Ann.* 553 'effudit voces' (Skutsch thinks that 'talis' ended the previous line). Rather than simply repeating the Virgilian phrase, Pedo might be expected to vary it more adventurously. Thus, with some hesitation, I follow Bursian, although there is no clear parallel for 'effundit pectora'—Statius, *Silv.* 5.1.111 'effuso . . . pectore' (lying prostrate on the ground) does not help. Occasionally the object of 'effundere' can be the vessel which is emptied rather than its contents (the earliest example in *TLL* is Pliny, *NH* 14.142 'tremulae manus effundentes plena vasa'); a metaphorical extension of that usage (as seemingly in Winterbottom's translation, above) might be considered. This could also suit 'obstructa'; when a blockage in e.g. a watering-can is freed the liquid comes out in a sudden rush.

obstructa: the verb can be used of stopping the nose or mouth, stifling the breathing (*OLD* 2(d)) or of choking, obstructing the faculties (*OLD* 5, citing this fragment). Pliny, *Epist.* 6.16.19 'crassiore caligine spiritu obstructo' (quoted by Courtney to support 'obstructo . . . pectore' here) describes the fate of his uncle after the eruption of Vesuvius.

16. quo ferimur?: for 'quo feror?' as an expression of bewilderment and loss of control, cf. *Aen.* 10.670 (Turnus), Lucan 1.678 (the inspired matrona); in different words, Horace, *Odes* 3.25.1 'quo me, Bacche, rapis . . .?'

17. ultima perpetuis claudit natura tenebris: *Suas.* 1.2 'quod humanis natura subduxit oculis, aeterna nox obruit'.

18–23. These lines (still within the ambit of the Alexander declamation and its theme of leaving the bounds of the world) contain a glorious mixture of ideas; we should not demand consistency of them. Britain is almost certainly in the foreground (see Tandoi, *SIFC* 36 (1964), particularly 144 ff.); during the interval between Julius Caesar and Claudius, this island gave room for hopeful prophecy and panegyric (e.g. [Tibullus], *Pan. Mess.* 149 'te manet invictus Romano Marte Britannus'). There may be hints of the Hyperboreans (Mela 3.5.36–7 'sub ipso siderum cardine . . . non bella novere'), even of the Happy Isles (islands in the Oceanus where war is unknown), although the locations and details do not all fit Germanicus' expedition.

18. alio . . . sub cardine: generally taken as 'region', 'district' (*OLD* 5, e.g. Silius 4.779–80 'quocumque in cardine mundi / bella moves'), but 'sub' rather suggests 'pole' (*OLD* 3), as in Seneca, *HF* 1139–40 'sub cardine / glacialis Ursae'.

ultra: beyond the Oceanus (*Suas.* 1.1 'aiunt fertiles in Oceano iacere terras, ultraque Oceanum rursus alia litora, alium nasci orbem').

gentes: for the theme of discovering and straightaway conquering nations that were previously unknown, see Tandoi, *SIFC* 36 (1964), 144, e.g. [Virgil], *Catal.* 9.53–4 (to Messalla) 'nunc aliam ex alia bellando quaerere gentem / vincere et Oceani finibus ulterius'.

19.   alium . . . orbem: compare Velleius Paterculus 2.46.1 'alterum paene . . . orbem' of Britain (with Woodman's commentary), *Suas.* 1.1 'alium . . . orbem'.

bellis intactum: the manuscripts have 'liberis' or 'libris'; for a list of conjectures see E. Pianezolla, *REL* 62 (1984), 192–205. Of these, 'bellis' (Meyer, and independently Tandoi) has most to commend it because of its frequent association with 'intactus' (e.g. Livy 3.26.2 'prope intacti bello fines', more in Dahlmann, *Cornelius Severus*, 132). The most serious competitor is 'nobis' (Burman, and independently Nisbet), which I would interpret as 'us Romans' rather than 'us men' (Bramble). I am not sure why Courtney considers *nobis* 'over-emphatic'.

quaerimus: contrast *Suas.* 1.2 'non quaerimus orbem sed amittimus'.

20–1.   di revocant rerumque vetant cognoscere finem / mortales oculos?: cf. *Suas.* 1.2 'quod humanis natura subduxit oculis'. I have postponed the question mark from the end of 19 to the middle of 21, so that 'di revocant—oculos' remains within the question, speculating rather than making a firm statement about the gods' motives. There is (quite elegant) asyndeton between 19 and 20.

21–3.   It is worth reading the younger Seneca, *QN* 5.18.5–10, much of which (including 8 'quid maria inquietamus?') could have been used in a declamation dissuading Alexander (mentioned in 10, 'sic Alexander ulteriora Bactris et Indis volet, quaeretque quid sit ultra magnum mare, et indignabitur esse aliquid ultimum sibi') from further exploration. Tacitus writes in a similar vein about Germanicus' father Drusus (*Germ.* 34.3): 'nec defuit audentia Druso Germanico, sed obstitit Oceanus in se atque in Herculem [who was held to have visited Germany too] inquiri. mox nemo temptavit, sanctiusque ac reverentius visum de actis deorum [Oceanus as well as Hercules] credere quam scire'—a fine *sententia* on which to end! The notion of impiety and violation is also present in Pedo (22 'violamus', 23 'turbamus') and in *Suas.* 1.4 'sacrum quiddam terris natura circumfudit Oceanum'.

21.   aliena . . . aequora: perhaps in contrast to the Roman Mediterranean, 'mare nostrum', rather than with reference to the idea that mankind was not intended to sail at all (see Nisbet and Hubbard's introduction to Horace, *Odes* 1.3 (pp. 43–4)).

22–3.   divumque quietas / turbamus sedes: we are reminded of the inviolate 'sedes . . . quietas' of the gods in Lucretius 3.18 ff. If the Epicurean gods lived in spaces between the worlds (*intermundia*, μετακόσμια), it is not unreasonable to find them here.

Before we leave Albinovanus Pedo, note the anonymous line extracted by Bentley from Seneca, *De ira* 2.15.5 'ingenia immansueta suoque simillima caelo' (**260** = fr. an. 24 Courtney). Many have thought of Albinovanus Pedo; Tac. *Ann.* 2.24 'truculentia caeli praestat Germania' might suggest a connection between the climate and character. See on **260**. Pedo is also a possible candidate for Adesp. **261**, 'iam madet adducta salsugine nubibus aether'.

Rabirius

229

(a) Ov. *Ex Ponto* 4.16.5–6: *cumque foret Marsus* [**172a**] *magnique Rabirius oris, / Iliacusque Macer sidereusque Pedo* [**225a**].

    (*b*) Velleius Paterculus 2.36.3: *paene stulta est inhaerentium oculis ingeniorum enumeratio, inter quae maxime nostri aevi eminent princeps carminum Vergilius Rabiriusque et consecutus Sallustium Livius, Tibullusque et Naso, perfectissimi in forma operis sui; nam vivorum ut magna admiratio, ita censura difficilis est.*

    (*c*) Quint. 10.1.90: *Rabirius ac Pedo* [**225d**] *non indigni cognitione, si vacet.*

(*b*) It is almost foolish to catalogue the great talents who are firmly within our sight: among these outstanding in our own age are Virgil, prince of poets, and Rabirius, Livy who succeeded Sallust, and Tibullus and Naso [Ovid], most perfect in the form of their work; as for living authors, while we admire them greatly, so critical estimation of them is difficult.

    (*c*) Rabirius and Pedo [**225d**] are worth getting to know, if you have the spare time.

230 (1 Bl., C.)

Idaeos summa cum margine colles

When with its topmost edge <? the sun strikes> the Idaean hills.

Charis., pp. 81–2 Barwick = GLK I, p. 65: *margo feminino genere, ut virgo imago Karthago et cetera similia quae ante o habent g; ideoque et Aemilius Macer ait* [**68**] *et Rabirius* [fort. <*feminine*>, Keil] *extulit:* 'Idaeos—colles'.

    extulit *Rabirio ipsi tribuit Barthius*

231 (2 Bl., C.)

hoc habeo, quodcumque dedi

Sen. *De ben.* 6.3.1: *egregie mihi videtur M. Antonius apud Rabirium poetam, cum fortunam suam transeuntem alio videat et sibi nihil relictum praeter ius mortis, id quoque si cito occupaverit, exclamare:* 'hoc habeo—dedi'.

It seems to me that, in the poet Rabirius, Mark Antony exclaims admirably 'I possess whatever I have given away', at a time when he sees his fortune passing to another and nothing remaining for himself except the right to determine his own death—and that too only if he seizes it without delay.

232 (3 Bl., C.)

ac veluti Numidis elephans circumdatur altus

. . . and, as when a lofty elephant is surrounded by Numidians . . .

Auctor De Dub. Nom., GLK V, p. 578: *elephantus generis masculini, ut Rabirius:* 'ac veluti—altus'.

altus *Haupt:* aliis *LV:* illis *M*   circumdatus alis *coni. Clericus*

233 (4 Bl., C.)

in tenue est deducta serum pars infima lactis

The lowest part of the milk is reduced to thin whey

Auctor De Dub. Nom., GLK V, p. 590: *serum lactis generis neutri, ut Rabirius:* 'in tenue—lactis'.

tenue *L. Mueller:* teneum *codd.:* tenerum *Haupt*   pars infima *Courtney:* pars intima *Haupt:* parsimonia *codd.*

234 (5 Bl., C.)

portarumque fuit custos ericius

. . . and guardian of the gates was the hedgehog.

Auctor De Dub. Nom., GLK V, p. 578: *erinacius, non ericius. tamen Rabirius:*
'portarumque—ericius'.

229

RABIRIUS is linked by Ovid (**229**a) to Domitius Marsus (*qua* epic poet, **172**a),
Macer (see Appendix, p. 424), and Albinovanus Pedo (**225**a). Ovid calls him
'grandiloquent Rabirius' ('magni . . . oris'), and Quintilian (**229**c) states that
he and Pedo are worth reading if you have the time. There is no hint of any
personal relationship between Ovid and Rabirius, by contrast with Macer and
Pedo—and also Cornelius Severus (**203–20**), another comparable poet of
approximately the same period. So Rabirius seems to belong to a group of
epic writers towards the end of Augustus' and the beginning of Tiberius'
reign; perhaps he came to prominence a little later than the others (hence no
personal dealings with Ovid). He must have been dead by AD 29, the year in
which Velleius (who declines to pass judgement on living writers) finished his
History (see A. J. Woodman, *CQ* NS 25 (1975), 282).

We at least have one substantial fragment of Cornelius Severus (**219**) and
Albinovanus Pedo (**228**) which allow us to see something of their quality and
individuality. For Rabirius there is no counterpart. Only **231** reveals that he
wrote on comparatively recent Roman history, and was capable of a *sententia*
which won the enthusiastic approval of the younger Seneca—the fact that this
was put into the mouth of Mark Antony might incline us to date it to the
principate of Tiberius rather than of Augustus. The other fragments (with the
possible exception of **230**) do not make a great impression. According to
Courtney (p. 332), Velleius rated Rabirius 'above Ovid and Tibullus', a sign
that V. 'was not intelligent enough to separate literary quality from subject-
matter'. That seems unfair: Velleius is clearly making separate judgements
according to literary genre. Tibullus and Ovid are his favourite elegists;
among recent epic poets Virgil is supreme ('princeps carminum', **229**b) but
Rabirius comes second. This may mean that Velleius preferred Rabirius to
Pedo (the pair bracketed by Quintilian, **229**c) and also to Cornelius Severus,
who could have claimed second place if he had completed his *Bellum Siculum*

to the standard of book 1 (see **203***e*). It is not clear whether Velleius would have regarded Ovid's *Metamorphoses* to be in direct competition with the epic poetry of Rabirius *et al.* (**229***b* probably refers only to O.'s elegiac verse).

On the basis of **231** some (e.g. G. Garuti, *C.* [?] *Rabirius, Bellum Actiacum* (1958), not convincing E. J. Kenney, *CR* N s 10 (1960), 138–9) have wished to ascribe the Herculaneum epic (*P. Herc.* 817, see Blänsdorf pp. 430–8, Courtney 334–40) to Rabirius; among other possible authors, Varius Rufus and Cornelius Severus (Courtney 334) have been suggested. Although of course the state of the text does not help, *P. Herc.* 817 seems to me to come from a very mediocre and unexciting composition, unworthy (certainly) of Varius Rufus and probably of Cornelius Severus too. Whether it was unworthy of Rabirius we are not in a position to say; I suspect that it dates from somewhat later in the first century. There is also the anonymous **262** 'armatum cane, Musa, ducem, belloque cruentam / Aegyptum' (cf. Courtney 334), which might belong to the Herculaneum epic / Rabirius, or be somebody's fraudulent idea of how such an epic ought to begin.

230 (1 Bl., C.)

Idaeos summa cum margine colles: some have included 'extulit' in the poetic quotation; in connection with 'colles' the verb might mean 'elevated', 'caused to rise'. But that is almost certainly wrong, since 'extulit' is a grammarian's technical term, 'to put (a word or root) into a given form, inflexion, etc.' (*OLD effero*, 7c), often used in this sense by Charisius (see V. Lomanto and N. Marinone, *Index Grammaticus* (1990), I, p. 728 s.v. *extulit*). Keil may have been right to suggest restoring the grammarian's original text as 'Rabirius <feminine> extulit', which would accord with Charisius' normal practice (e.g. p. 137 Barwick[2] 'Propertius feminine extulit', see app. crit. to **209**). The mere chance that 'extulit' could form the first foot of a hexameter before 'Idaeos' may have caused the loss of an equivalent metrical unit. Incidentally Charisius' implication that 'margo' is normally feminine (thus indeed Aemilius Macer, **68**) may be misleading; wherever the distinction can be made, Ovid has it masculine.

If this extract comes from a poem on Roman history, one may wonder about the relevance of 'Idaeos . . . colles'. I suspect that these words belong to a description of sunrise, that *cum* means 'when' rather than 'with', and that 'summa . . . margine' refers to the topmost edge of the sun's disc, as in Ovid, *Fasti* 3.361 'ortus erat summo tantummodo margine Phoebus'. Rabirius' sense could have been 'at the time when <the sun strikes> the Idaean hills with its topmost rim'; the initial dactyl might be supplied by e.g. 'percutit' or 'sol ferit' (cf. Ovid, *Met.* 9.93 'primo feriente cacumina sole'). Mount Ida in the Troad was thought to be the first place struck by the rays of the rising sun (Euripides, *Troades* 1066–8 Ἰδαῖα ... νάπη / ... / τέρμονά τε πρωτόβολον ἔωι). For the strange story that, from Mount Ida, one could see a new sun forming its orb every day, cf. Lucretius 5.663–5 'quod genus Idaeis fama est e montibus altis / dispersos ignis orienti lumine cerni, / inde coire globum quasi in unum et conficere orbem', with Bailey's commentary (pp. 1426–7, vol. III).

Perhaps Rabirius was describing some (?military) operation starting at the very first hint of dawn. A point of literary interest would arise. In place of the standard mythological account of dawn, involving Aurora and the bed of Tithonus or Oceanus (e.g. Furius Bibaculus, **72**), Rabirius has substituted something philosophical and scientific, recalling Lucretius.

231 (2 Bl., C.)

It seems likely that Seneca's words 'cum fortunam suam transeuntem alio videat et sibi nihil relictum praeter ius mortis, id quoque si cito occupaverit' are a paraphrase of the general context as expressed by Rabirius. Compare Pompey after the battle of Pharsalus in Lucan 7.647 ff., 'iam Magnus transisse deos Romanaque fata / senserat infelix ... / ...' (666) 'quid perdere cuncta laboras? / iam nihil est, Fortuna, meum', though Antony (unlike Pompey) was apparently delivering a self-epitaph shortly before his suicide.

hoc habeo quodcumque dedi: as Courtney says, this seems to be an adaptation of the Greek self-epitaph attributed to Sardanapallus, ταῦτ' ἔχω ὅσσ' ἔφαγον καὶ ἐφύβρισα καὶ μετ' ἔρωτος / τέρπν' ἔπαθον, τὰ δὲ πολλὰ καὶ ὄλβια κεῖνα λέλειπται (*Suppl. Hell.* 335.4–5 under Choerilus of Iasos, together with parallel texts). Cicero translated these two lines into 'haec habeo quae edi, quaeque exsaturata libido / hausit, at illa iacent multa et praeclara relicta' (Blänsdorf p. 178, from *Tusc. Disp.* 5.101). Rabirius' paradox, that one truly possesses only those things which one has given away, is elaborated by Seneca (loc. cit.) and is the subject of Martial 5.42, which ends (7–8) 'extra fortunam est quidquid donatur amicis; / quas dederis solas semper habebis opes' (Martial may still have read Rabirius). Antony's generosity is a constant theme in Plutarch's *Life* (e.g. 67.8).

232 (3 Bl., C.)

ac veluti Numidis elephans circumdatur altus: in order to show the mascu-
line gender, we need to accept one of two conjectures, either 'altus' (Haupt,
for 'aliis' or 'illis'), or Clericus' 'circumdatus' (which he coupled with 'alis',
another conjecture, making 'Numidis' adjectival) for 'circumdatur'. One
might naturally think of the Bellum Africum leading up to the battle of
Thapsus, in which both sides used elephants; e.g. [Caesar] *Bell. Afr.* 59
describes light-armed Numidian auxiliaries stationed behind elephants. This
is a simile; some other situation is being compared to an elephant surrounded
by Numidians. The point might be that the elephant is so much taller than the
men. Or perhaps the Numidians are hunting or attacking the elephant (a
parallel for some great fighter being attacked by lesser foes?). Bramble (*CHCL*
II, p. 486) cites Lucan 6.208 'sic Libycus densis elephans oppressus ab armis'.
For elephants in antiquity, see H. H. Scullard, *The Elephant in the Greek and
Roman World* (London, 1974).

233 (4 Bl., C.)

in tenue est deducta serum pars infima lactis: 'the lowest part of the milk is
reduced to thin whey'. Compare Pliny, *NH* 28.126 'discedit ['separates']
serum a lacte'. Courtney (who conjectured 'pars infima') suggests that this
line belonged to a simile; I cannot think of an epic parallel, or what the simile
might illustrate.

234 (5 Bl., C.)

portarumque fuit custos ericius: from one of the more bizarre entries in
Dub. Nom.—though it does at least deal with a noun (unlike several in GLK
V, p. 573), if not its gender. No less strangely Baehrens ('correxi' [!]) altered
'ericius' to the proper name 'Erycius'; admittedly we rather expect a proper
name after 'custos'—this may be a deliberate surprise from the poet.
Courtney is surely right: the reference is to a spiked defensive barrier, such as
the Pompeians used against Caesar in *BC* 3.67.5 'erat obiectus portae ericius',
in that case without success (ibid. 'exciso . . . ericio primo'). Compare Sallust,
Hist. 3.36, C. Cichorius, *Rh. M.* 76 (1927), 330.

ericius: 'hedgehog'. The animal name (cf. 'aries' and 'testudo' used for other pieces of military technology) helps the personification in 'custos'. A Greek form is χήρ (whence Nemesianus, *Cyn.* 57 'implicitumque sinu spinosi corporis erem'); in Latin we find also 'erinaceus' and 'iris' (Plautus, *Capt.* 184).

Adespota Selecta

235 (inc. 35 Bl., an. 10 C.)

Luna, deum quae sola vides periuria vulgi,
  seu Cretaea magis seu tu Dictynna vocaris

The figure of thought expressed by perplexity: 'Moon, you who alone of the
gods observe the common people's perjuries—or if you would sooner be
called Lady of Crete or Dictynna.'

1–2 Charis., p. 374 Barwick² = GLK I, p. 287: *schema dianoeas . . . per aporian*:
'Luna—vocaris'.

   2 Cretaea *nonnullis suspectum*: sive Hecate mavis . . . vocari *Naeke*

236 (inc. 36–37 Bl., an. 14 C.)

fortia neglecti velabant colla capilli,
  et per neglectos †velabant† colla capillos.
  a quotiens umbra porrexi bracchia mota!
  a quotiens umbra re<d>duxi bracchia mota!

Untended hair veiled his sturdy neck, and yet his neck <?gleamed> through
the untended hair. Ah, how often did I stretch out my arms when the
phantom stirred! Ah, how often did I withdraw my arms when the phantom
was removed!

1–4 Schol. Pers. 1.86 (85–6 'crimina rasis / librat in antithetis'), p. 268 ed. O.
Jahn (1843): *antitheta autem sunt haec*: 'fortia—mota'.

   2 †velabant†] lucebant *vel* candebant *Baehrens*   3–4 ah . . . / ah *Lindenbrog*:
aut . . . / aut *codd.*

237 (Aemilius Macer 11 Bl., an. 30 C.)

suspendit teneros male fortis aranea cassis
The feeble spider hangs out its soft nets.

Corpus Glossariorum Latinorum, vol. V, p. 175, ed. G. Goetz, 1894 (Gloss. Lat. I, p. 100 ed. Lindsay, 1926): *casses genus masculinum. Vergilius* <'laxos in foribus suspendit aranea casses' (*G.* 4.247) * * *> 'suspendit—cassis'.

hunc versum *G.* 4.247 esse vix credas; Aemilio Macro dedit H. Thomson, *AJP* 43 (1922), 352.

238 (inc. 33 Bl., an. 8 C.)

tuque Lycaonio mutatae semine nymphae
quam gelido raptam de vertice Nonacrino
Oceano prohibet semper se tingere Tethys
ausa suae quia sit quondam succumbere alumnae

And you, born from the Lycaon-sprung seed of the transformed nymph whom, after her abduction from the chill summit of Nonacris, Tethys forbade in perpetuity to bathe herself in Oceanus because she once had the audacity to supplant her nursling.

1–4 Hyg. *Fab.* 177: *Callisto Lycaonis filia ursa dicitur facta esse ob iram Iunonis quod cum Iove concubuit. postea Iovis in stellarum numero retulit, quae Septentrio appellatur, quod signum loco non movetur neque occidit. Tethys enim Oceani uxor nutrix Iunonis prohibet eam in oceanum occidere. hic ergo Septentrio maior, de qua in Creticis* [*versibus* del. Nisbet]: 'tuque—alumnae'.

Callisto daughter of Lycaon is said to have been turned into a bear on account of the anger of Juno because she lay with Jupiter. Later Jupiter included her among the stars, with the name Septentrio—a constellation which does not move from its position, nor does it set. This, then, is the Greater Bear, which is mentioned in the *Cretica*.

1 Lycaonio *Scheffer:* Lycaoniae *ed. Micylli 1535*   mutatae] mutate e *Heinsius* 2 Nonacrino *Muncker:* Nonacrinae *ed. Micylli*   3 thetis *ed. Micylli, corr. Muncker*

239 (inc. 34 Bl., an. 9 C.)

sed lucet in astris

Callisto renovatque suos sine fluctibus ignes

... but Callisto shines among the stars and renews her fires without help of
the waves.

1–2 'Lact. Plac.', Narr. Ov. *Met.* II.6 (p. 639 Magnus): *ut alii*: 'sed lucet—
ignes'.

240 (Bl. p. 196)

Lucili, quam sis mendosus, teste Catone
defensore tuo pervincam, qui male factos
emendare parat versus; hoc lenior ille
quo melior vir <et> est longe subtilior illo
qui multum puerum est loris et funibus udis 5
exhortatus, ut esset opem qui ferre poetis
antiquis posset contra fastidia nostra,
grammaticorum equitum doctissimus

Lucilius, how full of faults you are I will prove on the evidence of your
defender, Cato, who is preparing to correct badly written lines; in this respect
he is gentler, to the extent that he is a better man and far more refined, than
the one who has encouraged many a boy with straps and moistened ropes, so
that there should be someone capable of rescuing the old poets from our
disdain, most learned of the scholarly knights.

1–8 versus Hor. *Sat.* 1.10 praemissi

5 puerum est *Reisig*: puer et *codd.*: pueros *Nipperdey*   6 exhortatus ς, *Reisig*:
exoratus *Fλ*   8 *post* doctissimus *codd. habent* ut redeam illuc (*quod cum
praecedentibus vix cohaeret*)

241 (inc. 32 Bl., an. 3 C.)

iam puerile iugum tenera cervice gerebat

Already she was bearing the boy's yoke on her soft neck.

Isid. *Or.* 11.2.11: *puer autem tribus modis dicitur . . . pro aetate . . . unde est illud* 'iam—gerebat'.

242 (inc. 68 Bl., an. 6 C.)

aligeros conscendit equos

He mounted the winged chariot.

Isid. *Or.* 1.37.3: *fiunt autem metaphorae modis quattuor: ab animali ad animale, ut* 'aligeros—equos'. *metaphorice loquens miscuit quadrupedi alas avis*

de Varronis Atacini *Argonautis* dubitanter cogito, coll. Ap. Rh. 3.1235–7.

243 (inc. 63 Bl., an. 4 C.)

pontum pinus arat, sulcum premit alta carina

The pine ploughs the sea; its deep keel imprints a furrow.

Isid. *Or.* 1.37.3: *metaphorae . . . ab inanimali ad inanimale, ut*: 'pontum—carina'.

de Varr. At. *Argonautis* cogitavit iam Nettleship; confero Ap. Rh. 4.225–6.

244

Lactant. *De opificio Dei* 18.2: *idcirco animum et animam indifferenter appellant duo Epicurei poetae.*

Accordingly two Epicurean poets speak without distinction of mind (*animus*) and soul (*anima*).

poeta Epicureus alter plane Lucretius est (v. *DRN* 3.421–3); alterum Varium Rufum (*De morte*, cf. **147–50**) fuisse suspicor.

245 (Klotz, SRF I, p. 332)

ATREUS
en impero Argis; sceptra mihi liquit Pelops
qua ponto ab Helles atque ab Ionio mari
urgetur Isthmos

1–3 Sen. *Epist.* 80.7: *ille qui in scaena latus incedit et haec resupinus dicit:* 'en impero—Isthmos', *servus est; quinque modios accipit et quinque denarios.*
1 Quint. 9.4.140: *tragoedia*. . . ['locus desperatus', Winterbottom, cf. *Problems in Quintilian*, p. 186] . . . *spondeis atque iambis maxime continetur.* 'en impero—Pelops'.

(Seneca) He who walks with broad strides upon the stage and, throwing back his head, utters the following words: 'See, I rule over Argos: Pelops left to me kingly power, where the Isthmus is pressed by the Aegean and the Ionian sea' is a slave; he receives five modii and five denarii.

1 sceptra *Quint.*: regna *Sen.*

Fort. e Varii Rufi *Thyesta.*

246 (Klotz, SRF I, p. 349)

THYESTES
cur fugis fratrem? scit ipse

Sen. *Contr.* 1.1.21: *colorem ex altera parte, quae durior est, Latro aiebat hunc sequendum, ut gravissimarum iniuriarum inexorabilia et ardentia induceremus odia. Thyesteo more aiebat patrem non irasci tantum debere, sed furere. ipse in declamatione usus est summis clamoribus illo versu tragico:* 'cur fugis—ipse'.

(Seneca) He [Porcius Latro] used to say that the father should not merely get angry, but go mad, in the manner of Thyestes. He himself aroused the utmost enthusiasm by using in his declamation the famous tragic line 'Why do you flee from your brother? He himself knows.'

247 (inc. 40 Bl., p. 145 C.)

et verba antiqui multum furate Catonis,
Crispe, Iugurthinae conditor historiae

. . . and you, Crispus, composer of Jugurtha's history, who frequently stole the
words of old Cato.

1–2 Quint. 8.3.29: *nec minus noto Sallustius epigrammate incessitur:* 'et
verba—historiae'.
2 Mar. Vict. GLK I, p. 109: *tertia autem* [sc. species], *cum primus est dactylus
sequentibus duobus spondeis, anapaestis duobus in clausula positis, ut:*
'Crispe—historiae'.

248 (inc. 70 Bl.)

Musae Aonides

Boeotian Muses

Serv. GLK IV, p. 424: *quintus modus est, cum diphthongum vocalis sequitur; est
enim longa in hoc:* 'Musae Aonides' (fere eadem GLK IV p. 479, V p. 118, VI
pp. 230 et 242, VII p. 232).

249 (inc. 82 Bl., an. 32 C.)

Lactant. *Inst.* 1.11.1: *non insulse quidam poeta triumphum Cupidinis scripsit;
quo in libro non modo potentissimum deorum Cupidinem, sed etiam victorem
facit. enumeratis enim amoribus singulorum, quibus in potestatem Cupidinis
dicionemque venissent, instruit pompam, in qua Iuppiter cum ceteris diis ante
currum triumphantis ducitur catenatus.*

(Lactantius) It was not absurd for some poet to write of Cupid's triumph. In
that work he made Cupid not merely the most powerful of the gods, but even
their conqueror. For, after recounting the loves of individual gods (through
which they had come under the power and jurisdiction of Cupid), he sets up a
procession in which Jupiter, together with the other gods, is led in chains
before the chariot of the triumphant love-god.

250 (inc. 42 Bl, Maecenas 5–6 C.)

o qui chelyn canoram plectro regis Italo
O you who control the tuneful lyre with an Italian quill

[Caesius Bassus], GLK VI, p. 262: *Maecenas . . .* [**189**] *et Catullus* [63.2] *et ille* [sc. versus] *alterius auctoris*: 'o qui—Italo'.

251 (inc. 43 Bl., Maecenas 5–6 C.)

rutilos recide crines habitumque cape viri
Cut back your red hair and take on the clothing of a man.

Diom. GLK I, p. 514 [post Maec. **188**.1 et **189**]: *ceterum huic metro, quod enervatum diximus, simile est illud neotericum, quod est tale*: 'rutilos—viri'.

252 (an. 25 C.)

stat tamen et clamore iuvat
Yet he stands his ground and gives assistance by shouting.

Sen. *De tranquillitate animi* 4.5: *praecisis quoque manibus ille in proelio invenit quod partibus conferat qui* 'stat—iuvat'.

   Versum agnovit Weymann, *ALL* 15 (1908), 574.

253 (inc. 52 Bl., an. 19 C.)

magnae nunc hiscite terrae
Great Earth, now open wide

Quint. 9.2.26: *et irasci nos et gaudere et timere et admirari et dolere . . . fingimus. unde sunt illa: . . . et* 'magnae—terrae'.

254 (inc. 55 Bl., an. 12 C.)

Cyclops, Aetnaeus cultor, Neptunia proles
the Cyclops, Aetnaean dweller, offspring of Neptune

Charis., p. 10 Barwick=GLK I, p. 13 [post **259**]: *longa autem in hoc:* 'Cyclops—proles' (eadem Dositheus, GLK VII, p. 387).

255 (inc. 57 Bl.)

in medio victoria ponto
there is victory in the middle of the sea

Charis., p. 357 Barwick[2] = GLK I, p. 271: *de ellipsi. ellipsis est sententia verborum minus <habens> quam necesse est, salva tamen compositione verborum, ut per 'est':* 'in medio—ponto'.

256 (inc. 64 Bl., an. 5 C.)

te, Neptune pater, cui tempora cana crepanti
cincta salo resonant, magnus cui perpete mento
profluit Oceanus et flumina crinibus errant

. . . you, father Neptune, whose grey temples resound, encircled with roaring sea-swell, down the length of whose chin the great Ocean flows forth, and in whose hair rivers wander.

1–3 August. *De doctr. Christ.* 3.7.11: *sicut* [Neptunus] *a quodam poeta illorum describitur,* . . . *ita dicente:* 'te—errant'. Isid. *Or.* 1.37.4: *metaphorae* . . . *ab inanimali ad inanimale:* 'tu—errant'.

   1 te *August.:* tu *Isid.*

257 (inc. 60 Bl., an. 15 C.)

Iuppiter omnipotens, caeli qui sidera torques,
ore tuo dicenda loquar.

1–2 Diom., GLK I, p. 451: *cacozelia est per affectationem decoris corrupta*

sententia, cum eo ipso dedecoretur oratio quo illam voluit auctor ornare. haec fit
aut nimio cultu aut nimio tumore; nimio tumore 'Iuppiter—loquar'.

(Diomedes) Affectation ... is produced either by excessive refinement or
excessive bombast; by the latter in the case of 'All-powerful Jupiter, you who
make the stars of heaven revolve, I will speak words which should be uttered
by your mouth.'

258 (inc. 58 Bl.)

iam Danai nec si referunt

Not even if the Greeks are carrying back ...

Charis., p. 357 Barwick² = GLK I, p. 271 [post **255**]: *et* 'iam Danai—referunt',
pro 'ne si quidem referunt'.

nisi *codd., corr. Baehrens*

259 (inc. 54 Bl., an. 11 C.)

tune Clytaemestrae foedasti viscera ferro?

Did you befoul with your sword Clytaemestra's inmost parts?

Charis., p. 10 Barwick² = GLK I, p. 13 (eadem fere Dositheus, GLK VII, p. 387):
communes syllabae fiunt modis quinque. primo, si correpta vocalis excipiatur a
duabus consonantibus, quarum prior sit muta, sequens liquida; brevis enim est
in hoc 'tune—ferro?' [sequitur **254**].

260 (inc. 48 Bl., an. 24 C.)

ingenia immansueta suoque simillima caelo

Their character is wild, very like their own climate.

Sen. *De ira* 2.15.5: *in frigora septentrionemque vergentibus immansueta ingenia*
sunt, ut ait poeta, suoque simillima caelo.

Versum expedivit Bentley.

261 (inc. 65 Bl.)

iam madet adducta salsugine nubibus aether

Now the sky is soaked, after salt water had been sucked up to the clouds.

Comm. Berne (p. 124 ed. Usener (1869)) ad Luc. 4.82 'et caelo defusum reddidit aequor': †'iam adducata sal seginonubibus aetere'†.

Versum restituit Housman ad Luc. 4.82.

262 dub. (inc. 46a Bl., cf. Courtney 334)

armatum cane, Musa, ducem belloque cruentam
Aegyptum

Sing, Muse, of our Leader in arms, and of Egypt blood-stained with war.

1–2 Index Codicum A. Decembrii 1466 (ed. A. Capelli, Arch. Stor. Lombard 19 (1892), 114): *quoddam opusculum metricum, quod dicebatur esse Vergilii, de bello nautico Augusti cum Antonio et Cleopatra, quod incipit:* 'armatum— Aegyptum'.

THE ordering of these items (**235–62**) shadows the main section, attempting to assign them to a period and a genre and not eschewing hints about possible authorship (e.g. Aemilius Macer for **237**, Varro Atacinus for **241–3**, Varius Rufus for **244–6**). Chronological arrangement is indeed a slippery task (Courtney 455, who in some cases thinks of a date later than my period), but it seems worth making the effort. My selection differs somewhat from that of Courtney. I have not included any 'versus populares' (e.g. poems said to have been inscribed on walls, songs sung by soldiers at their general's triumph, epigrams attacking early Julio-Claudian emperors).

235 (inc. 35 Bl., an. 10 C.)

1–2. Luna, deum quae sola vides periuria vulgi, / seu Cretaea magis seu tu Dictynna vocaris: these lines have a neoteric feel about them, bringing to mind especially [Virgil], *Ciris* 303–5 (on the nymph Britomartis, who jumped from a Cretan mountain to avoid the amorous pursuit of King Minos), lines which—like these—breathe the atmosphere of the Alexandrian Museum:

unde alii fugisse ferunt et nomen Aphaei
virginis assignant; alii, quo notior esses,
Dictynnam dixere tuo de nomine Lunam.

In view of the fact that Valerius Cato wrote a poem entitled *Diana* or *Dictynna* (see on Cinna, **14**), scholars' thoughts have naturally turned in that direction; Lyne in his edition of the *Ciris*, p. 229, thinks that 303–5 (above) are 'more or less quotation (perhaps consecutive) from Valerius Cato'. Another possible author of our fragment is Catullus (Merkel), since it appears from Pliny, *NH* 28.19 that Catullus (fr. 4 Mynors, OCT) wrote a poem based upon Theocritus 2 (in which a lovesick woman addresses the Moon).

The 'periuria' witnessed by the Moon goddess (line 1) are likely to be those of love; 'sola' would have a point, since the gods in general and Jupiter in particular (e.g. Ovid, *AA* 1.633) were notoriously uninterested in lovers' oaths. For the moon, stars, or night as witnesses of love affairs, cf. e.g. Catullus 7.7–8 'aut quam sidera multa, cum tacet nox, / furtivos hominum vident amores', Horace, *Epodes* 15.1–4 'nox erat et caelo fulgebat luna sereno / inter minora sidera, / cum tu, magnorum numen laesura deorum, / in verba iurabas mea'. Consequently they are often invoked by lovers, e.g. in Theocritus 2.10–11 ἀλλά, Σελάνα, / φαῖνε καλόν, τὶν γὰρ ποταείσομαι ἅσυχα, δαῖμον, 69 etc. φράζεό μευ τὸν ἔρωθ' ὅθεν ἵκετο, πότνα Σελάνα, *Fragmentum Grenfellianum* 11 (Powell, *Coll. Alex.*, p. 177) Ἄστρα φίλα καὶ πότνια Νὺξ συνερῶσά μοι, Meleager, *Anth. Pal.* 5.191 (= 73 G–P). 1–2 Ἄστρα καὶ ἡ φιλέρωσι καλὸν φαίνουσα Σελήνη (more in Nisbet and Hubbard on Horace, *Odes* 2.8.11). According to a scholiast on Theocritus 2.10 (though the distinction cannot be maintained) women in love prayed to the moon, men to the sun. So our lines may be uttered by a woman, perhaps a betrayed woman. The coupling of passion with recondite learning (line 2) is not alien to Latin neoteric poetry (cf. Catullus 68.109–16).

2. Cretaea: 'Lady of Crete' (obelized by Courtney) is not a regular title of Selene/Artemis/Dictynna, but Britomartis/Dictynna is strongly connected with Crete (Callimachus, *Hymn* 3.189–205). Naeke's conjecture 'sive Hecate mavis . . . vocari' deserves to be kept in mind.

magis: 'for preference' (*OLD* 9). The deity is allowed a choice, as e.g. Horace, *Odes* 3.4.3–4 'seu voce nunc mavis acuta / seu fidibus citharave Phoebi'. A goddess may be addressed by all her alternative names (e.g. in Catullus 34.13 ff. Lucina/Trivia/Luna) with an invitation to choose whichever she prefers (ibid. 21–2 'sis quocunque tibi placet / sancta nomine').

236 (inc. 36–7 Bl., an. 14 C.)

One might reasonably suspect that these lines were manufactured as illustrations of *antitheta*. On the other hand (as Courtney says) the four lines together suggest quite a plausible scenario: the phantom of a handsome young man appears (to his wife or mistress?). As he moves towards her, she repeatedly makes to embrace him, but each time the phantom slips away. This situation would be applicable to e.g. the myth of Protesilaus and Laodamia, or Ceyx and Alcyone (Ovid, *Met.* 11.653–93), and no doubt to others—though the ghosts of those who have died violent deaths usually show signs of disfigurement (e.g. Hector in *Aen.* 2.270 ff.). Most editors have printed 1–2 and 3–4 as separate fragments, but the Persius scholion gives no indication of any gap between them. The couplets are lent sharpness by the emphatic 'et' (2) = 'and yet' (*OLD* 14)—despite the covering of disordered hair, the young man's neck could be seen gleaming through it—and the different senses of 'mota': 'stirred into movement' (3) but 'taken away' (4).

Courtney notes the form 'redduxi' as suggesting a writer 'no later than the generation of Lucretius' (see Bailey on 1.228 where we find both 'redducit' and 'redductum'). These lines display many neoteric features: they are all end-stopped and have a verb of molossic shape (three long syllables) after the masculine caesura (see Lyne's *Ciris*, pp. 21–4). 'Fortia neglecti velabant colla capilli' (1), with two nouns at the end, an adjective for each at the beginning, and a verb in the middle, forms a pattern frequently occurring in Catullus 64 (e.g. 39 'non humilis curvis purgatur vinea rastris') and the *Ciris* (e.g. 30 'magna Giganteis ornantur pepla tropaeis'). The interjection 'a!' (cf. Calvus, *Io*, **20**, Virgil, *Ecl.* 10.47 ff. = Cornelius Gallus, **141**) and in particular 'a quotiens' (e.g. Prop. 2.33.11 on Io), sometimes with the whole phrase repeated (e.g. Ovid, *Met.* 2.489, 491 on Callisto), sometimes just 'quotiens' (*Met.* 15.490, 492, cf. *Ciris* 81–2 with 'heu quotiens'), seems markedly neoteric. See Shackleton Bailey, *Propertiana*, 304.

Yet it seems to me that in our passage these neoteric mannerisms are exaggerated to the verge of absurdity. The almost exact repetition in pairs of lines looks like the extension of an Ovidian trick, e.g. *Met.* 9.488–9 'quam bene, Caune, tuo poteram nurus esse parenti; / quam bene, Caune, meo poteras gener esse parenti' (see Norden's list in his edition of *Aeneid* 6, p. 383, with some Hellenistic antecedents in my note on *Met.* 8.628–9). So, while these lines could have been written by a neoteric poet of the mid-first century BC, they might be at home a century later: some of the verses quoted and mocked by Persius show features which could be called 'neoteric', e.g. *Sat.*

1.93 'Berecyntius Attis', 94 'qui caeruleum dirimebat Nerea delphin', 99 'torva Mimalloneis inplerunt cornua bombis'.

1. neglecti ... capilli: cf. Ovid, *AA* 1.509–10 'forma viros neglecta decet; Minoida Theseus / abstulit, a nulla tempora comptus acu'. Phaedra felt the same as Ariadne: 'sint procul a nobis iuvenes ut femina compti; / fine coli modico forma virilis amat' (*Her.* 4.75–6).

2. †velabant†: obviously an intruder from the line above; 'lucebant' would do very well.

237 (Aemilius Macer 11 Bl., an. 30 C.)

suspendit teneros male fortis aranea cassis: it is hard to believe that this is just a misquotation of Virgil, *Georgics* 4.247 'laxos in foribus suspendit aranea casses'. Either the attribution to Virgil is a mistake, or the line of Virgil and the authorship of our line have fallen out of the text of the glossary (not an uncommon occurrence). H. Thomson in *AJP* 43 (1922), 352–4 argued ingeniously for Aemilius Macer (*Theriaca*, cf. **54–66**), and no other poet has so good a claim. 'Cassis' is not a normal word for a spider's web; the metaphor of a hunting net would be felt very strongly, and this could suggest the spider called ἀγρώστης, 'the hunter'. Compare Nicander, *Ther.* 734–6:

> Ἀγρώστης γε μὲν ἄλλος, ὃ δὴ λύκου εἴσατο μορφῇ
> μυιάων ὀλετῆρος, ὀπιπεύει δὲ μελίσσας,
> ψῆνας, μύωπάς τε καὶ ὅσσ᾽ ἐπὶ δεσμὸν ἵκηται.

Yet another is the Huntsman, and he is like the Wolf-Spider in form, the destroyer of blue-bottles; he lies in wait for bees, gall-insects, gadflies, and whatever comes into his toils. (G–S)

'Male fortis' and 'teneros' (whether *OLD* 4c 'fragile, frail' or 5a 'soft, yielding') well contrast the physical weakness of the spider—in Nic. *Ther.* 737 his bite is 'painless and without consequence' for a man—with his skill and cunning. If this line is really by Aemilius Macer, we would have here the only example of the relationship in detail which one might expect to find between Macer and Virgil (*Georg.* 4.247). Also one might recognize here the elegance without sublimity which Quintilian (**48***b*) detected in Macer.

Virgil's immediately preceding words 'invisa Minervae' (*Georg.* 4.246) seem to be the first surviving allusion to the contest between Arachne and Athena (cf. Ovid, *Met.* 6.1 ff.). I wonder whether Macer included that myth.

238 (inc. 33 Bl., an. 8 C.)

Exceptionally interesting verses. Courtney considered the possibility that they are simply a translation by Hyginus himself from a Greek poem entitled *Cretica*. But (as Courtney recognized) **239**, from a different source, may belong to the same Latin poem. Furthermore these lines are—in my judgement—of high quality and a distinctly neoteric cast: note the learned mythology, the spondaic fifth foot (2) and the fact that each line makes a sense unit (as for the most part in Catullus 64). Ovid appears to imitate this poem in his account (*Met.* 2.409 ff.), as the summary of 'Lactantius' (originally perhaps from a full commentary on the *Metamorphoses*) appears to recognize by quoting **239** verbatim. See below, and my article 'Traces of Ancient Commentaries on Ovid's *Metamorphoses*', in *PLLS* 9 (1996), 159–74 at 165–7; for a possible extra item see above on Cornelius Gallus, **144**.

Before quoting these four lines Hyginus named a source (but not, unfortunately, a Latin author), 'de qua in creticis versibus'. It seems likely that *Cretica* was the poem's title; a Greek Κρητικά was ascribed to Epimenides ([Eratosthenes], *Catasterismi* 27) and is probably referred to in Hyg. *Astr.* 2.5.1 'ut ait qui Cretica conscripsit'. This may have been the source for Aratus' Cretan version of the catasterism of the Bears (*Phaen.* 30 ff., see Kidd on 31). Professor Nisbet suggested to me that 'versibus' might be a later addition by someone who took 'in creticis' to refer to metre (not that 'cretici versus' was a regular term for 'verses in cretic metre'). Traces of such a misunderstanding remain even among modern scholars, e.g. in H. J. Rose's Hyginus, *Fabulae*, p. 123 ('non cretico metro ... sed heroico'). In *PLLS* 9 (1996), 167, I very tentatively suggested Varro Atacinus as a possible author of **238** and **239**. The style seems not inappropriate; one manuscript ascribes **120** to 'Varro in *Epimenide*', and one could imagine a double title '*Cretica* sive *Epimenides*'.

It seems possible that **238** and **239** come from a passage of learned mythological polemic, not unlike [Virgil], *Ciris* 54–91. At issue are the origin and identity of the constellations Great and Lesser Bear. Do they represent Callisto and Arcas, or the nurses of the infant Zeus? Were they raised to heaven from Arcadia or Crete? One is reminded of the dispute between Crete and Arcadia over the birthplace of Zeus in Callimachus, *Hymn* 1. In the case of the Bears, Arcadia was the firm favourite, but in Aratus, *Phaen.* 30 ff. (perhaps from Epimenides) the Bears are elevated from Crete, 'if indeed it is true' (εἰ ἐτεὸν δή, perhaps a hit at the Cretans' proverbial mendacity), and represent nurses of Zeus. This would be fit material for a *Cretica*. **238** follows the Arcadian tradition. Courtney (p. 457) fairly remarks that these lines do not look like the wording of a rejected version, but **239** could begin a rebuttal of the Arcadian myth on its own terms: even if we accept that the Great Bear is Callisto, and that she was barred from Ocean for the stated reason, the punishment did not achieve its purpose.

1. tuque: clearly addressed to Arcas. Any attempt to apostrophize Callisto herself (with vocative 'nympha' at the end of the line) would founder on 'se' (3) and 'sit' (4).

Lycaonio: for the patronymic adjective, cf. Callimachus, *Hymn* 1.41 Λυκαονίης ἄρκτοιο and fr. 110.66 (to judge from Cat. 66.66 'Callisto iuncta Lycaoniae'), Ovid, *Met.* 2.496 'Lycaoniae . . . parentis'.

mutatae: Heinsius (followed by Courtney) suggested 'mutate e', but the emphasis in these lines seems to be on the history of Callisto rather than that of her son Arcas. Perhaps one should print 'mutatae <e>', as in Statius, *Theb* 2.572 'Martisque e semine Theron', but Professor Nisbet suggests that, with 'Lycaonio' qualifying 'semine', '<e>' may not be necessary; he compares [Virgil], *Culex* 254 'discordantes Cadmeo semine fratres', recognizing that the case is unusual (progeny of sown dragon's teeth).

semine nymphae: a disturbing collocation (Courtney compares cases where 'satus' is coupled with the mother's name in the ablative), but perhaps made easier by 'Lycaonio' (rather than 'Lycaoniae'), which stresses the male descent. Lucretius can speak of 'materno semine' (4.1211).

2. raptam: 'carried off', to become a constellation ('raped' would not fit well with 'de vertice').

de vertice Nonacrino: compare Stat. *Theb.* 4.5 'de vertice Larisaeo' (echoing our poet?). 'Nonacrino' produces a hexameter with spondaic fifth foot (σπονδειάζων), a feature beloved of Hellenistic and Latin neoteric poets: thus Callimachus, *Aetia, Suppl. Hell.* 250.9–10 Νωνακρίνη / Καλλιστώ, probably *Hecale* fr. 140 H. = 352 Pf., Ovid, *Met.* 1.690, 2.409 'in virgine Nonacrina'.

Nonacrino: so Muncker. 'Vertice' then has two epithets (also 'gelido'), but that is not a serious objection since they are of different sorts (cf. Calvus, **23** 'frigida . . . Bistonis ora'), and 'vertice Nonacrino' functions as a unit. Micyllus gave 'Nonacrinae', which would require the mountain to be called 'Nonacrina'. In Callimachus, fr. 413 (from the prose Περὶ νυμφῶν) Νωνακρίνη is the name of an Arcadian city or region, in Pausanias 8.17.6 Νώνακρις of Callisto's mother (Lycaon's wife) and of a city called after her. Here it seems that 'Nonacrinus' is the adjective from a mountain Nonacris (Pliny, *NH* 4.21), mentioned by two sources probably dependent upon our passage: (*a*) Hyginus, *Astr.* 2.1.6 'in Nonacri monte Arcadiae' (see on line 4 'succumbere' for another reflection of this fragment in Hyg. *Astr.*) and (*b*) 'Lactantius Placidus'' summary of Ovid, *Met.* 2 (the source of **239**), p. 638

Magnus 'Iuppiter . . . cum circa Nonacrinum montem Arcadiae . . . vagaretur'. There is no mention of a 'mons Nonacrinus' in Ovid's own text of *Met*. 2.

3. prohibet: cf. *Met*. 2.528 (Juno to Tethys and Oceanus) 'gurgite caeruleo septem prohibete triones'.

se tingere: cf. *Met*. 2.530 'ne puro tingatur in aequore paelex'.

4. ausa . . . sit: 'she had the audacity . . .' It suits Juno (and hence Tethys) to lay all the blame on Callisto, rather than on her husband Jupiter. I suspect that Ovid is deliberately contradicting our fragment when he writes of Callisto's tremendous struggle in defence of her virginity (*Met*. 2.434–7):

> illa quidem contra, quantum modo femina posset,
> (adspiceres utinam, Saturnia, mitior esses!)
> illa quidem pugnat; sed quem superare puella,
> quisve Iovem poterat?

succumbere alumnae: a remarkable use of the verb + dative = 'to take the place of [a wife in her husband's bed]', paralleled only in Hyg. *Astr*. 2.1.5 (see above on line 2 'Nonacrino') 'Iunonis . . . cui Callisto succubuit ut paelex'. There is also a noun *succuba*, 'a woman who occupies a man's bed in place of his wife' (*OLD*, citing Apuleius, *Met*. 10.24, cf. 5.28). In Ovid, *Heroides* 6.153 editors print the unique 'subnuba', but 'succuba' is a well-supported variant ('aeque bene', Palmer).

alumnae: cf. *Met*. 2.527 'laesae . . . contemptus alumnae'. For the nurturing of Hera by Oceanus and Tethys, see *Iliad* 14.201 ff.

239 (inc. 34 Bl., an. 9 C.)

This verbatim citation from another Latin poet has no parallel in the prose summary by 'Lactantius Placidus' of the *Metamorphoses*; one might also wonder why such an obscure source should be quoted to illustrate such a well-known point of mythology. We have seen (above, on **238**.2 'Nonacrino') that 'Lactantius' seems to be aware of **238**, and I suggested (*PLLS* 9 (1996), 166–7) that an original fuller commentary might have quoted more extensively from the poem to which both **238** and **239** belong, in recognition of the fact that Ovid imitated and varied that account. Perhaps there was only a small gap (even as little as half a line) between **238** and **239**.

1. sed: possibly beginning the rebuttal of the mythological account which has just been presented in detail (**238**); cf. [Virgil], *Ciris* 62 ff. 'sed neque Maeoniae patiuntur credere chartae / nec . . .' etc.

1–2. lucet in astris / Callisto: cf. Ovid, *Met*. 2.508–9 'postquam inter sidera paelex / fulsit'.

240 (Bl., p. 196)

These lines, prefixed to Horace, *Sat.* 1.10 on one side of the manuscript tradition, clearly do not belong to that poem as we have it (some have considered that they might represent an early draft by Horace). On the other hand they reveal—and demand from the reader—a knowledge of the scholarly world in the third quarter of the first century BC which argues for a contemporary origin. Horace himself speaks of other satirists whom he felt able to outdo: 'hoc erat, experto frustra Varrone Atacino [**108**] / atque quibusdam aliis, melius quod scribere possem' (*Sat.* 1.10.46–7). It seems quite possible that this passage was written by one of the rival satirists (there is no particular reason to favour Varro Atacinus) and appended to the text of Horace because it represents another view on a subject which preoccupied all later satirists—the merits or demerits of their father-figure Lucilius. The final words of line 8 in the manuscripts, 'ut redeam illuc' ('to return to the point'), were perhaps added in an attempt to make a transition between our extract, which ended in mid-line, and the (genuine) opening of Hor. *Sat.* 1.10, 'I did indeed say . . .'

We know from Suetonius, *De gramm.* 2.2 (see Kaster, pp. 66–8) that Valerius Cato boasted of having read the *Satires* of Lucilius (probably in the 80s BC) under the tutelage of Vettius Philocomus, who had been personally acquainted with the great man. These lines indicate that Cato was preparing an edition of Lucilius in which he sought to 'correct' (*emendare*, 3) ill-fashioned verses. It is surprising that a neoteric poet of considerable influence and repute (see Appendix, p. 429) should have occupied himself with the satirist whom Horace (*Sat.* 1.4.11) compared to a muddy river in spate; the personal link through Philocomus may have influenced Cato.

Valerius Cato's desire to rescue Lucilius by 'improving' his text is contrasted with the approach of another scholar who preferred to beat a liking for old Latin poetry into his pupils (lines 5–8 of our passage). Most critics (including Nisbet, *Collected Papers*, 393) have seen here a portrait of Horace's teacher L. Orbilius Pupillus of Beneventum (Suetonius, *De gramm.* 9.1, with Kaster, especially pp. 125–37). His propensity for inflicting both corporal punishment ('plagosum') and old Latin poetry (the *Odyssey* of Livius Andronicus, perhaps in a modernized hexameter version) is attested by Horace (*Epist.* 2.1.69–71) and the first part also by Domitius Marsus (**177** 'si quos Orbilius ferula scuticaque cecidit'). Kaster, however, thinks (p. 129) that 'the identification has very little to recommend it'; in particular (p. 131) he disputes the general interpretation of *De gramm.* 9.1 'in Macedonia corniculo, mox equo meruit' as showing that Orbilius attained equestrian rank (which could be linked to line 8 'grammaticorum equitum doctissimus'). Nonetheless the evidence for identifying the second scholar as Orbilius remains powerful.

3. hoc lenior ille: because Cato seeks to win supporters for Lucilius by improving the text rather than by physical violence.

6–7. ut esset opem qui ferre poetis / antiquis posset: I would take the 'ut' clause as *Voluntas Fati*. Fate decreed that the old poets should have at least one champion, in the person of Orbilius.

7. contra fastidia nostra: suggesting that at this time the old Latin poets were generally held in low esteem. In 45 B C the 'cantores Euphorionis' (? people like Helvius Cinna and Cornelius Gallus) are said by Cicero (*Tusc. Disp.* 3.45) to despise Ennius (cf. p. 226 above on Cornelius Gallus).

8. doctissimus: so the characterization is not wholly negative.

241 (inc. 32 Bl., an. 3 C.)

iam puerile iugum tenera cervice gerebat: 'tenera cervice' suggests that the subject of 'gerebat' is a girl who by now ('iam') has succumbed to Cupid. 'Bearing the yoke' normally implies a sexual relationship, whether or not a formal marriage (Plautus, *Curculio* 50 'iamne ea fert iugum?', Catullus 68.118 'indomitam ferre iugum docuit', cf. Nisbet and Hubbard on Horace, *Odes* 2.4.1); here perhaps (so far) only an emotional attachment. Morel suggested that the reference might be to Medea in the *Argonautae* of Varro Atacinus. He compared Ap. Rh. 3.687 θρασέες γὰρ ἐπεκλονέεσκον Ἔρωτες (one might think of other passages in Ap. Rh. 3, such as 286 ff., 451 ff.). None of the parallels is very close, but Morel's idea is worth bearing in mind.

Isidore quotes this line as an (unnecessary) illustration of *puer* used 'de aetate'. It is clear from **242** and **243** that he had access to a document which divided metaphors into four categories, illustrating each by at least one poetic quotation; the same document was also used by Charisius (see my app. crit. for Varro Atacinus, **124**). Our present line would be much more pointful as an illustration of metaphor 'ab inanimali ad animale'; compare Charis. p. 358 Barwick², 'ab inanimali ad animale, sicut "si tantum pectore robur / concipis" [*Aen.* 11.368–9] a ligno ad hominem transtulit'. Here too 'iugum' would be transferred 'a ligno ad hominem', that is 'ab inanimali ad animale', which is the only category to lack a poetic example in Isid. 1.37.3–4. If **241** originally came from the classification of metaphors, it is worth noting that this document contained certainly one quotation from Varro Atacinus (**124**), perhaps a second (**243**) and conceivably a third (**242**).

242 (inc. 68 Bl., an. 6 C.)

aligeros conscendit equos: we may gather from Isidore's 'metaphorice loquens' that these horses were not literally 'winged' (unlike those of the Sun, for which see Bömer on Ovid, *Met.* 2.48 'alipedum . . . equorum'), but so called because of their speed. In view of the source's interest in Varro Atacinus (see above on **241**) my mind turns to the horses given to King Aietes by his father, the Sun god (Ap. Rh. 4.220–1 Αἰήτης ἵπποισι μετέπρεπεν οὓς οἱ ὄπασσεν / Ἥλιος πνοιῇσιν ἐειδομένους ἀνέμοιο). Presumably these would be the offspring of the Sun's stallions and ordinary mares, like those surreptitiously bred by Aietes' sister Circe (*Aen.* 7.282–3 'patri quos daedala Circe / supposita de matre nothos furata creavit'); it is reasonable that they should have inherited their sires' speed, but not their literal wings. The quoted words might correspond to Ap. Rh. 3.1235–7, where Aietes mounts the chariot which his son Apsyrtus/Phaethon has been holding in readiness for him:

τῷ δὲ καὶ <u>ὠκυπόδων</u> ἵππων εὐπηγέα δίφρον
ἔσχε πέλας Φαέθων ἐπιβήμεναι, <u>ἂν δὲ καὶ αὐτός</u>
<u>βήσατο.</u>

It would be rash to argue from D. Servius' note ('compositum a poeta nomen') on *Aen.* 1.663 'aligerum . . . Amorem' that the anonymous fragment must be later than Virgil—it seems very unlikely that D. Servius' database included the *Argonautae* of Varro Atacinus.

243 (inc. 63 Bl., an. 4 C.)

pontum pinus arat, sulcum premit alta carina: this line is obviously related to at least two of the *Aeneid*: 10.197 'longa sulcat maria alta carina' and 10.296 'sulcumque sibi premat ipsa carina'. There is also 5.158 'longa sulcant vada salsa carina'. The imitation could be either way; on general grounds perhaps it is slightly more probable that a single line of an earlier poet should produce several variations in a later one than *vice versa*. If Virgil is imitating the anonymous poet, there are subtleties of adaptation which might seem typical of the great master: *Aen.* 10.197 ends with the same two words (alta carina), but they do not agree with each other; the noun 'sulcum' is converted to the verb 'sulcat'. In *Aen.* 10.296 the situation is paradoxical: the ships are being driven on to the land, and so 'sulcum' there refers to a furrow made in the ground, not in the sea.

For the ultimate source of this fragment (a categorization of metaphors) and its knowledge of Varro Atacinus, see on **241** above. In my opinion there is a good chance that this line came from the *Argonauts*—as indeed was suggested (though without discussion or Greek parallel) by Nettleship in the Conington–Nettleship edition of Virgil on *Aen.* 10.294–6—corresponding to Ap. Rh. 4.225–7:

ὑπεκπρὸ δὲ <u>πόντον ἔταμνε</u>
<u>νηῦς</u> ἤδη κρατεροῖσιν ἐπειγομένη ἐρέτῃσι
καὶ μεγάλου ποταμοῖο καταβλώσκοντι ῥεέθρῳ

The single Latin line looks like the conclusion of a paragraph; I offer, purely *exempli gratia*, 'incumbunt remis, fluvioque urgente secundo / pontum pinus arat, sulcum premit alta carina'. The context in Ap. Rh. is that the Argo has already escaped from the mouth of the river Phasis before King Aietes has even launched his pursuing fleet upon the river.

pontum: if from the *Argonauts*, this would refer to the Pontus (Euxine, Black Sea) in particular.

pinus: the tree from which Jason's ship was made (e.g. Euripides, *Medea* 4, Catullus 64.1). For 'pinus' (singular, without epithet) = the Argo, compare Horace, *Epodes* 16.57 (written soon after the appearance of Varro's poem) 'non huc Argoo contendit remige pinus', Prop. 3.22.14, Tibullus 1.3.37 (if the reference is specific); for 'Thessala pinus' Ovid, *Her.* 18.158, Seneca, *Medea* 336.

arat: the figure of 'ploughing' the sea is already implicit in Homer's use of τέμνειν (e.g. *Od.* 13.88 θαλάσσης κύματ' ἔταμνεν); the first explicit occurrences are Aeschylus, *Supplices* 1007 and Euripides fr. 670 N². See Pfeiffer (Addenda, vol. I, p. 509) on Callimachus fr. 572 ἀρότας κύματος Ἀονίου.

sulcum: cognate with Greek ὁλκός, which can also be used of the sea (Ap. Rh. 1.1167 οἴδματος ὁλκούς). For 'sulcus', 'sulcare', 'sulcator' thus in later Latin poetry, see Spaltenstein on Silius 7.363 (add Manilius 1.708 'sulcum ducente carina').

premit: *OLD premo* 4, 'to make (marks, cavities, etc.) by pressing, digging or similar means, imprint'. One could regard this as a poetical use of the simple verb for the compound (*imprimo*), as e.g. in Ovid, *Met.* 1.48 'totidemque plagae tellure premuntur' ('are imprinted upon the earth').

alta carina: Argo has 'a good keel' in Ap. Rh. 1.401 ἐϋστείρης ... νηός and in Callimachus fr. 18.4. 'Alta' continues the ploughing image, as can be seen from Cicero, *De div.* 2.50 'cum ... sulcus altius esset impressus'.

244

There can be no doubt that the first Epicurean poet is Lucretius; indeed one can point to the particular lines which Lactantius (or his source) had in mind as *DRN* 3.421–3 'tu fac utrumque uno sub iungas nomine eorum, / atque animam verbi causa cum dicere pergam, / mortalem esse docens, animum quoque dicere credas'. But who is the second Epicurean poet? Lactantius himself might have been unable to tell us (if he simply took over the item from an earlier source). R. M. Ogilvie (*JThS* N s 26 (1975), 411–12) suggests Varro Atacinus. But there is no evidence that Atacinus was an Epicurean, and the text which Ogilvie relies on to show that a Varro wrote in verse *de rerum natura* more probably points to Varro of Reate. A much more plausible candidate is Varius Rufus, whose Epicurean leanings are firmly attested (see p. 260 above) and who wrote a hexameter poem *De morte* (**147–50**) which seems to have had something in common with Lucretius book 3. This topic would have given Varius plenty of opportunity to talk about *animus* and *anima*.

245

The speaker is clearly Atreus, and these appear to be his first lines on stage. Perhaps indeed the first lines of the whole play—that could explain why Quintilian chose line 1 to represent the standard iambic metre of tragedy. The play must have been very well known, since neither Seneca nor Quintilian feels any need to identify it. Could we have here the opening of Varius Rufus' celebrated *Thyestes* (as suggested by G. Jackmann, *Rh. M.* 70 (1915), 641–4)? Quintilian, who quotes the first line, is the only source to produce an ascribed fragment (**156**), and may have this play in mind when he refers to the tragic character of Aerope (11.3.73), quoted on p. 276 above). The handling of the metre (insofar as one can judge) is closer to Seneca than to Accius: note the fourth-foot tribrach in line 1 (L. Strzelecki, *De Senecae Trimetro Iambico* (1938), 42 Typus D) and the fifth-foot anapaest in 2 ('a preferred rhythm', E. Fantham, Seneca, *Troades* (1982), 109).

According to Seneca the actor 'latus incedit', occupying a wide space on the stage because of his tragic boot and excessively full clothing (*OLD latus* 3c), and throws back his head in a gesture of pride (*OLD resupinus* 2b).

1. sceptra: like Klotz (and Ribbeck before him) I prefer Quintilian's 'sceptra' to Seneca's 'regna'—both were probably quoting from memory.

2.   qua ponto ab Helles: here not the Dardanelles but the Aegean sea; Atreus must refer to the Corinthian isthmus which separates the Aegean from the Ionian sea (cf. Lucan 1.100 ff., Silius Italicus 15.154 ff.). See J. A. Nairn, 'The Meaning of *Hellespontus* in Latin', *CR* 13 (1899), 436–8 (starting from this fragment); Housman, *Classical Papers*, vol. II, p. 593 (on *Ciris* 411–13). Our poet may have in mind a line (Klotz p. 342, also unattributed) quoted by Cicero, *Orator* 163 'qua pontus Helles supera Tmolum ac Tauricos'. For splitting the elements of Hellespontus, cf. *Suppl. Hell.* adesp. 1132 ἡμεῖς δ' εἰς Ἕλλης πόντον ἀπεπλέομεν (= Call. fr. an. 392 Scheider = adesp. eleg. fr. 20 West, who suggests Antimachus). Ovid latinizes the pontus ('mare me deduxit in Helles', *Tr.* 1.10.15).

3.   urgetur Isthmos: I have not paralleled this use of the verb for water pressing against land, but *premere* is so used (e.g. Ovid, *Fasti* 1.292 'insula dividua quam premit amnis aqua', Stat. *Theb.* 5.49).

246

cur fugis fratrem? scit ipse: this tragic quotation was received with great enthusiasm when inserted into Porcius Latro's declamation about a young man trying to reconcile his father and uncle (we cannot expect the declamation to fit the original play in more than outline). This would suit a play that was currently all the rage, and several scholars have mentioned Varius' *Thyestes* (the case is weaker than for **245**). If the quotation is uninterrupted, it must come from a trochaic line (trochaic metres are rare in Seneca, but much commoner in the fragments of Ennius, Pacuvius, and Accius). We may deduce from 'Thyesteo more' (though perhaps not with complete certainty) that Thyestes was the speaker. In Seneca's *Thyestes*, Atreus makes a show of friendship and reconciliation in order to lure his brother to the fateful banquet; for this purpose he uses one of Thyestes' children as an unwitting accomplice. Thyestes is far from convinced, saying to himself 'reflecte gressum dum licet, teque eripe' (428), to which young Tantalus replies 'quae causa cogit, genitor, a patria gradum / referre visa?' (429–30). In the anonymous fragment (if the trochaic line could be split between two speakers) 'cur fugis fratrem?' might be spoken by Thyestes' son, or some other intermediary, to whom Thyestes replies 'scit ipse'. A declaimer like Porcius Latro would no doubt have sufficient histrionic ability to carry off the change of speaker. Alternatively the whole quotation might be given to Thyestes, repeating (verbatim or in paraphrase) the intermediary's question and then answering it: 'You ask me "why do you flee from your brother?" He himself knows the reason [*sc.* because of the terrible things which I did to him].'

247 (inc. 40 Bl., p. 145 C.)

This attack on Sallust mirrors part of what Suetonius, *De gramm.* 15 says about Pompeius Lenaeus, a freedman of Pompey the Great. He was so incensed by Sallust's description (in the *Histories*) of his former master than he tore him to pieces in the most bitter satire, calling him all sorts of rude names and furthermore 'priscorum Catonis verborum ineruditissimum furem'. If Lenaeus' satire was in hexameters, that cannot be the source of our elegiac couplet, which was apparently known to Ovid (*Tristia* 2.416 'Eubius, impurae conditor historiae', cf. *Ibis* 520). For the practice of Sallust and varying attitudes to literary *furta*, see Kaster, *Suet. De gramm.* p. 181. Suetonius, *De gramm.* 10.6 records with some surprise (because Pollio himself received quite different advice from Ateius) the belief of Asinius Pollio that Ateius Philologus had collected archaic words and figures for Sallust.

It seems likely that this incomplete epigram contained other criticisms (whether personal or literary) of Sallust, rather than criticism of other people. Sallust's *Bellum Iugurthinum* (*c.*41–40 BC) was written after the *Bellum Catilinae* (*c.*42–41); it is not clear whether the writer of this epigram considered the later work to be more reprehensible than the earlier with respect to *furta* from Cato.

248 (inc. 70 Bl.)

Musae Aonides: designation of the Muses as 'Aonides' (with or without the addition of e.g. 'sorores') is first attested in Ovid (*Met.* 5.333, 6.2, cf. e.g. Silius Italicus 11.463, 12.409). The epithet 'Aonian' = 'Boeotian' was popularized by Callimachus and first used in Latin by Catullus (see on Cornelius Severus, **209**); it was very probably to be found in Cornelius Gallus (Virgil, *Ecl.* 6.64–5 = **142** 'Gallum / Aonas in montis ut duxerit una sororum'). The grammarians who supply this quotation (no doubt all from the same ultimate source) treat a final diphthong separately from a final long vowel. Here -ae is neither elided nor shortened before 'Aonides', but allowed to retain its long quantity. The phenomenon can be paralleled (with a final long vowel rather than a diphthong) in Virgil, *Georgics* 1.437 'Glaucō et Panopeae et Inoo Melicertae', where Mynors notes the retention of the long quantity in 'thesis' as unique in Virgil. He compares *Iliad* 17.40 Πάνθῳ ἐν χείρεσσιν (where, however, Πάνθῳ represents older Πανθόῳ). Euphorion of Chalcis not infrequently allows hiatus (or lengthens irrationally) in the first syllable of a foot (see B. A. van Groningen's edition (1977), 262–3) but provides no parallel for what we have here. It is possible that 'Musae Aonides' represents a learned poet being metrically provocative—but the quotation could have been fabricated by a grammarian.

249 (inc. 82 Bl., an. 32 C.)

This poem must have been related to Ovid, *Amores* 1.2.23 ff., but the much greater detail (enumerating the loves of individual gods, and Jupiter in chains) makes clear that Lactantius, or his source, cannot have *Am.* 1.2 in mind. Some have believed that the poem was in Greek—a Hellenistic precursor to *Am.* 1.2 with the triumphal imagery added by a Latin paraphraser (cf. R. M. Ogilvie, *The Library of Lactantius* (Oxford, 1978), 18–19), but that seems very unlikely to me. Ogilvie regards 'quidam poeta' as proof that Lactantius had not read an original poem. That is probably so, though ancient writers (annoyingly for us) do on occasion refer to 'some poet' when they know the authorship full well. Blänsdorf includes the item in his section headed 'serioris aetatis versus' (pp. 444 ff.). It seems to me not impossible that the poem was pre-Ovidian (in **244** Lactantius preserves a unique nugget of information, perhaps relating to Varius Rufus, *De morte*). McKeown on *Am.* 1.2 (Ovid, *Amores*, vol. II, p. 31) refrains from speculation about date as well as authorship. 'Enumerating the loves of individual gods' would offer scope for mythological erudition and could produce a poem of considerable length; on both counts I think of Ovid, *Amores* 3.6, with its catalogue of enamoured river-gods.

250 (inc. 42 Bl., Maecenas 5–6 C.)

o qui chelyn canoram plectro regis Italo: perhaps deliberately imitated by Seneca, *Troades* 321 'levi canoram verberans plectro chelyn'. I would have followed Courtney in giving this galliambic line to Maecenas (cf. **188** and **189**), but for the way in which the grammarian presents it: 'Maecenas . . . [**189**] et Catullus [63.2] et ille [*sc.* versus] alterius auctoris [this line]' are cited in quick succession. 'Alterius auctoris' can hardly mean 'one or other of Maecenas and Catullus' (as if the grammarian were uncertain), and should denote an author other than the two just mentioned ('alterius' often stands for the genitive 'alius'); the only other poet whom we know to have written in galliambic metre is Varro Reatinus (see on **188**). The subject matter, as well as the metre, might suit Maecenas very well. As Courtney (p. 280) says, 'It may be addressed to someone who writes Latin poems in a Greek lyric metre, or possibly to a god who patronizes such an enterprise.' In the former case the first person to come to mind is of course Horace (the addressee of Maecenas, **185** and **186**). The grandiloquent tone (indeed, as if to a god) might be teasingly affectionate. This is an unusual galliambic, in that it is directed towards neither the Phrygian Magna Mater nor her devotees.

chelyn canoram: something of an oxymoron, since the tortoise was notoriously mute, gaining a voice only after death (e.g. Pacuvius, *Antiopa* 6 W. 'eviscerata inanima cum animali sono').

plectro ... Italo: another oxymoron, mixing Greek and Latin in a very Horatian manner (e.g. *Odes* 1.32.3–4 'age dic Latinum, / barbite, carmen', 2.16.38 'spiritum Graiae tenuem Camenae').

regis: 'control', 'direct', like *moderor* in Horace, *Odes* 1.24.14 'auditam moderere arboribus fidem' and *tempero* in 4.3.17–18 'o testudinis aureae / dulcem quae strepitum, Pieri, temperas'.

251 (inc. 43 Bl., Maecenas 5–6 C.)

rutilos recide crines, habitumque cape viri: a devotee of the Magna Mater is urged (whether by himself or by another) to abandon his lifestyle. Attis is struck by remorse in Catullus 63.73 'iam iam dolet quod egi, iam iamque paenitet'—but too late, since he has already castrated himself. For Diomedes' use of the term 'neotericum' here, see Alan Cameron, *HSCP* 84 (1980), 140 and Courtney 280.

rutilos ... crines: suggesting a Celtic origin for the Galli/Gallae?

252–262

These remaining items have an epic air.

252 (an. 25 C.)

stat tamen et clamore iuvat: Weymann's recognition of a verse citation is convincing. Courtney believes that in the original context these words referred to C. Acilius, whose right hand was cut off as he boarded a Massilian ship during the sea battle of 49 BC (Suetonius, *Div. Iul.* 68.4, Val. Max. 3.2.22, Plutarch, *Caes.* 16.2). But in Seneca the fighter has lost both hands; nonetheless he 'holds his ground', i.e. does not retreat (*OLD sto* 3a), which better suits a land battle. For 'clamore iuvat' Courtney compares Val. Flacc. 6.751 'solisque iuvant clamoribus agmen' (of soldiers on the edge of the battlefield). The addition of a bizarre element to the gruesomeness of battle accords with the epic tendency which culminated in Lucan.

253 (inc. 52 Bl., an. 19 C.)

magnae nunc hiscite terrae: quoted together with five bits of Cicero as examples of simulated emotion. Presumably the speaker has suffered some great disaster or disgrace. A wish to be swallowed up by the earth descends from *Iliad* 4.182 τότε μοι χάνοι εὐρεῖα χθών. Pease on *Aeneid* 4.24 has vast numbers of examples (including these very words from Vida, *Christias* 5.49). For the plural, cf. Virgil, *Georgics* 1.479 'terraeque dehiscunt'.

254 (inc. 55 Bl., an. 12 C.)

Cyclops, Aetnaeus cultor, Neptunia proles: an unusually spondaic hexameter, elevated in tone; twice employing an adjective ('Aetnaean inhabitant', 'Neptunian offspring') instead of the genitive singular. One pictures the formidable and monstrous Cyclops of the *Odyssey* rather than Theocritus' somewhat pathetic lover. Perhaps the Cyclops was the subject of the narrative, or perhaps he was mentioned incidentally in some poem involving Sicily— e.g. the *Bellum Siculum* of Cornelius Severus (see on **206–7**). There is an affinity between this line and [Tib.], *Pan. Mess.* 56 'cessit et Aetnaeae Neptunius incola rupis', where, although the reference is to Odysseus, there might be a secondary allusion to Messalla's service in the Sicilian war against another 'son of Neptune' (Sextus Pompeius).

　　Aetnaeus cultor: 'cultor'+adjective is not a normal way of saying 'inhabitant of . . .' I have found no real parallel beyond Martial, *Liber Spectaculorum* 3.3 'cultor Rhodopeius' (quoted by Courtney). Applied to the

Cyclops, the phrase is somewhat paradoxical, since the Cyclopes did not, in the literal sense, cultivate the earth (*Od.* 9.108 οὔτε φυτεύουσιν χερσὶν φυτὸν οὔτ' ἀρόωσιν).

255 (inc. 57 Bl.)

in medio victoria ponto: a hexameter with fourth-foot caesura after 'medio'. If we can trust the grammarian's statement that 'est' must be supplied, the clause may be complete in sense as it stands. Perhaps there is some contrast between victory at sea and victory (or the lack of it) on land. See on **258**.

256 (inc. 64 Bl., an. 5 C.)

Puzzling lines, which I include with a certain hesitation. We have found some reason to connect such illustrations of different types of metaphor with Varro Atacinus (compare **124**, perhaps also **242** and **234**). But I cannot see these lines as a counterpart to Ap. Rh. 1.13 πατρὶ Ποσειδάωνι—the degree of expansion seems inappropriate in context (note, however, Val. Flacc. 1.193 ff.). It has been suggested that they belong to the same poem as *Anth. Lat.* 720 = inc. 76 Blänsdorf (pp. 445–7), an overblown appeal to Venus for a safe voyage which in some manuscripts is attributed to Julius Solinus. Our passage has something in common with Virgil, *Aeneid* 4 and Ovid, *Metamorphoses* 1 (see below) and does not seem out of place in the late Augustan/ early Tiberian age.

Style and subject matter may put one in mind of the unnamed 'velivolique maris vates, cui credere posses / carmina caeruleos composuisse deos' (Ovid, *Ex Ponto* 4.16.21–2, see Appendix, p. 429). Perhaps that was a scientific poem rather than an epic about naval warfare. Our lines look like an invocation by the poet (at or near the beginning of his work?).

1. te: in the clash of saints I have preferred Augustine's 'te' to Isidore's 'tu', as fitting more naturally into an invocation.

The poet continually mixes anthropomorphic features of the god (his temples, chin, and hair) with different aspects of the water (billows of the sea, the Oceanus and rivers). The most famous passage of Latin poetry which employs this technique is *Aen.* 4.246–51 (the flight of Mercury):

> iamque volans apicem et latera ardua cernit
> Atlantis duri caelum qui vertice fulcit,
> Atlantis, cinctum adsidue cui nubibus atris

> piniferum caput et vento pulsatur et imbri,
> nix umeros infusa tegit, tum flumina mento
> praecipitant senis et glacie riget horrida barba.

Virgil continually shifts our attention between the giant and the mountain. Comparison of 'flumina mento / praecipitant' (250–1) with 'mento / profluit Oceanus' (2–3) suggests that our poet has Virgil in mind. There are traces of this technique in Hellenistic poetry (e.g. Call. *Hymn* 4.77–8, see my note on Ovid, *Met.* 8.549 ff.). Ovid takes it further in his allegorical personifications, particularly of Invidia (*Met.* 2.775 ff.) and Fames (8.801 ff.), though more like our fragment is the picture of Notus (1.266–7):

> barba gravis nimbis, canis fluit unda capillis;
> fronte sedent nebulae, rorant pennaeque sinusque.

For an even more elaborate development in Silver epic, see Statius, *Theb.* 9.408 ff. (the river-god Ismenus), with the commentary of M. J. Dewar. There is some affinity between these passages and the figure known as 'kenning', in which stones are 'earth's bones' and rivers 'earth's veins' (see Ingrid Waern, *ΓΗΣ ΟΣΤΕΑ: The Kenning in Pre-Christian Greek Poetry* (Uppsala, 1951), 96). Here the rivers are not quite 'Neptune's hair', but they wander about in his hair like snakes in a Gorgon's coiffure.

1–2. cana crepanti / cincta: very strong alliteration.

2. perpete mento: the adjective *perpes* (perhaps owing something to *praepes*) is found in Plautus and Pacuvius = 'continuous in time'. The expected sense here is of water issuing from Neptune's mouth which constantly flows into the Oceanus.

3. Oceanūs: the same lengthening before a single consonant occurs in [Virgil], *Ciris* 392 'miratur pater Oceanūs et candida Tethys'. Here placement at the masculine caesura makes the lengthening easier (as in *Aen.* 9.610 'terga fatigamūs hasta').

et flumina crinibus errant: the verb is used of meandering streams and loosely arranged hair (both *OLD* 1d); also of wriggling snakes (e.g. *Aen.* 7.353 'membris lubricus errat').

257 (inc. 60 Bl., an. 15 C.)

1–2. Iuppiter omnipotens, caeli qui sidera torques, / ore tuo dicenda loquar: the charge of affectation through excessive grandiosity seems more just than the grammarian's following condemnation of Ovid, *Met.* 2.107–9 as an example of *cacozelia* arising from excessive *cultus*.

1. Iuppiter omnipotens: = *Aen.* 2.689 = 5.687 (see further Courtney 66–8).

caeli qui sidera torques: going back to Ennius, *Ann.* 27 Skutsch 'qui caelum versat stellis fulgentibus aptum' (almost certainly of Atlas, as in *Aen.* 6.797 'axem umero torquet stellis ardentibus aptum'). Virgil replaces Ennius' *versare* with *torquere* (possibly remembering Varro Atacinus, **111**.1 'aetherio mundum torquerier axe') and, in *Aen.* 9.93 'torquet qui sidera mundi', changed the reference to Jupiter.

2. ore tuo dicenda loquar: so grand and weighty is the subject matter that only Jupiter could do it justice. Not a happy conceit—a little reminiscent of the unnamed poet of the sea 'cui credere posses / carmina caeruleos composuisse deos' (Ovid, *Ex Ponto* 4.16.21–2, see on **256** above).

258 (inc. 58 Bl.)

iam Danai nec si referunt: 'nec si' = 'not even if' like οὐδ' εἰ. Compare Catullus 66.73 'nec si me infestis discerpent sidera dictis', which Fordyce ad loc. claims at the earliest instance of 'nec' standing for 'ne . . . quidem'.

This is not a very good example of ellipsis. The quotation immediately follows **255**, and perhaps it is just worth considering that the two fragments might be from the same source and adjacent: e.g. <Troy's defeat on land will be avenged by> a victory at sea; even if the Greeks now are bringing back <Helen and the spoils of conquered Troy, their fleet will be wrecked on the return voyage by the great storm>.

259 (inc. 54 Bl., an. 11 C.)

tune Clytaemestrae foedasti viscera ferro?: clearly addressed to Orestes; traditional heroic subject matter continued to attract poets, as we can see from Ovid, *Ex Ponto* 4.16 (Appendix). There is no clue to the identity of the speaker (conceivably the poet apostrophizing his character). The tone seems to be one of disapproval, but even that is not certain.

foedasti ... ferro: the alliterative combination goes back to Ennius (Trag. 399 Jocelyn 'ferro foedati iacent'), cf. *Aen.* 2.55, 3.241. For the verb, cf. Cornificius **96**.

viscera: particularly shocking because she was the mother who bore him.

260 (inc. 48 Bl., an. 24 C.)

ingenia immansueta suoque simillima caelo: Bentley convincingly disentangled this line from Seneca's prose. Many have thought of Albinovanus Pedo's epic on Germanicus in Germany (see **228**); Tacitus, *Ann.* 2.24 'truculentia caeli praestat Germania' suggests a connection between climate and character. A less likely alternative might be the *Chorographia* of Varro Atacinus (**109–19**); Dionysius Periegetes in his Greek geographical poem sometimes talks briefly about inhabitants of the various lands. The absence of word-break after the first syllable of second, third, or fourth foot is not paralleled in the scanty remains of either poet, but the line is by no means inelegant.

    suoque simillima caelo: Virgil is the earliest poet (unless by chance this line predates him) to exploit the metrical convenience of the superlative thus placed: first in *Georgics* 2.131 'faciemque simillima lauro', never more beautifully than in *Aen.* 2.794 'par levibus ventis volucrique simillima somno'. Ovid, with his taste for the dactyl, is an enthusiastic follower.

    suo . . . caelo: compare Ovid, *AA* 2.320 'et vitium caeli senserit aegra sui' (she ascribes her ill health to the local climate).

261 (inc. 65 Bl.)

iam madet adducta salsugine nubibus aether: this fragment is cited (without comment or ascription) on Lucan 4.82, where a rainbow ('arcus', 80) has sucked up moisture (cf. Virgil, *Georgics* 1.381 with Mynors's note) from the salty waves: 'Oceanumque bibit, raptosque ad nubila fluctus / pertulit et caelo [ablative] defusum reddidit aequor' (81–2). An indication of authorship has probably fallen out (Albinovanus Pedo and Cornelius Severus are possible claimants). The corrupt quotation may represent a line which the commentator believed Lucan to have imitated. Housman's restoration seems as good a try as one could make ('nubilus' for 'nubibus' might also be considered) but is inevitably uncertain. 'Salsugo' = salty water, brine, is not otherwise attested in poetry.

262 dub. (inc. 46a Bl., cf. Courtney 334)

1–2. armatum cane, Musa, ducem belloque cruentam / Aegyptum: the credentials of this item are far from encouraging: a 1466 catalogue gives these as the first words of a poem (allegedly by Virgil) on the maritime war of Octavian against Antony and Cleopatra. One might think optimistically of

Rabirius (cf. **231** and on **229**), or of the Herculaneum epic (Blänsdorf pp. 430–8, Courtney 334–40) which some have ascribed to Rabirius. I suspect, however, that the quoted words represent a Renaissance idea of how such a poem ought to begin. Compare the alleged opening(s) of Ovid, *Fasti* 7 (in the Teubner *Fasti*, pp. v–vi).

Appendix

Named Poets of Whom No Verbatim Quotations Survive

This list could have been extended, but concentrates chiefly on poets named by Catullus, Virgil, Horace, Propertius, and Ovid. Many of these (at least in Catullus and Virgil) are mentioned only to be ridiculed, and their loss need not be regretted. One figure stands out because of the number, and the warmth, of the testimonia: Valerius Cato, whom I considered placing in the main section, but kept the minimum subscription at one word of text, with the result that Hortensius qualified but the much more important Valerius Cato does not.

By far the richest source of these poetic names is Ovid, *Ex Ponto* 4.16, where Ovid catalogues name after name in order to show that, despite the existence of so many notable writers, he himself had also won a reputation. Insofar as we can date them, the poets of *Ex Ponto* 4.16 seem to have flourished in the middle or later Augustan period—with the puzzling exception of Varius Rufus (see **153***a*), who may have returned to tragedy after completing his editorial labours on the *Aeneid*. The second most productive source lies in *Tristia* 2.421–42, a passage designed to prove that many Roman poets before Ovid had composed adventurous erotica.

ALBINOVANUS CELSUS: Warned against too close imitation of established poets in Horace, *Epist.* 1.3.15 ff. Also the addressee of *Epist.* 1.8; conceivably the Celsus whose death Ovid mourns in *Ex Ponto* 1.9. Albinovanus Celsus was probably related (father or brother?) to the epic poet Albinovanus Pedo (**225–8**). See Syme, *History in Ovid*, 90.

ANSER: We might have considered Anser to be a scholiastic fiction based upon Virgil, *Ecl.* 9.35–6 'nam neque adhuc Vario videor nec dicere Cinna / digna, sed argutos inter strepere anser olores' (taken up by Propertius, 2.34.84). But Ovid, *Tr.* 2.435 'Cinnaque procacior Anser' shows him to be real enough. Servius describes him as 'Antonii poetam [not necessarily a reason for Virgil's dislike at the time of the *Eclogues*], qui eius laudes scribebat', seeing an allusion to him (and a brother?) in Cicero, *Phil.* 13.11 'de Falerno Anseres depellantur'.

ANTONIUS IULLUS: Second son of Mark Antony and Fulvia; brought up in Rome by his stepmother Octavia—who became his mother-in-law—and highly favoured by Augustus (Syme, *Augustan Aristocracy*, 398) until his disgrace and enforced suicide in 2 BC for adultery with the emperor's daughter Julia. Horace (*Odes* 4.2) warns him against any attempt to emulate Pindar, and looks forward to an epic poem on Augustus' victory over the Sygambri. Nothing suggests that Antonius wrote such a work, but [Acron] on Hor. *Odes* 4.2.33 tells us that 'heroico metro Diomedias duodecim libros scripsit egregios'.

AQUINUS: Listed among bad poets in Catullus 14.18–19 'Caesios, Aquinos, / Suffenum'. Perhaps to be identified (but note the slight difference of name) with the Aquinius of Cicero, *Tusc. Disp.* 5.63 'adhuc neminem cognovi poetam (et mihi fuit cum Aquinio amicitia) qui sibi non optimus videbatur'.

BASSUS: Iambic poet. Together with the epic poet Ponticus he was a close friend of Ovid (*Tr.* 4.10.47–8 'Ponticus heroo, Bassus quoque clarus iambis / dulcia convictus membra fuere mei'). Quite likely to be the Bassus of Propertius 1.4, since Prop. also numbers Ponticus (in 1.7 and 1.9) among his friends. There is no reason to identify him with the declaimer Bassus of Seneca, *Contr.* 10 praef. 12.

BAVIUS: The target of Virgil, *Ecl.* 3.90 'qui Bavium non odit, amet tua carmina, Mevi', and also of Domitius Marsus' epigram (**174**) satirizing the break-up of his good relationship with his brother. Called a 'curator' by Philarg. on Virgil, *Ecl.* 3.90; he died in Cappadocia in 35 BC (Jerome, see on **174**).

CAECILIUS: From Novum Comum (modern Como). He made a nice start to a poem on the Magna Mater (Catullus 35.17–18 'est enim venuste / Magna Caecilio incohata Mater'), perhaps written in the galliambic metre proper to that subject (cf. Catullus 63, Maecenas **188–9**, Adesp. **250–1**). It seems to me an unwarranted inference (Thomson on Cat. 35.14 and Intr. to Cat. 63, p. 373) that the first words of Caecilius' poem were 'Dindymi domina(m)' (= Cat. 35.14), and hence that the metre was not galliambic. There is no mention of Caecilius elsewhere. Perhaps Catullus is being kind to a hopeful young friend; Caecilius' poem may never have been finished, let alone published. Certainly there is no justification for elevating Caecilius to full membership of a group of neoteric poets.

CAESIUS: A bad poet in Catullus 14.18 (coupled with Aquinus, see above).

CAMERINUS: Writer of an epic on Troy from the death of Hector (Ov. *Ex Ponto* 4.16.19 'quique canit domito Camerinus ab Hectore Troiam'). There is no reason to think that he is the consul of AD 9, though the dating would be reasonable.

CAPELLA: We know only that he was an elegist (Ov. *Ex Ponto* 4.16.36 'clauderet imparibus verba Capella modis').

CARUS: Author of an epic on Hercules (Ov. *Ex Ponto* 4.13.11–12 'produnt auctorem vires, quas Hercule dignas / novimus atque illi, quem canis ipse, pares', 4.16.7–8 'et qui Iunonem laesisset in Hercule Carus, / Iunonis si iam non gener ille foret'). We learn from *Ex Ponto* 4.13.47–8 that he was tutor to Germanicus' sons, and thus—Ovid must have hoped—someone who could put in a word for the exiled poet. See Syme, *History in Ovid*, 88, 156.

CASSIUS ETRUSCUS: Known only from Horace, *Sat.* 1.10.61–4 as a bad poet who composed at extraordinary speed and whose works provided combustion for his own funeral pyre. Not to be confused with the following.

CASSIUS PARMENSIS ('of Parma'): In a teasing response to Tibullus' frank criticism of Horace's *Satires*, the latter speculates that his friend may be engaged in writing 'quod Cassi Parmensis opuscula vincat' (*Epist.* 1.4.3). From this we may deduce that (in Horace's opinion) outdoing Cassius of Parma was no great achievement, and (probably) that Cassius composed elegies. He was one of the killers of Julius Caesar, executed by Octavian soon after the battle of Actium (Val. Max. 1.7.7). Suetonius (*Div. Aug.* 4.2) quotes from a letter of Cassius denigrating Octavian's ancestry. Porf. on Horace, *Epist.* 1.4.3 has a fair amount of nonsense.

CORNIFICIA: ' . . . cuius insignia extant epigrammata' (Jerome's *Chronicle*, ed. Helm², p. 159, on 41 BC). The entry no doubt comes from Suetonius, *De poetis*, and the continuing existence of Cornificia's epigrams thus refers to the first half of the second century AD. Sister of Cornificius the poet (**93–7**), Cornificia married a Camerius, possibly the addressee of Catullus 55 and 58a (see the inscription discussed on **93**).

The only surviving Latin poems written by a woman in this period are the six short elegies of Sulpicia, niece of Messalla Corvinus ([Tib.] 3.13–18). But we hear of several poetesses besides Cornificia and Ovid's step-daughter Perilla (below). According to Propertius, his Cynthia could rival Corinna and Erinna (who, I believe, was named in Prop. 2.3.22). When Ovid chose the pseudonym Corinna for his beloved, he may have implied that she too wrote verses. And e.g. the Catilinarian conspirator Sempronia was capable of doing so (Sallust, *Cat.* 25 'posse versus facere'). There is no evidence that any of the above wrote large-scale poems.

COTTA MAXIMUS: Second son of Messalla Corvinus (Syme, *History in Ovid*, ch. 7 'The Sons of Messalla', with pp. 125 ff. on Cotta). Together with his brother Messallinus, Cotta would have inherited the literary patronage of his father, and was still remembered for generosity in the time of Juvenal (5.109, 7.95). As well as his encouragement of others, Ovid mentions Cotta's own poetry (*Ex Ponto* 3.5.39 'recitas factum modo carmen amicis'), and cannot restrain himself from naming Cotta alone among the younger generation of poets (4.16.41–4).

It is curious that the Auctor de Dubiis Nominibus (GLK V, p. 587) ascribes the words 'nunc ad praesepia' (the quotation may originally have been longer) to Cotta rather than to his father's protégé Tibullus (2.1.7). But that treatise several times makes eccentric attributions of phrases found in standard authors.

FANNIUS: An inferior, publicity-seeking, poet whose ill opinion Horace can bear with equanimity (*Sat.* 1.4.21 and 1.10.79–80).

FONTANUS: A pastoral poet (*Ex Ponto* 4.16.35 'Naiadas a Satyris caneret Fontanus amatas'). I have not found Fontanus (see *OLD* for the god of springs) elsewhere as a personal name—though if Montanus, why not Fontanus? Some have suspected that here it may be a pseudonym, appropriate to the subject matter (Naiads). But the pseudonyms which can most plausibly be argued to represent contemporary literary figures are Greek: Codrus (Messalla Corvinus), Demophoon (Tuscus), Lynceus (conceivably Varius Rufus).

IULIUS CALIDUS: Cicero's friend Atticus rescued from proscription by the Second Triumvirate (among others) 'L. Iulium Calidum, quem post Lucreti Catullique mortem multo elegantissimum poetam nostram tulisse aetatem vere videor posse contendere, neque minus virum bonum optimisque artibus eruditum, post proscriptionem equitum propter magnas eius Africanas possessiones in proscriptorum numerum a P. Volumnio, praefecto fabrum Antonii, absentem relatum' (Cornelius Nepos, *Life of Atticus* 12.4–5). This L. Iulius Calidus may well be the L. Julius whom Cicero (without, it seems, personal knowledge) commended to the governor of Africa in 56 or possibly 55 BC (*Ad fam.* 13.6 = 57 SB).

The literary judgement is extraordinary from a man who had been the dedicatee of Catullus' collection (1.3 'Corneli, tibi') and should have known who was who and what was what. 'Nostram ... aetatem' should include at least the Virgil of the *Eclogues*. Part of the explanation might be that Nepos was out of sympathy with the more extreme Alexandrianizing ('cantores Euphorionis') that seems to have dominated Latin poetry for a decade after the death of Lucretius and Catullus, in the persons of e.g. Helvius Cinna and the up-and-coming Cornelius Gallus. Elevating a nonentity would also have the effect of disparaging more substantial talents. And we can find clues about the positive literary tastes of Nepos. He had thought well of Catullus' *nugae* (1.3–4 'namque tu solebas / meas esse aliquid putare nugas'); the collection dedicated to him can hardly have included Cat. 64. The words in which Nepos praises Calidus, 'multo elegantissimum poetam', likewise suggest epigrams (such as prominent Romans had written for several generations) and other short poems. Nepos also thought well of Calidus for his wide culture and (perhaps) his social and political attitudes: 'virum bonum optimisque artibus eruditum'.

IULIUS FLORUS: The recipient of Horace, *Epistles* 1.3 and 2.2, who served on Tiberius' staff during the Armenian expedition of 20 BC. According to Porf. on 1.3.1 he was a 'scriba' (personal secretary) and writer of satires. Horace's own words (1.3.20 ff. 'ipse quid audes? / quae circumvolitas agilis thyma? non tibi parvum / ingenium, non incultum est et turpiter hirtum. / (24) ... seu condis amabile carmen') rather suggests slighter and more refined genres. Syme (*Augustan Aristocracy*, 361) speculates that Florus may have come from one of the Gallic provinces.

LARGUS: 'Ingeniique sui dictus cognomine Largus, / Gallica qui Phrygium duxit in arma senem' (*Ex Ponto* 4.16.17–18). His *ingenium* was 'copious' (cf. Juv. 10.119 on Demosthenes and Cicero 'largus et exundans leto dedit ingenii fons'), and he wrote on the wanderings of Antenor who, despite *Aen.* 1.1 'primus', came from Troy even before Aeneas and founded Patavium. For all sorts of reasons (see Martin Helzle, *P. Ovidii Nasonis Epistularum ex Ponto Liber IV*, 187) one can rule out any possibility that this Largus was Valerius Largus, the disloyal friend who denounced Cornelius Gallus (Dio 53.23.6).

LUPUS: 'Auctor / Tantalidae reducis Tyndaridosque Lupus' (*Ex Ponto* 4.16.25–6). The return from Troy of Menelaus and Helen included a considerable entanglement in Egypt (*Od.* 4.78 ff.) which offered scope for Hellenistic learning (Nicander, *Ther.* 309 ff.).

MACER: Author of an epic on Troy (*Ex Ponto* 4.16.6 'Iliacusque Macer'), there coupled with Domitius Marsus *qua* epic poet (**172a**), Rabirius (**229a**) and Albinovanus Pedo (**225a**). While Rabirius and Pedo reach Quintilian's category of 'non indigni cognitione, si vacat' (10.1.90), the same is not true of Macer. In writing of his own current preoccupation with love poetry, Ovid reminds Macer that the Trojan saga contained similar material: 'et Paris est illic et adultera, nobile crimen, / et comes extincto Laodamia viro' (*Am.* 2.18.37–8). While in that poem Ovid writes of Macer's Trojan epic in general terms (1–2 'carmen ad iratum dum tu perducis Achillem / primaque iuratis induis arma viris'), by the time of *Ex Ponto* 2.10.13–14 he can be more precise: 'tu canis aeterno quicquid restabat Homero, / ne careant summa

Troica bella manu'. Macer's epic is revealed as a sequel to the *Iliad*, like that of Camerinus (above) and perhaps the *Amazonis* of Domitius Marsus (**173**).

This Macer, who is probably the addressee of Tibullus 2.6, was clearly a long-standing friend of Ovid, and perhaps a fellow member of the circle of Messalla; 'te duce' (*Ex Ponto* 2.10.21) suggests that Macer was somewhat older. Together with Ovid Macer made a grand tour which included Sicily and the cities of Asia (*Ex Ponto* 2.10.21 ff.)—perhaps also Athens and Alexandria (*Tristia* 1.2.77 ff.). It may have been from the Tetrasticha of this Macer that Ovid compiled a work 'In malos poetas' (see on **70**). The name 'Macer' is common, and attempts at identification have failed. He is definitely not Aemilius Macer (**47–70**) who was senior to Virgil and died in 16 BC (**47***d*). Some (e.g. Martin Helzle and others cited by him on *Ex Ponto* 4.10.6) have believed the poet to be 'Pompeius Macer', a fragile construction who has now been removed from Ovidian prosopography (P. White, *CQ* NS 42 (1992), 210–18, cf. McKeown, *Ovid. Amores*, III (1998), 382–3).

MAMURRA: 'Mentula conatur Pipleium scandere montem: / Musae furcillis praecipitem eiciunt' (Catullus 105).

MARIUS: 'et Marius, scripti dexter in omne genus' (*Ex Ponto* 4.16.24).

MELISSUS: 'et tua cum socco Musa, Melisse, levi' (*Ex Ponto* 4.16.30, contrasting with the tragic cothurnus of Turranius). This is C. Maecenas Melissus, freedman of Augustus' minister. Suetonius devotes a section to him (*De gramm.* 21). He invented a new kind of comedy in Roman dress (*togata*), which he called 'trabeata' from the *trabea* (a knee-length purple garment worn by *equites*). See further Kaster's commentary on *De gramm.* 21.

MEVIUS: Shot down in flames, together with Bavius (above), by Virgil, *Ecl.* 3.90 'qui Bavium non odit, amet tua carmina, Mevi'. We are probably meant to recognize him in the Mevius on whom Horace wishes a fatal shipwreck (*Epode* 10). One may accept (without great confidence) the statement of Porf. (p. 304 ed. Holder) on Horace, *Satires* 2.3.239 that Mevius too wrote about M. Clodius Aesopus dissolving in vinegar a fabulously expensive pearl which belonged to Metella, wife of Lentulus Spinther (cf. Nisbet, *Collected Papers*, 397–8). Parodies of Virgil were sometimes ascribed by scholiasts to Bavius and/or Mevius.

NUMA: Described in *Ex Ponto* 4.16.10 as 'subtilis', 'refined', an epithet probably meant to correspond to the λεπτός or λεπταλέος of the Callimachean school.

PASSER: From *Ex Ponto* 4.16.33 'Tityron antiquas Passerque rediret ad herbas'. The line is at first sight baffling, but explained by Housman, *Classical Papers*, 937 (vol. III) as = '<cum> Passer rediret ad Tityron antiquasque herbas'. He adds (pp. 937–8) that Propertius would have written 'Tityron antiquasque rediret Passer ad herbas', but Ovid disliked this rhythm more than he disliked entanglements of words. So we have a pastoral poet (cf. Fontanus above) called Passer; for the rare name Housman compared Petronius Passer in Varro, *De re rustica* 3.2.2 (*RE* Petronius 94, where a Caetronius Passer is also noted). It would seem that Passer recreated the manner and matter of Virgil's *Eclogues*; perhaps significantly Tityrus' name begins the line of Ovid as it does *Ecl.* 1.1. 'Returning to Tityrus' might pick up *Ecl.* 9.23 'Tityre, dum redeo', and 'herbas' the programmatic *Ecl.* 9.19–20 'quis humum florentibus herbis / spargeret ... ?' (Passer is prepared to resume where Virgil left off).

PERILLA: Ovid addresses a woman poet by this name in *Tristia* 3.7. Courtney (p. 229) guesses that she was a Greek freedwoman of Ovid who wrote poetry in Latin (whence line 12 'doctaque non patrio carmina more canis'). I prefer the traditional view that she is Ovid's step-daughter (cf. line 3 'dulci cum matre sedentem'); line 12 could well mean that she composed not in the manner of her stepfather (i.e. she avoided giving instruction in love, cf. 29–30). The reason for (presumably) her pseudonym is unknown—did Ovid choose it or she herself? In the circumstances it might have been more prudent to avoid a pseudonym which had been borne by the notorious Metella, celebrated by Ticida (**101***b*) and at least one other poet (see on **101**). Ovid, however, perhaps to avoid giving any such impression, stresses the 'mores ... pudicos' (13) of his Perilla.

PONTICUS (apparently his real name, not a pseudonym): An epic poet, linked with Bassus (above) as a friend of Ovid (*Tr.* 4.10.47–8). The same two names (no doubt the same people) appear individually in Propertius: Bassus in 1.4, Ponticus in 1.7 and 1.9. If we could take literally what Propertius says about Ponticus, he was engaged in a *Thebaid* (1.7.1–2 and 17; 1.9.9–10), and then fell in love, finding that his grand poetry helped him not at all. This is very similar to what Propertius says of Lynceus (who might just possibly be Varius Rufus) in 2.34; there too a *Thebaid* is adumbrated. Perhaps in both cases Thebes merely represents the highest kind of heroic poetry.

PRISCUS: There were two poets of this name (*Ex Ponto* 4.16.10 'Priscus uterque'). One of them could be the Clutorius Priscus of Tacitus, *Ann.* 3.49. He was given money by Tiberius in return for a poem on the death of Germanicus, but erred fatally by writing—and reciting—a poem on the death of Tiberius' son Drusus while Drusus was still alive (ibid.).

PROCULUS: 'Callimachi Proculus molle teneret iter' (*Ex Ponto* 4.16.32). Clearly an elegist ('iter' from Call. fr. 1.27–8 κελεύθους / ἀτρίπτους), with 'molle' suggesting love elegy.

PUPIUS: 'lacrimosa poemata Pupi' (Horace, *Epist.* 1.1.67). Said to have been a tragedian with a strong emotional impact. He was credited with a self-epitaph 'flebunt amici et bene noti mortem meam, / nam populus in me vivo lacrimavit satis', but, as Courtney says (p. 307), this was obviously written for him by others.

RUFUS: *Ex Ponto* 4.16.27–8 'et une / Pindaricae fidicen tu quoque, Rufe, lyrae'. To recreate Pindar in Latin was perhaps the greatest challenge that a poet could take up, because of Pindar's grandiloquence and complicated metres. The most likely result was total disaster, as Horace warns Iullus Antonius (*Odes* 4.2.1–4 'Pindarum quisquis studet aemulari, / Iulle, ceratis ope Daedalea / nititur pennis vitreo daturus / nomina ponto', cf. *Epist.* 1.3.9 ff. quoted on Titius below). 'Une' implies not necessarily that Rufus was the only one to make the attempt, but that he succeeded beyond all others and was in a class by himself.

SABINUS: Ovid's friend who had the ingenious idea of writing replies to some of the *Heroides*: in particular from Ulysses to Penelope (*Am.* 2.18.29, *Ex Ponto* 4.16.13–14), but also (*Am.* 2.18) from Hippolytus, Aeneas, Demophoon, Jason to Hypsipyle and Phaon to Sappho (this last stirs up a hornets' nest of controversy!). These replies could have stimulated Ovid to add his own three pairs of double letters (16–21).

Sabinus wrote other poems too: 'quique suam †trisomen† imperfectumque dierum / deseruit celeri morte Sabinus opus' (*Ex Ponto* 4.16.15–16). It looks as though when Sabinus died he was engaged in a poem which had something in common with Ovid's *Fasti*. The corrupt '†trisomen' in *Ex Ponto* 4.16.15 has generally been referred to an epic on the recovery of the Moesian town Troesmis from the Getae (cf. *Ex Ponto* 4.9.79–80; Syme, *History in Ovid*, 83). McKeown (*Amores*, vol. III, p. 384) is not convinced by this—and indeed it seems an unlikely subject for Sabinus. Ovid's fondness for syllepsis raises the possibility that, since the second object of 'deseruit' is an incomplete poem (*Ex Ponto* 4.16.15–16, on the Days), the first ('suam †trisomen†') was something rather different, e.g. a woman whom he loved (whether in life or literature), or a place which he cherished. But I have no emendation. An elision at the masculine caesura of an Ovidian elegiac hexameter would be very surprising.

SERVIUS: Coupled with Q. Hortensius Hortalus (**98–9**, probably not Cicero's colleague and rival, but the latter's son) as a noble who wrote adventurous love poems: 'nec minus Hortensi, nec sunt minus improba Servi / carmina. quis dubitet nomina tanta sequi?' (Ovid, *Tristia* 2.441–2). Also mentioned in Pliny's catalogue (*Epist.* 5.3.5) immediately after Q. Scaevola (**90–2**), and as one of the literary men whose judgement Horace values in *Sat.* 1.10.86 ('vos, Bibule et Servi'). In all likelihood the son of the consular (51 BC) jurist Ser.

Sulpicius Rufus (Cicero's antagonist in the *Pro Murena*); our Servius married a sister of Messalla Corvinus and fathered the poetess 'Servi filia Sulpicia' ([Tib.] 3.16 = 4.10.4). See Syme, *Augustan Aristocracy*, 205–6.

SUFFENUS: As dreary a poet as he is witty a conversationalist (Catullus 22); in a list of bad poets at Cat. 14.19. See Nisbet, *Collected Papers*, 411 for a speculation that Suffenus might be a pseudonym for none other than the addressee of Cat. 22, Alfenus Varus.

TITIUS: 'Quid Titius, Romana brevi venturus in ora, / Pindarici fontis qui non expalluit haustus, / fastidire lacus et rivos ausus apertos? / ut valet? ut meminit nostri? fidibusne Latinis / Thebanos aptare modos studet auspice Musa, / an tragica desaevit et ampullatur in arte?' (Horace, *Epist.* 1.3.9–14). For the dangers of trying to imitate Pindar in Latin, see above on Rufus, whom some have wished to combine with Titius as a putative Titius Rufus (Helzle on Ovid, *Ex Ponto* 4.16.27–8 is probably right to resist that idea).

TRINACRIUS: *Ex Ponto* 4.16.25 'Trinacriusque suae Perseidos auctor'. Clearly a pseudonym which one might expect to be borne by a pastoral poet (cf. Calpurnius Siculus); in [Virgil], *Cat.* 9.20 Theocritus is 'Trinacriae doctus . . . iuvenis'. Perhaps our poet started with pastoral and, like Virgil, moved on to greater things. A Latin epic on Perseus is quite credible in this period; cf. (above) Antonius Iullus on Diomedes and Carus on Hercules.

TURRANIUS: *Ex Ponto* 4.16.29 'Musaque Turrani tragicis innixa cothurnis', another tragedian to add to the not inconsiderable number in the triumviral and Augustan years: Asinius Pollio, Varius Rufus, Ovid (*Medea*), Gracchus, Pupius (above).

TUSCUS: 'Quique sua nomen Phyllide Tuscus habet' (*Ex Ponto* 4.16.20). 'Nomen habet' probably in two senses: (*a*) 'has won glory', (*b*) 'has taken his pseudonym'. 'Tuscus' was probably the poet's real name (though perhaps his Etruscan origin). Phyllis' mythical lover—one of the most notorious examples of male perfidy—was Demophoon son of Theseus, and Tuscus was probably so called in his own poems. He may well be the Demophoon of Propertius 2.22.

TUTICANUS: The addressee of *Ex Ponto* 4.12 and 4.14. In the former Ovid explains that, to accommodate Tŭtĭcānus, he would have to shorten either the first or the third syllable, or else to split the name between two lines (as e.g. Euphorion fr. 5 Powell did with his Apollo/dorus), none of which he wishes to do. In 4.12.27–8 Ovid mentions that Tuticanus had written a *Phaeacis*, on Odysseus' stay with King Alcinous and his Phaeacians (from *Odyssey* 6–8). This enables us to attach *Ex Ponto* 4.16.27 'et qui Maeoniam Phaeacida vertit' (without author's name or metrical apologies) to Tuticanus.

VALERIUS CATO: Although not one word verbatim of Valerius Cato has survived (some have wondered about Adesp. **235**), the number, and tone, of testimonies which he receives from fellow poets show him to have been a figure of considerable importance, both as a scholar and a poet. Most of these testimonia are preserved by Suetonius, *De grammaticis* 11 (see Robert A. Kaster's (Oxford, 1995) edition with commentary). Cato himself stated (Suetonius, ibid.) that he had been a *pupillus* (not more than 14) in the time of Sulla, i.e. during the Dictatorship of 82–80 BC; thus he was born not before 96 BC. Furius Bibaculus speaks of him approaching 'summam . . . senectam' (**84**.8) which suggests that he lived at least into his seventies, i.e. the 20s BC— though sometimes the ancients thought of old age as beginning much earlier (see Alan Cameron, *Callimachus and his Critics*, 174–81).

Suetonius attributes to Cato 'grammaticos libellos', and, according to the intrusive verses standing at the head of Horace, *Sat.* 1.10 (Adesp. **240**), Cato edited and 'improved' the satires of Lucilius. Two of his own poems became particularly famous: the *Lydia* (Ticida, **103**), and the *Diana* (so Suetonius) which Cinna (**14**) called *Dictynna*. Furius Bibaculus proclaims him 'optimum poetam' as well as 'summum grammaticum' (**85**.4). Equally important was his role as discriminating critic and encourager of young poets (Furius Bibaculus, **86**.2 'qui solus legit ac facit poetas'), determining who made the grade and who did not. Only because he had the co-authorship of the Muses could Cornelius Gallus face Cato's judgement with equanimity (Gallus, **145**.8–9). Valerius Cato was probably the recipient of Catullus 56 (cf. line 3 'ride, quidquid amas, Cato, Catullum') and Cornelius Gallus may be the 'Galle' to whom Bibaculus (**85**.1) laments Cato's impoverished old age. So these three poets at least (and probably others) would have counted themselves as Cato's personal friends. For more detailed commentary, see on the passages of other poets referred to above.

VOLUSIUS: Catullus 36.1 = 21 'Annales Volusi, cacata charta' and 95.7–8 'at Volusi annales Paduam morientur ad ipsam / et laxas scombris saepe dabunt tunicas'. Volusius is not heard of elsewhere. In Seneca, *Epist.* 93.11 we read 'annales Tanusii scis quam ponderosi sint et quid vocentur' (?? = 'cacata charta') on which Fordyce (*Catullus*, 179–80) comments very reasonably, 'the natural explanation is that the similarity of name tempted someone wickedly to apply to Tanusius what Catullus had said of Volusius'.

In Ovid, *Ex Ponto* 4.16 there are places where the subject of the poem is specified, but not the author. In one of these (line 27, 'et qui Maeoniam Phaeacida vertit') we have been able to identify the poet as Tuticanus (above). Since there was no reason for Ovid to conceal the author's name, we may guess that in the two other cases his reticence was likewise due to metrical intractability. First of all, a grandiloquent poem on the sea: 'velivolique maris vates, cui credere posses / carmina caeruleos composuisse deos' (21–2). This might have been scientific/philosophical, or else concerned with naval warfare; a very long shot would be to send Adesp. **256** in that direction. Secondly, line 23 'quique acies Libycas Romanaque proelia dixit'—possibly on the Punic wars, or on the Bellum Africum of Julius Caesar which culminated in the victory at Thapsus (46 BC).

Finally, I draw attention to the list of frivolous didactic poems in Ovid, *Tristia* 2.473–92. One of these poets (485 'ecce canit formas alius iactusque pilarum') has been plausibly identified as Dorcatius (**196**). Line 487 'composita est aliis fucandi cura coloris' may refer to Ovid's own *Medicamina Faciei Femineae*; some have applied 488 'hic epulis leges hospitioque dedit' to the *Hedyphagetica* of Ennius, but I suspect that Ovid had a more recent work in mind.

Select Bibliography of Secondary Sources

Adams, J. N., *The Latin Sexual Vocabulary* (1982).

Alexiou, Margaret, *The Ritual Lament in Greek Tradition* (1974).

Anderson, J. K., *Ancient Greek Horsemanship* (1961).

—— *Xenophon* (1974).

André, J., *Étude sur les termes de couleur dans la langue latine* (1949).

—— *La Vie et l'œuvre d'Asinius Pollion* (1949).

—— *L'Alimentation et la cuisine à Rome* (1961).

Ball, Sidney H., *A Roman Book on Precious Stones* (1950).

Ballaira, G., *Esempi di scrittura latina dell' età romana*, i (1993).

Bernabé, A., *Poetae Epici Graeci* (1988).

Bieber, Margarete, *The Statue of Cybele in the J. Paul Getty Museum* (J. Paul Getty Museum Publications, 3; 1968).

Birt, Theodor, *Kritik und Hermeneutik* (1913).

Bocuto, G., 'I segni premonitori del tempo in Virgilio e in Arato', *Atene e Roma*, 30 (1985), 9–16.

Boucher, J. P., *Gaius Cornelius Gallus* (1966).

Bowersock, G. W., *Augustus and the Greek World* (1965).

Brogan, O., *Roman Gaul* (1953).

Broughton, T. R. S., *The Magistrates of the Roman Republic*, iii (suppl.; 1986).

Cairns, Francis, *Generic Composition in Greek and Roman Poetry* (1972).

—— *Tibullus* (1979).

Cambridge History of Classical Literature, ii. *Latin Literature* (1982).

Cameron, Alan, *Callimachus and his Critics* (1995).

Casson, Lionel, *Ships and Seamanship in the Ancient World* (1971).

Cazzaniga, I., 'L'episodio dei Serpi Libici in Lucano e la tradizione dei Theriaca Nicandrei', *Acme*, 10 (1957), 27–41.

Chuvin, P., *Mythologie et géographie Dionysiaques* (1991).

Clausen, Wendell, *Virgil's Aeneid and the Traditions of Hellenistic Poetry* (1987).

Corpus Glossariorum Latinorum, ed. G. Goetz, 7 vols. (1892).

Courtney, E., *The Poems of Petronius* (1991).

Cova, P., *Il poeta Vario* (1989).

Dahlmann, H., *Cornelius Severus* (1975).

—— *Über Helvius Cinna* (1977).

—— *Über Aemilius Macer* (1981).

—— *Zu Fragmenten römischer Dichter* (1983).

Dahlmann, H. and W. Speyer, *Varronische Studien*, ii (1959).

Davies, Ceri, 'Poetry in the "Circle" of Messalla', *Greece and Rome*, 20 (1973), 25–35.

Davies, Malcolm, *Epicorum Graecorum Fragmenta* (1988).

Delia, Diana, 'Fulvia Reconsidered', in Sarah B. Pomeroy (ed.), *Women's History and Ancient History* (Chapel Hill, NC, 1991).

Diels, H., *Doxographi Graeci*[2] (1929).

Doblhofer, E., *Die Augustuspanegyrik des Horaz in formalhistorischer Sicht* (1966).

Dudley, D. R., *Urbs Roma* (1967).

Forbes, R. J., *Studies in Ancient Technology*, 9 vols. (1964–72).

Fraenkel, E., *Horace* (1957).

Fragmenta Poetarum Romanorum, ed. E. Baehrens (1886).

Fragmenta Poetarum Latinorum, ed. W. Morel (1927; revised by K. Büchner, 1982, and R. J. Blänsdorf, 1995).

The Fragmentary Latin Poets, ed. E. Courtney (1993; paperback version, with addenda, 2003).

Fränkel, H., *Einleitung zur kritischen Ausgabe der Argonautika des Apollonius* (1964).

Fraser, P. M., *Ptolemaic Alexandria* (1972).

Funaioli, H., *Grammaticae Romanae Fragmenta*, i (1907).

Gigante, M., *Ricerche filodemee* (1969).

Goodyear, F. R. D., *The Annals of Tacitus*, ii (1981).

Gowing, Alain M., *The Triumviral Narratives of Appian and Cassius Dio* (1992).

Griffin, Jasper, 'Horace in the Thirties', in Niall Rudd (ed.), *Horace 2000* (1993).

Grosser Historischer Weltatlas[2] (1954).

Hadley, Robert, 'Hieronymus of Cardia and Early Seleucid Mythology', *Historia*, 18 (1969), 142–52.

Hallett, Judith P., 'Perusinae Glandes', *AJAH* 2 (1977), 151–71.

Hardie, C. G., 'Octavian and Eclogue 1', in *The Ancient Historian and his Materials: Essays in Honour of C. E. Stevens* (1975).

Hardie, Philip, *Virgil's Aeneid: Cosmos and Imperium* (1986).

Harris, H. A., *Sport in Greece and Rome* (1972).

Harrison, S. J. (ed.), *Oxford Readings in Vergil's Aeneid* (1990).

Heath, T. L., *Aristarchus of Samos* (1913).

Henzen, W., *Acta Fratrum Arvalium* (1874).

Herescu, N. I. (ed.), *Ovidiana* (1958).

Hinds, Stephen, 'Carmina Digna . . .', *PLLS* 4 (1983), 43–54.

Hollis, A., 'Traces of Ancient Commentaries on Ovid's Metamorphoses', *PLLS* 9 (1996), 159–74.

—— 'Virgil's Friend Varius Rufus', *Proceedings of the Virgil Society*, 22 (1996), 19–33.

Hosius, C., 'Die literarische Stellung von Ausons Mosellied', *Philologus*, 81 (1926), 192–201.

Housman, A. E., *Classical Papers*, ed. J. Diggle and F. R. D. Goodyear (1971).

Hull, D. B., *Hounds and Hunting in Ancient Greece* (1964).

Irving, Forbes, *Metamorphosis in Greek Myths* (1990).

Jocelyn, H. D., *The Tragedies of Ennius* (1967).

Jocelyn, H. D. (ed.), *Tria Lustra* (Liverpool Classical Papers, 3; 1993).

Kaster, R. A., 'A Schoolboy's Burlesque from Cyrene?', *Mnemosyne*, NS 37 (1984), 457–8.

—— *Suetonius, De Grammaticis et Rhetoribus* (1995).

Kirwan, L. P., 'Rome beyond the Southern Egyptian Frontier', *Proceedings of the British Academy*, 63 (1977).

Klotz, A., *Scaenicorum Romanorum Fragmenta* (1953).

Knox, Peter, *Ovid's Metamorphoses and the Traditions of Augustan Poetry* (1986).

Kühner, C. F. L. A., and C. Stegmann, *Ausführliche Grammatik der lateinischen Sprache* (1914).

Kuiper, T. (ed.), *Philodemus over den Dood* (1925).

Lattimore, Richard, *Themes in Greek and Latin Epitaphs* (1942).

Lefèvre, E., *Der Thyestes des Lucius Varius Rufus* (1976).

Lightfoot, Jane, *Parthenius of Nicaea* (1999).

Lloyd-Jones, Hugh, *Academic Papers* (1990).

Lomanto, V., and N. Marinone, *Index Grammaticus* (1990).

Lowe, E. A., *Codices Latini Antiquiores*, iv (1947).

Lunelli, A., *Aerius* (1969).

Lyne, R. O. A. M., *Ciris: A Poem Attributed to Vergil* (1978).

Maass, E., *Commentariorum in Aratum Reliquiae* (1898).

Malcovati, H., *Oratorum Romanorum Fragmenta*[2] (1955).

Matthews, V. J., *Panyassis of Halikarnassus* (1974).

Mazard, J., *Corpus Nummorum Numidae Mauretaniaeque* (1955).

Morel, W., 'Iologica', *Philologus*, 83 (1927–8), 345–89.

Morford, M. P. O., *The Poet Lucan* (1967).

Moritz, L. A., *Grain-Mills and Flour in Classical Antiquity* (1958).

Most, Glenn (ed.), *Collecting Fragments* (Aporemata, 1; 1997).

Nairn, J. A., 'The Meaning of Hellespontus in Latin', *CR* 13 (1899), 436–8.

Nisbet, R. G., 'Voluntas Fati in Latin Syntax', *AJP* 44 (1923), 27–43.

Nisbet, R. G. M., *Collected Papers on Latin Literature*, ed. S. J. Harrison (1995).

Norden, E., *Agnostos Theos* (1923 reprint).

Ogilvie, R. M., *The Library of Lactantius* (1978).

Otto, A., *Die Sprichwörter der Römer* (1890).

Page, D. L., *Further Greek Epigrams* (1981).

Papathomopoulos, M., *Nouveaux Fragments d'auteurs anciens* (1980).

Pearson, A. C., *The Fragments of Sophocles* (1917).

Pelling, C. B. R., *Plutarch, Life of Antony* (1988).

Perutelli, A., *Frustula Poetarum* (2002).

Peter, H., *Historicorum Romanorum Reliquiae* (1914).

Pfeiffer, R., *History of Classical Scholarship: From the Beginnings to the End of the Hellenistic Age* (1968).

Pighi, G. B., 'De Nonnullis Veterum Romanorum Poetarum Fragmentis', in *Miscellanea di Studi Alessandri in memoria di Augusto Rostagni* (1963).

Platnauer, M., *Latin Elegiac Verse* (1951).

Pomeroy, A. J., *The Appropriate Comment: Death Notices in the Ancient Historians* (1991).

Powell, J. U. (ed.), *Collectanea Alexandrina* (1925).

Putnam, C. J., 'Propertius and the New Gallus Fragment', *ZPE* 39 (1980), 49–56.

Ramage, E. S., 'The *De Urbanitate* of Domitius Marsus', *CP* 54 (1959), 250–5.

—— *Urbanitas* (1973).

Rawson, Elizabeth, *Intellectual Life in the Late Roman Empire* (1985).

Ribbeck, O. (ed.), *Tragicorum Romanorum Fragmenta*[3] (1897).

Rosokoki, Alexandra, *Die Erigone des Eratosthenes* (1995).

Ross, David, *Backgrounds to Augustan Poetry* (1975).

Rostagni, A., *Virgilio minore*[2] (1961).

Schanz, M., and C. Hosius, *Geschichte der römischen Literatur*[4] (1927).

Scott, K., 'The Political Propaganda of 44–30 BC', *Memoirs of the American Academy in Rome*, 11 (1933), 7–49.

Scullard, H. H., *The Elephant in the Greek and Roman World* (1974).

Sear, D., *The History and Coinage of the Roman Imperators 49–27 BC* (1998).

Shackleton Bailey, D. R., *Propertiana* (1958).

—— *Cicero's Letters to Atticus*, v (1966).

—— *Onomasticon to Cicero's Speeches* (1988).

—— *Two Studies in Roman Nomenclature*[2] (1991).

Sherwin-White, A. N., *The Letters of Pliny* (1966).

—— *The Roman Citizenship*[2] (1973).

Skutsch, F., *Aus Vergils Frühzeit* (1901).

—— *Gallus und Vergil* (1906).

Skutsch, O., *Annals of Ennius* (1985).

Slater, W. J., 'Aristophanes of Byzantium and Problem-Solving in the Museum', *CQ* NS 32 (1982), 336–49.

Stahl, W. H., 'Astronomy and Geography in Macrobius', *TAPA* 73 (1942), 232–58.

Stinton, T. C. W., 'Si credere dignum est', in his *Collected Papers on Greek Tragedy* (1990), 236–64.

Sullivan, Richard D., *Near Eastern Royalty and Rome, 100–30 BC* (1990).

Sussman, Lewis A., *The Elder Seneca* (*Mnemosyne*, suppl. 51; 1978).

Sydenham, E., *The Coinage of the Roman Republic* (rev. edn. 1952).

Syme, R., *The Roman Revolution* (1939).

—— *The Augustan Aristocracy* (1986).

—— *History in Ovid* (1978).

Taplin, O., *The Stagecraft of Aeschylus* (1977).

Tarrant, R. J., *Seneca's Thyestes* (1985).

D'Arcy W. Thompson, *A Glossary of Greek Birds*[2] (1936).

—— *A Glossary of Greek Fishes* (1947).

Thomson, J. Oliver, *History of Ancient Geography* (1948).

Unger, R., *De Aemilio Macro Nicandri Imitatore* (1845).

Vitae Vergilianae Antiquae, ed. C. Hardie (1966).

Waern, Ingrid, ΓΗΣ ΟΣΤΕΑ: Τηε Κεννινγ ιν Πρε-Χηριστιαν Γρεεκ Ποετρψ (1951).

Warmington, E. H., *Remains of Old Latin*, 4 vols. (1979).

Watkins, C., 'Etyma Enniana', *HSCP* 77 (1973), 195–206.

Webster, T. B. L., *Tragedies of Euripides* (1967).

Weinstock, S., *Divus Julius* (1971).

White, P., ' "Pompeius Macer" and Ovid', *CQ* NS 42 (1992), 210–18.

Wigodsky, M., *Virgil and Early Latin Poetry* (1972).

Williams, Gordon, *Tradition and Originality in Roman Poetry* (1968).

Winterbottom, M., 'Problems in Quintilian', *BICS*, suppl. 25 (1970).

Wiseman, T. P., *Cinna the Poet and Other Roman Essays* (1974).

Index